T0313924

THE PROMISE AND PERIL OF CREDIT

HISTORIES OF ECONOMIC LIFE

*Jeremy Adelman, Sunil Amrith, and
Emma Rothschild, Series Editors*

*The Promise and Peril of Credit: What a Forgotten Legend about Jews and Finance
Tells Us about the Making of European Commercial Society* by Francesca
Trivellato

A People's Constitution: The Everyday Life of Law in the Indian Republic
by Rohit De

A Local History of Global Capital: Jute and Peasant Life in the Bengal Delta
by Tariq Omar Ali

The Promise and Peril of Credit

WHAT A FORGOTTEN LEGEND
ABOUT JEWS AND FINANCE
TELLS US ABOUT THE MAKING OF
EUROPEAN COMMERCIAL SOCIETY

FRANCESCA TRIVELLATO

PRINCETON UNIVERSITY PRESS
PRINCETON & OXFORD

Copyright © 2019 by Princeton University Press

Published by Princeton University Press
41 William Street, Princeton, New Jersey 08540
6 Oxford Street, Woodstock, Oxfordshire OX20 1TR

press.princeton.edu

Jacket Credit: Bills of exchange of the Isnard family of Marseilles, 1642-1643.
With permission from the Archives départementales des Bouches-du-Rhône,
Marseilles, 24E53.

All Rights Reserved

Library of Congress Control Number: 2018954761
ISBN 9780691178592

British Library Cataloging-in-Publication Data is available

Editorial: Eric Crahan and Pamela Weidman
Production Editorial: Leslie Grundfest
Production: Jacquie Poirier
Publicity: Tayler Lord
Copyeditor: Sarah Vogelsong

This book has been composed in Arno Pro

Printed on acid-free paper. ∞

Printed in the United States of America

10 9 8 7 6 5 4 3 2 1

CONTENTS

List of Illustrations vii

Acknowledgments ix

Preface xi

Introduction   1

1 The Setting: Marine Insurance and Bills of Exchange   19

2 The Making of a Legend   36

3 The Riddle of Usury   49

4 Bordeaux, the Specter of Crypto-Judaism, and the Changing
   Status of Commerce   66

5 One Family, Two Bestsellers, and the Legend's Canonization   99

6 Between Usury and the "Spirit of Commerce"   128

7 Distant Echoes   162

8 A Legacy that Runs Deep   197

   Coda   216

*Appendix 1: Early Modern European Commercial Literature:
   Printed Bibliographies and Online Databases* 227
Appendix 2: The Legend's Earliest Formulation 231
Appendix 3: Étienne Cleirac's Works: Titles, Editions, and Issues 239

Appendix 4: *The Legend in the Works of Jacques Savary and His Sons* 243

*Appendix 5: Printed Books in French that
Mention the Legend (1647–1800)* 249

*Appendix 6: Printed Books in Languages Other than French
that Mention the Legend (1676–1800)* 253

Appendix 7: Bibliographical References in Werner Sombart's
Die Juden und das Wirtschaftsleben *(1911)* 259

Notes 295

Index 395

ILLUSTRATIONS

1.1. Flow chart of a classic (four-party) bill of exchange 25

1.2. A classic (four-party) bill of exchange issued in Lyon in 1552 26

1.3. Transcription of the bill of exchange reproduced in figure 1.2 27

1.4. Stylized text of a classic (four-party) bill of exchange 27

1.5. Flow chart of a re-exchange contract 29

1.6. Flow chart of a dry-exchange contract 30

1.7. Multiple endorsements on the back of bills of exchange of the Isnard family of Marseilles, 1642–1643 33

2.1. Frontispiece of the manuscript version of *Us et coustumes de la mer* 42

2.2. Cleirac's commentary on the first article of the *Guidon de la mer* in the manuscript version of *Us et coustumes de la mer* 43

2.3. Gloss in the margin of Cleirac's commentary on the first article of the *Guidon de la mer* in the manuscript version of *Us et coustumes de la mer* 44

2.4. Detail of Paolo Uccello's *Miracle of the Profaned Host* (Urbino, 1460s) 46

4.1. The street in Bordeaux named after Cleirac 67

4.2. Map of France with the boundaries of the *parlements'* jurisdictions (mid-seventeenth century) 70

4.3. First page of a printed alphabetical list of all authors and texts cited in *Us et coustumes de la mer* 74

4.4. The Bay of Biscay (*Golfe de Gascogne*) in an eighteenth-century French map   76

4.5. The Portuguese shipwreck of January 12–14, 1627   77

4.6. Frontispiece of the 1647 edition of Cleirac's *Us et coustumes de la mer*   85

ACKNOWLEDGMENTS

THIS BOOK CAME ABOUT in bouts and breaks over the course of a decade during which I accumulated many intellectual, personal, and material debts. Several institutions subsidized my research trips and leaves from teaching: in 2012–2013, the John Solomon Guggenheim Foundation; in fall 2012, the Institute for Advanced Study in Princeton; in spring 2013, the American Academy in Berlin; and, on multiple occasions, the Provost's Office, MacMillan Center, and Program in Economic History at Yale University. While I made extensive use of digitized rare books, I could not have completed my work without the extraordinary physical repositories on the Yale campus—the Beinecke Library, Sterling Memorial Library, and Lillian Goldman Law Library—and their extraordinary librarians, including Susanne Roberts, Kathryn James, and Michael Widener. I also availed myself of the special collections of the Bibliothèque Nationale in Paris, the Municipal Library in Bordeaux, the Staatsbibliothek in Berlin, and many other storehouses of knowledge across Europe. During the Australian winter of 2016, the Toorak/South Yarra Public Library in Melbourne gave me shelter during many a cold afternoon and reminded me of what we stand to lose when we defund public libraries.

A number of research assistants, many now scholars and writers in their own right, have helped me at various stages to track down, swiftly search through, and translate material in multiple languages: Cornelia Aust, Aner Barzilay, Veronica Aoki Santarosa, Yemile Bucay, Gijs Dielen, Amanda Gregg, Charlotte Kiechel, Annalena Müller, Jesse Sadler, Miriam Salzmann, Maximilian Scholz, and Tijl Vanneste.

I am especially indebted to the many friends, colleagues, and passing interlocutors who asked questions, offered suggestions, corrected mistakes, replied to my queries, or simply provided food for thought along the way. In 2010 Caroline Walker Bynum responded positively to a talk in which I sketched out this project before I really knew what it was about, and her reaction gave me the confidence to continue my work. Later, she also gave me the benefit of her insight into a pile of untidy pages. Others were equally generous in reading portions of the manuscript (often in undigested form): Jeremy Adelman, William Caferro, Guillaume Calafat, Giovanni Ceccarelli, Simona Cerutti, Lauren Clay, David Garrioch, Oscar Gelderblom, Lynn Hunt, Ari Joskowicz, Naomi Lamoreaux, Sarah Lipton, Nadia Mantrige, Sarah Maza, Avinoam Naeh, Stefania Pastore, Derek Penslar, Sophia Rosenfeld, Maurice Samuels, Andrew Sartori, Roberto Savelli, Robert Schneider, Silvia Sebastiani, Kenneth Stow, Giacomo Todeschini, and Carl Wennerlind. Maxine Berg and two anonymous reviewers commented on the penultimate version of the book for the press and suggested ways of improving it.

I also wish to acknowledge the exceptional group of women and academics with whom I have shared work in progress on a few treasured occasions over the past several years: Amanda Claybaugh, Patricia Crain, Diana Fuss, Martha Howell, Heather Love, Sharon Marcus, and Judith Walkowitz. They have asked probing questions, put up with my clunky prose, and inspired me with their writing and their example.

Segments of the book have appeared in print in earlier incarnations: portions of chapters 1 through 3 were published in the *Journal of Modern History* (2011) and *Archives Juives* (2015), sections of chapter 4 in *Law and History Review* (2015) and *Tijdschrift voor Rechtsgeschiedenis / Revue d'histoire du droit / Legal History Review* (2015), and a version of chapter 6 in *French Historical Studies* (2016). The readers and editors for those articles improved the project when I most needed advice.

At Princeton University Press, Brigitta van Rheinberg and her staff, including her former assistant Amanda Peery, executive editor and editorial director for the humanities Eric Crahan, and senior production editor Leslie Grundfest, were a dream team. Sarah Vogelsong worked tirelessly to copyedit the manuscript, and David Luljak compiled the index. Their kindess and professionalism made all the difference. Brett Savage, academic assistant in the School of Historical Studies at the Institute for Advanced Study in Princeton, lent me his sharp eye while I was reviewing the proofs. Naturally, all errors are mine.

Once again, I owe more to Carolyn Dean than to anyone else.

IT WOULD BE MISLEADING to say that this book "found me." But the impetus behind it came as much from what was happening around me as from my academic interests. In September 2008 an endless stream of breaking news relayed bleaker and bleaker economic reports on the future of millions of ordinary people. Lehman Brothers collapsed. Home foreclosures became a daily event. Talk of greed resurfaced in public conversation. Even *usury* and *usurious,* words that I had not heard uttered outside of the classroom, reentered everyday vocabulary, alongside *loan shark* and *pawnbroker.* As financial mogul John Alfred Paulson admitted in April 2010, "We believed that the two-year adjustable rate mortgages made to lower income borrowers with poor credit history, little or no documentation, no downpayment and rates that would shortly reset at *usurious* interest rates set the stage for significant delinquencies and foreclosures, thus eroding the value of these securities."[1]

As a citizen, I was angry and anguished. As a historian of early modern European market organization and market culture, I was intrigued and felt slightly vindicated. Since the fall of the Berlin Wall, scholarly interest in the slow-paced economies of the preindustrial period had waned, and faith in the upward trajectory of modern financial capitalism had become nearly gospel. Now, it seemed, we were back to square one. No easy solution was in sight. In fact, the daily reports did not seem much clearer than seventeenth-century merchant manuals, which were filled with advice on how to make money as well as warnings against avarice and shady dealers.

While the global financial system stood on the brink of collapse after years of speculative frenzy, an old excerpt from Warren Buffett's 2002 annual letter to Berkshire Hathaway shareholders resurfaced and went viral. Sounding like Cassandra amid a cheerful crowd of Wall Street investors, Buffett had described credit default swaps as "financial weapons of mass destruction" carrying "dangers that, while now latent, are potentially lethal."[2] The statement remains controversial. Not everyone agrees with Buffett's judgment, and this skepticism affects the work of government and private agencies charged with regulating the industry to this day. What is remarkable about Buffett's warning is that the man who offered it was not a fierce opponent of corporate finance or a future leader of the Occupy Wall Street movement, but the richest man in the world at the time of its writing.

I mention these recent events not to suggest that we can link today's rapid "financialization" to earlier transformations of Europe's economy in simple terms, but to point out that even those who believe in the positive effects of expanding private and public credit, now as in the past, cannot easily agree on where to draw the boundaries of that expansion and what kind of oversight might best prevent fraud and the emergence of oligopolies. *The Promise and Peril of Credit* examines key episodes in the West's millennium-long struggle to delineate the place that finance ought to occupy in the social and political order. It does so by introducing readers to modes of thinking about the morality of credit that have become increasingly alien to us even as the questions that animated those early modern discussions remain as vital now as they were then.

After decades of retreat from the mainstream, economic history is making its way back to college curricula and scholarly publications. Today as always, present concerns stimulate academics' choice of subject matter and approaches to historical inquiry. Income and wealth inequality, the connection between slavery and capitalist modes of production and consumption, the impact of cultural traditions on economic performance, and the timing and consequences of globalization top the list of current research topics pursued by economic historians of various persuasions. A sense of urgency infuses this research—a welcome and energizing change after decades during which North American history departments' interest in economic history lay dormant. However, one should not forget that each of these themes has its own long and distinguished scholarly pedigree; nor should we risk falling into the old trap of searching for the origins of contemporary phenomena—Marc Bloch's "idol."[3] While I readily admit, and indeed embrace, the influence that present concerns exert on my scholarly work, my aim in this book is to bring back to life ways of thinking about the economy that have become increasingly foreign to the mainstream of the academy and to interrogate the sources of our amnesia about topics and problems that not long ago occupied a central place in debates about the development of European capitalism.[4]

In Anglophone historiography in particular, the demotion of the preindustrial period to second-rank importance in examinations of Europe's economic takeoff has often been compounded by the enduring legacy of the Protestant

Black Legend, according to which Catholic societies after the Reformation eschewed profit and indulged in idleness. This twin tendency has affected even serious scholarship and detracted from the study of economic transformations in Catholic Europe from the medieval commercial revolution to the industrial revolution. To be sure, one can always find staunch enemies of all forms of commercialization among Catholic authors, but more interesting—and, by the sixteenth century, often more influential—were those theologians, lawyers, judges, philosophers, statesmen, merchants turned writers, and polymaths who did not oppose financial dealings as such but disagreed on the written and unwritten rules that ought to govern the marketplace for the benefit of Christian and polite commercial society.

Credit was central to those intellectual debates. Derived from the Latin verb *credere*, "to believe" and "to trust," the noun *credit* and its cognates during this period had economic, legal, political, social, and cultural connotations. Used less frequently, *finance* referred primarily to government finances. The more capacious and common *commerce* was adopted by early modern commentators not only in reference to the activities of retail and wholesale merchants, but also to describe the economic policies governing those activities. But *commerce* had even wider meanings that transcended the economic realm. In the Italian city-states of the fifteenth century, the Latin word *commercium* denoted the material transactions conducted for the purpose of earthly gain and gratification, but it was used just as often in reference to the relationship between believers and the divine, the exchange of ideas among humanists, the social bonds linking all humans (or at least those men who saw each other as peers), and even prostitution (carnal commerce). Although the word *commerce* had a somewhat narrower meaning by the eighteenth century, it continued to be applied to the entire gamut of human activities and beliefs. It follows that technical disquisitions about credit instruments, and what might make them go astray, were never abstracted from moral, political, and social considerations.

Thus framed, the subject of my inquiry would be boundless, since the search for a well-tempered commercial society was at the heart of too many consequential intellectual and political projects in preindustrial Europe to be examined in any depth in a single study. In this book, I turn to one little-known but revealing chapter in these heated debates about the morality of credit: a narrative that for a good 250 years, from the mid-seventeenth to the early twentieth century, attributed to medieval Jews the invention of marine insurance and bills of exchange, two key instruments of European private finance. There is no truth to this tale, since both financial tools emerged slowly out of previous arrangements, and Jews had no special role in the process, yet it proved surprisingly resilient—which is why I believe it warrants the designation of *legend*. Over time, this unfounded and today largely forgotten origin story punctuated many and varied literatures about commerce. By working with and around this narrative about Jews and credit, I discuss how numerous Christian authors—some famous, some fallen into oblivion—articulated their vision for a morally acceptable and productive commercial society.

I take representations of Jews' economic roles to be symptomatic of larger claims: implicitly or explicitly, they conveyed hard-to-define ideals of a Christian-inflected marketplace rather than describing the actual involvement of Jews in the economy. This approach has been adopted almost exclusively in reference to the Middle Ages because of the widely held assumption that in the mid-seventeenth century, the "science of commerce" began to shed its religious concerns about merchants' moral integrity.[5] Here, I show instead that late medieval representations of Jews and their alleged modes of handling credit, recast in new guises at various junctions, continued to be central to the definition of European commercial society through the French Revolution and that the founders of modern social thought—Karl Marx, Max Weber, and Werner Sombart—incorporated these representations of medieval Jews' economic roles into their grand narratives.

In the pages that follow, readers will encounter familiar names and famous moments in European history, such as those I just mentioned, but will also be introduced to a host of unknown figures and unpredictable connections across themes and periods. In trying to make sense of fragments of the past that our blind spots have led us to neglect, I weave together strains of scholarship that have been growing further and further apart. That is why this book does not fall squarely into any single field of historical inquiry but is rather an exercise in demonstrating the potential (and, no doubt, the pitfalls) of roaming across times and places, blending economic and religious history, approaching the history of economic thought from new angles, and integrating Jewish history more fully into the narrative of Europe's past.

In piecing together the traces left by the legend that attributed to medieval Jews a foundational role in the creation of modern private finance, my ultimate aim is to demonstrate that throughout European history, debates about the market's reach have been inseparable from the construction of legal and symbolic hierarchies of inclusion and exclusion. The impersonality of the market is a recent ideal and remains an elusive reality.

THE PROMISE AND PERIL OF CREDIT

Introduction

FEW TODAY KNOW WHAT bills of exchange are or how they worked. But from the sixteenth through much of the nineteenth century, bills of exchange were ubiquitous across Europe. Around 1615, an English traveler visiting Venice counseled those interested in following his itinerary on how to obtain ready cash in local currency: "Returne thy money in England by bill of exchange that thou maiest receive it againe in Venice."[1] So many used these bills as remittances that they soon acquired metaphorical meanings. An Anglican preacher, for example, declared, "Our prayers are our bills of exchange; and they are allowed in Heaven, when they come from pious and humble hearts: But if wee bee broken in our religion, and bankrouts of grace, God will protest our bills, hee will not bee wonne with our prayers."[2] A century later, in the mid-eighteenth century, this system of payment fueled the darkest side of the booming Atlantic trade: the majority of slave cargoes in the British Caribbean were sold for bills of exchange redeemable in London.[3]

Credit default swaps, an innovation of the 1990s and the target of Buffett's censure, are only the latest creation of financial engineering, developed in order to facilitate both risk management and speculation. The rate of innovation in the financial sector of preindustrial Europe was slower than that seen today, but not imperceptible. Between 1250 and 1650, bills of exchange introduced considerable novelties, which is why they once were a venerable topic in economic and legal history. In those centuries, they boosted long-distance trade and international finance, and they remained the lifeblood of European and colonial commerce even after corporate stocks began to be sold in Amsterdam and London in the early seventeenth century. During the period of their use, bills of exchange garnered considerable attention among enthusiasts and critics alike, not only for their ability to move and generate wealth in seemingly mysterious ways, but also for their potential to trick naïve investors. As such, they epitomized the promise and the peril of early modern commercial credit.

What was so admirable and yet controversial about bills of exchange? Almost everything, especially in the eyes of the inexperienced. Materially, these bills (from the Latin word for "letter," *bulla*) were slips of paper, smaller than today's personal checks, on which someone who was legally or socially recognized as a merchant scribbled a few coded words before adding his (or, more rarely, her) signature. With these coded words, he ordered his agent to pay a specified amount, in a set currency and at a set date, to a third party. The original and principal function of bills of exchange was to transfer funds to distant locations where they could be redeemed in local currency and thus used to purchase goods or pay down a debt. They offered merchants a safe alternative to the transport of minted coins, protecting their wealth from pirates, corrupt customs guards, storms, and landslides. Over time, bills of exchange also came to be used for purely speculative purposes. Experienced and savvy bankers could buy and sell these instruments without any intent of acquiring merchandise but merely to profit from fluctuating currency exchange rates. In this respect they signaled private finance's incipient autonomy from commodity trade.

Bills of exchange were the invisible currency of early modern Europe's "international republic of money."[4] No formal membership was needed to join this commonwealth, which was made up of merchants who cooperated and competed with one another, spoke different languages, and hailed from different regions. A mixture of informal oversight and legal sanctions held this commonwealth together, and after the sixteenth century its boundaries expanded in conjunction with Europe's first period of sustained economic growth since the Black Death and the aggressive overseas expansion that accompanied it. What assured the circulation of bills of exchange among the members of this amorphous republic of money, as an eighteenth-century jurist noted, was "a merchant's reputation, the extent and solidity of his business, the wisdom of the banker ensuring the creditworthiness of those letters."[5] Given how little public information about the assets of private merchants was then available, anyone engaging in transactions involving these bills depended first and foremost on channels of epistolary communication, occasional informers, relatives, and distant friends. A commercial bank chartered in Vienna in 1787 demanded that Greek merchants provide three sound trading houses as guarantors if they wished to cash a second bill of exchange—a measure of the bank's difficulty in ascertaining the solvency of its clients.[6]

By the time their invention was attributed to Jews, bills of exchange were frequently endorsed and passed on from one holder to another. Consequently, they were often confused with money. However, unlike commodity money or minted coins, bills of exchange had no intrinsic value. Unlike paper money designated as legal tender (whether backed by precious metals or land or, more rarely in the early modern period, issued as fiat money), they were secured not by sovereign authorities but solely by the individuals who signed them. While a state that accepts paper money as a form of tax payment can oblige taxpayers to use that same paper money in their private transactions, the circulation of bills of exchange was entirely voluntary, and a merchant retained the right to refuse to pay a bill drawn on his name.

Naturally, bills of exchange had multiple connections to public finance. State agents, such as tax collectors or army suppliers, used them regularly to move funds from one region to another. More importantly, variations in currency exchange rates depended on the bullion reserves in the region, which in turn depended to a significant extent on a state's monetary and trade policy (although private merchants themselves sometimes moved bullion from one location to another in order to alter exchange rates). But unlike state bonds, annuities, and the stocks that financed chartered corporations, bills of exchange were primarily an instrument of private finance, and to study them challenges the conventional nexus drawn by historians between money and sovereignty.

The usefulness of bills of exchange was matched only by their opacity. This combination ensured that they came to symbolize what was most appealing and most anxiety generating about private credit. By moving funds in invisible ways across mountains and oceans, bills of exchange functioned as the lubricant of the "reciprocal commerce" celebrated by many Enlightenment thinkers. At the same time, the lack of transparency with which they fulfilled their functions caused many to worry that cliques of traders possessed undue advantages over others. Moreover, by abstracting value from any tangible referent, bills of exchange amplified widespread fears about social disintegration and the erosion of traditional hierarchies that accompanied the expansion of commerce.

Ultimately, bills of exchange represented the ability of merchants to regulate their own activity. Adam Smith regarded this self-regulation as beneficial to society at large, but he was neither the first nor the last to address the topic. This book examines some of the strongest reactions that bills of exchange, as emblems of merchants' self-regulation, generated among the learned public. It focuses on the metaphorical associations between these bills and Jews because this connection was frequently drawn in expressions of suspicion about the growing expansion and autonomy of private finance in early modern Europe.

Starting in the mid-seventeenth century, a number of authors, first in France and then across Europe, maintained that those Jews who had been expelled from the kingdom of France at various points in time between the seventh and fourteenth centuries had devised bills of exchange in order to evade the confiscation of their properties and to smuggle their wealth abroad. The guile of Jews and the resourcefulness of fugitives in general were the two lessons most commonly extracted from this narrative. From Old Regime France, the legend attributing to medieval Jews the invention of bills of exchange spread widely, with echoes heard as far as Brazil and Russia. Subsequently it was resurrected in the nineteenth century, when it informed some of the most influential narratives about the so-called Rise of the West and provoked harsh reactions among scholars of the Middle Ages during the interwar period.

Today, one is hard-pressed to find anyone who recognizes the existence (let alone deciphers the meaning) of this tale of origins, both within and beyond academia. I know of only one recent attempt to interrogate its significance: an article published in Hebrew in 2004 by Benjamin Arbel. The article's chief goal is to set the record straight and dispel any residual claim that Jews possessed superior financial prowess, although in the process Arbel unearths important and little-known facts about Jews' handling of bills of exchange in the sixteenth-century Mediterranean.[7]

My goal is different. Of course, I stress the lack of any empirical basis for the legend that pointed to Jews as the originators of European financial development. I insist, however, on treating the legend for what it is: a legend. I reconstruct the aspirations and collective fears of those who invoked it, the reasoning of those who contested it, and the agenda of those who reassembled its moving parts into ever more variations on a theme. In so doing, I map changing and conflicting attitudes toward commercial credit and discuss why Jews, who in the legend are figments of the Christian imagination, provided a broad spectrum of tropes through which those attitudes could be articulated.

The legend today is so mystifying that I have felt the need to unpack all its constitutive elements in considerable detail and to recount just how many forms it took and how many authors contended with it. The result is the long journey from the Middle Ages through the twentieth century traced in the coming pages. My larger ambition, put succinctly, is to show the heuristic value of Christian representations of Jewish economic roles for probing long-held narratives about the power and limits of the market to create more equal societies. I am not concerned with the question of whether or not Jews ever had a putatively special relationship with capitalism—a question that, incidentally, I do not believe can be treated separately from its intellectual genealogy. Nor do I posit that in early modern Europe it was impossible to talk about credit without talking about Jews. That would simply not be true. Rather, I draw attention to one consistent assumption that ran through different European cultures from the fourteenth to the twentieth centuries: the idea that Jews were nowhere and everywhere. This idea is at the heart of the legend of the Jewish invention of bills of exchange.

The theme of Jewish invisibility took different forms across time and space depending on the models of interaction with the majority-Christian society to which Jews were subjected: forced conversion, acculturation, or legal equality. After the mass conversions that followed the pogroms perpetrated in Spain in 1391, the difficulty of distinguishing Jewish converts to Catholicism from the rest of the population became the focus of ecclesiastical and secular efforts, which culminated in the "purity of blood" statutes (1448) and the establishment of a modern Inquisition (1478).[8] The decrees ordering the expulsion or forced conversion of Jews in Castile and Aragon (1492), Portugal (1497), and Navarre (1498) escalated the paranoia that surrounded these presumed "crypto-Jews." The legend of the Jewish invention of bills of exchange was born in the one region of Europe other than Iberia where, after the mid-sixteenth century, crypto-Judaism was a de facto reality: the southwest of France. There, Iberian refugees were welcomed as "Portuguese merchants" and, until 1723, were prohibited from practicing Judaism in the open but always suspected of doing so in secret. These so-called New Christians, the wealthiest of whom were concentrated in professions connected with maritime and regional trade, were treated as invisible Jews: their inner religious convictions (whatever they were) had to conform to the outward practice of Catholicism, but their allegiance to Catholicism and to the kingdom of France was constantly doubted; Jews were nowhere to be seen, but their financial power was assumed to be everywhere.

The invisibility of Jews in those port cities of western and Mediterranean Europe where Iberian converts were allowed to make a home as Jews after the late sixteenth century—notably Venice, Livorno, Amsterdam, Hamburg, and, later on, London—was of a different sort. It was neither theological nor complete but the result of a long process of acculturation and deliberate efforts to integrate this group into the fabric of commercial society. In those areas of Europe, Sephardic merchants acquired unprecedented contractual equality in the commercial sphere at the very same time that all merchants who were involved in long-distance trade largely abandoned guilds. The weakness of corporate organizations within the upper echelons of private international trade together with ad hoc policies designed to attract New Christian refugees with fortunes and trading connections meant that Sephardic merchants could now join the international republic of money in ways that they had not been able to do before. They could now enter into contracts with anyone of their choosing, uphold their property rights before secular courts, and even buy state bonds—a privilege that came with financial and symbolic benefits that had earlier been denied to Jewish bankers in medieval Italian city-states with a public debt.[9]

In many other respects, Sephardim continued to endure restrictive legal measures and to serve as the targets of scorn and mistrust. But their newly acquired economic privileges put pressure on existing corporate structures and engendered changes that extended well beyond the economic sphere. In both southern and northern Europe, Sephardic Jews cultivated the collective self-image of a respectable merchant community, subordinated some of their religious norms to the demands of commerce with non-Jews, and drew sharp lines between themselves and other Jewish groups that more visibly conformed to Christian stereotypes. Acculturated by choice or by necessity, these postexpulsion communities of New Christians and New Jews, small as they were, were prized for their commercial skills, better liked than their Ashkenazi brethren (because they were more in tune with the local customs), and yet still not fully trusted to play by the rules of Christian commerical society. As a result, they represented both the progress and the dangers of market exchanges that increasingly transcended the traditional hierarchies of clearly demarcated corporate entities.

After the French Revolution granted Jewish men citizenship rights, making them legally indistinguishable from their peers, Jews' invisibility assumed yet another guise—and the most paradoxical to date. Assimilation bred new fears of Jewish separatism. Indistinguishable from the broader polity but supposedly clannish, Jews were now seen as willing and able to undermine the nation from within in ways that were particularly difficult to unmask. This view soon became the mantra of conservative thinkers, but it appeared with different intensities across a large spectrum of authors and framed the legend's postemancipation meanings. In Old Regime corporate societies, the fears caused by the emergence of an increasingly impersonal commercial world could be pinned on a group that was highly acculturated but still legally and socially distinct from the dominant one. (Marriages between Jews and Christians, for example, required the conversion of one or the other spouse.) Later, in the postemancipation regimes' atmosphere of aspiring universalism, those who did not trust the invisible hand to control misbehavior could resurrect ancient tropes and identify Jews as the obscure force behind economic abuse and corruption. During the democratic age, a new essentialism regarding Jews' collective traits took shape, which, like so-called scientific racism, hardened those hierarchies that legal equality had sought to soften.

The legend of the Jewish invention of bills of exchange emerged and evolved as part of the collective suspicion produced by forced baptism, acculturation, and assimilation—three very different phenomena, but all accompanied by apprehensions about moral contagion and the subversion of the established order. Throughout this book, I will illustrate how easily the anxieties created by Jews' potential invisibility in the marketplace could be mapped onto the increasing abstraction of the paper economy. The legend's myriad threads, in other words, bring to the fore the misgivings that went hand in hand with the rise of capitalism and formal equality as pillars of European modernity.

———

Turning from topic to approach, I wish to single out three broad historiographical debates on which my analysis impinges. The first is the question of what constitutes "the economy" as a field of inquiry and what is included in the canon we use to access this field, a concern that has become particularly relevant in light of the impact of the digital revolution on the study of Europe's past. The second is the relationship between what we might call "practices" and "representations" and the tendency some scholars have had to pit the two against each other. Finally, the third is the perennial question of periodization, which Jewish history and Christian prejudice toward Jews bring into sharp relief, especially when, as I do, we examine a singular but mutable figure, the Jewish usurer, across several historical periods. The next three sections expand on each of these problems.

The *Ars Mercatoria*: Sources and Canons

I first encountered what I later started to call the legend of the Jewish invention of bills of exchange while rereading Jacques Savary's *Le parfait négociant* (1675), the single most influential merchant manual of early modern Europe. I was looking for something else, but a chapter on the origins of bills of exchange caught my attention. It stated that Jews expelled from France between the years 640 and 1316 had invented these bills as a way of sheltering their assets when fleeing the kingdom.[10] I was surprised. The story was riveting, and in spite of many years spent reading about commerce and Jews, I had never heard of it. *Le parfait négociant* was a blockbuster, so influential and rich in information that it is difficult to imagine an economic historian of preindustrial Europe without at least a cursory knowledge of it. So why had I never heard of this story? Arguably, economic historians ignored it because it was unfounded, while Jewish historians, who might have noticed it, were unlikely to peruse such a source.

Since I was sitting near a computer linked to my university's library system, I typed a few keywords into an online database, *The Making of the Modern World*, to see if I could find other mentions of the story and, ideally, its provenance. It did not take long at all before I identified a title I was not familiar with and that, it turned out, none of the colleagues I consulted knew either: Étienne Cleirac's *Us et coustumes*, a compilation of maritime laws accompanied by extensive commentary printed in Bordeaux in 1647.[11] The first steps of my research went quickly. It took much longer to reconstruct the genealogy of what I now describe as a legend and to unravel its meanings and ramifications.

In 1977, Albert Hirschman opened his *The Passions and the Interests*, a brilliant work that is critically important for my purposes, by noting that during the seventeenth and eighteenth centuries, "with the 'disciplines' of economics and political science not yet in existence at the time, there were no interdisciplinary boundaries to cross."[12] This observation captures not only the spirit of its author, impatient as Hirschman was with all disciplinary strictures, but also the amorphous nature of the sources on which my investigation is based. Today a number of electronic repositories of printed material from early modern Europe permit us to re-create the vastness of the archives that Hirschman had in mind and to mine them beyond the key texts he sampled in support of his influential account of the emergence of the idea that commerce promoted proto-democratic political regimes.

My book is proof that digital libraries can serve as a powerful corrective to anachronism insofar as they broaden the canon of texts and authors that we can scrutinize. Countless scholars before me undoubtedly read the chapter in Savary's *Le parfait négociant* that ascribes to medieval French Jews the invention of bills of exchange. Savary cites no source for this narrative. Short of monstrous erudition or a stroke of good luck, how could anyone trace the roots of his account or its evolution over time? It is thanks to *The Making of the Modern World* that I was able to bring Cleirac's *Us et coustumes de la mer,* a work that few today have heard of, back into the fold of the writings on all things relating to commerce and the economy, or *ars mercatoria*, where it once held pride of place. Inquiries about the boundaries of the canon are certainly not new; traditional bibliographical and reading methods have already yielded consequential insights, and I am hardly the first to rely on digital libraries.[13] But digital collections and their potential grow by the day, and they have been used less in European economic history than in other fields (see appendix 1).

There are, of course, serious limits to the productive disturbance that data-mining tools can produce. In the case of *The Making of the Modern World*, the exclusion of manuscript sources, the overrepresentation of English-language texts, and the imperfection of its optical recognition devices caution us against using it as the referential universe for a statistical analysis of the incidence of certain keywords. For this and other reasons, I chose to cast "distant reading" aside—that is, not to resort to quantitative treatments of published titles but to rely instead on a more conventional combination of close and contextualized reading.[14]

The availability of digital platforms has nonetheless been critical to my ability to map the legend's transmission and sketch the larger labyrinth of textual worlds within which it traveled. Since early modern authors (with the exception of biblical and legal scholars) made sparing use of footnotes or other bibliographical reference systems, full-text keyword searches are crucial to identifying chains of intertextuality. Moreover, to speak of a canon is to refer not only to a set of texts and authors, but also to their classification into schools of thought—in our case, those of mercantilism, anticommercial classical republicanism, *doux commerce*, the Gournay circle, and physiocracy, to cite only the most well-known trends within French economic thought from the late seventeenth century to the Revolution. Of course, many scholars have challenged the stability of these "schools." Scans of searchable digital libraries challenge these traditional interpretive frames even more. References to the legend of the Jewish origins of bills of exchange are sometimes the result of intentional borrowings and other times the byproduct of uncritical copying. They cross genres and widely accepted ideological fault lines to the point of blurring those lines.

Images as Practices, Practices as Images

In addition to questions about sources and reading modalities, I was drawn to this project because the study of both commercial credit and Jewish life in premodern Europe defies the traditional division of labor between intellectual and cultural historians, on the one hand, and social and economic historians, on the other. The so-called "history wars" of the last quarter of the twentieth century raised important epistemological questions about the relationship between discourse, power, and social change, but also built high walls between practitioners of different areas of historical inquiry. The chapters that follow constitute my effort to surmount these walls, even as I am all too aware of the reasons why they exist and the difficulty of meshing dissimilar approaches.

My inquiry began not with any specific interest in the legend of the Jewish invention of bills of exchange, but with a puzzle: early modern merchant manuals and dictionaries of trade aimed at legitimizing commerce and laid out the norms that facilitated engagement in commercial transactions beyond close-knit groups, but they were also peppered with stereotypes about certain communities of traders. Why did these stereotypes multiply alongside the effort to broaden the boundaries of European commercial society? What was the meaning of these biases? Did they inform a proto-sociology of merchants, or did they serve a different function? And what accounted for the attributes ascribed to each group? Savary and many other commentators, as we will see, compared Jewish merchants to those from eastern churches, such as Armenians and Greeks, and even to some groups from Central and South Asia. How did these seeds of Orientalism emerge, evolve, and crystallize in European commercial literature, which sometimes contrasted one group with another and other times lumped all of them together as paragons of economic slyness? What impact did these images have on merchants' strategies? That is, what kind of signals, if any, did labels such as "Jews," "Greeks," and "Armenians" send in competitive marketplaces plagued by a scarcity of information about the creditworthiness of individual actors, especially those coming to town from afar or moving within separate circles?

A related and complementary set of questions concerns the status and credibility of women. In eighteenth-century Paris, for example, it became easier for aristocratic women to obtain credit in the growing number of shops where the latest fashionable garments were sold, even if in reality they were not always in a position to repay their debts—an indication that rank remained a pivot of economic reputation.[15] Contemporary Enlightenment texts often identified women as avatars of luxury and consumption, whether to condemn the volatility and corruption of commercial society or, by contrast, to exalt its expanding possibilities. There are obvious parallels between women and Jews and their respective positions in credit markets, not least because both groups were deprived of legal equality during the Old Regime. There are also many differences in the access that each group had to credit and to legal recourse, as well as obvious differences in the economic power enjoyed by a variety of Jewish and Christian women. In eighteenth-century France, only women who were members of a guild or merchants' widows who were "publically known as merchants" could legally sign bills of exchange, but there is evidence that transgressions of this norm occurred. When and how were women able to obtain commercial credit? How did social perception affect their reputation in the sphere of market transactions? Although I am unable to take up these issues in this book, I spell them out because they animate my broader agenda and might provide the impetus for further comparisons of the legal and social purchase of different marginalized groups.

Cultural constructions of propriety in credit markets do not speak solely to questions of representation but also fulfill regulatory functions, albeit in ways difficult to measure. A merchant's reputation was the black box of premodern commercial credit. It follows that the reputation of Jewish merchants in Christian Europe, like that of other stigmatized minorities, was normally a product of both documented individual behavior and collective stereotyping. The goal of my analysis is not to calculate the degree to which belief in the legend of the Jewish invention of bills of exchange affected credit relations between individual Jews and non-Jews, but to show that the legend's intellectual evolution was nourished by and gave voice to preoccupations that were real and tangible. Rightly or wrongly, an individual's public conduct was usually taken to be a reflection of his or her aptitude and financial standing. But could all individuals control their public image—or were some seen through a collective lens? Who was subjected to this vetting and when?

As a general rule, the greater the uncertainty under which credit relations are established, the more tempting, and arguably sensible, it is for lenders to resort to collective stereotypes in judging potential borrowers. Imperfect as they are in measuring an individual's competence and rectitude, collective stereotypes in premodern societies reflected the existence of segmented communities, each of which was the object of greater or lesser mistrust and more or less able to monitor its members. The notion that collective stereotyping in credit markets is discriminatory is very recent, both culturally and legally. Even in today's markets, which are comparatively more open and freer from overt discrimination, actors often resort to what economic sociologists call "status signals" in order to advertise their performance and products.[16]

A simple fact is indicative of the legend's normative function in the commercial sphere: the tale did not first appear in the sermon of a Franciscan friar, an Elizabethan play, an anti-usury tract, or a Christian polemic against the so-called "errors of the Jews"—all genres that abounded at the time and reveled in antisemitic tropes. Rather, its earliest and principal vehicles were compilations intended to valorize the role of commerce in a feudal society and to offer merchants concrete guidance. Occasionally, we also find mentions of the legend in the everyday documents drafted by French Catholic merchants. A report submitted in 1702 by the Deputies of Commerce, a council of twelve merchants from the kingdom's major cities charged with advising the crown, asked the king to curb the "abuses" committed by tax farmers and state financiers who surreptitiously exported funds by means of bills of exchange. The report was far from an indictment of bills of exchange as such, but by opening with a recapitulation of their supposed invention by the Jews expelled from France "on account of their usuries," it arguably appropriated the legend in order to introduce the notion that there were more and less legitimate ways of handling those bills.[17]

This is a striking example of the fact that we cannot assume that a sort of pragmatic tolerance infused merchant culture. The moralizing and sometimes venomous tone of petitions and didactic literature produced by and/or for merchants had a clear prescriptive value. After all, the parameters of public action that rulers set for different merchant groups responded to the public perception of each of these groups and a generalized distrust of Jews' loyalty to the state and to society. In the absence of a modern conception of separation between church and state, Jews' rejection of Christian revelation cast them in the eyes of elites and the uneducated alike as infidels lacking *fama* and *fides*, that is, public reputation and trustworthiness. For this reason, although the legal status of Jews varied greatly from place to place, nowhere could they hold public office, join craft guilds, or give testimony against Christians in a court of law.

Negative group stereotypes tend to be remarkably impermeable to reality, even as they possess a striking ability to conjure new meanings out of a finite repertoire. This twin characteristic is a distinctive feature of Christian prejudice against Jews and is apparent in the legend under investigation, which fused medieval clichés about Jewish usury and seventeenth-century exaggerated admiration for Jewish commerce. Jewish lending to Christians in the late Middle Ages was largely confined to pawnbroking for the poor and loans to rulers. Bills of exchange, by contrast, were icons of the early modern paper economy, capable of moving funds across distances in invisible ways, yielding profits with no direct connection to the sale of material goods, and proving susceptible to equally mysterious defaults. In spite of new regulations issued after the sixteenth century by municipal, state, and fair authorities, bills of exchange were difficult to monitor, and in the matter of their management, expert merchants somehow always knew better than lawyers, judges, and government officials.

By pointing to Jews as the inventors of bills of exchange, the legend did not identify any specific type of abuse that was occurring but rather cast suspicion on commercial credit in general by playing into widely shared cultural assumptions about Jews' unscrupulous dealings. In so doing, the legend became a substitute for hard-to-define normative criteria for the rightful handling of bills of exchange. Its subsequent adaptations, then, recombined different elements of the sketchy historical narrative on which it was grounded for different ends. Some of these accounts were closer to the original version than others, but all grappled with the aspirations and fears generated by the paper credit instruments' abstraction of wealth from tangible assets.

In this respect, my approach echoes William Sewell, Jr.'s self-consciously oxymoronic quest to write "a concrete history of social abstraction," that is, a history of those practices and institutions that created the conditions for more anonymous market exchanges and were thus part of the process by which the market became a metaphor for a democratic political order.[18] Bills of exchange lend themselves particularly well to this task. As material artifacts, they had no intrinsic value. Their monetary worth was the measure of the credibility assigned to the chains of signatories who backed them, rather than of any sovereign authority. At the same time, because they had to be physically transported from one place to another in order to be redeemed, their circulation depended on concrete communication infrastructures and was embedded in personal networks of recognition, which relied on epistolary exchanges and other verification systems.

But I also insist more than Sewell probably would on the asymmetric nature of the exchanges that these abstract credit instruments promoted. His interest in isolating the social practices that underpinned the eruption of egalitarianism during the revolutionary years has led him, in my view, to overestimate the transparency and openness of Parisian coffeehouses and promenades, which he regards as spaces where men and, to an increasing degree, women disguised their legal identities in ways that subverted a cardinal principle of Old Regime hierarchies: status. Recovering Jürgen Habermas's explicitly neo-Marxist approach (which previous Anglophone appropriations of Habermas had largely eschewed), Sewell overplays the egalitarian ethos of the proto-capitalist classes.[19] I believe that we ought to take his invitation to locate the material bases of emerging social abstraction and democratic politics seriously, but that we cannot overlook the apprehension that anonymity generated or the lack of fairness that plagued competitive markets of the time.[20]

Bills of exchange are ideal objects for this type of analysis because they embody the tension that existed between egalitarianism and oligopolies in early modern commercial credit markets. Their diffusion was greeted by praise of their utility but also denunciations of the potential harm they could inflict. Jonathan Sheehan and Dror Warman have recently argued that the South Sea Bubble of 1720 triggered a Europe-wide intellectual and cultural shift that displaced both providentialism and mechanical materialism in favor of the concept of self-organization in many spheres of intellectual inquiry.[21] There may be an interesting coincidence between the 1720 financial crash and a host of philosophical trends, but in the realm of economic thought, broadly conceived, self-organization had by this time already been recognized as a powerful force. Self-organization is in fact what bills of exchange epitomized and to what the legend of the Jewish invention of bills of exchange responded. Merchants' autonomy and self-organization were both desirable and unsettling. The legend offered no solution to this conundrum but, in most of its permutations, acted as a warning, because Christian observers agreed that to trade bills of exchange "in the Jewish manner" meant something dangerous and unwelcome.

Continuities and Change

Formulated in the mid-seventeenth century as money markets were becoming more and more impersonal, the legend of the Jewish origin of bills of exchange grafted medieval clichés about Jewish pawnbroking onto the early modern reality of new instruments of credit. By the early twentieth century, then, this story became a pseudo-fact in credible academic accounts. This exceedingly long chronology raises questions about the permanence and reconstitution of stereotypes. These questions in turn prompt us to probe the pertinence of labels such as "medieval," "early modern," and "modern" for Jewish and European history at large.

Those scholars of European Jewry who are wedded to a "lachrymose" narrative are also prone to emphasize continuity, in the form of persecution, rather than change (although considerable disagreement exists about whether racialized antisemitism in the second half of the nineteenth century constituted a new phenomenon or a mere evolution of preexisting themes). By contrast, confronted with the variety of manifestations of Jewish life and thought, many historians tend to stress adaptation more or at least as much as discrimination.[22]

Every inquiry into Christian representations of Jews, however, shows that this contrast is overly simplistic. Prejudice is at once tenacious and protean. It builds on motifs from earlier times that are transmitted through both learned and popular culture and at the same time gives voice to tensions that are locally bound and highly specific. This dual nature of prejudice is fully reflected in the legend of the Jewish invention of bills of exchange. That is also why by the mid-eighteenth century, different characterizations of the economic roles played by Jews began to correspond to larger narratives about continuity and change between what today we refer to as the "medieval" and "early modern" periods in European history. Montesquieu's *The Spirit of the Laws* (1748) linked the notion of Jews as forerunners of European capitalism to the view of the medieval church as an anticommercial institution and in so doing cast a long shadow over future scholarly endeavors and lay conceptions alike. For the French philosophe, in the Middle Ages Jews dominated commerce because the church demonized commerce and therefore good Christians shunned it. In his view, Jews invented bills of exchange at the time of Europe's maritime explorations and colonial expansion—the onset of what today we would call early modernity—and thus helped inaugurate a new epoch during which the influence of the church receded and commerce promoted "softer" politics and social mores.

For generations to come, progressive liberal historians seized upon the caesura that Montesquieu posited between a Catholic obscurantist Middle Ages and a secular early modernity propelled by commerce, and branded it into a standard periodization. Marxist and conservative social theorists also embraced the philosophe's discontinuity between the Middle Ages and the sixteenth century, albeit with different cultural and political valences. In the interwar period, however, specialists of medieval Europe challenged this paradigmatic chronology by dating the origins of modern European capitalism to the twelfth and thirteenth centuries and portraying it as a notable achievement of Christian communal civilization, untainted by Jewish influence. Since the 1970s, the marginalization of the sixteenth century—the period when bills of exchange gave rise to new forms of financialization—in the historiography of European economy and economic thought has reintroduced the idea of a sharp break between late medieval and early modern financial institutions.

Through a different set of reflections, scholars of European Jewry have also come to emphasize discontinuity and now recognize three distinct moments in Christian thought about Jews' economic roles across the medieval and early modern periods, each with its own temporal and geographical specificities. The first moment, which coincided with the economic boom of Italian city-states and culminated in the norms issued at the Fourth Lateran Council (1215) to regulate the Jewish presence amid Christians, was dominated by writings on usury by moral theologians and canon lawyers. There are two sides to the thirteenth-century conception of usury, which shaped European representations of Jews and credit for centuries to come. On the one hand, Jews were thought to embody the practice of usury. Having denied the divinity of Christ, they were presumed to feel no allegiance to the Christians among whom they lived and whom they cheated at liberty. As proof and consequence of Jews' theological infidelity, secular rulers assigned to them the function of pawnbrokers and allowed them to charge high interest rates. On the other hand, both religious and lay commentators defined usury (the opposite of charity) as the ultimate antisocial behavior, one that was not a prerogative of Jews. Franciscan friars, in particular, who proved instrumental in devising a Christian ethic for the urban renewal of late medieval Italy, formulated a conception of Jewish usury as a metric against which to measure everyone's conduct. If Jews were programmed to exploit Christians, all economically exploitative behavior could be portrayed as metaphorically Jewish.[23]

After the mid-sixteenth century, in pockets of Europe there emerged a second discourse, which was also linked to a new set of policies, dubbed "philosemitic mercantilism" by Jonathan Israel.[24] These policies favored greater inclusion for Jews on the grounds that they possessed unique commercial skills that could benefit both the state and society in an age of growing competition between European powers for the control of overseas resources and territories. Although far more inclusive of real-life Jews than their medieval antecedents, seventeenth-century doctrines of toleration inspired by philosemitic mercantilism still regarded Jews as a discrete and potentially oligopolistic group that required ad hoc regulation within a corporate social order. These doctrines left no room for ideals regarding the anonymity of the market and all-around free competition. In Bordeaux, where Cleirac lived and wrote, the French crown implemented policies founded on a peculiar version of these beliefs.

Finally, a third discourse on the connection between Jews and the monied economy appeared along the Franco-German border in the last quarter of the eighteenth century. This late Enlightenment discourse is the most familiar to us because it still informs a good portion of modern historiography. It postulates that Jews' hyperspecialization in commerce was the result of historical circumstances rather than nature. According to this account, since the fall of the Second Temple in 70 CE, centuries of persecution and exclusion from other economic sectors imposed by Christian rulers forced Jews to devote themselves to commerce; in the process, Jews came to excel at it. This discourse has been called a "new paradigm" because, unlike previous ones, it relieved Jews of any blame, condemned their oppressors, assumed the reversibility of Jews' economic proclivities, and went further than any existing theory of toleration in advocating Jewish civic and political equality.[25]

There are good reasons to stress the differences among these three discourses, including the rejection of a "lachrymose" narrative of fixed enmity against Jews. At the same time, this tripartite scheme errs on the side of discontinuity, eliding the facility with which elements from each of these discourses migrated from one to the other and were recycled in new syntheses. The fusion of the figure of the medieval Jewish pawnbroker with that of the all-powerful early modern Jewish merchant, for example, became complete in France during the last quarter of the eighteenth century in the course of debates about whether or not to grant equal rights to Jewish men. No champion of the Jewish cause advanced an argument based on Jews' commercial prowess or heralded as models the highly acculturated Sephardim of Bordeaux, although some scholars today argue that this group's success provided reformers with the rationale for granting French Jews legal equality. In fact, the process leading to the first emancipation of Jews in Europe reveals that ostensibly positive assessments of Jewish contributions to commerce never rendered medieval images of Jewish usurers obsolete.

The tripartite scheme that currently dominates scholarship on Christian images of Jews' economic roles also leaves out an important chapter in the history of early modern European economic thought: sixteenth-century debates on legitimate and illegitimate forms of credit and the role that representations of Jews played in them. Europe's greatest economic thinkers in the sixteenth century were Scholastic moral theologians who sought to adapt Aristotle's preference for a natural economy of subsistence to the contemporary growth of international trade. The result was the condemnation of those merchants whose sole purpose was to "fructify" wealth and the valorization of those merchants who redressed the God-given unequal distribution of resource endowments across the planet by carrying goods from one region to another. Contrary to the claims of an older historiography, Scholastic condemnations of usury were rarely generalized, blanket statements, if only because the church was itself involved in financial affairs by its administration of immense landed and movable wealth. Even in the medieval Catholic tradition, the vilification of improper credit practices coexisted alongside positive depictions of respectable merchants, who were often portrayed as upright leaders of civic and political institutions. The early modern period inherited from the thirteenth century not only the difficulty of distinguishing wicked from reputable financial transactions, but also the habit of resorting to images of Jews to draw such distinctions.

The tenacity of this double construction of usury, with its literal and figurative cogency, not only reinforced the assumption that Jews would always act unfairly in credit markets but also ensured that they became synonyms for self-serving economic practices in general. Ultimately this capacious definition of Jewish usury would be used to police membership in the medieval *civitas*, the eighteenth-century *société*, and the postemancipation nation-state.

1

The Setting

MARINE INSURANCE AND BILLS OF EXCHANGE

Insurance policies and bills of exchange were unknown to ancient Roman
jurisprudence and are the posthumous invention of Jews, according to the
remarks of Giovan[ni] Villani in his universal history.[1]

THOUSANDS HAVE READ this passage since it first appeared in print in 1647,
yet we still do not know what to make of it. The statement is patently false:
Jews invented neither marine insurance nor bills of exchange. Nevertheless,
for nearly three centuries, it captured the imagination of a great many authors—some famous and others today regarded as inconsequential but once
read widely. My aim in this book is twofold: to demonstrate that this tale of
origins was once so well known that it can justly be called a legend and, by
understanding its significance and reverberations, to shed new light on Europe's cultural and intellectual entanglements with economic modernity.[2]

The quotation claiming that Jews invented marine insurance and bills of
exchange is lifted from a compilation of maritime laws assembled with commentary by a provincial French lawyer, Étienne Cleirac, published in Bordeaux
under the title *Us et coustumes de la mer* (*Usages and Customs of the Sea*). Forgotten as much as the story it relays, this volume, as we will see, was a
seventeenth-century publishing success. In this and the next two chapters, I
peel back the layers of each historical and textual reference made by Cleirac in
the three lines cited above and in the longer segment of commentary—roughly
seven pages of printed text—to which they belong. In so doing, I unlock the
explicit and, even more crucially, implicit meanings that contemporary readers

would have gleaned from this narrative. I begin by describing the characteristics of the two financial instruments that Cleirac invokes, marine insurance and bills of exchange, in order to make clear what his audience would have known about them. Chapters 2 and 3 will then review the bewildering assortment of citations that Cleirac weaves into this tale of origins, including his false attribution of it to the medieval Florentine chronicler Giovanni Villani (d. 1348).

Cleirac's prose is undisciplined even by period standards, as the short excerpts included in the next several page indicate (and they are the least meandering in his commentary!). It is for this reason that I parse his words almost one by one. My exegesis will show that out of a hodgepodge of citations, which range from St. Paul to Matthew Paris, from French chroniclers to Jesuit theologians, from Dante to Ariosto and beyond, his consistent preoccupation emerges: how to distinguish good from bad creditors, and good from bad credit instruments, in an increasingly impersonal market. The legend that Cleirac committed to the printed page proved to be a gripping, if inadequate, answer to the thorny problem of where to draw the line between illegitimate and appropriate credit relations, a problem that the commercial revolution of the Middle Ages had raised and the further diffusion of new credit instruments in the sixteenth century had made impossible to avoid.

My interpretative practice is loosely indebted to symptomatic reading, that is, a reading modality that urges critics to unveil the latent meanings that lie beneath the surface of a text.[3] In so doing, I uncover a powerful discourse that drew from Catholic definitions of usury and adapted them to a seventeenth-century reality in which marine insurance and bills of exchange were widely used. The result, as I will elucidate, had a seductive rhetorical purchase.

Why Marine Insurance and Bills of Exchange?

The passage quoted at the opening of this chapter, which sums up the legend of these financial instruments' Jewish origins, appears in Cleirac's commentary on the first article of the *Guidon de la mer* (*The Standard of the Sea*), a set of maritime rules promulgated in Rouen in the mid- to late sixteenth century and reprinted in *Us et coustumes de la mer*. The *Guidon*, as the title of its first article—"On the contracts or policies of insurance: Their definition, conformity, and differences from other maritime contracts"—suggests, was devoted to marine insurance. It made no mention of bills of exchange. It was Cleirac who linked the two credit instruments to one another. His argument was historically baseless but had its own logic: after inventing bills of exchange, he claimed, Jews also had to invent marine insurance in order to protect the value of the assets they had left behind—value on which they expected their bills of exchange to be drawn.

Marine insurance and bills of exchange were among the most prized by-products of the commercial revolution of the twelfth and thirteenth centuries, which, unlike the industrial revolution that followed half a millennium later, was propelled by institutional more than technological change. They made it easier for investors to conduct their business without leaving their home base and formed the connective tissues of European long-distance trade.[4] At the same time, both marine insurance and bills of exchange became the objects of intense theological and canonistic debates concerning usury.

No single person or group invented either of these instruments. Both went through a long period of incubation and incremental evolution, which reached maturity in the sixteenth century.[5] Three trends characterized this formative period in the history of European commercial credit instruments. First, although marine insurance and bills of exchange were designed to facilitate transactions conducted at a distance, considerable variations existed in the local norms that regulated their issuance and use. These variations inevitably generated uncertainty. Second, while marine insurance and bills of exchange became more and more standardized, ordinary, and common over time, they also increased in complexity and sophistication. These developments rendered them opaque in the eyes of the uninitiated. Last, by the early modern period, merchants no longer needed to notarize these (and other) business contracts. In continental Europe, notaries were public officials who charged small fees in return for issuing documents that courts would accept as evidence. Both rich and poor went to notaries to protect their property rights. An exception was made for merchants, who processed too much paperwork to be bothered to notarize each of their obligations, and so their signature appended to a contract styled in conformity with written norms and accepted practices came to suffice as legal proof. After the mid-fourteenth century, bills of exchange, too, ceased to be notarized.[6]

For our purposes, the latter shift had two important consequences. It granted European merchants an unusually high degree of self-regulation, since no other social group in Roman law countries was equally able to certify its own property rights. Moreover, in the cities of western Europe where Jews were allowed to reside as international merchants rather than as pawnbrokers after the late sixteenth century, Jewish merchants were permitted to forgo notarization like all other merchants and to bring their papers before Christian tribunals. This legal framework, designed to make access to the market more generalized, eased commercial credit relations between Jews and non-Jews; at the same time, it also blurred the distinction between the two groups in the eyes of those who did not wish to see that distinction undone.

Marine Insurance

Marine insurance contracts grew out of previous risk-sharing contracts, notably sea loans, which had existed in the Mediterranean since antiquity with the dual function of financing overseas trade and reducing its uncertainty.[7] Premium-based insurance was an innovation of the mid-fourteenth century that soon spread from the Italian maritime republics to other regions of Europe. Its principles were analogous to those of today's insurance. The premium was expressed as a percentage of the declared value of the items that were being insured and generally included the broker's fees. In case of a legitimate loss, the underwriter owed the insured party the declared value of the items that had been insured. By the time Cleirac composed his commentary, it was possible to insure not only cargo but also the ship and its infrastructure, as well as passengers (in case they fell prey to infidel captors), and even to resell the insurance contract to another underwriter.[8]

While sea loans were issued against collateral (whether the ship or its cargo), the price of marine insurance was determined by underwriters on account of their knowledge of vessels, captains, routes, wars, piracy, and other elements affecting the likelihood of an accident at sea. Information was thus key to making a profit, but it was unevenly distributed. Although actuarial computation of mortality trends appeared in the seventeenth century, no public statistics were available for calculating insurance premiums. The incremental standardization and professionalization of the purchase, sale, and litigation of marine insurance offered only partial solutions to structural risks.

Long before Cleirac declared marine insurance a Jewish invention, the terms of most insurance policies were outlined in preprinted forms. In 1524, Florence mandated the adoption of a standard formula and the registration of all policies.[9] After considerable debate over its specifics, a model contract was issued in Antwerp in 1571.[10] In many port cities, licensed bodies of specialized brokers developed alongside courts devoted to adjudicating disputes concerning insurance policies, while statutory norms, treatises, and ordinances on the subject proliferated. A tribunal for lawsuits concerning marine insurance

(*Kamer von assurantie en avarij*, or Chamber of Insurance and Average) was instituted in 1598 by the Amsterdam municipal council and approved by the States of Holland in 1612. Analogous institutions were subsequently created in London (1601), Rotterdam (1614), Marseilles (1669), and Paris (1671).[11] In 1673, France's finance minister, Jean-Baptiste Colbert, proposed the establishment of a chamber of insurance in Bordeaux, where Cleirac resided.[12]

The circulation of printed premium quotations between set locations arguably led to price convergences, and some merchants and ship owners purchased their policies abroad at competitive rates. Modern calculations based on surviving documents suggest that experienced brokers and underwriters knew how to price insurance by the mid-sixteenth century.[13] Expertise, however, varied greatly. Lorraine Daston concludes that "the system for determining the premium . . . relied on a combination of experience, intuition, and conventions," rather than on actuarial models. Looking at the very text we are examining here, she observes that "nowhere . . . in his comprehensive survey of maritime insurance does Cleirac offer any specific guidelines to pricing."[14] In other words, in the absence of hard facts, an underwriter's know-how, which was largely a measure of his local connections and access to reliable correspondents abroad, mattered a great deal.

Conventional as it was, this system elicited concerns about honesty and transparency. Some merchants tried to insure ships they knew had already been lost, hoping the news had not yet reached their underwriters. Some underwriters spread rumors about the capture of valuable vessels in order to induce ship owners to accept higher premiums. As the speculative character of marine insurance increased, overly confident but sometimes ill-informed investors were drawn into the field and lost fortunes, as happened in Bordeaux during the Franco-Dutch War of 1672–1678.[15] In short, even as it became a fixture of overseas trade, marine insurance continued to disquiet observers. While the instrument helpfully distributed risks across individuals and groups, it retained a similarity to gambling and never dispelled the legitimate fear that certain individuals and groups possessed a disproportionate amount of information on the basis of which they could adjust prices.

Compared to more sober sources, Cleirac's commentary, full of digressions and hyperbole, may appear to exaggerate this fear, but its rhetorical excess is better understood in the context of contemporary regulatory institutions' inability to enforce proper conduct. Even in Amsterdam, the seventeenth-century financial capital of Europe and the city that most resembled an open-access commercial society with equal protection for all its participants, worries that expertise could lead to the emergence of oligopolies surfaced frequently. Until 1772, individual underwriters and brokers dominated the insurance market, while attempts to set up large companies or a centralized office were struck down for fear that they would give rise to serious market manipulation. A guild of insurance brokers was created in 1578, although unlicensed brokers still continued to operate after its appearance. Jewish merchants, who had a significant presence in Amsterdam, were permitted to join the guild only in fixed numbers. In spite of this restriction, some Christian brokers described their Jewish colleagues as either inept or unfair—two common refrains of anti-Jewish polemics of the time.[16] In contrast to these guild records, however, notarial deeds show Jewish merchants to have been well integrated into an insurance market dominated by Christian underwriters.[17] This discrepancy suggests that even in the most tolerant European city, where Jews enjoyed unparalleled freedom of thought and economic action, they still symbolized dishonest competition.

Bills of Exchange

If marine insurance prompted qualms about abuses and oligopolies, bills of exchange elicited even greater apprehension. Singular instruments in the landscape of premodern finance, bills of exchange functioned simultaneously as credit contracts and as means of currency exchange. Those who used them testified to their intricacies. Writing in the mid-fifteenth century, the Veneto-Dalmatian merchant-writer Benedetto Cotrugli (1416–1469) noted that it had taken him two years of practice to learn how to use them.[18] In the 1630s, an English merchant of the Levant Company took it upon himself to jot down "the explanation of the mystery of exchange." His phrasing was perhaps aimed at wooing readers, but since the book was reissued in 1671, 1677, and 1700, there was clearly an audience for such an explication.[19] Even to a jurist as versed in commercial law as Sigismondo Scaccia, bills of exchange appeared to be an "obscure, difficult, and dangerous subject," something akin to "alchemy."[20]

By the time Cleirac set out to write his commentary, bills of exchange were no longer a novelty but had become even more complex than marine insurance. As remittances, their primary function was to transfer funds to a distant location while also ensuring that those funds were made available in the desired local currency. Over time, as we shall see, international bankers also used these bills as speculative instruments involving complicated transactions.

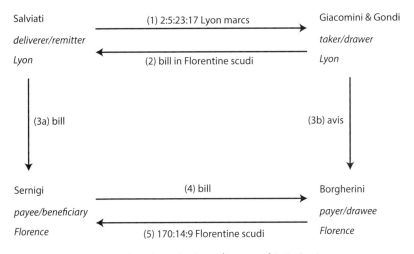

FIGURE 1.1. Flow chart of a classic (four-party) bill of exchange

Figure 1.1 illustrates the flow of money in a classic bill of exchange using a bill issued in Lyon in January 1552 and reproduced in figure 1.2. A classic bill of exchange was also known as a "four-party bill" because it involved four parties in two locations. In this case, Averardo Salviati of Lyon needed to remit funds to Rinieri Sernigi in Florence for the purchase of some goods or the settling of a debt. Instead of sending a bag of minted coins across the Alps or down the Rhone River and then on to a ship from Marseilles to Livorno, choices that ran the risk of losing the money either at sea or to robbers, Salviati (the deliverer or remitter) purchased a bill of exchange in Lyon marcs from a local banker, Giacomini & Gondi (the takers or drawers), who had close ties to Florence. The bill ordered the takers' agent in Florence (Niccolò Borgherini, the payer or drawee) to pay a set sum in Florentine currency to Salviati's agent, Sernigi (the payee or beneficiary).

All this elaborate information was condensed into a series of cryptic words on a thin slip of paper that resembled a modern personal check (figure 1.2). A nineteenth-century commentator called these bills "laconic" texts.[21] To many, they also appeared enigmatic. They all followed a technical vocabulary (much indebted to vernacular Italian) and a standardized format (figures 1.3 and 1.4). The expression "per questa prima," for example, meant that this was the first of several copies of the same bill to be issued; each copy was sent via an alternative route to augment the chances that at least one would arrive at its destination, but only one could be cashed. The exchange rate was set at the start of the transaction, even if the payment always occured at a later moment in

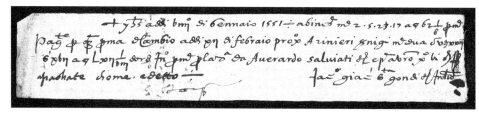

FIGURE 1.2. A classic (four-party) bill of exchange issued in Lyon in 1552. With permission from the Beinecke Rare Book and Manuscript Library, Yale University.

time—in this case, after thirty-four days. Sometimes a bill would indicate that the payment had to occur *at usance* (the English rendering of "ad uso," from the Italian word for "custom," *usanza*), which meant the standard number of days after which a bill came due in each pair of European cities, as reported in printed sheets, commercial newspapers, and merchant manuals.[22]

The meaning of certain bills' coded terms could be even more obscure and eluded most people's understanding. Thus, while the synthetic quality of these instruments enhanced their expediency, their lack of transparency made them seem potentially dangerous weapons in the hands of a coterie of bankers in a position to manipulate them in secretive ways. Moreover, the immaterial quality of these pieces of paper could give the impression that they were devoid of all tangible value. Exacerbating that impression was the fact that by the mid-sixteenth century, merchants rarely deposited a bag of coins when purchasing or paying a bill of exchange. By this time, the banking system had become sufficiently sophisticated to allow merchants to settle their payments via bookkeeping transactions, especially when they engaged in multiple dealings with one another.[23] Thus, in the example, Borgherini paid the bill to Sernigi after receiving a note (*avis*) from Giacomini & Gondi and cancelled one of the latter's obligations from his account book without cashing the corresponding value in coin. Even Salviati could make the initial payment to Giacomini & Gondi by a mere stroke of the pen in an account book rather than by depositing a sack of coins.

Front:

+ Yesus addì viiii di gennaio 1551 ab incarnacione marchi 2:5:23:17 @ scudi $62^{1/8}$ per macho

Pagate per questa prima di cambio addì xxi di febraio proximo a Rinieri Sernigi marchi dua once v denari xxiii grani xvii a scudi lxii $^{1/viii}$ d'oro in oro per marcho per la valuta da Averardo Salviati e compagni e ponete a vostro. Christo vi guardi.

Jacopo Giacomini, Giovambattista Gondi e compagni in Lione

Paghate chome è detto ---
Aceptata.

Back:

Ser Niccolò Borgherini e compagni in Firenze.
Prima.
scudi 170:14:9 d'oro

FIGURE 1.3. Transcription of the bill of exchange reproduced in Figure 1.2

Front:

[Christian Cross] Date when bill is issued – Amount and currency exchange rate

Pay this [first] letter on DATE [or within X number of days at maturity / on sight / at usance] to PAYEE'S NAME a certain amount in set currency, which we were given by DELIVERER'S NAME and charge it to your account there. May God protect you.

DRAWER'S SIGNATURE. Location

Paid to the above mentioned payees.
Accepted [sometimes on DATE].

Back:

PAYER'S SIGNATURE. Location.
First [or other] bill.
Total amount paid.
[sometimes multiple endorsers]

FIGURE 1.4. Stylized text of a classic (four-party) bill of exchange

In all these respects, bills of exchange were the quintessential instruments of commercial credit. Unlike a pawnshop, a mortgage contract, or even a marine insurance policy, they were backed not by collateral but by the perceived solvency of their signatories. For this reason, merchants were also the only group in French society that could still be imprisoned for debt when no criminal intent had been ascertained. As the contemporary expression *contrainte par corps* implies, their body stood in place of the collateral in commercial credit operations (chapter 4). An authoritative French dictionary of 1690 put the situation plainly: credit in the commercial sphere was extended "on the basis of a merchant's reputation for *probity* and *solvency*."[24] Probity is a moral trait, solvency a financial condition. Neither implies the other, even if under the best of circumstances the two go hand in hand. Perceptions and hard facts were not easily separable in preindustrial Europe, because verifiable information about borrowers' solvency was scarce and actuarial models still in their infancy. Imprecise as they were, word of mouth and business letters were the best sources one could rely on to assess a fellow merchant's financial standing. No less important than an individual's perceived probity and solvency were his rank (an aristocrat enjoyed higher credibility than a commoner) and religious affiliation (an infidel was less trustworthy than a good Christian).

Both the absence of pledges in commercial credit and the conflation of economic, legal, and moral credibility are essential to understanding the reactions that bills of exchange provoked among many observers, and the narrative of the putative Jewish invention of these credit instruments more specifically. We will return to these issues over and over in the course of the book. Here it is useful to consider several additional features that made bills of exchange increasingly complex financial tools as the sixteenth and seventeenth centuries progressed.

A bill's conversion rate was established in the market of origin in advance of the bill's maturity. Here lay these bills' speculative quality as well as a common defense against charges of usury. To merchant-bankers who possessed thick webs of knowledgeable agents and correspondents abroad, bills of exchange offered new speculative opportunities. Divorced from the economy of production and commodity trade, bills during the sixteenth and seventeenth centuries could be used solely for currency arbitrage, that is, betting on the differential values of one currency over another at any location (*agio*). Figure 1.5 illustrates the mechanisms of re-exchange, through which, under ideal conditions, a merchant from Bordeaux could make a 10 percent profit on a hypothetical sequence of conversions between the local currency and Amsterdam's currency.

Although exchange dealings between early modern European cities became more and more frequent, unpredictable events, such as the sudden breakout of war or the shipwreck of a galleon carrying bullion from the Americas, could alter the money market in ways that left the lender highly exposed. As a result, the profits derived from such dealings varied greatly. In the mid-fifteenth century, re-exchange contracts between Venice, London, and Bruges brokered by the Medici family, who served as Europe's chief bankers, yielded annual profits

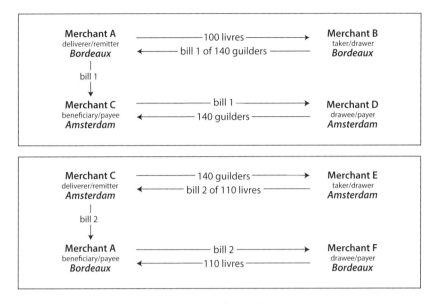

FIGURE 1.5. Flow chart of a re-exchange contract

ranging between a loss and 28.8 percent, with a median value of roughly 14 percent, which equaled the commercial rate of interest at the time.[25] But even the most experienced bankers could not expect to reap consistently high profits. The Lyon branch of the Salviati bank, a key protagonist of the sixteenth-century fairs described in the next section, aimed to net a profit of 2.5 percent on most bills and as much as 16 percent on a few others.[26] But its agents also described exchange dealings as "a matter of fortune" (*cosa di ventura*) for the high degree of uncertainty they involved.[27]

Dry exchange was the name used for a speculative loan that involved only a fictional currency conversion (figure 1.6).[28] In 1582 the Florentine writer Bernardo Davanzati explained this name by recourse to a body metaphor. In a healthy commercial society, he reasoned, four-party bills of exchange would act as the veins that fueled the blood (money) of commodity trade, thus working to "universal benefit." By contrast, bills traded against other bills would dry up the blood from the veins because they could not sustain "the utility of trade" but "only the utility of money."[29] A learned polymath, Davanzati incorporated into his explanation the views of theologians and canon lawyers, who referred to bills of exchange that did not involve the remittance of any funds as "fictitious exchange." His moralizing tone, infused with nostalgia for the good old days when merchants traded goods rather than paper bills, places

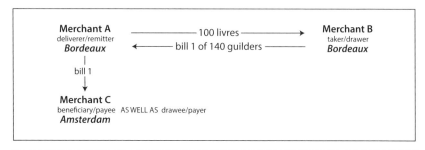

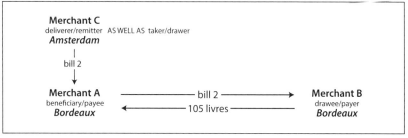

FIGURE 1.6. Flow chart of a dry-exchange contract

him in a long and illustrious line of commentators, stretching from Aristotle to Adam Smith, who pitted the ethical industriousness of commodity trade against the parasitical profits derived from financial speculation. Of course, metaphors associating money and blood were never too far from images of Jews. In Franciscan sermons, Jewish moneylending was frequently described as sucking the blood of the town, with the town symbolizing the earthly incarnation of the body of Christ and thus the common good of Christian society and institutions.[30]

Financial Fairs

Early modern financial fairs witnessed the first major divergence between capital and commodity markets in preindustrial Europe. Davanzati also referred to dry exchange as "bills of Besançon," after the French city where one of the most renowned of these fairs was held. An innovation of the sixteenth century, financial fairs hosted specialized bankers and designated brokers who devoted themselves exclusively to the negotiation of bills of exchange. The Lyon gathering was the most important of these fairs, and Florentine bankers acquired a dominant position there. To counter their influence, Genoese bankers established rival fairs in Besançon (1535), which later relocated to Piacenza (1579) and Novi Ligure (1622). Meanwhile, a number of smaller seasonal gatherings of this sort cropped up in various other towns.[31]

Several defining characteristics of these capital markets can help us understand how an informed but distant observer like Cleirac might have perceived them. First, financial fairs were the dominion of big businessmen, who set the calendar and the exchange rates. Although admission to them was not formally restricted, only a small number of operators cycled through them.[32] Davanzati depicted the fairs as assemblies of fifty to sixty men walking around carrying notebooks in which they recorded bills drawn and cashed across Europe and settled on an appropriate currency exchange rate (unsettled balances could be transferred to the next seasonal fair, with four held annually in Lyon).[33] At their peak in the early seventeenth century, the financial fairs in Piacenza hosted some 145 bankers, chiefly from Florence, Lucca, Genoa, and Milan, in any given year.[34]

Second, these international fairs were events during which particularly arcane financial instruments were developed, including a variant of the dry exchange known as *pacte de ricorsa*, which involved multiple transactions, with the parties to a bill at every seasonal gathering rolling over any accrued interest to the next arbitrage operation.[35] Third, all transactions were made in money of account (called *écu de marc* or *scudo di marche* in Lyon and Besançon), a virtual currency that did not exist as minted coins but was used for accounting purposes to convert all bills in foreign currencies and settle accounts.[36] Finally, while local authorities had to agree to host financial fairs in their territories and oversaw their tribunals, they largely left the regulation of disputes between participants to the fairs' organizers.[37]

More than any other sphere of international commerce, the fairs at which bills of exchange were traded thus represented the degree of self-governance enjoyed by an in-group of well-connected merchant-bankers. At the same time, these rarefied capital markets were not entirely self-contained, as stay-at-home investors with varying amounts of disposable wealth and financial literacy, including noblemen with no direct experience in trade, funded some of their operations. A swathe of commentators that extended beyond intransigent moral theologians feared that financial fairs had become sites of what today we would call insider trading and predatory lending. Aristocrats as well as members of the middle classes engaged in such speculation, lured by the prospect of easy profits. When all went well, investors could reap a 12 to 14 percent profit. But nothing was guaranteed. In 1608 a chain of bankruptcies was caused by young men who, hoping to gain independence from their families, entrusted their savings to agents trading in *pactes de ricorsa* they did not fully understand. Ruined by their misguided speculations, the young men turned to the Venetian Senate and even accused Jews of being involved in the failure of their investments.[38]

The features of bills of exchange summarized so far explain why they enjoyed a mixed reputation. Before the spectacular stock market crash of 1720, which opened the door to cheap print campaigns against the "follies" of financial speculation, they epitomized the alchemical ability to multiply money or, conversely, to dissipate large fortunes. The author of a mid-fifteenth-century manual described exchange operations as "a passing bird which, if not caught as it lights for a moment, will fly away and be gone for ever."[39] Two hundred years later, in a melancholic meditation on the passing of the glories of Italian (and especially his own city's) trade, the Genoese merchant-writer Giovanni Domenico Peri lamented the ease with which capital was squandered at financial fairs, provoking serious liquidity crises even among rich bankers.[40] A staunch defender of the legitimacy of exchange dealings and the similarity of money to any other merchandise, Peri was nonetheless acutely aware of the risks involved in trading bills of exchange. He warned that those risks were growing by the day because a few great merchants had cornered the market and begun selling complex instruments to the unsuspecting managers of women's or wards' estates.[41]

Alongside financial fairs, two other innovations affected the workings and perception of bills of exchange: their transferability and the practice of discounting. While to most people financial fairs were esoteric markets in which an expert elite operated according to its own rules, these two innovations accelerated the geographical and social diffusion of bills of exchange and made them an everyday presence in the cities and towns of early modern Europe.

The transferability of bills of exchange was first introduced in the late fourteenth century but became more common after the early seventeenth century. In this kind of transaction, a payee could endorse a bill and thus transfer the claim to another individual, who now had the right to collect the debt.[45] Figure 1.7 shows bills that, unlike the one reproduced in figure 1.2, carried the signatures of multiple endorsers on the back. In principle, endorsements could be repeated indefinitely because any signatory would assume that previous endorsers had done due diligence and assessed the reliability of the other countersigners. In practice, long chains of endorsers were not the norm. The cost of acquiring information on the solvency of previous endorsers was lower in hubs like Amsterdam, which had highly developed information and legal sys-

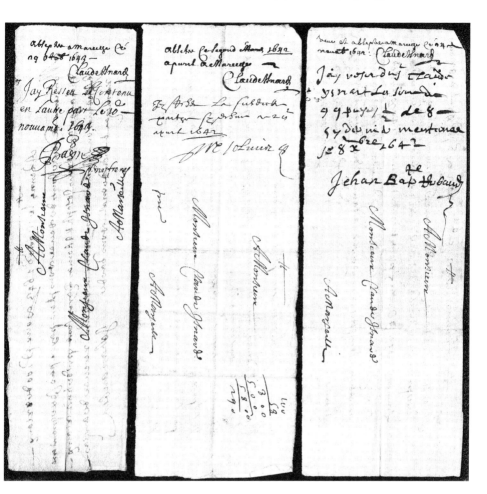

FIGURE 1.7. Multiple endorsements on the back of bills of exchange of the Isnard family of Marseilles, 1642-1643. With permission from the Archives départementales des Bouches-du-Rhône, Marseilles, 24E53.

tems.[46] By contrast, when merchants used bills of exchange to trade between distant regions where they relied on a limited number of correspondents, chains of endorsers were typically shorter.[47]

By the early seventeenth century, traders in large commercial hubs could also sell these obligations at a discounted price to a third party in anticipation of their maturity.[42] If a bill's beneficiary was in urgent need of cash, he could endorse the bill to a banker in exchange for the immediate payment of a lower sum of cash than the bill's face value. This transaction clashed with usury prohibitions because it guaranteed a profit to the banker, as the jurist Scaccia reminded readers in 1619.[43] But by then, discounting bills of exchange had become standard practice, and, in some places, public banks had been set up for this purpose. After the creation of the Exchange Bank (*Wisselbank*) in Amsterdam in 1609, anyone wishing to negotiate or discount bills worth more than 600 guilders (300 guilders after 1700) had to open an account with that bank. Since foreign traders from all over complied with this demand, the *Wisselbank* became a clearinghouse for bills issued across Europe. During liquidity crises, those account holders who were not strapped for cash could speculate by purchasing bills at a discount.[44]

Conclusion

By adding bills of exchange to his commentary on marine insurance, Cleirac paired two credit contracts that by the mid-seventeenth century had become indispensable to long-distance trade and were handled by merchants of all sorts. Of the two, marine insurance was the least murky. By this time, as the next chapter explains, this collateralized speculative instrument was no longer considered usurious. Bills of exchange, by contrast, came in different guises, baffled all but a few adepts, and continued to ignite fierce debates over usury. For these reasons, the majority of authors who engaged with Cleirac's attribution of the invention of both credit instruments to Jews focused primarily on bills of exchange; this is also why marine insurance will recede into the background as the book progresses.

The ease with which bills of exchange could be passed from one person to another generated the erroneous but indelible impression that they were like paper money. Some eighteenth-century French authors even referred to bills of exchange as *papier-monnoye*.[48] Aside from the fact that paper money was rare in Europe before 1800, bills of exchange were not backed by land or bullion managed by the state or a central bank.[49] Unlike banknotes, they were not fully negotiable, nor were payers obliged to accept them.[50] Rather, their value was the direct measure of the faith that endorsers placed in one another and could only be redeemed if acquired in good faith. In sum, the guarantor of a bill of exchange was a signatory's reputation. Today, cashless payments are routine because verification systems have become sufficiently advanced and automated. In the late medieval and early modern periods, behind these enigmatic slips of paper lay a highly personalized, if no longer face-to-face, market in which dense networks of epistolary correspondents marshaled the information necessary to evaluate an endorser's credibility.

Such were the mechanics behind the circulation of bills of exchange, but we cannot ignore the perception produced everywhere by the rapid pace at which these bills circulated: the sense that they could be bought and sold by anyone, with little oversight. Indeed, these bills' social and geographical reach grew rapidly during the mid-sixteenth century. James Steven Rogers describes this development as moving them "from the exotic to the everyday."[51] By the time Cleirac composed his commentary, discounting bills and transferring their assignability were ordinary operations in France.[52] Not only tax collectors but also local traders and members of the urban middle classes used them on a day-to-day basis.[53]

Propelled by Europe's colonial and commercial expansion, bills of exchange also traveled farther and farther, in the sense that the geographical distance separating the parties involved in any single bill grew considerably. Even in the absence of an institution like the *Wisselbank*, a multiplicity of sources—oral, written, printed—helped merchants who might not have known each other to conduct the background checks necessary to endorse a bill. Private business correspondence was essential to this task, which is one of the reasons why it remained a vital tool of long-distance trade.[54]

If tight interpersonal networks were the best assurance against fraud, they could also fail colossally. Collusion among speculators could lead to lives being ruined and households dispossessed. Alarmist commentators were proven right more than once in Old Regime France. In 1728, a group of Parisian bankers filed a suit claiming that the signatures on the bills they had purchased had been forged.[55] In the 1760s, when Turgot was the royal official (*intendant*) charged with overseeing the region of Limoges, which included some of the poorest areas of the kingdom, members of the local population in Angoulême fell prey to a group of investors. When the deceived parties sued in court, panic spread in the city and interest rates shot up.[56]

Regulatory powers proved weak in the face of such financial crimes. For this reason, self-policing by merchants and bankers was essential but naturally raised questions about foxes guarding the henhouse. This is one of the reasons why, no matter how distorted it was, the legend of the Jewish invention of bills of exchange attracted attention: by recourse to the old trope of Jewish deceit, it articulated concerns about the morality of credit that were very real and yet difficult to pin down. By the time Cleirac inked his account of this legend, bills of exchange had become both more prevalent and more elaborate, instruments that laws and tribunals struggled to regulate.

2

The Making of a Legend

AFTER STATING THAT "insurance policies and bills of exchange were unknown to ancient Roman jurisprudence and are the posthumous invention of Jews," Étienne Cleirac continues his commentary on the first article of the *Guidon de la mer* with a long, if fallacious, historical excursus meant to illustrate his point:

> When these abominable circumcised were banned from France because of their wrongdoings and their execrable crimes, and their assets were seized, at the time of King *Dagobert*, King *Philip Augustus*, and King *Philip the Tall*, in order to retrieve their commodities and money, which they had consigned to or hidden in the hands of their friends before leaving, necessity taught these malicious men lacking public trust to use secret letters and bills written with few words and little substance, as bills of exchange still are, addressed to those who had received and concealed their stolen goods and given Jews a hand. Jews carried out these tasks by employing travelers and foreign merchants.[1]

He resumes the digression later in the same section of the commentary:

> The Italian Lombards, witnesses of and actors in this Jewish intrigue, after they retained the models of these letters, learned to use them effectively when in Italy the unhappy sects of Guelfs and Ghibellines, meaning the followers of the Pope and the Emperor, respectively, threatened each other, so to endeavor to supplant one another and put Christianity through great troubles and tumult.

Finally, Cleirac concludes:

... it follows that German and Flemish people call all exchange dealers, bankers, dirty usurers, and resellers of whatever background *Lombards*; and for the same reason the square in which the market for currency exchange and second-hand goods is located in the city of Amsterdam has kept the name of *Lombard Square* until today.

Fact and Fiction

These excerpts encapsulate the gist of the story that Cleirac bequeathed to his many readers and that this chapter and the next seek to elucidate. In brief, we are told that the Jews expelled from France in subsequent waves under the kingdoms of Dagobert (r. 629–634), Philip Augustus (r. 1180–1223), and Philip the Tall (r. 1316–1322) invented marine insurance policies and bills of exchange in order to salvage their assets when fleeing to "Lombardy," that is, to northern and central Italy. There, Guelfs and Ghibellines, supporters of the pope and the Holy Roman Emperor, respectively, were embroiled in protracted wars for political control and found those inventions to be very useful every time they were expelled from their own city-states. As a result, Italian refugees exported the newly invented financial instruments north of the Alps, the Guelfs mostly to France and the Ghibellines mostly to Germany and Flanders, where bankers and moneylenders were called "Lombards," a name eventually given to a public square in Amsterdam.[2]

Cleirac's account is an astonishing mix of fact and fiction, a mix that ensured it a long life. The mention of the Merovingian and Capetian kings by name suggests that Cleirac borrowed whatever little knowledge of medieval French Jews he had from the numerous histories of France that circulated in his lifetime, in which the medieval expulsions were the only mentions of Jewish life (even if in most of those histories more attention was given to Philip the Fair's general ban on Jews in 1306 than to the persecutions enacted by Philip the Tall).[3] The reference to specific French kings seems to have lent credibility to his tale, because scores of later writers repeated those names (and occasionally added others) when reiterating versions of the legend. For their part, medieval chroniclers kept alive the genre of the vitriolic anti-Jewish polemic. Recalling the expulsions from France of 1182 and 1306, a Spanish Franciscan friar in 1674 borrowed the motifs of earlier chronicles when he justified the expropriations ordered by Philip IV, known as "the Fair," "because he discovered that they [the Jews] owned nearly all of Paris through their usury and that they held as their captives ... the remainder of the population."[4]

Like his account of the timing of the Jews' expulsions from the kingdom of France, Cleirac's depiction of the role of Italian merchants in disseminating banking and accounting techniques throughout the Low Countries contains a kernel of truth but also distorts essential facts. It portrays Amsterdam (the capital of the world economy in Cleirac's lifetime) rather than medieval Bruges as the Lombards' prime destination north of the Alps.[5] Moreover, no place called "Lombard Square" existed in the Dutch city, contrary to what Cleirac states. Rather, a pawnbroking establishment called "Bank of Loan or Lombard" (*Bank van lening ofte Lombard*) had been in operation in Amsterdam since 1550, and in 1614, in response to complaints about the abuses to which private moneylenders subjected their customers, the city council turned it into the civic equivalent of the *Monti di Pietà*, the Italian pawnshops set up by friars that extended consumer credit to the poor at very low interest rates.[6] Cleirac may have confused this minor Amsterdam establishment with the city's magnificent stock exchange (*Beurs*), where after 1611 merchants gathered in a courtyard surrounded by arcades to conduct financial transactions. In fact, although crowded together in a small urban area, each of these spaces—the commodity marketplace, the municipal pawnshop, and the stock exchange—was distinct from one another and catered to different clienteles.

Whether deliberate or the result of unfailingly muddled prose, Cleirac's merging of these spaces has the effect of tracing a direct line between fourteenth-century Lombards and seventeenth-century Amsterdam, and makes pawnbroking appear contiguous with the most sophisticated forms of financial credit developed during the sixteenth century. The legend, that is, purposefully conflates what today we call the "medieval" and "early modern" periods. This chronological compression is crucial to Cleirac's rhetorical strategy of making medieval Jewish moneylenders, the object of scorn and prejudice, interchangeable with the international merchant-bankers of the seventeenth century.

Why Jews?

The historical excursus Cleirac lays out for his readers teaches this first lesson: "It follows that bills of exchange and insurance policies are Jewish from birth, both in their invention and denomination." With expulsion came confiscation, and Cleirac writes that in order to save their assets, Jews consigned "commodities and money . . . in the hands of friends before leaving." To redeem the value of these goods abroad, they invented bills of exchange. It is the cryptic quality of these bills, "written with few words and little substance," that Cleirac emphasizes and that would become a staple of later literature.[7]

We have seen how the thin slips of paper that constituted bills of exchange encapsulated myriad rights and obligations. This was the advantage of merchant documents: they omitted the lengthy and convoluted formulas used by lawyers and notaries. But the opacity of bills of exchange separated insiders from outsiders in credit markets. In the eyes of Christians, opacity was also a defining trait of Jews, one that blended their religious and economic infidelity and rendered them suspect of in-group maneuvering.[8] Jews seemed as impenetrable to Christians as bills of exchange. They had rejected the divine nature of Christ and continued to follow traditions and rites that Christians found mystifying and irrational. The publication in 1637 of the first explication of Jewish religious rituals for a Christian audience, *The History of the Rites, Customes, and Manners of Life, of the Present Jews*, by the Venetian rabbi Leon Modena, did little to dispel this perception.[9] On the eve of the French Revolution, ardent gentile supporters of equal rights for Jews called for the elimination of Yiddish (sometimes described as a "Tudesco-Hebraico-Rabbinical jargon"), which they regarded as a sign of ignorance but also, wrongly, as the source of endless tricks committed by Jewish moneylenders at the expense of local peasants ignorant of that language.[10]

Once they invented these portentous bills—a claim that apparently required no further corroboration—Jews, Cleirac tells us, deployed their superior financial skills to make sure they would not "be deceived on the exchange rate" and would in fact be able "to make a profit." In his story, Jews and a few fellow Christian moneylenders were the sole repositories of all knowledge concerning both foreign currency conversions and the intrinsic value of metallic coins, including that related to debasement, government revenues on new minting issues (*seigniorage*), and clipping.[11] Cleirac assumes that Jews possessed the expertise required to tame the volatility of financial markets. A special interest group endowed with a talent for commerce, they were seen as wielding undue advantage over their competitors and thriving by cheating ill-informed customers.

Accusations of religious infidelity and economic cunning were mutually reinforcing. Cleirac seems to have chosen his words carefully: those he uses in reference to Jews are theologically loaded, even if they had become common parlance by the time of his writing. He tells us that Jews were banned from France "because of their wrongdoings and execrable crimes," the latter phrase being an expression commonly applied to Jews and heretics.[12] He describes

Jews as "malicious men lacking public trust" and "people without a con-science." For Cleirac, Jews always stood apart from the world that surrounded them: they felt "mistrust" even toward those who assisted them in their escape, and it was their ability to turn "the risks and dangers of a voyage" into "a gift or a modest price" that assured them a profit. But Jews' obsession with self-interest, which was a sign of their separateness from Christian society, meant that their financial skills did not contribute to the common good.

In a later booklet devoted exclusively to bills of exchange (then still a rela-tively new genre), titled *Usance du négoce* and published a year before his death, Cleirac's language is even more theologically charged. He labels Jews as "infa-mous," that is, as lacking *fama*, public trust or reputation, and thus the quality that one needs to belong to a community.[13] The trade in bills of exchange is said to retain "its original sin, that is, Jewish perfidy."[14] *Perfidia* is a keyword that would have hit its mark at the time. A Latin term denoting Jews' refusal to recognize Christ's divine nature, it acquired a more capacious and ominous meaning in European vernaculars. At a minimum, it denoted Jews' untrust-worthiness and exclusion from the Christian commonwealth.[15] *Perfidia* was also closely linked to usury. Canon 67 (*Quanto amplius*), the section of the decrees issued at the Fourth Lateran Council (1215) devoted exclusively to Jewish usury and cited by Cleirac in his commentary on marine insurance, began with the premise that "the perfidy of Jews" (*Iudaeorum perfidia*)—that is, their intention to extract money from the Christian community through high interest rates—grew in proportion to the ability of Christians to restrain themselves from lending at interest and thus drained resources from the Chris-tian community.[16]

Shortly after the Fourth Lateran Council, a lavishly illustrated manuscript commissioned by the king of France translated those doctrinal precepts into a sinister visual repertoire.[17] Cleirac's commentary reveals the astounding lon-gevity of such medieval anti-Jewish rhetoric and imagery. Even as late as the mid-seventeenth century, it was still possible to draw on a host of entrenched associations in order to depict marine insurance and bills of exchange as "Jew-ish from birth" and instruments of "Jewish intrigue"—that is, as synonyms of usury.

Why Villani?

Twice in his commentary on the *Guidon de la mer* Cleirac attributes the legend to Giovanni Villani's "universal history," or *Nuova Cronica*, one of the most famous medieval chronicles written in Italian vernacular. Villani's account of the history of Florence from its legendary beginnings in biblical times to 1346, two years before the author's death from plague, includes no claims about a Jewish invention of marine insurance and bills of exchange.[18] So why did Cleirac invoke it? The answer, speculative as it must remain, likely lies again in Cleirac's tendency to mix fact and fiction. Cleirac had read more than a fair share of Villani's chronicle and there found several ingredients for his story: the power struggle between the Guelfs and the Ghibellines for the control of Florence and its nearby territories, the city's banking activities, and Jewish usury. Villani's firsthand experience as an apprentice and later partner in two of the city's main trading and banking companies, both of which suffered catastrophic bankruptcies in the 1340s, left a contradictory mark on the chronicle. On the one hand, Villani's work celebrates the economic ingenuity of the Florentines. On the other hand, his narrative is imbued with a moralizing critique of avarice that derives as much from the religious thought of the time as from the devastating effects of the collapse of the city's leading banks.[19]

Both themes are echoed in Cleirac's commentary. In the manuscript draft of what became *Us et coustumes de la mer*, a gloss located in the margin of the first article of the *Guidon de la mer* attributes the invention of bills of exchange to Florentine Guelf and Ghibelline expatriates and mentions Villani as the source of information about medieval Florentine and Genoese banking in general (figures 2.1–2.3).[20] This gloss does not mention Jews. It is impossible to ascertain what happened as Cleirac turned the manuscript into a printed volume or what role, if any, his publisher, Guillaume Millanges, played along the way.[21] Two things are certain: Cleirac read large portions of Villani, and, once he committed the legend to print, he did not doubt its veracity. In fact, he expanded it in the second edition of *Us et coustumes de la mer*.[22] He also repeated it in his later work, *Usance du négoce*, although he did not there attribute it to Villani.[23]

The perennial struggles between the Guelfs and the Ghibellines, which ordinarily ended with one of the two banned from serving in the municipal government, and the workings of Florentine banks are themes that run through Villani's chronicle and are echoed in Cleirac's work. In *Usance du négoce*, the French lawyer cites Villani on the history of the minting of the twenty-four-carat golden florin starting in 1251.[24] Other references to the fortunes of Tuscan expatriates are less accurate but likely borrowed from Villani, whose history emphasizes the Guelfs' role in disseminating banking techniques throughout France.[25]

Villani's chronicle mentions usury in several contexts: sometimes simply to describe private or public credit in general, other times to censure unfair lending practices.[26] It also records specific ecclesiastical doctrines on usury,

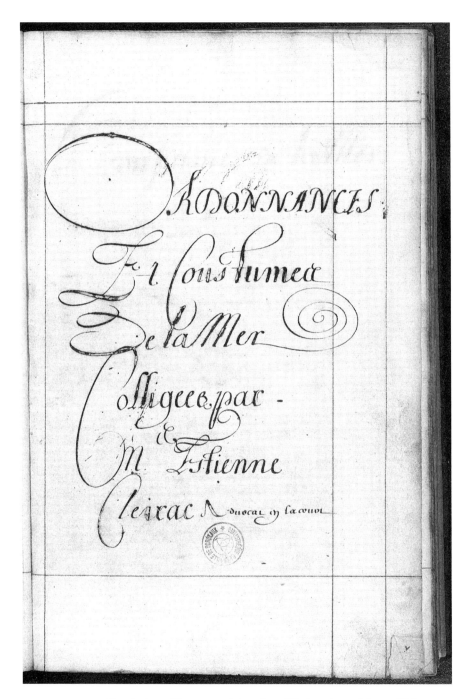

FIGURE 2.1. Frontispiece of the manuscript version of *Us et coustumes de la mer*. With permission from the Bibliothèque Municipale, Bordeaux, Ms. 381, title page.

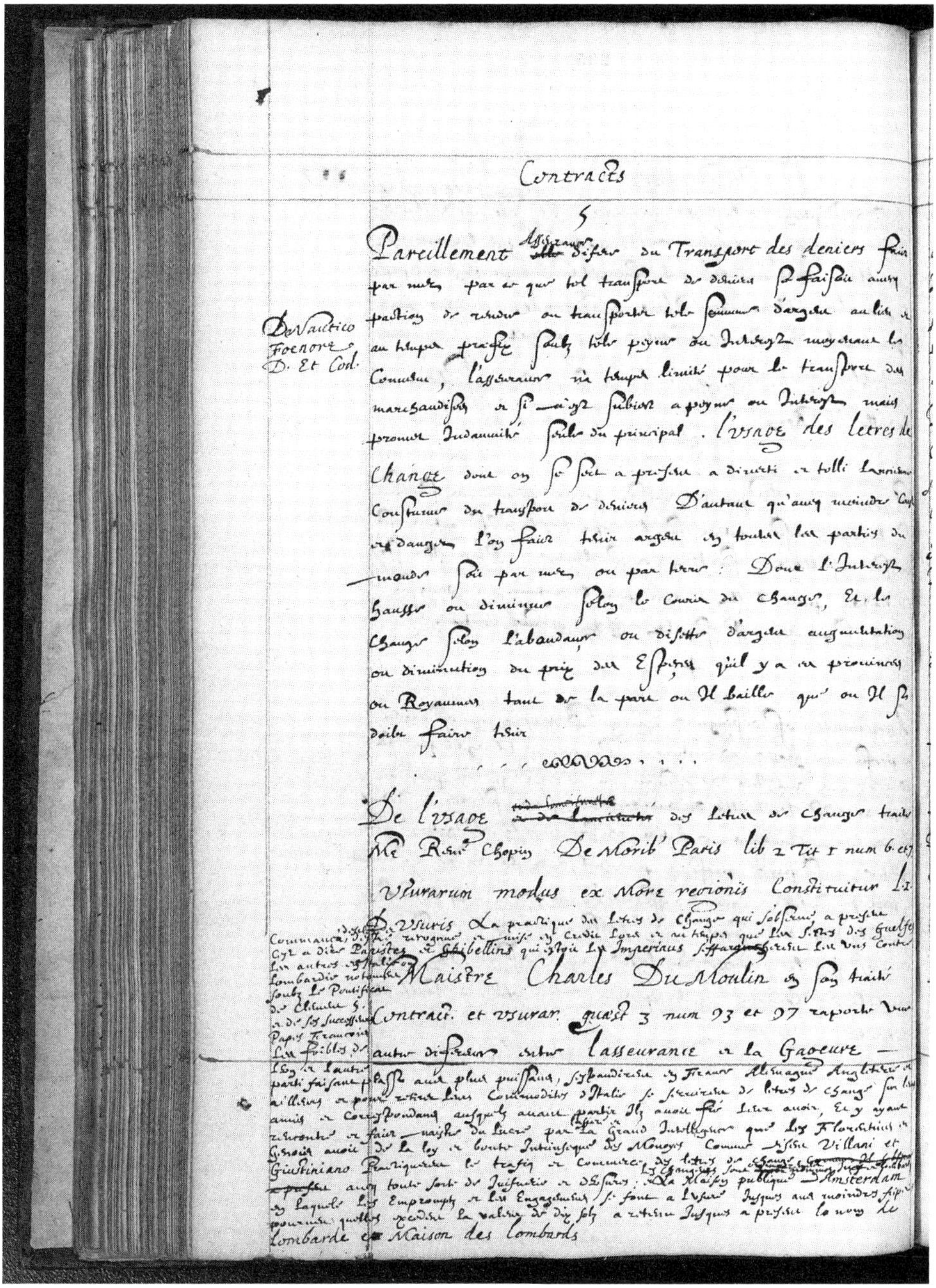

FIGURE 2.2. Cleirac's commentary on the first article of the *Guidon de la mer* in the manuscript version of *Us et coustumes de la mer*. With permission from the Bibliothèque Municipale, Bordeaux, Ms. 381, fol. 117v/p. 236.

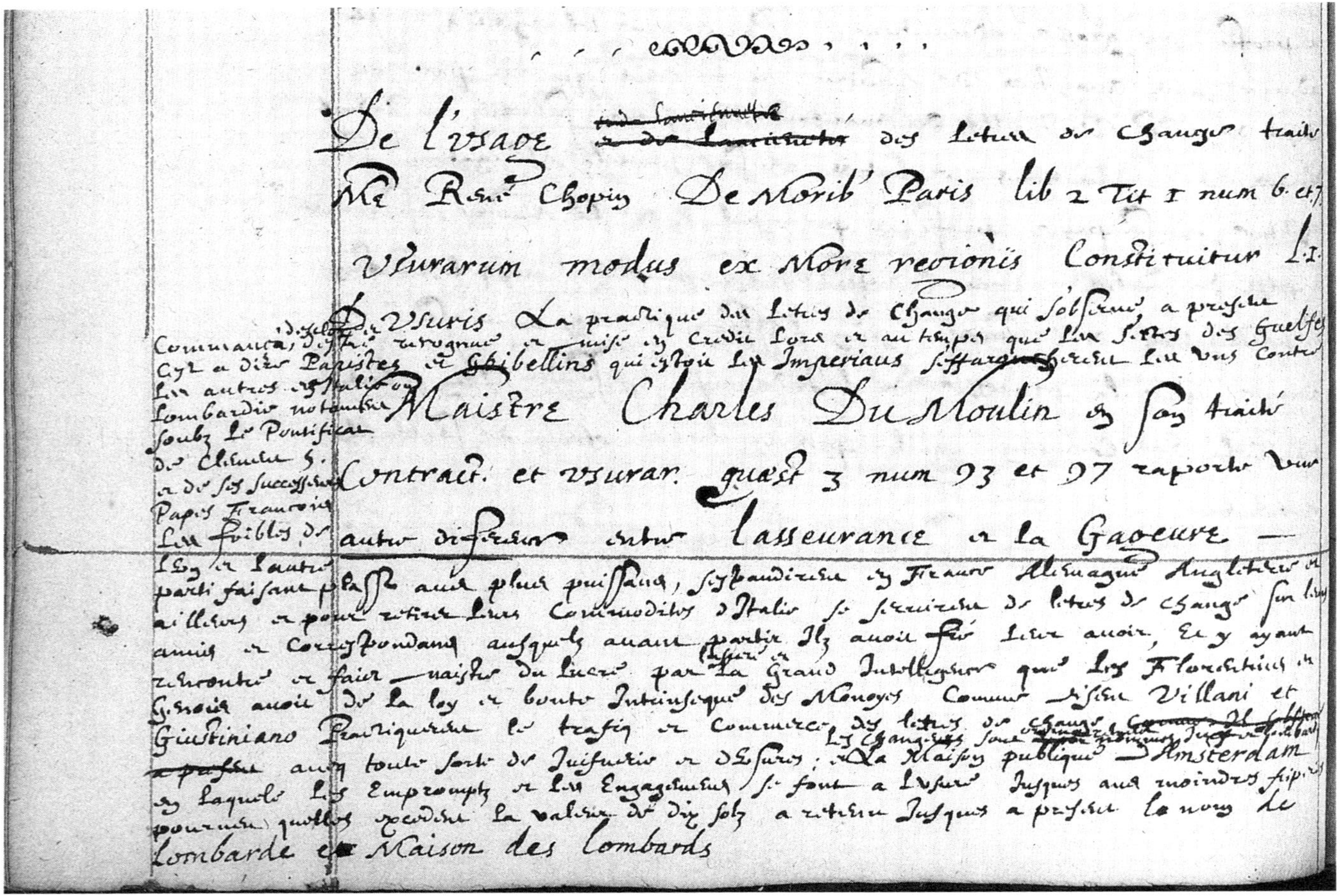

FIGURE 2.3. Gloss in the margin of Cleirac's commentary on the first article of the *Guidon de la mer* in the manuscript version of *Us et coutumes de la mer*. With permission.

including the Second Council of Lyon's condemnation in 1274 of Christian (rather than Jewish) usury, a piece of information that Cleirac would later relay in *Us et coustumes de la mer*, although without any specific mention of Villani.[27] Significantly, Villani also describes the expulsion from France of Italian moneylenders ("Lombards") at the hands of Philip the Fair in 1277, which, as we will see, plays a central role in Cleirac's argument.[28]

Most revealing of all is a citation from Villani that Cleirac inserts into his commentaries on the *coustumier de Guyenne*, a collection of legal customs from the region of Bordeaux dating from the fourteenth century that underwent reforms in 1520 (Cleirac claims to have consulted the version of the *coustumier de Guyenne* found in the library of Michel de Montaigne).[29] The citation is from book VII, chapter 136, of Villani's chronicle, a section that contains the most influential version of the story of the miracle of the profaned host, an episode that allegedly occurred in Paris in 1290 and thereafter provided fodder for tales of ritual murder.[30] In this account, a Christian woman brings the host to a Jewish pawnbroker, who tosses it into the fireplace, where it spills blood—clear proof that it had been consecrated (in Catholic doctrine, the bread of the host through the ritual of the mass miraculously becomes the body of Christ). The rescue of the host and the (different) punishments inflicted on the Christian woman and on the Jewish pawnbroker wrap up the story, which has since been told and retold in myriad texts, paintings, and cheap prints, including, most famously, a sequence of images painted by Paolo Uccello on a predella commissioned by the Confraternity of the Corpus Domini in Urbino in the 1460s (figure 2.4).

The Jewish pawnbroker's sacrilegious act of throwing the host into the fireplace forges a nexus between Jewish usury and Jews' denial of Christ's divine nature. For this reason, the alleged miracle of the profaned host nourished some of the most inimical fantasies of medieval antisemitism.[31] We know that Cleirac came across the miracle in Villani's chronicle. And although he never mentions it explicitly in his writings about commerce and banking, the narrative of the host's profanation was entirely congruent with the legend's logic. Following Davanzati's metaphor, the Jewish pawnbroker misused the host's blood in the same way as dry exchanges drained blood from the healthy body of the Christian economy.

Cleirac's tendency to digress and insert untenable stories into his commentaries has discredited his legacy among the few specialists of the history of commercial and maritime law who still recognize his name. At the very least, he has a reputation of being unreliable (his only biographer to date sought to

FIGURE 2.4. Detail of Paolo Uccello's *Miracle of the Profaned Host* (Urbino, 1460s). With permission from De Agostini Picture Library, Bridgeman Images.

rescue him from the charge that he was a *fantaisiste*, a fanciful writer).[32] These criticisms obscure the fact that, by means of a thick web of seemingly disjointed citations (almost all of which, it must be noted, are more accurate than the one attributing the legend to Villani), Cleirac wove together a coherent story. In fact, his erroneous ascription to Villani of the statement that Jews invented marine insurance and bills of exchange is less perplexing than the paucity of objections that the statement elicited. It was not until the mid-twentieth century that a scholar of maritime law thought to verify the textual reference to the Florentine chronicler and found it missing.[33] For all too long, Villani was seen as a plausible source of the legend, and the link that Cleirac posited between Jews and usury was regarded as so self-evident that no one challenged the mistaken attribution and, with it, the gist of the story.

Conclusion

Cleirac's explicit and implicit allusions, scattered throughout his tale of origins, constitute a coherent allegory of bad credit as "Jewish." I call this tale a legend rather than a myth because Cleirac casts it as a historical narrative; I call it a legend rather than an anecdote because, as the rest of the book shows, it had

an astounding resonance over the following centuries among writers who touched on economic themes in France and across Europe.

Warning his readers of the terrible consequences of shady (but hard-to-specify) handling of bills of exchange, Cleirac moves from the realm of the law to that of history—or, better, to that of fictional history. His Middle Ages are half real and half imaginary. No medieval author would have proclaimed marine insurance and bills of exchange to be Jewish inventions, because these obligations were then understood to be the prerogative of the elite Christian merchant-bankers who were also the political and civic leaders of the city-state. For the renowned fifteenth-century mathematician and Franciscan friar Luca Pacioli, "exchange dealers should be blessed instead of being called usurers, Jews, and even worse."[34] Jewish moneylenders at that time were largely confined to lending to the state in return for basic guarantees or to the poor in return for pawns. Medieval Jews ignited Cleirac's imagination because he saw them as the embodiment of "manifest usurers" (*usurarii manifesti*): they carried marks of distinction on their clothes, set up their shops in prescribed spaces, and offered their lending services to the public like prostitutes.[35]

In recent decades, scholars have demonstrated that moneylending was not the prevalent, let alone exclusive, economic activity in which Jews were involved in medieval France, and that where it occurred, Jewish moneylending could bind Christians and Jews together as much as it could pit them against each other.[36] These findings are important correctives to previous misconceptions of European economic and Jewish history, but they do not assist us in the effort to illuminate how contemporary readers might have approached Cleirac's text. The image of Jewish moneylending that emerges from his commentary reminds us that centuries of verbal and visual indoctrination shaped the views of learned and illiterate Christians alike, no matter what their lived experience might have been.

Cleirac's Jews were phantoms of a past that allowed his readers to make sense of the present, and the legend he fashioned, or at least broadcast, owed its success to the fact that it used medieval representations of the Jewish usurer to express early modern anxieties about the intricacy and ubiquity of bills of exchange. In it, Jews are first described as the target of expulsions ordered by medieval French kings and an allusion is made to the thirteenth-century miracle of the consecrated host. Then, through a fast-paced narrative, an ostensibly Jewish invention, bills of exchange, is said to have reached its pinnacle in Amsterdam, the seventeenth-century capital of the world economy, a hub of commercial credit (rather than pawnbroking), and home to the most interdenominational of all early modern European commercial societies. In piecing this story together, Cleirac falls back on the figure of the Jewish usurer as a defensive mechanism at a time when the increasing impersonality of market exchanges was perceived as threatening established social hierarchies and traditional forms of authority. The next chapter will illustrate how the figure of the Jewish usurer seized by Cleirac was at once tenacious and malleable, dual qualities that account for the legend's persistence and plasticity.

3

The Riddle of Usury

THE NOTION THAT the church stalled economic development in Catholic Europe and, conversely, that a few brave merchants succeeded in business by ignoring Catholic doctrines about usury, at least until their last confession, long dominated lay and scholarly views of the Middle Ages, particularly in the Anglo-American world. But a fertile field of historiographical research in the past half century has put these views to rest and made us fully aware of what Étienne Cleirac and his contemporaries knew all too well: the Catholic Church neither opposed all forms of profit and entrepreneurship nor turned a blind eye to infringements of its own doctrines; instead, it struggled to reach a consensus regarding acceptable forms of wealth and wealth management. From this perspective, we can recognize Cleirac's tirades against Jews and usury as vernacular expressions of learned debates about which contracts were illegitimate and which agreeable, as well as about who could permissibly be party to either.[1]

The next chapter will situate Cleirac and his works in the context of their time. For now, I will resume my analysis of his text where I left it. Cleirac's words locate him at an important and little understood historical junction, when the late medieval habit of treating money and the economy as part of the moral and theological universe intersected with the emerging "science of commerce," that is, the increasingly secularized literature that discussed commerce as a profession and an object of government policies.[2] This literature assigned multifarious meanings to the word *usury*. Church doctrines about usury were neither uniform nor uncontested. Different definitions of the practice coexisted, and clergymen granted considerable leeway to ecclesiastical or secular tribunals investigating those charged with the sin (a sin that in some polities had been made into a crime). The most salient phase in these debates, for the purpose of understanding Cleirac's musings on the topic, occurred in the sixteenth century, when Catholic theologians devised new and subtle arguments about the legitimacy of various financial contracts, including marine insurance and bills of exchange, in order to control but not hamper the expansion of European commercial society.

By the eighteenth century, writers of the *ars mercatoria* treated the term *usury* as a placeholder for all sorts of unsavory economic behaviors, and because of the enduring influence of an earlier discourse, they often assumed that Jews personified such behaviors. As a result, allusions to Jews continued to function as symbolic standards against which economic conduct could be measured long after the Middle Ages.

Usury and Its Enigmas

Historians cannot determine the interest rates charged on bills of exchange because they were included in the currency conversion rate. The stratagem was similar to the one that a series of recent consolidated class actions alleged Visa, Mastercard, and Diners Club had engaged in as a way of hiding foreign transaction fees behind currency conversion rates.[3] Some scholars assume that in the premodern period this expedient allowed merchants and bankers to avoid charges of usury and represented the ingenuity of Catholic merchants wishing to bypass canon law. In reality, theologians and canon lawyers were not easily fooled. As the complexity of bills of exchange grew, so did the financial expertise of those intent on combating usury and the intricacies of church rules condemning it. That is why, a few specialists aside, "usury is perhaps the most ridiculed, but least understood, idea in the history of economics."[4]

The Old Testament (Exodus 22:24–25, Leviticus 23:33–37, Deuteronomy 23:19–20, Psalms 15:5), one passage in the Gospel of Luke (6:34–35), and several Patristic texts provided authoritative scriptural foundations for the strictest position articulated in Gratian's *Decretum*, according to which "any sum returned in excess to the principal is usury."[5] Thomist theologians meanwhile rediscovered Aristotle's doctrine of the sterility of money (*Politics* 1:10, *Nicomachean Ethics* 5:5), which they adopted as a complementary anti-usury argument.[6] But even before Reformed leaders in the sixteenth century questioned strict Scholastic interpretations of usury, Catholic moral theologians and canon lawyers had already devised two sets of responses to this thorny problem, both of which are reflected in Cleirac's commentary: the first developed new taxonomies of legitimate and illegitimate credit contracts; the second approached charges of usurious behavior on an ad hoc basis, judging conduct case by case and issuing exceptions rather than sweeping condemnations. All anti-usury injunctions, in any case, only applied to Christians. Excluded from the community of believers, Jews were allowed to charge interest and soon became widely accepted symbols of rapacious moneylending.

Cleirac derives his equation of Jews and usury from some of the most bellicose Christian depictions of this equivalence, notably those by Church Father Ambrose of Milan and Canon 67 of the Fourth Lateran Council.[7] In 1215, the Fourth Lateran Council required Jews living amid Christians to wear distinctive clothing and crystallized the association between Jews and usury in Canon 67, which described Christian society and church properties as being devoured by Jews, who were said to extort "heavy and immoderate usuries" (*graves immoderatasque usuras*).[8] At the time, some Jewish scholars who were fully versed in Scholastic thought challenged church doctrine and Christian hypocrisy in matters of Jewish moneylending.[9] But these texts were neither accessible nor of interest to Cleirac. His training and his faith took him elsewhere—specifically, to the new ethics developed by moral theologians and canon lawyers, especially Franciscan friars, for mercantile urban elites in the wake of the commercial revolution of the Middle Ages and to the writings of their sixteenth-century successors.

Unlike earlier medieval monks who railed against the moneyed economy, Franciscan friars did not condemn all forms of profit. Rather, they scrutinized each and every business contract, outlined theories of just prices and private property, and devised ingenious justifications of the church's management of its own large landed and movable wealth. Aiming to regulate the market according to its moral principles, the church strove to distinguish between usury and beneficial credit transactions rather than banning all profit-making activities. Bernardino da Siena (d. 1444), the vocal Franciscan preacher later proclaimed a saint and a leader of antisemitic persecutions, was among the many in his order who not only denounced fraud and avarice but also stressed the positive impact that trade had on civic life: "Nothing contributes to the Commune so much as the profit of the guilds and of the merchandize that is bought and sold," he declared.[10] Literal readings of scripture never went away, but the doctrines of the Roman Catholic Church came to encompass a variety of competing definitions of usury, and theologians, moral philosophers, and canon and civil lawyers debated which credit instruments were legitimate and which were not.

Marine insurance was among the first credit contracts to find wide acceptance. Pope Gregory IX's decretal *Naviganti* (1236) denied that the assumption of risk (*periculum sortis*) justified charging any interest, but its wording left the door open to protracted disquisitions about the nature of usury.[11] Only a few decades later, the noted Franciscan John Duns Scotus admitted that professional merchants were allowed to derive a profit in exchange for servicing society at large (as long as their commercial activities involved neither fraud nor duress) and, more specifically, that they could be paid a premium to cover the risk of transporting goods.[12] By the early fifteenth century, the Florentine lawyer Lorenzo Ridolfi and others had proposed a different but even more powerful counterargument to the papal injunction of 1236: marine insurance was acceptable because it was not a loan but a type of contract unknown in ancient Roman law (*contractus innominatus*), a form of lease in which the insurer took on the assumption of risk from the merchant and was entitled to demand remuneration in exchange.[13]

The recognition that marine insurance provided collective benefits and its classification as a lease paved the way for the full legitimation of premium insurance. During the next period of rapid economic growth, the sixteenth century, the most influential moral theologians at the University of Salamanca, including two Dominicans, Francisco de Vitoria (1492–1546) and Domingo de Soto (1495–1560), and the Jesuit Luis de Molina (1535–1600), reaffirmed the legitimacy of marine insurance. In *Us et coustumes de la mer*, Cleirac cites a well-known Spanish confessional manual of the time to support his statement that marine insurance is an asset to the flourishing of the state.[14] Molina proved particularly influential in this regard because he argued that marine insurance was a purchase-and-sale contract, rather than a credit contract, and thus not susceptible to usury charges.[15] Jurists embraced his definition, which the Genoese commercial law expert Sigismondo Scaccia repeated in 1619.[16]

Cleirac knew this argument well, since it constituted the core principle of the first article of the *Guidon de la mer*, the object of his commentary.[17] He was even familiar with pertinent jurisprudence that adopted this definition. Indeed, before introducing the extravagant tale of the Jewish invention of marine insurance and bills of exchange, Cleirac notes that the high civil court of Genoa, the *Rota*, defined marine insurance as a purchase-and-sale contract in which the price was justified and determined by the risk involved ("emptioni & venditoni propter prætium quod datur ratione periculi").[18]

The same logic came to be applied to bills of exchange.[19] They passed muster as long as, following Aristotle and Roman law, they were classified not as money (which could be loaned) but as nonfungible goods like horses and real estate, which were not susceptible to a loan contract (*mutuum*) because they could be returned in the same condition as when they were given.[20] Sustained through longer and fully-articulated disquisitions, the argument was widely accepted by the time Cleirac penned his commentary, with one important caveat: whereas marine insurance was no longer suspected of being usurious, different types of bills of exchange still stirred considerable controversy. The majority of churchmen accepted as legitimate four-party bills, which they described as "real exchanges," but suspicion continued to follow more complex instruments, such as dry exchange, that had come to the fore at the financial fairs of Lyon and Besançon and in Europe's major commercial hubs.

Cleirac appears to have been well acquainted with these technical debates and the leading voices of Second Scholasticism, who had updated Franciscan teachings to address the increasing financial sophistication of the time. With unusual clarity, he synthesizes the views of two leading Catholic theologians of the sixteenth century: "In reality, those banking activities and insurances that are treated as honorable, upright, and legal activities are greatly useful and helpful to business, even according to the opinion of Thomas de Vio, known as Cardinal Cajetan, in his *Tractatus de cambijs*, chapter 5, and Navarrus, in his *Enchiridion*, chapter 17, no. 284."

The Dominican Tommaso de Vio, better known as Cardinal Cajetan (1469–1534), is usually remembered as a commentator of Aquinas's *Summa* and a fierce opponent of the Reformation (he questioned Luther at the Diet of Augsburg in 1518–1519 and refused to annul Henry VIII's marriage to Catherine of Aragon). But he was also the author of several treatises on the economy, including one on exchange dealings, *De cambiis*, written in 1499 and first published in 1506, which sought to categorize licit and illicit forms of exchange and concluded that neither moneychanging involving real coins nor classic bills of exchange were usurious, only re-exchange contracts and dry exchange. Having rejected the notion that four-party bills of exchange were loans, Cajetan's treatise, in the chapter that Cleirac cites, affirmed the usefulness of honest moneychangers who acted for the well-being of society (*civitas*).[21]

Cleirac's other reference in this passage is to Martín Azpilcueta, also known as Doctor Navarrus (1491–1586), another towering figure of Second Scholasticism. The *Enchiridion*, Navarrus's handbook for confessors and penitents, distilled subtle moral and economic arguments about topics such as usury, ecclesiastical properties, and money, and became an extremely popular publication. Chapter 17 of the *Enchiridion* was a commentary on the seventh commandment, "Thou shalt not steal," and delivered a harsh condemnation of usury. Cleirac zooms in on a section that Navarrus added to the revised Latin edition of his handbook focusing on dry exchange as opposed to the four-party bill of exchange. There, agreeing with Cajetan, de Soto, and others, Navarrus declared dry exchange to be against natural, divine, and human justice.[22]

It was precisely this differentiation between unmitigated censures of usury and condemnations of certain types of bills of exchange that interested Cleirac and that he helped popularize. Like most of his contemporaries, however, he clearly found the taxonomy of contractual forms to be insufficient for establishing what constituted acceptable credit practices. To complement the frameworks proposed by moral philosophers and canon and civil lawyers, Cleirac turned to a familiar cultural referent: the figure of the Jewish usurer.

The oblivion into which the legend we are grappling with has fallen today has much to do with the fact that modern scholars of commercial and maritime law are accustomed to thinking that by the seventeenth century, this field of inquiry had entered the sphere of politics and left that of theology. In reality, the figure of the Jewish usurer hardly disappeared from the early modern imagination and impressed on readers the notion of improper financial behavior more effectively than did arguments based on casuistry and canon law. A 1585 French manual of practical arithmetic instructed merchants to calculate compound interest at the same time as it denounced compound interest as "usury of usury" and a Jewish habit that was "execrable" and "abominable" (two adjectives that, as we saw in chapter 2, were typical of anti-Jewish Christian polemics).[23] Forty years later, a treatise on bills of exchange called dry exchange "adulterous," conflating sexual transgression with financial immorality.[24] Cleirac concurred and added that dry exchange was "pure Jewishness" (*pure Iuifverie*).[25]

Even if he was particularly insistent in linking usury to Jews, Cleirac was not alone in this tendency among the authors of early modern didactic texts about merchant practice, whom we might otherwise assume would have taken a more neutral stance. In order to pinpoint specific contracts as acceptable or unacceptable, these texts resorted to the same association between Jews and usury. They thus demonstrate the power of language and tradition to police the boundaries of proper credit and to define, at least in negative terms, ethical standards of behavior and sources of collective identification.

From Jews to Lombards and Cahorsins

Midway into the narrative of what I am calling the legend of the Jewish invention of marine insurance and bills of exchange, Cleirac shifts his target, if not his tone. Having called both credit instruments "Jewish from birth, both in their invention and denomination," he explains that Jews were not the worst culprits in the crime of lending at interest. Even more repugnant, he claims, were those Christians who adopted "this Jewish intrigue" and, "after they retained the models of these letters [i.e., bills of exchange], learned to use them effectively." He refers to these individuals as "Lombards and Cahorsins."

> The unexpected arrival of this sort of usurers from south of the Alps caused them [i.e., the Jews] great discontent and pain, because they [i.e., the Jews] saw that their imitators, their disciples, their acolytes, and their wretched clerks had mastered the art of usury to an even greater extent than they did; they [i.e., Lombard bankers] had become even more evil and malicious insofar as usury and rapaciousness were concerned; they bent and concocted their practices, and extracted from people greater profits and loot than Jews dared to aim for or demand; and those scoundrels were now being treated as noblemen, held in esteem as men of honor and merit, and considerably well-placed in their favors—*e lodati ne van, non che impuniti*— whereas Jews were hated, treated as jackanapes, and continuously ridiculed with contempt and affront, marked with a yellow hat, harassed as pages and lackeys at every occasion.

Lombards, originally hailing from Asti in Piedmont, were licensed Christian moneylenders and bankers whose presence became particularly visible in those regions of Europe from which Jews had been expelled. By 1323, Paris had a Rue des Lombards. The town of Cahors, north of Toulouse, was also invariably associated with devious Christian bankers. Specialists have since corrected several misconceptions concerning the alleged rapaciousness of Lombards and Cahorsins.[26] Here, however, it is the traditional image of these groups as incarnations of avarice and duplicity that matters more than the reality of their lending practices. In this portrayal, the terms *Lombards* and *Cahorsins* lost all geographical specificity and became stands-in for usurious Christian moneylenders. A businessman defending the noted Tuscan merchant Francesco Datini after he joined the guild of bankers and money-changers (*Arte del Cambio*) in 1398, for example, declared: " 'They will say, he is a *caorsino*' and I reply, 'He does not do it to be a usurer, for he will leave all he has to the poor!' "[27] A near contemporary of Cleirac wrote that *Lombard* announced the presence of usury in the same way as *Monte di Pietà* signaled the absence of usury.[28]

In canto XI of Dante's *Inferno*, Cahors takes the place of Gomorrah next to Sodom—a passage that Cleirac cites in full.[29] Following the Aristotelian view absorbed by Thomist theology that "money is barren," sodomy became a synonym for usury. Cleirac finds confirmation of the analogy between Jewish usury and nonreproductive sex in Paul's epistle to the Ephesians (5:3–5), which branded all "fornicators" as "idolaters."[30] The Benedictine monk and English chronicler Matthew Paris (d. 1259), Cleirac's most trusted guide in matters of usury (he is cited a total of five times), denounced not only Jews but also those Christian merchants and bankers who succeeded in "cloaking their usury under the shadow of trade" ("usuram sub specie negotiationis palliantes").[31] Usury, like sodomy, was viewed as an antisocial behavior, and Jews were alleged to excel at it. Blaming Jews for all the evils that had befallen Christian society, a seventeenth-century Portuguese polemicist accused them of having introduced sodomy and incest in Portugal and Africa and described them, drawing on a popular trope of the day, as dogs and horses that could not control their instincts ("cães ou cavalos desenfreados").[32]

In Cleirac's words, Lombards and Cahorsins "mastered the art of usury to an even greater extent than they [the Jews] did" and "extracted from people greater profits and loot than Jews dared to aim for or demand." Having learned to use bills of exchange ("these Jewish inventions"), Christian bankers now only handled "the feather and the sheet of paper," that is, intangible credit instruments rather than minted coins. In so doing, they confounded debtors and preyed on them more easily.

In Cleirac's assessment, Lombards not only had "become even more evil and malicious insofar as usury and rapaciousness were concerned" but were also, concerningly, "treated as noblemen, held in esteem as men of honor and merit." In this serious indictment of Christian rulers and society, Cleirac's humanistic education comes to his rescue, affording him a touch of humor in an otherwise grim portrait. He turns to the Renaissance Italian poet Ludovico Ariosto, who satirized the frequency with which Jews were "harassed . . . at every occasion" (*I suppositi*, III.1) and denounced the hypocrisy of punishing women for adultery while praising men for the same sin (*Orlando Furioso*, IV.66.8).[33] In spite of the comic relief provided by Ariosto, Cleirac still insists on the gravity of the problem. At least "Jews were hated, treated as jackanapes, and continuously ridiculed," he notes. The requirement that they be "marked with a yellow hat" literalized their status as outcasts. But what, if anything, could cordon off Lombards from other Christians? All other measures having failed, the 1274 church canon entitled *The Abyss of Usury* (a document mentioned by Villani) demanded that Christian rulers expel foreign Christian moneylenders from all their domains (chapter 2).

Cleirac gives the following summary of those historical events: "Eventually, these Lombard bankers became so intolerable due to their exorbitant usurious charges, exactions, extortions and illicit profits, that they were treated in France in the same fashion as Jews were." He recounts the sequence of expulsions of Lombards from medieval France in greater detail than he provides for their Jewish equivalents, singling out those ordered by Saint Louis (r. 1226–1270) and Philip the Fair (r. 1285–1314). Cleirac also laments that Lombards ("these rustics") continued to wield considerable influence at court and in 1311 were readmitted to the kingdom "on condition that they would become honest in the future and would abstain from all their bad practices." That did not happen. In fact, "instead of reforming themselves, these parasitical hypocrites became even more dissolute." King Philip VI of Valois (r. 1328–1350) had no choice but to expel them. Finally, in 1347, he "purged his kingdom of them and drove them out of France."[34]

When relaying the chronology of Jews' expulsions from medieval France in the first part of his narrative, Cleirac makes no reference to specific chronicles or other sources of information. By contrast, when outlining the actions taken by French kings against foreign Christian moneylenders, he offers more details and relies not only on older narratives by the chronicler Jean Froissart (c. 1337–c. 1405) and the royal secretary and historian Nicole Gilles (d. 1503), but also on more recent writers, including Étienne Pasquier (1529–1615), a historian one generation younger than Cleirac who based his work on documents he had examined firsthand while an officer in the royal treasury.[35] A compilation by French lawyer and jurist Adam Théveneau serves as a further reminder that public authorities had taken steps to curb usury in France since the fourteenth century.[36] Catholic authors like Cleirac, in other words, had access to considerably less factual information about the Jewish past than the Christian past, but this imbalance did not prevent them from using a few known episodes in Jewish history for didactic purposes.

Jewish Usury: Theology, Law, and Metaphor

In the end, the primary targets of Cleirac's spiteful portrayal of Jews are not Jews themselves but Lombards, Cahorsins, Guelfs, and all other Christian bankers: "These malicious liars, whose frauds are aimed to take people by surprise and to pillage their fortunes, . . . enriched themselves at the expense of their debtors, whom they initially pretended to wish to assist charitably in their adversities, only to lure them into their net." The ill intent of those able to manipulate credit instruments with ease was viewed as even more lamentable because it exploited naïve borrowers whose needs were pressing. Cleirac describes Christian bankers who had perfected the art of trading in bills of exchange as predatory lenders:

> Having hooked their debtors, they became even more eager to seize every possible gain, to exact usury, exchange and re-exchange rates, stipulate fines, expenditures, damages and interest, and other such shameful incremental charges, so that they never wanted to receive back the principal as long as the debtor was left solvent. They were elated by the facility with which deeds of protest and overdue terms could apply. When a debtor was weak or in difficulty, they never left him in peace, but tormented him at every scheduled date when interest payments came due, that is, every month (because in these matters *usance* and month are synonyms, in the sense that usury means interest payments stipulated by month) and they never ended their harassment until they had taken everything from their debtors.

Layered with technical language, this merciless denunciation of Lombards and Cahorsins indicates that, no matter how extravagant his commentary may appear to us, Cleirac assumed his readers were well versed in the financial intricacies of bills of exchange. He also counted on them to recognize the description of Christian bankers as "imitators," "disciples," "acolytes," and "wretched clerks" of Jews. As Léon Poliakov noted more than fifty years ago, to say " 'Jewish usury' does not necessarily mean that it is or was carried on by Jews."[37] *Peius iudaizare*, or "behaving in a manner even worse than the Jews," is how the Cistercian monk Bernard of Clairvaux (1090–1153) famously described the conduct of Christian moneylenders, adding that it would be more appropriate to call them "baptized Jews" than Christians.[38] In the early Christian church, the sin of "Judaizing" described the actions of those Jews who had recently converted to Christianity but continued to observe certain rites of their former religion, such as fasting and circumcision. During the medieval commercial revolution, the verb "to Judaize" ceased to carry a literal meaning and became the cornerstone of a discursive edifice in which Christian usurers were cast as "baptized Jews."

Wherever Jewish converts to Christianity were a lived reality, the insidious analogy between Christian usurers and "baptized Jews" acquired particular poignancy.[39] It was in the aftermath of the mass conversions that occurred in Spain after the violent pogroms against Jews of the 1390s that the Valencian Dominican preacher Saint Vincent Ferrer (1350–1419) railed: "Today, nearly everything is avarice, for almost everyone commits usury, which used not to be done except by Jews. But today Christians do it too, as if they were Jews."[40] This rhetorical casting of Christian merchants who engaged in unacceptable behavior as Jews gained enormous traction and lived on well beyond the confines of those locations where the recently converted Jews were the object of policing and suspicion.[41]

To call a dishonest Christian a Jew was the easiest answer to a wrenching question: What defined a good merchant? No single or uniform Catholic theory of usury existed. Even theologians' obsessive attempts to create typologies of credit contracts, such as those formulated by Cajetan and Navarrus, did not resolve the matter. Part of the ambiguity was intentional. Thirteenth-century theologians and canon lawyers had devised a vast array of "exceptions" to the stringent norm that "any sum returned in excess to the principal is usury." These exceptions were not aberrations but rather constitutive elements of a moral and theological paradigm designed to make the reputation (fama) of contracting parties a defining criterion of the legitimacy of credit contracts and thus to understand market exchanges as mirrors of social relations and hierarchies that existed outside of the marketplace.[42] In this sense, the antisocial nature of usury retained its versatile symbolic power well beyond the historical context in which it emerged (the moral theology of the early thirteenth century). That is why Cleirac could still mobilize the trope of Jewish usury in the seventeenth century, when commercial society was acquiring more pronounced contractual features.

Government tribunals did not offer clearer directives on usury than the church. Secular authorities turned many sexual and economic sins into crimes, but in matters of usury, it was the latitude, rather than strictures, of theological and canonical definitions that influenced civil law and jurisprudence, especially in Catholic states.[43] France long resisted setting a cap on the interest allowed on private loans, and both norms and customs of lending varied greatly across the kingdom. During Cleirac's lifetime, royal legislation still formally forbade lending at interest and reiterated the state's opposition to all forms of usury.[44] A special regime was devised for certain types of long-term credit instruments backed by collateral, which normally took the form of real estate; such instruments were in essence private annuities that demanded the repayment of low rates of interest (*rentes perpétuelles* and *rentes viagères*).[45] The crown capped interest rates on annuities at 6.25 percent per annum in 1601 and lowered this ceiling to 5 percent in 1655, where it stayed for most of the eighteenth century.[46]

Meanwhile, royal authorities exhibited considerable hesitation about setting similar terms for commercial credit. The city of Lyon was the exception. There, royal edicts spoke of "interest" rather than "usury" in reference to bills transacted at the fairs to shield them from criticism.[47] Jean-Baptiste Colbert sought to codify a lawful 5 percent interest rate for commercial loans, but the committee he charged with drafting the 1673 ordinance on commerce rejected his proposal for fear of antagonizing the Faculty of Theology at the Sorbonne, which opposed the measure because it put a price on usury. As a compromise, the final 1673 ordinance (title VI, art. 1) allowed merchants and others dealing in bills of exchange to charge interest, but not to hide it behind the principal (which is what all merchants did).[48] The discrepancy between law and practice, however, soon gave way to rampant abuses and inspired reformers like Étienne Bonnot de Condillac and Anne-Robert-Jacques Turgot in the 1770s to call for legitimizing interest-bearing loans and letting the market equalize their rates.[49] The arbiters who adjudicated lawsuits over bills of exchange for the commercial court of Paris sometimes detected an injury (*lésion*) in the exchange rate and recommended compensation.[50] Only the Revolution lifted all legal restrictions on charging interest on loans and moved to regulate interest rates on October 12, 1789.[51] Until then, though they were never numerous, usury trials were held and offenders punished with bans and rites of public humiliation reminiscent of earlier times, in which they were made to kneel in public squares holding a sign labeling them "manifest usurers."[52]

Evidently, it was not to positive law or to the courts that one could turn in the mid-seventeenth century for clear-cut answers about the legitimacy of all forms of bills of exchange. Merchant manuals and legal commentaries sought to fill the void. The extent to which these texts, which varied in scope, originality, and precision, were meant and able to impart practical knowledge to aspiring or experienced practitioners remains debatable. Most certainly, they fulfilled a different but essential function in the self-regulation of European commercial society: they forged a shared understanding of the cultural underpinnings that sustained the more or less detailed formal norms of the credit contracts they illustrated.

Cleirac partook in this effort. His predecessors, including Jean Trenchant and Mathias Maréschal, had followed more conventional paths, adopting the taxonomy of legitimate and illegitimate bills of exchange established by moral theologians.[53] A trained lawyer, Cleirac oscillates between an all-encompassing meaning of usury as improper economic practice and a narrower jurisprudential approach. In *Us et coustumes de la mer*, in addition to citing the opinions of theologians like Cajetan, Navarrus, and Coli, who all declared dry exchange to be usurious, he mentions a sentence (*arrêt*) issued by Bordeaux's royal appellate court (*parlement*) on July 16, 1637, confirming an earlier ruling of the city's commercial tribunal against someone caught using dry exchange.[54] Cleirac exhibits a more contradictory attitude toward marine insurance. He dismisses those who still regarded it as a form of speculation rather than as the price of risk, but he also stresses the uncertainty under which premiums were negotiated and enforced (e.g., the difficulty of verifying when a shipwreck occurred, the incompetence of ship captains who prolonged a voyage) and calls underwriters "truly usurious and Jewish" for speculating on this uncertainty.[55] Rather than expressing unrelenting opposition to all credit contracts, these accusations confirm the facility with which Cleirac summoned the figure of the Jewish usurer to condemn economic practices that he judged to be unfair but the dubiousness of which he could not better articulate.

In his treatise on bills of exchange, *Usance du négoce* (a shorter work than *Us et coustumes de la mer* and a standalone piece rather than a commentary), Cleirac also alternates between description and moralizing admonishment, between crude attacks against usury and subtler accounts of specific credit contracts, between accurate citations and fanciful readings. In addition to Cajetan and Navarrus, he invokes a noted Florentine merchant in Flanders, Ludovico Guicciardini, to argue that four-party bills of exchange are "useful and genuine, when used with moderation and loyalty."[56] He stresses the need to combine the knowledge of customary norms related to bills of exchange with "human prudence."[57] Unable to define how exactly "human prudence" affects credit operations, he singles out people whom he asserts obviously lack this quality: Jews, to be sure, since they were "cheaters" and thus willing to take advantage of any opportunity regardless of its consequences, but also "Mohammedans," "Turks," and "Saracens," all of whom lagged behind the Jews in financial sophistication.[58] With rare precision, in one instance, he gives a number to the practices he describes: 12 percent annual interest, by his estimation, was the standard rate charged by "bankers, Jews, and dirty usurers."[59] Reverting to old habits, he calls dry exchange "a business of Jews and Cahorsins."[60]

In so many words, Cleirac reveals the impossibility of giving a precise and exhaustive definition of "good business." Nowhere does he define usury in unambiguous terms. Rather, usury is how he refers to everything he regards as the opposite of prudent, upright, and legal ways of handling bills of exchange. As the next chapter will show, Cleirac's marketplace promoted talent and created new riches, but it was also full of menaces and villains, replete with jealousy between groups, and haunted by the possibility of fraud. It was anything but an ecumenical meeting place of faceless merchants, seafarers, and underwriters. Regulation mattered (that is why Cleirac chose to study maritime and commercial law in the first place), yet regulation alone could not guarantee the fair conduct of trade. Cleirac resorted to stereotyping not only because prejudice against Jews was rooted in the mentality of the time, but also because written norms about bills of exchange and other financial instruments were still sparse during the first half of the seventeenth century. By conjuring "Jewish extortion" (*Iuifve tortionaire*), he could explain the ineffable: objectionable ways of handling bills of exchange that went undetected.[61]

Should Cleirac's railing against Jews and others he lumps together with them ultimately surprise us? The answer is yes and no. His words are more venomous than those that punctuate other merchant manuals, legal commentaries, and dictionaries of trade, and his work is sometimes amateurish. But his habit of alternating between technical disquisitions about credit instruments, tenets of moral theology, and invocations of Jewish usury as the archetype of financial misconduct would have been entirely recognizable to his readers. In this respect, *Us et coustumes de la mer* belongs to the continental literature on commercial and maritime law of the sixteenth and seventeenth centuries, which, Rodolfo Savelli reminds us, displayed a distinctive osmosis of law, theology, and merchant culture.[62] As the language of commerce became more and more secular, it did not shed its didactic invocations of Jewish usury.

Conclusion

This chapter and the previous one have parsed Cleirac's jumbled arguments in an effort to render them as intelligible as I believe they would have been to his many seventeenth-century readers. In the process, I have set aside an important detail to which we must return. Cleirac maintains that "insurance policies and bills of exchange were unknown to ancient Roman jurisprudence." This portion of his otherwise outlandish account of the emergence of Europe's financial instruments is truthful and, far from representing a mere legal technicality, gestures toward a pivotal component of the logic that undergirds the legend.

Medieval and early modern legal scholars searched long and hard for the Roman origins of both marine insurance and bills of exchange and eventually concluded that premium-based insurance, the forerunner of our modern forms of insurance, as opposed to other risk-sharing agreements, did not exist in antiquity and that examples of credit transfers noted by classical authors did not amount to proper bills of exchange. The sentence of the Genoese Rota with which Cleirac opens his commentary on the first article of the *Guidon de la mer* defined marine insurance as a *contractus innominatus* ("nameless contract"), a category developed by medieval jurists to indicate contracts that did not have a specific equivalent in the Roman civil law of obligations. Thus called because they lacked a name in the authoritative ancient sources, nameless contracts were voluntary bilateral agreements in which each party, acting with equal contractual power, promised to do his part to fulfill the agreement.[63] Marine insurance and bills of exchange fell into this category, which Cleirac, a graduate of law, knew well.[64]

Improbable as their designation sounds, nameless contracts belong to a momentous chapter in the history of European law, one during which new legal classifications emerged as expressions of the political and social order of city-states where, after the late eleventh century, urban elites tied to commercial interests affirmed their independence from the feudal aristocracy. The late medieval growth of long-distance trade demanded that full contractual rights be given to social groups that until then had been regarded as inferior to the titled nobility. It also demanded the recognition of new financial contracts and the development of new doctrines and customary practices to absorb those contracts into existing legal systems. The two requirements were really one. Reciprocity, consensus, and good faith were the defining elements of the new contracts, which were in turn predicated upon the legal ability of some (though not all) individuals to enter into voluntary contracts with one another. The men at the helm of the medieval city-states and those who belonged to the high-ranking guilds were the primary beneficiaries of these new legal doctrines. The poor, slaves, captives, unfree domestic labor, male rural workers, and the vast majority of women remained severely restricted in their contractual autonomy.

Confronted with the expansion of credit instruments during the commercial revolution of the Middle Ages, jurists and lawyers were tasked with reconciling the conception of social groups as belonging to a fixed natural hierarchy with the recognition of the freedom of consenting individuals to enter into voluntary commercial agreements with their peers.[65] Debates of enormous consequence for the course of European history focusing on the interplay of an individual's legal status (as defined by birth or, more rarely, through a rite of passage) and his freedom to choose among a broader or narrower set of contractual options infused the legalistic disquisitions that between the eleventh and thirteenth centuries began to redefine the law of obligations on the Continent. During the sixteenth century, a time of rapid demographic and economic growth, the pace of these legal and social transformations accelerated and provoked a crisis of legibility in the market. In this early phase of European globalization, international merchants increasingly operated with "the feather and the sheet of paper," that is, immaterial payment and credit instruments. They were no longer required to enroll in guilds (unlike artisans) and thus escaped guilds' supervision.[66] As merchant guilds, the institutions that had traditionally guaranteed the good standing of their members, lost ground, traders involved in transactions across long distances had to resort to other means to prove their good reputation. Rank alone had never been a sufficient metric of credibility, but the expansion of the boundaries of commercial society represented something new: the promise of broader participation in market exchanges and the peril of the indiscriminate mixing of actors using increasingly abstract credit instruments.

How were investors and entrepreneurs wishing to enter into a voluntary bilateral agreement with someone outside of their immediate circle to verify the integrity and expertise of the contracting party? The legend of the Jewish invention of marine insurance and bills of exchange, erroneous as it was, provided an answer to this vital and yet intractable question. The legend evoked risks that could not be calculated easily and drew symbolic boundaries in a world in which intangible financial instruments and the erosion of merchants' corporate status made the impersonality of the market as threatening as it was potentially beneficial.

On a discursive level, a striking continuity linked the twelfth-century French abbot of Clairvaux to the seventeenth-century lawyer of Bordeaux: the frequent semantic slippage between Jews and untrustworthy creditors in general. Visual and textual examples of this analogy survive in artifacts from the seventeenth-century Spanish Low Countries, where no Jews had resided since the Black Death and where "Lombards" replaced them until 1618. In paintings large and small, Christian moneylenders were depicted with recognizable

"Jewish" attributes.[67] On the level of everyday reality, by the mid-sixteenth century, the notion of "baptized Jews" was as much a lived experience as a metaphor in Bordeaux, since many of the Jews who were fleeing the Iberian inquisitions passed through or settled in the region north of the Pyrenees. Not the world of the ghetto, but the conversion crises of the 1490s, as the next chapter will show, loomed large in the pages of *Us et coustumes de la mer*.

4

Bordeaux, the Specter of Crypto-Judaism, and the Changing Status of Commerce

THE PREVIOUS TWO CHAPTERS have treated Cleirac's annotations as "a tissue of quotations drawn from the innumerable centers of culture" and shown that, out of this "tissue," a new narrative came to life.[1] The next chapters will survey the fate of this narrative—a fate that surely surpassed its author's expectations and embedded variants of the original formulation into a chain of intertextual transmission. For now, I wish to illustrate the circumstances in which Cleirac composed his writings. I do so not in the name of the illusion against which Roland Barthes famously protested: "When the Author has been found, the text is 'explained.'"[2] Rather, by immersing the legend of the Jewish invention of marine insurance and bills of exchange in the time and place in which it was first committed to print, I continue in my effort to recover some of the implicit connections that readers would likely have made at the time and that today elude us.

Étienne Cleirac (1583–1657) was born, lived, and died in Bordeaux, where a street is named after him (figure 4.1). Then a mid-ranking urban center, Bordeaux was the site of an important humanist secondary school and a law school, a burgeoning Atlantic port and banking center, and one of only two French cities (the other was Metz, annexed to France in 1552) where a Jewish minority resided. Bordeaux's Jewish minority, however, was unusual in the sense that, unlike Metz's, it was not openly Jewish. In 1550, the French crown invited "merchants and other Portuguese known as New Christians" to settle in the southwestern region of the kingdom, exempting them from the need to

FIGURE 4.1. The street of Bordeaux named after Cleirac

request naturalization letters. This invitation automatically guaranteed these immigrants' families the same privileges as all French subjects, including freedom of movement, full property rights, and the ability to conduct any economic activities they wished.[3] By this measure, "his most Christian majesty," as the French king was addressed at the time, aimed to inject capital and talent into his trading system. The ordinance's beneficiaries, though unnamed, were unmistakable: those former Jews who, having been forcibly converted to Catholicism in Spain and Portugal during the 1490s, wished to escape. Even more specifically, the ordinance targeted those New Christians who lived in Portugal, for whom the recent creation of a national inquisition in 1536 constituted a mounting threat.

In the mid-sixteenth century, other towns in Europe, including Florence, Ferrara, and Antwerp, also welcomed New Christians in spite of the Catholic Church's objection to leniency toward baptized Jews, whom Rome regarded as prone to living secretly as Jews in defiance of the sanctity of baptism. But this type of accommodation was short-lived. By the 1590s, secular authorities preferred to invite Iberian émigrés to settle in their territories as Jews, rather than as New Christians, in order to dispel any residual ambiguity surrounding their religious identity. As a result, new Sephardic Jewish communities were established in Venice, Livorno, Hamburg, and Amsterdam. In Bordeaux, however, the institutional arrangement devised in 1550 continued for more than a century and a half. The absence of any modern inquisition tribunal in France allowed for the emergence of a regime of toleration in which crypto-Judaism was an open secret. The theological notion of "baptized Jews" thus found its most lasting institutional incarnation outside of Iberia in southwestern France. While few in number, "Portuguese merchants" were overrepresented among Bordeaux's international traders and well established in certain manufacturing sectors (silk and Moroccan leather in particular), local retail markets, and the medical profession.[4] For all the reasons we have recounted, New Christians' concealed religious identity not only troubled religious authorities but also heightened fears that behind any reputable merchant might lurk a "Jewish usurer."

The consolidation of the Portuguese community in Bordeaux after the Wars of Religion (1562–1598) coincided with a period of economic and legal changes that tested the traditional division in Old Regime French society between noblemen and merchants. Historians have written extensively on the venality of France's legal and administrative offices, first institutionalized under Francis I (r. 1515–1547), and on the creation of the "nobility of the robe" (as opposed to the "nobility of the sword"), a title and idea that undermined genealogical conceptions of nobility.[5] They have also dissected the appearance of "merit" in the aristocratic language of the seventeenth century and the need to reconcile merit with deep-seated notions of lineage and the hereditary quality of "honor."[6]

We know much less about the changing legal and cultural status of commerce in the seventeenth century, especially during its first half, before Jean-Baptiste Colbert, who served as Louis XIV's controller-general of finance from 1665 until his death in 1683, initiated a series of consequential reforms. Idiosyncratic as they are, Cleirac's writings afford us a unique entry point into this transformative and yet neglected phase of French history, offering the view of a sympathetic but distressed participant-observer at a time when ongoing economic changes and the crown's political ambitions were putting pressure on long-held ideas about the place of commerce in a well-ordered corporate society. The meaning of the word "merchant" had evolved over the years: it no longer exclusively denoted someone affiliated with a guild but referred to anyone who carried out a range of commercial transactions. As a result, both noblemen and Jews could be designated as merchants. New symbolic hierarchies, Cleirac implies, had to be erected as legal ones were being eroded.

After graduating from the Collège de Guyenne, one of the kingdom's most renowned humanist secondary schools (both Michel de Montaigne and Joseph Scaliger had been educated there), Cleirac studied law and spent the rest of his life working as a barrister (*avocat*) at the royal appellate court (*parlement*) of Bordeaux and, briefly, as a royal legal official (*procureur du roy*) in the city's admiralty (figure 4.2).[7] In 1616 he acquired the status of *bourgeois*, a title that at the time granted not only social recognition but also fiscal exemptions, and two years later he married.[8] While many in his profession embraced the Calvinist faith, Cleirac remained fiercely Catholic and monarchist, whether out of conviction or necessity. His professional career suffered from his son's prominent involvement in the Ormée (1651–1653), Bordeaux's radical arm of the Fronde, which rallied many artisans, merchants, lawyers, low-ranking magistrates, and a few clergymen to revolt against the monarchy.[9] Forced to retreat to his residence in the countryside as a result of his son's activities, Cleirac immersed himself in reading and writing. At the time of his death, he had amassed a vast collection of 671 books.[10]

Unusually for a man of his time and background, Cleirac turned his attention not to the *ius commune* or the French *coutumes*, subjects that animated both theorists and critics of absolutism, but to maritime law. He approached the topic from a stance steeped in humanistic learning and Roman law but also armed with firsthand experience, having participated in complex deliberations involving shipowners, captains, sailors, merchants, and underwriters. Probably driven by self-promotion, he aimed to produce a text that would be of practical use to judges and administrators. Today virtually unknown outside a small

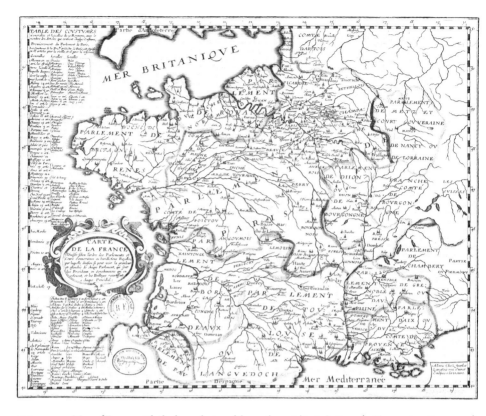

FIGURE 4.2. Map of France with the boundaries of the *parlements'* jurisdictions (mid-seventeenth century). With permission from the Bibliothèque Nationale de France, Paris.

circle of experts, *Us et coustumes de la mer* proved a remarkable publishing success.[11] An arcane and specialized subject, then as now, maritime law in the early seventeenth century overlapped with multiple spheres of knowledge, life, and government. It was not a topic of instruction in law schools, but since the mid-sixteenth century it had generated a few important scholarly treatments, which served as guides to magistrates who adjudicated commercial and financial litigation. Meanwhile, the growing centrality of overseas trade in the international system of great powers put maritime and commercial law squarely at the center of emerging interstate and domestic politics.

The two best-known French contributions to European statecraft in these fields are the royal ordinances on commercial (1673) and maritime (1681) law. Both of these ordinances were the fruit of a long period of legal, political, and intellectual gestation. It was during that period and against the backdrop of the peculiar composition of Bordeaux's commercial society that Cleirac included the legend of the Jewish invention of marine insurance and bills of exchange in his commentary on Rouen's rules of marine insurance.

A Forgotten Bestseller of the *Ars Mercatoria*

Nothing like *Us et coustumes de la mer*—a vernacular publication that assembled, translated, and commented on legal norms of maritime trade developed in western and northern Europe since the twelfth century—existed in Europe when it first appeared in Bordeaux in 1647.[12] Judging by its publication record, it filled a void. Printed in-quarto (roughly 10 × 8 inches), the 1647 edition is a voluminous text of 576 pages, plus index and appendices. An expanded version appeared in Bordeaux in 1661 in a print run of at least 1,200 copies, an extraordinarily high run for any nonreligious book, and all the more so for one devoted to maritime law.[13] For purposes of comparison, consider that in 1528, the first edition of Baldassare Castiglione's *Courtier*, one of early modern Europe's veritable bestsellers, comprised 1,030 copies.[14] Print runs grew over time, but in the early seventeenth century it was still rare for more than 1,000 copies of nonreligious books to be printed; publishers only made some 2,000 to 3,000 copies of certain dictionaries and Roman or canon law compilations.[15]

The 1661 edition of *Us et coustumes de la mer* replaced the first and was reissued with minimal alterations four more times: in Paris in 1665, in Rouen in 1671 and 1682, and in Amsterdam in 1788.[16] The choice to publish the work in the vernacular set Cleirac apart from other jurists and proved a recipe for success, albeit one that largely bypassed him, since he died four years before the second edition went to press. Until the appearance of Jean-Marie Pardessus's monumental compilation in the mid-nineteenth century, *Us et coustumes de la mer* was the single most comprehensive collection of European maritime laws published in the vernacular.[17]

The volume is divided into three sections. The first comprises the Judgments of Oléron, the Laws of Wisby, and the rules of the Hanseatic League from 1591, which Cleirac incorrectly dates to 1597 (although the mistake is perhaps simply due to a typographical error). The second section focuses on marine insurance, reproducing the *Guidon de la mer* as well as the norms on marine insurance promulgated by Philip II in Antwerp in 1563 (inaccurately dated to 1593) and an ordinance published in Amsterdam in 1598, together with the relevant formulas. Finally, the third section consists of a redacted and copiously annotated assemblage of French royal ordinances pertaining to internal and seaborne navigation in times of war and peace issued between 1400 and 1584. It expands, reorganizes, and comments on all decrees concerning the jurisdiction of the admiralty of France listed in the most extensive collection of French royal ordinances to date, the so-called "Code Henri," after King Henry III (r. 1574–1589), who had commissioned it.[18] At the end of the volume, Cleirac appends an earlier minor work, *Explication des termes de marine* (1636), a short text that belonged to the emerging genre of maritime and naval dictionaries and contained a rudimentary glossary of terms pertaining to maritime trade and contracts, followed by a description of flags used by ships of different states.[19]

Only the book's first section was translated into English in 1686, when it appeared as *The Ancient Sea-laws of Oleron, Wisby and the Hanse-towns Still in Force* and was immediately reprinted together with Gerard Malynes's *Consuetudo, vel Lex Mercatoria, or, The Ancient Law-Merchant* (first published in 1622), one of the most popular English-language merchant manuals of the period.[20] The English translation omitted the *Guidon de la mer*, and thus Cleirac's commentary that featured the pseudo-historical narrative of the Jewish invention of marine insurance and bills of exchange. The omission was logical, since the Judgments of Oléron, the contested authorship of which elicited competing patriotic accounts from French and English writers, and the Laws of Wisby, which influenced the rules of Dutch and Baltic navigation, were the most interesting texts edited by Cleirac for English-speaking readers.[21] This editorial choice, however, affected the legend's reception in England (chapter 7).

The seven pages of *Us et coustumes de la mer* that recount when and why Jews invented marine insurance and bills of exchange and how misguided Christian bankers adopted those credit instruments are unusually unwieldy. All of Cleirac's commentaries, however, juxtapose predictable and legitimate sources with more improbable ones. The result is a mishmash of citations from the Hebrew Bible, the New Testament, and the writings of greater and lesser Roman and Greek authors, Church Fathers, saints, theologians, antiquarians, geographers, medieval chroniclers, towering humanists like Gerolamo Cardano and Scaliger, novelists and poets like Dante, Boccaccio, and Ariosto, and historians like Nicole Gilles and Étienne Pasquier, as well as collections of proverbs and travelers' accounts. Only when he added citations from the Qur'an and *The Prophecies of Merlin* to the second edition did Cleirac feel compelled to explain that he chose to include the works of such "ignorant and ridiculous" authors not because he believed their superstitions but because they were their own worst enemies, in the sense that they could not hide their fallacies.[22]

The eclecticism of *Us et coustumes de la mer* gives it a flavor of dilettantism and has earned its author a mixed reputation among modern specialists, yet this characteristic was arguably one of the primary ingredients of its appeal. The work translated and digested for a broad reading public concerns about the world of commerce that were located at the intersection of law, theology, humanism, and practical merchant culture. At least one person studied the book sufficiently seriously to compile a (generally accurate) printed list of all the authors cited in it (figure 4.3).[23]

Us et coustumes de la mer was and remains difficult to classify. A nearly exact contemporary of Hugo Grotius (1583–1645), Cleirac lacked that scholar's original mind and eloquence. He drew from established models of legal scholarship, but the muddled nature of his annotations departs from the rigor of Latin treatises on commercial and maritime law by jurists like the Anconetan Benvenuto Stracca, the Portuguese Pedro de Santarém, the Roman Sigismondo Scaccia, and the Genoese Raffaele della Torre, not to mention Grotius and his rival John Selden.[24] More than any of those treatises, *Us et coustumes de la mer* abounds in practical instructions, examples of contracts, and moralizing tales about credit, yet it is neither a merchant handbook nor a confessor manual. Leaning on his training, Cleirac repeatedly references Roman law, jurisprudence, and French regional customs. And while he turns regularly to prominent legal scholars like Andrea Alciato (1492–1550), Charles du Moulin (1500–1566), Jacques Cujas (1522–1590), and Charles Loyseau (1566–1627), he does not disdain more modest French jurists and lawyers with expertise in local statutes and customs.[25]

Cleirac's sparing use of practical or normative books about trade is symptomatic of his position as a half-removed observer of the world of maritime trade. The list of his citations from this genre is short even if we consider that he wrote before Jacques Savary produced his masterpiece in 1675 (chapter 5); it is limited to the works of Jean Trenchant, Juan de Hevia Bolaños, Mathias Maréschal, Peter Peck, and Pedro de Santarém, as well as the sentences of the Genoese Rota.[26] While he quotes Italian poets and playwrights, Cleirac makes no reference to the robust Italian literature on commerce and exchange dealing that was widely accessible at the time. There is no mention of Bernardo Davanzati's treatises on bills of exchange, Giovanni Domenico Peri's merchant manual, or even Benedetto Cotrugli's *Della mercatura*, which had been

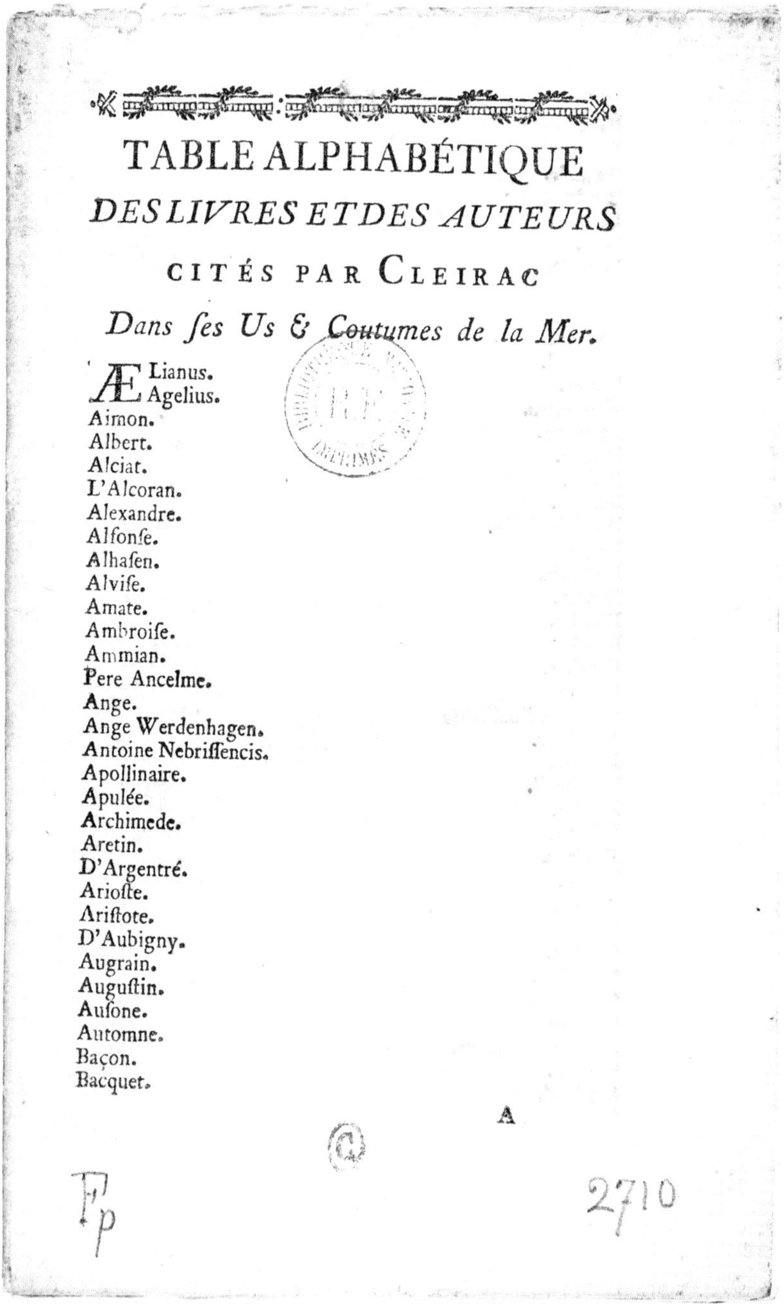

TABLE ALPHABÉTIQUE

DES LIVRES ET DES AUTEURS

CITÉS PAR CLEIRAC

Dans ses Us & Coutumes de la Mer.

Æ Lianus.
Æ Agelius.
Aimon.
Albert.
Alciat.
L'Alcoran.
Alexandre.
Alfonse.
Alhasen.
Alvise.
Amate.
Ambroise.
Ammian.
Pere Ancelme.
Ange.
Ange Werdenhagen.
Antoine Nebrissencis.
Apollinaire.
Apulée.
Archimede.
Aretin.
D'Argentré.
Arioste.
Aristote.
D'Aubigny.
Augrain.
Augustin.
Ausone.
Automne.
Baçon.
Bacquet.

A

FIGURE 4.3. First page of a printed alphabetical list of all authors and texts
cited in *Us et coustumes de la mer*. With permission from
the Bibliothèque Nationale de France, Paris.

translated into French. The absence of these Italian classics helps explain why Cleirac attributes to medieval Jews, rather than to Florentines, as Cotrugli did, the invention of marine insurance and bills of exchange.[27]

In spite of its inaccuracies and distortions, readers flocked to *Us et coustumes de la mer*. At the time of its publication, maritime law was attracting the increasing attention of statesmen, publishers, scholars, and practitioners alike. In the 1570s, a merchant from Marseilles, Guillaume Giraud, had commissioned the translation and printing of Barcelona's *Libre del consolat de mar* (composed around 1340 and first printed in Catalan in 1494), the best-known medieval collection of maritime customs from southern Europe.[28] In the 1620s and 1630s, preeminent man of letters Nicolas-Claude Fabri de Peiresc (1580–1637) displayed more than a passing interest in maritime law in his wide-ranging inquiries into overseas trade.[29] The aggressive military policies pursued by Cardinal Armand du Plessis, Duke of Richelieu and chief minister of the French crown from 1624 to 1642, required that France defend its prerogatives over the sea, especially in the English Channel and the Mediterranean. An expansive treatise published in Latin in 1643 by Claude Barthélemy de Morisot (1592–1661), of which Cleirac makes use, outlined the evolution of maritime and commercial law and articulated a distinctive synthesis of the doctrines of *mare liberum* (the right to free circulation on the high seas) and *mare clausum* (a state's sovereignty over the sea).[30]

This literature was as much the result of emerging political and intellectual concerns as a response to specific incidents at sea that demanded that state officials be given new legal weapons with which to embark on elaborate diplomatic negotiations. In 1627, one of these potentially explosive events endangered relations between France and Spain at a delicate moment. Years later, when he sat down to compile *Us et coustumes de la mer*, Cleirac still had a vivid memory of his involvement in this tragic incident.

Crisis on the Guyenne Shore

In mid-January 1627, two enormous Portuguese cargo ships, the *São Bartolomeu* and the *Santa Helena*, as well as five of the six armed galleons that escorted them, sank in the Bay of Biscay (figures 4.4 and 4.5). A survivor called the naval disaster the greatest loss Portugal had sustained since the time of King Sebastian—a comparison that was not meant lightly, given how largely the loss of independence that followed the death of King Sebastian in 1578 loomed in the Portuguese imagination.[31] In the winter of 1627, the royal

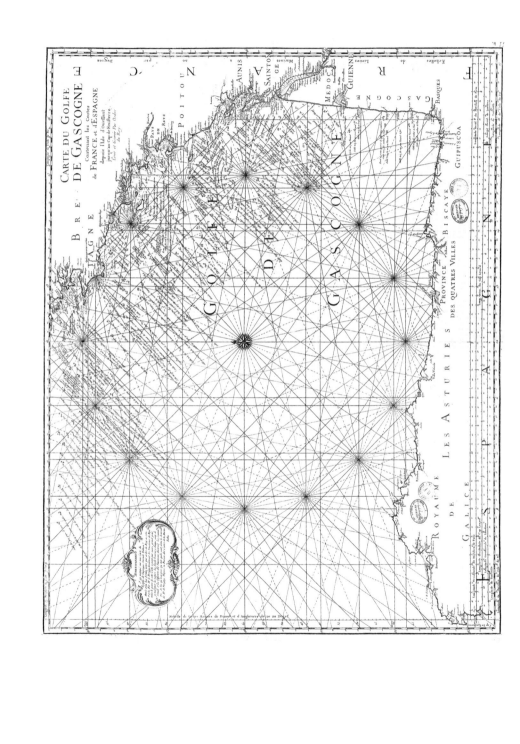

CARTE DU GOLFE DE GASCOGNE

Contenant les Costes de FRANCE et d'ESPAGNE depuis l'Isle d'Ouessant jusqu'au Cap de Finisterre.
Levée et dressée par Ordre du Roy

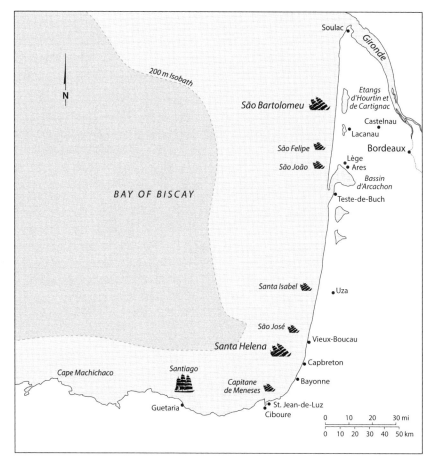

FIGURE 4.5 The Portuguese shipwreck of January 12-14, 1627. Redrawn by William Nelson from Jean-Yves Blot and Patrik Lizé, eds., *Le naufrage des portugais sur les côtes de Saint-Jean-de-Luz et d'Arcachon (1627)* (Paris: Chandeigne, 2000), 174.

convoy was returning to Lisbon, as it did every year, from Goa, the capital of the Portuguese Empire in India, to discharge its precious cargo of spices, ivory, ebony, ceramics, wax, coconut, silk, Chinese wooden cabinets, Indian cotton textiles, precious stones, ambergris, bezoar, and other prized imports from Asia, Ethiopia, and the interior of Africa. Exact figures for the 1627 losses differ from one source to another, but all of the numbers provided are staggering. Perhaps as many as 2,000 men perished, including high-ranking noblemen, and only 215 members of the crew survived. The total cargo was valued at between 6 and 8 million ducats—an extraordinary sum that equaled the official value of all annual imports from Spanish America in that same year.

The timing and location of the shipwreck could not have been less propitious for Richelieu. Earlier that January, he had begun to deploy his diplomatic talent to persuade the king of Spain, Philip IV, to lend him military aid against the English and the Huguenots at La Rochelle.[32] Now Philip IV demanded the return of the spoils of the wreckage that were turning up along the beaches of southwestern France. In seeking to comply with the request, the cardinal discovered the limits of his own domestic power. That peasants and villagers looted whatever they found was only part of the problem. Royal legislation in matters of wrecks (*droit de bris et naufrage*) assigned a third of all unclaimed recovered goods to those who salvaged them, a third to the admiral of France (a role that Richelieu had recently assumed), and a third either to the king or to local feudal lords.[33] The latter provision was the vestige of an old customary right (*le droict de coste*, or *varech* in Normandy). It was to this right that the powerful governor of Guyenne, Jean-Louis Nogaret de La Valette, duc d'Épernon (1544–1642), appealed when claiming possession of several diamonds that washed ashore and obstructing the cardinal's initiatives.

In order to sort out these legal controversies and placate both domestic and foreign stakeholders, Richelieu sent two envoys to the region, first François de Fortia and then Abel de Servien.[34] Cleirac was then the chief legal appointee (*procureur du roy*) at the admiralty of Bordeaux, which adjudicated conflicts over shipwrecks and maritime trade, and in that capacity assisted Fortia and Servien (he later used his privileged access to admiralty documents when composing *Us et coustumes de la mer*).[35] Meanwhile, Richelieu also charged a learned member of the Parisian republic of letters, Théodore Godefroy (1580–1649), with assembling the existing doctrine and jurisprudence concerning the law of wreck. By the time Godefroy handed in his report in January 1630, the dispute had been resolved and Richelieu was absorbed by the War of Mantua Succession. As a result, to this day, Godefroy's work remains unpublished.[36]

Unlike Godefroy, Cleirac took to writing on his own initiative, seeing his work as a tool of social affirmation. He seems never to have been in Paris, never to have corresponded with the capital's literati, and never to have joined any of the kingdom's emerging scholarly academies. Isolated even in his own Bordeaux, he poured his energies into compiling *Us et coustumes de la mer*. To redeem his reputation from the scandal provoked by his son's leadership in the Ormée, he peppered the work with laudatory remarks about Richelieu (who did not live long enough to see it). But he accomplished much more than rehabilitating his image. The law of wreck exposed the patchwork nature of

French absolutism, tying the hands of the monarch.[37] Cleirac offered theorists and administrators of royal rights useful legal weapons and an elegant justification of their prerogatives in matters of wreckage. He highlighted the edicts that Richelieu had issued in the wake of the 1627 disaster, which strengthened the position of the crown vis à vis coastal lords, and cast these edicts' protection of the property rights of seagoers as a civilizing mission against the "cruelty" of earlier times, when wreckages of naval disasters were invariably pillaged.[38]

Two sets of debris became the object of particularly tense negotiations in the aftermath of the Bay of Biscay disaster: cannons and diamonds. Pressing needs added to the perennial military value of artillery. In May 1627 Richelieu began to mount preparations for the siege of the Huguenot bastion of La Rochelle, which was attacked throughout the summer and capitulated in October of the following year. His emissaries in Bordeaux raked up all military equipment in the region, while the local population felt aggravated by the mobilization. With the cooperation of some local lords, the royal envoys succeeded in recovering about fifty cannons from the naval wreckage that negotiations with Spain allowed them to retain for the purpose of attacking La Rochelle. Governor d'Épernon was less obliging with regard to some of the precious stones that had survived the wreck. He had acquired a large castle on the Garonne through marriage, which gave him seigniorial rights over a stretch of the coast of Médoc, and the Spanish envoy accused him of hiding diamonds in his castle.[39]

Richelieu, in other words, had to negotiate on two fronts for the recovery of the goods that had come ashore in January 1627: with Spain on the one hand, and with his own regional governor and a few recalcitrant lords on the other. Diamonds and precious stones added complications of their own. Shipwrecks eroded what one historian has called the "wall of secrecy" that Portuguese merchants built around the intercontinental trade of precious stones, a trade in which New Christians participated in great numbers and that often involved smuggling.[40] According to an official list, diamonds and other stones made up 18.5 percent of the declared value of the cargo of the *São Bartolomeu* and *Santa Helena*, or slightly more than the 14 percent average that the same historian estimated to be the fraction of this merchandise on board all Portuguese vessels returning from India between 1580 and 1640.[41] One diamond listed among the 1627 cargo was a gift to the Spanish queen from the king of Bijapur. All the other stones, unlike pepper and spices in general, which were subject to the Portuguese crown's monopoly, were the legitimate property of private merchants, who were allowed to transport them in so-called "liberty boxes." Many of these private merchants were descendants of baptized Jews. By one estimation, in 1630 Lisbon's principal New Christian merchant families controlled about 80 percent of the registered private merchandise on board the *carreira da Índia*.[42] Though inevitably imprecise, this figure points to a phenomenon that caught contemporaries' attention, in part, to be sure, because of the tendency of Christian observers (and some modern scholars too) to inflate Jewish economic influence.

At the time of the disaster along the coast of Guyenne, both French and Spanish authorities sought to conceal the involvement of New Christian traders and financiers in order to protect their own and those traders' interests. The French crown officially tolerated the presence of "Portuguese merchants" in the southwestern part of the kingdom as long as they renounced all traces of their Jewish identity. For his part, Spain's chief minister, Count-Duke Olivares, was particularly attentive to the interests of New Christian financiers. Shortly after the shipwreck, on January 31, 1627, he declared state bankruptcy, suspended payments to long-standing Genoese creditors, and replaced most of them with Portuguese lenders. This move inaugurated the fifteen-year golden age of New Christian banking in Madrid, which lasted until (and contributed to) Olivares's demise in 1643.[43]

In February 1628, Richelieu prevailed over d'Épernon and promised to return the recovered goods to Spain, but inquiries to determine property rights continued. Given the investigations conducted by the Spanish Inquisition and the hostility of common folk in the French coastal villages toward Spaniards and Jews, it is not surprising that only a thin and oblique paper trail of the New Christians' ownership of the diamonds on board the sunken ships and those individuals' possible role in the recovery operations exists among government records. Unfortunately, private business papers have not survived. Here and there, however, official documents mention, albeit *sotto voce*, a host of Iberian *conversos* from Bordeaux and Paris who facilitated the efforts to retrieve the merchandise by transmitting information and anticipating the sums needed to ransom the goods from looters. They included a "Portuguese" named Diego da Costa, a Castilian merchant in Bordeaux named Antonio Enrique, a Portuguese merchant in Paris named Enrique Alvarez ("portugues de nación, mercader en Paris"), and the enigmatic informer of Richelieu and diamond dealer Alphonse Lopez.[44] Frustrated by the slowness of the salvage and restitution process, the Spanish royal envoy suggested that "the Portuguese merchants who reside in Bordeaux" could help expedite the mission.[45] These and other clues have led the authors of a study of the 1627 shipwreck to conclude that Portuguese New Christians were "the most secret protagonists, and possibly the most powerful ones" in the story.[46]

New Christians, Crypto-Jews, and New Jews in Bordeaux

Although Cleirac makes no explicit reference to New Christian merchants, there can be no doubt that he met some of them in the course of his life in Bordeaux, whether in the classroom, in the now-demolished Palais de l'Ombrière (then the site of the admiralty court), or even in his parish church. Questions of religious conflict and toleration were then the subject of daily negotiation in a region that had become a bulwark of Protestantism and the destination of Jewish refugees from Iberia. The Collège de Guyenne, which Cleirac attended in his youth, had been co-founded by a Portuguese New Christian, André Govea, attracted both local and Iberian pupils, and included several teachers and students of Huguenot confession. After the *parlement* of Bordeaux ratified the Edict of Nantes in 1599, Calvinist students were excused from the requirement of signing the cross at the beginning of classes. Cleirac's classmates thus comprised both professing Catholics of Jewish descent and openly practicing Calvinists.[47] At the same time, the ritualistic or sacramental nature of the Eucharist remained a lightning rod in theological disputes that were no less explosive in Bordeaux than elsewhere.[48] And it was in Bordeaux that in 1643 the heterodox Calvinist scholar Isaac La Peyrère anonymously published his unusual appeal to the French king to join forces with the Jews in order to hasten the coming of a Judeo-Christian messianic age.[49]

Since 1550, Bordeaux and the smaller town of Bayonne, located along the Franco-Spanish border, as well as outposts in the interior like Bidache and Peyrehorade, had served as temporary stops for many New Christian families fleeing the Iberian inquisitions and for some had become permanent homes. In line with its conception of Gallican liberties, the French crown had been able to choose a form of accommodation for the exiled that its Catholic competitors on the Italian peninsula, all regional states that hosted a branch of the Roman Inquisition, had been forced to reject as too destabilizing. Between 1589 and 1593, the rulers of Venice and Livorno created incentives for Jews of Iberian descent, all of whom had been baptized as infants, to embrace Judaism (with all the restrictions that that choice entailed) in exchange for protection from the accusation of apostasy, a charge that could be fatal.

In Bordeaux, by contrast, it was not until 1723 that the crown allowed the open practice of Judaism in the region, and so until then Portuguese and Spanish merchants were asked to live and die as good Catholics: they married in church, baptized their children, and buried their loved ones in Catholic cemeteries. Their inner feelings are lost to us, while their religious practices ranged from sincere Catholicism to syncretic crypto-Judaism. The tenor of municipal ordinances from this period admonishing those who harassed "Portuguese merchants" suggests that the label remained a euphemism for much of the local population, with many regarding these individuals as impious and less than welcome.[50]

The crown's interest in protecting New Christians was rooted in the expectation that they would contribute to the growth of Bordeaux's international trade. The 1550 decree that invited "Portuguese merchants" to settle in the region exempted them from the punitive *droit d'aubaine*, the king's right to confiscate the assets of any foreigner who died on French soil.[51] These immigrants were thus styled as naturalized French subjects with full property rights. The measure paid off. In 1636, by official count, Bordeaux had 260 Portuguese and Spanish residents, although they constituted less than 1 percent of the city's population, estimated at 30,000–35,000.[52] With the rise of Bordeaux into a major hub of Atlantic trade in the eighteenth century, the New Christian population also expanded, increasing by midcentury to roughly 1,500 Iberian immigrants (or more than 2 percent of the inhabitants of a town that by then had some 65,000 residents), with the richest among them living next to affluent Catholic merchants in the Chartrons neighborhood in the northern section of the city.[53]

Both rival merchants hostile to Jews and royal authorities intent on protecting the Portuguese newcomers likely exaggerated the New Christians' economic influence, albeit for opposite reasons. It is, however, indisputable that, while never a dominant economic group, the New Christians stood out for their commercial dynamism. In 1675, Bordeaux's municipal government (*jurade*) pleaded with Colbert for protection of the city's Portuguese merchants, who were threatening to leave Bordeaux on account of riots that were endangering their trade. Their departure, the local authorities feared, would inflict great losses on the city.[54] In 1686, the chief royal officer (*intendant*) in Guyenne, Louis Bazin de Bezons, advised against imposing a special tax on New Christians and urged them not to emigrate while also reminding them of the necessity of living as Old Catholics (*anciens catholiques*).[55] Between 1718 and 1722, another crown official (*sous-intendant*) defended Jews' reputation against a complaint submitted to the Chamber of Commerce that lamented their supposed monopoly on the brokerage of bills of exchange: without Jews, the official maintained, commerce in the region would perish.[56]

The Franco-Spanish border was easy to cross along the Atlantic shoreline. This geographical reality had both religious and economic consequences. New Christian families with fluid religious identities lived on both sides of the frontier.[57] At the expiration of the Twelve Years' Truce between Spain and the United Provinces (1609–1621), when trade between the two countries was made illegal once again, southwestern France became a strategic area for the smuggling of goods between the Iberian Peninsula and northern Europe and its colonial markets. New Christians from the region became heavily involved in both lawful and illicit trade with the Sephardic community of Amsterdam.[58] Inquisition records offer biased but valuable information about these relationships. Many of those whom the tribunal of Lisbon tried for apostasy after finding that they had resided in southwestern France during the seventeenth century were involved in commercial activities, and are described in records as *comerciante, tratante, homem de negócios,* and *mercador.*[59]

Once the Spanish Inquisition resumed its crackdown on presumed crypto-Jews in the 1630s and 1640s, it was quick to find many of them on the French side of the border, including a sizable group in Rouen.[60] During his interrogation in 1637, the Portuguese merchant Juan Núñes Saraiva admitted to following the Jewish rites "as they are observed in France" and confessed that he had lured a rabbi from Holland to Bordeaux so that his father could be circumcised before he died there.[61] In the same year, a Portuguese *marrano* born in Biarritz handed the Toledo Inquisition a list of 155 crypto-Jews whom he denounced for residing in or traveling back and forth to southwestern France.[62] At least one official French document referred to "the Jews resident in Bordeaux under the name of Portuguese" in 1686.[63] After the open practice of Judaism was permitted in Bordeaux in 1723, Parisian merchants jealous of the Jews of Bordeaux's success accused them of "a double apostasy": in Portugal, they were Jews turned Christians; in France, they were Christians turned Jews.[64]

Arguments used in favor of and against the presence of "Portuguese merchants" in Bordeaux suggest that Cleirac's vision of Jews was nurtured in an environment in which New Christians were perceived as the embodiment of economic prowess and slippery religious identity. France's geographical proximity to Spain and the repeated wars between the two countries (in Cleirac's lifetime alone, such conflicts occurred in 1595–1598, 1628–1631, and 1635–1659) added a political dimension to the traditional motifs of Christian anti-Jewish sentiments. Even in peacetime, a counselor to the French king denounced all Portuguese residents of southwestern France as traitors.[65] Two hundred miles north of Bordeaux, in Nantes, economic rivalries mixed with religious and political aversions exploded into anti-Jewish riots during the winter of 1636–1637.[66] And during the Spanish siege of Bordeaux in 1653, "Portuguese merchants" were deemed to be disloyal subjects and spies.[67]

Fears that Jews and Christians could become indistinguishable permeated European Christian culture at large during this period. The regime of toleration that prevailed in seventeenth-century Bordeaux heightened rather than quelled fears about the porousness of the boundaries between Jews and Christians. There, more than in any other city of the kingdom, a small but proactive group of New Christian merchants was at once visible and invisible. Whether valued or condemned, their economic activities were not confined to a separate corporate body, with its own place in the hierarchical society of the time. They walked the same docks as other merchants and sat in the same church pews as other Catholics. For Cleirac and his readers, the lack of precise boundaries between Jews and non-Jews mirrored the erosion of age-old divisions between merchants and noblemen at a time when a major restructuring of the legal and social order, and the place of commerce within it, was underway in France.

Commerce in a Changing Legal and Social Order

The frontispiece of Cleirac's 1647 edition of *Us et coustumes de la mer*, an otherwise unadorned volume, displays a rare illustration and inscription. The motto "Potent over sea and over land" accompanies the coat of arms of Anne of Austria, the regent queen of France from 1643 to 1651 (during the minority of Louis XIV), to whom the book is dedicated (figure 4.6).[68] France was then entering the competitive arena of European commercial expansion and overseas territorial conquest. Maritime law was an essential tool of this expanding international politics. At home, interest in this branch of law was inseparable from broader concerns about the reordering of social hierarchies. Cleirac points to these broader concerns in his dedication, in which he lays out two reasons for assembling his compilation: the wish to furnish judges of ordinary courts like him, with little or no direct experience of maritime trade, with a reference book that would assist them in adjudicating disputes in matters of navigation; and the desire to elevate the reputation of all people working at sea ("fils de Neptune"), so that instead of being regarded as unrefined and loath-

VS,
ET COVSTVMES
DE LA MER,

DIVISE'ES EN TROIS PARTIES,

I. De la Nauigation. II. Du Commerce
Naual, & Contracts Maritimes. III. De
la Iurifdiction de la Marine.

Auec vn Traicté des termes de Marine, &
Reglemens de la Nauigation des Fleuues
& Riuieres.

ΤΗΝ ΓΗΝ ΚΑΙ ΘΑΛΑΣΣΑΝ ΥΠΗΚΟΟΝ ΕΧΩΝ

Vndarum Terræque Potens.

A BOVRDEAVX,
Par GVILLAVME MILLANGES Imprimeur
Ordinaire du Roy, 1647.

FIGURE 4.6 Frontispiece of the 1647 edition of Cleirac's *Us et coustumes de la mer.*
With permission from the Bibliothèque Nationale de France, Paris.

some ("grossiers et méprisables"), they could acquire the dignity accorded to those working the land ("fils de la Terre").[69]

Cleirac was not alone in his desire to enhance the respectability of "Neptune's sons." His contribution, however, is notable for its early date and for its emphasis on maritime law. When examining the corrosive effects of commerce on traditional concepts of honor and nobility, scholars of Old Regime France have focused on the debates on luxury and the so-called "commercial nobility" that became incendiary in the mid-eighteenth century. Shifting the attention to an earlier moment, Amalia Kessler illuminates the importance of the legal reforms that accompanied these debates, particularly those initiated by Colbert in the administration of commercial justice. One such reform, in which Colbert made all individuals involved in commercial transactions, regardless of their rank, accountable before merchant tribunals, was nothing less than epochal. In the jurisprudential terminology of the time, the 1673 *ordonnance de commerce* turned commercial law from a personal-status law (*ratione personae*) into a subject-matter law (*ratione materiae*), that is, into a body of norms and procedures that applied not to a legally defined group (whoever was categorized as a merchant) but to everyone who entered into a specific set of contracts (those regulated by the ordinance itself).[70] Needless to say, French commercial society was not suddenly transformed into a contractual society as a result of a royal edict. But historians have focused more on the protracted resistance to this innovation, whether by noblemen or by rival courts, than on its significance for the formation of a commercial society that downplayed, at least formally, the importance of personal status.

Cleirac's writings are better understood in relation to these developments, which trace their origins to a royal edict of November 1563 that established a specialized merchant tribunal (*juridiction consulaire*) in Paris, following earlier experiments with courts at commercial fairs in other cities of the kingdom, notably Lyon.[71] Only a year later, the same institution existed in all major French cities, and Bordeaux had elected its first *juges-consuls*.[72] By 1710, there were fifty such tribunals across the kingdom, with twenty more created in that year.[73] These courts were presided over by one head judge and four elected consuls, all of whom were merchants, native subjects of the French crown, residents of the city where the tribunal operated, and elected by an assembly of peers. These *juges-consuls* were ordered to decide cases without charging any fees, with minimal recourse to lawyers or other legal experts, and with fast and summary proceedings ("sommairement & sans figure de procès") that stood in contrast to those of the civil courts, which were frequently decried for their length, intricacy, and cost. The *juridictions consulaires* relied primarily on merchants' oral testimonies and admitted only certain written evidence (such as merchants' declarations of what constituted standard practice in any given time and place).[74] Rapid and cheap, this procedure was designed to lower the costs of administering and obtaining justice in the realm of commerce.

The 1563 edict took pains to define the jurisdictional purview of the newly created courts: the *juges-consuls* were to adjudicate "disputes that from now on will arise between merchants, solely for what pertains to commercial matters, between their widows (when the latter are publicly known as merchants), their employees, and their agents," as long as the litigation concerned obligations, receipts, bills of exchange, insurance, debts, and partnership agreements (art. 3).[75] Merchant courts had no authority over matters pertaining to bankruptcy, navigation (a subject delegated to the admiralty courts), and existing fair courts, including those of Lyon.[76]

In its original conception, then, the *jurisdiction consulaire* was a corporate tribunal, just another piece in the jurisdictional tapestry of Old Regime privileges: it carved out a sphere of autonomy for merchants and bankers within clearly demarcated boundaries. In practice, however, the 1563 edict altered the status quo because of the growing range of people who utilized credit instruments that were once the prerogative of professional merchants. A century after their creation, in 1651, an informed commentator wrote that merchant tribunals had jurisdiction over all disputes over bills of exchange regardless of the "quality" of the persons involved, including clergymen or noblemen.[77] The observation was technically inaccurate but speaks to the ambiguity generated by the legal and social transformations that were underway in the realm of commercial credit. In 1675, a rare voice among the clergy argued that lending at interest fulfilled a particularly "pure and Christian function" when it allowed those who were not merchants "to live honorably in their condition."[78] Confusing as these comments may appear, they show that many people in the mid-seventeenth century were grappling with the promise and disruption that credit was bringing to traditional ways of life.

The ambiguity surrounding commercial tribunals' jurisdictional boundaries engendered prolonged battles with rival civil courts—an important subject that scholars have yet to fully illuminate. Nowhere were these battles more strenuously fought than in Lyon, a hub of international finance and silk manufacturing, where in 1463 the king had created a court, the *Conservation des privileges royaux des foires*, tasked with settling disputes among merchants attending the seasonal fairs, French and foreign alike, by means of summary procedures and holding the right to enforce its rulings across the kingdom.[79] Over time, the tribunal sought to broaden its authority to adjudicate all commercial lawsuits, whether or not they arose during the fairs and whether or not they involved merchants. With an edict of July 1669, the monarchy tilted the balance in favor of the *Conservation* by granting it jurisdiction over all disputes regarding commerce and finance ("le fait du négoce et commerce de marchandises"), including bankruptcies, that occurred at any time of the year. The transition to a subject-matter jurisdiction, defined by the nature of the controversies rather than the status of the plaintiffs or the defendants, seemed complete. The edict's formulation, however, was typically imprecise. One article established that the *Conservation* was to adjudicate cases involving those who traded in commodities, kept their account books, and stipulated payments during the fairs.[80] Did this capacious category of people extend to nonprofessional merchants, such as noblemen, magistrates or clergymen, who signed bills of exchange and participated in wide networks of commercial credit?

This question goes to the heart of a central feature of Old Regime France: this society's ancient disdain toward manual professions and trade was not only deeply rooted in the culture of the time (a theme famously satirized by Molière in his 1670 *Bourgeois gentilhomme*), but also inscribed in the law. According to the 1563 edict (art. 12) and the 1673 ordinance on commerce (title VII, arts. 1–2), for example, those unable to repay their bills of exchange were sentenced to prison. Imprisonment for debt (*contrainte par corps*) was not allowed in regular jurisdictions but was made available to commercial tribunals on the grounds that loans between merchants were not backed by collateral. This norm had severe implications. A titled lord who failed to pay a bill of exchange was now judged by a commercial tribunal and might end up going to prison for debt, sentenced by a court of commoners.[81]

Such a scenario was so threatening to the established social order that from the sixteenth century onward the titled nobility sought to counter it by hardening existing hierarchies.[82] Most cities of the kingdom experienced an aristocratization of their political life, with commercial elites sidelined in favor of the nobility and royal officials. In Bordeaux, the municipal council of aldermen saw its influence progressively weakened during the last quarter of the seventeenth century, and Colbert abolished the fiscal privileges associated with the status of *bourgeois*.[83] The "nobility of the robe," a rank that could be acquired via the purchase of certain offices, gained ground over the merchant class.

The rise of moneyed elites and the legal profession during the sixteenth century also reinvigorated debates over the so-called *loi de dérogeance*, which deprived those aristocrats who engaged in mechanical arts, commercial activities, and public administration of their privileges, including their coveted fiscal immunities. In 1610, the noted jurist Loyseau listed the occupations that caused the forfeiture of noble titles: "prosecuting attorney, clerk of a court, notary, serjeant, clerk in general, merchant, and artisan of any trade, except hunting." The reason was simple: all these occupations, he explained, are done "for profit." He added: "It is *base and sordid gain* that derogates from nobility. The proper course for nobility is to live on one's rents, or at least not to sell one's efforts and one's labor."[84] Profit derived from commerce and banking was considered particularly "base and sordid," and Loyseau placed merchants one step below judges and lawyers in the hierarchy of non-noblemen.

This forceful defense of *dérogeance* was a conservative, even reactionary, stance, one that certain circles at court wished to combat because it tied the fortunes of the aristocracy to the land and curbed the state's ability to bolster French power in the race for overseas expansion and conquest. Richelieu emphasized the dignity of commerce in several initiatives designed to promote France's ability to compete economically with its rival and foe, the United Provinces. He encouraged the nobility especially to invest in newly chartered (if still fragile) trading companies, such as the *Compagnie de la Nouvelle France* (1627–1663), which he hoped would expand France's colonial and commercial presence in North America.

In 1629, two years after the shipwreck in the Bay of Biscay, the crown urged the Parisian and provincial *parlements* to ratify a comprehensive reform project, known as the Code Michau, that had been in the making for more than a decade. While it reaffirmed the principle of *dérogeance* for all noblemen (art. 198), the Code Michau included an important exception for those who invested in overseas wholesale trade (art. 452). It also allowed for the ennoblement of those merchants who manned a vessel weighing no less than 200 tons for at least five years, as well as anyone who served as a consul or magistrate, as long as he did not engage in petty trade (art. 452). Most of these recommendations, however, remained dead letters, because several provincial *parlements* refused to ratify the Code Michau in its entirety.[85]

It took until 1669 for Colbert to succeed where Richelieu had not. A month after issuing the July edict that expanded the *Conservation*'s jurisdiction in Lyon, the crown crafted a wide-ranging legitimation of commerce, which it described as an essential source of public and private wealth and "one of the most honest occupations of civil life." The August 1669 edict further declared that overseas (though not overland) commerce was compatible with the status of nobility and suspended the *loi de dérogeance* whenever a nobleman engaged in maritime trade.[86] Those aristocrats who wished to conduct wholesale maritime trade now had to list their names on a public board provided by the merchant tribunal in their town. Four years later, the 1673 *ordonnance de commerce* made everyone who signed a bill of exchange subject to the jurisdiction of merchant-run tribunals (title XII, art. 2). Commenting on this norm 100 years later, a jurist put it bluntly: by signing a bill of exchange, "even noblemen, office-holders, and clergymen" lost their "quality."[87]

He was hardly the only one to stress the extent to which the creation of a *noblesse commerçante* and the emergence of subject matter, rather than personal status, as the determinant of jurisdictional prerogatives in commercial disputes were altering time-honored hierarchies. As a lawyer in the Paris *parlement* wrote in 1710, rank had ceased to be a person's exhaustive and stable descriptor. Someone who held the title of *bourgeois* of Paris but was neither an artisan nor a merchant, he noted, would still be considered a merchant if he bought and sold merchandise for profit. Royal officials, jurists, and clergymen tacitly renounced some of their privileges if they engaged in trade. Even agricultural workers were equated with merchants if they bought tools and goods for their occupation and sold the fruit of their labor. Anyone could call himself a banker: there was no guild to confer that title.[88] By 1740, a comprehensive treatise on commercial jurisprudence posited that "anyone who mingles in wholesale trade, traffic, artisanal activity, in any merchandise or manufacture is considered a merchant or an artisan, even if he is not an apprentice, has not passed a master test or is in a profession different from that of commerce."[89]

Predictably, the resistance to these changes was considerable.[90] In 1722, those Bordeaux merchants who had recently acquired a noble title asked to march ahead of regular merchants in public processions. The central authorities, however, rejected their claims, presumably in an effort to protect the *négociants*.[91] The same incident also exposes the persistence of anticommercial prejudice. Contributors to Diderot's *Encyclopédie* a few decades later still felt the need to affirm that "the merchant profession is honorable."[92] Words matter, and yet they cannot engineer cultural change alone. The violent response to a pamphlet published in 1756 by the Jesuit Gabriel-François Coyer that exhorted aristocrats to abandon ancient preconceptions and engage in wholesale trade was the aftershock of an earthquake set in motion a century earlier by Colbert's reforms.[93]

"The fire of chicanery"

As every good jurist knows, laws are only operational as far as general consensus allows. Several decades before the crown sanctioned the honorability of those activities that came under the purview of maritime law, Cleirac was already broaching this delicate subject. More than adhering to the strain of "commercial humanism" that Henry Clark has located in early-seventeenth-century France, his commentaries reveal the interdependence of the legal and cultural foundations of the process of conferring dignity on commerce.[94]

To justify the importance of his own writing, the Bordeaux lawyer praises the value of all knowledge associated with the art of navigation, notably mathematics and cosmography, which he refers to as "noble sciences."[95] He even bemoans the tendency among talented young men to pursue the medical profession after graduating from humanist schools and universities and reproaches those who aspire to live as *rentiers*. To counter these propensities and channel French youth toward commerce and marine service, he advocates free public education in the art of navigation.[96] Competence went hand in hand with respectability. While the Portuguese and Dutch appeared to Cleirac to be fluent in all matters pertaining to overseas trade, the inhabitants of the French Atlantic coast were in his estimation more similar to the Swedes and Germans whom he met when employed at the admiralty of Bordeaux: they drank and smoked excessively and lacked knowledge of navigational instruments.[97]

Here and elsewhere Cleirac echoes a growing literature on the developing middle classes. In a timely, encyclopedic, and moralizing book in Italian vernacular first published in 1585, Tommaso Garzoni catalogued the virtues and vices of 400 "professions," most of which demanded manual labor. The sheer scope of the project was a tribute to the industriousness of these groups, while the author's repeated warnings against the corruption into which laborers could sink reflected the genre's conventions. His treatment of merchants popularized a three-tier classification of this group, with wholesale traders at the top, retail traders (*piccoli merciari* and *fondaghieri*) in the middle, and "bankers" at the bottom, indistinguishable from "usurers."[98] Overall, Garzoni's compilation was filled with both admiration and disdain for merchants: they were described as literate and knowledgeable (well versed in a wide range of goods, weights, measures, and currencies) but also as quick to manipulate the market to their advantage, sell counterfeits, and trick regular folks with incomprehensible commercial papers, causing their ruin. Bankers, in his view, were even worse, with no redeeming qualities.

Cleirac takes for granted the tripartite scheme that Garzoni propagated. He places "mercers" below wholesale merchants, whom he calls "honorable," but above "those who trade in money alone, that is, usurers." In fact, he doubts that usurers—that is, bankers—are merchants at all ("ceux-là ne sont pas veritablement marchands").[99] In the real world, the boundaries between wholesale merchants and bankers were blurred, since no long-distance trade was possible without the use of financial instruments, and few if any international bankers specialized exclusively in finance. The fact that bills of exchange could now be traded as if they were commodities made such rigid classifications meaningless.

Adopting a Thomistic trope, Cleirac also applauds "the flourishing of commercial exchanges, that is, the reciprocal, fraternal, and fertile communication between all Nations."[100] In the mid-seventeenth century, to say as much did not imply an endorsement of free trade as a means to promote world peace and tame religious wars, nor did it constitute a programmatic *politique* position that quietly criticized bellicose Catholicism.[101] In search of social affirmation and political redemption after the Fronde, Cleirac takes a far more conventional and practical stance. In his writings he commends the "good and noble qualities" of those "who furnish bills of exchange when they are needed and make sure they are delivered and paid with probity."[102] But he draws a line at those bankers whose "gluttony" (*ingordigia*), as the Florentine Davanzati had called it, led them to transform bills of exchange from means of remitting payments into purely speculative instruments.[103]

To lawyers, solicitors, and savants like Cleirac, the venality of offices brought no benefits, since those offices could neither be held in perpetuity nor bequeathed to heirs. Excluded from the nobility of the robe, these professionals were also less threatened by the valorization of commerce. Written before Colbert expanded the purview of commercial and maritime law, and quirky as it is, *Us et coustumes de la mer* suggests that the everyday experience of individuals was as important as top-down reforms in paving the way for the normative adoption of more positive attitudes toward commerce. For a trained legal professional, the intellectual project of conferring respectability on commerce and navigation was inseparable from the effort to establish the legal rules that would undergird the performance of those activities. Yet this effort was littered with obstacles. Far from being homogenous and self-enforcing, as some legal theorists and social scientists want them to be, maritime laws remained uneven and contested, both within and beyond the borders of the kingdom.[104]

At the same time that Cleirac advocates greater regulation of overseas trade, he implicitly acknowledges the limitations of the written word of the law in taming the dangers of commercial credit. Legal norms, he implies over and over, are a necessary but insufficient tool to curb merchants' trickery. He expresses pride in France's welcoming attitude toward foreign merchants but also worries about their undue influence, which he assumes to be at the root of the increase in commercial fraud.[105] Foreigners, he claims, would impoverish France and its native subjects with "their malicious schemes, swindles, plots, monopolies, cabals, and Jewish ways of dealing (*Iuifveries*)."[106] His estimate that these "worm-like activities" of foreign merchants had fleeced 300 or 400 million livres from the province of Guyenne is so exaggerated that it surpasses what scholars assess to be the value of all precious metals that arrived in France from the Americas in 1715.[107]

The other villains in Cleirac's story are the financiers and tax farmers of the French monarchy, said to operate as a "secret and sacred cabal" that sought to manipulate the trade in bills of exchange.[108] Everybody despised tax farmers. In 1637, even the levy of the *taille*, the most widespread direct land tax in the kingdom, was farmed out. Acerbic criticisms of these financiers dotted various genres, from moralizing plays to libels (*mazarinades*), in which they are depicted as archetypes of greed.[109] Falling back on his old habit, Cleirac chooses a term with an unmistakable Jewish association, *cabale*, to describe these individuals' dealings—a word that other texts of the period used to designate conspiratorial associations of merchants who manipulated prices or defrauded consumers.[110] Backing up his arguments with the usual eclectic mix of citations, Cleirac denounces state financiers for their propensity to "turn public poverty into private wealth."[111] This portrait evinces no confidence in the ability of economic actors to self-regulate but also displays limited faith in the power of public authorities to defend themselves (and their subjects) from cunning speculators.

Ultimately, Cleirac oscillates between faith in the "medicine" that regulation provides (in his account, the Hanseatic League is the best "doctor" for healing the diseases of commerce) and a more general sense of despair in the face of the various subterfuges that invariably strip good laws of their efficacy. He recalls the creation in 1576 of a new guild of brokers (*corratiers*) to oversee all transactions negotiated by foreigners, whether in cash or by credit.[112] These brokers were made collectively liable for all payments in the hope that this obligation would lead them to scrutinize the affairs of their clients while simultaneously protecting those guild members who took on ill-fated business unintentionally. As Cleirac reports, abuses soon abounded: some foreigners, for example, joined the brokers' guild and colluded with merchants abroad. With characteristic pessimism about merchants' dispositions, he concludes that everyone put his personal gain above that of the collective and blames the guild's board for lacking the will and the ability to contain fraud.[113]

If neither self-interest nor legal enforcement kept merchants in line, what could? Cleirac never supplies a straightforward answer. The legend of the Jewish invention of bills of exchange and marine insurance filled this void in a symbolically prescriptive way that was more intelligible then than now. Cleirac's verbal attacks against "foreigners" and tax farmers are less virulent than those against Jews, but they respond to the same logic. In both cases, he defines proper commercial conduct by pointing to its opposite. And yet, to repeat, he was no enemy of the embryonic French commercial society. He refuses to degrade merchants as a whole, arguing: "The lowly birth of a craft . . . or the mischievousness of those who abuse it do not diminish the integrity, do not pollute the candor, do not darken the glaring reputation of upright workers."[114] He declares his respect for "honorable bankers, those who practice their financial businesses (*négoce pecuniaire*) with loyalty and in good faith like respectable people (*gens de bien*)."[115] But he warns too that "credit insinuates itself in commerce only to introduce bankruptcy and the fire of chicanery."[116] His didactic impulse always brings him back to the same point: honorable merchants are the opposite of "Jews, Lombards, Cahorsins, and those who go bankrupt."[117]

Conclusion

The decree of March 31, 1492, that expelled Jews from the kingdoms of Castile, Aragon, and Granada granted them a window of four months during which they were allowed to sell their property. They were forbidden from taking gold, silver, minted coins, and outlawed merchandise out of the country but permitted to export the proceeds of their sales either in kind or through bills of exchange (*canbios*).[118] Indeed, some Spanish Jews succeeded in carrying liquid assets (the value of which was arguably much diminished by the forced sales) to safety by buying bills of exchange from Genoese merchants, who made those bills payable to them abroad.[119]

We have no way of knowing whether the memory of these events may have stimulated the imagination of those who witnessed the arrival of Iberian refugees in Bordeaux before and after 1550. But at the end of a reasonably exhaustive search, we can conclude that no formulation of the legend of the Jewish invention of bills of exchange and marine insurance appeared in print prior to *Us et coustumes de la mer*. Why, then, did Bordeaux in the mid-seventeenth century prove to be a fertile ground for the fantasy that placed Jews at the center of the development of modern credit instruments in Europe? We cannot pinpoint a precise incident or encounter that might have triggered the creation of this legend—not even Cleirac's participation in the disputes over property rights concerning the surviving cargo of the *São Bartolomeu* and *Santa Helena*. But whether Cleirac coined or merely repeated it, the legend of the Jewish invention of marine insurance and bills of exchange was his attempt at making sense of the changes in the legal, political, and social orders that the expansion of overseas commerce set in motion.

Cleirac's life unfolded in a city where Jews were indistinguishable from local and foreign Christian merchants involved in long-distance trade, many of whom no longer belonged to a guild. It would not have surprised anyone in seventeenth-century France that New Christians, Catholics, and Protestants signed each others' bills of exchange and underwrote each others' marine insurance policies. The private records of a prominent Tuscan banking family, the Salviati, show that its Lyon branch assisted the legendary Beatriz Mendes, also known as Doña Gracia Nasi (c.1510–1569), by transacting bills of exchange on her behalf under various pseudonyms so that she could transfer funds to her family members across Europe and to fellow baptized Jews in Portugal as she fled the Inquisition.[120] Unfortunately, no collection of private business papers from Bordeaux survives from the first half of the seventeenth century, even if there is evidence that New Christians were embedded in confessionally and religiously diverse commercial networks.[121] Merchants' letters dating from 100 years later show that both those "Portuguese" who remained ostensibly Catholic and those who began to practice Judaism in the open traded in bills of exchange with merchants, officials, and clergymen of all religions and confessions.[122]

Until 1723, however, crypto-Judaism was an institutionalized reality in Bordeaux. The consequence of this state of affairs was an escalation of the crisis of legibility in the boundaries separating Jews and Christians that had begun after the mass conversions of Spanish Jews during the 1390s and the forced baptisms administered across Iberia a century later. The specter of crypto-Judaism infuses Cleirac's narrative of the origins of marine insurance and bills of exchange. In this tale, he demonizes an imagined medieval world in which Jews supposedly outmaneuvered Christian kings, traders, and poor folks with their financial savvy but also longs for those times when one could tell a Jew from a Christian, when visible exterior markers set roguish money-lenders apart from respectable merchants. In reality, visible markers had never been sufficient standards of respectability. But appearances admittedly became more fluid in the early modern period. Compared to medieval Jewish pawn-brokers, the "Portuguese merchants" of Bordeaux and the Sephardim who were involved in the Atlantic economy of the seventeenth century lived by all measures a less segregated life.

Questions about who was a Christian and who was a Jew were not entirely separate from better-known debates about what criteria made a person noble, debates that often considered the types of economic activities that were and were not compatible with an aristocratic status. In a fictional dialogue written in Florence around 1440, the humanist Poggio Bracciolini pitted nobility of virtue against nobility of birth. Defending the latter, one of his characters objected that if "paintings, sculptures, elegance, wealth, and ample possessions, as well as public offices and positions of authorities" might confer noble status, then "even moneylenders, no matter how wicked and abominable, would be noble just by being rich and holding public office."[123] Nowhere in early modern Europe, not even in eminently mercantile societies like Holland and England, did individual merit and the pursuit of profit fully displace older notions of heritable honor. But wherever feudalism had deeper roots, as in France, resistance to the conferral of respectability onto merchants was stronger. An ancient morality still suffused this battle between mercantile and aristocratic cultures, a worldview based on Aristotle's argument that condemned the traffic in money but conceded the utility of international trade between regions with different natural endowments and industries, as well as on the Stoic distinction between wholesale trade (which was regarded as acceptable) and retail trade (which was deemed degrading).[124]

More than a century before the 1789 Revolution, the French crown purposefully inserted a fissure in the feudal structure by creating incentives for aristocrats to invest in overseas trade without being stigmatized for doing so. Implementation of such initiatives was slow and hampered by opposition, because they hit at the heart of long-established legal and cultural hierarchies. Coupled with Colbert's reforms of the jurisdictional reach of commercial tribunals, these measures broadened significantly the definition of who was a merchant. After 1673, the public performance of a contract altered an individual's relation to the state and society, even if it did not altogether override the formal assignment of a rank (whether that assignment had been made at birth or through a formal change of status, such as that associated with the nobility of the robe).

Scholarship critical of progressive theories of European state-building has long emphasized the insufficiency of rank as an operative category of historical analysis on the grounds that Old Regime institutions were too weak to enforce all the norms they produced and that social action altered the meanings of the formal hierarchies designed by the state. Simona Cerutti makes a compelling case for the role that social recognition played in the definition of a claimant's legal status. She shows that in eighteenth-century Turin, the medieval notion of a "foreigner" as someone who had weak social ties to local society and was therefore potentially suspicious continued to inform how judges deliberated and how plaintiffs approached the court.[125] Such work has the merit of bridging legal and social history to produce a less anachronistic understanding of actors' sense of belonging in urban communities in the highly stratified societies of Old Regime Europe.

If we consider the terms under which Jews were allowed to reside in different European cities after the sixteenth century, this perspective raises additional questions that matter to both Jewish and European history. From a strict legal perspective, Jews were not always the paradigmatic foreigners. In Livorno, for example, Sephardic merchants were subjects of the grand duchy. Elsewhere, they possessed the same contractual rights as other merchants. Yet on a symbolic level, they never shed their own cultural foreignness entirely. Cleirac's commentaries on maritime law illuminate some little-known aspects of the cultural process that accompanied the redefinition of legal and social hierarchies during the last two centuries of the Old Regime.

New Christians in Bordeaux lived as naturalized subjects of the crown and planted deep roots but, as a collective, were never trusted. The peculiar regime of toleration that the monarchy adopted in southwestern France sought to conceal the presence of Jews and at the same time intensified public fears of a Jewish presence. Meanwhile, the expansion of commercial society in seventeenth-century France meant that the institutions that once defined its membership, imperfect as they were, were being chipped away, and traditional markers of status were receding in the marketplace. It was in this environment that the legend of the Jewish origins of marine insurance and bills of exchange emerged.

A host of fanciful but evocative analogies arguably fostered the association between Jews and immaterial credit instruments. Like baptized Jews who fled the Inquisition, bills of exchange moved across geopolitical borders with great ease. Bills of exchange, like Jews, operated on the basis of a secret language unintelligible to outsiders. Like New Christians who passed themselves off as devout Catholics, fraudulent use of bills of exchange was not easily detectable.

Baffling as these analogies may appear today, they help us make sense of how contemporaries approached the key problem raised by the contractual equality and self-regulation of commercial society, namely, how to detect a dishonest merchant when he operated outside a corporate regime of verification. Modern readers may be disoriented by Cleirac's approach to this problem because standard accounts have expunged Jewish metaphors from the history of European economic thought of the seventeenth and eighteenth centuries and concentrated instead on other intellectual and institutional ways of grappling with the same issue. In the last quarter of the seventeenth century, Colbert believed the solution to the problem of merchants' greed consisted of stronger state regulatory structures and a capillary system of inspection (chapter 5). A century after Cleirac, Montesquieu's concept of *doux commerce* allowed for greater optimism about the natural tendency of commerce to "soften" merchants' bad proclivities and turned attention instead to the dilemma of how to contain rapacious rulers (chapter 6). Later in the eighteenth century, Adam Smith denounced monopolies and offered a full-blown formulation of the benefits of free trade based on the notion that the prospect of future gains would keep traders from misbehaving. Many have tendentiously interpreted Smith's thesis to be the definitive answer to the problem of self-interest and corruption. In the next chapters, we will see that salient features of these better-known paradigms ought to be revisited in light of their treatment of a legend that we have forgotten but that early modern authors knew well.

5

One Family, Two Bestsellers, and the Legend's Canonization

Cherafs: Banyan money-changers established in Persia, especially in Shamakhi, on the Caspian Sea, in comparison with whom Jews appear to be dilettantes in commerce.

—DIDEROT & D'ALEMBERT, *ENCYCLOPÉDIE*[1]

JACQUE SAVARY's *Le parfait négociant*, first printed in 1675, was the manifesto of seventeenth-century French commercial society. It was also the most reprinted, translated, and plagiarized merchant manual of early modern Europe. A far more experienced and effective writer than Cleirac, Savary shared with his predecessor a commitment to setting new legal and cultural standards for private trade and finance. With a deft editorial hand, he repeated the fictional account of Jews' invention of bills of exchange while also streamlining and purging the seven relevant pages of *Us et coustumes de la mer* of their overt anti-Jewish language. In so doing, Savary singlehandedly ensured the legend's propagation. In its abbreviated and sanitized form, the tale was picked up by several other authors. After Savary's death, two of his sons published a massive dictionary of commerce, the first of its genre, which proved to be another bestseller of the *ars mercatoria* and disseminated the legend even further. Taken together, the complete works of the Savarys, father and sons, constitute the most articulate explication of the norms and ethos that infused the practice and politics of commerce under the reigns of Louis XIV (r. 1643–1715) and Louis XV (r. 1715–1744).

Several reasons account for the fortune of these publications. They contained an unprecedented amount of practical information and summarized government regulations on trade, although the extent to which merchants availed themselves of printed instructions when making strategic decisions about their businesses remains unclear.[2] Above all, the Savary family stepped in at the right moment and gave the new figure of the wholesale merchant the respectability it needed. Louis XIV's trusted minister of finance, Jean-Baptiste Colbert, sought to reinvigorate trade and manufacturing by reforming the legal, fiscal, and administrative apparatus of the French economy. In 1669, as we saw, he allowed, and in fact encouraged, noblemen to engage in long-distance trade and subjected them to the same legal framework that governed commoners involved in maritime commerce. It is difficult to overestimate the significance of these reforms in a society dominated by the notion of rank and in which rank was inseparable from the administration of justice. But it is equally important to realize that these reforms would have been moot without an accompanying reorganization of societal values.

Le parfait négociant did more than any other publication to address the cultural shift that Colbert's legal innovations implied and demanded. The book's title captured the essence and magnitude of this shift. It dispensed with the generic term *marchand*, which denoted both wholesale and retail traders, as well as some artisans, and echoed a corporate terminology of ancient pedigree (the original six guilds of Paris were called *corps des marchands*, and their head was the *prévot des marchands*).[3] Savary chose instead the word *négociant*, which beginning in the seventeenth century referred exclusively to a merchant involved in wholesale and overseas trade who was versed in the financial transactions that exchanges over long distances required. Moreover, a *négociant* was not necessarily a guild member but rather someone known publicly as a merchant—a connotation that broadened the range of those who might be qualified as such.[4]

The Scholastic economic theory in which Cleirac was schooled conceived of guilds as repositories of the knowledge necessary to ensure the fairness of market exchanges. When moral theologians spoke of the "general estimation" (*communis aestimatio*) that ought to determine what prices were just and thus acceptable, they assumed the existence of a specialized professional group, whose boundaries were traditionally defined by guild membership, that had the ability to evaluate the process of price formation.[5] By testing apprentices' skills, inspecting raw materials, and vouching for the quality of the goods put on sale, guilds were supposed to protect consumers while also shielding workers and merchants from unfair competition. In reality, more often than not, guilds turned into corrupt cartels. Yet the alternative—open and free competition—was not a universal remedy either, not so much because it did not belong to the ideological landscape of the time as because it was (and is) equally imperfect: there is no market in which everyone possesses the same information or wields identical influence. The erosion of the corporate structure that governed those merchants who were involved in long-distance trade and private finance during the sixteenth century and the emergence of the *négociant* as a key figure left authorities and the public alike in need of a new institutional framework to oversee and regulate trade and its practitioners.

How were young men to learn the rules of the game when guild apprenticeship was no longer mandatory and only minimal public instruction was offered? How were established merchants to monitor each other's behavior as more and more actors flooded the marketplace? Now that foreign merchants paced the Bourse of Bordeaux and noblemen could invest in the Atlantic trade, a freer and more mobile commercial society promised to unleash new talent and resources (at least for the privileged few capable of availing themselves of these opportunities). But this fluidity also harbored new dangers. How was it possible to keep those dangers in check without curtailing entrepreneurship? How could traders who did not belong to a guild ensure that everyone operated intelligently and honestly?

Colbert regarded commerce and manufacturing as sources of national power but was exceedingly fearful of merchants' autonomy. He did not believe that entrepreneurs had the desire or ability to curb their most extravagant ambitions. He therefore promoted as a counterbalance parallel organizations, including royal manufacturing establishments and state-funded commercial companies, and appointed royal inspectors to monitor the manufacturing, commercial, and fiscal sectors.[6] These regulatory initiatives, however, ran the risk of stifling entrepreneurship and creating new forms of dependency on the central government. Works like Savary's were designed to lend respectability to *négociants* and to strike a balance between autonomy and regulation through the definition of informal yardsticks against which merchants could measure their behavior.

As royal decrees injected elements of contract into a society of status, new written and unwritten norms were needed to police the marketplace. In this unsettling transitional moment, authors like Cleirac and Savary appealed to the figure of the Jewish merchant to convey universal standards of how *not* to handle commercial and financial transactions. The thirteenth-century association between Jews and usury was so profoundly imprinted on Christian minds that it remained meaningful even as Jews became connected with commercial credit rather than pawnbroking. With Marseilles and the Mediterranean at the epicenter of Savary's *Parfait négociant*, the fears about the hidden influence of New Christians that had haunted Cleirac in Bordeaux gave way to a different, though not incompatible trope: that of the all-powerful Jewish trader who outmaneuvered rivals by virtue of his supposedly domineering position in the exchanges between Christian Europe and the Muslim Mediterranean. A proto-Orientalist discourse added a new dimension to this trope. In travel accounts and commercial literature, different segments of the Jewish diaspora were lumped together with other ethnoreligious minorities. Jews came to be mentioned frequently alongside Armenians and, by the eighteenth century, Greeks. Christian observers praised all of these groups as the opposite of the allegedly indolent and unskilled Muslims and yet demonized the subterfuges that they all supposedly used to trick French merchants.[7]

The new trope of the omnipotent Mediterranean Jewish trader infused the legend of the Jewish invention of bills of exchange and marine insurance with new meaning. In this chapter and the next, I chart the legend's reception in France from the mid-seventeenth century to the Revolution. I identify four phases in its propagation, separated by two moments of discontinuity (the list of French titles that mention this legend is found in appendix 5). The "consecration" phase (1647–1690) was interrupted by the earliest refutation of the legend's validity in 1690. While the rebuff was not universal, skepticism toward Cleirac's narrative emerged and nurtured alternative origin stories, including one connecting the invention of bills of exchange to Florentine expatriates in Lyon. The "dissemination" phase (1700–1748) culminated in a second break, this time brought about by Montesquieu's novel interpretation of the legend in 1748, and its consequences were more profound. I then divide the second half of the eighteenth century into a "bifurcation" phase (1748–1775), during which Montesquieu's more positive version of the legend coexisted alongside the earlier and darker one proposed by Cleirac and Savary, and a final phase (1775–1791), during which this darker version entered the prerevolutionary debates about Jewish emancipation.

In recounting the legend's permutations, I stress both the persistence and the malleability of Christian images of Jewish economic roles. I also assess the role that context and intertextuality played in the reproduction and elaboration of certain tropes and not others. Ultimately, my analysis aims to broaden the current map of French economic thought and puts pressure on accepted historical accounts of the relationship between economic, social, and—by the late eighteenth century—political order that regard commerce as a progressive force.

Phase I (1647–1690): Consecration

If the gist of the convoluted pages of *Us et coustumes de la mer* endured the passing of time and left a mark on the European imagination, it is first and foremost thanks to Jacques Savary (1622–1690), the bestselling author of the early modern European *ars mercatoria* and the mastermind behind the 1673 *ordonnance de commerce*, the first European national code of commercial law. Shortly after its publication, *Le parfait négociant* was translated into German (1676) and Dutch (1683). By 1800 it had appeared in at least twenty-nine French editions, some of which considerably expanded on the first one.[8]

More extensive and accurate than any of its antecedents, Savary's manual walked a merchant through every bit of information he needed to succeed, from weights and measurements to partnership contracts, bookkeeping, and more. It borrowed from previous Italian examples, such as Peri's *Il negotiante*, from its author's personal experience, and from a wealth of legal documents. The 1679 edition, which would become the canonical one, also reproduced many reports (*mémoires*) written by merchants, travelers, and government officials, often anonymously and usually at the request of state agencies, which constituted a distinctive genre documenting commerce and its policing in Old Regime France. No doubt Cleirac's *Us et coustumes* lay on Savary's desk, even if it went unmentioned in the latter's work; after all, period standards for citations and plagiarism did not demand bibliographical references.[9]

Bills of exchange were an obligatory topic of any merchant manual, and Savary introduced the subject with a chapter on their "origin and usefulness for commerce." There he offered a condensed version of the legend. He omitted any mention of marine insurance, a subject that his book did not treat. He also eliminated all vituperative invective regarding Jews and usury, but by affirming the Jewish origin of bills of exchange, Savary cast a shadow over the morality of those credit instruments. The setting of this pseudo-history in France and its apparent richness of factual details elevated the tone of the tale. In place of Cleirac's meandering narrative, he presented a synthetic and ostensibly linear chronicle of events. Cleirac had indicated the names of the three kings responsible for the medieval expulsions that supposedly led Jews to invent bills of exchange. Savary added the dates of each expulsion ordered by those kings: Dagobert I in 640, Philip Augustus in 1182, and Philip the Tall in 1316.[10] These dates arguably boosted the legend's credentials; not surprisingly, multiple authors thereafter repeated them (with occasional additions and modifications).

Savary followed Cleirac in affirming that "Italian Lombards," having found "the invention of bills of exchange to be very useful to cover up usury," took up the habit of using those bills and carried them wherever they went. But Savary also gave the narrative a new and lasting twist: he attributed to the Ghibellines, not to the Jews, the invention of re-exchange, the more sophisticated credit instrument that permitted merchant-bankers to use bills of exchange to engage in currency arbitrage rather than simply use them to pay for goods abroad (chapter 1). Though re-exchange was among the new financial instruments that troubled theologians the most, it was also a tribute to the cleverness of international merchants and bankers, who took advantage of the asymmetry of information in currency markets to reap profits—something ordinary observers found baffling but that Savary eulogized. The twist that Savary added to the story was not entirely novel. Half a century earlier, another French author, Mathias Maréschal, had maintained that Italian rather than French merchants had devised the mechanism of re-exchange. But Maréschal did so because he did not want the French to be tainted by business practices that theologians despised.[11] Savary magnified this seemingly minor detail and put it in a positive light. Instead of condemning re-exchange, he used it to restore Italian merchants to a more important position in the historical arc of European finance.

Why did Savary endorse the story of the Jewish origin of bills of exchange, at least in their earliest and most rudimentary form, with such conviction? Born four decades after Cleirac, Savary still lived at a time when commerce's reputation in France was both fragile and contested. His family had lost its noble status in the fifteenth century because of its involvement in trade.[12] By his mid-thirties, Savary had reached the top tier of the mercer guild in Paris, where he worked as a wholesale merchant (*mercier-marchand en gros*) and accumulated a considerable fortune.[13] Encouraged by Nicolas Fouquet, Louis XIV's superintendent of finance, he purchased a royal office for the management of custom duties. After the fall of Fouquet, Colbert overlooked his resentment toward his predecessor and, recognizing Savary's talent, tapped him to chair the commission charged with drafting a comprehensive royal ordinance on commerce.[14]

Together, this piece of legislation and *Le parfait négociant* laid the legal and cultural foundations for a commercial society based on contract rather than rank. But the aristocratic tradition that Savary challenged could not be over-turned instantaneously. A far more successful public servant and writer than Cleirac, Savary outlined his goals for *Le parfait négociant* very clearly. He wished to provide a pedagogical instrument for those embarking on a career in long-distance trade and to legitimize the merchant profession as "useful" (*utile*) and "honorable" (*honorable*). Both words are crucial. Other French authors before him, including Cleirac and Jean Eon, had also seized on the term "honor," the quintessential aristocratic quality and a supposedly inherit-able characteristic, speaking of "honorable merchants" and "honorable com-merce."[15] Savary specified that a noble pedigree ought not impede a career in commerce and, conversely, praised everyone's quest for profit and desire to better themselves ("le profit et le desir de s'élever").[16] Although no longer based on birth, hierarchies were still essential. Savary drew a sharp distinction along Ciceronian lines between ordinary traders involved in local retail and brokerage and more elite *négociants* active in transregional exchanges and fi-nance. Advocates of the nobility's involvement in commerce latched onto this new hierarchy as a way to confer dignity on long-despised activities. A clergy-man from Marseilles, François Marchetty, argued that noblemen engaged in long-distance trade ("nobles marchands") should not be confused with regular merchants ("simples bourgeois & des autres negociants").[17]

The other half of Savary's formula for legitimating commerce in the age of Colbert was utility, or the alignment of private and public interests. Savary's entire body of work argued for the interdependence of the monarchy's mer-cantilist interests and merchants' private interests. In this view, a stronger and more respectable merchant class was needed if the monarchy wished to prevail in the increasingly competitive arena of international trade. Savary's patron, Colbert, however, was wary of private merchants. In a letter of 1679 to the *in-tendant* in the region of Marseilles, he denounced their selfishness and lack of concern for the welfare of the state: "The Marseillais merchants, who care for nothing but the little profit they can make, and who abuse the liberty that they have been given up to now to ship money as they like to the Levant, do so against . . . the universal and fundamental law of all states, which prohibits the transport of gold and currency on pain of death."[18]

Le parfait négociant struck a less pessimistic chord. Like Cleirac, Savary denounced successful merchants' habit of purchasing offices that conferred a noble title ("charges de la robe") for their sons. But compared to Cleirac and

Colbert, Savary had a less bleak view of merchants and their ambitions. He even referred to the "sweetness of commerce" ("c'est ce commerce aussi qui fait toute la douceur de la vie"), although the phrase still did not have the larger meaning that Montesquieu later attributed to it.[19] The goal of *Le parfait négociant*, Savary reassured his readers and the public authorities, was not to divulge trade secrets learned on the ground but rather to establish the conditions under which individuals would not engage in reckless behavior and easily squander fortunes.[20] Savary remained concerned with the nefarious effects that commerce could unintentionally produce. In his view, only the state could reduce these potentially negative effects, and the state, not private individuals, should remain the primary driver of commercial expansion.

Mercantilism (which is itself not an early modern term) is how scholars have labeled the political economy promoted by Colbert, which Savary translated into everyday practice for French *négociants*. If we wish to retain that label, we ought to understand it not only as a set of policies molded on a conception of international commerce as a zero-sum game that privileged exports over imports, but also as a belief in the need for a centralized visible hand to orchestrate merchants' actions. This doctrine placed little faith in merchants' ability to self-regulate.[21]

Bills of exchange played an important role in theories and practices of mercantilism, broadly defined. By moving large sums in and out of the kingdom, private merchants and the crown's financiers altered exchange rates between French and foreign currencies and thus affected France's position in international commerce.[22] At this time, there was no central coordinating institution able to stabilize financial markets in moments of crisis. Savary emphasized both the logic of a self-policing commercial society (merchants would be likely to show prudence in using bills of exchange because they depended on them) and the need for surveillance (by rulers who wanted to prevent improper manipulations and the outflow of capital).[23]

In his chapter on the "origin of bills of exchange and their commercial usefulness," Savary affirmed, not once but twice, that "there is nothing more useful to the State and to the public than the use of bills of exchange." To this emphatic endorsement, however, he added a cautionary note: "But it should also be admitted that there is nothing more dangerous than this commerce, which produces a great deal of usury and bankruptcies when bankers, merchants, and traders practice it with lust and imprudence." What constituted "lust and imprudence" ("convoitise & imprudence"), and how was it possible to inhibit these vices? For Savary, the architect of the 1673 code, re-exchange contracts in themselves were neither lustful nor imprudent. Better equipped than Cleirac to answer technical questions and less dependent on theologians, he nonetheless shared with his Bordelais predecessor a heightened concern for the hidden ways in which bills of exchange could engender ruinous effects. Elsewhere he noted that dry exchange, condemned by canon law as usurious, was responsible for the greatest number of bankruptcies.[24] New decrees and jurisprudence, Savary implied, did not contain sufficiently firm benchmarks for limiting "lust and imprudence." Written laws inevitably included loopholes and had to be complemented by shared cultural norms to become enforceable.

In an effort to lay out those cultural norms, Savary oscillated between didactic invocations of Jews as dishonest traders and a matter-of-fact recognition of the degree to which Jewish merchants participated in Europe's commercial society. This ambivalence came into full view in his *Parères*, a compilation of his legal opinions on seventy lawsuits over matters of commerce. Commenting on an intricate case concerning the fine imposed on a broker for handling a bill of exchange improperly, Savary pointed to Jews as the medieval inventors of classic four-party bills of exchange.[25] Here the legend, mentioned casually, functioned as a placeholder. The linkage cast a shadow on financial practices that, while widespread, could derail honest businesses. The 1673 ordinance prohibited brokers from issuing or cashing bills of exchange in their own names, but not from using their insider knowledge to their customers' advantage. Brokers, Savary claimed, were responsible for the majority of bankruptcies of merchants and large commercial houses.[26] Since real-life Jews could not be brokers in early modern France, the tale of the Jewish origin of bills of exchange functioned as a warning: some people could take advantage of those bills to the detriment of others in ways that the written law could not regulate. In another legal opinion, however, Savary addressed actual Jews (albeit not Jews from France). His clients, French Catholics, had issued bills for Jewish agents in Antwerp who had failed to follow the proper procedures to protest those bills they did not wish to accept. Savary used no denigrating words in reference to these individuals. At most, he called his clients by name while referring to their Antwerp correspondents as "the Jews."[27]

In other words, Savary exemplifies a tendency that we find across the literature on commerce from the last quarter of the seventeenth century on: Jews and other minorities were sometimes matter-of-factly referred to as a presence in European and global marketplaces and other times were depicted as sinister characters not to be trusted. Jews in particular provided a yardstick against which all of the evils that lurked behind the growing paper economy could be measured. They could perform this allegorical role because of the assumptions that authors and readers shared. Some of these assumptions that appeared in *Le parfait négociant* were the same as those that informed *Us et coustumes de la mer*. In spite of his more detached tone, Savary nevertheless described Jews as ominous characters who devised letters "of very few words and little substance," reiterating the notion that the cryptic language of bills of exchange could trick nonexperts. He also portrayed Jews as going out of their way to squeeze as much profit as possible from foreign transactions: "Because this sort of people is so attuned to opportunities for gain and profit, they make every effort to acquire knowledge about the intrinsic value and possible impurities of all currencies in order to avoid any mistakes in calculating monetary transactions."

At the same time as it relied on age-old negative associations between Jews and credit, *Le parfait négociant* also incorporated new variants of these motifs, with the figure of the Jewish pawnbroker making way for that of the formidable Jewish international merchant. On the surface these two archetypes might appear to contradict one another: we associate the former with an economy of scarcity and the latter with abundance and commercial credit. In fact, usury linked the two in both the learned tradition and the popular imagination. Literally, *usury* meant the charging of interest, but since to charge interest was to exploit borrowers, *usury* was also used to denote unfair economic practices more generally. The perceived overrepresentation of Jews in certain areas of Mediterranean and colonial trade was easily construed as a case of usury because Jews were seen as an oligopolistic group able to extract unreasonable prices from non-Jews.[28]

Savary made sparing use of the word *usury*, but when he did use it, he evoked its more capacious meaning. Discussing various forms of credit, he advised wholesale merchants not to charge higher interest on late payments, a practice he called "a horrific usury," because to do so increased the chance that debtors would go bankrupt.[29] The logic was airtight: proper ethics and self-interest would yield the same outcome. In the 1676 Franco-German edition of *Le parfait négociant*, he added a few more pieces of advice, urging wholesale merchants not to lend on collateral to avoid the wrath of God and not to charge interest when lending to close friends because to do so would mean to behave like Jews ("car ce seroit imiter les Juifs").[30] Here Jews stood in for the heartless moneylender who put his interest ahead of human sympathy and the common good.

Elsewhere in Savary's work, Jewish merchants acquired new sociological features that were part reality and part fantasy. Savary portrayed those operating in northern Europe, and especially in Amsterdam, as rivaling Christian commercial elites, not only in wealth but also in worldly sophistication. Those operating throughout the Mediterranean, however, he depicted as untrustworthy wheelers and dealers and the keepers of secret information on how to conduct business with Arabs and Turks. In the first edition of *Le parfait négociant*, the inclusion of the legend was Savary's only significant engagement with a Jewish-related theme. But as French experts' reports on Mediterranean trade were incorporated into the 1679 expanded edition, Jews began to figure more prominently. Those in Livorno were said to monopolize all trade.[31] In Smyrna and other Ottoman ports, French merchants were described as being at the mercy of Jews and Armenians, from whom they borrowed at exorbitant interest rates.[32] Given the market power of these people, there were great profits to be made by trading with them, Savary told his readers, but one had to be ready to take risks that were even greater than normal circumstances would demand because of "the bad faith that there may be in Jews and Armenians."[33]

This shift in the portrayal of Jews from pawnbrokers to the dominant merchant group in the Mediterranean mixed old clichés with new conditions in Marseilles, Savary's adoptive town. Unlike Cleirac's Bordeaux, Marseilles was not home to a New Christian community and became instead a battleground in the dispute between the crown and the local merchant elite over whether to extend commercial privileges to Jews, Armenians, Calvinists, Muslims, and foreigners more generally. In April 1669, Colbert declared Marseilles a free port. His intention was not only to attract merchandise by way of low tariffs but also to lure Jewish and Armenian merchants to the region in an effort to capitalize on their extensive trade networks in the Mediterranean. But he met with staunch opposition from the local merchant oligarchy, organized in the kingdom's first Chamber of Commerce (created in 1650), which ultimately prevailed. The edict was revised to restrict low customs duties to French merchants and shipowners while imposing significantly higher tariffs on all foreigners and their ships.[34]

Armenians and Jews were the primary targets of this mercantilist legislation. While numerically few in Europe, Armenians nevertheless loomed large in the French imagination, principally because of their important role in exporting Persian raw silk, a highly prized commodity, but also because in the 1670s they opened some of the first cafés in Paris, in the area of Saint-Germain-des-Prés, where customers were surrounded by Turkish decor and black servers.[35] In Marseilles, French merchants feared the competition of Livorno's Jews, who had established themselves as influential intermediaries with North Africa and the Levant. In 1682, the crown gave in to the pressure of the Chamber of Commerce and expelled all Jews from Marseilles. That the injunction had to be reissued in 1690 and 1758 suggests that a few Jewish merchants continued to operate underground, although their numbers dwindled eventually.[36]

These conflicts were ongoing while Savary was composing and revising his *Parfait négotiant*. From his place of observation in Marseilles, he not only identified Jews with oligopolies and dishonesty but juxtaposed Jews and Armenians and exaggerated their market power. In so doing, he created a new trope in European commercial literature, one that his sons' dictionary would crystallize. From now on, Jews and Armenians—assumed to be cohesive and clearly demarcated groups—would be frequently mentioned together in Orientalizing travel and commercial literature. In the mid-eighteenth century, David Hume, the Scottish skeptic and champion of the virtues of commerce and moderation, famously rejected the fixity of "national characters" for Europeans, though not for black Africans; for Jews, whom he described as "noted for fraud"; or for Armenians, who were supposedly characterized by "probity."[37] He was not alone in reserving gentler words for Armenians (most of whom were eastern Christians, though some had converted to Catholicism), but they, too, emerged as shady figures in several accounts.

Savary's depictions of Armenians and Jews hardly amounted to dispassionate proto-ethnography.[38] He made little effort to identify the many social realities that lay behind the generic terms of "Jews" and "Armenians," in spite of the fact that such information was available and would have benefited readers in search of advice about how best to conduct their businesses. Different subgroups of Jews and Armenians occupied different niches of the Mediterranean trade and possessed different legal privileges, which in turn affected their ability to enter certain markets. In 1621, for example, Marseilles banned all Armenians and their goods. Yet only fifteen years later, after France signed a peace treaty with the Safavid Empire, Richelieu encouraged Persian Armenians (but not those who were subjects of the Ottoman Empire) to trade with Marseilles. Predictably, Ottoman Armenians looked for opportunities to secure safe-conduct passes and other identification papers that would allow them to be treated as Persians.[39] Religious affiliation mattered too. Catholic Armenians were more welcome in Venice and Livorno than those belonging to the Armenian Church, but they had to conceal their faith in Amsterdam, where Catholics were banned from worshiping. It is fair to assume that the traders who crisscrossed the Mediterranean were cognizant of the varying religious and political affiliations of the Armenian diaspora and that such information would have been of interest to Savary's intended readership. *Le parfait négociant*, however, overlooked these differences, simply mentioning that Armenians carried silk from Persia to Smyrna and a few resided in Venice. For the most part, it paired Armenians and Jews and referred to both as epitomes of commercial guile.

In short, tradition and socially constrained perceptions informed Savary's characterization of merchant groups more than his (limited) direct experience. This was particularly true when it came to non-French and non-Catholic traders. In a chapter devoted to French trade in Egypt, Savary noted that small quantities of Asian goods still arrived in Cairo via caravan routes, and that "Turks, Jews, and Armenians" rushed to buy them and bring them back to the "Turkish Empire."[40] These groups, he claimed, served as the exclusive intermediaries between French traders and "Arab brokers." The inflated power Savary attributed to Jews is even more evident in his report that the Egyptian city on the Nile had 4 to 5 million inhabitants, 23,000 mosques, and 12,000 Jewish residents—all wildly exaggerated numbers.[41]

Overall, *Le parfait négociant*'s mentions of Jews conjured up images of both usurious lenders and almighty merchants. It was against this background that readers made sense of the legend that Savary relayed. Less moralistic in language and tone than Cleirac, Savary nevertheless shared with his predecessor two aims: asserting the honorability of commerce and cordoning off disreputable types of commercial activity from permissible ones. During the quarter century that separated the publication of *Us et coustumes de la mer* and *Le parfait négociant*, the boundaries between the feudal aristocracy and the mercantile elite grew more porous. The two-way process of legal and cultural transformation accelerated after the August 1669 decree on the *noblesse commerçante* and demanded the erection of new symbolic benchmarks of commercial morality. Once again, Jews performed an important function in this regard, illustrated by Savary's mixing of the medieval figure of the usurious Jew with the new Jewish merchants operating in the seventeenth-century Mediterranean.

In light of what I have said so far, it will not come as a surprise that the two texts that further disseminated the legend of the Jewish invention of marine insurance and bills of exchange throughout France during the late seventeenth century were legal commentaries on recent royal edicts designed by Colbert.

Philippe Bornier (1635–1711), a nobleman and royal official in Montpellier, was charged by the king with producing a systematic collection of all recent royal decrees on civil, criminal, and commercial law. His commentary on the 1673 ordinance traced the invention of both bills of exchange (title V, art. 1) and marine insurance (title XII, art. 7) to Jews, borrowing generously from (but not citing) Cleirac's *Us et coustumes de la mer*. Bornier reiterated a point made by both Cleirac and Savary: that bills of exchange "are very useful, as long as no one commits any abuse in handling them and they involve real exchange."[42] Building on his university training more than on practical experience, he invoked the distinction drawn by theologians between real and fictive exchanges, that is, between bills employed to transfer funds from one city to another and bills that functioned exclusively as financial instruments, a distinction that Savary had largely abandoned. More than Savary, Bornier also adopted Cleirac's religiously charged language when speaking of Jews ("leur crimes execrables," "retirer à la Juive") and cited Giovanni Villani as an unquestioned authority.[43]

The other legal commentary of those years in which the legend figures prominently was written not at the bequest of the crown but upon the initiative of a commoner, Jean Toubeau, the former head of the merchant guild of Bourges, a town in what was then the province of Berry, in the heart of France. Unjustly overlooked by most scholars, Toubeau's *Les institutes du droit consulaire* (1682) solely concerned the *ordonnance de commerce* of 1673 and is a key text for understanding the social and legal entanglements of Old Regime commercial society. Dedicated to Colbert, the work vigorously asserted the honorability of commerce and defended the autonomy of merchants' tribunals against trained justices and lawyers, whom Toubeau denounced as "idolaters of Roman law."[44]

The first part of Toubeau's treatise was devoted to consular jurisdictions, the definition of a merchant, and noblemen's involvement in commerce. By the late seventeenth century, noblemen and clergymen were frequently trading or endorsing bills of exchange, but they resented having to renounce their immunities to appear before a merchant judge. To defend the principle established by the 1673 ordinance, according to which the nature of the disputed transaction rather than the status of the parties involved in it determined whether a lawsuit would be adjudicated before a commercial or a civil court, Toubeau turned to legal authorities (jurists like Andrea Alciato, Jacques Cujas, and Sigismondo Scaccia) and to history (notably the cities of Venice and Genoa) in order to demonstrate that commerce was a dignified activity that was entirely congruent with noble status. He rejected Cicero's distinction between wholesale and retail trade, arguing that noblemen should feel entitled to engage in all forms of trade. This strong antihumanist position departed from earlier, more conciliatory statements by authors of the *ars mercatoria* and signaled a greater reliance on law than on tradition in legitimizing commerce.

In the second part of *Les institutes du droit consulaire*, which concerned exchange dealings, Toubeau expressed his impatience with all religious condemnations of credit. Following Savary, he attributed the invention of re-exchange to the Ghibellines who fled Florence for Amsterdam and defended this type of transaction against those, like Maréschal, who had deemed it to be usurious.[45] In spite of his full vindication of commercial credit in its most sophisticated forms, Toubeau still followed in the footsteps of Cleirac, Savary, Bornier, and even Villani (whom he had evidently not read) in maintaining that Jews invented both bills of exchange and marine insurance.[46] Only thirty-five years after the publication of *Us et coustumes de la mer* and seven years after the first appearance of *Le Parfait négociant*, the legend was thus referenced as a matter of fact.

Toubeau's treatment signals the normalization of the legend. In 1690, an authoritative French dictionary repeated it in relation to both marine insurance and bills of exchange without a shadow of a doubt.[47] At the same time, Toubeau's reference to Jews as inventors of marine insurance was not entirely casual. Questioning the existence of marine insurance in Roman law, he anticipated the trend, especially pronounced among eighteenth-century German and Italian jurists, of searching for the antecedents of credit contracts in Roman law and the classical tradition (chapter 7).[48] In the short term, however, it was Toubeau's belief in the legend that attracted attention. A review of his treatise published in the *Journal des sçavans* singled out the Jewish invention of bills of exchange as one of the curious ideas that one could glean from it.[49]

The First Moment of Discontinuity (1690): Refutation

In 1690, in his *L'art des lettres de change*, the first French treatise devoted entirely to bills of exchange, Jacques Dupuis de la Serra made Cleirac's account the object of a frontal attack—a measure of the reputation the legend had developed since 1647. Bills of exchange had become so widespread that everyone handled them, the author declared, but they remained "mysterious and only intelligible to those who specialize in this trade, known as bankers."[50] By his estimation, this informational asymmetry between insiders and outsiders was particularly dangerous when disputes over bills of exchange ended up in appellate courts (*parlements*), because the judges who presided over these courts, as Cleirac had also noted, were ignorant of the ways in which these instruments worked and therefore often unable to issue fair sentences. To close the gap between the practical knowledge of merchants and the bookish culture of men of law, Dupuis de la Serra went further than any previous author in assembling French and foreign legislation concerning bills of exchange.

As had become customary, he opened his treatise with a taxonomical distinction between different types of exchange: moneychanging involving foreign coins, four-party bills of exchange, dry exchange, and bills traded at the fairs of Lyon. In the second chapter, he turned to a historical account of the emergence of bills of exchange. Here he departed from his predecessors. Together with a strong assertion of the usefulness of bills of exchange and their unique contractual nature (which differentiated them from usurious loans), Dupuis de la Serra marshaled a robust rejection of the idea that Jews had invented those bills. He agreed with Cleirac only that no comparable contracts had existed in ancient Roman law. Otherwise, he challenged the Bordeaux lawyer on two grounds. First, he reasoned that inventions materialize quickly, not over 600 years, the interval between the expulsion decrees of 640 and 1316 cited by Cleirac and Savary as having inspired Jews to conceive these new credit devices. Second, he stressed the hatred toward Jews that pervaded the periods of their expulsion. According to the legend, the Jewish invention of bills of exchange required the assistance of gentile neighbors who took Jews' money and property and fulfilled the promise to remit cash payments to them abroad. In Dupuis de la Serra's view, such relationships of cooperation and trust could not have emerged amid public hostility.[51]

The logic of both objections was persuasive and provided fodder for those wishing to refute the legend of the Jewish invention of bills of exchange in the decades and centuries to come. Not even this challenge, however, delivered the fatal blow to the legend. Dupuis de la Serra argued against the account's coherence but did not question the reliability of the sources that Cleirac had invoked. Poor source criticism, that is, insulated the legend from further scrutiny. Villani, in particular, was a legitimizing source, and Dupuis de la Serra failed to verify what his chronicle said about the matter. Ironically, Villani, albeit indirectly, was also the inspiration for Dupuis de la Serra's alternative hypothesis, which credited "those Florentines who had been expelled by the Ghibellines and found refuge in France" with inventing bills of exchange.[52]

Had Dupuis de la Serra probed the sources he was citing, he would have found that Villani made no such claim about the Jewish invention of bills of exchange and blown Cleirac's cover. Even so, he corrected Savary's inflation of the role played by Ghibellines in the instrument's invention, which rested on a garbled rendering of medieval Florentine history, since the wealthiest bankers had in fact been Guelfs. More significantly, he triggered the first consequential moment of discontinuity in the legend's reception. Overall, he stressed the uncertainty surrounding the origins of bills of exchange, expressed his preference for attributing their invention to Florentine exiles in France, and reinforced the link between the resourcefulness of refugees and the opportunity bills of exchange offered exiles to move funds surreptitiously under the eyes of their oppressors. We will encounter this theme of the economic ingenuity of persecuted minorities, heralded sometimes in jubilant tones, other times in more somber ones, again later in the book.

Short and lucid, *L'art des lettres de change* was another publishing hit. Reprinted in seven standalone French editions (1693, 1706, 1750, 1767, 1783, 1789, 1792), it was translated into Latin in 1712 and Italian in 1718, and enjoyed seven more Italian reprints (1740, 1750, 1761, 1772, 1785, 1803).[53] In 1828 it was incorporated into a new edition of Daniel Jousse's eighteenth-century commentary on the 1673 *ordonnance de commerce*.[54] It is particularly interesting to note that Dupuis de la Serra was a close collaborator of Savary, and it is to him and to Claude Naulot that we owe the most technical sections of *Le parfait négociant* in its revised 1679 edition.[55] Moreover, beginning in 1697, Dupuis de la Serra's treatise was included at the end of every new edition of Savary's manual—another indication that factual consistency was hardly a priority in the *ars mercatoria*, since the two texts offered contradictory accounts of the origins of bills of exchange.

Dupuis de la Serra's slim booklet reached a broad audience and planted the seeds of an alternative origin story, one that touted Florentine bankers as the inventors of bills of exchange and resonated especially with Italian and German scholars (chapter 7). Remarkably, however, the legend lived on in spite of having being shown to be utterly implausible.

Phase II (1700–1748): Dissemination

At this point in the story, mentions of the legend become too frequent to be discussed one by one. Two aspects of the second phase in the legend's dissemination in France are noteworthy, however. While the merchant literature remained the narrative's primary vehicle of diffusion, the alleged Jewish invention of bills of exchange (and sometimes marine insurance) began to crop up in texts unrelated to commerce and soon became a cliché more than an occasion for reflection—a trend that accelerated with the proliferation of serial and encyclopedic works in the eighteenth century. At the same time, this cliché took on different meanings depending on the discursive context in which it was invoked. My interpretative effort therefore consists in examining how the legend squared with other Christian representations of Jews and how a range of symbolic associations between Jews and credit could be combined and recombined over and over to suit changing circumstances.

Predictably, Savary's *Parfait négociant* became the blueprint for a growing number of handbooks on trade. Its most successful imitation, Samuel Ricard's *Traité general du commerce*, written and published in Amsterdam, appeared in multiple editions and inspired other French and Dutch writers. Ricard affirmed that bills of exchange belonged to the realm of natural law (*droit des gens*), rather than to canon or civil law, and judged them to be economically useful and morally legitimate. His brief and sober reference to the Jewish invention of bills of exchange appeared as an uncontested fact alongside praise for Italian contributions to commercial techniques.[56]

To these ideas inherited from Savary, Ricard added a distinctive Dutch perspective. Channeling a common sentiment, he reserved his praise for Spanish and Portuguese Jews and expressed uncharitable views of Ashkenazim, whom he called by the pejorative names of *Tudesques* (Germans) and *Semowfies* (Smousen) and depicted as engaged in the petty exchange of foreign coins.[57] Eastern European Jewish immigrants to Amsterdam at the time were indeed mostly poor, even if a few soon challenged the primacy of Sephardim in international trade and finance. Here we need to stress that even in the most tolerant of all early modern European cities, the practical commercial literature freely mixed factual statements (Ricard, for example, listed accurately the presence of 375 Christian and 20 Jewish licensed brokers in Amsterdam) with value judgments that reflected received wisdom more than direct observation.[58] The net result of this tendency was the widespread belief that different merchant communities enjoyed different degrees of collective credibility.

In Ricard's work and a host of other merchant manuals from the early eighteenth century, the legend only merited brief mention. Its appearance was sometimes incidental; other times it was more prominently placed. Sometimes the tale was left uncontested; other times it was accompanied by alternative explanations for the origin of credit instruments.[59] For whatever reason, perhaps because of their concise and parenthetical nature, modern scholars have overlooked these statements. But their recurrence suggests that they were placeholders for deep-seated associations between Jews and credit that readers at the time would have been quick to spot.

The second bestseller of the French *ars mercatoria*, the monumental dictionary of commerce compiled by Savary's two sons, is an excellent guide to the web of references to Jews and credit that pepper this literature. Its primary author was Jacques Savary des Brûlons (1657–1716), a royal official and inspector-general of manufacturing goods at the Custom House of Paris. After his death, his brother Philémon-Louis Savary (1654–1727), a cleric and canon of Saint-Maur-des-Fossés, a church under royal patronage in the greater Parisian region, completed the work. The first edition of the *Dictionnaire universel de commerce* appeared in three volumes between 1723 and 1730 and enjoyed enormous success. It was followed by several expanded and abridged editions in French and was imitated, adapted, and pirated in multiple languages.[60] To assemble their vast compilation, the two brothers drew from multiple sources: unpublished notes left by their father; travel accounts and official government papers ranging from surveys of specific trades and industries (such as spices or textiles) to memoranda (*mémoires*) written by merchants, sea captains, consuls, and others; legal inquiries (*procès-verbaux*) relating to commercial and maritime affairs; and finally, a vast printed literature, beginning with their father's *Parfait négociant* and extending to publications such as Ricard's *Négoce d'Amsterdam* (1700).[61]

Dictionaries and encyclopedias became the preferred and authoritative ways of organizing knowledge in the eighteenth century. They were not meant to be read cover to cover, and no matter how clear their programmatic aim and how strict their editorial oversight, they were inevitably inconsistent. The Savary brothers' dictionary was no exception. Yet with regard to the associations between Jews and credit, it displayed remarkable coherence.[62] References to Jews throughout the dictionary were far more numerous than in *Le parfait négociant*. To start, Savary's sons included an entry for "Jew" that encapsulated the entire discourse that revolved around the term: "Jews have the reputation of being very skilled at commerce but they are also suspected of trading without the maximum of honesty and probity."[63] This perceived combination of commercial acuity and treachery was at the heart of the interlocking stereotypes concerning Jews and helps us identify four themes that characterize the many references to Jews and credit throughout this voluminous dictionary.

First, the Savary brothers used the word *usury* both in a technical sense (lending at interest) and with a generic meaning of economic malpractice.

Both meanings were explicitly linked to Jews, who across multiple entries were described as guilty of charging exorbitant interest rates, hoarding, counterfeit, and deceit. Second, Jews were portrayed as alternately poor and exceedingly wealthy. This dyad had emerged in the sixteenth century and remained a staple of economically motivated anti-Jewish sentiments until the modern period. Oxymoronic only on the surface, it derived its appeal from the notion that both the poor and plutocrats existed on the margins of society and regularly engaged in fraud.[64]

A third theme connected Jews to all forms of commercial malpractice. The Savary brothers put it starkly: "The word 'Jew' has several meanings in relation to commerce, but almost all negative." Note that the emphasis was on the *word* Jew, that is, on the figurative rather than the sociological qualification of Jewishness. Examples of this usage were included: "A merchant is said to be rich like a Jew when he is believed to have amassed great fortunes, especially if he is suspected of some usurious traffic." What, then, was "usurious traffic"? A "merchant usurer" was someone who pillaged (*rançonne*) those he traded with and was called "a real Jew." It followed that "to fall in the hands of Jews" was to deal with traders who were harsh and tenacious in their negotiations. The Paris guild of secondhand dealers (*marchands fripons*) was mentioned to illustrate the point: it included many "honest people and good Catholics," the dictionary declared, but its members were often called "Jews," either because the populace regarded them as especially duplicitous or because they were suspected of being of Jewish descent.[65] To be a *fripon* was to behave like a Jew regardless of one's religious affiliation. The term could be applied to all sorts of characters: Greek and Armenian textile workers in Smyrna were said to be *grand fripons*, compelling merchants to put a special seal (*boul*) on the calicoes they painted to limit the chances of fraud.[66]

Fourth and last, the *Dictionnaire universel de commerce* regarded Jews (or, more precisely, certain segments of the Jewish diaspora) as wielding excessive influence in world finance and international commerce and linked this phenomenon to specific policies, including Colbert's brand of mercantilism. His effort to promote the inclusion of Jews or Armenians, whom he regarded as capable of enriching the royal coffers, unsettled the status quo. In 1615 Antoine de Montchrétien, to whom we owe the expression "political economy," had struck an early blow to the Aristotelian theory of international commerce by portraying it as an agonistic arena rather than as a system of balance and reciprocity. But Montchrétien was vehemently hostile to all foreigners, whom he regarded as spies and unfair competitors rather than as potential contributors to the national economy, and he was particularly averse to Jews, whom he saw as pouring into the kingdom with only their own interest at heart.[67] Colbert rejected this vision and attempted to turn exaltations of Jewish economic talents into reasons to grant them special privileges in exchange for their economic services but failed to persuade the commercial elites of Marseilles.

None of the views relayed by the Savary brothers was new, but they gave more space than previous authors to the different types of Jewish settlements that European rulers permitted in order to take advantage of Jews' ostensible commercial prowess. Even the "nations that are most ill-disposed toward Jews," the dictionary explained, were interested in "learning their business secrets and sharing their profits." The numbers adduced in support of this claim were more reliable (though still inflated) for Amsterdam than for Livorno, with Jews in the former divided into two "tribes": Portuguese Jews, who were richer, worked as bankers and merchants, and counted roughly 5,000 individuals, and German Jews, who were only 1,200 in number.[68] In Livorno, the Savary brothers wrote, there were "more than ten thousand" Jews—a figure three times larger than the actual one that they likely derived from the travel literature. According to the *Dictionnaire*, Jews controlled the majority of trade in both locations, but those in Livorno were truly hegemonic: they left only 2 percent of the Levant trade to be shared between the French, Italians, Dutch, English, and Armenians residing in the Tuscan port city.[69] Needless to say, this estimate bore no relation to reality.[70]

Livorno posed a greater threat to French expansion in the Mediterranean than Amsterdam did in the Atlantic and the Indian Ocean. Perhaps this situation, together with the Savary brothers' reliance on their father's work, led them to vastly overestimate the role of Livorno's Jews as intermediaries in the trade with the Ottoman Empire. Who exactly the Savarys thought these Jews were is not clear. They often treated Jewish and Christian subjects of the Ottoman Empire interchangeably. An anonymous *mémoire* on the commerce of Marseilles reprinted in the *Dictionnaire* explained that "all trade in Turkey is in the hands of Greeks, Armenians, Jews, and Syrians. These people, oppressed by the Turks, have lost their natural pride, but crushed under the yoke of a rapacious and despotic empire, seek repayments for their misfortunes from foreigners."[71] Muslim indolence and Ottoman despotism were fixtures of the Orientalist discourse that had matured since the publication of *Le parfait négociant* (Montesquieu's *Persian Letters* had appeared to great acclaim in 1721, just two years before the first volume of the Savary brothers' dictionary was issued).[72] Now the *Dictionnaire* added Greeks to the list of merchant groups from the southern and eastern shores of the Mediterranean that deceived Westerners and held undue market power.

As Jews became part of this Orientalist discourse, they morphed into an undifferentiated group, one among other Levantine communities. At the same time, Jews continued to be cast as paragons against whom every phenomenally talented merchant group was to be judged. The leitmotif figured in both French travel and commercial literature, which worked as echo chambers. Only a year after the publication of *Le parfait négociant*, the famed Huguenot traveler Jean-Baptiste Tavernier described Indian moneychangers (*Banianes*) as "devouring pests and vipers" and "worse usurers than the Jews," reflecting that they would have swallowed all of Persia's wealth had the shah not expelled them.[73] A later edition of the Savarys' dictionary added that "the Banyans and the Chinese are the most important merchants in the [East] Indies, to whom we could add the Jews and the Armenians, who are also scattered everywhere." The entry went on to claim: "We can associate [Banyans] with Armenians and Jews for their experience and their ability in all sorts of trades."[74] More often, Armenians were dropped from the equation. A French Huguenot exile in Berlin wrote that no people understood commerce better than the Chinese, who for this reason should be referred to as "the Jews of the Orient."[75]

Bankers and traders living in the town of Shamakhi, in today's Republic of Azerbaijan, near the Caspian Sea, were said to possess such rare financial abilities that they surpassed the Jews.[76] Through multiple intertextual borrowings, Shamakhi and its traders acquired iconic status in the European perception of Central Asia.[77] The entry in Diderot and d'Alembert's *Encyclopédie* cited as the epigraph at the start of this chapter assured the traders of Shamakhi a place in Enlightenment thought but also sealed the fate of the Jews as the ultimate symbol of commercial prowess.[78]

Scholars who have examined the writings of the Savary family or used them as sources of information about the history of European trade and merchant culture have neglected their multiple references to Jews. In fact, the figure of the Jew was essential to definitions of market ethics, if only because Jews served as abstract referents that exemplified improper behavior. In some cases, they also marked the proper boundaries of state commercial policies. The interlaced themes of the Savarys' dictionary illustrate that utility, a positive and necessary principle for any ruler, had to be weighed against usury, the most negative of all attributes of Jews and a wickedness from which Christians were not immune. In spite of its didactic tone, none of the literature produced by the elder Savary or his sons explained just how to achieve the proper balance between utility and usury.

By now, the difficulty of defining this elusive equilibrium should not surprise us. Arguments about the morality of commerce during this time were made through associations rather than precise demarcations, and such associations proved long lasting. Since the late Middle Ages, the notion of Jewish usury had been linked to Jews' ostensibly antisocial behavior and exclusion from the Christian covenant. These presumptions informed the entire spectrum of stereotypes about Jewish economic roles, ranging from the image of Jewish moneylenders choking Christian borrowers sanctioned at the 1215 Fourth Lateran Council to the figure of the all-powerful Jewish merchant forged in the seventeenth- and eighteenth-century Mediterranean and even the theme of Jewish pauperism that was emerging in central and eastern Europe. Political pragmatism allowed Jews a new and special space in those cities of Europe where Sephardim were welcomed with the expectation that they would boost trade and finance. But this newly gained position only applied to a subset of the Jewish diaspora and, more importantly, never counteracted a persistent source of hostility toward the entire group. Precisely because they were allegedly so skilled, Jews were bound to be perceived as trespassing the boundaries of the physical and symbolic spaces assigned to them.

The images of Jews that we find in the early modern French commercial literature absorbed and elaborated on widespread religious motifs. The symbiosis of religious and economic infidelity was crystallized in an episode recounted in the so-called "courtroom literature," which collected and commented on both famous and obscure trials. One of the first to experiment with this genre was the lawyer and polymath François Gayot de Pitaval (1673–1743), who assembled accounts of a vast number of sensational trials in a collection titled *Causes célèbres et interessantes*. The first edition appeared in twenty volumes between 1734 and 1743, and was reprinted in multiple formats. Among the notable trials selected for inclusion in this collection was that of Raphäel Levi, sentenced to death for ritual murder in Metz in 1670.[79]

Pitaval in this work for the first time embedded the legend of the Jewish invention of bills of exchange in an account of blood libel, the ultimate crime of which Jews were accused.[80] Cleirac had hinted at the analogy between usury and the desecration of the host (and thus ritual murder, since in Catholic doctrine the consecrated host is the body of Christ) through his reference to Villani (chapter 2). Transposed to the northeastern region of France, the analogy became explicit. Echoing the language of Canon 67, Pitaval maintained that "these abominable Jews" committed "all sorts of impieties" and oppressed Christians "with their excessive usuries" in times of both war and peace. He described in detail a scheme for fooling local peasants into buying low-quality horses imported from Germany as an instance of "the usuries and pillages perpetrated by the Jews of Metz."[81]

Causes célèbres et interessantes left behind the buoyant port cities of Bordeaux and Marseilles to situate the legend of the Jewish invention of bills of exchange in Lorraine, where Jews were impoverished and segregated, and mostly made a living as lenders to the poor peasants who despised them. Pitaval also resurrected the name of Giovanni Villani, which the Savarys had elided and which was indirectly tied to ritual murder. In the same years during which *Causes célèbres et interessantes* first appeared, more enlightened philosophes portrayed Jews as sympathetic victims of the Inquisition and used blood libels as weapons of anticlerical propaganda even as they continued to indulge in spiteful representations of rabbinical Judaism and Jewish society (chapter 6). *Causes célèbres et interessantes* did not embrace this antipapal agenda, constructing instead the most sinister version of the legend to date, one that did not become mainstream but arguably found an audience, especially among the legal professionals who were its principal readers.

Conclusion

Depicted by the Annales school as a century of famines, deflation, and rebellions, the French *grand siècle* long suffered bad press among economic historians. More recently, scholars of the seventeenth century (particularly Anglophones) have insisted on a portrayal focusing less on pauperization and more on the degree of commercialization that all strata of French society experienced during this time. The peasantry, once believed to have been caught in a perpetual Malthusian trap, has emerged from this revisionist literature as capable of rational economic decisions.[82] The opulent aristocracy, once portayed as parasitical in its conspicuous consumption, is now widely considered to have been able to make long-term investments, and all the more so after the introduction of the venality of certain offices.[83] French port cities, from Saint-Malo to Bordeaux, where merchants involved in overseas trade invariably handled bills of exchange, were early participants in the rising Atlantic economy.[84] Even the least prosperous French men and women did not live autarkic lives. According to a study of marriage and property disputes among families of artisans, shopkeepers, and laborers in Lyon and Nantes, "litigation over debt was the single largest category in court case loads" in seventeenth-century France.[85] In short, noblemen, bourgeois, artisans, peasants, and peddlers, whether in remote rural villages or in thriving coastal cities, all grew dependent on the thick economic networks linking Paris to the provinces and the entire kingdom to its colonial outposts.

What mechanisms existed at this time to match creditors and lenders? How were those who possessed capital able to evaluate a potential borrower's reputation? Merchant handbooks like those by the elder Savary dispensed practical instructions on how to minimize risk—for example, by tending to one's accounts and correspondence—while also outlining in broad strokes the profile of a virtuous merchant and his opposite: Jews and Armenians. The little attention that economic historians have paid to these stereotypes suggests that they regard them as irrelevant to the period's mercantile culture, mere vestiges of the religious prejudice of the time. In fact, the recurrence of these stereotypes in early modern commercial literature was neither casual nor superfluous. A presumed homology between religious and economic trustworthiness informed works such as those by the Savary family, in which Jews and non-Catholics symbolized economic guile. Not normally considered a source for the study of European attitudes toward Jews, in reality these early texts of the "science of commerce" reveal the extent to which old and new clichés about Jewish usury informed the culture of early modern European merchants.

By the late seventeenth century, the word "Jew" in France carried an array of meanings, all hostile in tone, that could be applied to individuals who were not themselves Jewish. They ranged from the medieval trope of the Jewish pawnbroker and rag dealer to the figure of the omnipotent Jewish merchant who undercut his competitors in the Levant. Antoine Furetière's dictionary asserted that "by a man rich like a Jew, we mean a very rich man." It added that "we call usurer a merchant who cheats or extorts, [or we call him] a Jew, because Jews are notable usurers, double-dealers, and deceptive" ("usuriers, frippiers, & trompeurs").[86] The same dictionary proposed an expansive definition of usury that encompassed not only the charging of interest (following the strictest precept of canon law) but also "an illicit profit that derives from using money in ways contrary to the laws."[87]

The definition was hardly clear-cut. Civil laws defined usury in the context of noncommercial loans (*rentes*) but were famously vague in all other respects (chapter 3). The 1673 *ordonnance de commerce*, which Savary was instrumental in drafting, forbade merchants from building interest rates into the principal when issuing bills of exchange and from charging compound interest (title VI, arts. 1–2), but both infractions were difficult to detect and reflected practices so common as to make the law meaningless. Regrettably, no systematic studies have been done on commercial litigation in Old Regime France. Judging from existing collections of jurisprudence, however, the adjudication of disputes over bills of exchange remained contentious and was complicated by a lack of firm criteria.[88]

In any case, a punitive judicial system cannot be the only foundation for a commercial society. Written and unspoken norms also guide merchants' behavior. In early modern France, inevitably some merchants tested the normative consensus and the reach of the law when they acted in bad faith. At the time of Savary's composition of *Le parfait négociant*, Colbert's mistrust of merchants was inspiring highly centralized commercial policies, including the creation of a network of royal inspectors charged with reporting back to Paris. Ultimately, it was impossible for the state to control every production site and marketplace in the kingdom. Top-down regulation anywhere requires internalized cultural norms of conduct in order to achieve its intended aims. In this fragile institutional environment, merchant manuals and legal commentaries spelled out not only the written rules of conduct, but also a broader range of shared values necessary to sustain the operations of respectable and successful *négociants*. These works combined advice and prescriptions with spurious information, including anecdotes that served as warnings. Such was the function of the legend of the Jewish invention of bills of exchange, a poignant narrative meant to convey the dangers that lurked behind the exceedingly complex financial instruments on which the market increasingly relied.

Nurtured by prejudice, the legend was canonized by some of the very works of Europe's *ars mercatoria* that imparted practical teachings on how to succeed as a *négociant*. It even survived almost intact the objections raised in 1690 by Dupuis de la Serra, who exposed serious flaws in the story. Savary's credentials were undoubtedly greater than Dupuis de la Serra's, although the latter also enjoyed remarkable success. A fertile cultural terrain supported the legend's diffusion. Accusations about the usurious character of Jews issuing bills of exchange could even be introduced in court as aggravating charges, as happened in Toulouse in 1745.[89] Although the most influential and reckless treasurers of eighteenth-century France—John Law (1671–1729), Samuel Bernard (1651–1739), and Jacques Necker (1732–1804)—were all Calvinists, and thus controversial in their own right, moralizing tales about the destructive character of credit more often centered on Jews. The fate of Bernard, the single largest financier of the crown during the War of Spanish Succession, is emblematic in this regard. As France's mounting public debt led to a dramatic currency depreciation and lenders ceased to accept Bernard's bills of exchange, rumors spread that he was Jewish (a false claim facilitated by Huguenots' frequent use of Old Testament names). Through a dazzling series of textual distortions and cross-references, which began with a comment by Voltaire, Bernard was turned into the iconic figure of the devious Jewish banker who undermined the well-being of the state in order to enhance his own interests.[90]

The transformation of the figure of the Jewish usurer into that of the Jewish financier unfolded against the backdrop of the general diffusion of the paper economy. Local context, too, colored the process. The works of Savary father and sons placed the legend of the Jewish invention of bills of exchange in the context of changing power dynamics in the Mediterranean. French trade in the Levant was on the ascent in the last quarter of the seventeenth century, especially after 1673, when the crown brokered a more advantageous diplomatic and commercial treaty with the Ottoman Empire than those negotiated by rival European powers. Marseilles, France's foremost Mediterranean port and Savary's window onto the world of overseas trade, was dear to Colbert but resisted his plans for the settlement of foreign communities there. In 1669, the same year that the edict promoting the greater involvement of noblemen in overseas trade was enacted, Colbert granted exclusive control over French trade in the Mediterranean to the Chamber of Commerce of Marseilles, which thereafter also elected the French consuls who assumed diplomatic roles in North Africa and the Middle East.[91] This oligopolistic body, which represented the interests of local shipowners, wholesale merchants, and bankers, opposed Colbert's desire to attract Jews and Armenians to Marseilles and ultimately won.

The figure of the dominant Jewish merchant who allegedly cheated and outmaneuvered the *négociants* of Marseilles was a Provençal variant on a widespread theme. Once again, existing tropes about Jews and commerce were adapted to local conditions and contingent struggles. Far from being mere ways of speaking, inimical representations of minority groups also provided a rationale for exclusionary legislative measures. Representations of Jewish and Armenian traders as unfair competitors were in line with the xenophobic commercial policies promoted by the Chamber of Commerce of Marseilles, which was fiercely jealous of its sphere of influence. Five years after Jews were expelled from Marseilles, Armenians who were Ottoman subjects were forbidden from selling silk (their principal trading item) there on the grounds that their textiles were of inferior quality.[92]

Jews were seen as more threatening than any other minorities because many assumed that their wicked habits could contaminate the rest of society. In Cleirac's tale of the Jewish invention of marine insurance and bills of exchange, the real danger was that "Lombards and Cahorsins" were imitating Jews' worst behavior. The logic reverberated with particular strength in Bordeaux, where crypto-Judaism was an institutionalized phenomenon, but it appealed to Christians' imagination the world over. In the 1670s, an anonymous report addressed to the municipal government of Marseilles described Jewish merchants as practicing usury, employing counterfeit currencies, and overcharging customers. To these accusations, it added a more damaging claim: the presence of Jews "Judaified" young men in Marseilles to the "disgrace of our religion."[93] This example shows that the specter of Judaism could be invoked as an argument for regulation in the commercial sphere even in places where crypto-Judaism was not a lived reality.

In spite of many objections, Colbert hoped to persuade the Chamber of Commerce of Marseilles of the utility of enticing Jews and Armenians to settle there. His plan was neither unique nor radical. Livorno, Marseilles' main rival, was only one among other European port cities, including Venice, Amsterdam, Hamburg, and London, that had given Jews (particularly those fleeing Iberia) exceptional privileges on account of their perceived commercial and financial competence. The reason of state arguments that inspired these policies became so widely accepted that Jewish leaders learned to spin them to their own advantage. In Venice, Rabbi Simone Luzzatto (1583–1663) penned the best-known early modern defense of Jewish commerce and successfully fended off an impending decree of expulsion. To persuade the Senate of the republic of the Jews' utility to the state, he inflated their economic contribution by more than doubling the number of Jewish residents in the city (to 6,000, from the actual number of 2,400) and used the resulting number as the multiplier for his estimates of the taxes and custom duties that he claimed Jews paid.[94] Moreover, Luzzatto reasoned, Jews were more valuable and less ominous than other communities of foreign merchants because they lacked the backing of a state and could not wage military or commercial wars on their own: because they were not in direct competition with Catholic subjects of the republic, they could only help them flourish. Shortly thereafter, the Amsterdam rabbi Menasseh ben Israel (1604–1657) adopted an analogous strategy to plead with

Oliver Cromwell to readmit Jews to England in 1655–1656—a request that was tacitly granted.[95]

At this mid-seventeenth-century moment, it was reasonable for Colbert to argue for the benefits of inviting foreigners to settle in Marseilles. He likely assumed that the corporatist structure of Old Regime France and the system of royal oversight would tame any potential disruption generated by the contractual equality he would extend to Jewish and Armenian merchants. But it appears that he underestimated the backlash generated by the legal and social reforms that he had set in motion, reforms that chipped away small but significant building blocks of the very corporatist architecture designed to distinguish a merchant from a nobleman, a foreign merchant from a native guild member. The city's commercial elites were thus placed on the defensive. In this conflict, Marseilles could count on more than its fierce municipal tradition to oppose Colbert's plan. Advocates of economic protectionism also marshaled widely held religious stereotypes as weapons of resistance. Jews and Armenians could open doors in the Levant, these opponents argued, but could they be contained—or would they insinuate themselves among the upstanding *négociants* of the free port that Colbert wished to create? Commercial credit and, more than any other instrument of the sort, bills of exchange epitomized the voluntaristic character of a commercial society in which the economic power of an individual mattered more than his personal status. The disruption they engendered was more than financial: it went to the heart of ingrained notions of hierarchy and authority, including political authority, as the next chapter will show.

6

Between Usury and the "Spirit of Commerce"

TWO DATES DOMINATE THE history of French Jews in the eighteenth century: January 28, 1790, and September 27, 1791. In the span of eighteen months, for the first time in the history of Europe, Jewish men acquired the same civil and political rights as their non-Jewish peers. A small fraction of the population of the kingdom (some 35,000, or 0.125 percent of all inhabitants), Jews on the eve of the Revolution loomed far larger in the French collective imagination than their demographic presence warranted. Hardly a homogenous group, French Jews formed a mosaic of different communities, each with its own traditions, privileges, and degrees of acculturation to Christian society. We have already encountered the richest, though not the largest, Jewish group living in and around Bordeaux, a group prominently represented among the merchants involved in the Atlantic trade. These Sephardic traders were also the French Jews who most adopted the habits and manners of their Catholic peers. By contrast, their more numerous brethren in Alsace and Lorraine were largely confined to peddling and small-scale moneylending in the countryside, were frequently accused of practicing usury, and lived more insular lives. Paris had only a tiny Jewish community, which was not distinguished by particular cultural or economic achievements, and the poorest of the Jews of Avignon sought better fortunes in Bordeaux to no avail. One of the questions this chapter addresses is the extent to which these different social realities informed new iterations of the legend and the views of advocates and opponents of the expansion of Jewish rights.

Emancipation was a watershed moment in both Jewish history and the history of Western liberalism. By conferring formal equality in the legal and political order on a group long deemed unworthy of it, it reshaped the meaning of Jewish identity. Treatments of Jewish emancipation, however, are quite different in the historiography of European Jewry and that of France. Accounts of the Jewish past almost invariably pause at emancipation, while most studies of the French Revolution relegate it to a footnote.[1] This split is curious. A great deal of ink has been spilled on the fact that women did not achieve equality during the Revolution and African slaves in the French Caribbean were freed only temporarily. Historians rightly take eighteenth-century conceptions of women and blacks and, more recently, the interplay of gender and race as illustrations of the patent limits of the notions of progress and universalism conceived by the Enlightenment and the Revolution.[2] Jews rarely figure in this early history of human rights, but their fate is instructive. Compared to women and the black population of the French colonies, adult Jewish men of some means gained the most from the Revolution. The process through which a group that for centuries had been regarded as inimical to Christian society came to be granted civil and political rights therefore sheds light on the contradictions of the nascent egalitarianism of the revolutionary period.

Among scholars of European Jewish history, emancipation remains a controversial topic. Most studies concentrate on its consequences for Jewish life, notably the restructuring of the institutional relations between the state and Jewish organizations, the changing place of religion in Jewish self-definition, and the false promises that formal equality made to those Jews who sought to assimilate. No less relevant and contentious is the question of how Jews came to be perceived as worthy of equality—that is, the social and intellectual changes that led to this turning point. Most historians today favor a gradualist interpretation and insist on the variety of paths emancipation followed across Europe. Within this camp, an influential argument emphasizes the politics of commerce espoused by certain western European states, France included, as the principal driver of integration of segments of the Jewish diaspora into Christian society. David Sorkin argues that for the "port Jews" of Sephardic extraction, who in the course of the eighteenth century developed cultural traits and a legal status that set them apart from their Ashkenazic brethren, emancipation was "not a rupture or radical departure but merely a completion of a process that had begun two centuries before." The Sephardic Jews of southwestern France are a case in point because they "were already living beyond the autonomous community in merchant corporations or voluntary communities" and therefore "gained emancipation through a confirmation of their existing privileges" rather than by the removal of legal disabilities.[3]

My reading of the place occupied by the legend of the Jewish invention of bills of exchange in eighteenth-century French debates puts this gradualist thesis to the test. It does so not only by considering alternative interpretations of Jewish history, but also by bringing French and Jewish history to bear on one another more than has been done so far.[4] Now that the anti-Marxist impetus that dominated the revisionist historiography on the French Revolution during the last quarter of the twentieth century has lost steam, the economic life and institutions of Old Regime France have sparked new interest, especially among Anglophone historians. Like earlier work, however, this recent scholarship overlooks the roles that Jews played in the marketplaces of the kingdom and in eighteenth-century economic thought.[5]

What I propose in this chapter should prompt historians of Jewish emancipation to square the faith they often place in commerce as a driving force in the transition from toleration to equality with the limited and contentious scope that commercial interests played in revolutionary rhetoric.[6] Historians of the French Enlightenment, for their part, will find that depictions of Jewish economic roles test the inclusivity of the Enlightenment trope of commerce as sociability. A number of eighteenth-century French authors regarded commerce as a capacious category that transcended mere economic exchanges and, in its broadest sense, represented bonds of sociability that, though compatible with absolutism, cut across geographical frontiers and legally sanctioned social ranks. Even when singled out as the spinners of far-flung commercial webs, Jews remained marginal to this Enlightenment portrait of commercial society, and no debate ensued about the degree to which Jewish merchants actually belonged to those voluntary, interest-based associations that were said to foster new bonds between strangers.[7]

To recover the centrality of Jewish emancipation to the history of the Revolution demands not only that we examine how Enlightenment concepts of commerce fared once the hierarchical society to which they were tailored came tumbling down, but also that we consider the fears that newly emancipated Jews elicited. In so doing, we can appreciate the extent to which Jewish emancipation served as a litmus test for the Revolution as a whole insofar as this event marked the formal transition from a society of status (in which an individual's rights and obligations were tied to the corporate group to which he was assigned, usually at birth) to a society of contract (in which, in principle, every eligible man was free to enter into contract with other equally free male individuals and to choose from a large menu of contractual choices). Rival visions of Jews and of commerce, I wish to show, are excellent guides for reassessing the inconsistencies of this transition and its longer-term legacies.

This chapter hinges on two moments: the reworking of the meaning of the legend of the Jewish invention of bills of exchange by Montesquieu in the 1740s and the debates on emancipation that occurred during the last quarter of the century. I argue that the discursive and political contexts in which the legend was evoked account for the vastly different meanings that it acquired at those two moments. Montesquieu praised Jews for forging new credit instruments that benefited everyone because he assumed that Jews inhabited a society of status that kept them in a subordinate position. When equality emerged later in the century as a concrete and, for some, desirable possibility, Jewish commercial and financial dexterity was once again perceived as a threat rather than a boon to state and society. On the eve of the Revolution, both friends and enemies of Jews depicted them as burning with the desire to extract excessive profits from Christians, even as they differed about whether any remedy for this moral failing was possible.

While Montesquieu drew a sharp line between commercial credit and usury, the two were conflated once again during the emancipation debates, as they had been in Cleirac's commentary. The prospect of legal equality once again made Jews an emblem of the disruptive character of credit, and particularly of oligopolies. Baptism had rendered Jewishness invisible in societies that prized clearly demarcated religious boundaries. Citizenship now rendered Jews legally indistinguishable in a political and economic order that proclaimed its preference for individualism over corporatism but in fact remained wary of the leveling of differences it had produced.

Because of the scope of my inquiry, I focus on Christian representations of Jewish economic roles, with a nod to the responses that they elicited from a few Jewish writers and community leaders.[8] I show that eighteenth-century Christian views of Jewish commerce and usury developed at the intersection of discursive traditions and the lived experience of different Jewish communities in France. Montesquieu's positive characterization of Jewish commerce owed at least something to the more inclusive Bordelais context. His more generous disposition did not endure once it was transplanted into a different time and place a quarter century later. At this time, acrimonious debates about the civic and political status of Jews broke out not in and around Bordeaux, but in the northeastern regions of France, where masses of poor Jews and a few wealthy moneylenders and army contractors were regarded by the Christian population as exploitative usurers. The economic side of the emancipation debates thus brings to the fore yet another configuration of a Christian discourse in which Jews symbolized the hidden dangers of credit markets in which contractual equality masked an a priori power differential between economic actors.

The Second Moment of Discontinuity (1748): Montesquieu

Two books of Montesquieu's *Spirit of the Laws* were devoted to commerce, and one to money. Additional reflections about how the economy intersected with politics, society, and culture peppered the entire work. Book XXI described the history of commerce from antiquity to the (then) present. A climactic turning point appeared in chapter 20, which bore the dramatic title "How Commerce Broke Through the Barbarism of Europe" ("Comment le commerce se fit hour en Europe à travers la barbarie") and traced the waning of medieval anti-usury sentiments and the rise of *l'esprit de commerce* ("the spirit of commerce"). Around the time of Europe's first transoceanic voyages, Montesquieu wrote, commerce ceased to be "the profession only of mean persons," and thus the exclusive province of "a nation covered with infamy" (by which he meant Jews), and "re-entered . . . the bosom of probity."[9] In this account, Jews were the frontrunners in the transformation of commerce from a despised occupation associated with usury and moneylending to a dignified and valuable activity. In this way they spearheaded a veritable political and cultural revolution through which commerce, for the first time, "became capable of *eluding violence*" (XXI, 20, my emphasis). (I draw attention to the words "*eluding violence*" because in the course of the chapter, we will see that they played a particularly important rhetorical function.)

How were Jews able to engineer such a monumental transformation and bequeath to Europe a modern, safe, and secular commercial society? To this complex question, Montesquieu gave a deceptively simple answer: "The Jews invented letters of exchange" (XXI, 20). Scores of scholars, many imbued with great learning, have read this statement, yet very few have reflected on its meaning. Studies of Montesquieu have generally glossed over it.[10] There are various reasons for this neglect: the relative marginality of Jews and Judaism in Montesquieu's thought, a general disregard for these themes among main-stream scholars of the French Enlightenment, and a deep investment in the irenic and inclusive quality of *doux commerce*.[11] Even specialists of Montesquieu's economic thought normally treat his mystifying statement as a self-evident assertion that requires little more than some paraphrasing. They spend more time on other subjects, such as Montesquieu's opposition to the nobility's involvement in trade, his critique of mercantilism ("jalousie sur le commerce"), his preference for commercial over territorial empires, and his contrast between "commerce de luxe" (which he regarded as typical of monarchies) and "commerce d'économie" (a feature of republics). Those who cite Montesquieu's passage about the Jewish invention of bills of exchange, regardless of their ideological tendencies, do so incidentally or without inquiring into its sources.[12]

One name stands out in this scholarly landscape: that of Albert Hirschman, the first modern critic to draw attention to Montesquieu's claim about the Jewish invention of bills of exchange and to make it a cornerstone of his reading of *The Spirit of the Laws* as a case for commerce as a check on despotism and unbridled passions.[13] By virtue of his own biography, Hirschman may have been more predisposed than others to recognize the pride of place that, uncharacteristically for his time, Montesquieu assigned to Jews in his narrative of the civilizing process. Yet even Hirschman displays little interest in probing the provenance of Montesquieu's statement about the Jewish invention of bills of exchange or the reception it may have had. Rather, he uses it to support his strikingly original reading of *The Spirit of the Laws*, which emphasizes the nexus between anti-authoritarian politics and commerce as a prefiguration of the interdependence of democracy and capitalism.

The evidence uncovered in this chapter will question this reading. For now, as further testament to the divergent patterns of French and Jewish historiography, we may note that Montesquieu's passage relaying the legend of the Jewish invention of bills of exchange has drawn more attention from historians of early modern Jews, who treat it as evidence that Montesquieu was one of the few eighteenth-century French philosophes sympathetic to Jews, than from scholars in any other field.[14] When, in 1968, Arthur Hertzberg made the controversial case for the Enlightenment roots of modern antisemitism, he also singled out Montesquieu as a skeptical anti-Voltaire, a philosophe benignly predisposed toward Jews.[15] Subsequent studies of the French Enlightenment's engagement with Jews and Judaism have taken issue with Hertzberg's portrait and offered more nuanced interpretations of it, but these works have also contributed little to our understanding of Montesquieu's view of the relation-ship between Jews and the spirit of commerce.[16]

In modern critical scholarship, therefore, Montesquieu's contention that "Jews invented letters of exchange" is treated alternately as too obvious or too enigmatic to engage. By now, however, we know that these words contain more than meets the eye and that they would not have passed unnoticed at the time. The footnote that Montesquieu added in support of his assertion will ring all too familiar to readers of this book: "It is known that under Philip Augustus and Philip the Tall, the Jews who were chased from France took refuge in Lombardy, and that there they gave to foreign merchants and travellers secret letters, drawn upon those to whom they had intrusted their effects in France, which were accepted" (XX, 20, note *o*). By introducing his corroborating evi-dence with the turn of phrase "it is known," Montesquieu was not merely adopting a common rhetorical device. The legend, we now realize, had been in circulation for a whole century when he reiterated it. While the prevailing standards for attribution at the time did not demand that he offer a biblio-graphical reference, it is clear that *Us et coustumes de la mer* and *Le parfait né-gociant* provided Montesquieu with the gist of the story.[17] And yet the spin he gave to it was utterly new.

The Spirit of the Laws introduced the second moment of discontinuity in the legend's reception, one that was more disruptive than Dupuis de la Serra's refutation of its credibility (chapter 5). Attention-grabbing stories and influ-ential authors are a combustive mix, no less so when the stories are specious. Montesquieu lent his authority to the legend of the Jewish invention of bills of exchange, but he also altered its meaning. Gone were the didactic aims of Cleirac and Savary, intended to draw a line between shady speculators and upright merchants. By inventing bills of exchange, Montesquieu posited, Jews introduced new dynamism into Europe's economy and became harbingers of modernity. By devising a credit instrument that enabled them to outsmart their oppressors, they resisted persecution and curbed the reach of despotism. Thanks to these bills, "commerce . . . became capable of *eluding violence . . .* ; the richest merchant having none but invisible effects, which he could convey imperceptibly everywhere he pleased" (XXI, 20, my emphasis).[18]

A putatively Jewish invention, we are told, engineered a cultural and politi-cal revolution that altered the course of European history. A despot, perhaps seeking to placate popular anti-Jewish sentiments, might have been tempted to confiscate land, homes, ingots, or cargoes, but not pieces of paper that he could not redeem. Once limited in their ability to plunder, princes realized that they "should govern with more prudence than they themselves could ever have imagined"; thus might Europe "be cured of Machiavelism" (XX, 20). Meanwhile, the church, which equated commerce with "knavery," lost its grip on society and "the Theologians were obliged to limit their principles" (XXI, 20). With the rise of the spirit of commerce, moderation triumphed in the spheres of government and social mores: "Happy is it for men that they are in a situation in which, though their passions prompted them to be wicked, it is, nevertheless, to their interest to be humane and virtuous" (XXI, 20).

Montesquieu's account of the emergence of commercial society in this chapter of *The Spirit of the Laws* proved extremely influential in France and abroad in two primary ways. First, it provided the most authoritative rendition of the theory of *doux commerce*, which supporters repeated over and over and critics derided no less insistently. The chapter was in many respects a rebuttal of *The Adventures of Thelemachus* (1699), a novel written by the Archbishop of Cambrai, François de Salignac de La Mothe-Fénelon, that has been deemed "the most read literary work in eighteenth-century France (after the Bible)."[19] Montesquieu shared with Fénelon a disdain for the Machiavellianism of Louis XIV and his entourage but lacked Fénelon's nostalgia for ancient agrarian republicanism. Second, *The Spirit of the Laws* outlined a chronology of European history that gained enormous traction, pitting a dark medieval past against the increasing progress of what today we call the early modern period. Montesquieu did not dwell on precise dates (his reference to Philip Augustus and Philip the Tall would place the invention of bills of exchange between 1180 and 1322, while the gist of his narrative clearly postpones it to a later moment), but the picture he painted leaves no doubt that he viewed the Middle Ages as a period dominated by the barbarian invasions, Scholasticism, economic stagnation, and tyrannical rulers. An enemy of the Roman Church, he portrayed medieval Catholic doctrine as hostile to all profit-seeking enterprises. Needless to say, this picture left a deep mark on scholarly and popular understanding of both the Middle Ages and the Jewish past.

With no small touch of irony, Montesquieu placed Jews at the center of his narrative of the triumph of the spirit of commerce over medieval Christian obscurantism. For Cleirac 100 years earlier, the supposedly historical account of how Jews devised marine insurance and bills of exchange to protect their assets forged a link between medieval usury and seventeenth-century commercial credit. For Montesquieu, who glorified commercial credit, bills of exchange became the antithesis to, rather than the sequel of, the pawnshop. As such, after the publication of *The Spirit of the Laws*, they began to figure alongside the three great inventions of the printing press, the compass, and firearms that, following Francis Bacon, were said to have made the modern world.[20] Proponents of the Napoleonic Code of Commerce would later describe the invention of bills of exchange, whether by Jews or by Florentines, as "comparable to the discovery of the compass and of America."[21] Opponents of Montesquieu's thought were even quicker to seize on his words. The Sorbonne theologians found the entire chapter in which they appeared so scandalous that they demanded its expurgation. At issue was both Montesquieu's disparagement of medieval church views of the economy and his casting of Jews not just in a positive light, but as *dei ex machina* behind the creation of a new European commercial society in which credit flowed freely, secure from government prying.[22]

Montesquieu's rendition of the oft-repeated legend of the Jewish invention of bills of exchange must have appeared as novel to eighteenth-century readers as Machiavelli's nonreligious definition of *virtù* had appeared to readers of *The Prince* 200 years earlier. Jews, however, were incidental to Montesquieu's valorization of the spirit of commerce, and they remained so in all other arguments in which he deployed them. In 1723, two years after the appearance, to great acclaim, of the *Persian Letters*, the Jews of Bordeaux were officially allowed to practice their religion. There is no doubt that Montesquieu was acquainted with some of these individuals and met other Jews during his travels.[23] In the three-quarters of a century that followed the publication of Cleirac's *Us et coustumes de la mer*, fears of religious dissimulation continued to haunt Catholic believers, but crypto-Judaism in reality progressively declined. During the years that Montesquieu served in the city's *parlement* (1716–1726), Jews "were coming into the open," ceasing to marry in church or baptize their children.[24] Meanwhile, Bordeaux became France's chief Atlantic port together with Nantes and one of Europe's main commercial hubs. There, New Christians and New Jews, alongside native Catholic and Huguenot merchants and resident Dutch, English, and Hamburgers, built large commercial houses and the most well-to-do absorbed the *rentiers'* habits of conspicuous consumption.[25] These merchants of various religions and confessions endorsed each other's bills of exchange and underwrote each other's marine insurance as a matter of course.[26]

Without reducing the novelty of Montesquieu's version of the legend to a reflection of this reality, we can still suspect that the important economic roles played by Jewish merchants in his native Gascony and the social standing that some of them achieved influenced his views. However, his version of the legend did not signal an all-embracing appreciation of Jews by either Montesquieu or his followers. Unlike Voltaire, whom Ronald Schechter has described as "obsessed with the Jews," Montesquieu had only a side interest in the subject.[27] But like Voltaire and other philosophes, from time to time, Montesquieu, too, drew from his understanding of Jewish history and religious books to marshal anecdotes in the service of his critique of European history and culture. Using a technique already tested in the *Persian Letters*, Montesquieu in *The Spirit of the Laws* put his harshest indictment of the Iberian inquisitions in the mouth of an imaginary Portuguese Jew who allegedly witnessed the burning at the stake of "an eighteenth-year-old Jewess" in Lisbon (XXV, 13).[28]

Aside from this well-known vignette, references to Jews in *The Spirit of the Laws* are few and far between, if generally sympathetic. The ancient Israelites, following Josephus, are said to have been an agricultural nation, the opposite of the Phoenicians (XXI, 6)—an argument that Christian reformers would deploy later in the century as evidence of the possibility of "regenerating" a people that had not always devoted itself to usury.[29] In only one other instance did Montesquieu refer to the plight of Jews as evidence that commerce was incompatible with despotism. In Russia, he wrote, all subjects of the empire were forbidden from conducting any import and export trade, and the expulsion of Jews in 1745 followed accusations that they were smuggling money out of the country and to those banished to Siberia by means of bills of exchange (XXII, 14). Blind despotism, Montesquieu intimated, was a cause of economic underdevelopment.

The evaluation of Jews' economic functions across Montesquieu's works is not consistent. The *Persian Letters* indulged in stereotypes about Jews' unchanging nature and avarice while also praising their diminishing persecution in Europe.[30] In addition to containing conflicting judgments, Montesquieu's oeuvre is also full of missed opportunities. The relationship between commerce and toleration is never discussed specifically with respect to Jews. Some of the most oft-quoted lines from *The Spirit of the Laws* are emblematic of the theory of *doux commerce*: "Commerce is a cure for the most destructive prejudices; for it is almost a general rule, that wherever we find agreeable manners, there commerce flourishes; and wherever there is commerce, there we meet with agreeable manners" (XX, 1). The phrasing is powerful and the thesis famous, but readers are left guessing who the victims of these "destructive prejudices" are and how exactly self-interest curbs those prejudices. Allusions make room for expansive and ideologically laden readings.[31]

Alongside its admiration for the effects of commerce, *The Spirit of the Laws* also registered certain qualms. Elaborating on a motif then in wide circulation,

Montesquieu expressed no doubt that "the history of commerce is that of the communication of people" (XXI, 5). But commerce could also tear apart the social fabric, he noted: mercantile societies often lacked hospitality, asking monetary compensation for what used to be offered for free (XX, 2). An astute observer and privileged nobleman, Montesquieu expressed his staunch opposition to the *noblesse commerçante* for both political and ethical reasons (V, 8; XX, 21–22). "Commerce," he pronounced resolutely, "is the profession of equal people" (V, 8).[32] Fully immersed in the society of orders of his time, Montesquieu embraced a concept of equality that meant equality of rank, rather than wealth. Merchants' fortunes, as he realized, could vary enormously. But even more than the nobility's oligopolistic position, he abhorred the idea that commerce might erode traditional hierarchies and aristocratic honor.

Departing from more conventional interpretations, some scholars insist that Montesquieu feared both the excesses of consumption and "the spirit of extreme equality" into which democracy could degenerate (VIII, 2).[33] This is also how certain noblemen read Montesquieu at the time. In a petition addressed to Marseilles' city government, the nobility of the sword, which had been excluded from power in favor of the local commercial elite in 1660, demanded reinstatement in the municipal council, noting that, as "the author of the *Spirit of the Laws* has written, 'in countries where people are moved solely by the spirit of commerce, they sacrifice everything humane, all moral virtues.'"[34] This is a fair citation of passages that are not normally highlighted in modern scholarship on Montesquieu, which tends to stress the positive rather than the detrimental consequences of the spirit of commerce.

Where does all this leave us with regard to the Jews? Did Montesquieu conceive of those in his own Bordeaux as "equal people" within commercial society even if, for example, they were barred from leadership positions in the city's Chamber of Commerce? And in his view, did Sephardic merchants, like all Jews allegedly, "display for their religion an obstinate, invincible loyalty which borders on fanaticism," or were they full participants in "the communication of people"?[35] Montesquieu never pursued these questions because, as even an admirer of his views on Jews admitted, he "was fundamentally not interested in Jews as such, but only to the extent that they provided him startling examples of the relationship between intolerance and proselytism."[36] In this indifference, Montesquieu was hardly alone. Voltaire was only the most eloquent of the philosophes who invoked Jews for the purpose of making abstract pronouncements about commerce as an engine of religious toleration, in spite of his antipathy toward Jews and Judaism. His *Lettres philosophiques* of

1734 contained an iconic description of the London Royal Exchange as a place where "representatives of all nations gather for the utility of mankind; there, the Jew, the Mohammedan and the Christian behave towards each other as if they were of the same religion, and reserve the word 'infidel' for those who go bankrupt."[37]

Literary critic Erich Auerbach, writing in exile from Nazi Germany, noted that Voltaire's vignette "was not really written for a realistic purpose," but rather "to insinuate certain ideas" about the subordination of religious belonging to the logic of the market.[38] Others have since identified earlier Dutch and English variants of this cameo.[39] In the same vein, Montesquieu's rendering of the legend of the Jewish invention of bills of exchange was more concerned with offering a vivid critique of despotism and the Catholic Church than engaging with the actual status of Jewish merchants or interrogating the role of commerce in Jewish history. The moral of his tale was thus bounded by a political order that made no space for equal rights for Jews.

Phase III (1748–1775): Bifurcation

In the aftermath of *The Spirit of the Laws*, the legend's textual transmission split along two paths. Some authors absorbed Montesquieu's interpretation of the alleged Jewish role in propelling the development of a commercial society in which bills of exchange linked merchants together in defiance of despotic rulers. Others followed in the footsteps of Cleirac and Savary, portraying Jews as having invented an instrument that allowed ill-intentioned merchants to accumulate wealth by duplicitous means. A boom in serial publications and an expansion of the reading public facilitated the diffusion of both strands of this story, which occasionally merged in surprising ways.

Diderot and D'Alembert's *Encyclopédie* illustrates all these trends vividly. With some 74,000 entries written by more than 130 contributors, this grand intellectual project inevitably fell short of consistency. In the *Encyclopédie* the legend appeared in reference to both marine insurance and bills of exchange, in both abbreviated and extended form, and sometimes accompanied by an endorsement and other times by doubts or revisions.[40] Among the entries that mentioned the legend, two relied mostly on Montesquieu and one primarily on Cleirac and Savary. The entry for "Lettre de change," authored by Antoine-Gaspard Boucher d'Argis, a noted lawyer whose writings were used in the failed attempt to exonerate the Huguenot merchant Jean Calas in an infamous trial in 1762, borrowed from both *Us et coustumes de la mer* and *Le parfait négociant*, lifting entire sections from each. Boucher d'Argis raised questions about the legend's truthfulness, but in the end he did not embrace the objections proffered by Dupuis de la Serra about the narrative's plausibility. Instead, after acknowledging the inconsistencies in the historical account of the Jewish invention of bills of exchange, he concluded: "It would nonetheless be difficult to imagine that the Jews did not take any precautions to salvage their goods when fleeing to Lombardy—something that could only be accomplished by means of bills of exchange. Therefore, there are reasons to believe that they were the first inventors of these instruments."[41]

This passage reveals how Jewish cunning was the one attribute that no one disputed. For Boucher d'Argis, the legend contained a kernel of truth because he assumed that Jews possessed superior economic skill. His readers appreciated the comparison that he left implicit: other groups had been subjected to expropriation before, but the Jews were "the first" to have devised the means to "salvage their goods." Dupuis de la Serra had questioned the historical account passed on by Cleirac on logical grounds. Boucher d'Argis proceeded in the opposite way: he recognized several flaws in that historical account but found part of its logic unassailable. The compromise he reached is instructive of a broader trend: in the second half of the eighteenth century, the Enlightenment's emphasis on the historical and circumstantial causes of Jews' economic shrewdness coexisted with a belief in their essential character as wily speculators.[42]

The other two entries in the *Encyclopédie* that recounted the legend with regard to bills of exchange instead bore Montesquieu's imprint: they used the tale to denounce the exploitative policies of arbitrary rulers and to exalt the ingenious resistance of a persecuted minority. Both François Véron de Forbonnais's entry on "commerce" and Chevalier Louis de Jaucourt's "Juif" depicted the Middle Ages ("the barbarous centuries") as a time when trade was in the hands of Jews, referring to them as "a wandering people" and as "infamous usurers," respectively. But if Forbonnais treated Jews as incidental to the rise of commerce, Jaucourt praised their skills and art of survival in the face of oppression and embraced the mainstream position of defenders of Jewish rights: external constrictions rather than natural proclivity explained why Jews flocked to commerce, an economic activity that Christians loathed.[43]

Curiously, Forbonnais and Jaucourt were even more adamant than Montesquieu in singling out Jews' financial inventiveness compared to other trading communities that suffered persecution. The *Persian Letters* foreshadowed the sociological theory of "middleman minorities," merchant groups that strove to be indispensable to those societies that denied them full opportunities.[44] *The Spirit of the Laws* stressed the economic proficiency not only of Jews but of all hounded groups.[45] No close comparison between Jews and other trading communities figured in any of these authors' works. Rather, skillfully elaborating on Montesquieu's ideas, Jaucourt penned a passage that the consortium of printers who owned the rights to this and associated publications reproduced several times. It is worth citing the segment in full because of its curious fate:

> In the end, constantly expelled from every country, they [the Jews] found the ingenious means to save their fortunes and to ensure their withdrawals. Banned from France under Philip the Tall in 1318, they found refuge in Lombardy and there, they gave merchants letters drawn upon those to whom they had entrusted their goods before leaving, and these letters were settled. The admirable invention of bills of exchange was born out of desperation and only thanks to them was commerce able to *elude violence* and sustain itself across the globe.[46]

The absence of modern copyright laws combined with the acumen of those in charge of what Robert Darnton calls "the business of enlightenment" ensured that these lines were reproduced verbatim in numerous publications sponsored by the fictional *société de gens de lettres*, a label that was meant to convey the collective effort of those writers engaged in the project of enlightening the public.[47] The passage even appeared in a spurious entry on Jews in several posthumous editions of Voltaire's *Dictionnaire philosophique*, which, in four loosely related sections, meshed together antiquarian knowledge with tendentious readings of the Bible to produce a baffling account of the alleged absurdity of Jewish rites and the obtuseness of Jewish people. Buried amid derision and hostility was an ambivalent appreciation of Jews' commercial prowess, contained mostly in the third section ("On the dispersion of Jews") and derivative of Montesquieu's thought in both argument and form. Though inauthentic, the entry is consistent with Voltaire's negative views of Spain as a place where the Catholic Church and the nobility despised Jews and commerce alike. However, while its admiration for the purported Jewish invention of bills of exchange fits with Voltaire's belief in Jews' commercial aptitude, the passage is first and foremost a careless repetition of an authoritative cliché.[48]

The legend revealed once again its protean qualities. The spurious text attributed to Voltaire radiated contrarian meanings, but its putative author's fame ensured that the echoes of this sketchy and untenable historical account traveled fast and widely. More generally, during the second half of the eighteenth century, admirers of Montesquieu followed him in evoking the legend without making scornful reference to Jews. But since they trusted their muse, they also did not question his reliability. The massive and incredibly popular *Histoire philosophique et politique des deux Indes* (1770) incorporated the legend as transmitted by Montesquieu in order to press one of its favorite themes, the triumph of ingenuity over church superstition.[49] In a contemporaneous "universal history" presented as the collective labor of *une société de gens de lettres*, the legend resurfaced in the narrative of the massacre of the Jewish community of Munich in 1285. The authors defended the innocence of the Jews emphatically and depicted avarice as a Christian crime, portraying commoners, clergymen, and ruling authorities as blinded by their hatred of Jews and their desire to seize Jews' wealth. The legend was thus reframed as a tale of survival and Jewish inventiveness: when armed Christians stormed Jewish homes ready to steal their belongings, all they found were slips of paper—the bills of exchange that Jews had devised in order to protect their assets; given that they could not redeem those bills, the Christian looters had to live with the shame of having killed for nothing.[50]

Intent on using the legend as a redemptive allegory, Montesquieu's followers showed little interest in disputes over its veracity and repeated it in all sorts of genres, including memoirs and travel accounts.[51] By contrast, the French commercial and legal literature of the second half of the eighteenth century propagated a more negative view of Jewish usury, derived from the accounts of Cleirac and Savary, while also cultivating doubts about the tale's accuracy and offering alternative narratives of the invention of medieval financial instruments. An authoritative commentary on the 1681 *ordonnance de la marine* published in 1760 oscillated between confirming the assertion by Franz Stypmann (1612–1650), a leading writer of maritime law, that marine insurance first emerged in medieval Italy and following the common view according to which "the Jews, who are usurers by nature," invented marine insurance and used it to make inequitable loans.[52] Jews' usurious character was often taken for granted in the literature on commerce. Cleirac had captured this belief in a dictum that resurfaced in the eighteenth century: in the Levant, he wrote, "Jews, Turkish merchants, Armenians, Persians, Arabs, those from Alexandria and the Moors" charged so-called "lunar interests."[53] Since lunar months are slightly shorter than those of the Gregorian calendar, the expression indicated the charging of higher interest rates than normal.

Meanwhile, an antiquarian search for the earliest documentary evidence of medieval marine insurance and bills of exchange further undermined the legend, with France's leading Roman law jurist, Robert Joseph Pothier (1699–1772), presenting textual evidence from classical antiquity and the Middle Ages that challenged its validity.[54] Other sources of growing skepticism were natural law accounts of the emergence of commerce. Those for whom necessity was the mother of invention found it superfluous to search for an individual or group responsible for any pathbreaking innovation. Following this logic, the need to make payments at a distance and mitigate the risks of long-distance trade spurred a spontaneous development of new solutions to address those needs. One comprehensive treatise on marine insurance dismissed as futile the debate over whether Italians or Jews had contributed most to the creation of marine insurance, "a contract that was born out of the nature of things."[55] A few sixteenth-century Italian authors had already described these credit instruments as the result of cumulative and collective knowledge rather than the genius of a single people.[56] One merchant manual expressed the belief that only a dramatic event could have given rise to bills of exchange but credited "the spirit of commerce," which encouraged creativity and led to useful discoveries, with their invention.[57]

In sum, by the last quarter of the eighteenth century, the legend was in wide circulation and was being subjected to considerable scrutiny. More than anyone else, Montesquieu gave it a new and positive meaning by linking commerce to toleration. However, when the debate on Jewish emancipation erupted in the French public sphere, the legend reappeared in an older, less favorable light.

Phase IV (1775–1791): Usury, the Spirit of Commerce, and Emancipation

Hertzberg maintains that in the late eighteenth century, "Montesquieu was consistently quoted by all those who were on the side of the Jews."[58] In fact, Montesquieu's influence over the debates on emancipation was more ambiguous. Jews' involvement in moneylending and commerce became a touchstone in those debates as they unfolded in the northeastern regions of France during the last quarter of the eighteenth century. In that environment, which was quite unlike that of southwestern France, where Montesquieu had recast the legend in positive terms, Cleirac's and Savary's cautionary tales of the pernicious effects of Jewish usury still resonated.

Demands to extend full civic rights to Jewish men were first voiced in earnest during the 1770s in Alsace and Lorraine, and provoked no small outcry. The largest portion of France's Jews (roughly 30,000 individuals) resided in this region. Their economic status and social makeup differed markedly from those of the Jews in Bordeaux. Never forced to conceal their religious identity, Franco-Ashkenazim spoke Yiddish, maintained their religious traditions, and were limited in their economic and legal freedoms. They were banned from all cities, except Metz, unless they paid a humiliating personal transit tax. Forbidden from owning real estate, cultivating the land, joining craft guilds, or hiring non-Jewish help, most of them lived in small enclaves in the countryside and earned their living as peddlers, moneylenders, sellers of used goods and clothes, or workers in the cattle trade; only the most affluent were involved in provisioning the army with horses and other necessities.[59]

In these adverse circumstances, the earliest gentile advocate of Jewish rights was also the most radical. In 1775, Pierre-Louis Lacretelle (1751–1824), an audacious lawyer and later a moderate revolutionary, called for the full equality of Jews as men (*hommes*) and as subjects of the kingdom (*régnicoles*).[60] Less bent than others on demanding that Jews be "regenerated," he nonetheless advocated passing special laws to limit Jews' economic activities.[61] Although Lacretelle denounced the contemporary public hatred of Jews, he attributed it in no small part to their practice of usury and *friponnerie*.[62]

A catchword used by both Cleirac and the Savarys, the term *fripon* became a staple of all eighteenth-century gentile descriptions of Jews' economic roles, regardless of the author's ideological leaning. A *fripon* was a rogue or, as a period French-English dictionary defined it, "an unworthie fellow, one that useth, or is given to, base trickes, and . . . hath no inclination to any goodness."[63] Bernard Mandeville's *Fable of the Bees, or, Private Vices, Public Benefits* (1714) was rendered into French as *La fable des abeilles, ou, Les fripons devenus honnestes gens*. In Antoine Furetière's dictionary (1690), a *fripon* was someone who could not be trusted ("fourbe, qui n'a ni honneur, ni foi, ni probité") but also a near synonym for Jews, described as "great usurers, cheaters, and double-dealers" ("les Juifs sont de grands usuriers, frippiers, & trompeurs").[64] The recurrence of the terms *fripon* and *friponnerie* in eighteenth-century French references to Jews is significant because it underscores the constraints that language imposed on the emergence of a counterdiscourse premised on a more positive relationship between Jews and credit.

If the words "usury" and *friponnerie* were invariably conntected to Jews, "commerce" and "credit" were not, as evidenced, for example, in the definitions of these terms in contemporary French dictionaries. In the economic reality of the time, Jews could be pawnbrokers, lending on collateral to the poor, or merchants negotiating bills of exchange for the conduct of long-distance trade. In the discursive themes of the time, by contrast, Jews belonged almost exclusively to the former domain. The medieval characterization of usury as an antisocial economic activity monopolized by religious infidels persisted, even as the term acquired a more secular connotation of "illicit profit." Arguing that the spirit of commerce could tame a despotic monarch in a society of orders, Montesquieu could point to Jews as the origins of the new spirit without questioning established hierarchies. However, once egalitarian demands grew louder, the champions of Jewish rights were at pains to distinguish between usury and commerce and not at all inclined to attribute to Jews a positive role in initiating the development of commercial society.

For Lacretelle, the sorry state of French Jews compared unfavorably with that of the Jews of Holland, parts of Italy and Germany, and especially the American colonies, where "commerce brought them a bit closer to the ordinary human condition," making them "more honest and more faithful in their dealings."[65] In revising his works for posterity, Lacretelle stressed this point by turning to a familiar subject: the legend, as recounted by Montesquieu.[66] Yet even Lacretelle, who attributed to commerce a more positive role than later supporters of Jewish civic and political rights, failed to uphold French Sephardim as models. His plea for Jewish civic rights anticipated the unresolved tension between moneylending and commerce that would characterize all emancipation debates. "Usury," Lacretelle wrote, "seems to have made Jews, at all times, into its loyal agents."[67] As he reasoned, Jews had been banned from artisanal and commercial activities because Christians feared competition; as a result, Jews had specialized in moneylending, which had corrupted their moral fiber. Here and there, Lacretelle held up the Sephardim as proof of the beneficial effects of commerce, but he did so tangentially and without conviction. More often, he associated Jews with retail trade and moneylending.

The thread that linked seventeenth-century philosemitic mercantilism to Montesquieu's *doux commerce* became looser and looser as the emancipation debates progressed. In actuality, Jewish lending activities in Alsace had little in common with their critics' portrayal of them. Notarial records show Jews to have been a minority among the creditors in the region, even if they were overrepresented among rural moneylenders.[68] In spite of these facts, Christian resentment against Jewish moneylending in Alsace ran deep. In 1777–1778, a crown official with an aversion to Jews and a gift for inflammatory rhetoric named François-Joseph-Antoine Hell engineered an unprecedented defamation campaign against the region's Jews. He persuaded Alsatian peasants not to repay their debts to Jews and distributed forged receipts attesting to the extinction of those debts.[69]

The ease with which Hell seized on peasants' hatred of Jewish moneylenders alarmed the Alsatian Jewish leader Cerf Berr (1730–1793), who hired a Prussian civil servant with radical inclinations, Christian Wilhelm von Dohm (1751–1820), to pen the most vigorous defense to date of Jewish civic and political rights. Dohm recommended that Jews shift their economic endeavors away from trade and toward manufacturing and agriculture.[70] A century earlier, the ecclesiastical historian Claude Fleury had expressed admiration for the simple life of ancient Israelites, whom he believed had been devoted to cultivating the land in Palestine, while condemning the corruption, greediness, and duplicity of postexilic Jews in the diaspora.[71] By the 1780s, this narrative had become a leitmotif among gentile backers of Jewish rights.[72]

Dohm depicted the Middle Ages in terms not dissimilar to Montesquieu's, describing them as a time when church persecutions had forced Jews into shameful businesses, but, unlike Montesquieu, he did not attribute to Jews the ability to free society at large (or themselves, for that matter) from the evil effects of their specialization in the moneyed economy thanks to the invention of bills of exchange. Only after the fall of the Roman Empire, Dohm wrote, did the Jews turn to commerce. Though the byproduct of persecution, overspecialization in commerce meant that fraud and usury became distinctive traits of the Jewish character.[73] In order to "cure this corruption," Dohm proposed not only to open all professions to Jews, but also to institute specific measures to "distance Jews from the *profession of commerce* and to seek to lessen its influence on their character."[74] In Jonathan Karp's analysis, Dohm decried Jews' concentration in mercantile professions "not because he was opposed to commerce per se but because . . . he believed that commerce was too important to be left to Jews."[75] In this view, a universalist commercial society was one in which Jews neither held an oligopolistic position nor tainted gentiles involved in the same activities.

This reading, however, obscures the blurring of commerce and usury in Dohm's seminal text. Although a deist, Dohm was deeply influenced by Christian theological and popular notions that saw usury as the antithesis of commerce, which was understood as a social bond, and reaffirmed the Jews' exclusion from French society. If Dohm blamed centuries of harassment for "the moral depravity of Jews," he also depicted the effects of harassment in familiar terms: a Jew could not be "a good citizen, a sociable fellow" ("un bon citoyen, un homme sociable").[76] Echoing a thirteenth-century trope, he added: "Their [the Jews'] character tends to lead them to commit usury and fraud in commerce. . . . [T]heir religious biases render them asocial."[77]

A critic of the deleterious influence that commerce supposedly exerted on the collective character of Jews, Dohm did not celebrate the Sephardim. He borrowed from a Sephardic author the belief that Jews "were the first to establish banks" in Bordeaux and Bayonne but buried the statement in a footnote and did not otherwise praise Sephardic commercial talent.[78] The same statement would resurface in other texts in the years to come, but no author linked Montesquieu's version of the legend to the idea that Jews founded the first banks in southwestern France in order to downplay the equation of Jews and usury or to argue that Jews' financial contributions benefited the country at large.

Dohm's pamphlet provided the blueprint for the French-language debates that ensued, and particularly for the submissions to an essay competition sponsored by the Royal Society of Arts and Sciences in Metz in 1785, a contest that Hertzberg calls "the central event in the battle of opinion [about Jews] in the last years before the Revolution."[79] The competition took as its theme the question: "Are there ways of making the Jews more useful and happier in France?" There were three winners: Claude-Antonie Thiéry, a Protestant barrister from Nancy; Zalkind Hourwitz, a Polish Jew who had recently immigrated to Paris and would soon be hired by the Bibliothèque du Roy as an interpreter of Oriental languages; and Abbé Henri Grégoire (1750–1831), a priest who later overshadowed the other two. All three concurred that education and economic activities were vital tools to "regenerate" Jews and thus make them eligible for full citizenship.[80] All three also associated Jews with usury. The only Jewish voice, Hourwitz, boiled down all Christian accusations against Jews to two: usury and *friperie* ("they are usurers & *fripons* because they are oppressed").[81] The latter term and its cognates also appeared frequently in Grégoire's moral characterization of the Jews.[82]

All advocates of emancipation conceived of Jewish usury as a product of history rather than nature, but none of them made a concerted effort to distinguish between commerce and moneylending. Thiéry lamented that Jews "soon forgot their primitive simplicity and renounced life in the fields in favor of arts and commerce."[83] In a chapter titled "In What Manner the Jews Became a Commercial People and Usurers," Grégoire repeated the narrative that ancient Israelites had been farmers, declaring that they had even "neglected commerce, though they inhabited a maritime country, abounding with excellent harbours."[84] Postexilic Jews, according to this account, had been forced into commerce, and commerce had corrupted them. Here commerce was no longer, as in Montesquieu's narrative, the steppingstone toward a new, less rapacious and divisive form of sociability, and bills of exchange were no longer the antithesis of medieval usury.

When Grégoire resurrected the legend of the Jewish invention of bills of exchange, he was aiming to cast Jewish economic talents in a thoroughly negative light. His was no casual remark. So resolved was Grégoire to assert the legend's authenticity that he went out of his way to dismiss alternative accounts pointing to Florentines or Germans as the inventors of bills of exchange.[85] Borrowing Montesquieu's phrase, he maintained that by inventing bills of exchange, Jews could "*elude violence* and support themselves by means of riches almost invisible."[86] But the meaning he attributed to the phrase was unlike that which Montesquieu had intended. Rather than benefiting commercial society as a whole, for Grégoire, this invention furthered the interests of Jews alone. Jewish commerce was usurious because it fulfilled an egotistic purpose.

Born to a modest family in a small village in Lorraine, Grégoire keenly felt the plight of the peasantry, who railed against Jewish moneylenders.[87] In his appropriation of the legend, he turned Montesquieu's narrative on its head and demonstrated that Cleirac's earlier rendering remained alive. In fact, the entire section of Grégoire's *Essay* devoted to Jews' economic activities was in many ways a dialogue with Montesquieu. For the priest, during the Middle Ages commerce was synonymous with Jews: "Every commercial resource was found naturally in their hands."[88] While he emphasized the harms caused by Christian persecution, he also described Jews as possessing (or having developed—the reasoning is unclear) qualities that over time became innate, such as "a thirst for gain," "an acuteness which in an instant could see what profits were to be made," and a "genius for calculation" (*génie calculateur*).[89] Secular authorities who deprived Jews of alternative means of livelihood in the interest of securing their financial services were to blame for Jews' association with commerce, but the fact remained that Jews "worship no other idol but money, and are infested with no other leprosy but usury."[90] Like other fervent partisans of Jewish rights before and after him, Grégoire easily slipped into essentialized views of Jewish economic cunning at the same time that he sought to undo them.

In a subtle rebuttal of Montesquieu, Grégoire volunteered "a remark, which no person, perhaps, [has] ever yet made," namely, that as Christians began to engage in commerce in the late Middle Ages, they provided competition for the Jews and thus reined in "the robbery of the Jews." As the pursuit of profit became acceptable among Christians, "security" and "sincerity" came to be increasingly valued because of their importance in guaranteeing respect for contractual obligations. Among Christians, he added, the spirit of commerce led to the development of a self-policing commercial society: "The rays of reason, enlightening the mazy path of usury, taught the people to be on their guard against the frauds of the usurer."[91] For reasons that Grégoire did not elucidate, the spirit of commerce did not transform Jews in the same way. His logic echoed earlier hostile views of Jews as rivals of Christian merchants. But now, with the ascent of nationalism, these arguments acquired new potency. If all merchants were suspected of being unpatriotic ("the merchant, become a citizen of the world, . . . is seldom a zealous patriot"), Jews were unredeemable: rootless people ("not attached to the soil"), they would be perceived as always willing to sell out to the highest bidder.[92]

This was a different sort of cosmopolitanism from the one captured in Voltaire's romanticized description of the London Royal Exchange, and one with considerable purchase. In 1767, in a corporatist defense of their privileges against the incursion of Jews, the representatives of the six guilds of Paris, an ancient institution that still wielded some influence, defined usury as the tool Jews used to oppress Christians (after all, the Bible allowed Jews to charge interest to non-Jews). As a result, Jews were said to be unable to join any other "nation" because their aim was always to dissolve rather than unite an existing "political society." That is also why they were not, the petition continued, "cosmopolitan": "They belonged to nowhere in the universe," rather than to everywhere.[93] Jewish asociality, in other words, was a direct extension of Jews' religious infidelity, and usury was the confirmation of their proclivity to exploit Christian society. As patriotism became the foundation of the new political order, the trope of Jews' multiple allegiances was used to render them unfit for citizenship and became a weapon in the hands of those opposing Jewish emancipation.[94]

At the onset of the Revolution, Grégoire moved to Paris and abandoned apologetics in favor of political action, embracing radical positions in the National Constituent Assembly. In October 1789, his *Motion en faveur des Juifs* laid out the arguments for granting Jews full equality. Grégoire's political activism was not aimed at Jews alone. In fact, he fought equally if not more fervently for the emancipation of African slaves in the French Caribbean. I will return to this point in the next section, but it needs to be noted here if we are to understand Grégoire's statements about Jews as evidence of the possibilities of and constraints placed on minority groups' participation in an egalitarian (Christian) society. Grégoire's activism was conditional on Jews' shedding what he regarded as moral, social, and religious liabilities that were incompatible with those of citizens. His view of usury as constitutive of Jewish character was one of the pillars of this conditional approach to emancipation.

In his *Essay*, Grégoire had borrowed from Dohm the claim that Jews brought banking to Bordeaux and Bayonne. But the contention, in light of Grégoire's use of the legend, was not meant as a compliment.[95] Perhaps impressed by his encounter with a delegation of Jews from southwestern France, in his *Motion* the revolutionary priest hailed the respectability of the Jews of Amsterdam, The Hague, Berlin, and Bordeaux, describing them more generously than he had in his *Essay*. In the *Motion*, however, Grégoire resorted once again to the legend as evidence of the interdependence of Jewish commerce and usury.[96] More generally, throughout his work, he sometimes referred to "the Jews" collectively and sometimes contrasted the Sephardim and Ashkenazim, although ultimately he hoped for the conversion of all of them.[97]

How did Jews respond, rhetorically, to these indictments? Among the entrants in the Metz contest, Hourwitz alone came close to singling out the Sephardim as the living example of regeneration. But he too alternated between distinguishing Sephardic commerce from Ashkenazic moneylending and conflating the two. In both cases, he indicated that usury separated Jews from the rest of the population. To remedy the situation, Hourwitz advocated Jews' admission to craft guilds and liberal professions and recommended that they be allowed to cultivate the land—all measures that would decrease the number of merchants among them "and thus the number of *fripons*."[98] He urged Jews to take concrete steps to abandon all particularism, to develop closer ties to gentile customers, and to submit themselves to "the inspection of *la police*" in order to diminish opportunities "to cheat and steal" and thus enhance the chances that merchants among them would turn "into more honest men."[99] If they followed his recommendations, he concluded, the Jews of the eastern regions would "over time, become as happy and as useful to the state as their coreligionists from Bordeaux and Bayonne."[100] Nevertheless, Hourwitz's depiction of Jewish economic activities displeased the leaders of Bordeaux's Jewish community, who were offended by his essay's call for regulation and likening of commerce to usury.[101]

Other Jewish advocates also hinted at the utility of Jewish commerce or the beneficial effects that commerce had on the Sephardim of southwestern France, but unlike their seventeenth-century predecessors, they did not obtain new rights on the grounds that Jews' skills in commerce and finance were useful to France. In 1788, the Sephardim petitioned Chrétien Guillaume de Lamoignon de Malesherbes, the minister charged with reforming the status of non-Catholic French subjects, to be admitted to the chambers of commerce of the kingdom on account of what they "contribute[d] to the progress of commerce."[102] Their request was denied. There was a historical reason for this refusal. The stakes were different from those of 150 years earlier, when privileges—rather than rights—were the cardinal principles of politics. In the seventeenth century, Simone Luzzatto and Menasseh ben Israel could win their cases with Christian rulers by overstating Jews' economic contributions. After the Revolution began, such arguments were no longer tenable. The deputies of the Jewish community of Bordeaux, addressing Grégoire in August 1789, cited "a multitude of associations devoted to trade and charity" as examples of the "fraternity between Christians and Jews" that entitled them to equal rights yet refrained from elaborating any further on their economic activities.[103]

Jews' advocacy of their rights at this time no longer revolved around claims of commercial utility. In January 1790, three representatives of the Spanish and Portuguese Jews of Bordeaux sent a letter to the National Constituent Assembly detailing how the Jews of the southwest differed from those of the rest of France and Europe at large. The letter argued that the Sephardim "were both *négociants* and farmers" and contributed to the flourishing of the region where they lived. But more than anything else, it stressed the civic equality that the Jews of southwestern France enjoyed with all other "co-citizens" thanks to the privileges granted to them by the crown in 1550 and again in 1776. It was on the basis of those privileges that they had been allowed to participate in the elections for the National Assembly. There was no difference, the representatives wrote, between the Jews of southwestern France and "French Catholics," either in the "civil order" or in the "moral order."[104] The battle for citizenship was a political struggle fought on legal and moral grounds rather than economic ones.

Jewish authors from northeastern France used different slogans to advance their cause and put even less faith in the emancipatory effects of commerce.

In a memo drafted to recruit Dohm to take on the cause of the Jews, the Strasbourg leader Cerf Berr touted freedom of commerce as an antidote to the causes of Jewish moneylending in Alsace. But he also exalted the economic functions of court Jews like himself, who served the economic needs of the state, more than he reaffirmed the tenets of *doux commerce*.[105] In October 1789, Isaac Berr-Bing was even more cautious in demanding the lifting of all restrictions on Jewish occupations and property rights in Alsace and Lorraine. While celebrating the orderly society of the regions' Jews, he lamented that petty trade (*la petite friperie*) was the only occupation that sustained the two-thirds of the community who lived in poverty and stressed that no Jew in the area had ever engaged in wholesale trade in grain, "because our religion condemns those who amass this basic food staple."[106] The grain crisis of the summer prior had been the first major test of the revolutionary government, and Berr-Bing knew well the fears of oligopolies and famines that it had provoked. He chose to make the case for Judaism as a religion that inspired charity rather than emphasizing the virtues of large-scale commercial transactions handled by Jews.

Gentile observers were even more prone to conflate commerce with usury. In Alsace, an anonymous voice sympathetic to Jews praised their economic contributions to society and the state but equated "commerce" with "moneylending."[107] In a famous speech to the National Assembly on December 23, 1789, the Count of Clermont-Tonnerre said little of substance about the economic roles of Jews. He blamed the state's restrictions on Jews' professions, not their character, for their habit of lending at interest but lumped all moneyed professions together, without distinguishing between commerce and pawnbroking.[108] At the opposite end of the political spectrum, Abbé Maury denied that Jews had ever been an agricultural people ("They were laborers neither under King David nor under King Solomon") and equated them with the Barbary pirates, who were "occupied solely in commerce" and lived off robbery at sea.[109]

Jews and Other Minorities

In the revolutionary battle for equality, male Jews emerged as the winners while other disadvantaged groups were left behind. No single reason explains why Jewish men gained equality while women and blacks did not, although the temporary abolition of slavery (1794–1802) and Jews' emancipation reveal the republican belief in the capacity of the Revolution to change the nature of men—although not women, who were never seen as real candidates for equality. Rather, the process of Jewish emancipation helps us better understand the limits of the Revolution's universalism—limits derived not only from the perceived innate characteristics of each group that demanded inclusion in the new legal and political order but also from the need to reaffirm differences in this more egalitarian order. From both a historical and a theoretical perspective, women posed the greatest challenge to the universalism of human rights (not coincidentally called "the Rights of Man and of the Citizen" in the 1789 Declaration).[124] A rare champion of women's political equality, the Marquis of Condorcet was uncompromising in his defense of "natural rights" and the perfectibility of all humans. Yet he, too, had his favorite causes: he wrote more strenuously on behalf of slaves than Jews.[125] Grégoire, by contrast, fought for active political rights for blacks and Jews but saw women as inherently unable to hold government and administrative positions.[126]

While he did not explicitly compare Jews and blacks, Grégoire relied on the same reasoning when he argued that both groups deserved inclusion in the body politic: as Christian persecutions hampered Jews, he noted, so "accidental circumstances and local causes have prevented or impeded the progress of civilization in Africa."[127] In this view, centuries of European exploitation rather than nature explained why free and enslaved blacks lingered in an inferior "degree of civilization": "The natives of Africa and America would long ago have risen to the highest level of civilization if this good purpose would have been supported by a hundredth part of the efforts, the money, and the time that have been given over to tormenting and butchering many millions of these unfortunate people, whose blood calls for vengeance against Europe."[128]

For all the similarities of Grégoire's arguments in favor of blacks and Jews, the *bon curé* patently considered it easier to "regenerate" the former than the latter. It has even been noted that during an animated session of the National Assembly in December 1789, Grégoire remained silent on the question of the fate of the Jews, perhaps for fear of endangering the antislavery cause.[129] For sure he was generous in enumerating the "moral qualities of the negroes," their "upright character" and "true bravery," "their talents . . . for arts and craftsmanship," and the sophistication of their "political societies" in Africa.[130] By contrast, one is hard pressed to find any praises of Jews' cultural achievements in his Metz *Essay*. Rejecting Isaac de Pinto's arguments, Grégoire was also skeptical of the existence of substantial differences between Ashkenazic and Sephardic Jews and more inclined to think that "the Jewish nation has been the most like itself, at all times, both in beliefs and usages." Surely, he claimed, "there is more resemblance between the Jews of Ethiopia and those of England, than between the inhabitants of Picardy and those of Provence."[131] This was a low bar, which left no room for appreciating the Sephardim's achievements in long-distance trade.

The lingering particularism that inflected revolutionary ideals is arguably the thorniest legacy that the events of the 1790s have bequeathed to Western liberalism, setting up a clash between an abstract aspiration to equality and the irreducible existence of differences, including the affirmation of those differences by legal and demographic minorities themselves.[132] As Maurice Samuels has recently reminded us, the 1791 decree that emancipated all Jews in France included none of the conditions that theorists of "regeneration" had demanded, and yet, at times, their desire that Jews shed any residual particularism seems to have been fulfilled.[133] In 1792, a Hebrew version of the *Marseillaise* was sung in the synagogue of Metz to celebrate the victory of the republican army at Thionville, the Lorraine town from which Lacretelle had first launched the pro-Jewish cause.[134] In that same year, while battling militarily for survival, the French Republic included a recently emancipated Jewish citizen among its army suppliers.[135] Episodes such as these are cited as evidence of the "compatibility of republicanism and Judaism."[136] But that compatibility was short-lived. Subsequent incarnations of French secularism (*laïcité*) reserved the blending of patriotism and the public display of religion for the majority of French citizens who, whether practicing Catholics or not, were (and still are) neither Jewish nor Muslim.

Conclusion

In his classic *The Passions and the Interests*, Hirschman departs from mainstream scholarship on Montesquieu to call attention to the contention that Jews invented bills of exchange. For his purposes, the validity and genealogy of that contention are irrelevant. Whether real or imaginary, the claim exemplifies Montesquieu's argument that commercial expansion is incompatible with autocratic government. The legend is thus central to Hirschman's overall thesis as captured by its subtitle: *Political Arguments for Capitalism Before Its Triumph*, with an emphasis on the word *Political*. Without denying the naïveté of some of Montesquieu's generalizations, Hirschman finds that *The Spirit of the Laws* planted the seeds for a fully developed theory of the interdependence of commerce and democracy that deserves as much attention as the paradigms proposed by Adam Smith and Karl Marx. Brilliant and penetrating, if inevitably partial, *The Passions and the Interests* has been hugely influential, to the point of obscuring how *The Spirit of the Laws* was read at the time, certainly with regard to the assertion that Jews invented bills of exchange. In fact, commerce played a minor role, if any at all, in the political emancipation of Jews.

Montesquieu set up a dichotomy between bills of exchange as new and fundamentally positive credit devices and usury as a medieval and nefarious credit practice. Historians of eighteenth-century French Jews have mapped this dichotomy onto the Sephardim/Ashkenazim divide and emphasized the divergent socioeconomic profiles of the Jewish communities in the southwestern and northeastern regions of the kingdom. The Sephardim engaged in long-distance trade and international finance and were better integrated into the fabric of local society, while the Ashkenazim, who were overwhelmingly occupied in moneylending and petty trade, experienced social isolation and were the targets of overt Christian hostility.

In the accepted account of emancipation, articulated in both academic and popular histories of the Jews, this divide had direct political consequences because commerce made the Sephardim of Bordeaux into more respectable members of the wider community, paving the way for citizenship. In the early twentieth century, the author of a brief outline of the history of Jewish emancipation in France could write: "I dwell somewhat upon the Bordeaux Jews, for . . . it was their position more than any other single fact or argument whatsoever which carried the Jews of France past the crisis of their faith." Although a few pages later he describes the debates in the National Assembly as "a chaos of ideas and motives," the same author celebrates the Sephardim as pathbreakers.[110] More recent scholarship refines but does not alter this picture and even suggests that the Sephardim of Bordeaux sought to distance themselves from their Ashkenazic brethren in 1789–1790 (and perhaps even to stall the latter's emancipation) for fear of compromising their own chances.[111]

This widely shared view of emancipation implies the existence of an invisible link connecting Montesquieu's celebration of Jewish commercial activity, captured by his positive spin on the legend of the Jewish invention of bills of exchange, to the extension of citizenship to the Sephardim in January 1790, granted eighteen months before the same rights were conferred on all Jewish men of France. One scholar, making that link explicit, even wonders why Montesquieu fell short of advocating full equality for Jews.[112] The analysis I have provided thus far demonstrates that the question is misguided.

My case rests on my reading of the French Enlightenment, variegated as the phenomena that fall under this rubric are. Schechter has already demonstrated that interest in Jews in eighteenth-century French thought far exceeded what their numbers might logically call for, with images of Jews serving as vehicles to articulate concepts that had little or nothing to do with Jews.[113] However, neither he nor any of the numerous scholars who have written about eighteenth-century French commerce broadly conceived have paid much attention to the historical and figurative presence of Jews in that realm. Given the centrality of *doux commerce* in French economic and political thought, it is important to highlight the role that Montesquieu attributed to Jews in the development of the spirit of commerce, as well as the "moderate" political implications of his account.[114] He never argued explicitly in favor of a nonconfessional commercial society and believed that merchants should operate within the confines of a corporatist framework that constrained any potentially disruptive effects on existing hierarchies. Montesquieu's unshakable belief in a society of orders allowed him to celebrate Jewish commerce in ways in which more egalitarian thinkers would not.

His novel interpretation of the legend presupposed a discontinuity between medieval usury and early modern forms of credit but was far from a cry for equality. By the mid-eighteenth century, it had become a cliché for theorists of commercial society to maintain, as Forbonnais did, that commerce bound people into "reciprocal communication."[115] This communication was understood as compatible with the existence of inherent differences and hierarchies. In the 1760s, both the *Encyclopédie* and the Jewish authors who rebutted Voltaire's anti-Jewish writings could celebrate Jewish merchants as "pegs and nails" in the edifice of global trade as well as emphasize the status of the Jews of Bordeaux and Bayonne as subjects of the crown (*régnicoles*) rather than foreigners. In 1765, when Jacob Rodrigues Péreire (1715–1780), a leader of the then official Sephardic community, republished the *lettres patentes* that had granted the "Portuguese merchants" of Bordeaux their privileges from 1550 to 1723, he extolled these individuals' "talent in making commerce flourish and their genius at creating new trade branches."[116] But emancipation was not even on the horizon in those years. In the most consistent defense of Jews' contributions to commerce in the 1760s, the Parisian Jew Israël Bernard de Vallabrègue used the generic meaning of the word "citizen" in his argument for Jewish civic equality, without making any reference to active political rights.[117]

Commerce, in other words, was undoubtedly the linchpin of early modern toleration policies that offered New Christians and New Jews in southwestern France privileges that their brethren in Alsace and Lorraine could not aspire to attain. Commerce also embedded Jewish and Christian merchants in networks of economic dependence (often connected via bills of exchange), both in Bordeaux and overseas. These privileges, and the social interactions they generated, however, were only acceptable in a society in which the majority population was clearly separated from Jews and the latter could not aspire to full membership in it. When equality became a possibility, few heralded the Jews of southwestern France as archetypes of the virtues of commercial credit in contrast to the Jews of northeastern France, who remained emblems of usury.

No matter how diverse they may be, all the texts examined here dating to the last quarter of the eighteenth century failed to differentiate between commerce and usury. *Friponnerie* was viewed as the hallmark of both. Usury and bad faith were understood to be the antisocial faces of commerce, and, in the eyes of even the most sympathetic observers, they remained historically (if not theologically) associated with Jews.[118] The frequent blurring of the boundaries between commerce and usury in eighteenth-century French representations of Jewish economic roles not only proves the tenacity of discursive traditions, sometimes even when authors consciously tried to break with those traditions, but also demonstrates that the exaltation of Jews' commercial prowess was a more effective rhetorical strategy in the context of Old Regime policies of toleration than it was during the struggle for emancipation. The lexical and conceptual slippage between commerce and usury that is detectable from Lacretelle onward signals the tenuousness of the line separating Ashkenazic moneylending from Sephardic commerce in the Christian imagination. That the Revolution emancipated the Jews of France in two steps, those of the southwest in January 1790 and all others in September 1791, arguably suggests that the Sephardim were regarded as more acculturated. But the 1790 decree, in line with the demands of Sephardic leaders, who clung to the hope of preserving their corporate autonomy, portrayed emancipation as the confirmation of preexisting privileges. When such language expressing continuity with the Old Regime disappeared from the 1791 decree, it was not—*pace* Hirschman—because commercial "interests" had displaced prevailing "passions" about Jews.[119]

Amid the "cacophony of arguments" marshaled in favor of emancipation, the virtues of commerce were never used as weapons by pro-Jewish advocates.[120] Only the little crossover that exists between French and Jewish historiographies and the scant attention that both pay to the language used by the champions of Jewish rights to describe Jews' economic roles can explain why many scholars still regard Sephardic merchants as the driving force in the emancipation process. Perhaps nowhere is the disconnect between scholarship on Jewish emancipation and scholarship on the Revolution more pronounced than in the treatment of Honoré-Gabriel de Riqueti, Count of Mirabeau (1749–1791), son of the noted physiocrat and the most influential politician of the first year of the National Assembly (1789–1790). Historians of European Jewry know him for his laudatory portrait of Moses Mendelssohn and his support of Jewish rights in a pamphlet that was modeled largely on Dohm's ideas.[121] Historians of the Revolution know him as a master orator, the fierce and opportunistic adversary of Finance Minister Jacques Necker, and the writer of a "climactic pamphlet," *Dénonciation de l'agiotage* (*Denunciation of Speculation*), which belonged to a series that, while serving the interests of a circle of bankers and friends who gambled in stocks and foreign currencies, condemned the crown's handling of the public debt and financial markets.[122]

In fact, the two Mirabeaus have a lot in common. Both of his influential pamphlets, the one on Jews and the one on speculation, were written in 1787 when Mirabeau was in Berlin, where Mendelssohn had lived until his death the year before. Both conveyed the same message, one resonant of physiocratic principles, which favored economic liberalization, including the abolition of guilds and other corporate institutions that had long restricted Jews' economic activities, but deplored commerce and banking. In this formulation, in order to become citizens and patriots, Jews had to recover the supposedly rural way of life of the ancient Israelites and sever their long-held ties to commerce, which Mirabeau called "the veritable, or rather the only cause of the corruption of the Jews."[123] Montesquieu had denounced John Law but did not see private credit as existing on a continuum with public finance. On the eve of the Revolution, however, the awareness of how easily private speculators could alter the value of the royal treasury made it more difficult to sustain the difference between private and public finance.

Overall, the economic dimension of Jewish emancipation exposes the limits of French universalism. In the aftermath of the Revolution, the poor economic condition of the majority of French Jews and entrenched suspicions about their usurious character had a decisive effect on the stalling of the advancement of formal equality. Responding to the popular hostility unleashed by the emancipation decrees and persistent complaints that Jews in the northeastern regions "followed no other profession than that of usurers," in 1806

Napoleon convened the Assembly of Jewish Notables, later constituted as the Grand Sanhedrin, to address problems raised by the imperfect assimilation of Jews. In the meantime, he suspended repayments of all loans made by Jews to "husbandmen, not traders," for a year's time.[137] Usury, alongside marriage, divorce, rabbinical authority, and military service, figured prominently among the controversial questions that Jews were asked to answer as evidence of their willingness to assimilate.

With the cooperation of the Assembly's head, Abraham Furtado, who was, conveniently, a leading Sephardi from Bordeaux and a former Girondin, Napoleon secured assent to what came to be known among French Jews as the "infamous decree." Promulgated on March 17, 1808, it ruled invalid all loans made by Jews with interest rates above 10 percent a year or issued to minors, women, and soldiers. The state imposed further restrictions on Jews who wished to engage in commerce: they had to obtain a special license, which required a review of their character and verification that they had not previously engaged in usurious activities. These measures, together with other limitations on Jews' civil rights, applied only to the Jews of Alsace and Lorraine, were set to last for ten years, and aimed to alter not only the socioeconomic profile but also the inner character of the newly emancipated group. The Jews of southwestern France were spared these humiliating restrictions but were also much fewer in number than their Ashkenazic brethren and did not loom as large in the French imagination.

Once again, usury was the symbol of something bigger—namely, the suspicion that Jews might be unable to partake in civil and political society as fair players. Forced into (or assumed to occupy) an economic position from which they could take advantage of everyone else, Jews were regarded by most as unable to meet the demands of equality. The transformation of their legal status that occurred during the Revolution was enormous, but representations of Jews after emancipation continued to be predicated on a centuries-long discursive tradition. In the late Middle Ages, economic and religious infidelity were cited as reasons for excluding Jews not only from the urban patriciate that ruled commercially minded city-states, but also from the ideology of the common good more generally. In the newborn French nation-state, Jews' usurious character was perceived as deriving from a lack of patriotism.

The transition from a medieval to a modern conception of political belonging was gradual—and accompanied by changes in the meaning of the word "nation"—but it did not dispense with persistent fears of economic oligopolies and conspiracies. Among the reasons given by the six guilds of Paris for rejecting the membership of Jewish merchants in 1767, one turned to an alchemical metaphor: Jews were like particles of quicksilver, which run in all directions but ultimately always unite in one single block. Whereas French Catholic merchant houses operated as individual units in fair competition with one another, every single Jew, the Parisian merchants claimed, was inseparable from his larger "nation," and therefore each one could destabilize "the harmony of political societies."[138] The same logic was articulated in new language after the Revolution. In 1810, even Grégoire accused the Jews of disloyalty to France: "The Jew has his eyes constantly turned toward Jerusalem, desiring only it for his *patrie* [motherland]."[139] The charge that Jews constituted "a nation within the nation" became a leitmotif.[140]

By following the winding paths of the legend of the Jewish invention of bills of exchange across eighteenth-century France, I have revisited key moments in the history of the Enlightenment and the Revolution. In contrast to the tendency of most histories of economic thought to slice up the eighteenth century into discrete, if sometimes temporally overlapping, doctrines, ranging from the anticommercial stand of Fénelon's classical republicanism to the physiocrats' call for the liberalization of trade and manufacture and for the primacy of agriculture over public and private credit, I have stressed the extent to which the legend traversed such partitions. Its malleability allowed it to serve multiple purposes. Montesquieu appropriated it in order to develop a critique of despotism and religious intolerance that hinged on an exaggerated image of Jewish commercial ingenuity. Later in the century, Grégoire evoked it to reinforce a historical connection between Jews and rapacious moneylending that at times veered toward essentialism.

It is not a coincidence that Montesquieu wrote in Bordeaux and Grégoire in Lorraine, but the trajectory of the legend that identified Jews as the originators of modern European financial instruments suggests something deeper. The revolutionary promise of equality carried with it the prospect of a fully realized society of contract, in which credit markets would shed their religious and corporatist biases in favor of anonymous competition. Equality and anonymity in turn carried with them new risks: How could one discern which economic actors were reputable and which duplicitous in an impersonal market? As emancipation promised to eliminate every last vestige of formal discrimination against Jewish economic actors, Cleirac's concerns from a century and a half earlier about the inability to detect fraud in the new paper economy regained purchase. At the dawn of the democratic age, emancipation was an indisputable achievement, yet the backlashes it generated echoed older responses. Christian abhorrence for crypto-Judaism resurfaced in new guises. The demand for one form of regeneration, the economic, replaced the original religious concept of spiritual rebirth. Even more important, citizenship replaced baptism as the requisite rite of passage but remained equally unpersuasive in dispelling Christian mistrust of the newly emancipated Jews. Equality at once expanded the boundaries of commercial society and rendered Jews more and more indistinguishable from all other citizens. Once again, Jews' invisibility intensified fears of contamination, and their perceived ubiquity continued to serve as a metaphor for the perils lurking behind ever more complex financial markets.

7

Distant Echoes

THE REWORKING OF THE legend of the Jewish invention of bills of exchange by Montesquieu proved the most influential reinterpretation of Étienne Cleirac's 1647 narrative and injected new life into the tale. The fact that the same narrative of Jewish ingenuity could radiate diverse, even contradictory, meanings is one of the reasons why it traveled so far and retained its power for so long. In the pages that follow, I analyze the legend's echoes beyond France up to 1800 and how they intersected with a variety of discourses about the morality of commercial credit. For the sake of clarity, the chapter is organized by politico-linguistic regions, although intellectuals and state administrators in eighteenth-century Europe borrowed ideas from one another and crossed borders more easily than they would after the advent of the nation-state. I organize the traces left by the legend across Europe by the regions in which it appeared in print in order of frequency: England/Britain, the Holy Roman Empire, the Italian and Iberian peninsulas, and the United Provinces.[1] A final section examines the first published appropriation of the legend by an Anglo-Jewish author.

By using the legend as my Ariadne's thread across the Continent and beyond the Channel, my purpose is neither to compile an exhaustive list of all authors who discussed the idea that Jews invented marine insurance or bills of exchange nor to force those authors into preestablished schools of thought. Rather, I wish to tackle the three broad issues that I outlined in the introduction: the definition of a canon, the relationship between images and practices, and the continuities and changes in Christian representations of Jewish commerce. Along which routes did the tale of the Jewish invention of Europe's financial instruments travel beyond France, and how did it acquire local purchase? And what does the legend tell us about the persistence of discursive traditions that associated Jews and money and the ways in which those traditions intersected with or skirted specific polemics about the status of commerce in the social and political order? As we progress into the eighteenth century, we also need to address an additional topic: changing scholarly procedures of verification. Did the least plausible aspects of the legend set in motion the process of formulating new standards of proof, or did they remain impermeable to them?

As noted before, statistics are not adequate tools with which to answer these questions. Even if we wanted to verify the incidence of the legend in quantitative terms, a comprehensive bibliography of all European books only exists for the period before 1600, rendering it nearly impossible to calculate the frequency of words, passages, or even titles in the material printed during the two centuries that followed.[2] Nor does a capacious and clearly demarcated corpus exist against which to measure the legend's recurrence within all works dealing with the economy writ large.[3] The higher incidence of references to the alleged Jewish invention of marine insurance and bills of exchange that can be seen in English works might be related to the output of English-language printed media, which we can reasonably assume to have been higher than that of Portugal, for example, or to the likely overrepresentation of English-language material in the rare book collections currently available online. Only further expansion of these collections will permit us to test some of the arguments I present in this chapter.

One point is indisputable: it would be misleading to focus only on canonical works. Savary and Montesquieu were exceptional amplifiers of the legend, but genres during this period were by definition blurred, and now-forgotten texts such as Cleirac's *Us et coustumes de la mer* continued to be read widely. During the eighteenth century, accounts of the origins of bills of exchange and marine insurance figured in an increasingly wide spectrum of works, ranging from merchant handbooks to treatises like *The Spirit of the Laws*, encyclopedias, legal commentaries, novels, and more.[4] Moreover, it was primarily in lesser-known publications that the legend's credibility was scrutinized and challenged. And because even works that sought to debunk the legend indirectly propagated it, appendix 6 lists all printed works that mentioned the legend regardless of whether they endorsed it or not. Appendix 6, however, cannot do justice to the myriad ways in which the legend was rewritten or the varied discursive contexts in which it was embedded. That is the task of this chapter.

As I have done with regard to France, I scan the broader environment of the legend's reception. Multiple factors affected its dissemination, standing, and reworking, including authorial credibility, the effects of serial publication and intertextual transmission, the local politics of commerce and finance, and reform projects aiming to improve the conditions of Jewish life. Given the vastness of the terrain I cover, my analysis is more cursory than it has been in the previous chapters. It nonetheless yields several important findings that challenge received wisdom about how both real and imaginary Jews figured in the making of European commercial society.

First, the legend that pointed to Jews as the creators of European private finance did not travel along confessional lines. Developed in Catholic France, the legend also appeared in England, the Reformed areas of the Holy Roman Empire, and the United Provinces. The Catholic–Protestant divide, to which scholars of Western capitalism have attributed great significance, turns out not to be a pertinent axis along which to organize our inquiry. Second, although they were shaped by an arsenal of Christian representations of Jews that traversed periods and cultures, public debates about Jews' economic credibility were more intense where cultural acceptance of the merchant profession and the place of commerce and finance in national politics was most contentious. This explains why we detect the lowest incidence of the legend in both the most and the least tolerant areas of Europe: the United Provinces and the Iberian peninsula, respectively. These were also the two regions where commerce enjoyed the highest and the lowest levels of legal and cultural recognition. As in France, then, elsewhere in Europe the legend conveyed the most elusive critiques of the evils of credit in those contexts where the expansion of credit was underway. Third, we cannot establish a simple correlation between the degree of a society's commercialization and positive images of Jews. In England and the United Provinces, the emergence of the stock market (rather than bills of exchange) was the catalyst for an increase in hostile views toward Jews, who symbolized the dangers brought by financial speculation. It is thus not surprising that arguments about Jewish commercial prowess did not advance the cause of Jewish emancipation in these countries.

A lag of more than fifty years separates the legend's appearance in French and its circulation in other languages, in part because of the time it took for the translation of Savary's *Le parfait négociant* to permeate the foreign commercial literature. Translations of works by the Savary family and Montesquieu were the legend's most influential vehicles of diffusion and transmutation. Most non-French versions of the legend, however, adapted the tale to make it palatable to new readerships. Montesquieu's status certainly contributed to the legend's credibility in the eighteenth century. At the same time, an increasing number of writers challenged the legend's accuracy. They did so from an array of perspectives. Some simply picked up on earlier doubts about its logic. More deployed new evidentiary tools, including source criticism, to dispute the legend's historical veracity and debunk its assertions. Others continued to believe that particular merchant communities were responsible for world-changing innovations but disputed the idea that the invention of marine insurance or bills of exchange should be attributed specifically to Jews.

The legend's reception thus provides a lens through which to analyze the impact of changing scholarly practices in the age of colossal encyclopedic projects, world histories of commerce, and renewed interest in studying Roman law. It also demonstrates how, as it traveled to different parts of Europe during the eighteenth century, the legend was absorbed into emerging proto-nationalist discourses. Many Italian authors insisted that Florentines rather than Jews had been the first to devise bills of exchange and to propel Europe's commercial expansion, just as the glorious voyages undertaken by famous explorers and pathfinders had. Certain English and German authors also argued for alternative historical trajectories, although they could not attribute the invention to their ancestors as easily. In Germany during the latter part of the eighteenth century, the reworking of the legend even stimulated the emergence of a new and influential narrative about the economic function of Jews. According to this narrative, Christian resentment of Jews' alleged domination of commerce spurred Europe's late medieval economic growth by encouraging Christian merchants to take control of the financial innovations that Jews had presumably devised and, until then, monopolized. By the last quarter of the nineteenth century, this narrative had become a pillar of some of the most influential academic accounts of European economic history (chapter 8).

For all of these reasons, the reception of the legend of the Jewish invention of marine insurance and bills of exchange anticipates some and even constitutes one of the most important developments in European economic thought up through the nineteenth century. Though my focus is necessarily on Christian images of Jews, I also discuss a few Jewish authors at the end of the chapter in order to assess their reaction to Christian presumptions about Jews' ostensible commercial dexterity. One author in particular, Isaac D'Israeli (1766–1848), stands out not only because he was the first Jewish writer to mention the legend in print but also because, borrowing from Montesquieu, he endorsed it emphatically. How to explain D'Israeli? Admittedly, few Jewish authors wrote in vernacular about economic matters during the early modern period. But a body of Jewish apologetic writings did stress Jews' economic talents (to the point of exaggeration) in order to secure more favorable treatment from Christian rulers interested in expanding their commercial reach (chapter 5). Had the legend primarily carried the positive meaning that Montesquieu attributed to it, Jewish authors, I suspect, would have evoked it in their pleas to secular authorities. Yet they did not. As we examine the first, hesitant introduction of the legend to Jewish self-representations at the end of the eighteenth century, we also need to interrogate this silence.

England/Britain

If we exclude the translations of Savary's *Le parfait négociant* into German (1676) and Dutch (1683), to which I will return, England (Great Britain after 1707) is the European country outside of France where we find the earliest mentions of the legend of the medieval Jewish invention of marine insurance and bills of exchange. There, the legend joined a variety of allegorical mentions of Jews that functioned as vehicles of expression for anxieties about the morality of private and public credit.

If credit permeated all strata of English society even more than in France, the institutions that promoted and regulated it were considerably different from their French counterparts. Lower courts offered cheap remedies to litigants seeking to settle small debts. At the opposite end of the credit market, after 1613, the East India Company used equity rather than debt to finance its operations, issuing shares of its stock and paying dividends periodically. During the second half of the seventeenth century, a private and public securities market flourished, and the financial revolution of 1688–1694 joined the interests of the state and individual investors as never before in European history. In London, the number of individuals who owned and traded companies' shares increased fivefold between the 1690s and the 1720s.[5] The legal and cultural barriers to the nobility's involvement in commerce and finance were considerably lower in England than in France. The status of Jews in these countries was also remarkably different. After the 1656 tacit readmission, the Jewish community in England evolved from a tiny Iberian New Christian presence to a growing and economically polarized group. As a result of these intersecting trends, in eighteenth-century England "Jewishness" assumed connotations that were not present in France, including the association of Jews with the stock market rather than with bills of exchange.[6]

Post-Reformation England regulated usury in ways not dissimilar from those found in Catholic France: in 1571 annual interest rates of up to 10 percent were permitted on mortgages, a ceiling that by the early eighteenth century had declined to 5 percent.[7] Meanwhile, the rampant need for credit during the sixteenth-century economic boom coincided with a shortage of minted coins. This situation was sometimes blamed on bills of exchange, which unsettled the balance of trade. In the short term, preoccupations about rapacious moneylending intensified. The discursive equation of usurers and Jews that we have examined at length was very much alive in Tudor and Stuart England. Francis Bacon opened his "Of Usury" (1625) by drawing on a trope we have encountered many times: "Usurers should have orange-tawney bonnets, because they do judaize."[8] As it had centuries earlier, the verb "to Judaize" singled out those who were construed as imitating Jews, rather than Jews themselves, and who therefore needed to wear a distinctive sign marking them apart from fair economic actors. Thomas Wilson's *A Discourse upon Usury* (1572), a widely reprinted fictional dialogue about the merits and dangers of moneylending and credit, had relied on the same discursive equation of usurers and Jews. Wilson's text, punctuated by religious sermons, was made up of opinionated exchanges between a merchant, two lawyers, and a preacher. In it, the latter (an "enemy to usurie") rails against Jews' penchant for usury in language reminiscent of Matthew Paris: all those Englishmen who "lende their money or their goods whatsoever for gain, I take them to be no better than Iewes." One lawyer agrees with the preacher on this point: "No better do I call them [i.e., merchants] then Iewes, yea, worse than any infidel, that wittingly lvye by the onely gayne of their money."[9]

After Lord Protector Oliver Cromwell quietly agreed to allow the practice of Judaism in London in 1656, Jews became a lived reality in England for the first time since the royal expulsion of 1290. The size of the Jewish community remained relatively small until the mid-eighteenth century, when refugees from central and eastern Europe arrived in large numbers and tested the cohesion of Anglo Jewry as well as its collective image. In England, the divide between Sephardim and Ashkenazim was no less pronounced than in France, but unlike in France, it did not correspond to an equivalent degree of geographical segregation. Most Jews lived in London. Sephardim counted among themselves few wealthy traders, financiers, and army suppliers, but those who reached that level of economic success were highly visible. Most Ashkenazic Jews, by contrast, were poor, sometimes extremely so, and regarded as petty criminals. Evidence from the historical insurance market gives us a measure of their bad repute. In 1786, after a fire destroyed the house of some people referred to as "the lower Order of Jews," the surveyors reported back to the underwriters that "from every appearance of the persons and inhabitations of many of the claimants, they had the greatest reason to suspect their accounts to be false and fraudulent."[10] The insinuation was that members of "the lower Order of Jews" had likely set fire to the house themselves in order to cash in on the rewards. We have no way of determining whether the allegation was true. The point is rather that the lack of credibility associated with Jews (or at least Ashkenazim) not only served as an ethical yardstick against which to judge everyone's behavior but could also have a tangible effect on Jews' daily lives.

For all the enthusiasm that surrounded the rapid commercialization of seventeenth- and eighteenth-century England, an equally profound awareness existed that, as Julian Hoppit puts it, "credit had negative as well as positive features," and not all of those features were easily measurable.[11] Concerns about the potentially destructive consequences of reckless speculation, the moral corruption generated by excessive spending, and the devious motives of those who pumped cash into the pockets of needy borrowers accompanied the expansion of private, public, and corporate credit.

Literary scholars have detected a pronounced gender bias in the language with which these concerns were expressed, exemplified by Daniel Defoe's "Lady Credit," who personified the flimsy, irrational, and improper character of Britain's booming financial speculation.[12] However, these scholars have rarely looked at literary figures of Jews alongside those of women in English representations of credit. In London and other cities, credit and its discontents were the talk of the town. Surveying the polemical and practical literature on credit between 1680 and the 1790s, Hoppit corrects the progressive perspective that places Adam Smith at the apex of a long-term transformation of English (later British) social and economic thought and concludes that most ordinary commentaries on credit throughout the period were informed "by ideas that were more often backward than forward looking."[13] Among these backward-looking ideas he notes the association of Jews with pawnbroking, an association that inflated Jewish involvement in that activity at the time but served as a criticism of financial extortion conducted by well-known political figures.[14]

Legislation to regulate financial markets, and stockbrokers in particular, was proposed numerous times during the eighteenth century but dismissed in the interest of protecting the fiscal needs of the state.[15] This legislative vacuum opened the door for symbolic regulatory tools: out-groups such as Huguenots, Jews, and the Dutch, who populated but did not dominate the London financial market, were constructed as personifications of oligopoly and deceit.

Trapped in a half-real and half-imaginary medieval past, the figure of the Jewish usurer continued to exert considerable influence in early modern England, as it did in France. Invoking this figure allowed one to draw the moral line between merchants contributing to the common good and those seeking to enrich themselves at all costs.

Meanwhile, a new theme marked the conversion of the Jewish pawnbroker into the Jewish financier in England: the association of the latter with trading in stocks rather than in bills of exchange. Amid the thousands of pages Defoe wrote on commerce, he spoke sparingly of Jews, but when he did, it was primarily to denounce them as the epitome of unrestrained speculation.[16] His depiction of Exchange Alley, the area of narrow streets and coffeehouses where brokers who had been expelled from the Royal Exchange traded in stocks, centered on the repellent character of Jewish dealers: "The Alley throngs with Jews, Jobbers and Brokers, their names are needless, their Characters dirty as their employment, and the best thing that I can yet find out to say of them, is, that there happens to be two honest Men among them."[17]

The collapse of the speculative frenzy known as the South Sea Bubble in 1720 brought to the surface thinly veiled resentments against Jews, which, as we will see, had already emerged in the United Provinces after the Amsterdam stock market took a sudden plunge in 1688.[18] In times of exuberant speculation, exaltation of the virtues of commerce often gave way to conservative critiques: opportunists tricked naïve investors, gambled on the fictional value of paper instruments, and endangered the well-being of the country for the sole purpose of advancing their station. Theatrical representations satirized the promise of social mobility that credit offered and often resorted to Jewish characters to do so.[19] Many of these critiques had clear political connotations. As Jonathan Karp has noted, the Tory Party—the defender of landed interests and values—turned the figure of the Jewish "stockjobber" (a term heavily used in the public sphere after 1720) into a weapon of propaganda against Whig campaigns in favor of expanding overseas trade and the power of the Bank of England.[20]

Lord Bolingbroke and his Tory supporters were the most vocal but not the only detractors of the paper economy. David Hume, like Montesquieu, famously despised the public debt more than private credit.[21] Adam Smith, who had witnessed the effects of the Panic of 1772 in Scotland, described in detail the advantages of banknotes and bills of exchange but also warned about the risks brought by the "excessive circulation of paper money," that is, the imbalance between banknotes and bills of exchange in circulation and a country's bullion reserves. In condemning such excesses, Smith invoked Greek mythology rather than anti-Jewish clichés, contrasting "the Dædalian wings of paper money" with "the solid ground of gold and silver."[22] Those who espoused the anticommercial ethos of classical republicanism were more likely to borrow from the stockpile of anti-Jewish rhetoric. Writing from London in 1786, John Adams urged Thomas Jefferson to strengthen Congress' control over public finance. His outsized fear that European speculators might bring the United States to its knees found expression in terms that we have come to recognize: "Jews and Judaizing Christians are now scheming to buy up all our continental notes at two or three shillings in the pound, in order to oblige us to pay them at twenty shillings. This will be richer plunder than that of Algerines, or Lloyd's coffee houses."[23] Here, as in other instances, the boundaries between private and public credit were blurred.

In England as in France, metaphorical invocations of Jews not only greatly exaggerated Jews' economic roles but also obscured real differences within Jewish society, and especially the gulf that separated affluent from impoverished Jews. The "Jew" in these narratives was either a treacherous moneylender or a masterful bond manipulator, both of which were seen as varieties of usurers. It was arguably with these images in mind that readers made sense of the references to the medieval Jewish invention of bills of exchange they encountered in English-language texts. Elizabethan literature, in which usury loomed large, did not attribute the invention of marine insurance or bills of exchange to Jews. Nor was the Jewish origin of these instruments mentioned in the earliest English treatises devoted solely to bills of exchange.[24] Rather, more or less literal translations of the Savarys and Montesquieu were the primary sources of the tale across the Channel.[25] The authority of these French texts and the ways in which translators adapted them thus proved decisive in shaping the legend's reception. The writing of early modern merchant manuals and related works was not unlike that of encyclopedias: it relied on educated plagiarism. Some English merchant manuals translated Savary's chapter on the origins of bills of exchange faithfully.[26] Others produced imitations and pastiches that generated new twists in the legend.[27] Still others omitted the tale altogether.[28]

The delayed blossoming of English dictionaries of trade made them less susceptible to tales of origins. By the mid-eighteenth century, the evolution of European commercial society from a barter system to one based on money and finally paper credit instruments such as bills of exchange was an accepted narrative, even if exactly how the latter had come into being remained the subject of much speculation. Wyndham Beawes's *Lex mercatoria rediviva*, one of the most frequently reprinted English merchant manuals of the period, was agnostic about whether marine insurance had been invented by Roman emperor Claudius (as per Suetonius) or by French Jews in 1182 (as the Savarys claimed) but was certain that it had been brought into England "by some Italians from Lombardy, who at the same time came to settle at Antwerp" (the standard assumption to this day).[29] With regard to bills of exchange, Beawes was equally torn, debating whether they had been invented by Jews banished from France under Philip Augustus and Philip the Tall or, "with a greater appearance of probability," by the Florentine Ghibellines who sought refuge in Lyon.[30]

The most authoritative and original engagement with the legend by a British author came from the pen of the prominent judge and jurist Sir William Blackstone (1723–1780). In his *Commentaries on the Laws of England*, he accepted the gist of the tale (that persecution had led to invention) but claimed a role for the English crown. The invention of bills of exchange, Blackstone wrote, occurred when Jews were "banished out of Guienne in 1297, and out of England in 1290." At the time of the supposed events, the duchy of Guyenne was an English possession. By juxtaposing the two regions and the two dates, Blackstone sought to bring the story into an English domain and ensured that his account was incorporated into the *Encyclopædia Britannica*.[31]

Overall, the legend met with considerable skepticism in England. One author qualified it as a product of French patriotism and declared it "extremely improbable."[32] The first comprehensive English treatment of marine insurance, published in 1787, relayed the versions given by both the Savarys and Montesquieu but concluded that the origin of marine insurance "is involved in so much obscurity" that no satisfactory explanation could be offered.[33] Following unusual reasoning, another author described the development of bills of exchange as "a little uncertain" but ultimately backed the idea that Jews were their inventors, "because I have observed that, generally speaking, the Jews to this day practice this kind of commerce most, and understand it best of any people in the world."[34] This is the only instance I have encountered of an author invoking firsthand experience to maintain that Jews' commercial conduct was consistent with the spirit of the legend and thus confirmed its veracity. Meanwhile, a translation of a German work at the close of the century introduced a new criterion for dismissing the legend: empirical verification. In 1690, Jacques Dupuis de la Serra had questioned the tale on account of its incoherence (chapter 5); now the legend was rejected because "no proof" supported it.[35]

Only the followers of Montesquieu, fewer in Britain than on the Continent, clung to the positive depiction of Jews as having devised financial instruments able to undercut autocratic rulers and promote the flow of private credit. The translation of Montesquieu's *The Spirit of the Laws* into English (1750) and the simultaneous publication of Beccaria's *A Discourse on Public Œconomy and Commerce* (1769) in Italian, French, and English popularized the nexus between Jews' persecution and their inventiveness, a connection that economic writer Thomas Mortimer (1730–1810) repeated without any shadow of a doubt.[36] Montesquieu's version of the legend was also echoed in several prefaces to technical works on bills of exchange, on which it conferred a historical veneer.[37] But its real megaphone was Sir James Steuart (1713–1780), a Jacobite lord who lived in exile until 1763. Steuart's treatise on political economy could not compete in originality with the economic writings of such giants of his time as Quesnay, Cantillon, Turgot, Hume, and Smith, but it is estimated that outside of Britain, through the 1780s, it was better known and more frequently cited than *The Wealth of Nations*.[38] Steuart followed Montesquieu's version of the legend closely, but he too added his own touches: while Montesquieu regarded bills of exchange as the preeminent credit instrument of private merchants who sought to escape the rapaciousness of despotic rulers, Steuart included the legend in a vigorous defense of public credit.[39]

In short, the legend met a dual reception in England, as it had in France: works indebted to Cleirac or the Savarys cast Jews in a negative light but also led to a search for more stringent empirical verification, while those that followed Montesquieu placed Jews on a pedestal and dispensed with the need for accuracy. In England, however, Montesquieu's version was marginalized and the legend never figured in contentious debates about the political status of Jews. In fact, by comparing the fate of the legend in France and Britain, we find that the political impact of representations of Jews' economic roles on the two sides of the Channel was not as divergent as is usually believed.

John Toland, the earliest proponent of granting prosperous Jews who relocated to Britain the status of subjects of the crown ("naturalization"), insisted that Jews made vital contributions to international trade and did not demand that they be "regenerated," but he was an unconventional figure. In 1714, Toland, an Irish Catholic who first converted to Anglicanism and later renounced Christianity altogether, published a pamphlet marshaling economic arguments in favor of allowing all Jews in the kingdom to be recognized as subjects of the crown.[40] He was writing at a time of fierce disputes about the terms under which foreign Protestants should be naturalized. His pamphlet appeared in the same year that the Whigs regained control of Parliament. In 1753,

Parliament passed the "Jewish Naturalization Act" allowing affluent foreign-born Jews to become subjects of the crown without taking the sacrament (a privilege that would entitle them, among other things, to enter all branches of trade and own ships). Another defender of this act, the Anglican reverend Josiah Tucker, who was also an effective polemicist and economic writer, spilled considerable ink to argue, counter to prevailing views, that this policy promoted British commercial interests.[41]

Naturalization in mid-eighteenth-century Britain was an elite phenomenon rather than a political and legal status analogous to postrevolutionary French citizenship, yet it succeeded in stirring up an enormous uproar. Those opposing it mounted a vicious public campaign, waged by means of pamphlets, newspaper articles, sermons, plays, etchings, and public gatherings. In the end, the so-called "Jew Bill" was revoked. Neither its promoters nor its detractors seem to have invoked the legend of the Jewish invention of financial instruments in favor of or against it, but the resistance to the act proved ingrained stereotypes about Jewish usury to be stronger than the efforts to yoke Jewish commercial prowess to pro-naturalization arguments. In the many satires that circulated at the time, "Jews were widely represented as speculators and plundering usurers."[42] The protagonist of one sketch, "Mr. Judas the Broker," is illustrative of such representations: a shadowy figure, Mr. Judas is willing to sell stocks in defiance of the Bubble Act, which in the aftermath of the 1720 crash forbade joint-stock companies lacking a royal charter from trading their shares.[43]

In France, as we saw, advocates of Jewish emancipation avoided pro-commercial arguments in making their case (chapter 6).[44] In Britain, such arguments were marshaled in favor of the more modest proposal of granting naturalization to a select group of prosperous Jews, but they backfired because large segments of the public perceived Jews as selfish speculators. Only in 1867 did adult male Jews gain the right to vote in Britain.

Holy Roman Empire

Savary's *Le parfait négociant* appeared in German translation in 1676, a year after the French original, and became the earliest vehicle for the legend's transmission into the German-language commercial and legal literature.[45] Montesquieu's influence followed in time. With regard to the claim that Jews might have invented marine insurance and/or bills of exchange, eighteenth-century German economic writers confirmed their well-known debt to French authors. But by reconstructing the trajectory of the legend and the objections to it, we can go a step further to map the landscape of German debates on the morality of commercial society and its relationship to the state during the eighteenth century. In the Holy Roman Empire, as elsewhere, this issue was treated in different, if overlapping, genres: merchant handbooks, which were most directly modeled on that of Savary; legal disquisitions on the origins of mercantile contracts, a literature largely unknown in Britain because of the feebler influence that Roman law exerted there; encyclopedias, some devoted to universal knowledge, others to trade alone; Cameralism, an amorphous and distinctively German tradition of academic writing on the economy and the fiscal needs of the state aimed at administrators and government officials; and, finally, treatises on the emerging "science of commerce" by Francophile admirers of Montesquieu.

Mentions of Jews crop up in all of these genres and yet have been overlooked by scholars of both German political economy and central European Jews. These mentions are indebted to the manifold traditions we have examined so far but also reflect the conditions of regional and international trade in central Europe and the circumstances in which Jews lived and worked there. The stock market, essentially a London and Amsterdam institution (the Paris Bourse took off slowly only during the last quarter of the eighteenth century), was absent from central Europe during this time. Overall, the Jewish presence in Prussia, Austria, and the smaller German principalities and city-states was spotty and marked by tense relations with sovereigns and neighbors. Hamburg was the exception: in 1612 the Senate won its battle with the Lutheran clergy and allowed a small number of Sephardic merchants engaged in Atlantic trade to settle in the city-state with their families. A few Jewish merchants, most of them from Germany or Poland, were also active at the international fairs of Leipzig and Frankfurt am Main, which experienced a revival in the eighteenth century.[46]

The social structure of the Jewish communities in the Habsburg Empire was strictly pyramidal, with the mass of poor folks excluded from artisanal professions and confined to small-scale retail topped by a few so-called court Jews, wealthy financiers and army suppliers who negotiated basic privileges for the entire community in return for their services to the ruler. Jews across the German-speaking territories were thus vulnerable to the will of the sovereign and were largely identified with poverty and criminality. In spite of these conditions, Christian merchants perceived even the poorest Jewish shopkeepers, salesmen, and peddlers as competitors and lamented their ostensibly excessive economic power, as shown by the 1672 "Petitions of the Estates to the Great Elector" of Brandenburg-Prussia.[47] A century later, a prominent economic writer condemned all peddlers, and Jews in particular, for the poor quality of their merchandise.[48]

More than their contemporaries elsewhere, German Orientalists and Biblical scholars produced virulent attacks on Judaism under the guise of learned exposés, joining new scholarly expertise with older theological polemics. Johann Andreas Eisenmenger's 1700 *Entdecktes Judenthum* (*Judaism Unmasked*) was the most hateful of these works, but many more, including one by the noted Johannes David Michaelis, relied on Hebraica to demonstrate Jews' alleged inferiority and lack of respect toward Christians.[49] In less scholarly publications, the portrait of Jews was rarely more favorable. By the late 1740s, writers like Christian Fürchtegott Gellert and, more famously, Gotthold Ephraim Lessing were offering positive representations of virtuous Jewish merchants. However, these works have stood the test of time not only because of their literary achievements but also because they rejected the then-dominant association of commerce with fraud, and with the Jews who symbolized it. Now forgotten are many more unremarkable texts that aired more conventional views.[50] To a certain Johann Ludolf Holst, a law graduate and resident of Hamburg, the city with the largest resident community of international Jewish merchants in the Holy Roman Empire, we owe an extensive and unsympathetic treatment of the economic roles of Jews.[51]

Emancipation was not imminent in central Europe. The 1782 Edict of Toleration of Habsburg emperor Joseph II paled in comparison to the privileges that Catholic states like Venice and Tuscany had granted Jews two centuries earlier. But because of the insistence of a few reformist voices, Jewish and gentile alike, the question of the "civic improvement" of Jews made its way into German-language works. Written on behalf of the Jews of Alsace, Christian Wilhelm von Dohm's case for granting civic and political rights to Jews was more audacious than any other to date, and it was built on knowledge and arguments that German authors had debated for half a century.[52] Dohm's treatise, however, had a more immediate impact in France, where it inspired debates in favor of and against Jewish emancipation (chapter 6), than it did in the Holy Roman Empire.[53]

Seeking to instruct future administrators on how to strengthen the welfare of their polities, Cameralist textbooks outlined methods to boost demographic growth (which was seen as the source and proof of all riches) and improve output in agriculture, manufacturing, and mining. Neither private nor public finance was key to Cameralist authors. Private finance appeared to them extraneous to the economic sphere of government administration, while the public debt was a moot topic because German rulers borrowed from bankers rather than subjects. By contrast, private credit was a more important theme in merchant handbooks, which owed a great deal to Savary and his sons. Two authors were instrumental in disseminating the legend of the Jewish invention of bills of exchange as part of their efforts to emulate French compilers of dictionaries of trade: Paul Jacob Marperger (1656–1730) and Carl Günter Ludovici (1707–1778).[54] A member of the Prussian Royal Society of Sciences, Marperger served as a commercial court judge and took upon himself the task of assembling "the unwritten merchant laws or their so-called style" in order to guide judges like himself and other bureaucrats overseeing commercial disputes and councils. A professor of philosophy and later rector of the University of Leipzig, Ludovici invested considerable energy in large editorial projects, including the completion of a dictionary conceived by Johann Heinrich Zedler (1706–1763) that proved a monument of eighteenth-century German encyclopedic knowledge.[55] All these projects relied greatly on the Savary brothers' *Dictionnaire universel de commerce*.

Through the usual mixture of deliberate plagiarism and thoughtless reproductions, the legend of the Jewish origin of bills of exchange that the Savarys had canonized infiltrated these German-language works. But German writers also expressed more doubts about it than their French counterparts. In 1709 Marperger relayed the legend of the Jewish invention of bills of exchange in full (including the names of the medieval French kings cited by Savary as responsible for banishing Jews from the Kingdom) but concluded that "it is more likely that the Ghibellines, who were expelled from Italy by the Guelph faction and for the most part moved to Germany and to the Low Countries, were responsible for the first real beginning of the trade in bills of exchange."[56] He gave a clearer reason for preferring an Italian source over a Jewish one a few years later in a book dedicated specifically to the history and functions of banks. There, he added that he was "certain that, as the Italians are clever tradesmen down to this very day and since most of the institutions that serve and facilitate maritime commerce come from them, the useful practice of banks must, too."[57] Zedler's *Lexicon* took notice of Marperger's update but also asserted that medieval French Jews invented marine insurance.[58] When Ludovici undertook his adaptation of the dictionary compiled by the Savary brothers, he drew from the *Lexicon* as well.[59]

Overall, German authors tended to credit Italians rather than Jews with having expanded medieval commercial and banking activities. Today we know that their hypothesis is sounder than the rival interpretation focusing on Jews, but we also reject the wisdom of looking for a single point of origin for any complex phenomenon. Early signs of diffidence toward this search became visible at the beginning of the eighteenth century. As the proliferation of didactic multivolume compilations led to the mechanical reproduction of various tales of origins, German authors questioned the legend's soundness more than readers elsewhere. A prolific author, Marperger changed his mind on the matter: only five years after he endorsed the idea that Ghibellines had invented bills of exchange, he aired an altogether different theory, arguing that these credit instruments were born out of the needs of long-distance trade.[60] In yet another major compilation about "the science of commerce," Ludovici, under the influence of Dupuis de la Serra, followed suit: while endorsing a probable Florentine origin, he also insisted that all financial contracts were a spontaneous response to the increasing complexity of international commerce.[61]

Legal scholars also injected a healthy dose of skepticism about the putatively Jewish invention of marine insurance and bills of exchange into the debate. Steeped in Roman law, German jurists before and after the Reformation were equally versed in Scholastic and canonistic debates on usury. Those of Protestant confession, including the noted Wolfgang Adam Lauterbach (1618–1678), a member of the faculty of law in Tübingen, were more likely to reject Aristotelian doctrines about the sterility of money and defend the legitimacy of credit instruments.[62] More generally, all jurists scrutinized the contractual nature of marine insurance and bills of exchange. By stating that "insurance policies and bills of exchange were unknown to Roman jurisprudence," Cleirac had intervened—correctly—in lively and consequential debates about the existence or absence of Roman law antecedents of the contractual obligations that fueled Europe's commercial expansion (chapter 3). German jurisprudence refined this point of contention. Discussions of maritime and commercial law, the bulk of which appeared in Latin dissertations, generally omitted any reference to the legend. Instead, they offered lengthy digressions on the dubious use of Cicero and other classical authors as evidence of the Roman origins of modern credit instruments.[63] As part of these inquiries, a few German jurists discovered Cleirac's *Us et coustumes de la mer* and, with it, the fabled story of the Jewish invention of marine insurance and bills of exchange, but their interest in the Bordelais author had more to do with the range of legal sources for the study of maritime law he provided, particularly the first modern edition of the Laws of Oléron.[64]

While German authors subjected the legend to empirical scrutiny, Montesquieu's influence once again pushed interpretation in the opposite direction, encouraging the view that the tale was unquestionably true and conveying an uplifting message. Even before *The Spirit of the Laws* was translated into

German in 1782, many German scholars had read it in French.[65] No one drew more inspiration from it than Jakob Friedrich von Bielfeld (1717–1770), a graduate of Leiden University and court master of Prince Augustus Ferdinand of Prussia. In reproducing Montesquieu's account of the Jewish invention of bills of exchange, Bielfeld applauded those "good princes" who chose to protect the tiny pieces of paper that had become "sacred" to the entire *Europe commerçante*.[66]

As a result of these multiple influences, by the end of the eighteenth century a broad spectrum of theories about the origins of European credit instruments characterized German economic literature, ranging from full endorsements of the legend[67] to the preference for an Italian beginning[68] and the outright rejection of the possibility of pinning down a single inventor.[69] One prolific mathematics teacher in Hamburg, Johann Georg Büsch (1728–1800), held different views over the course of his lifetime.[70]

Out of this heterogeneity, one adaptation stands out because less than a century later it would become a commonplace explanation among German academics of the decline of Jews' presumed economic supremacy in the early Middle Ages and the rise of postmedieval Europe (chapter 8). The Cameralist writer Friedrich Christoph Jonathan Fischer (1750–1797) sought to claim pride of place for medieval German merchants in the history of the origins of bills of exchange and, possibly, marine insurance. He argued that those inventions appeared at a time when the ingenuity of Christian merchants had been stimulated by a desire to free themselves from the domination of "Jews and Lombards." For Fischer, "Christians could not watch indifferently the benefits that Jews and Lombards derived from their trade in money and from their business in bills of exchange [*Wechselgeschäft*]."[71] As the next chapter will show, the doyen of the German Historical School, Wilhelm Roscher, would later elaborate on this idea that, having copied Jews' financial devices, Christians grew envious of their skills. One of the most influential narratives of the rise of European commerce and antisemitism therefore had its roots in a twist of the legend with which we are grappling.

Italian Peninsula

In spite of the wide resonance that Montesquieu's work had with Italian Enlightenment figures, the legend of the Jewish invention of bills of exchange left only scant footprints on the Italian peninsula. There, a long tradition of merchant manuals and treatises on maritime and commercial law dating back to the late Middle Ages had fostered considerable knowledge of these credit instruments and their historical evolution. In 1641, six years before the publication of Cleirac's *Us et coustumes de la mer*, a Latin treatise on exchange dealings likened their development to a river formed from a multiplicity of small contributory streams—a metaphor that signaled the impossibility of determining with precision where the river originated.[72] The Jewish presence on the peninsula was also radically different from that in southwestern France. During the sixteenth century, under the dual pressure of ecclesiastical and state authorities, Iberian Jews fleeing to Venice, Livorno, and the Papal States were given shelter as long as they relinquished their Christian identity. As a consequence, crypto-Judaism was a relatively short-lived phenomenon in Italy.

The tendency of Italian writers to claim the invention of bills of exchange for their ancestors also contributed to their rejection of the legend. In the earliest refutation of Cleirac, in 1690, Dupuis de la Serra proposed that the honor of having invented early credit instruments go to Florentine émigrés to Lyon. Predictably, this hypothesis met with a warm reception in Italy, where its spread was aided by a Latin and Italian translation of Dupuis de la Serra.[73] Giuseppe Lorenzo Maria Casaregi (1670–1737), a jurist and preeminent scholar of commercial law, followed Dupuis de la Serra's account in attributing the invention of bills of exchange to Guelf expatriates in Lyon, thus correcting the references that peppered the French literature treating Guelfs and Ghibellines as interchangeable groups.[74] Several other Tuscan commentators naturally welcomed this theory. Some stressed the Florentines' refugee status. Others, like Giovan Francesco Pagnini (1714–1789), a scholar of agrarian reforms and finance and a high official in the Tuscan Habsburg government, emphasized their leadership in international banking.[75]

In Livorno, the Italian city with the highest proportion of Jewish residents and the most tolerant policies toward them, the brothers Pompeo and Ascanio Baldasseroni, authors of treatises on exchange dealings and marine insurance, respectively, confirmed their preference for the Florentine origin of bills of exchange. Pompeo declared that Tuscany should count not only Galileo Galilei and Amerigo Vespucci among its "glories," but also the inventors of bills of exchange.[76] For Ascanio, Savary and Beawes were not to be trusted. Although he argued that Jews displayed a "natural inclination" for trade in bills of exchange and excelled at that activity, he asked that equal if not more credence be given to the Florentine hypothesis.[77] A Genoese author had little to add except to mark his territory in the perpetual rivalry between Italian city-states, paying homage to the role that the Genoese, not just the Florentines, had played in spreading the invention of bills of exchange.[78]

Despite the mounting dismissal of the legend by those most versed in the legal and practical facets of commerce, Montesquieu's version of the tale of Jewish invention insinuated itself into the works of the most influential figures of the Italian Enlightenment. Between 1754 and 1779, five academic chairs in what came to be known as political economy, which at the time was described alternately as "the science of commerce," "mechanics and commerce," "economic sciences," or "civil economy," were established in Naples, Milan, Modena, Catania, and Palermo. The occupants of the first two, Antonio Genovesi in Naples (1712–1769) and Cesare Beccaria in Milan (1738–1794), were also the most notable. They differed in their depiction of Jews' role in the making of European commercial society, but both discussed the topic.

Genovesi was, along with Ferdinando Galiani (1728–1787), the leading figure of the Neapolitan Enlightenment. His *Delle lezioni di commercio* (1765–1767) represented the culmination of an effort to synthesize a traditional eighteenth-century conception of commerce as promoting friendship between peoples and nations with the growing impetus, modeled on Newtonian science and pioneered by Galiani, to devise universal laws for the economy. The book was very well received and, as its numerous translations testify, earned Genovesi a place in the European pantheon of scholars who broke ground in the emerging field of political economy. In a chapter devoted to paper money ("Della moneta di carta"), he praised bills of exchange for supporting foreign trade and paper money for facilitating domestic trade. He also maintained that persecuted Jews at the time of the Crusades began to use bills of exchange in order to bring their assets abroad safely, implying that they had had a role in the early use of those instruments but also that it was a role that did not coincide with the Christian goal of reconquering the Holy Land.[79]

Other references to Jews in the rest of Genovesi's work revealed a darker view of their economic roles than had been found in Montesquieu, whom he echoed only in assuming that "during the barbarous times that followed Greek and Latin politeness [*politezza*]," Jews dominated trade. Genovesi took it upon himself to enumerate the evils of Jewish moneylending, which he declared "reached up to 30 and 40 and 100" percent interest rates until charitable lending institutions set up by Franciscan friars (the *Monti di pietà*) put an end to those "bloody usuries."[80] Writing from Naples, a city that had chased Jews out in the early sixteenth century (except for a brief interlude in the 1740s), Genovesi depicted Jews as parasitical pawnbrokers and thus deviated from Montesquieu's template.

Not so Cesare Beccaria, the celebrated author of the first European treatise condemning torture and the death penalty, who did not stray far at all from Montesquieu, offering an equally positive portrait of Jewish involvement in the creation of modern commercial society. On the occasion of his appointment to his chair in Milan in 1769, Beccaria delivered a speech that painted in broad strokes the historical process by which European commerce had achieved its dominance. Published simultaneously in Italian, French, and English, this brief text circulated widely. Beccaria glossed over the details and resorted to a more cautious formulation whereby Jews did not necessarily invent but certainly "*had recourse to* [*ricorrono* in the Italian original, *recourent* in the French translation] the invention of bills of exchange to save their treasures from the rapaciousness of tyrannical inquisitions."[81] Paraphrasing Montesquieu, Beccaria also praised bills of exchange for their ability to "augment to a great degree the certainty and readiness of communication among the trading nations."[82] He used commerce and communication as synonyms and viewed bills of exchange as the pillars of both. Like Montesquieu, Beccaria portayed Jews as having invented a tool of resistance against tyranny.[83] Adapting another adage dear to Montesquieu, he grouped bills of exchange with the compass and the Spanish and Portuguese transoceanic explorations, the two other apexes of Western civilization, and added a patriotic touch by singling out the contributions of the Italian "genius" Christopher Columbus.

Montesquieu's authoritativeness at this time was so great that few dared to disprove him. One exception was the Tuscan physician, botanist, and geographer Giovanni Targioni Tozzetti (1712–1783), who challenged the philosophe's account of the birth of bills of exchange and did so, unlike Dupuis de la Serra, on strictly empirical grounds. Describing a manuscript containing the works of the noted thirteenth-century Pisan mathematician Leonardo Fibonacci, Tozzetti remarked that bills of exchange had been well known in Pisa at that time and concluded that both Montesquieu's anecdote and any accounts attributing the invention of bills of exchange to Florentine émigrés in Lyon were proven wrong by this text.[84] When Domenico Alberto Azuni (1749–1827), a foremost jurist and theorist of commercial law, took on the task of updating the Savary brothers' dictionary of commerce, he incorporated Tozzetti's correction.[85] In so doing, he not only exalted Tuscany's precocious capitalist development, but also proved the value of source criticism.

Both the supporters and the detractors of the legend of the Jewish invention of bills of exchange in eighteenth-century Italy discussed the tale with little regard for the actual status of Jews living on the peninsula. The one exception was a debate that ensued in Mantua, a town then under Habsburg rule that in the 1770s and 1780s became the fulcrum of reformist initiatives and bitter counterattacks on them. The Jewish community in Mantua traced its origins to the twelfth century and boasted scholars and rabbis of great repute who epitomized the Ashkenazic-Italian tradition predating the arrival of Iberian refugees in the sixteenth century. Thanks to a rich manufacturing tradition, they were not as impoverished as the Jews of Alsace and Lorraine; nevertheless, they were poorer and less acculturated than the Sephardic merchants living in Venice and Livorno.[86] In the early 1780s, the local nobleman Giovanni Battista Gherardo D'Arco (1739–1791) and the Jewish physician and *maskil* (Enlightened scholar) Benedetto Frizzi, also known as Benzion Rafael Kohen (1756–1844), engaged in an acrimonious debate about the Jews' civic rights (or lack thereof) and in the process rehearsed trite arguments about the economic functions of Jews in Christian society.

A self-styled physiocrat, D'Arco submitted a formulaic tribute to the civilizing properties of commerce to a prize competition sponsored by the Royal Academy of Marseilles. Denouncing the harm caused by monopolies, he pointed to Jewish businesses as his prime example.[87] After his work was rejected by the French committee, D'Arco expanded on his view of Jews' pernicious economic dominance, which he regarded as inseparable from their deviant religious beliefs, in a book with the ominous title *On the Influence of the Ghetto on the State*, which advocated curbing Jewish self-government in the wake of the 1782 Habsburg Edict of Toleration. Borrowing arguments that we have encountered before, and which the Turin jurist Giuseppe Sessa had recently reiterated, D'Arco praised Maria Theresa's decision to expel Jews from Prague in 1745 as a way of eradicating their "asocial egotism" (*egoismo insociale*).[88]

This was the central accusation that Frizzi sought to rebut. Persecution, he maintained, had made Jews circumspect rather than fraudulent, and commerce had instilled in them moderation and allowed them to perform multiple services to the state. He praised Jews not only for excelling at but also for inventing banking activities when expelled from France, as well as for spreading those techniques to all maritime states, including Venice, Amsterdam, and Bordeaux.[89] Writing after Dohm, Frizzi went further than other contemporary Jewish apologists to extol the financial skills of Jews, but he did so in a context in which full emancipation was not on the table (indeed, he argued for more rather than less Jewish corporate self-government). He did not, however, go as far as taking credit for his people's supposed invention of bills of exchange— a telling omission.

Iberia

The legend reached Iberia late and had only a slight influence on Spanish and Portuguese debates on the morality of commerce. There are many reasons for its low profile. Early modern Iberian economic thought arguably peaked in the sixteenth century, when moral theologians and a few lay authors produced some of the most sophisticated explanations of the growing credit economy. As in Italy, these writers had a deep knowledge of exchange dealings, the emergence of which they attributed to the natural progression from barter to money and the need to find alternatives to the transport and conversion of minted coins.[90] During the economic decline of the seventeenth century, advisors and critics of the crown, the so-called *arbitristas*, concentrated on proposing reforms of fiscal and commercial policies. By the eighteenth century, Spanish and Portuguese economic literature had become more dependent on foreign currents of thought and focused on the governance of mainland and imperial territories.

Imported from abroad, the legend arrived in Iberia via the translations of Bielfeld and Genovesi. A brief if affirming reference to it appeared in terms that echoed Montesquieu in a compilation of the Catalan polymath and editor of medieval Barcelona's *Libro del consulado del mar*, Antonio de Capmany y Montpalau (1742–1813).[91] A different treatise, devoted entirely to bills of exchange, cited Savary and Villani alongside the refutation of their narrative by Dupuis de la Serra.[92] Bernardo Danvila, a Valencian jurist and scion of a mercantile family, listed multiple possibilities for the origin of bills of exchange, including the Jewish hypothesis, in a chapter on money in his lectures on commerce.[93]

In the Portuguese world, as elsewhere, scholars rediscovered Cleirac in the last quarter of the eighteenth century, when Enlightenment reformists were advocating the passage of new comprehensive codes. While reading Cleirac as a source of earlier maritime laws, some were also drawn to the legend. The Brazilian economist, jurist, and historian José da Silva Lisboa, Baron and Viscount of Cairu, relied on Cleirac's *Us et coustumes de la mer* to compile his own principles of maritime law, in which he recalled various theories about the origins of bills of exchange, including the one attributing their invention to Jews fleeing France in 1182.[94]

Proponents of economic liberalization at the close of the eighteenth century also clung to the legend, with some embracing more benign versions than others. A treatise inspired by French physiocrats criticized the Spanish crown for expelling Moriscos, whom it described as refined artisans and farmers. Surveying the sources of a state's wealth (agriculture, taxes, the arts, industry, money, and coinage), that work referred to the legend to account for the shift from metal currency to bills of exchange and singled out Jews who were forced to flee England and France in the twelfth and thirteenth centuries. They deposited their assets with people they trusted, the author relayed, and thus drew up written documents that served as models for bills of exchange. In a seemingly neutral tone, he concluded that "the discovery of this secret, which probably existed before among the Jews because of their usuries, facilitated commercial operations."[95] The laissez-faire economist José Alonso Ortiz also noted that most of the authors he consulted attributed the invention of bills of exchange to persecuted Jews from the times of the Crusades. Ortiz did not defend the idea that Jews invented these bills but expressed certainty that they were among the first to have used them. How could he be so sure? Because Jews' permanent displacement ("la condición errante de estas gentes") and continuous persecution had led them to specialize in commerce, he declared, so much so that "they have always been the richest merchants in Europe."[96]

This assumption went unchallenged in a region that had freed itself of Jews 300 years earlier and where commerce and finance had gained only partial acceptance. Sporadic as these mentions of the legend were on the Iberian peninsula, they were never accompanied by demands for evidence, a reflex that elsewhere in Europe was corroding the credibility of the idea that the most advanced credit instruments were the brainchild of persecuted medieval Jews.

United Provinces

Once they gained independence from the Spanish Low Countries, the Calvinist United Provinces went further than any other early modern European state in removing usury from the domain of moral theology and ecclesiastical power and placing it in the sphere of civil law. In 1658, the estates of Holland and West Friesland ruled that "the question of moneys loaned by banks does not fall within the jurisdiction of church boards, classes, or synods, but comes under the supervision of the civil government," which takes it upon itself to protect the poor and "to ensure profit for the majority of the population."[97] As the phrasing of this norm implied, civil authorities saw themselves as being able to both let merchants lending at interest and shield the poor from economic exploitation. Did they succeed?

The artwork of the Dutch Golden Age, Simon Schama has shown, not only celebrated opulence but also offered an opportunity for reflection on the ills of profligacy.[98] But the visual arts were only the most striking vehicle used by elite Dutch culture to express moral concerns about the ubiquity of credit. The printing press did its part, too. The legend of the Jewish invention of marine insurance and bills of exchange, however, did not establish a firm footing in the Dutch commercial literature. This is all the more remarkable given that Dutch was the second language after German into which Savary's *Le parfait négociant* was translated in 1683.[99] It is tempting to jump to the quick conclusion that Amsterdam, the most tolerant city in early modern Europe, offered unparalleled safeguards to its Jewish population and therefore proved impermeable to a legend that, in most renditions, vilified Jews. The hypothesis is plausible, but we need to consider at least two other elements when trying to make sense of the lack of traction that the legend gained in the United Provinces. The first is the relative paucity of handbooks and dictionaries about trade that were written and published in Dutch compared to English, in spite of the pervasiveness of commerce in both societies. The second is the tendency of Dutch authors to invoke Jews to express disapproval of the excesses of the stock market rather than bills of exchange, a trait more consonant with a phenomenon we have already seen in England.

The United Provinces, a major hub of international trade, produced a remarkably small fraction of the Continent's *ars mercatoria*. The Dutch population had generally high literacy rates and consumed a great deal of printed economic information in the form of broadsheets, price and stock lists, auction sale advertisements, and other ephemera. Moreover, some of Europe's most influential theorists of republicanism and international and natural law, from the De La Court brothers to Hugo Grotius, not only were born in Holland but also voiced the intellectual and political predicaments of the milieus in which they lived. Nevertheless, eighteenth-century Dutch printing houses issued fewer merchant dictionaries and manuals than their English, French, and German counterparts, and most of those that were issued offered hands-on instructions rather than investigating the historical and philosophical aspects of commerce.[100]

Among the exceptions is a manual compiled by the Huguenot refugee Jacques Le Moine de L'Espine, which appeared simultaneously in French and Dutch in Amsterdam in 1694 as *La négoce d'Amsterdam/Den koophandel van Amsterdam*. Ten years later, a revised Dutch edition opened with a chapter on the origins of bills of exchange that mixed together bits and pieces from

Cleirac and Savary to relay the legend as a matter of fact.[101] This text proved to be incredibly popular, with a total of twelve Dutch editions repeating the story of how Jews expelled from France invented bills of exchange. But aside from its inclusion in this well-liked merchant manual, the legend did not figure in many other works, except for the anonymous *De koopman* (*The Merchant*), a collection of commonplaces that appeared later in the century.[102] Nor did it enter the learned disquisitions of legal scholars.[103]

This is not to say that references to Jews were absent from Dutch public commentaries on commerce and finance. For both those who welcomed it and those who resented it, the presence of a sizable Jewish community in the heart of Holland was predicated on its real and preceived economic contributions to the commonwealth. In 1692, an anonymous piece published in the Dutch periodical *Histoire des ouvrages des savants* (1687–1709) put it bluntly: Jews "are tolerated for no other reason than the advantages that they bring to commerce," in spite of the fact that "there is nothing that is more odious to Christianity."[104] Others voiced more benevolent opinions of Jews' economic influence, if only to advance their own political agenda. In 1673, an English pamphleteer expressed his admiration for Dutch political economy by praising Amsterdam as a city that used to have nothing by way of commerce until it welcomed the Jews expelled from Iberia.[105]

In times of financial crisis these stereotypes quickly acquired a more menacing tone, and Jews were accused of cornering the market. Still a small presence, they received little blame for the bust in tulip bulb prices in 1637, the most massive early speculative scheme gone awry.[106] By contrast, the Amsterdam stock market crash of 1688 exposed what Jonathan Israel has called "a new strain of economic anti-Semitism rooted in the mystique of the stock market."[107] The 1720 South Sea Bubble sent shockwaves through Holland. Amid an explosion of printed material satirizing the "trade in wind," caricatures of Jews vilified the unsavory financial deals in which they allegedly engaged. Part of the blame for the South Sea disaster fell on foreigners, English and Frenchmen in particular. But the greatest blame was placed on Jews, who were accused of having swindled honest and naïve Dutchmen into making foolish investments. Faced with a possible financial meltdown, Dutch society ceased to distinguish between refined Sephardim (still the majority of Jewish stock traders in 1720) and uncouth Ashkenazim.[108]

"Smous Levi" and "Greedy Judases" became staple characters in pamphlets and theater plays.[109] One of these works depicted Harlequin, the duplicitous if endearing character of the *commedia dell'arte*, selling "wind" (instead of victuals) to a ship captain headed south: "Profit is expected in exchange for Wind; as Jew and Moonlighter try, out of selfishness, to confuse everything."[110] The trope was repeated in 1773 at the time of another financial crisis, when *De koopman* accused Portuguese Jews of encouraging rampant speculation in wind (*windhandel*) rather than commodities.[111] So widespread were these allegations that scholars have recently singled out Jean-Frédéric Bernard and Bernard Picard's multivolume book on world religions, *Ceremonies et coutumes religieuses de tous les peuples du monde*, published in Amsterdam between 1723 and 1737, as an exception to the tendency to attribute the 1720 stock market crash to Jews.[112]

In the United Provinces, the stock market was the source of much contention. The earliest European book entirely devoted to the subject appeared in Amsterdam, with the title *Confusión de confusiones*, in 1688. Its author was a Sephardic Jew, Joseph Penso de la Vega, born in Andalusia but raised in Amsterdam, where he achieved considerable notoriety. In de la Vega's lifetime, Sephardim became more and more involved in the secondary market of East India Company stock, although they never dominated it. When rumors spread that Stadholder William III was planning to invade England, ranking officials in the city of Amsterdam (all by definition Christian) were equally if not more ready than Sephardic Jews to use insider information in order to sell their East India Company stocks before they took a dive.[113]

In *Confusión de confusiones*, "a naïve Philosopher" and a "discrete Merchant" seek to understand "the mysterious affair" of the stock market; a "knowledgeable Shareholder" answers their questions in four "curious dialogues."[114] Jonathan Israel reminds us that Amsterdam Jews strongly favored (and supported financially) William of Orange's military plans but were frequently portrayed as unpatriotic. In his reading, de la Vega started to write his book precisely when news of William's expedition became public, in May 1688, and completed it after stock values plummeted in August. For Israel, one of de la Vega's aims was to cleanse the reputation of Jews, who were seen as having been instrumental in luring a great many modest people into the stock market under the false promise of certain gains.[115] Others argue instead that *Confusión de confusiones* lacked any original economic insights and aimed solely at entertaining its readers while leaving them with the sense that the stock market was a dangerous place.[116] In fact, the two interpretations are not incompatible. In the highly charged atmosphere of the time, de la Vega had every reason to embed his defense of Jews' involvement in the stock market in an entertaining text that portrayed all shareholders and brokers as callous.

In truth, there are scant explicit references to Jews in the book, which, in the words of a specialist of Dutch Jewry, "contains no reference whatsoever to halakhic issues, and in fact totally ignores any specific Jewish questions" because "the stock exchange was considered to be outside the bounds of Jewish life."[117] An indirect reference can be found in the last chapter, arguably written after the dramatic stock dive of the summer of 1688, in which de la Vega describes "the climax of the exchange transactions" and deplores a new type of share called the *ducaton*, which Jewish brokers apparently used disproportionally and which had enticed "so many men with small means" to invest in stocks and lose everything.[118]

Written in Castilian and dedicated to a fellow Sephardi, *Confusión de confusiones* made for a more entertaining read than the standard manual of instructions but was also longwinded and enigmatic. Neither a merchant nor a stock trader, de la Vega had no direct knowledge of business or its relevant technical literature.[119] Ultimately, he exploited the literary device of the dialogue as a way to avoid dogmatism and air opposing views. To counter the Philosopher's scorn of the "frightful folly" in which "gamblers and speculators" are all "double-dealers," he had the Shareholder make a detailed case for how it is possible to invest with moderation and avoid "excesses."[120]

For our purposes, it is important to note that de la Vega never hinted at the legend that attributed to medieval Jews the invention of marine insurance and bills of exchange. To set up his case, the treatise had the Merchant praise the stock market for avoiding the complications of commodity trade ("the importunities of instructions, the shipment of goods, and the circulation of bills of exchange are all so burdensome").[121] In any case, in 1688, five years after the translation of Savary's *Le parfait négociant* into Dutch, the legend only carried negative connotations in the United Provinces, so mentioning it would not have provided a defense of Jews' financial roles. That said, we should dig deeper into the ways in which early modern Jewish authors did—and did not—grapple with the legend as it spread across Europe.

Jewish Voices

Silence is difficult to interpret, but it can be loud. Few Jewish writers before emancipation broached economic subjects in works written in European vernaculars. In the seventeenth century, two rabbis, Simone Luzzatto and Menasseh ben Israel, took it upon themselves to address Christian secular authorities in Venice and London, respectively, with eloquent defenses of Jewish commerce (chapter 5). A century later, in Amsterdam, the Sephardic layman Isaac de Pinto (1717–1787), an author even more prominent than de la Vega, wrote several works in Portuguese and French. None of them, however, alluded to the possibility that Jews might have invented marine insurance or bills of exchange. Their reticence should not go unnoticed.

To counter the threat of expulsion faced by Venetian Jews in the 1630s, Luzzatto exaggerated the influence of Jewish merchants beyond any reasonable degree to demonstrate Jews' utility to society and the state. In the process, he anticipated later arguments by attributing Jews' contributions to the Venetian economy to structural conditions rather than innate skills: their geographical dispersal, exclusion from artisanal guilds and real estate ownership, and access to Ottoman markets, he posited, led Jews to specialize in overseas trade.[122] A decade before Cleirac put the legend into circulation, Luzzatto cleverly appropriated negative stereotypes about Jews' economic conduct to defend their basic existence in a seventeenth-century mercantilist state.

Luzzatto had considerable knowledge of the financial instruments used by international merchants, including bills of exchange. He probably issued the most lenient ruling a rabbi had delivered up to that moment in favor of those credit instruments that, according to stricter interpretations of Jewish law, infringed on usury prohibitions.[123] However, he did not mention the Jewish invention of bills of exchange when describing Jews' commercial talents in his plea to the Venetian authorities. Nor did Menasseh ben Israel in his "Humble Addresses" to Oliver Cromwell, which borrowed generously from Luzzatto's arguments. Ben Israel's silence is even more revealing than Luzzatto's, because his apologetics stressed the "naturall instinct" for commerce with which "Providence and mercy of God" had endowed the Jews in the diaspora.[124] His choice was in sync with that of most supporters of the 1656 readmission of Jews, among whom many were Puritans, who shunned economic arguments in favor of those predicated on religious millenarianism.[125]

Best known for his rebuttal of Voltaire's disparaging attacks on Jews, de Pinto moved in high social and literary circles in Amsterdam, Paris, and London, and even tried his hand at international diplomacy.[126] His economic writings in French, aimed at a gentile audience, largely avoided any specifically Jewish themes.[127] However, they offered forceful and learned defenses of the economic policies and attitudes that favored the types of activities in which Jews were most involved. Weighing in on a controversy that was raging at the time, de Pinto denounced the equation of luxury with corruption and challenged the physiocratic doctrines of the Marquis of Mirabeau, the Count of

Mirabeau's father, which put agriculture ahead of commerce, as well as Hume's denunciation of spiraling national debt.[128] Instead, he glorified both public and private credit. In passing, he praised Iberian Jews as honest, industrious, and good subjects, but mostly left it to his readers to infer that Jews made positive contributions to the economic activities for which he advocated.[129]

As noted earlier, we have no way of knowing whether the legend of the Jewish invention of bills of exchange existed in oral form before Cleirac published his commentary on the Rouen rules about maritime insurance. What we do know is that even if it did, Jewish authors did not embrace it as a weapon of self-defense. We also know that they hesitated to use it even after Montesquieu gave the tale of Jewish financial creativity a positive spin. De Pinto cited or echoed Montesquieu more than once in his arguments in favor of commerce but never recounted the version of the legend that appeared in *The Spirit of the Laws*. A century and a half would pass after the appearance of Cleirac's commentary of 1647 before a Jewish author felt he could commit the narrative to print.[130]

That task fell to Isaac D'Israeli, father of the future British prime minister Benjamin Disraeli, in his *Vaurien*, a minor satirical novel published in 1797 that was meant to expose the superficiality of his age. Finance was one of the novel's targets, alongside French "philosophie" and republicanism. "Enormous wealth is obtained by speculations; we have become a nation of jobbers," the book declared.[131] Unlike his Tory predecessors, D'Israeli used the term "jobbers" to refer to all Britons, not Jews alone. A fierce critic of traditional Judaism, he described Vaurien, the novel's main character, as a "Jewish philosopher," a pork-eating fellow and admirer of Moses Mendelssohn who exposes the absurdity of many prejudices targeting Jews while expressing other prejudices of his own, such as the alleged contrast between "the physiognomy as well as the customs" of Sephardic and Ashkenazic Jews.[132] For Vaurien, the Jews' "commercial character" is the result, not the cause, of their dispersal and suffering: "Christian injustice produced Jewish usury" and turned Jews into "objects of national pillage."[133] In a historical commentary appended to this fictional speech, D'Israeli added: "Despair with the Jews was the parent of invention, and bills of exchange were imagined by them."[134]

In short, D'Israeli embraced and magnified Montesquieu's positive depiction of the Jewish invention of bills of exchange. More than Montesquieu, he linked Jews' persecution explicitly to their creativity. Writing only a few years after the emancipation of French Jews, however, he did not attach any political valence to the legend, in spite of the fact that Jews in Britain remained legally disadvantaged. His contribution resided elsewhere. A Jewish author, D'Israeli espoused and amplified Montesquieu's idea that Jews had played a pivotal role in the arc of European civilization. He thus advanced a current of Jewish scholarship that flourished throughout the nineteenth and early twentieth centuries and that had as its objective the enumeration of "Jewish contributions to civilization."[135] In a later publication titled *The Genius of Judaism* (1833), D'Israeli expanded on his earlier argument: forced into "the most humiliating industry," that is, "the commerce of money," he declared, Jews were able to bring it "to a noble perfection"; by rendering fortunes invisible, "their genius produced the wonderful invention of bills of exchange," which, together with "the art of printing . . . are sources of civilization, and connect together, as in one commonwealth, the whole universe." Eventually, though, he added, the Jews' "successful pursuits worked their own fatality."[136] Resentment followed triumph and led Christians to victimize those who had given them access to the most useful financial tools.

In the end, D'Israeli's treatment of the legend of the Jewish invention of bills of exchange sheds new light on two important discourses. Once introduced into the genre of Jewish contributions to civilization, the legend came to occupy a niche in Jews' collective self-fashioning. In the 1820s, for example, in a petition to Pope Leo XII, the Jews of Rome listed their ancestors' invention of bills of exchange and banking as evidence of the positive influence Jews had on industry and commerce everywhere, as well as their ability to incite emulation among non-Jews.[137] Furthermore, D'Israeli's emphasis on Christian resentment of Jewish financial inventiveness—an emphasis that, as we saw, the German Cameralist Fischer had recently aired—replaced Montesquieu's version of the legend and became a new topos. As Michael Toch has demonstrated, and as the next chapter will show, nineteenth-century German academic works, whether by antisemitic scholars or Jewish apologists, cultivated the idea that Jews had dominated international trade in the early Middle Ages before being reduced to the status of pawnbrokers in the thirteenth century.[138] The systematic reconstruction of the legend's meandering paths that this and earlier chapters have pursued thus reveals something new about how this well-known scholarly consensus came to be.

Conclusion

Geologists designate as karstic certain landscapes, such as the borderlands between Italy and Slovenia, in which surface and groundwaters shape the terrain of soluble rocks by carving out large caves beneath the soil. Karstic landscapes are a topography of sinkholes and streams that disappear abruptly where they seep into the ground. Most streams continue to flow underground, but occasionally, some reemerge and erode the surface, only to run underground again at a later point—a process that is repeated over time. Scientists have only a modest ability to predict the courses of these aquifers—that is, when and where they will resurface and how they will mold the soil. By analogy, we can think of the discursive and material contexts covered in this chapter as soluble rocks and the manifold versions of the legend of the Jewish invention of bills of exchange as the corrosive streams that plunge underground and reappear from time to time—never in exactly the same guise, sometimes leaving only a minor trace, and other times creating more durable paths.

This analogy brings into relief some of the challenges we confront when we attempt to uncover how ideas are forged, disseminated, and refashioned. A number of cultural and intellectual historians have made creative use of the term "morphology," a neologism coined by Goethe while touring the botanical gardens of southern Italy and now the name of a branch of biology and linguistics, in order to make sense of similarities between ideas and cultural forms that manifest in disparate times and places and that, in the absence of direct lines of transmission, might otherwise seem unrelated. Critics have faulted these efforts for their tendency to recognize certain equivalences and not others or to overplay analogies between different versions of the same trope in spite of the fact that those differences might be equally revealing.[139]

By choosing karstic topography rather than morphology as a metaphor, I emphasize the intricate and sometimes unpredictable webs of meaning that connected a wide range of associations between Jews and credit across the landscape that I have surveyed. I do so to account for a central struggle of my inquiry: after the late Middle Ages, Christian associations of Jews with money displayed remarkable stability because they combined and recombined a set of preexisting tropes, yet these associations were not immutable. Our task is to interpret small differences, the hardest ones to decipher. To do so requires that we stress the permanence of discursive traditions alongside local struggles and the intentional disturbance introduced by certain authors while simultaneously making room for contingency—a balancing act that is hard to capture in a single formula but that I attempt to perform throughout the entire book.

Not every narrative of the development of European commercial society, even those found in merchant handbooks, focused on the introduction of bills of exchange. In the stadial conception of history embraced by John Locke, Hume, and Smith, the key moment in this narrative hinged on the earlier transition from barter, the hallmark of primitive societies, to market exchanges mediated via money (initially understood as a metallic currency), a transition that was less the result of state intervention (a later thesis known as Chartalism) than the continuation of the natural progressive arc of commerce's civilizing mission. Espoused and advanced by the Scottish Enlightenment, this influential account also explains why the legend of the Jewish invention of bills of exchange never took center stage in the eighteenth century's most canonic works of "economics," which focused on the transition from barter to money and on the public debt more than on paper instruments of private credit.[140] In Gerard Malynes's widely read compilation of merchant customs and norms, for example, the appearance of metallic money (there dated to 300 BCE Rome) marked the momentous beginning of a new historical phase. The subsequent creation of "exchange by bills for moneys" was simply a response to the dual challenge of carrying precious metal and converting the huge variety of currencies that were then in circulation.[141]

Interest in the transition from barter to money has similarly preoccupied modern scholars, even if they have debunked the idea that barter ever existed as a primordial and self-contained historical stage, and has thus distracted their attention from the existence of contemporaneous debates on the origins of what were once the most sophisticated paper instruments of private credit, notably premium insurance and bills of exchange. What this scholarship has failed to note is that, for a great many early modern writers, and obviously for Montesquieu, it was the transition from metallic currencies to bills of exchange that inaugurated a new era in the history of European commercial society—a transition depicted in unconditionally positive terms by the French philosophe and in more sober tones by those who praised the virtues of bills of exchange but worried about their unfettered diffusion.

The significance attributed to the replacement of coins with bills of exchange predated the fictitious account penned by Cleirac. By the mid-sixteenth century, Italian and Spanish authors had outlined an enduring counternarrative of this shift: merchants' industriousness, not the prodigious talents of one refugee group or another, had led to the creation of new instruments capable of transferring money across regions for the purpose of moving goods from where they were abundant to where they were scarce, thus multiplying the beneficial effects of trade.[142] In Germany possibly more than elsewhere, works of jurisprudence and merchant handbooks both adopted this naturalist thesis. A young German jurist wrote in 1646 that "the law of nations and necessity introduced exchange operations, which civil law confirmed and customs approved of."[143] A German guide to commerce drew a parallel with biological reproduction: "The bill of exchange with its laws was born from commerce like a child from his mother."[144] Recapitulating existing theories on the origins of marine insurance, a jurist and civic leader in Lübeck, a Hanseatic town with a long maritime and commercial tradition, noted that some believed it existed in Roman law under different names, while others dated it to the the fourteenth or fifteenth century.[145]

A lively discussion about the process through which credit instruments emerged and developed was thus already underway when Cleirac entered it, but his influence on the debate remained conspicuous for a good 250 years. After the mid-seventeenth century, the majority of European authors who discussed the origins of bills of exchange or marine insurance mentioned medieval Jews as being among the possible candidates for these instruments' inventors—whether the discussions sought to endorse that hypothesis, disprove it, or, most often, contemplate it alongside others. If early modern debates about the emergence of bills of exchange are our karstic landscape and the various theories about their origins are the aquatic streams, then Cleirac, Dupuis de la Serra, and Montesquieu can be seen as headwaters, because each of them put forward a strong theory with which others contended. But because of the mysteries of karstic connections, we also need to pay attention to the multiple and intersecting streams that molded a landscape that in the eighteenth century became more trafficked and intricate.

The multiplication of printed works, including serial publications such as encyclopedias and dictionaries, occurred at a time of weak standards for plagiarism and paved the way for the propagation of a trope that sometimes appeared as little more than a casual reference. All in all, authorial credibility was paramount in the dissemination of ideas, and few authors were seen as so authoritative as Montesquieu. His was indeed the most consistent stream through which the legend infiltrated different corners of Europe. The Scottish Jacobite exile to France James Steuart, the German Cameralist Bielfeld (who wrote in French), the son of a leading Huguenot pastor living in Berlin Louis de Beausobre (1730–1783), and the Milanese professor of political economy Cesare Beccaria (whose disquisition on the subject appeared simultaneously in Italian, French, and English) did more than any others to embed the legend of the Jewish invention of bills of exchange in a progressive narrative of European commercial society inspired directly by Montesquieu. Like their muse, they were less concerned with the history of Jews than with the allegorical power of the episode.

Not everyone agrees with me on this point. Beausobre included the fictional narrative of the invention of bills of exchange at the hands of medieval Jews fleeing France in his treatment of the history of banking.[146] Miriam Yardeni takes him literally and, ignoring the derivation of his passage, interprets it as "a factual report, devoid of ethical considerations of persecution as such." Instead of viewing his account of Jews' financial talent as a tale with a long past, she considers it exemplary of a growing tendency among second-generation Huguenot exiles, particularly those in Berlin, who had not experienced persecution firsthand, to be "more level-headed and perhaps more objective" with regard to Jews.[147] From everything I have said thus far, it is clear that the legend relayed by Beausobre hardly warrants this literal interpretation. There is no doubt that Huguenot exiles such as Pierre Bayle (1647–1706) and Henri (1615–1710) and Jacques (1653–1723) Basnage de Beauval advanced the cause of religious toleration more than most in their time, but neither their work nor Montesquieu's portrayal of Jews as the engines of commercial society qualify as examples of objective inquiry.

The legend's formulations clearly did not reflect the local conditions of Jewish life mimetically, even when they adapted and incorporated local themes. Overall, I do not detect an increasingly dispassionate ethnographic style in the treatment of Jews in merchant handbooks and commercial literature, in contrast to other genres of Christian writing about Jews.[148] In fact, the most serious blows to the historical account on which the legend rested came from French, German, and Italian authors writing in contexts in which Jews were less accepted and were inspired by either regional pride or antiquarian tendencies rather than by any desire to right the record regarding Jewish history. Meanwhile, the legend continued to appear in those contexts in which the place of commerce in national politics and the status of merchants in the social hierarchy remained contested. As its association with bills of exchange evolved to include other financial instruments, the view of Jews as shady manipulators of the stock market solidified even in those places where the degrees of religious toleration were highest—Amsterdam and London (although admittedly England was a distant second best to Amsterdam for Jews in the eighteenth century).

Generations of historians, anthropologists, and literary critics have demonstrated the importance of understanding tales that once held sway over people's imagination because they disclose forgotten cultural models and their demise. By the close of the eighteenth century, the treatment of the origins of the credit instruments that had propelled European finance to new levels of sophistication was evidence of an enduring dilemma in academic scholarship. Two competing logics—the dogma of Jewish guile and the rise of positivist historical methods—played themselves out as scholars contended with multiple accounts of Europe's capitalist modernity and the place of Jews in those accounts. As we will see, the tale of the Jewish invention of bills of exchange became a lightning rod in rival narratives of the so-called Rise of the West in the early days of modern European academia.

8

A Legacy that Runs Deep

Bills—convenience to the mercantile world,
for which, I believe, we are originally indebted
to the Jews, who appear to me to have had
a devilish deal too much to do with them ever since . . .

            —CHARLES DICKENS, *DAVID COPPERFIELD* (1850)[1]

The bill of exchange is the Jew's real god.
His only god is the illusory bill of exchange.

            —KARL MARX, "ON THE JEWISH QUESTION" (1844)[2]

THE HABIT OF ATTRIBUTING to Jews the invention of bills of exchange reached its zenith in the nineteenth century and percolated into an ever-broader variety of literary and scholarly genres. It left more than a trace in Victorian novels, which often portrayed Jews as usurers and callous social climbers, as the epigraph from Charles Dickens's *David Copperfield* indicates.[3] It was also a bone of contention for both French enemies and defenders of Jews in the 1880s and 1890s, the period leading up to the Dreyfus affair.[4] The possible Jewish origin of European financial instruments was mentioned even more frequently in countless works on maritime and commercial law, bills of exchange and marine insurance, and currency and paper money—a booming literature that encompassed historical studies of the evolution of private contracts for use in long-distance trade and legal treatises designed to clarify the nature of these contracts for either pedagogical purposes or domestic and international codification projects. This nineteenth-century body of work would demand a separate investigation.[5]

In closing, I will depart from my penchant for lesser figures and focus instead on three giants of modern social thought: Karl Marx (1818–1883), Max Weber (1864–1920), and Werner Sombart (1863–1941). In their efforts to define what constituted *modern* capitalism and how it came into being, each proposed a different role for Jews. Although only Sombart transformed Jews into key actors in the genesis of Western capitalism, all three thinkers appealed to Jews to define how modern capitalism differed from earlier forms of commercialization. As part of this quest, Sombart proposed yet another version of the legend of the Jewish invention of bills of exchange, which figured front and center in his *Die Juden und das Wirtschaftsleben* (*The Jews and Economic Life*), a text that most economic historians justly dismiss but that has exerted an enormous, troubling, and—as of late—contradictory influence on the field of Jewish history.[6]

My treatment of these complex authors bears directly on the three broad themes that I identified in the introduction and have addressed throughout the book. The first is the question of what constitutes a canonical work in the history of economic thought and how those works shaped European ideas about the birth of capitalism. The previous chapters have demonstrated that Étienne Cleirac's *Us et coustumes de la mer* (1647), now almost completely forgotten, once represented a crucial point of reference that spun the legend of the Jewish invention of marine insurance and bills of exchange in myriad directions. A short piece on the economic role of Jews in medieval Europe published in 1875 by Wilhelm Roscher (1817–1894) met a similar fate: although today only a few specialists know it, the theory it advanced became canonical in the last quarter of the nineteenth century. One simply cannot understand Sombart's views of Jews and capitalism without reference to Roscher's.

A deeper link than their relative obscurity connects Cleirac to Roscher. In light of the analysis of the place of Jews in the economic literature that I have conducted this far, Marx, Roscher, and Sombart appear as the heirs of, or at least as profoundly influenced by, early modern economic debates. From that previous era they inherited both their familiarity with the legend of the Jewish invention of bills of exchange and their tendency to stress the "Jewishness" of early capitalism. Weber broke with this tendency and inaugurated the process of the Christianization of capitalism that became dominant in the twentieth century. By the interwar period, leading medievalists of all persuasions— Marxists and non-Marxists, some more indebted to Weber than others, many (but not all) Catholics, and a few flirting with fascism—reacted against the then-emergent consensus that relegated the Middle Ages to a precapitalist phase of European civilization. These scholars reaffirmed the importance of late medieval economic growth in several ways, simultaneously rejecting the significance their predecessors attributed to medieval Jews in the making of modern capitalism.

This observation feeds into my second concern, which is with periodization, and specifically with competing views of the way in which the transition from the medieval period to (early) modernity unfolded. The historical narrative of the supposed invention and dissemination of bills of exchange relayed by Cleirac implied a continuity between the medieval expulsions of French Jews and the seventeenth-century primacy of Amsterdam as a financial center. In both contexts Christian finance was seen as tainted by its Jewish origins. By contrast, Montesquieu's refashioning of the legend presumed a sharp break between a medieval period during which the despised activities of trade and moneylending were understood as the prerogatives of Jews and a new phase in European history, located around the time of the transoceanic voyages by Columbus and Vasco da Gama, when the church retreated from the influential position it held in politics and society and commerce gained both independence from rulers' arbitrary power and respectability.

Although the social theorists whose work I examine here never mentioned Montesquieu, they replicated his view of the Middle Ages as a time of economic autarky and of the sixteenth century as the beginning of the triumph of commerce as a superior civilizational stage. For all their differences, Marx, Sombart, and Weber agreed that the European economy during the Middle Ages did not meet their respective definitions of modern capitalism (even if Weber's early work on medieval trade and urban society should lead us to qualify this statement). Different in temperament, political views, and scholarly approaches, all three thinkers experienced the epochal changes of rapid industrialization, mass migration to cities, and the consumerism and pauperism that accompanied these phenomena. The scale and pace of these upheavals were enormous and impressed academics, writers, and artists alike. Most scholars stressed what was new in modern capitalism—whether to praise or to demonize it—more than they dwelled on long-term continuities. The search for origins was part and parcel of this emphasis on ruptures.

Sombart parted ways with the general trend among both Christian and Jewish scholars by focusing not on medieval moneylenders but on Jewish merchants of the sixteenth century, and those of Iberian descent in particular. In keeping with his focus on the Western Sephardic diaspora, he provided a new iteration and date for the supposed Jewish invention not of bills of exchange *tout court*, but of endorsable bills, which had come to circulate more widely because they passed from one holder to the next (chapter 1). Sombart turned that Jewish invention into a cornerstone of his narrative about the nexus between Jews and modern capitalism. His portrayal of the international webs of Sephardic trade and finance, however, was not a tribute to Jews' ability to integrate into a diverse commercial society and contribute to its expansion. Instead, his account mixed an outsized celebration of Sephardic commerce with a conservative disdain for capitalism that went beyond the nostalgia of widespread antimodernist positions. Read against the turn toward ethnonationalism and the social strife of Wilhelmine Germany, his argument about Jews and captialism contained a more menacing message.

This point leads me to the last major issue with which I have been wrestling throughout this book: the relationship between the discursive representations of Jews and commerce by various authors on the one hand and the immediate historical circumstances in which those representations took shape on the other. I started by describing in detail the financial mechanisms underpinning bills of exchange and marine insurance in order to reveal the precise mixture of admiration and backlash that these instruments engendered when they were still relatively new (chapters 1–3). I then situated the emergence and evolution of the tale attributing to Jews the invention of bills of exchange in relation to the social and political tensions that characterized Old Regime France, through the Revolution and beyond (chapters 4–6). Similarly, in mapping the legend's diffusion across Europe from the mid-seventeenth to late eighteenth centuries, I examined the intellectual and material environments in which that tale was received, challenged, or rejected (chapter 7). I cannot provide an equally granular description of the historical contexts in which the grand theories we have inherited from Marx, Sombart, and Weber came into being, but I will hint at the extent to which contemporary events, including rising nationalism and authoritarianism, the politics of antisemitism, racial theories, and Zionism, mapped onto scholarly pursuits concerning the history and definition of modern capitalism.

Emancipation is commonly recognized as the dividing line between the period we have examined up to this point and the historical backdrop to this chapter. In each European country, emancipation during the nineteenth century was a process rather than an event. During Marx's youth, the legal equality of Jewish men in Prussia was still a matter of dispute. Between 1867 and 1871, however, most restrictions on Jews' rights to residence, professional practice, and real estate ownership were lifted, at least on paper, across the German Empire. In other words, by the time Weber and Sombart wrote about Jews, the legal equality of male Jewish citizens had been inscribed into law. This legal revolution was a major stepping-stone toward a more equal society. Curiously, while it marked a profound break from the social and political structures of the Old Regime, emancipation also prolonged and transformed anxieties that had once been associated with a diametrically opposed measure, namely, forced baptism. The majority-Christian population feared that recent converts and newly emancipated Jews, although formally embracing the rules of their new fellowship, harbored a secret desire (as well as the power) to undermine the community that they had joined. The fear that former Jews continued to adhere to their ancient beliefs and allegiances after being baptized had been particularly acute in those regions of early modern Europe, including Iberia and southwestern France, where forced conversions were a fact of life. Under new guises, in those areas where emancipation erased most legal barriers between Jews and Christians, the view of Jewish citizens as a "fifth column" fueled new theories about the proper place that Jews should be assigned in delineating the historical trajectory of Western civilization.

Marx, Sombart, and Weber

In the fall of 1843, at age twenty-five, Marx penned a review of two pieces on the so-called Jewish question that the atheist theologian and radical Young Hegelian Bruno Bauer had just published. In so doing, he joined a lively public debate on the subject. Bauer had challenged the Prussian Liberal Party, which demanded legal parity for Jews, by arguing that as long as Prussia remained a Christian state, Jews would always be second-class citizens, even if they were relieved of all legal disabilities. In support of his argument, Bauer had pointed to the French example: there, citizenship rights had not helped Jews improve their general conditions after 1790–1791, and in any case, religious discrimination had not been eradicated.[7] Marx agreed on this point but went further. For him, the 1789 Declaration of the Rights of Man and of the Citizen equated "the rights of man" with political rights, said nothing about social rights, and merely ushered in a new property regime from which all other rights derived.

"The practical application of the right of man to freedom is the right of man to *private property*," he wrote. "Therefore, not one of the so-called rights of man goes beyond the egotistic man, . . . namely an individual withdrawn into himself, his private interest and his private desires and separated from the community."[8]

Read alongside his "Critique of Hegel's Doctrine of the State," completed just a month or two earlier, "On the Jewish Question" (1844) was an early articulation of Marx's conception of private property as the fundamental logic that animates modern civil society. By focusing on the so-called Jewish question, it elaborated a "criticism of the political state" and tackled the "relationship of political emancipation to human emancipation."[9] Even a fully secular (i.e., non-Christian) republican state, Marx reasoned, could not protect its citizens from the power of money. Even once property qualifications for voting were lifted, private property, occupation, and education would still define social relations. To counter these forces, Marx famously demanded not the political emancipation of Jews, but "the emancipation of society from Judaism," in the sense of mankind's emancipation "from haggling and from money."[10] Jews stood in for what Marx would later call "the cash nexus"; they represented the "anti-social element" that, he claimed, had by then reached its historical peak.[11]

In Marx's conception, Jews worshiped the bill of exchange; they did not invent it. The difference should not go unnoticed. By making Judaism a synecdoche of humanity (a humanity incessantly occupied by buying, selling, bartering, and hustling), Marx treaded waters all too familiar, identifying Jewish usury as an attribute of both Jews and non-Jews and accusing Christian merchants of behaving like Jews in order to denounce their crookedness. But Marx also departed from this trope in a remarkable way. Rather than identifying Jewishness as a marker of certain flawed individuals, groups, or economic techniques, he presented the Judaization of (Christian) society as a process that was now completed: "The practical Jewish spirit has become the practical spirit of the Christian people," he wrote—or, in other words, all "Christians have become Jews," not only some of them.[12]

A quick comparison of Marx's notion that greed had become an inescapable social condition affecting everyone with more traditional views of Jewish usury as depicted by Honoré de Balzac in those same years brings the difference between the two into relief. One of the Jewish characters in Balzac's *La comédie humaine*, Gobseck, a "banknote man" (*homme-billet*), is an aged and clever usurer born in Antwerp around 1740 and living in Paris during the Restoration. Gobseck is not without qualities, but he has little regard for his fellow human beings ("If humanity, if sociability were a religion, he could be considered an atheist," Balzac wrote). Unlike Shylock, the anachronistic pawnbroker of sixteenth-century Venice, Gobseck speculates on bills of exchange (many signed by women, another sign of the lamentable expansion of commercial society). He also belongs to a conspiratorial clique:

> There are a dozen of us here in Paris, all silent unknown kings, the arbiters of your destinies . . . we meet on certain days of the week at Café Thémis, by the Pont Neuf. There, we uncover the mysteries of finance. There is no fortune that can keep the truth from us; we know every family's secrets. We keep a kind of black book where we track the most important bills issued and redeemed, drafts on the public credit system, on the bank, in trade.[13]

In short, Balzac's Jewish moneylender and sly financier lives on the margins of Christian society, whose resources he is ready to siphon off in collusion with other Jews. Not so Marx's Jews: they were understood to represent society in its totality. That is why there was no room in Marx's work for the narrative of the Jewish invention of bills of exchange as we have come to know it, because in whatever version, that tale implied an initial separation between, rather than a convergence of, Jews and Christians. Jews bequeathed to non-Jews a financial innovation, and only after they adopted that innovation did Christian merchants become either potential "Judaizers" (as per Cleirac) or individuals able to use those bills to rein in the despot (according to Montesquieu). For Marx, instead, all of Christian capitalist society was "Jewish" from the start. Bills of exchange were Jews' only real god in the sense that they were everyone's only real god.

Marx's identification of Jews with capitalism did not raise eyebrows then as it did later, when his antisemitic imagery ("Money is the jealous god of Israel"; "The chimerical nationality of the Jew is the nationality of the merchant") generated no shortage of puzzlement, mistrust, and even revulsion among his readers.[14] It is impossible to pinpoint a single source of influence on Marx's choice of the injurious language of economic antisemitism as a tool of critique. That language permeated the contemporary political discourse of both the Left and the Right. His readings of Hegel and Feuerbach made Marx arguably better versed in Christian than Jewish thought. His biography, too, certainly played a part and has been used either to exculpate him or to depict him as a self-hating Jew who provided ammunition to the enemies of Jews for generations to come.

Born of Jewish parents, Marx was baptized shortly after his father and not long before his mother, while both his paternal grandfather and uncle were rabbis in his native Trier. He grew up a Lutheran, a member of the reformed German Evangelical Church, the confession of Prussian rulers, in the predominantly Catholic region of the Rhineland, just after Prussia wrested it from Napoleon in 1814. Trier, on the Moselle River, was less than fifty miles from Thionville, where in 1775 Pierre-Louis Lacretelle launched the first campaign for Jewish emancipation (chapter 6). Ruled by France from 1795 to 1814, the left bank of the Rhine was the easternmost region to experience the Revolution's repercussions: its largely impoverished Jewish population was emancipated, subjected to new restrictions under Napoleon, and perpetually resented by the no less disadvantaged Catholic majority that was often indebted to Jewish moneylenders. We can only speculate about the impact that these circumstances had on the young Marx.[15] What is certain is that, unlike contemporary socialist antisemitic writings, chief among them Alphone Toussenel's *Les juifs, rois de l'époque* (*The Jews, Kings of the Time*), Marx's work eschewed historical Jews and Judaism in favor of a metaphorical invocation of both.[16]

For reasons that Marx never elucidated, he soon relinquished the equation of Jews and capitalism.[17] In its place, he put history into the service of theory in order to outline the transition from feudalism to capitalism in Europe's past, with a focus on England. His evolutionary conception of history was reminiscent of the Enlightenment's stadial theory insofar as it regarded urbanization and foreign trade as the two engines of the transformation of what Adam Smith called "the age of agriculture" into the "age of commerce." Yet Marx differed from Smith not only in his insistence on land as a source of primitive accumulation but also in his belief that "the age of commerce" was neither the pinnacle of civilization nor its endgame. Whereas for Smith, "commerce and manufactures gradually introduced order and good government, and with them, the liberty and security of individuals," Marx believed that capitalism negates individuals' freedom.[18] Adapting the Hegelian dialectic to his theories, he transcended the thesis and antithesis of feudalism and capitalism with a new synthesis: socialism. In both Smith and Marx, the historical chronology was hazy, but the sixteenth century was identified as the definite turning point. In the first volume of *Capital*, Marx maintained that "trading nations," which included the Jews, "exist[ed] in the ancient world only in its interstices," while "the modern history of capital dates from the creation in the 16th century of a world-embracing commerce and a world-embracing market."[19]

Although Sombart and Weber rejected Marx's materialist explanation for the rise of modern capitalism, they both retained his basic chronology dating the causal forces that unleashed capitalism to the sixteenth century. Weber focused on the Reformation and Sombart insisted on depicting the Middle Ages as precapitalist.[20] Jewish history played a role in both authors' conceptualizations of modern capitalism—a famously central role in Sombart's and as an important counterexample in Weber's. In fact, while on the surface their respective interpretations of Jews' economic roles throughout history appear antithetical, on closer scrutiny, they can be seen to share important traits.

Both Weber and Sombart absorbed Roscher's portrait of the medieval economy, and Sombart took more than a cue from Roscher's depiction of Jews as the driving force behind the development of Western capitalism. Often referred to as the father of the German Historical School, Roscher exerted enormous influence on German academia through his writings and his students, notably Gustav von Schmoller (1838–1917). In a landmark 1875 essay, he proposed a simple thesis: "Among the Germanic peoples the Jews were better treated during the earlier than the later Middle Ages" (with the Black Death as the rough cutoff date). For Roscher, in the earlier period, Jews were the only ones "carrying on a professional trade in goods"; for several centuries, they were thus "the commercial guardians of the young nations," that is, of medieval Christian powers. "The Jewish persecutions of the later Middle Ages," he continued, "are in large measure a product of trade jealousy."[21]

What made "the young nations" feel they could turn against their economic benefactors without committing suicide? Roscher explained that medieval Jews introduced three innovations, and once Christians learned to handle them, they were free to rid themselves of their teachers. These "three important steps of economic progress" devised by medieval Jews were "the introduction of interest on capital," "the protection of the possessor of an object illegally alienated but taken into possession in good faith by the receiver" (e.g., the full negotiability of stolen cash, as long as the receiver was unaware of its illicit provenance), and "the invention of bills of exchange."[22]

As was usual at the time, footnotes in Roscher's article were sparse.[23] It is therefore impossible to trace exactly how the legend that first appeared in the pages of Cleirac's *Us et coustumes de la mer* in 1647 made its way into this text of the last quarter of the nineteenth century. To be sure, Roscher's interpretation of the alleged invention of bills of exchange by Jews was antithetical to

Montesquieu's and closer to Friedrich Christoph Jonathan Fischer's rendition of the legend (chapter 7). While in *The Spirit of the Laws* Christian nations were depicted as putting the Jewish invention to such good use that commerce bettered social and political relations for everyone, in Roscher's account Christians' appropriation of the same Jewish invention inspired "jealousy" toward those who devised it, leading to antisemitic hatred and persecution.

Sombart absorbed this lesson. As in Roscher's essay, the association between Jews and bills of exchange figured prominently in his 1911 *The Jews and Economic Life*. For modern capitalism to emerge, Sombart noted in a core chapter of the book, credit had to evolve "from being a personal matter into one of an impersonal relationship," a historical evolution that occurred once stocks and securities became tradable and payments began to be made in banknotes. In all the stages that accompanied this development, he wrote, "the Jew was ever present with his creative genius."[24] Through a series of distorted citations and ludicrous statements (often rhetorically phrased as inferences but meant as assertions), Sombart proceeded to enumerate instances in which Jews had been the protagonists of all Europe's private and public financial innovations. His treatment of bills of exchange encapsulated the two horns of his argument: Jews brought capitalism to its mature form during the sixteenth century, but they had been merchants since antiquity and personified commerce throughout the ages. The reason for this long-term specialization in trade resided in Judaism itself, which Sombart described as having a contractual and legalistic conception of the relationship between humans and the divine, a conception that preceded Protestantism and was similarly congruent with the calculative logic of capitalism.

By the time Sombart wrote *The Jews and Economic Life*, a number of scholars, including the towering German specialist of commercial law Levin Goldschmidt (1828–1897), had rejected the possibility that Jews might have invented bills of exchange and argued instead that those bills were the product of a slow evolution of the legal and financial systems.[25] In a formulation typical of his reasoning, Sombart claimed that these scholars "do not render testimony strong enough for the statement that the Jews were *not* the inventors of bills" during the Middle Ages.[26] His real subject, he added, was "the modern endorsable bill" rather than the simple four-party bill of medieval derivation. Noting that Goldschmidt had traced the origins of negotiable bills of exchange to sixteenth-century Venice and that a reference to bills in general was made in a petition addressed by Christian merchants to the Venetian Republic in 1550, when the government was discussing the possibility of expelling crypto-Jews from the city, Sombart concluded: "It is fairly certain that the use of circulating endorsable bills in Venice must have been first commenced by Jews."[27] The logic exceeded the evidence in a way that was characteristic of the entire book's argumentative style. A reviewer at the time derided the faulty syllogism underlying this logic: banking was highly developed in Venice; sixteenth-century Venice housed a sizable Jewish community; therefore, Jews invented banking.[28]

Sombart transplanted Roscher's tale of the Jewish invention of bills of exchange from late medieval Europe to the sixteenth-century Adriatic, where those bills became negotiable—and thus emblems of the ultimate abstraction of modern capitalism—before migrating to Holland and across the Atlantic. Not even this inflated historical arc, however, satisfied him. Drawing on biblical and Talmudic citations that specialists immediately demonstrated to be spurious, Sombart went on to state that "modern credit instruments [derived] from Rabbinic law."[29] His argument thus came full circle, fusing the image of the sixteenth-century Jewish capitalist with that of the Jew as the eternal merchant.

More preposterous than Roscher's essay of 1875, *The Jews and Economic Life* was also more heavily annotated. And more than Roscher, Sombart owed an immense debt to the then-nascent field of academic scholarship on the Jewish past, which he pillaged and distorted. Of the more than 500 bibliographical citations that appeared in its footnotes (in a book that contained 434 pages of text), 83 percent were published after 1850 and 70 percent after 1875 (appendix 7). The majority of these recent publications represented what was then a new phenomenon: the rapid increase in the number and quality of works of Jewish history written by Jewish authors. Sombart relied on Heinrich Graetz's landmark multivolume *History of the Jews* more than on any other reference, citing it seventy times.[30] The choice was not surprising: Graetz (1817–1891) was indisputably the most renowned Jewish historian of the nineteenth century. But it was also a curious choice, because Graetz, a religious traditionalist, had little to say about the economic life of past Jewish societies and, to the extent that he addressed the topic, emphasized Christian persecution as the cause of Jews' specialization in moneylending and commerce. That was not Sombart's view. *The Jews and Economic Life* stipulated that the expulsions from Iberia in the 1490s catalyzed Jewish capitalist potential, whereas Graetz did not see any progress in the conditions of Jewish life after 1492, and certainly did not celebrate the expansion of Jewish commerce in the sixteenth-century Atlantic. Sombart thus treated Graetz as a repository of information that he could fit into his predetermined scheme. Contrary to anything Graetz would have advocated, he even argued that the "spirit of capitalism" had belonged to the Jews from the start. Espousing the specious notion that "for some twenty centuries the Jews have kept themselves ethnically pure," Sombart affirmed that their "characteristics were constant" and that Jews had "devoted themselves to trade" throughout their history.[31]

The treatment of Graetz is telling of how Sombart used the sources he cited. Another of his favorite authors was Meyer Kayserling (1829–1905), a rabbi and prolific amateur historian who wrote with fervor on a great many topics, from Jewish women to Moses Mendelssohn, but turned his attention in particular to Iberian Jews. In Kayserling's work Sombart encountered claims he subsequently made his: that the fortunes seized from Jews had financed Christopher Columbus's Atlantic voyages and that forcibly converted Jews ("Marranos") had flocked to the Americas, where they came to dominate trade.[32] In the nineteenth century, cultivated German Jews admired the literary, aesthetic, and philosophical achievements of their ancestors in medieval Iberia, whom they regarded as antithetical to the inward-looking, uncultivated, Yiddish-speaking eastern European Jews who surrounded them. Kayserling's work was part cause and part effect of this "allure of the Sephardic," whose idealization of the harmonious relations among Jews, Christians, and Muslims in pre-1492 Iberia was a measure of elite German Jews' desire to assimilate while retaining their identity.[33] Sombart absorbed this cultural trend and turned it on its head: against the consensus that the Iberian "golden age" ended in 1492, he exalted sixteenth-century Sephardic Jews, a group scorned by Orthodox Jews for having converted (albeit under pressure) and thus unlikely heroes of Jewish history. His exaltation obviously was not meant to restore the greatness of Western Sephardim and in fact represented a distorting caricature of it.

No less telling of Sombart's attitudes toward his sources is the list of those he did not credit or consult, omissions that cannot be attributed solely to the imprecise citation standards of the time. The list begins with Roscher, who was never mentioned in the book. If his theories were sufficiently known to be recognizable to contemporary readers, the same cannot be said for the Christian anti-Jewish polemicist Johann Andreas Eisenmenger (1654–1704), whom Sombart echoed without explicit acknowledgement.[34] With no command of Hebrew, he can be excused for ignoring an intra-Jewish literature absorbed in debating matters of philanthropy and economic solidarity that would have clashed with his views.[35] No linguistic barrier, however, separated him from credible Jewish scholarship in German and French that engaged with the economic roles of Jews but did not square with his conclusions; he either discounted this scholarship altogether or treated it as the source of minor details cited out of context.[36]

At the very same time, Sombart cherry-picked from abundant midcentury Jewish scholarly and lay publications by liberal and assimilated rabbis and writers, notably Ludwig Philippson (1811–1889), who used "a decidedly triumphalist tone" to celebrate Jews' successes in commerce in ways that resonated positively among segments of the German bourgeoisie.[37] Here and there, this apologetic literature also included proud references to the Jews' invention of bills of exchange.[38]

After the 1873 stock market crash in Germany, however, antisemitism and nationalism were on the rise, and this kind of Jewish liberal triumphalism was no longer viable. The publication of *The Jews and Economic Life* in 1911 met with strikingly different responses among the German Jewish public, ranging from outraged hostility to enthusiastic embrace. For the most part, liberal Jews were angered by the work, while committed Zionists rejoiced at Sombart's portrait of the brave new economic man as Jewish.[39] Speaking to a large Jewish audience, Eugene Fuchs, leader of the moderate Central Union of German Citizens of Jewish Faith (*Centralverein deutscher Staatsbürger jüdischen Glaubens*), which worked for the integration of Jews into German society, denounced Sombart as the most insidious type of antisemite: someone who mixed traditional elements of Jewish hatred with seemingly philosemitic praises. Not only did he fail to convince his audience, which included a group of zealous Zionists, but "the meeting, to Fuchs' dismay, ended in near riot."[40] Exceeding the expectations of his Jewish admirers, the following year, in 1912, Sombart published a short pamphlet titled *Die Zukunft der Juden* (*The Future of the Jews*), which denied that Jews could assimilate but conceded that they formed a nation of their own—a claim well received by Zionist separatists.[41]

The reception among Jewish historians was more sober and more sobering. By and large, they were closer to Roscher than to Sombart in their emphasis on persecution as the chief explanation for Jews' commercial specialization, but their framework could accommodate elements of Sombart's thesis. Georg Caro (1867–1912) and Ignaz Schipper (1884–1943), the authors of two recent and authoritative large-scale histories of the Jews, paid more attention to the economy than did Graetz. Sombart, however, lifted from these surveys a mere couple of anecdotes to back up his claims and failed to engage with their arguments.[42] It fell upon Jewish textual scholars, who were philologists more than historians, to tear apart the building blocks of Sombart's account by demonstrating the inaccuracy of his biblical and Talmudic citations, beginning with those related to the alleged Jewish invention of bills of exchange, stocks, obligations, and banknotes.[43] These damaging criticisms by Jewish textual scholars, however, did not forge a coherent alternative to the narratives offered by either Graetz or Sombart.

That kind of work only appeared later, inspired at least in part by Weber's very different treatment of Jewish economic history. In his college thesis, completed under Goldschmidt's supervision, Weber identified legal innovations that had promoted capitalism in the late medieval Italian communes.[44] But he never focused on bills of exchange, whose Jewish origin Goldschmidt had contested.[45] Weber also soon abandoned the study of Italian communes and is better remembered for the work that he produced in dialogue with Sombart.

It is well known that Sombart's *The Jews and Economic Life* was a response to Weber's *The Protestant Ethic and the Spirit of Capitalism* (1904–1905).[46] Weber's *Ancient Judaism* (1915–1919), in turn, was a response to Sombart's *The Jews and Economic Life*. In that work, as well as in the university lectures that he delivered the semester before his death in June 1920 and in the pages later collected in *Economy and Society*, Weber singled out Jews and Judaism as the opposites of modern capitalism and its spirit (as he defined it). He repeated Roscher's thesis when he stated that "the first wave of anti-Semitism" at the time of the Crusades was "a symptom of the development of a national commercial class."[47] But he thoroughly rejected the way in which Sombart had spun Roscher's thesis and specifically the identification of Judaism with the ethics of capitalism. For Weber, Jews possessed loyalty only to other Jews and were thus unable to participate in impersonal market transactions. Introducing the notion of Jews as pariahs and their dual in-group/out-group morality, Weber spoke of Jews' "voluntary ghetto" as predating "compulsory internment."[48] He then concluded that "since antiquity, Jewish pariah capitalism . . . felt at home in the very forms of state- and booty-capitalism along with pure money usury and trade, precisely what Puritanism abhorred."[49]

Weber disagreed with Sombart on several other issues concerning the origins and achievements of Western capitalism. Given his greater textual meticulousness and his rejection of any affinity between Judaism and the spirit of modern capitalism, he made no reference to the alleged Jewish invention of bills of exchange, which both Roscher and Sombart had highlighted. That said, in spite of all the important differences between Weber's and Sombart's characterizations of past Jewish economic contributions, the two shared a conception of Judaism as a religion that favored self-segregation—a belief that allowed both of them to downplay persecution and to portray Judaism as exogenous to the arc of Western history. For Weber, modern capitalism was *"uniquely Occidental"* and Judaism an "Oriental" religion.[50]

The Revolt of the Medievalists

One of the unintended consequences of the heated debates spurred by Weber's and Sombart's rival interpretations of the causes of Europe's economic ascent beginning in the sixteenth century was a call to arms by economic historians of the Middle Ages. The expression "the revolt of the medievalists" was coined by Wallace Ferguson in 1948 to describe the contributions of those scholars who, during the interwar period, had subverted Jacob Burckhardt's legacy in the study of the Renaissance and proclaimed the twelfth century to be the foundational moment of European civilization.[51] In fact, a parallel revolt of other medievalists, different from but not unrelated to the one Ferguson identified, had been underway since 1914, when the Belgian historian Henri Pirenne (1862–1935), objecting to both Sombart and Weber, wrote: "All the essential features of capitalism—individual enterprise, advances on credit, commercial profit, speculation, etc.—are to be found from the twelfth century on, in the city republics of Italy—Venice, Genoa, or Florence."[52] Around the same time, the German Catholic liberal historian Lujo Brentano (1844–1931) not only belittled Sombart's account but also maintained that the warlike mentality of feudalism and the church during the High Middle Ages were responsible for transforming commerce (which had not disappeared after the fall of Rome) into modern capitalism. In his words, "The beginning of modern capitalism does not date from the Fourth Crusade [1204]; had it not already developed long before, the Fourth Crusade would not have been thinkable."[53]

Far from being a mere quibble over periodization, the revolt of these medievalists had far-reaching consequences for twentieth-century scholarly debates about the so-called Rise of the West. Until the 1970s, the alternative chronology it proposed for Europe's economic takeoff had mainstream purchase. Moreover, the Middle Ages that the opponents of Weber and Sombart portrayed as the incubators of Western capitalism were thoroughly Christian; Catholic historians in particular detected in these societies a positive alliance between moral theologians and political elites, between Scholasticism and the ethics of merchant-bankers who were also civic leaders.

The economic historians of the interwar period who saw capitalism taking shape in the Middle Ages came from a wide political spectrum, but all relegated Jews to the margins of their inquiries, if they discussed them at all. In France, they included anti-Marxists like Henri Sée (1864–1936) and André-E. Sayous (1873–1940), as well as Marxists like Henri Hauser (1866–1946).[54] In Italy, a legal-economic school anticipated the early revolt of the medievalists with pioneering studies of medieval commercial law, including several focusing on marine insurance and bills of exchange. Predictably, once they scrutinized archival records in Genoa, Venice, and other Italian medieval cities, these scholars, some of whom, notably Alessandro Lattes (1858–1940) and Arturo Segre (1873–1928), were Jewish, found no trace of a supposed Jewish invention of bills of exchange. More generally, they repudiated the idea that Jews had been key players in medieval international trade and finance.[55]

A different group of Italian medievalists proved even more influential. Intent on stressing the compatibility of Christianity and capitalism, they denied Jews any role in the genesis of the latter. The two best-known of these scholars were Amintore Fanfani (1908–1999), who replaced the esteemed Jewish medievalist Gino Luzzatto (1878–1964) at the University of Venice while the Racial Laws of 1938 were in effect and served five times as Democratic Christian prime minister of the postwar Italian Republic, and Armando Sapori (1892–1976), a senator from the non-Communist Left and a scholar who wielded tremendous academic power from his position at the Università Luigi Bocconi in Milan. While Fanfani criticized Weber's emphasis on Protestantism, Sapori took issue with Sombart. Both insisted that the origins of modern capitalism resided in the Italian medieval communes and were infused with Christian ethics and a sense of solidarity—a depiction designed to lessen the atomized character of early capitalism. In order to buttress their thesis, they pushed Jews to the fringes of medieval urban economies by portraying them as pawnbrokers rather than international traders. In a 1964 volume of reflections on Sombart's wide-ranging work and its Italian reception that Fanfani edited, no mention was made of the *The Jews and Economic Life*.[56]

Medievalists led the way among British economic historians of the interwar period but they also sidelined the topic of Jewish economic activities, in part because their studies privileged agriculture over long-distance trade and in part because they focused on England, which had expelled Jews as early as 1290.[57] Robert Sabatino Lopez (1910–1986), an Italian Jewish refugee to the United States, where he arrived soon after losing his university position in Genoa under Fascism, shared Pirenne's interest in the revival of late medieval European cities.[58] His many studies of Genoese and Mediterranean trade culminated in *The Commercial Revolution of the Middle Ages, 950–1350* (1971), which made the most powerful statement to date about the direct descent of modern capitalism from its medieval predecessor: "And if medieval growth was not fast, it was altogether irreversible; it created the indispensable material and moral conditions for a thousand years of virtually uninterrupted growth; and, in more than one way, it is still with us."[59]

The book included a brief section on "the Jews," which described them as the only group that from the ninth to the early eleventh centuries was "left to provide a link, however tenuous, between Catholic Europe and the more advanced countries beyond it: the Islamic world, the Byzantine Empire, even India and China"; in Europe, too, Lopez added, "for certain villages, the resident or transient Jews represented the only window open onto the world."[60] But in Lopez's overall narrative, the lead characters were the Italian merchants of the late Middle Ages. The Belgian accountant-turned-historian Raymond de Roover (1904–1972), who had coined the expression "commercial revolution of the Middle Ages," concurred entirely.[61] And in his studies of Scholastic economic thought, he went even further in Christianizing medieval capitalism.[62]

After this fertile season of scholarship, research on medieval commercial contracts, including marine insurance and bills of exchange, and their evolution in the sixteenth century retreated into a corner of the academy. Today, the most influential narratives about Europe's takeoff focus on the seventeenth and eighteenth centuries, and the leading causes to which various scholars attribute the primacy of Europe over Asia (public finance and representative institutions, colonialism and slavery, high wages and technological innovation) do not include the fruits of the medieval commercial revolution, for reasons I will return to in the coda.[63]

Conclusion

That the founders of modern social theory were well acquainted with the legend of the Jewish origin of bills of exchange—and that some of them embraced it outright—should be cause for reflection. By the late eighteenth century, the notion that medieval Jews might have been responsible for devising key European financial instruments had come under increasing scrutiny for its evidentiary fallacies and inconsistent storyline. One might well have expected the rise of academic scholarship in the nineteenth century to seal the fate of the legend. To the contrary, the improbable tale experienced a rich afterlife in the age of positivism. In spite of attempts to set the record straight, notably Goldschmit's authoritative study of commercial law, the account attributing to Jews the invention of bills of exchange entered a new phase when, in 1875, Roscher transformed that moral tale into a pseudo-fact. He did so without invoking any source, as if the notion that Jews invented bills of exchange needed no corroboration, wiping out nearly two centuries of debate over the meaning and plausibility of Cleirac's tale of origins. Ultimately, Roscher turned a fantasy about the past into a legitimate and commanding academic statement, which, in Sombart's hands, fueled new fantasies.

And insidious fantasies they were. Today it is common practice to take Weber to task for his Orientalist distortions, which led him to portray all premodern Islamic societies as lacking both entrepreneurship and robust political institutions. But when measured against the available secondary literature and the prevailing standards of source criticism of the time, Sombart's scholarly practice must be judged to be far shoddier than Weber's. And yet there has been a recent revival of interest in his thesis about Jews and capitalism, as if its more damaging and problematic implications could be set aside (coda).

More than the veracity of the legend itself, the place of Jews in the historical arc of Western modernity became the subject of intense debate throughout the nineteenth and early twentieth centuries. During this period bills of exchange were still ordinary modes of payment, especially in international trade, and most of the scholars discussed in this chapter no doubt had direct or indirect knowledge of how they worked. But with the second industrial revolution underway, new economic and financial institutions, including factories, deposit banks, the corporation, and the stock market (rather than bills of exchange), became the focus of contemporary discussions of the productive and destructive forces of modern capitalism. The legend thus ceased to be a compass of the morality of credit, as it had been in the Old Regime, but entered the academic grand narratives about the emergence of Western capitalism.

Different definitions of capitalism and different evaluations of the historical trajectories leading to it meant that Jews were assigned different positions in these grand narratives. For the young Marx, Jews and Judaism did not represent a stage in capitalist development but rather personified modern capitalism *tout court*. By contrast, Weber was not only more interested in capitalism than in Jews, but also intent on salvaging what was good in capitalism as a hallmark of Western civilization. With that intent, he purged his account of any Jewish traces, regarding Jews and Judaism as inferior and extraneous to that civilization. For Sombart, in contrast, capitalism bred moral decline, which is why it had a Jewish face.

Sombart stood out in the increasingly crowded field of scholars debating "Jewish contributions to Western civilization" because he glorified not the achievements of medieval Iberian Jewries but the commercial and financial networks of those Jews who had been expelled or forced to convert in the 1490s. This shift of focus also meant that he treated all New Christians as crypto-Jews whose economic cunning was even more insidious than that of practicing Jews, because the true nature and genuine allegiances of those who possessed it were hard to discern. The inability to distinguish baptized Jews and their descendants from the rest of the population had rendered these individuals particularly suspicious in Old Regime Bordeaux, where they were suspected of paying only outward homage to their new religion while commanding significant economic influence and allying with hostile political forces. This blurring of the line dividing Jews from non-Jews remained the source of lingering reservations after Jews were granted political equality. At the turn of the twentieth century, so-called scientific racism, which promised to render Jews visible after they had become legally indistinguishable from their Christian peers, tainted all discussions of what bonded Jews together (regardless of whether or not one agrees that Sombart embraced a racial theory of Jews).

The medievalists who rebuffed the assertion that economic modernity started with the Jewish invention of bills of exchange agreed on one thing: Marx, Sombart, and Weber underestimated the many and lasting contributions that the Middle Ages made to the so-called Rise of the West. But the Middle Ages these scholars had inherited from previous generations was stained by accounts that posited oversized roles for Jewish usury. From the mid-seventeenth to the early twentieth centuries, scores of writers had battled over the proper place of commerce, and Jewish commerce in particular, in European (i.e., Christian) societies. In their revolt, interwar medievalists pushed Jews to the margins of their investigations as a way of cleansing the stain that any associations of capitalism with Jews carried. In the process, they also contributed to pushing Jewish history out of the mainstream, consigning it to a subfield of academic inquiry into which few nonspecialists roam.

Coda

No retrospect will take us to the true beginning.

—GEORGE ELIOT, *DANIEL DERONDA* (1876)[1]

THIS BOOK BEGAN with a chance encounter. A few lines in the best known of all seventeenth-century European merchant manuals jumped off the page because they made little sense to this modern reader. Over the years, curiosity and stubbornness prompted me to stay with these lines. In the end, I was able to document how a forgotten tale of the origins of European financial capitalism constituted conventional wisdom from the 1650s to the 1910s to such a degree that those who did not believe in it had to go out of their way to contest it.

Throughout these 250 years, what I have called the legend of the Jewish invention of bills of exchange absorbed and at the same time transformed conceptions of Jewish usury that had emerged in the thirteenth century. Resilient as those conceptions proved to be across time, they also evolved and adapted in response to new realities and competing discursive traditions. In fact, the legend analyzed here, as capacious and malleable as any other, served multiple, sometimes even conflicting, agendas. By mapping the routes of its transmission, I have shown why this tale became a powerful tool for debating and policing the boundaries of European commercial society and why it planted deeper roots in France than in the rest of Old Regime Europe. Finally, I have concluded with an excursus on the afterlife of the legend in the nineteenth and early twentieth centuries, which has revealed how central to European economic history this narrative was until a century ago.

One question remains: If the legend was as significant and widespread as I claim, why do we not know about it today? At the most basic level, its disappearance was to be expected: we no longer use bills of exchange, so we no longer worry about who invented them. Within the academy, however, the silence is less self-evident. The fact that the legend's validity has been debunked does not explain its fall into oblivion. Origin stories continue to fascinate historians, anthropologists, and literary critics, less for the veracity of their content than for what they tell us about shared beliefs of societies different from ours. Scholars of humanism and early modern thought have documented the inexorable tendency of European chroniclers and historians to mix demonstrable facts, forgeries, and myths. In the seventeenth and eighteenth centuries, more consistent protocols of authentication and verification of textual and material pieces of evidence emerged, but they continued to coexist alongside utterly unsubstantiated reconstructions of the past.[2] We thus remain interested in the so-called battle between the ancients and the moderns, whose competing claims about the value of imitation or originality responded to logics we no longer share; similarly, eighteenth-century projects of encyclopedic knowledge continue to intrigue us even if they fall short of modern evidentiary standards.

By contrast, we pay little attention to the combination of fact and fiction that punctuates the literature written by and for merchants, for the simple reason that we tend to assign to this literature a pragmatic function even as we recognize that merchant ethics was not easily separable from religious morality or that political imperatives tilted recommendations in favor of one economic solution over another. The legend I have examined throughout this book relied on a mixture of selective memory (Christian authors knew little about the Jewish past) and sheer fabrication (Jews in late medieval France and Italy had nothing to do with the invention of bills of exchange). This mixture helped make the legend an allegory of the hopes and fears brought about by the expansion of credit relations between people near and far, relations that were deemed to be at once extraordinarily beneficial and threatening to the established social and political order.

The recent process of forgetting the legend in turn prompts us to review a number of trends, particularly pronounced in Anglophone scholarship, that have been underway within the academy over the past fifty years. I have already hinted at some of these trends when analyzing the disconnect between historians of the French Revolution and historians of Jewish emancipation in France: even when they examine the same events or the same authors (notably the Count of Mirabeau), they pass each other like ships in the night (chapter 6). To evaluate more systematically the reasons for the amnesia that surrounds the legend of the Jewish invention of bills of exchange is also to reflect on past and current modes of writing about European economic history, as I began to do at the end of the previous chapter, and to explain why my inquiry intersects with several fields, disciplines, and intellectual traditions and fits neatly into none.

Bills of exchange once held pride of place in economic and business history. In nineteenth-century German universities, economic history was taught in faculties of law. Legal and economic history were strongly linked in sectors of the French and Italian academies as well. From that perspective, bills of exchange were an ideal object of analysis: scholars disagreed sharply about the nature of the legal and financial arrangements that underpinned these bills and their historical evolution, but they all treated bills' increasing complexity from the late medieval period to the seventeenth century as symptomatic of larger transformations in European history. No doubt an introduction to the history of bills of exchange was part of the training in economic history that Max Weber and Werner Sombart received. Both also absorbed the lessons of the German Historical School, which pitted historical specificity, and particularly the nexus between cultural, legal, and economic norms, against the emerging formalism of the Austrian School and the laissez-faire dogmatism of the Manchester School. In retrospect, the founders of German social theory appear overly bent on describing historical change as a series of progressive stages of development and civilizational blocks, but we ought to appreciate their precocious interest in the legal framework of economic organization, an interest that today is once again at the heart of the social sciences.

In the mid-twentieth century, business history was still integral to the study of the Renaissance. If the Renaissance was the cradle of modernity, many scholars asked, what role did the development of financial instruments play in that story? And if individualism was an essential trait of modernity, which economic institutions most fostered it? In mining volumes of business correspondence and the bookkeeping registers of Italian merchants, both ordinary and exceptional (the Medici Bank being among the latter), Raymond de Roover devoted particular attention to bills of exchange.[3] Few followed in his footsteps, and even fewer matched his ability to paint a broad canvas using minute reconstructions of early banking techniques and intricate theological diatribes about usury and just price. In the meantime, the center of gravity in the economic history of preindustrial Europe began to move away from southern Europe and further along in time. In the process, the sixteenth century slipped under economic historians' radar, and with it, the golden age of bills of exchange and financial fairs.

In North America in the past fifty years, economic history has migrated from history to economics departments (although recently this trend has been partially reversed). Among economists, economic historians are a minority, and those interested in preindustrial Europe are an even tinier group. Large-scale datasets suitable for statistical treatment are a near-requirement in the discipline but are harder to come by or to construct for earlier periods. To the extent that the military and fiscal expansion of Europe in the sixteenth century remains a subject of inquiry, it is studied via secondary sources. For the brave few who still venture into the archives, the pressure to identify antecedents to present-day financial institutions means that the public debt and stock markets of northern Europe are better-trodden paths of scholarship than bills of exchange.[4]

Meanwhile, social scientists' propensity to measure economic indicators such as wages, stock prices, and tax revenues has been coupled with a renewed interest in culture as a causal motor of change. In some areas, notably the study of technological innovation, that interest had never faded. But in others, the affirmation of rational choice theory as the dominant interpretative paradigm in the social sciences had expunged culture from the list of variables to be taken into consideration when analyzing the causes of past economic growth and decline. Even as interest in cultural determinants resurfaces, however, disciplinary and methodological balkanization between humanistic and social scientific research persists and has even created new chasms in the very terrain where one could in principle expect greater collaboration. Economists and political scientists are comfortable with a static notion of cultural blocks (e.g., Europe vs. China, Latin Europe vs. the Islamic world, Catholics vs. Protestants) that is anathema to historians and tend to emphasize persistence rather than change over time.[5] Naturally, this is not the type of scholarship that would call attention to a seemingly idiosyncratic narrative like the legend of the Jewish invention of bills of exchange.

The history of economic thought has experienced its own mutations and in the process has sidelined the kind of questions that would lead us to pay attention to a legend like this. With a few exceptions, found mostly in Marxist-leaning citadels, the history of economic thought is no longer part of the mandatory curricula of economics doctoral programs and is taught in only a handful of history departments in North America. The marginalization of the field has had some refreshing effects, including the broadening of the range of texts and authors that now come under its purview. All in all, however, this rejuvenation has not affected all areas of inquiry equally: the Middle Ages and the sixteenth century have largely been relegated to the periphery, while the Enlightenment and eighteenth-century political economy have come to occupy center stage. The impetus for this resurgence of interest owes a great deal to influential works of the Cambridge School. Yet these works give primacy to politics over the economy, and consequently, the focus has shifted to public finance or the balance of trade at the expense of credit instruments that wove together the everyday lives of ordinary people and private entrepreneurs.[6]

Because moral theologians and canon lawyers who debated usury were also among the major economic theorists before 1600, the thinning of scholarly work on the economic history and history of economic thought of that period during the second half of the twentieth century has meant fewer opportunities for mainstream historians of early modern Europe to encounter scholarship on Christian debates about Jews and usury. Meanwhile, the growing affirmation of Jewish history as a legitimate academic subject with its own separate institutional infrastructure, a phenomenon seen especially in North America, has tended to widen rather than narrow the gap between its practitioners and historians of Europe. Admittedly, one can count on one's hand the early modern Jewish authors, such as the Amsterdam merchant-turned-philosophe Isaac de Pinto, who engaged in conversation with non-Jewish writers regarding the place of commerce in politics and society. But the elision of Jewish topics from the history of early modern European economic thought and economic history is first and foremost the result of the segmentation of academic fields— a tendency this book has sought to combat.

A bit more needs to be said about both the fate of economic history and the fate of the legend itself among scholars of European Jewry. To start, we ought to recognize that economic history has long had a mixed reputation among Jewish scholars. The first grand narrative of Jewish history to displace the primacy of religion and foreground a sociological approach was the work of the Russian Jewish scholar and advocate Simon Dubnow (1860–1941).[7] In the interwar period, the doyen of twentieth-century Jewish historians, Salo W. Baron (1895–1989), completed the first version of his massive and massively influential history of the Jews from antiquity to the modern age. Titled *A Social and Religious History of the Jews*, it devoted limited space to economic phenomena.[8] In 1942, Baron called for a "dispassionate examination of the historic relationships between modern capitalism and the Jews," yet his own broad sketch was more intent on stressing the detrimental effects of "individualism and materialism" on Jewish tradition than on producing the kind of "dispassionate examination" he advocated.[9]

In the aftermath of World War II, few were ready to pick up Baron's undertaking where he had left it. The prominence of economic themes in the murderous persecutions of Jews carried out by totalitarian regimes in the mid-twentieth century made most Jewish scholars wary of delving into the subject. A general discomfort surrounded the scholarly treatment of all economic activities by Jews, and the commercial roles Jews played in premodern Europe in particular.[10] As a result, the four decades after the Holocaust were not a period of innovation in the field of Jewish economic history. To the extent that Zionist historians were interested in the topic, they turned to agriculture and industrialization as the two defining phenomena of past and modern Jewish societies. The standard narrative remained the same: only under the mounting pressure of persecution after the destruction of the Second Temple in 70 CE had Jews flocked to commerce, an activity in which they came to excel not because of innate characteristics but because of a lack of alternative opportunities.

This was the consensus that Jewish historians took for granted when they wrestled with the possibility that Jews might have invented bills of exchange, a claim that cut both ways: it valorized Jews' resilience in the face of inauspicious external circumstances, but it also risked casting them as perennial and omnipotent merchants. At the turn of the twentieth century, *The Jewish Encyclopedia*, the English-language monument to the recent achievements of Jewish scholarship, relayed the views of those who ascribed to Jews the invention of bills of exchange, but it gave more credence to the idea that Muslim traders devised these financial instruments in the eighth century and that Italian merchants later perfected them.[11] In the 1930s, Baron had no doubt that "the vital innovations of paper currency, international bills of exchange, the stock exchange, etc., reveal little, if any, Jewish influence in their early stages."[12]

The authoritativeness of Baron's statement did not mean that lay and academic Jewish audiences ceased to come across the legend of the Jewish invention of bills of exchange. In a pioneering history of the Jews of his native Thessaloniki, Isaac Samuel Emmanuel (1896–1972), a German-educated historian and ordained rabbi, connected the tale with his ancestors: in his telling, bills of exchange had been invented by Jews fleeing Spain in 1492, who hid those pieces of paper in their prayer books and were thus able to save a great deal of their assets.[13] With Sephardic Jews still occupying a marginal position in

Jewish academic institutions, this further elaboration of the legend did not gain traction.

It was Montesquieu's version of the legend that enlisted the most supporters and detractors. In a fast-paced lecture in London on the emancipation of European Jewry and the rise of capitalism, the renowned book collector, scholar, and polymath Chimen Abramsky (1916–2010) took the time to debunk Montesquieu's idea and explain instead that "Lombard merchants and bankers" had introduced bills of exchange.[14] When Shmuel Ettinger (1919–1988), a lapsed communist and secular Zionist professor of history at Hebrew University, painted the economic history of Jews in broad strokes in a brief essay, he greatly downplayed the link between commerce and emancipation, but even he could not resist relaying Montesquieu's exaltation of Jews' financial skills as rare praise amid the generally unsympathetic Enlightenment treatment of the Jews.[15] Ettinger was not the only faculty member in Jerusalem who incorporated the legend into his teaching and writing. In the 1960s, a student at Hebrew University could still be taught that medieval Jews invented bills of exchange as part of the narrative that celebrated Jews' outstanding commercial skills as a form of survival in adverse circumstances.[16]

It took an outsider to shatter the historiographical consensus. In his *European Jewry in the Age of Mercantalism, 1550–1750*, first published in 1985, Jonathan Israel focuses on Sombart's post-1492 chronology but rejects his framework entirely by attributing the reversal of the fortunes of both eastern and western European Jews in the period between 1550 and 1713 to the "political and spiritual upheaval which engulfed European culture as a whole at the end of the sixteenth century."[17] Israel's wide-ranging synthesis aims to show that a singular convergence of the doctrines of toleration that emerged from the French Wars of Religion, the surge of interest in the Hebrew Bible among Christian scholars, and new economic policies designed to attract Jews and other foreign merchants to Christian communities in order to boost commerce favored Jews' reintegration into parts of Europe from which they had been expelled in the Middle Ages. Not any inherent facility with money, but a tendency to adapt to local structures they could not control led Jews to take up different economic roles in different regions of the Continent: in western Europe, Sephardim seized opportunities created by sweeping maritime empires; in central Europe, a few wealthy financiers negotiated privileges for fellow Jews in exchange for providing princes with the resources and services they needed to fund their war efforts; in the Polish–Lithuanian Commonwealth, absentee feudal lords relied on Jews to tend to their estates. When political and economic conditions in each region changed, so did the economic profile of the Jews there.

Although Israel does not discuss the commercial techniques utilized by Jewish merchants and brokers, he implies that these individuals conformed to the forms of business organization that prevailed in the surrounding societies. Obviously, there is no place in his approach for the legend or any other special ties between Jews and bills of exchange. Nor does he feel the need to mention Sombart. His goal is to weave Jewish history into the fabric of European history, not to confine it to a separate sphere. In Israel's perspective, the singularities of the Jewish experience serve to illuminate broader dynamics that affected early modern Europe at large and offer grounds for further comparisons more than they are significant in and of themselves.

This disregard for Sombart, however, has been far from universal. At the turn of the twenty-first century, the old discomfort toward economic history has given way to a spike in interest in the subject among historians of past Jewish societies.[18] And with it, Sombart has been resurrected, alternatively as the dead horse that still needs beating or as a hidden muse. Breaking the usual reticence that many display in broaching the subject of Jews and capitalism, some scholars today justify their approach in relation to Sombart, and others even find redeeming qualities in his work. Yuri Slezkine joins a long line of thinkers for whom "the Jews epitomize Western civilization—as its original creators, best practitioners, and rightful beneficiaries."[19] At the same time, for fear that these assertions might be misconstrued, he distances himself from Sombart.[20] In a prize-winning book, two economists, Maristella Botticini and Zvi Eckstein, argue that the compulsory religious education of Jewish men transformed Jewish society from an agricultural to a commercial one during the first millennium and a half of the Common Era. Their approach is reminiscent of Sombart's in two respects: it downplays persecution as an explanatory factor and stresses the persistence of Jewish cultural traits across time and space.[21] In a recent essay, Adam Sutcliffe recounts the controversies surrounding the publication of *The Jews and Economic Life* in 1911 and situates the work in the intellectual climate of the time but also urges us not to dismiss Sombart too easily, suggesting that he was neither "as straightforwardly hostile [to Jews] as many critics have assumed" nor "altogether wrong."[22]

The partial rehabilitation of Sombart, whose "filtration with fascist ideology after World War I" was until recently deemed to have "irreparably tarnished his reputation," is perplexing.[23] If the goal is to revitalize interest in economic themes among scholars of past Jewish societies, Sombart is not the right starting point. *The Jews and Economic Life* should be read as a flawed empirical account and as a chapter in modern intellectual history, not as an imperfect model.[24] Sombart's insistence on the unusual economic occupational structure of most postexilic Jewish societies was nothing new at the time of its publication, and his explanations for this phenomenon were indefensible even by the standards of historical inquiry in his day.

Extreme as he was, Sombart was also the heir to a long tradition of referencing (more or less imaginary) Jews in order to make arguments for (and more often against) capitalism—to gloss once more the subtitle of Albert Hirschman's influential work *The Passions and the Interests: Political Arguments for Capitalism Before Its Triumph*, this time putting the emphasis on *Arguments*.[25] This long tradition was already fading when Hirschman detected one of its traces. In 1977, his evocation of Montesquieu's version of the legend of the Jewish invention of bills of exchange briefly revived positive receptions of that tale and incorporated it into an argument about the future of modern capitalism and democracy that was more uplifting than the one articulated by Sombart. But the reference to Montesquieu's tale of Jewish inventiveness and survival fell on deaf ears, as the many readers of *The Passions and the Interests* did not recognize the legend's complicated history and significance.

This example is indicative of a larger phenomenon: the decline in invocations of figures of Jews as forms of social and political critique. As I write these pages, antisemitism in the United States and especially in Europe is again on the rise, and insidious references to domineering Jewish capitalists—references that in some cases translate into hostile actions—are not confined to the fringes of media and society. Meanwhile, Islam has begun to provide another foil against which the West defines itself, primarily among the political Right, but even in sectors of the Left. Today as in the past, antisemitism and Islamophobia are neither mutually exclusive nor necessarily in competition with one another; in fact, they coexist in locally distinctive forms, particularly across parts of Europe, where images of Jews and Muslims are sometimes used interchangeably in debates about credibility, integrity, and civic loyalty.[26] But if Hirschman's reference to the legend of bills of exchange could be so easily disregarded, it is also because, thanks to meaningful changes in attitudes and to a new awareness of the power of language to cause harm, representations of Jews are no longer a preferred vehicle for mainstream Western culture, let alone scholars, to express their deepest worries and aspirations.

By contrast, as this book has shown, that habit of mind was not only pervasive in the Middle Ages and at the height of racist antisemitism in modern

Europe but also widespread in the post-Reformation period, that is, at the very time when European merchant culture is generally assumed to have begun to free itself from religious dictates. By establishing an intimate connection between Jews and bills of exchange, the legend did not censure all commercial pursuits. Rather, it reworked ingrained images of Jews as trickster lenders and disloyal subjects of Christian rulers who were capable of siphoning wealth out of the realm. In so doing, it projected onto imaginary figures generalized fears that the transformation of bills of exchange into both ordinary and incredibly complex operations made more and more acute in the course of the sixteenth and early seventeenth centuries.

The putative Jewish invention of these bills became a way of addressing questions about the increasing abstraction of credit relations, the beneficial and corrupting consequences of their expansion, the limits of regulatory institutions, and even the nature of political power. Although not as autonomous from state financial policies as Bitcoins claim to be today, bills of exchange were primarily an instrument of private finance. They represented the ability of far-flung merchants to move funds, speculate on currency arbitrage, and potentially subvert states' and empires' monetary policies. In the 100 years before the French Revolution, they also became a fairly common form of payment among men and, to a lesser extent, women whose financial literacy was not always commensurate with the complexity of the speculative schemes into which they entered. During the nineteenth century, as new capitalist institutions from the factory to the corporation displaced commercial credit as the primary subjects of cultural and political struggle, the legend lost its immediacy as a moral tale and entered a new chapter of its existence as a pseudo-fact at the heart of influential accounts of the historical trajectory of Western capitalism.

There are many reasons why representations of Jews—and specifically of Jews' alleged ways of handling money in the late Middle Ages—have had such an incredible pull on European authors of the most diverse dispositions and backgrounds. At bottom, all those representations have something in common: the assumption that historically, Jews behaved in the marketplace according to attributes that defined them outside of the marketplace. Not everyone agreed on what those attributes were and whether they were immutable or reformable. That is why we have encountered a plurality of representations of Jews and their economic roles, even if the most persistent was that of a devious Jewish usurer hiding behind an honest façade, ready to exploit credulous and upright Christian borrowers. The ubiquity of this image was a measure of the pull of the fantasy that market society, before and after it was called capital-ism, might be constructed as a neutral zone, one unaffected by outside influ-ences and where only those forces generated within market exchanges them-selves meet and clash on a level playing field.

All the authors we have read and interrogated throughout this book wres-tled with variations of the same question: How do legal, economic, and sym-bolic hierarchies that precede one's entry into a financial transaction with someone from outside one's immediate circle affect those transactions? By the seventeenth century, certain European governments had designed regimes of toleration that promised to treat Jewish merchants like all other merchants with regard to their trading and banking activities. Later, emancipation lifted all legal restrictions on Jewish men operating in the market. Different as these historical moments were, they both produced a more egalitarian structure within which Jewish economic actors could interact with non-Jews. Yet figures of Jews that owed more to long discursive traditions than to real-life struggles stripped even these more egalitarian forms of coexistence of their full meaning. That is why the ease with which Jews have been perceived as at once invisible and distinctive, marginal and yet centrally disruptive, ought to be part of how we understand the development of Western commercial society.

Early Modern European Commercial Literature

PRINTED BIBLIOGRAPHIES AND ONLINE DATABASES

A SPECIALIST OF SIXTEENTH-CENTURY western European merchants, the late Pierre Jeannin launched a laudable project at a time when historians still took notes on 6 × 8 index cards: an inventory of all economic treatises and manuals printed in Europe during the early modern period. Thanks to the collaboration of two colleagues, Jochen Hoock and Wolfgang Kaiser, the first volumes of this ongoing project have appeared, covering the period up to 1700. Jeannin and his collaborators titled their work *Ars Mercatoria*. By choosing a Latin expression, they gave the impression that they were using early modern terminology. In fact, they turned a rare expression into a staple phrase, at least among specialists. *Ars Mercatoria*, the art of commerce, is a felicitous title because it is capacious: it captures the amorphous boundaries of the literature it seeks to map in ways other modern terms, such as "economic treatises" or "manuals," cannot.[1] Bulky and only available in the traditional form of the bounded book, these volumes are an invaluable source: while expensive, their cost is not prohibitive; they are present in many libraries and can be ordered even by those with access only to interlibrary loan; and, most important of all, they list the library holdings of each bibliographical item. I have consulted them many times but could not rely on them alone in writing this book because at present they do not go beyond the year 1700.

Far smaller and partial, but also handier and more accessible, is the corpus of "economic bestsellers" published in Europe before 1800 redacted by Kenneth

E. Carpenter, the former librarian of the Harvard Business School's Kress Library of Business and Economics (now part of Baker Library). This list identifies forty titles of political economy, published between 1588 and 1848, primarily in English, French, German, Spanish, and Italian, on the basis of the estimated number of editions published in the original language and in translation. It is an eclectic list, one that begins with Bernardo Davanzati's *Lezione delle monete* and ends with Karl Marx's *Manifesto*, and excludes "practical works of the how-to-do-it" variety, such as Jacques Savary's *Parfait négociant*.[2] I made little use of this catalogue because of the few titles it includes and its a priori division between high- and low-brow economic bestsellers. Sophus Reinert, by contrast, relied entirely on Carpenter's corpus for his analysis of the canon of European political economy and its translation from one language to another; consequently, he also omitted the less canonical handbooks that I considered here.[3]

Given the focus of this book, I should mention one more traditional scholarly work: Jean-Claude Perrot's pioneering essays on the economic literature published in Old Regime France. Perrot was the first to attempt to quantify the size of this phenomenon, although the basis for his calculations is not always clear.[4] Moreover, although he labeled his subject the study of "political economy," a term coined in 1615 that gained currency in the following century, Perrot covered in detail texts such as Savary's *Parfait négociant* and the Savary brothers' *Dictionnaire universel de commerce*, which fit neither the contemporary nor the modern definition of "political economy."[5]

The online database that best succeeds in embracing the wide assortment of publications available to early modern readers, ranging from price sheets to treatises of political economy, merchant manuals, commentaries on maritime law, and more, is *The Making of the Modern World*. This project began with the digitization of the two largest collections of printed material pertaining to all things economic from the invention of the printing press until the mid-nineteenth century: the Goldsmiths Library of Economic Literature at the University of London and the Kress Collection of Business and Economics at Harvard Business School. Since its creation, it has incorporated additional material from the Seligman Collection of the Butler Library at Columbia University and Sterling Memorial Library at Yale University. It is bound to expand further. As a result, multiple copies of the same title have sometimes been digitized.

The main advantage of this database is that it comes closest to capturing the definition of "the economy" as it existed in the minds of the readers and writ-

ers of the time. It does not exclude material by subject: everything from de-
mography to trade, finance, agriculture, administration, and law comes under
its purview. Nor does it make any formal or hierarchical distinctions between
bound books, serial publications, pamphlets, or loose-leaf pages containing
pieces of legislation, price lists, and more. Given the expansion of European
commerce and colonial rule over this period, it also contains useful, if selective, information about other regions of the world. In short, it does not rely on
a preestablished notion of what "the economy" meant at a given time, although
its strengths reflect those of the library collections it uses and are thus tilted
toward core areas of western Europe.

The main drawback of this resource is its price. *The Making of the Modern
World* (*MMW*) is sold by Gale in three packages (*Part 1: 1450–1850, Part 2:
1851–1914*, and the recently added *Part 3: 1890–1945*). The company's website
shows that in 2015, out of a total of 166 institutional subscribers to at least one
of the digital collections produced by Gale, 49 percent were in the United
States and 24 percent in Japan. Across Europe there were only twenty-nine
institutional subscribers (of which eight were in the United Kingdom and another eight in Switzerland).[6] Of the ten universities with the largest endowments in the United States in 2016 (Harvard, Yale, Stanford, Princeton, the
Massachusetts Institute of Technology, the University of Pennsylvania, Texas
A&M–College Station, the University of Michigan–Ann Arbor, Columbia,
and Notre Dame), two (Texas A&M–College Station and the University of
Pennsylvania) do not subscribe to *MMW*.[7]

Among the other electronic databases that I used most often, three require
a subscription: the *Early English Books Online* (*EEBO*) and the *Eighteenth-
Century Collections Online* (*ECCO*), both of which only include English-
language texts, and the *Sabin Americana, 1500–1926*, which, like *MMW* and
ECCO, is also produced by Gale.

To combat the prohibitive costs of for-profit online resources, a number of
libraries have partnered to produce open-access platforms that are more func-
tional than Google Books. Particularly relevant to my work is the Hathi Trust
Digital Library, which collects millions of digitized books, journals, and other
materials (including pilot projects that extend to digital audio and image content, as well as digital-born publications). French rare book material can be
accessed via Gallica, which makes available part of the digitized collections
of the Bibliothèque Nationale de France, even if it is rather clunky, and the
Project for American and French Research on the Treasury of the French

Language (ARTFL), which includes several old dictionaries as well as Diderot and D'Alembert's *Encyclopédie* and has user-friendly search tools. Artworks, video, and sounds figure more prominently in Europeana Collections, an open-access interface that makes available millions of rare books, images, and other sources from European digital collections.

The Legend's Earliest Formulation

WHAT FOLLOWS IS MY English translation of the text that forms the basis of the legend of the Jewish invention of marine insurance and bills of exchange as it appears in Étienne Cleirac's 1661 *Us et coustumes de la mer*. I chose the second rather than the first (1647) edition of this book because it offers an extended version of the legend and because it circulated more widely than the first, as the number of surviving copies in rare book libraries attest. (Today, readers can access both editions online through Gallica.) Note that there exist two prints of the 1661 edition, both issued in Bordeaux, both with the same title and the same pagination. One version has a colored frontispiece and more decorations; it was printed "En la boutique de Millanges chez Guillaume Taupinard, marchand libraire." The other has a black-and-white frontispiece and fewer decorations; it was printed "Par Iacques Mongiorn Millanges, imprimeur ordinaire du roy."

I have underlined those words and sentences that do not appear in the 1647 edition and were added in 1661. I have retained italics, capital and small letters, and most of the punctuation as they figure in the original. I have chosen to stay as close to the text as possible except when a literal translation would be unintelligible.

Source: Estienne Cleirac, *Us et coustumes de la mer, divisées en trois parties: I. De la navigation. II. Du commerce naval & contracts maritimes. III. De la iurisdiction de la marine. Avec un traicté des termes de marine & reglemens de la navigation des fleuves & rivieres: le tout reveu, corrigé & augmenté par l'autheur en cette derniere edition* (Bordeaux: Millanges, 1661), 217–223.

The Standard of the Sea[1]

Chapter 1: On insurance contracts or policies, their definition, their similarities with and differences from other contracts pertaining to maritime affairs. First Article: *Insurance* is a contract through which one promises the indemnity of the goods that are transported from one country to another, especially when they are transported by sea; and it works by means of a price calculated as a percentage of the insured goods' value and agreed upon between the insured, who carries the goods or has them transported by a third party, and the insurer, who promises the indemnity.

[CLIERAC'S COMMENTARY]

Contractus assecurationis id est avertendi periculi, dicitur contractus innominatus. FACIO UT DES, DO UT FACIAS, unde debet regulari iuxta naturam contractuum quibus assimilatur, assimilatur autem emptioni, & venditoni propter prætium quod datur ratione periculi, quia qui assecurationem facit propter prætium dicitur emere eventium periculi. Decisio Rotæ Genuæ tertia, num. 28 & decis. 39, no. 9.[2]

Insurance policies, and bills of exchange, were unknown to the ancient Roman jurisprudence and are the posthumous invention of Jews, according to the remark of *Giovan Villani* in his universal history.[3]

When these abominable circumcised[4] were banned from France because of their wrongdoings and their execrable crimes, and their assets were seized, at the time of King *Dagobert*, King *Philip Augustus*, and King *Philip the Tall*,[5] in order to retrieve their commodities and money, which they had consigned to or hidden in the hands of their friends before leaving, necessity taught these malicious men lacking public trust to use secret letters and bills written with few words and little substance, as bills of exchange still are, addressed to those who had received and concealed their stolen goods and given Jews a hand. Jews carried out these tasks by employing travelers and foreign merchants.

And having succeeded in this scheme, in order not to be deceived on the exchange rate, or in order to make a profit, they kept themselves informed *au pair & à la touche*, that is to say, about the intrinsic goodness, the metal purity and impurity of currencies,[6] so that they would not be mistaken about the value and reduction of the different exchange rates of each currency, whose rates have always changed and varied in each province, much more in the past than at present; and this was the origin of bills of exchange, as *Villani* says.

In order to retrieve their movable goods, their commodities, and their other belongings in the Jewish fashion and to the risk and danger of those who performed that service for them, their mistrust suggested to them the invention of a rudimentary beginning of what became insurance certificates or policies, through which all the risks and dangers of a voyage fell onto those who had insured the goods, on condition that a gift or a modest price, which today is called *premium*, be paid; it follows that bills of exchange and insurance policies are Jewish from birth, both in their invention and name. *Polizza di cambio, Polizza di sicuranza.*

The Italian Lombards, witnesses of and actors in this Jewish intrigue, after they retained the form of these letters, learned to use them effectively when in Italy the unhappy sects of Guelfs and *Ghibellines*, meaning the followers of the Pope and the Emperor, respectively, threatened each other, so to endeavor to supplant one another and put Christianity through great troubles and tumult.

The weakest, or the most timid among each party, took refuge in those places that they estimated to be safest or most favorable, where, in order to survive in the absence of other professions, they practiced usury and these Jewish inventions. And in order to protect themselves from ecclesiastical censure, which has always condemned every sort of usury and usurers, they skillfully succeeded in having their practices recognized—not just tolerated by connivance, but recognized as highly necessary to the exercise and maintenance of commerce and traffic. *Usuram sub specie negotiationis palliantes,*[7] as in reality those banking activities and insurances that are treated as honorable, upright, and legal activities are greatly useful and helpful to business, even according to the opinion of Cardinal Cajetan, the great theologian Thomas de Vio, in his *Tractatus de cambijs,* ch. 5,[8] and *Navarrus, in his Enchiridio, ch. 17, no. 284.*[9]

The Guelfs who found refuge in France, Avignon, England, and in the countries of obedience[10] were initially favored and supported, notably at the [papal] court of Avignon, in the name of which they had been exiled from their homes; they succeeded in obtaining the grace and the dispensations of the [papal] court of Rome, thanks to which they attributed to themselves and took the venerable title of *Domini Papæ Mercatores et Scambiatores, ob murmurantibus tamen Iudæis,* as Matthew Paris says in his history of England, *in vita Regis*

Henrici terij.[11] We ought to consider that in those times as well as today usury was strictly prohibited before *the tribunal of conscience*,[12] and it was only tolerated for the miserable Jews, as people without conscience. *Cap. quanto amplius. De usuris extra.*[13] The unexpected arrival of this sort of usurers from south of the Alps caused them [i.e., the Jews] great discontent and pain, because they [i.e., the Jews] saw that their imitators, their disciples, their acolytes, and their wretched clerks had mastered the art of usury to an even greater extent than they did; they [i.e., Lombard bankers] had become even more evil and malicious insofar as usury and rapaciousness were concerned; they bent and concocted their practices, and extracted from people greater profits and loot than Jews dared to aim for or demand; and those scoundrels were now being treated as noblemen, held in esteem as men of honor and merit, and considerably well-placed in their favors—*e lodati ne van, non che impuniti*[14]—whereas Jews were hated, treated as jackanapes, and continuously ridiculed with contempt and affront, marked with a yellow hat, harassed as pages and lackeys at every occasion, in the same way as it is described in the search that the Master cook does of his waiter or gourmet in the comedy *I supposti*, written by *Messer Ludovico Ariosto*: *Sera rimasto a dare caccia à qualche cane, ad ogni cosa che truova per via se ferma, se vede facchino, o vilano o Giudeo, non lo terriano le cattene, che non li andasse à fare qualche dispiacere.*[15]

　　But the hypocrisy or fake probity of these Guelf bankers was soon recognized and condemned by the people, who named them *Caorsini* as a considerable offense and insult. *Caursini, et caursinorum pestis abominanda*,[16] Boccaccio, *Deorum Genealogiæ, book 14, ch. 11.*[17] [See also] master Adam Théveneau in his learned and serious treatise about the laws on usury, article 1.[18] It is from them [usurers] that the Italian noun *scarcità, cio è avaricia, scarci, avari, scarcella* derives: the bag or purse[19]; the said epithet or nickname *ca[o]rsins* was given to them from the town of Cahors in Quercy, where this vermin reached its highest level under the pontificate of Pope John XXII, who was a native of that town.[20] This fact was a big scandal and gave a bad reputation to the town of Cahors, which was under a curse because of those usurers and was considered to be as abhorrent as *Sodom*. On this subject the poet *Dante* in his Inferno, *canto* XI, puts in the same circle those who suffered bad luck, those burning from sulphur, those suffering in anguish and eternal sorrow, *Sodom and Cahors*, together with all the biggest scoundrel cheaters, dishonest people,[21] teasers, charlatans,[22] those who went bankrupt, insolvent debtors condemned to wear a green hat,[23] fraudulent sellers,[24] usurers who count every month and every

cent,[25] sybarites, sycophants, calumniators, rodents,[26] scrubbers,[27] counter-
feiters, inventors of taxes and subsides, impostors, holders of unlawful claim
forms,[28] tax collectors, those who purchase and collect remittances of money
and other things of no worth,[29] prison guards,[30] troublemakers,[31] servants and
attendants,[32] *diviners of the future*,[33] poisoners, werewolves, and sorcerers, and
all other damned people whose reputation is tainted by the horrible sin against
nature, mortal enemies of all human kind, who will never be part of the kingdom of God. *Saint Paul's Epistle to the Ephesians, ch. 5, verses 3–5.*[34]

E Sodoma e Caorsa
Et chi spregiando Dio, col cor favella,
La frode, on'ogni coscienza è morsa.[35]

Eventually, these Lombard bankers became so intolerable due to their exorbitant usuries, exactions, extortions, and illicit profits,[36] that they were
treated in France in the same fashion as Jews were. *Kings Saint Louis and
Philip the Fair*[37] banished them and made them leave the kingdom in disgrace. Nevertheless, these rustics had so many friends at court, their money
wielded so much power, and that good *King Philip the Fair* was so strongly
pressured by the princes and the potentates of Italy, that in consideration of
their requests, after some time he allowed them to return. But he permitted
them to do so on condition that they would become honest in the future and
would abstain from all their bad practices. *The edict or letters of readmission
of 1311 are included in tertia parte stili parlamenti Tit[ulo] 40, De usuris, sect. 3,
no. 9.*[38]

But once these Lombard bankers returned, instead of reforming themselves, these parasitical hypocrites became even more dissolute. As a result, in
the end King *Philip of Valois*[39] finally purged his kingdom of them and drove
them out of France, confiscating their goods and loot. *Nicole Gilles* in his
Chronicles attributes the rationale for their expulsion to *the considerable draining of French finance that they inflicted, which caused the kingdom's impoverish-
ment, because after all debtors were dismissed, the king was left with the largest
burden; when they come to France they never carry a ducat but only a sheet of paper
in one hand and a feather to write in the other, and thus they put a leash on the back
of the French people and impose a tax on their money, etc.*[40]

The feather and the sheet of paper designate the bills of exchange, the insurance policies, the signatures and official documents[41] of the court of Rome,
which they acquired and then sold at high prices. *Pasquier in his Recherches,*

book 2, chap. 3, claims to have seen among the records of the treasury of Paris[42] the order sent to that court by King *Philip of Valois,* dated 12 August 1347, requesting the trial of the Lombard usurers.[43]

These malicious liars, whose frauds are aimed to take people by surprise and to pillage their fortunes, and who enriched themselves at the expense of their debtors, whom they initially pretended to wish to assist charitably in their adversities, only to lure them into their net, are ingenuously described with the forms of their usurious contracts[44] by *Matthew Paris* in his History of England: *ad annum 1235 circumveniebant enim in necessitatibus indigentes, usuram sub specie negotiationis palliantes, non ut alienæ succurrerent inediae, sed ut suæ consulerent avariciæ.*[45] [See also] *Ambrose* in his book *De Tobia, chap. 3.*[46] These boors had considerable appeal and fallacious lure that allowed them to attract debtors; and after having hooked the latter, they became even more eager to seize every possible gain, to exact usury, exchange and re-exchange rates, stipulate fines, expenditures, damages and interest, and other such shameful incremental charges,[47] so that they never wanted to receive back the principal as long as the debtor was left solvent. They were elated by the facility with which deeds of protest and overdue terms could apply. When a debtor was weak or in difficulty, they never left him in peace, but tormented him at every scheduled date when interest payments came due, that is, every month (because in these matters *usance* and month are synonyms, in the sense that usury means interest payments stipulated by month) and they never ended their harassment until they had taken everything from their debtors, *quanto perditior quisque est, tanto acrius urget: quo quisque infirmior eo prædæpatet.*[48]

We need not speak about discounting, which they always received as usury disguised as spending and to an excessive degree, because at that time all forms of usury were forbidden by the Decretals and Clementines.[49] There existed neither tariffs nor laws about interest rates; the only rule was whether or not the greediness and rapacity of some creditors from south of the Alps was tolerated. In this and other malpractices, they were much more ruinous than the Jews, according to the remarks of the same Matthew Paris, *quae conditio gravior est quam Iudeorum, quia quandocunque sortem Iudeo attuleris recipiet, cum tanto lucro, quod tempori tanto se commensurat.*[50]

As far as the Ghibellines are concerned, they worked their way into all parts of Germany and the regions that were either subject to, recognized by or confederated of the Empire, and were called *Lombards* [according to] *Froissart* in *chapter 85 of volume 4,*[51] where it is maintained that they practiced similar sordid usuries, with less support or favors, because in the end they were big skimps, mean-minded, dealers of old clothes, merchants of second-hand goods, mercers of old merchandise and monopolists[52]; from this it follows that German and Flemish people call all exchange dealers, bankers, dirty usurers, and resellers of whatever background *Lombards*; and for the same reason the square in which the market for currency exchange and second-hand goods is located in the city of Amsterdam has kept the name of *Lombard Square* until today.

Étienne Cleirac's Works

TITLES, EDITIONS, AND ISSUES

In Manuscript

Coustumier de Guyenne nommé Roolle de la ville de Bourdeaus, contenant partie des privilèges, franchises, lois, mœurs et formes de vivre des anciens Bordelais, sur lequel la coustume réformée en l'an 1520 a été extraite. Tiré de l'estude de Messire Michel de Montaigne, autheur des Essais, avec quelques notes pour l'intelligence et l'explication tant du langage que de l'histoire, adjoutées par Monsieur Estienne Cleirac, advocat au Parlement. Bibliothèque de l'Université Montesquieu-Bordeaux 4, Ms. 5. This is a nineteenth-century copy of the original.

Ordonnances et coustumes de la mer colligées par Monsieur Estienne Cleirac, advocat en la court. Bibliothèque Municipale, Bordeaux, Ms. 381.

In Print

Explication des termes de marine

Explication des termes de marine employez dans les edicts, ordonnances, & reglemens de l'Admirauté. Ensemble les noms propres des nauires, de leur parties, & l'usage d'icelles, l'artillerie navale, les livrees ou couleurs des estendards & pauillons de ceux qui voguent sur les mers. Dedié a Monseigneur l'Archevesque de Bordeaux. Paris: Chez Michel Brunet, 1636.

Us et coustumes de la mer

Us et coustumes de la mer, divisées en trois parties: I. De la navigation. II. Du commerce naval & contracts maritimes. III. De la iurisdiction de la marine. Avec un traicté des termes de marine & reglemens de la navigation des fleuves & rivieres. Bordeaux: Par Guillaume Millanges, imprimeur ordinaire du roi, 1647.

Us et coustumes de la mer, divisées en trois parties: I. De la navigation. II. Du commerce naval & contracts maritimes. III. De la iurisdiction de la marine. Avec un traicté des termes de marine & reglemens de la navigation des fleuves & rivieres: le tout reveu, corrigé & augmenté par l'autheur en cette derniere edition. Bourdeaux: En la boutique de Millanges chez Guillaume Taupinard, marchand libraire, 1661.

Us et coustumes de la mer, divisées en trois parties: I. De la navigation. II. Du commerce naval & contracts maritimes. III. De la iurisdiction de la marine. Avec un traicté des termes de marine & reglemens de la navigation des fleuves & rivieres: le tout reveu, corrigé & augmenté par l'autheur en cette derniere edition. Bourdeaux: Par Iacques Mongiorn Millanges, imprimeur ordinaire du roy, 1661.

Les us et coutumes de la mer, divisées en trois parties: I. De la navigation. II. Du commerce naval, & contrats maritimes. III. De la jurisdiction de la marine, Avec un traitté des termes de marine, reglemens de la navigation des fleuves & rivieres; et les nouveaux edits, reglemens, arrests & iugemens rendus sur le fait du commerce de la mer. Paris: Chez Denis Becket, 1665.

Les us et coutumes de la mer, divisées en trois parties: I. De la navigation. II. Du commerce naval & contrats maritimes. III. De la jurisdiction de la marine. Avec un traitté des termes de marine, reglemens de la navigation des fleuves & rivieres; et les nouveaux edits, reglemens, arrests & iugemens rendus sur le fait du commerce de la mer. Rouen: Chez Jean Berthelin, ruë aux Juifs, prés le Palais, 1671, avec privilege du roy.

Les us et coutumes de la mer, divisées en trois parties: I. De la navigation. II. Du commerce naval & contrats maritimes. III. De la jurisdiction de la marine. Avec un traitté des termes de marine, reglemens de la navigation des fleuves & rivieres; et les nouveaux edits, reglemens, arrests & iugemens rendus sur le fait du commerce de la mer. Rouen: Chez Jean Viret, imprimeur ordinaire du roy, au haut des degrez du Palais, 1671, avec privilege du roy.

Les us et coutumes de la mer, divisées en trois parties: I. De la navigation, II. Du commerce naval & contrats maritimes, III. De la jurisdiction de la marine. Avec un traitté des termes de marine, reglemens de la navigation des fleuves & rivieres, et les nouveaux edits, reglemens, arrests & jugemens rendus sur le fait du commerce de la mer. Rouen: Chez Jean Lucas derrier le Palais, prés S. Lo., avec privilege du roy, 1671.

Les us et coutumes de la mer, divisées en trois parties: I. De la navigation, II. Du commerce naval & contrats maritimes, III. De la jurisdiction de la marine. Avec un traitté des termes de marine, reglemens de la navigation des fleuves & rivieres, et les nouveaux edits, reglemens, arrests & jugemens rendus sur le fait du commerce de la mer. Rouen: Par la Compagnie des Imprimeurs-Libraires au Palais, 1682.

Les us et coutumes de la mer, divisées en trois parties: I. De la navigation, II. Du commerce naval & contrats maritimes, III. De la jurisdiction de la marine. Avec un traitté des termes de marine, reglemens de la navigation des fleuves & rivieres, et les nouveaux edits, reglemens, arrests & jugemens rendus sur le fait du commerce de la mer. Amsterdam: n.p., 1788.

Usance du négoce

Usance du negoce ou commerce de la banque des lettres de change colligé par M.e Estienne Cleirac advocat en la cour de parlement de Bordeaux, ensemble les figures des ducats de Guyenne, & des anciennes monnoyes bourgeoises de Bordeaux pour le menu change. Bourdeaux: Par Guillaume da Court, imprimeur ordinaire du roy & de l'université, 1656.

Usance du negoce, ou, Commerce de la banque des lettres de change colligé par M.e Estienne Cleirac adovcat en la court de parlement de Bordeaux, ensemble les figures des ducats de Guyenne, & des anciennes monnoyes bourgeoises de Bordeaux pour le menu change. Paris: Chez Charles Angot, 1659.

Usance du negoce, ou, Commerce de la banque des lettres de change colligé par M.e Estienne Cleirac ... Veu, corrigé & augmenté. Bourdeaux: Par Guillaume de la Court, imprimeur ordinaire du roy & de l'université, 1670.

The Ancient Sea-Laws of Oleron, Wisby and the Hanse-Towns

Guy Miege, *The Ancient Sea-Laws of Oleron, Wisby and the Hanse-towns Still in Force: Taken out of a French Book, Intitled, Les us & coutumes de la mer and Rendred into English, for Use of Navigation...* London: J. Redmayne for T. Basset, 1686.

The Legend in the Works of Jacques Savary and His Sons

Le parfait négociant

Source: Jacques Savary, *Le parfait négociant, ou, Instruction générale pour ce qui regarde le commerce de toute sorte de marchandises, tant de France, que des pays estrangers* (Paris: Chez Louis Billaine, 1675), 121–124.

[Book 1] Chapter XIX: On the origin of bills of exchange and their commercial usefulness.

Before discussing bills of exchange and *billets de change* in detail,[1] it seems appropriate to examine their origin and the time period when their commerce began in France in order to satisfy the curiosity of those who do not know about these matters.

A thousand years ago no one in France knew what bills of exchange were; they were invented by the Jews who were expelled from France during the reigns of Dagobert I, Philip Augustus, and Philip the Tall, in the years 640, 1181, and 1316. They [the Jews] took refuge in Lombardy and in order to withdraw the money and the goods that they had left in France in the hands of their friends, necessity taught them to use letters and bills of very few words and little substance, as bills of exchange still are today, addressing those bills to their friends; and in order to carry out this task, they relied on travelers, pilgrims, and foreign merchants. Through this means they succeeded in retrieving all their assets, but because this sort of people has infinite genius for anything regarding gain and profit, they made every effort to acquire knowledge about the intrinsic value and possible impurities of all metallic currencies in order to make no mistakes in calculating the alloy of different coins, which at the time was highly volatile.

The Italian Lombards found the invention of bills of exchange to be very useful to cover up usury; and the Ghibellines who were exiled from Italy by the Guelph party, having settled in Amsterdam, followed the example of the Jews and [used] this instrument to retrieve the assets that they had in Italy and established the commerce of bills of exchange, which they called *polizza di cambio*. It was they who invented the re-exchange, when the bills that were sent to them came back protested and they pretended to be suffering losses, expenses, damage, and interest rates.

Merchants and traders found this invention very useful in order to facilitate their business in foreign countries, and because they derived considerable profits from these bills, they began to deal in these bills honestly. Princes and kings assisted them in this effort because the use of bills rendered superfluous the export of silver, diamonds, and precious stones out of their states for the purpose of buying merchandise, something that they always found important to prevent. For this reason princes and kings granted ample privileges to these merchants, designating squares and other public spaces to the conduct of exchange dealings. Still today the square in Amsterdam is called *Lombard square* owing to the fact that the Ghibellines gathered there in order to carry out their exchange dealings.

The merchants of Amsterdam spread the commerce of bills of exchange all over Europe, and particularly in France, through their correspondents; as a result our kings conceded ample privileges to merchants, especially to those in Lyon, where it seems that the commerce of bills of exchange began. These privileges gave rise to the establishment of the jurisdiction that in that city is called *Conservation* and the jurisdiction known as *Consulaire*, which was created by Charles IX in 1563 and which is now established in all the cities of the kingdom where commerce is considerable, so that all disputes between merchants and traders over bills of exchange and other commercial matters[2] be adjudicated on the spot, without any legal formalities except for the simple issuing of a libel, and without recourse to lawyers or other legal intermediaries.[3] The hope is that in this manner justice be provided free of charge and by judges who are chosen from among merchants and traders for their knowledge of all matters concerning commodities and bills of exchange.

It is certain that there is nothing more useful to the state and to the public than the use of bills of exchange. But it should also be admitted that there is nothing more dangerous than this commerce, which produces more usury and bankrupts when bankers, merchants, and traders practice it with lust and imprudence. Moreover, merchants ought to keep good records of their business in order to know its condition quickly and at any time. Because banking is an activity practiced by bankers and merchants of all the cities in the kingdom [of France] where manufactures are established, and is usually conducted in cooperation with foreigners, bills of exchange are of utmost necessity for the maintenance of commerce and in order to receive or pay the sums of money that bankers, merchants, and traders draw on each other and remit reciprocally for the purchase and sale of their merchandise; even for matters others than commerce, bills of exchange are very useful to the state and the public.

The etymology of the word "bill of exchange" is easily understood: it means nothing else than to convert the money that a merchant has in one city and sends it to be received in another city by a merchant who has a stable business there and has available a similar sum, which he gives in exchange in the city where he resides, from where the bill is drawn. This exchange is equally advantageous to both parties because the one who will have the money in a city without this convenience would otherwise be obliged to make the money come in specie through couriers and chariots and the one who would need it in the same city to conduct his business would otherwise be obliged to transport it from the place of his residence.

The word "exchange" also derives from the fact that the profit or interest that is received and the one that is produced when a bill is drawn or remitted are never the same: the profit can be high or low; sometimes there is a loss, other times a gain; occasionally the exchange is even, that is, there is nothing to lose or to gain among those involved in these exchange dealings: the commerce of bills of exchange gives rise to a perpetual transformation.

It is important to stress that different exchange rates from one country to the other are what determines the currency conversions. For instance, if a merchant wants to remit to Amsterdam one écu of France currency that is worth 3 livres, he won't receive more than 96 deniers de gros, which are worth 48 sols (presuming that the exchange is at this rate because it always fluctuates, as I said above); because 120 gros make one écu, which are 3 livres in France, it follows that the merchant will lose 12 solds per écu, or 20%, in the exchange. This loss is to be attributed to the fact that the currency is weaker in Holland than in France: the same happens with issuances and remittances to and from foreign countries where the currency is weaker than in France. Indeed, if all currencies were valued at the same rate as in France in every European state, all exchange would be equal: that is, a merchant would give one golden Louis in a French city in order to receive another currency of equivalent value in a foreign location. In that case, there would be neither loss nor gain for either party, and all gains or losses in the exchange dealings would result from the abundance or scarcity of money in the places where issuances and remittances would be carried out. For example, in France, where all moneys have the same exchange rate, if the Parisian money market only needed 1,000,000 to pay what it owed in Lyon for its payments of the month of August, and if the Lyon money market also only needed 1,000,000 in Paris, the exchange would even itself out because both cities had the same need; by contrast, if Paris needed 1,500,000 livres to pay in Lyon at the time of the aforementioned payments, while Lyon only needed 1,000,000 in Paris, bills of exchange would be rare, and the money paid in Paris in order to draw bills in Lyon would be devalued, and bills would appreciate; and if the abundance of money were in Paris and the scarcity in Lyon, the bills would lose in value and money would appreciate in value.

The usefulness that merchants found in the commerce of bills of exchange gave rise to the so-called *billets de change*, delivered or deliverable, payable to the order or to the bearer, which greatly facilitate payments and do not oblige [merchants] to keep all their money idly in the cashier without the possibility of generating any gains, as well as other bills that are considered as money that were lent or merchandise that was sold, payable to the order or to the bearer, which are a class of credit instruments different from simple bills with value of money or merchandise.

I will explain in the following chapters the many types of bills of exchange and the endorsements that we write on their back. Regarding the different types of trade handled with these bills, I will also discuss the duration of the credit; whether it expires on a certain date or after a standard period (*at usance*); a bill's acceptance, whether it is oral or written; how bills were practiced before the *Ordonnance* of March 1673; how protests work; and what diligence should be undertaken to avoid not being able to bring exchanges to a good end. I will also explain all sorts of bills, whether bills of exchange or other types, with the diligences that should be undertaken in case of default according to the *Ordonnance*; and I will give the formulas in which these instruments should be written in order to avoid the risk that they be annulled for not following the form prescribed by the *Ordonnance*. I do so in the hope that merchants' factors and commission agents will learn all these differences and acquire the skill to carry out this business, in the service of their principals or of themselves when they will practice this commerce on their own.

Dictionnaire universel de commerce

Source: *Dictionnaire universel de commerce: contenant tout ce qui concerne le commerce qui se fait dans les quatre parties du monde. Ouvrage posthume du Sieur Jacques Savary des Bruslons ... Continué sur les memoires de l'auteur, et donné au public par M. Philemon Louis Savary*, 3 vols. (Paris: Chez J. Estienne, 1723–1730), 1:180, s.v. "assurance," and 2:503, "lettre de change."

Insurance: ... The origins of insurance come from the Jews: they were its inventors, when they were expelled from France in 1182 during the reign of Philip Augustus. They used insurance to facilitate the transport of their assets. They used it again in 1321, under King Philip the Tall, when they were once again expelled from the Kingdom.

Bills of exchange: ... Bills of exchange were unknown to ancient Roman jurisprudence: according to the prevalent opinion, they were invented by Jews, who, after being banned from France for the horrible crimes of which they were accused, and having found refuge in Lombardy during the reigns of Philip Augustus in 1181 and Philip the Tall in 1316, found the way of salvaging the assets that they had left in their friends' hands through the use of secret letters and notes drafted in short and precise terms, as bills of exchange still are today, and did so through the intervention of travelers and foreign merchants.

After being expelled from Italy by the Guelph party, the Ghibellines, having reached Amsterdam, used the same instruments as the Jews in order to retrieve the goods that they had been forced to leave behind in Italy; it therefore seems plausible that it was them [the Ghibellines] who instilled the first knowledge of bills of exchange into the minds of Amsterdam's traders and merchants, who have since spread it across Europe with the sole goal of making their own commerce easier.

It is maintained that those very same Ghibellines also invented the re-exchange, to account for their losses and interests in those instances when bills of exchange (which they called *polizze di cambio*) were not cashed and were sent back via a protest.

Others maintain that merchants from Lyon were the first to circulate bills of exchange in France as a result of the considerable trading relations that they had with merchants from Amsterdam and Italy.

Bills of exchange are of great utility in commerce as long as merchants do no commit any abuses and that the exchange is real, especially because thanks to these bills it is possible to receive money everywhere one needs it without any trouble and without any risk. It is more or less certain that without the aid of these bills, commerce and all forms of business would languish.

Printed Books in French that Mention the Legend (1647–1800)

EC	Author	Title	Year of Publication	Place of Publication	Language	Inclusion of Legend	Dubious
	Cleirac, Estienne	Us et coustumes de la mer	1647	Bordeaux	French	BE + MI	N
	Cleirac, Estienne	Usance du négoce	1656	Bordeaux	French	BE	N
	Savary, Jacques	Le parfait négociant	1675	Paris	French	BE	N
	Bornier, Philippe	Conférences des nouvelles ordonnances de Louis XVI	1681	Paris	French	BE + MI	N
	Toubeau, Jean	Les institutes du droit consulaire	1682	Bourges	French	BE + MI	N
	Savary, Jacques	Parères	1688	Paris	French	BE	N
	Dupuis de la Serra, Jacques	L'art des lettres de change	1690	Paris	French	BE	Y
	Furetière, Antoine	Dictionnaire universel	1690	The Hague	French	BE + MI	N
	Ricard, Samuel	Traité général du commerce	1700	Amsterdam	French	BE	N
	Gobain, Pierre	Le commerce en son jour	1702	Bordeaux	French	BE	Y
	Moulinier, Jean	Le grand trésor des marchands, banquiers et négocians	1704	Bordeaux	French	BE	N
		Dictionnaire universel françois et latin (Dictionnaire de Trévoux)	1704	Trévoux	French	BE + MI	N
	Ricard, Samuel	L'art de bien tenir les livres de comptes en parties doubles	1709	Amsterdam	French	BE	N
	Biarnoy de Merville, Pierre	Ordonnance de la marine du mois d'août 1681	1715	Paris	French	MI	N
	Gobain, Pierre	Questions les plus curieuses	1717	Bordeaux	French	BE	Y
	Savary des Brûlons, Jacques; Savary, Philémon-Louis	Dictionnaire universel de commerce	1723–1730	Paris	French	BE + MI	N
	Bléville, Thomas de	Le banquier françois	1724	Paris	French	BE	N
	Aubin, Nicolas	Dictionnaire de marine	1736 (2nd ed.)	Amsterdam	French	MI	N
	Gayot de Pitaval, ed.	Causes célèbres et interessantes	1739–1750	Paris	French	BE	N
		Histoire universelle	1742–1802	Amsterdam	French	BE	N
	Montesquieu, Charles de Secondat	De l'esprit des lois	1748	Geneva	French	BE	N

	Author	Title	Date	Place	Language	BE / MI	Y (BE) / N (MI)
	Diderot, Denis; Alembert, Jean	Encyclopédie, ou, Dictionnaire raisonné des arts et métiers	1751–1765	Paris	French	BE	N
Y	de Forbonnais, François Véron Duverger	Elémens du commerce	1754	Leiden, but Paris	French	BE	Y
Y	Valin, René-Josué	Nouveau commentaire sur l'ordonnance de la marine du mois d'août 1681	1760	La Rochelle	French	MI	N
	Bielfeld, Jakob Friedrich	Institutions politiques	1760–1772	The Hague	French	BE	N
	Lacombe de Prézel, Honoré	Dictionnaire du citoyen	1761	Paris	French	BE	N
	Paganucci, Jean	Manuel historique, géographique et politique des négocians	1762	Paris	French	BE	N
	Roux, Augustin et alii	Dictionnaire domestique portatif	1762–1764	Paris	French	BE	N
	Pothier, Robert Joseph	Traité du contrat de change	1763	Paris	French	BE	Y
	de Beausobre, Louis	Introduction générale	1764	Berlin	French	BE	N
		Le grand vocabulaire françois	1767–1774	Paris	French	BE	N
	Beccaria, Cesare	Discours … pour le commerce & l'administration publique	1769	Lausanne	French/ trans.	BE	Y
	Raynal, abbé	Histoire philosophique et politique des établissemens & du commerce des Européens dans les deux Indes	1770	Amsterdam	French	BE	N
	Eon de Beaumont, Charles	Les loisirs du chevalier	1774	Amsterdam	French	BE	N
	Guyot, Pierre Jean	Répertoire … de jurisprudence	1775–1783	Paris	French	BE	Y
	Nicodéme, Paul Joseph	Exercice des commerçans	1776	Paris	French	BE	Y
	Lacretelle, Pierre Louis	Plaidoyer pour deux Juifs de Metz	1777	[Metz?]	French	BE	N
	Origny, Antoine Jean Baptiste Abraham d'	Dictionnaire des origines	1777	Paris	French	BE + MI	N
	Robinet, Jean Baptiste	Dictionnaire universel	1777–1783	London	French	BE	Y
		Code de l'humanité	1778	Yverdon	French	BE	Y
	Cloots, Jean-Baptiste	Lettre sur les juifs	1783	Berlin	French	BE	N

EC	Author	Title	Year of Publication	Place of Publication	Language	Inclusion of Legend	Dubious
	Émerigon, Balthazard-Marie	Traité des assurances et des contrats à la grosse	1783	Marseille	French	MI	Y
	Rousselot de Surgy, Jacques-Philibert	Encyclopédie méthodique: Commerce	1783–1784	Paris/Liège	French	BE	N
	Rousselot de Surgy, Jacques-Philibert	Encyclopédie méthodique: Finances	1784–1787	Paris/Liège	French	BE	N
	Lacretelle, Pierre Louis	in "Mercure de France"	1786		French	BE	N
	Mayer, Charles J. de	Voyage … en Suisse	1786	Amsterdam	French	BE	N
	Grégoire, Henri	Essai sur la régénération … des Jufs	1789	Metz/Paris/Strasbourg	French	BE	N
	Grégoire, Henri	Motion à faveur des Juifs	1789	[Paris]	French	BE	N
Y	Steuart, James Sir	Recherche des principes de l'économie politique	1789	Paris	French/trans.	BE	N
	Voltaire	Dictionnaire philosophique	1789	Amsterdam	French	BE	N
	Arnould, Ambroise Marie	De la balance du commerce et des relations commercia-les exterieures de la France	1791	Paris	French	BE + MI	N
	Gaignat de L'Aulnais, C.-F.	Guide du commerce	1791	Paris	French	BE	N
	Peuchet, Jacques	Dictionnaire universel de la géographie commerçante	1799	Paris	French	MI	N

Notes: EC = Works listed in Kenneth E. Carpenter, *The Economic Bestsellers Before 1850* (see Appendix 1); BE = bills of exchange; MI = marine insurance.

Printed Books in Languages Other than French that Mention the Legend (1676–1800)

EC	Author	Title	Year of Publication	Place of Publication	Language	Inclusion of Legend	Dubious
	Forbes, William	A Methodical Treatise Concerning Bills of Exchange	1703	Edinburgh	English	BE	Y
	Chambers, Ephraim	Cyclopaedia	1728	London	English	BE + MI	Y
	Montesquieu, Charles de Secondat	The Spirit of the Laws	1750	London	English/trans.	BE	N
	Barrow, John	A New and Universal Dictionary of Arts and Sciences	1751	London	English	BE	N
	Beawes, Wyndham	Lex mercatoria rediviva	1751	London	English	BE + MI	Y
	Postlethwayt, Malachy	The Universal Dictionary of Trade and Commerce	1751–1755	London	English/trans.	BE	N
	Rolt, Richard	A New Dictionary of Trade and Commerce	1756	London	English	BE	N
	Cunningham, Timothy	The Law of Bills of Exchange	1760	London	English	BE	Y
	Stevenson, William	A Full and Practical Treatise upon Bills of Exchange	1764	Edinburgh	English	BE	Y
	Blackstone, William	Commentaries on the Laws of England	1765–1769	Oxford	English	BE	Y
	Mortimer, Thomas	A New and Complete Dictionary of Trade	1766	London	English	BE + MI	Y
	Steuart, James	An Inquiry into the Principles of Political Œconomy	1767	London	English	BE	N
		The General Principles of Commerce	1767	n.p.	English	MI	Y
	Beccaria, Cesare	A Discourse on Public Œconomy and Commerce	1769	London	English/trans.	BE	Y
	Mortimer, Thomas	The Elements of Commerce, Politics and Finance	1772	London	English	BE	N
		Encyclopaedia Britannica	1778–1783 (2nd ed.)	Edinburgh	English	BE + MI	N
	Weskett, John	A Complete Digest of the Theory, Laws, and Practice of Insurance	1781	London	English	MI	Y
	Millar, John	Elements of the Law Relating to Insurances	1787	Edinburgh/London	English	BE	Y
	Park, James Allan	A System of the Law of Marine Insurances	1787	London	English	BE + MI	Y
	Hall, William Henry	The New Royal Encyclopedia	1788	London	English	BE	N
	Kyd, Stewart	A Treatise on the Law of Bills of Exchange	1790	London	English	BE	N

	Author	Title	Date	Place	Language	Type	Incl.
	Grégoire, Henri	An Essay on the Physical, Moral, and Political Reformation of the Jews	1791	London	English/trans.	BE	N
	Tisdall, John	Laws and Usages Respecting Bills of Exchange	1795	Philadelphia	English	BE	N
	D'Israeli, Isaac	Vaurien; or, Sketches of the Times	1797	London	English	BE	N
	Beckmann, Johann	A History of Inventions and Discoveries	1797	London	English/trans.	MI	Y
	Savary, Jacques	Der vollkommene Kauff- und Handelsmann	1676	Geneva	German/trans.	BE	N
	Marperger, Paul Jacob	Neu-eröffnetes Handels-Bericht	1709	Hamburg	German	BE	Y
	Marperger, Paul Jacob	Beschreibung der Banqven…	1717	Halle; Leipzig	German	BE	Y
	Zedler, Johann Heinrich	Grosses vollständiges Universallexicon aller Wissenschafften und Künste	1732–1755	Leipzig	German	MI	Y
	[Ludovici, Carl Günter]	Allgemeine Schatz-Kammer der Kauffmannschafft	1741–1743	Leipzig	German	BE	Y
	Ludovici, Carl Günter	Eröffnete Akademie der Kaufleute	1752–1756	Leipzig	German	MI	Y
Y	de Forbonnais, François Véron Duverger	Der vernünftige Kaufmann	1755	Hamburg; Leipzig	German/trans.	BE	N
	Ludovici, Carl Günter	Grundriß eines vollständigen Kaufmanns-Systems	1768	Leipzig	German	BE	Y
	Bielfeld, Jakob Friedrich	Des Freyherrn von Bielfeld Lehrbegriff der Staatskunst	1768–1773	Breslau; Leipzig	German/trans.	BE	N
	Steuart, James sir	Untersuchung der Grundsätze der Staatswirthschaft	1769–1770	Hamburg	German/trans.	BE	N
	Kruenitz, Johann Georg	Oeconomische Encyclopädie	1773–1858	Berlin	German	MI + BE	Y
	Genovesi, Antonio	Grundsätze der burgerlichen Oekonomie	1776	Leipzig	German/trans.	BE	N
	Deym, Friedrich von	Kurzgefaßte gründliche Einleitung in die Commerz und Handlungswissenschaft	1779	Frankfurt u.a.	German	BE + MI	N
	Mortimer, Thomas	Grundsätze der Handlungs- Staats- und Finanzwissenschaften	1781	Leipzig	German/trans.	BE	N
	Montesquieu	Das Geist der Gesetze	1782	Altenburg	German/trans.	BE	N
	Beckmann, Johann	Beyträge zur Geschichte der Erfindungen	1783–1805	Leipzig	German	MI	Y
	Büsch, Johann Georg	Handlungsbibliothek	1785–1797	Hamburg	German	BE	Y
	Euler, Martin	Allgemeine Wechselencyclopädie	1787	Frankfurt am Main	German	BE	Y

EC	Author	Title	Year of Publication	Place of Publication	Language	Inclusion of Legend	Dubious
	Püttmann, J.L.E.	*Der Stadt Leipzig Wechselordnung*	1787	Leipzig	German	BE	Y
	Büsch, Johann Georg	*Theoretisch-praktische Darstellung der Handlung in deren mannigfaltigen Geschäften*	1791–1792	Hamburg	German	BE	Y
	Martens, Georg Friedrich von	*Versuch einer historischen Entwicklung des wahren Ursprungs des Wechselrechts*	1795	Göttingen	German	BE	Y
	Püttmann, J.L.E.	*Grundsätze des Wechsel-Rechts*	1795	Leipzig	German	BE	Y
	Musäus, Johann Daniel Heinrich	*Anfangsgründe des Handlungs- und Wechsel-Rechts*	1799	Hamburg	German	BE	Y
	Dupuis de la Serra, Jacques	*Trattato delle lettere di cambio*	1718	Florence	Italian/trans.	BE	Y
	Montesquieu, Charles de Secondat	*Lo spirito delle leggi*	1750	Napoli	Italian/trans.	BE	N
	Pagnini, Giovanni Francesco	*Della decima e di varie altre gravezze*	1765–1766	Florence	Italian	BE	Y
Y	Genovesi, Antonio	*Delle lezioni di commercio*	1765–1767	Naples	Italian	BE	N
	Targioni Tozzetti, Giovanni	*Relazioni d'alcuni viaggi*	1768 (2nd ed.)	Florence	Italian	BE	Y
	Beccaria, Cesare	*Prolusione letta il giorno 9 gennaio 1769*	1769	Milan	Italian	BE	Y
	Baldasseroni, Pompeo	*Leggi e costumi del cambio*	1784	Pescia	Italian	BE	Y
	Baldasseroni, Ascanio	*Delle assicurazioni marittime trattato*	1786	Florence	Italian	MI	Y
	Azuni, Domenico Alberto	*Dizionario universale ragionato*	1786–1788	Nice	Italian	BE	Y
	Muzio, Giovanni Francesco	*Principi di aritmetica e commercio*	1790	Genova	Italian	BE	N
	Bielfeld, Jakob Friedrich	*Instituciones politicas*	1767–1801	Madrid	Spanish/trans.	BE	N
	Muñoz, Antonio	*Discurso sobre economía política*	1769	Madrid	Spanish	BE	Y
	Danvila y Villarrasa, Bernardo J.	*Lecciones de economía civil, o de el comercio*	1779	Madrid	Spanish	BE	Y

EC	Author	Title	Year	Place	Language	Type	
	de Capmany y de Montpalau, Antonio	Memorias históricas sobre la marina, comercio y artes	1779–1792	Madrid	Spanish	BE	N
	Suárez y Nuñez, Miguel Gerónimo	Tratado legal theórico y práctico de letras de cambio	1788–1789	Madrid	Spanish	BE	Y
	Alonso Ortiz, José	Ensayo económico	1796	Madrid	Spanish	BE	N
Y	Genovesi, Antonio	Lecciones de comercio, ó bien de economía civil	1785–1786	Madrid	Spanish/trans.	BE	N
	Savary, Jacques	De volmaakte koopman	1683	Amsterdam	Dutch/trans.	BE	N
	Le Moine de L'Espine, Jacques; Lelong, Isaac	Den koophandel van Amsterdam	1704	Amsterdam	Dutch	BE	N
		De koopman, of, Bydragen ten opbouw van Neerlands koophandel en zeevaard	1768–1776	Amsterdam	Dutch	BE	N
	Heineccius, Johann Gottlieb (*)	Grondbeginselen van het wisselrecht in 't Latyn saamgesteld	1774	Middelburg	Dutch/trans.	BE + MI	N
	Dupuis de la Serra, Jacques	Tractatus de arte litterarum cambii	1712	Köln	Latin/trans.	BE	Y
	Manni, Domenico Maria	De Florentinis inventis commentarium	1731	Ferrara	Latin	BE	Y
	Ayrer, Georg	De cambialis instituti vestigiis apud Romanos	1743	Amsterdam	Latin	BE	Y
	Cairu, José da Silva Lisboa	Principios de direito mercantil e leis de marinha	1798	Lisbon	Portuguese	BE	Y
Y	de Forbonnais, François Véron Duverger	Elementos do commercio	1766	Lisbon	Portuguese/trans.	BE	Y
	Савари де Брюлон Ж [Savary des Brûlons]	Экстракт Саварриева лексикона о комерции [Ekstrakt Savarieva leksikona o komertsii]	1747	St. Petersburg	Russian	MI	N

Notes: EC = works listed in Kenneth E. Carpenter, *The Economic Bestsellers Before 1850* (see Appendix 1); BE = bills of exchange; MI = marine insurance; * = mention appears in editorial notes, not in translated text.

Bibliographical References in Werner Sombart's *Die Juden und das Wirtschaftsleben* (1911)

Number of citations	Author	Book/Article Title	Periodical/Multivolume	Place of Publication	Year of Publication
2		Kiddushin			
3		Pesachim [Talmud]			
	Cicero	Pro Flacco			[1st century BCE]
	Tacitus	The Annals			[1st century CE]
		[Shulchan Aruch] Orach Chajim			
2	[Saravia de la] Calle	Institutione de' mercanti che tratta del comprare et vendere, et della usura che può occorrere nella mercantia insieme con un trattato de' cambi		[Venice]	[1561]
	Stracca	[De mercatura seu mercatore tractatus]			1568
	Brunner	Francofordiense emporium sive Francofordienses nundinae quam varia mercium genera in hoc emporio prostent pagina septima indicabit			1574
2	San Juan	Examen de ingenios para las ciencias			1575
	Luzzato	Discorso circa il stato de gl'Hebrei et in particolar dimoranti nell'inclita città di Venetia			1638
	Müller	Judaismus, oder Jüdenthumb		[Hamburg]	1644
	Guicciardini	Totius Belgii descriptio		[Amsterdam]	1652
	Altzema, Lieuwe van	Historia pacis a foederatis Belgis ab anno 1621 ad hoc usque tempus tractatae			[1654]
	Ligon	A True and Exact History of the Island of Barbados		[Barbados]	1657
	Barrios	Historia universal Judayca			[c. 1670]
2	Moscherosch	Wunderliche und warhafftige Gesichte Philanders von Sittewald		[Strasbourg]	1677
4	Child	A New Discourse of Trade		[London]	[1693]

	Mission	*Reise nach Italien: Mit vilen neuen anmerckungen und figuren vermehret*		[Leipzig]	1713
7	Schudt	*Jüdische Merckwürdigkeiten*		[Frankfurt]	[1714–1717]
	Lau	*Einrichtung der Intraden und Einkünffte der Souverainen und ihrer Unterthanen*		[Frankfurt]	1719
	[Defoe]	*The Anatomy of Exchange Alley, or a System of Stock Jobbing*		[London]	1719
2	Ricard	*Le Négoce d'Amsterdam*		[Amsterdam]	1723
	Hönn	*Betrugs-Lexicon: worinnen die meiste Betrügereyen in allen Ständen*			1724
4	Savary	*Dictionnaire universel de commerce*		[Paris]	1726
2	Defoe	*The Complete English Tradesman: In Familiar Letters*		[London]	1726–1727
	Mélon	*Essai politique sur le commerce*		[Amsterdam]	1734
4	Tovey	*Anglia Judaica: Or, The History and Antiquities of the Jews in England*		[Oxford]	1738
	du Hautchamp	*Histoire du système des Finances sous la minorité de Louis VX*		[The Hague]	1739
		Juden	Allgemeine Schatzkammer der Kaufmannschaft order vollständiges Lexikon aller Handlungen und Gewerbe		1741
12		*Allgemeine Schatzkammer der Kaufmannschaft oder vollständiges Lexikon aller Handlungen und Gewerbe*			1741–1742
	Thurloe	*A Collection of the State Papers of John Thurloe*			[1742]
	Schwartz	*Historische Nachlese zu denen Geschichten der Stadt Leipzig*			1744
			The Spectator		1749

Number of citations	Author	Book/Article Title	Periodical/Multivolume	Place of Publication	Year of Publication
	L'Estocq	Exercitatio de indole et jure instrumenti Judaeis usitati cui nomen "Mamre" est			1755
5	Postlethwayt	Universal Dictionary of Trade and Commerce		[London]	1757
	de Gouvest	Ephraim justifié: memoire historique et raisonne sur l'etat passe, present, et futur, des finances de Saxe			1758
	von Justi	Staatswirtschaft oder systematische Abhandlungen aller oekonomischen und Kameralwissenschaften			1758
2	Griesheim	Anmerkungen und Zugaben über den Tractat: die Stadt Hamburg		[Hamburg]	1759
	Du Bois	Vies des gouverneurs généraux, avec l'abrégé de l'histoire des établissemens hollandois aux Indes orientales		[The Hague]	1763
4	Pinto	Traité de la circulation et du crédit		[Amsterdam]	1771
	Kant	Von den verschiedenen Racen der Menschen: zur Ankündigung der Vorlesungen der physischen Geographie im Sommerhalbenjahre 1775	edited volume Hartenstein		1775
3	Romani	Eines edlen Wallachens landwirtschaftliche Reise durch verschieden Landschaften Europens			1776
	Smith	The Wealth of Nations			[1776]
	Fermin	Tableau historique et politique de l'état ancien et actuel de la colonie de Surinam, et des causes de sa décadence		[Maestricht]	1778
	Sérionne	La richesse de la Hollande: ouvrage dans lequel on expose l'origine du commerce & de la puissance des Hollandois		[London]	1778
4	Risbeck	Briefe eines reisenden Franzosen über Deutschland an seinen Bruder zu Paris		[Paris]	1780

3	Pinto	*Apologie pour la nation juive ou Reflexions critiques sur le premier chapitre du VII. tome des Oeuvres de monsieur de Voltaire, au sujet des juifs*	Lettres de quelques juifs	[Paris]	1781
	Besekes	*Thesaurus juris cambialis*			1783
0	Krünitz	*Juden*	Oekonomische Encyklopädie, oder allgemeines System der Staats-, Stadt, Haus- u. Landwirthschaft in alphabethischer Ordnung	[Berlin]	[1784]
	[Knüppeln]	*Charakteristik von Berlin: Stimme eines Kosmopoliten in der Wüsten*		[Philadelphia]	1784
3	[La Platière]	*Encyclopédie méthodique ou par ordre de matières*			[1785–1828]
3	Mercier	*Tableau de Paris*		[Paris]	1788
	Nassy	*Essai historique sur la colonie de Surinam*	Paramaribo	[Amsterdam]	1788
7	König	*Annalen der Juden in den preußischen Staaten besonders in der Mark Brandenburg*		[Berlin]	[1790]
2	Kortum	*Über Judenthum und Juden, hauptsächlich in Rüksicht ihres Einflusses auf bürgerlichen Wohlstand*		[Nürnberg]	1795
	Moseley	*Abhandlung über den Zucker*		[Berlin]	1800
	[Stetten]	*Geschichte der Juden in der Reichsstadt Augsburg*		[Ausburg]	1803
2		*Juden, sind sie der Handlung schädlich?*		[Frankfurt am Main]	1803
	Diebitsch	*Kosmopolitische, unpartheyische Gedanken über Juden und Christen*		[Berlin]	1804
	[Rohrer]	*Versuch über die jüdischen Bewohner der österreichischen Monarchie*		[Vienna]	1804
	Lamb	*[Seasonal Observations (1659), in] Somers' Tracts*			[1811]
2	[Guénée]	*Lettres de quelques juifs portugais, allemands et polonais à M. de Voltaire*		[Paris]	[1815]
4	[Holst]	*Über das Verhältnis der Juden zu den Christen in den deutschen Handelsstädten*		[Leipzig]	1818

Number of citations	Author	Book/Article Title	Periodical/Multivolume	Place of Publication	Year of Publication
3	Holst	Judentum in allen dessen Theilen aus einem staatswissen-schaftlichen Standpuncte betrachtet		[Mainz]	1821
3	Gönner	Von Staats-Schulden, deren Tilgungsanstalten und vom Handel mit Staatspapieren		[München]	1826
3	Bender	Der Verkehr mit Staatspapieren		[Göttingen]	1830
	Geiger	Jüdische Zeitschrift für Wissenschaft und Leben		[Nürnberg]	[1835]
		Jahresbericht des historischen Vereins in Mittelfranken			[1837]
			Allgemeine Zeitung des Judentums		1837–
	Ritter	Über die geographische Verbreitung des Zuckerrohrs	Abhandlungen der Königlich Preussischen Akademie der Wissenschaften	[Berlin]	1839
	Carmoly		Revue Orientale	[Bruxelles]	1841
	McCulloch	A Dictionary, Practical, Theoretical, and Historical, of Commerce and Commercial Navigation		[Philadelphia]	[1841]
	Richter		[Allgemeine Judenzeitung]	[Leipzig]	1842
4	Wertheimer	Die Juden in Oesterreich: vom Standpunkte der Geschichte, des Rechts und des Staatsvortheils		[Leipzig]	1842
7	Koenen	Geschiedenis der Joden in Nederland		[Utrecht]	1843
	Rönne and Simon	Die früheren und gegenwärtigen Verhältnisse der Juden in den sämmtlichen Landestheilen des Preußischen Staates		[Breslau]	1843
	Marx	Zur Judenfrage	[Deutsch-französischen Jahrbüchern]		1844
	Brant	Das Narrenschiff		[Stuttgart]	[1845]

	Scheible	Das Kloster, weltlich und geistlich; meist aus der ältern deutschen Volks-, Wunder-, Curiositäten-, und vorzugsweise komischen Literatur		[Stuttgart]	[1845]
2	Frankel	Der gerichtliche Beweis nach mosaisch-talmudischem Rechte		[Berlin]	1846
	Lassen	Indische Altertumskunde: Geschichte des chinesischen und arabischen Wissens			1847
2	Reils	Beiträge zur ältesten Geschichte der Juden in Hamburg	Zeitschrift des Vereins fur Hamburgische Geschichte		[1847]
2	Fassel	Tugend- und Rechtslehre, bearbeitet nach den Principien des Talmuds und nach der Form der Philosophie		[Vienna]	1848
4	Lindo	The History of the Jews of Spain and Portugal		[London]	1848
2	Saalschütz	Das mosaische Recht: mit Berücksichtigung des spätern Jüdischen		[Berlin]	1848
2	Francis	Chronicles and Characters of the Stock Exchange		[Boston]	1849
	Bruch	Weisheitslehre der Hebräer: ein Beitrag zur Geschichte der Philosophie		[Strasbourg]	1851
	Halphen	Recueil des lois, décrets, ordonnances, avis du conseil d'état, arrêtés et règlements concernant les Israélites depuis la révolution de 1789		[Paris]	1851
	Schröder	Satzungen und Gebräuche des talmudisch-rabbinischen Judenthums		[Bremen]	1851
			Monatsschrift fur Geschichte und Wissenschaft des Judentums		1851–
2	Netscher	Les Hollandais au Brésil: notice historique sur les Pays-Bays et le Brésil au XVIIe siècle		[The Hague]	1853
	Cochut	Law, son système et son époque		[Paris]	[1853]
	Frankel	Die Diaspora zur Zeit des zweiten Tempels	Monatsschrift fur Geschichte und Wissenschaft des Judentums	[Paris]	[1853]
	Sommerhausen	Die Geschichte der Niederlassung der Juden in Holland und den holländischen Kolonien	Monatsschrift fur Geschichte und Wissenschaft des Judentums	[Leipzig]	[1853]
	Weiss	Histoire des réfugiés protestants		[Paris]	1853

Number of citations	Author	Book/Article Title	Periodical/Multivolume	Place of Publication	Year of Publication
33	Graetz	*Geschichte der Juden von den ältesten Zeiten bis auf die Gegenwart* [*no vol. specified*]			[1853–1876]
12	Graetz	*Geschichte der Juden von den ältesten Zeiten bis auf die Gegenwart* (vol. 9)		[Leipzig]	[1853–1876]
3	Graetz	*Geschichte der Juden von den ältesten Zeiten bis auf die Gegenwart* (vols. 7–8)		[Leipzig]	[1853–1876]
3	Graetz	*Geschichte der Juden von den ältesten Zeiten bis auf die Gegenwart* (vol. 10)		[Leipzig]	[1853–1876]
4	Graetz	*Geschichte der Juden von den ältesten Zeiten bis auf die Gegenwart* (vol. 9)		[Leipzig]	[1853–1876]
2	Graetz	*Geschichte der Juden von den ältesten Zeiten bis auf die Gegenwart* (vol. 6)		[Leipzig]	[1853–1876]
3	Graetz	*Geschichte der Juden von den ältesten Zeiten bis auf die Gegenwart* (vol. 5)		[Leipzig]	[1853–1876]
4	Graetz	*Geschichte der Juden von den ältesten Zeiten bis auf die Gegenwart* (vol. 4)		[Leipzig]	[1853–1876]
4	Graetz	*Geschichte der Juden von den ältesten Zeiten bis auf die Gegenwart* (vol. 2)		[Leipzig]	[1853–1876]
4	Graetz	*Geschichte der Juden von den ältesten Zeiten bis auf die Gegenwart* (vol. 3)		[Leipzig]	[1853–1876]
	Graetz	*Geschichte der Juden von den ältesten Zeiten bis auf die Gegenwart* (vol. 11)		[Leipzig]	[1853–1876]
2	Fassel	*Das mosaisch-rabbinische Zivilrecht*		[Groß-Kanizsa]	1854
5	Mommsen	*Römische Geschichte*			[1854–1885]

#	Author	Title	Publication	Place	Year
	Renan	Histoire générale et système comparé des langues sémitiques		[Paris]	1855
	Bodemeyer	Die Juden: ein Beitrag zur Hannoverschen Rechtsgeschichte		[Göttingen]	[1855]
	Capefigue	Banquiers fournisseurs, acquéreurs des biens nationaux		[Paris]	1856
	Handelmann	Geschichte der Insel Hayti		[Kiel]	1856
		Juden	Allgemeine Encyclopädie der Wissenschaften und Künste		[1856]
4	[Steinmann]	Das Haus Rothschild: seine Geschichte und seine Geschäfte		[Prague & Leipzig]	1857
	Döllinger	Heidentum und Judentum: Vorhalle zur Geschichte des Christentums		[Regensburg]	1857
4	Kuntze	Die Lehre von den Inhaberpapieren			1857
		Zur Geschichte der Juden in Danzig	Monatsschrift für Geschichte und Wissenschaft des Judentums		1857
2	Buckle	Geschichte der Zivilisation in England			[1857–1861]
	Vallée	Les manieurs d'argent: Études historiques et morales (1720–1857)		[Paris]	1858
	Euler	Zur Geschichte der Inhaberpapiere	Zeitschrift für das Gesamte Handelsrecht		[1858]
	Ben Israel	Humble Address [1656]	Jewish Encyclopedia		1859
2	Biener	Wechselrechtliche Abhandlungen		[Leipzig]	1859
	Jost	Geschichte des Judenthums und seiner Sekten		[Leipzig]	1859
	Kayserling	Zur Geschichte der jüdischen Ärzte : Die Familien de Castro	Monatsschrift für Geschichte und Wissenschaft des Judentums		1859
	Manasseh ben Israel	Bericht, 1655	Jewish Chronicle		1859

Number of citations	Author	Book/Article Title	Periodical/Multivolume	Place of Publication	Year of Publication
2	Wolf	Ferdinand II. und die Juden		[Vienna]	1859
			Jewish Chronicle	[London]	1859
2	Handelmann	Geschichte von Brasilien		[Berlin]	1860
	Manasseh ben Israel	Bericht, 1655	Jahrbuch des Literar Vereins		1861
4	Kayserling	Geschichte der Juden in Spanien und Portugal			1861–1867
2	Kuntze	Zur Geschichte der Staatspapiere auf Inhaber	Zeitschrift für das gesamte Handelsrecht		[1862]
	Colmeiro	Historia de la economia politica en España		[Madrid]	[1863]
2	Laspeyres	Geschichte der volkswirtschaftlichen Anschauugen der Niederländer und ihrer Litteratur zur Zeit der Republik		[Leipzig]	1863
	Macleod	Bank of Venice	Dictionary of Political Economy	[London]	[1863]
	Güdemann	Zur Geschichte der Juden in Magdeburg	Monatsschrift für Geschichte und Wissenschaft des Judentums		1865
2	Auerbach	Geschichte der israelitischen Gemeinde Halberstadt		[Halberstadt]	1866
	Reed	The History of Sugar and Sugar Yielding Plants		[London]	1866
	Rénan	Les Apôtres		[Paris]	1866
	Stobbe	Die Juden in Deutschland während des Mittelalters in politischer, socialer und rechtlicher Beziehung		[Braunschweig]	1866
2	Haenle	Geschichte der Juden im ehemaligen Fürstenthum Ansbach		[Ansbach]	1867
	Bastian	Das Beständige in den Menschenrassen und die Spielweite ihrer Veränderlichkeit. Prolegomena zu einer Ethmologie der Culturvölker		[Berlin]	1868
	Fürst	[Der Kanon des alten Testaments nach den Überlieferungen in Talmud und Midrasch]		[Leipzig]	1868

	Kayserling	Zur Geschichte der jüdischen Ärzte	Monatsschrift für Geschichte und Wissenschaft des Judentums		1868
	Wagner	Die Darwinsche Theorie und das Migrationsgesetz der Organismen		[Leipzig]	1868
4	Büchsenschütz	Besitz und Erwerb im griechischen Alterthume		[Halle]	1869
	Hecht	Ein Beitrag zur Geschichte der Inhaberpapiere in den Niederlanden		[Heidelberg]	1869
	Lattes	La libertà delle banche a Venezia dal secolo XIII. al XVII. secondo i documenti inediti del R. Archivio dei Frari		[Milano]	1869
2	Auerbach	Das jüdische Obligationenrecht nach den Quellen und mit besonderer Berücksichtigung des römischen und deutschen Rechts		[Berlin]	1871
	Ferrara	Gli antichi banchi di Venezia	Nuova Antologia		[1871]
	Ferrara	[Documenti per servire alla storia dei banchi veneziani]	Archivio Veneto		[1871]
3	Friedländer	Darstellungen aus der Sittengeschichte Roms in der Zeit von August bis zum Ausgang der Antonine		[Leipzig]	[1871]
3	Geiger	Die Geschichte der Juden in Berlin		[Berlin]	1871
	Grünebaum	Der Fremde nach rabbinischen Begriffen	Jüdische Zeitschrift für Wissenschaft und Leben		1871
	Saling	Die Norddeutschen Börsenpapiere		[Berlin]	[1871]
	Wagner	Über den Einfluß der geographischen Isolierung und Kolonienbildung auf die morphologischen Veränderungen der Organismen		[München]	1871
	Chwolson	Die Semitischen Völker: Versuch einer Charakteristik		[Berlin]	1872
	Meyer	Die Aktiengesellschaften			1872–1873
2	Scheube	Aus den Tagen unserer Großväter			1873
2	Endemann	Studien in der romanischkanonistischen Wirtschafts und Rechtslehre		[Berlin]	1874

Number of citations	Author	Book/Article Title	Periodical/Multivolume	Place of Publication	Year of Publication
	Hotten	The Original Lists of Persons of Quality: Emigrants, Religious Exiles, Political Rebels, Serving Men Sold for a Term of Years, Apprentices, Children Stolen, Maidens Pressed, and Others, Who Went from Great Britain to the American Plantations, 1600–1700		[New York]	1874
	Zimmerman	Josef Süss Oppenheimer, ein Finanzmann des 18. Jahrhunderts		[Stuttgart]	1874
3	Graetz	Die Familie Gradis	Monatsschrift für Geschichte und Wissenschaft des Judentums		1874–1875
	Guillard	Les opérations de bourse: histoire, pratique, législation, jurisprudence, réformes, morale, économie politique			1875
6	Malvezin	Histoire des Juifs à Bordeaux			1875
4	Picciotto	Sketches of Anglo-Jewish History		[London]	1875
2	Sampson	A History of Advertising from the Earliest Times, 1875		[London]	1875
	Rios	Historia social, política y religiosa de los Judíos de España y Portugal		[Madrid]	1875–1878
	Glagau	Der Börsen- und Gründungschwindel in Berlin		[Leipzig]	1876
	Gosselin	Documents inédits pour servir à l'histoire de la marine normande et du commerce rouennais pendant les XVI et XVII siècles			1876
2	Knies	Der Credit		[Berlin]	1876
	Marquardt	Römische Staatsverwaltung		[Leipzig]	[1876]
2	Pimentel	Geschiedkundige Aantekeningen betreffende de Portugesche Israelieten in Den Haag en hunne synagogen aldaar		[The Hague]	1876

	Sammter	Talmud Babylonicum: Tractat Baba Mezia mit deutscher Übersetzung und Erklärung		[Berlin]	1876
	Glagau	Der Börsen- und Gründungschwindel in Deutschland		[Leipzig]	1877
	Barbeck	Geschichte der Juden in Nürnberg und Fürth		[Nürnberg]	1878
2	Brunner	Zur Geschichte des Inhaberpapiers in Deutschland	Zeitschrift für das gesamte Handelsrecht		[1878]
	Brunner		Zeitschrift für Rechtsgeschichte		1878
	Grünebaum	Die Sittenlehre des Judenthums andern Bekenntnissen gegenüber			1878
	Rabbinowicz	Législation civile du Talmud		[Paris]	1878
4	Brunner	Das französische Inhaberpapier des Mittelalters und sein Verhältniss zur Anwaltschaft, zur Cession und zum Orderpapier		[Berlin]	[1879]
3	Herzfeld	Handelsgeschichte der Juden des Alterthums			[1879]
	Nasse	Das venetianische Bankwesen im 14., 15., und 16. Jahrhunderts	Jahrbücher für Nationalökonomie und Statisik		[1879]
4	Weber	System der altsynagogalen palästinischen Theologie : aus Targum, Midrasch und Talmud		[Leipzig]	1880
	Endemann	Handbuch des deutschen Handels-, See- und Wechselrechts		[Leipzig]	1880–1881
2	Cahen	Les Juifs de la Martinique au XVIIe siècle	Revue des études juives	[Paris]	[1881]
	Jellinek	Der jüdische Stamm in nichtjüdischen Sprichwörtern	Revue des études juives	[Vienna]	1882
4	Cahen	Les juifs dans les colonies français au XVIII siècle	Revue des études juives	[Paris]	[1882]
	Back	Die Entstehungsgeschichte der portugiesischen Gemeinde in Amsterdam		[Frankfurt am Main]	1883
	Ehrenberg	Die Fondsspekulation und die Gesetzgebung		[Berlin]	1883
	Gumplowicz	Der Rassenkampf: Sociologische Untersuchungen		[Innsbruck]	1883

Number of citations	Author	Book/Article Title	Periodical/Multivolume	Place of Publication	Year of Publication
	Wirth	Geschichte der Handelskrisen			1883
	Hamburger	Real-Encyclopädie des Judentums: Wörterbuch zum Handgebrauch für Bibelfreunde, Theologen, Juristen, Staatsmänner, Gemeinde- und Schulvorsteher, Lehrer, Schulinspektoren u. a. m.			[1883–1886]
	Lewin	Der Judenspiegel des Dr. Justus, ins Licht der Wahrheit gerückt		[Frankfurt am Main]	1884
	Bonnaffé	Dictionnaire des amateurs français au XVIIe siècle		[Paris]	[1884]
	Schiffer	Das Buch Kohelet, nach der Auffassung der Weisen des Talmud und Midrasch und der jüdischen Erklärer des Mittelalters I		[Frankfurt am Main]	1884
2	Schlessinger	Buch Ikkarim, Grund- und Glaubenslehren der Mosaischen Religion, von Rab. Joseph Albo		[Frankfurt am Main]	1884
	Deutsch	Die Sprüche Salomo's nach der Auffassung im Talmud und Midrasch dargestellt und kritisch untersucht		[Berlin]	1885
2	Hoffmann	Der Schulchan-Aruch und die Rabbinen über das Verhältnis der Juden zu Andersgläubigen		[Berlin]	1885
	Philippovich	Die Bank von England im Dienste der Finanzverwaltung des Staates			1885
	Tawrogi	[Der talmudische Tractat Derech Erez Sutta nach Handschriften und seltenen Ausgaben: mit Parallelstellen und Varianten kritisch bearbeitet, übersetzt und erläutert]		[Königsberg]	1885
2	Ranke	Französische Geschichte vornehmlich im sechzehnten und siebzehnten Jahrhundert			[1885]

	Salvioli	*I titoli al portatore nella storia del diritto italiano*	Zeitschrift für das gesamte Handelsrecht und Wirtschaftsrecht	[Stuttgart]	[1885]
	Maulde	*Les Juifs dans les Etats français du Saint-Siège au moyen age*			1886
	Weyl	*Les juifs protégés français aux échelles du Levant et en Barbarie*	Revue des études juives		1886
2	Schürer	*Geschichte des jüdischen Volkes im Zeitalter Jesu Christi*			[1886–1890]
	Drumont	*La France juive: essai d'histoire contemporaine*		[Chicago]	[1886]
	Macaulay	*The History of England from the Accession of James the Second*		[Chicago]	[1886]
	Reeves	*The Rothschilds: the Financial Rulers of Nations*		[Chicago]	1887
	Wahrmund	*Das Gesetz des Nomadentums und die heutige Herrschaft jüdischer Kader*		[Leipzig]	1887
2	Ranke	*Der Mensch*			[1887]
	Pigeonneau	*Histoire du commerce de la France*			[1887–1889]
	Markens	*The Hebrews in America: a Series of Historical and Biographical Sketches*		[New York]	1888
	Neumann	*Volk und Nation: eine studie*		[Leipzig]	1888
	Wolf	*The Middle-Age of Anglo-Jewish History (1290–1656)*	Publications of the Anglo-Jewish Historical Exhibition	[London]	1888
	Wolf	*The Resettlement of the Jews in England* / *Papers Read at the Anglo-Jewish Historical Exhibition*	Publications of the Anglo-Jewish Historical Exhibition	[London]	1888
	Goldschmidt	*Inhaber-, Order- und exekutorische Urkunden im classischen Alterthum*	Zeitschrift der Savigny-Stiftung für Rechtsgeschichte		1889
3	Ratzel	*Völkerkunde*		[Leipzig]	[1888]
	Brüll		Populär-Wissenschaftliche Monatsblätter		1888–
	Kahn	*Les Juifs à Paris depuis le VIe siècle*		[Paris]	1889

Number of citations	Author	Book/Article Title	Periodical/Multivolume	Place of Publication	Year of Publication
	Kaufmann	Die letzte Vertreibung der Juden aus Wien und Niederösterreich, ihre Vorgeschichte (1625–1670) und ihre Opfer		[Budapest]	1889
2	Schaffer	Das Recht und seine Stellung zur Moral nach talmudischer Sitten- und Rechtslehre		[Frankfurt am Main]	1889
	Schechter	The Dogmas of Judaism	The Jewish Quarterly Review		1889
	Wagner	Die Entstehung der Arten durch räumliche Sonderung		[Basel]	1889
	Wellhausen	Medina vor dem Islam		[Berlin]	1889
	Wolf	Jessurun Family	Jewish Quarterly Review		1889
2	Braunschweiger	Die Lehrer der Mischnah, ihr Leben und Wirken		[Frankfurt am Main]	1890
4	Lippmann	Geschichte des Zuckers		[Leipzig]	1890
7	Mensi	Die Finanzen Österreichs von 1701 bis 1740		[Vienna]	1890
	Sattler	Die Effektenbanken		[Leipzig]	1890
			Revue historique		1890
	Ehrenberg		Jahrbücher für Nationalökonomie und Statistik		[1890s]
	Fraser	Memoirs of the Rev. James Fraser of Brea, A.D. 1639–1698		[Edinburg]	[1891]
6	Goldschmidt	Universalgeschichte des Handelsrechts		[Stuttgart]	1891
	Knapp	Ursprung der Sklaverei in den Kolonien	Archiv für soziale Gesetzgebung und Statistik		[1891]
	Oehler	Theologie des Alten Testaments		[Stuttgart]	1891
	[Perles]	[Ahron ben Gerson Aboulrabi: la légende d'Asnath, fille de Dina et femme de Joseph]	Revue des études juives	[Paris]	1891

	Puigcerver	*Los Judios en el Nuevo Mundo*		[Mexico]	1891
	Sumner	*The Financier and the Finances of the American Revolution*		[New York]	1891
2	Wahl	*Traité théorique et pratique des titres au porteur français et étrangers*			1891
	Zittel	*Die Entstehung der Bibel*		[Leipzig]	1891
			Jewish Quarterly Review		1891
2	Campbell	*The Puritan in Holland, England, and America*		[New York]	1892
2	Kahn	*Les Juifs de Paris sous Louis XV (1721–1790)*		[Paris]	1892
	Kaufmann	*Urkundliches aus dem Leben Samson Wertheimers*		[Vienna]	1892
3	Nowack	*Handkommentar zum Alten Testament*			[1892]
	Schaps	*Zur Geschichte des Wechselindossaments*		[Stuttgart]	1892
	von Luschan	*Die anthropologische Stellung der Juden*			1892
			Korrespondenzblatt für Anthropologie, Ethnologie und Urgeschichte		
2			La Révolution Française: Revue d'histoire moderne et contemporaine	[Paris]	1892
2	Bäck	*Die religionsgeschichtliche Literatur der Juden in dem Zeitraum vom 15.-18. Jahrhundert*			1893
			Die jüdische Literatur seit Abschluss des Kanons		1893
	Daly	*History of the Settlement of Jews in North America*		[New York]	1893
	Daly	*Settlement of the Jews in North America*		[New York]	1893
	de Swarte	*Un Banquier du trésor royal au XVIIIe siècle: Samuel Bernard, sa vie, sa correspondance (1651–1739)*		[Paris]	1893
	Dembitz	*Jewish Beginnings in Kentucky*			[1893]
			Publications of the American Jewish Historical Society		

Number of citations	Author	Book/Article Title	Periodical/Multivolume	Place of Publication	Year of Publication
	Friedenwald	Jews Mentioned in the Journal of the Continental Congress	Publications of the American Jewish Historical Society		[1893]
	Hollander	Some Unpublished Material Relating to Dr. Jacob Lumbrozo	Publications of the American Jewish Historical Society		[1893]
	Jones	The Settlement of the Jews in Georgia	Publications of the American Jewish Historical Society		[1893]
2	Kohler	Beginnings of New York Jewish History	Publications of the American Jewish Historical Society		[1893]
2	Leroy-Beaulieu	Israël chez les nations		[Paris]	1893
2	Lipsius	Von der Bedeutung des griechischen Rechts		[Leipzig]	[1893]
3	Modona	Gli Ebrei e la scoperta dell'America		[Casale]	1893
	Neubaur	Die Sage vom ewigen Juden		[Leipzig]	1893
			[Publications of] the American Jewish Historical Society		[1893–1961]
	Baasch	Hamburgs Seeschiffahrt und Warenhandel vom Ende des 16. bis zur Mitte des 17. Jahrunderts	Zeitschrift des Vereins fur Hamburgische Geschichte		1894
3	Beer	Das Staatsschuldenwesen und die Ordnung des Staatshaushalts unter Maria Thereisa		[Vienna]	1894
	Brunner	Forschungen zur Geschichte des deutschen und französischen Rechts: Gesammelte Aufsätze		[Stuttgart]	1894
	Datz	Histoire de la publicité, depuis les temps les plus reculés jusqu'à nos jours		[Paris]	1894
	Felsenthal	On the History of the Jews in Chicago	Publications of the American Jewish Historical Society		[1894]

#	Author	Title	Series / Journal	Place	Year
	Guttmann	Über Dogmenbildung und Judenthum		[Breslau]	1894
3	Kahn	Les juifs de Paris aux XVIIIe siècle		[Paris]	1894
4	Kayserling	Christopher Columbus and the Participation of the Jews in the Spanish and Portuguese Discoveries		[New York]	1894
	Kayserling	The Colonization of America by the Jews	Publications of the American Jewish Historical Society	[New York]	[1894]
2	Klerk de Reus	Geschichtlicher Überblick der administrativen, rechtlichen und finanziellen Entwicklung der Niederländisch-Ostindischen Compagnie		[Batavia]	1894
2	Markgraf	Zur Geschichte der Juden auf den Messen in Leipzig von 1664–1839		[Leipzig]	1894
	Ouverleaux	Notes et documents sur les juifs de Belgique	Revue des études juives		[1894]
	Wolf	Geschichte der Juden in Wien (1156–1876)		[Vienna]	1894
	Wolf	The First English Jew	Transactions (Jewish Historical Society of England)		[1894–1895]
	Winter and Wünsche	Die jüdische Litteratur seit Abschluss des Kanons		[Trier]	[1894–1896]
	Budde	The Nomadic Ideal in the Old Testament	[The New World]		1895
	Denekamp	Die Amsterdamer Diamantindustrie			[1895]
3	Dyer	Points in the First Chapter of New York Jewish History	Publications of the American Jewish Historical Society		[1895]
4	Kohler	Phases of Jewish Life in New York Before 1800	Publications of the American Jewish Historical Society	[New York]	[1895]
	Lehmann	Die geschichtliche Entwicklung des Aktienrechts bis zum Code de Commerce		[Berlin]	1895
	Model	Die grossen Berliner Effektenbanken: Aus dem Nachlasse des Verfassers			1895
	Monod		Revue historique		1895
2	Reinach	Textes d'auteurs grecs et romains relatifs au judaïsme	[Fontes Rerum Judaicarum]	[Paris]	1895
	Remedios	Os Judeus em Portugal		[Coimbra]	1895

Number of citations	Author	Book/Article Title	Periodical/Multivolume	Place of Publication	Year of Publication
	Wolf	Crypto-Jews under the Commonwealth	Transactions (Jewish Historical Society of England)		1895
	Wolf	The American Jew as Soldier and Patriot	Publications of the American Jewish Historical Society		[1895]
2	Bertholet	Die Stellung der Israeliten und der Juden zu den Fremden		[Leipzig]	1896
4	Brunschvicq	Les Juifs en Bretagne au XVIIIe siècle	Revue des études juives		1896
	Cohen	The Jews in Texas	Publications of the American Jewish Historical Society		[1896]
12	Ehrenberg	Das Zeitalter der Fugger: Geldkapital und Creditverkehr im 16. Jahrhundert		[Jena]	1896
4	Kahn	Les Juifs de Montpellier au XVIIIe siècle	Revue des études juives		1896
	Meyer	Die Entstehung des Judenthums: eine historische Untersuchung		[Halle]	1896
	Fagniez	L'économie sociale de la France sous Henri IV, 1589–1610		[Paris]	1897
	Funke	Die Leipziger Messen		[Leipzig]	1897
	Cohen	Henry Castro, Pioneer and Colonist	Publications of the American Jewish Historical Society		[1897]
	Friedenwald	Some Newspaper Advertisements of the Eighteenth Century	Publications of the American Jewish Historical Society		[1897]
	Kohler	The Jews in Newport	Publications of the American Jewish Historical Society		[1897]

	Author	Title	Publication	Place	Year
	Kohler	Civil Status of the Jews in Colonial New York	Publications of the American Jewish Historical Society	[Philadelphia]	[1897]
	Hilprecht	The Babylonian Expedition of the University of Pennsylvania			1898
	Jacobs	Typical Character of the Anglo-Jewish History	The Jewish Quarterly Review		1898
	Kollmann	Lehrbuch der Entwicklungsgeschichte des Menschen		[Jena]	1898
	Lévy	Notes sur l'histoire des Juifs en Saxe	Revue des études juives		1898
		Les Juifs et les communautés d'arts et métiers	Revue des études juives		1898
	Martin	La grande industrie sous le règne de Louis XIV		[Paris]	1898
2	Roubin	La vie commercial des juifs comtadins en Languedoc	Revue des études juives		[1898]
7	Bloch	Les Juifs et la prospérité publique à travers l'histoire		[Paris]	1899
	[Ehrenberg]	Börsenwesen	Handwörterbuch der Staatswissenschaften		[1899]
3	Buhl	Die sozialen Verhältnisse der Israeliten		[Berlin]	1899
	Cohen	Das Problem der jüdischen Sittenlehre: eine Kritik von Lazarus' Ethik des Judenthums	Monatsschrift für Geschichte und Wissenschaft des Judentums		[1899]
	Eberstadt	Das französische Gewerberecht und die Schaffung staatlicher Gesetzgebung und Verwaltung in Frankreich vom dreizehnten Jahrhundert bis 1581		[Leipzig]	1899
3	Feilchenfeld	Anfang und Blütezeit der Portugiesengemeinden	Zeitschrift für Hamburgische Geschichte		1899
	Feilchenfeld	Die älteste Geschichte der deutschen Juden in Hamburg	Monatsschrift für Geschichte und Wissenschaft des Judentums		1899
3	Godart	L'ouvrier en soie: monographie du tisseur lyonnais, étude historique, économique et sociale		[Lyon]	1899
2	Kracauer	Beiträge zur Geschichte der Frankfurter Juden im dreißigjährigen Kriege	Zeitschrift für die Geschichte der Juden in Deutschland		1899

Number of citations	Author	Book/Article Title	Periodical/Multivolume	Place of Publication	Year of Publication
2	Müller	Aus fünf Jahrhunderten: Beiträge zur Geschichte der jüdischen Gemeinden im Riess	Zeitschrift des historischen Vereins für Schwaben und Neuberg	[Ausburg]	1899
2	Sieveking	Genueser Finanzwesen mit besonderer Berücksichtigung der Casa di S. Giorgio			1899
2	Brann	Eine Sammlung Fürther Grabschriften	Gedenkbuch zur Erinnerung an David Kaufmann	[Breslau]	1900
	Friedenthal	Über einen experimentellen Nachweis von Blutsver-wandtschaft			1900
	Goldschmidt		Zeitschrift für das gesamte Handelsrecht		[1900]
	Hüher	Asser Levy: A Noted Jewish Burgher of New Amsterdam	Publications of the American Jewish Historical Society		[1900]
3	Kayserling	The Jews in Jamaica and Daniel Israel Lopez Laguna	Jewish Quarterly Review		1900
2	Levy	Geschichte der Juden in Sachsen		[Berlin]	1900
	Martin	La grande industrie en France sous le règne de Louis XV		[Paris]	1900
	Philipson	The Jewish Pioneers of the Ohio Valley	Publications of the American Jewish Historical Society		[1900]
	Stark	Das biblisch-rabbinische Handelsgesetz		[Vienna]	[1900]
	Lederer	Lehrbuch zum Selbstunterricht im babylonischen Talmud			1900–1906
	Chamberlain	Die Grundlagen des 19. Jahrhunderts			1901
	Adler	Auto da Fé and Jew	Jewish Quarterly Review		[1901]
2	Freudenthal	Leipziger Meßgäste: Die judischen Besucher der Leipziger Messen in den Jahren 1675 bis 1764	Monatsschrift für Geschichte und Wissenschaft des Judentums		1901
	Gottheil	Contributions to the History of the Jews in Surinam	Publications of the American Jewish Historical Society		[1901]

	Hüher	Whence Came the First Jewish Settlers of New York?	Publications of the American Jewish Historical Society		[1901]
4	Kaufmann	Die Vertreibung der Marranen aus Venedig im Jahre 1550	Jewish Quarterly Review		1901
2	Kiesselbach	Die wirtschafts- und rechtsgeschichtliche Entwicklung der Seeversicherung in Hamburg		[Hamburg]	1901
	Muret	L'esprit juif: essai de psychologie ethnique		[Paris]	1901
	Necarsulmer	The Early Jewish Settlement at Lancaster, Pennsylvania	Publications of the American Jewish Historical Society		[1901]
	Sayous	Le fractionnement du capital social de la Compagnie Néerlandaise des Indes Orientales aux XVIIe et XVIIIe siècles	Nouvelle revue historique de droit français et étranger		1901
3	Demolins	Comment la route crée le type social		[Paris]	[1901–1903]
		Abensur, Daniel	Jewish Encyclopedia		[1901–1906]
		Alabama	Jewish Encyclopedia		[1901–1906]
		Albany	Jewish Encyclopedia		[1901–1906]
		America	Jewish Encyclopedia		[1901–1906]
		Art Brokers	Jewish Encyclopedia		[1901–1906]
2		Banking	Jewish Encyclopedia		[1901–1906]
		California	Jewish Encyclopedia		[1901–1906]
		Commerce	Jewish Encyclopedia		[1901–1906]
		Commerce	Jewish Encyclopedia		[1901–1906]
		Netherlands	Jewish Encyclopedia		[1901–1906]
		Salvador	Jewish Encyclopedia		[1901–1906]
		South Africa	Jewish Encyclopedia		[1901–1906]
		South Carolina	Jewish Encyclopedia		[1901–1906]

Number of citations	Author	Book/Article Title	Periodical/Multivolume	Place of Publication	Year of Publication
2	Aronius	Regesten zur Geschichte der Juden im fränkischen und deutschen Reiche bis zum Jahre 1273		[Berlin]	[1902]
5	Grunwald	Portugiesengräber auf deutscher Erde		[Hamburg]	1902
	Gumplowicz	Die soziologische Staatsidee		[Innsbruck]	[1902]
	Holmes	Sketch of the Origin Development and Probable Destiny of Men	American Anthropologist		1902
	Hüner	The Jews of Georgia in Colonial Times	Publications of the American Jewish Historical Society		[1902]
3	Kohler	Jewish Activity in American Colonial Commerce	Publications of the American Jewish Historical Society	[New York]	1902
	Sievking	[Aus venezianischen Handlungsbüchern: Ein Beitrag zur Geschichte des Großhandels im 15. Jahrhundert]	Schmollers Jahrbuch für Wirtschafts- und Sozialwissenschaften		1902
	Sombart	Der moderne Kapitalismus			[1902]
	Weber	Depositenbanken und Spekulationsbanken: ein Vergleich deutschen und englischen Bankwesens		[Bonn]	1902
3	Wolf	The Jewry of the Restoration	Transactions (Jewish Historical Society of England)		1902
	Bloch	Der Mamran, der Jüdisch-Polnische Wechselbrief	Berliner Festschrift	Berlin	1903
	Crump	The Theory of Stock Exchange Speculation		[London]	1903
	Eliassof	The Jews of Chicago	Publications of the American Jewish Historical Society		[1903]
2	Elzas	The Jews of South Carolina		[Charleston]	1903

	Author	Title	Journal	Place	Year
	Friedländer	Geschichte der jüdischen Apologetik als Vorgeschichte des Christentums		[Zürich]	1903
	Gottheil	The Jews and the Spanish Inquisition	Jewish Quarterly Review		1903
	Hilprecht	Explorations in Bible Lands During the 19th Century		[Philadelphia]	1903
3	Judt	Die Juden als Rasse: eine Analyse aus dem Gebiete der Anthropologie		[Berlin]	1903
	Kober	Studien zur mittelalterlichen Geschichte der Juden in Köln am Rhein, insbesondere ihres Grundbesitzes		[Breslau]	1903
8	Liebe	Das Judentum in der deutschen Vergangenheit		[Leipzig]	1903
6	Maignial	La question juive en France en 1789		Paris	1903
2	Mayer	Die ökonomische Entstehung der Wiener Judenschaft	Monatsschrift der Oesterreichisch-Israelitischen Union		[1903]
	Messerschmidt	Die Hettiter		[Leipzig]	1903
	Plenge	Gründung und Geschichte des Crédit Mobilier		[Tübingen]	1903
	Stratz	Was sind Juden? Eine ethnographisch-anthropologische Studie		[Vienna]	1903
	Traband	Les origines de la loi mosaïque	[Revue de théoloque et de philosophie]		1903
	Verax	La Roumanie et les Juifs		[Bucarest]	1903
	Volz	Jüdische Eschatologie von Daniel bis Akiba		[Leipzig]	1903
	Wenger	Papyrusforschung und Rechtswissenschaft		[Graz]	1903
	Wilser	Die Germanen: Beiträge zur Völkerkunde		[Leipzig]	1903
	Woltmann	Politische Anthropologie: Eine Untersuchung über den Einfluss der Descendenztheorie auf die Lehre von der politischen Entwicklung der Völker		[Jena]	1903
	Elkind	Die Juden: Eine vergleichend-anthropologische Untersuchung, vorzugsweise auf Grund von Beobachtungen an polnischen Juden	Archiv für Rassen- und Gesellschafts-Biologie		1904

Number of citations	Author	Book/Article Title	Periodical/Multivolume	Place of Publication	Year of Publication
5	Grunwald	Hamburgs deutsche Juden bis zur Auflösung der Dreigemeinden 1811		[Hamburg]	1904
	Hertz	Moderne Rassentheorie: Kritische Essays		[Vienna]	1904
	Hüher	The Jews of South Carolina from the Earliest Settlement to the End of the American Revolution	Publications of the American Jewish Historical Society		[1904]
5	Lazarus	Die Ethik des Judentums		[Frankfurt am Main]	1904
2	Mandl	Das Wesen des Judentums: Dargestellt in homilitischen Essais		[Frankfurt am Main]	1904
	Merriam	The Classification and Distribution of the Pit River Indian Tribes of California	Science		1904
	Michaelis	Prinzipien der natürlichen und sozialen Entwicklungsgeschichte des Menschen	Natur und Staat	[Jena]	1904
	Moody	The Truth about the Trust: A Description and Analysis of the American Trust Movement		[New York]	[1904]
2	Sandler	Anthropologie und Zionismus		[Brünn]	1904
	Starr	The Relations of Ethnologie	Congress of Art and Science, publication of the Universal Exposition in St. Louis of 1904	[St. Louis]	1904
	Stein	Materialien zur Ethik des Talmud			1904
6	Stern	Die Vorschriften der Thora, welche Israel in der Zerstreuung zu beobachten hat: ein Lehrbuch der Religion für Schule und Familie		[Frankfurt am Main]	1904
6	Wellhausen	Israelitische und jüdische Geschichte		[Berlin]	[1904]
	Amitai	La sociologie selon la législation juive		[Paris]	1905

4	Cunningham	Growth of English Industry and Commerce		[Cambridge]	1905
	Ehrenberg	Große Vermögen: ihre Entstehung und ihre Bedeutung, Die Fugger—Rothschild—Krupp		[Jena]	1905
	Fishberg	Beiträge zur physischen Anthropologie der nordafrikanischen Juden	Zeitschrift für Demographie und Statistik der Juden		1905
	Frankl	Der Jude in den deutschen Dichtungen des 15., 16. und 17. Jahrhunderts		[Leipzig]	[1905]
	Fromer	Das Wesen des Judentums			1905
	Grunwald	Mitteilungen zur jüdischen Volkskunde		[Berlin]	1905
	Heinemann	Jewish Beginnings in Michigan Before 1850	Publications of the American Jewish Historical Society		[1905]
	Henriques	The Return of the Jews to England: A Chapter in the History of English Law		[London]	1905
	Hertz	The Jew in South Africa		[Johannesburg]	1905
2	Lucas	A Historical Geography of the British Colonies		[Oxford]	1905
	Michaelis	Die jüdische Auserwählungsidee und ihre biologische Bedeutung	Zeitschrift für Demographie und Statistik der Juden		1905
	Nossig	Die Auserwähltheit der Juden im Lichte der Biologie	Zeitschrift für Demographie und Statistik der Juden		1905
	Peters	The Jews in America: A Short Story of their Part in the Building of the Republic, Commemorating the Two Hundred and Fiftieth Anniversary of Their Settlement		[Philadelphia]	1905
6	Pollak	Rabbi Nathans System der Ethik und Moral		[Frankfurt am Main]	[1905]
	Riesser	Zur Entwicklungsgeschichte der deutschen Großbanken mit besonderer Rücksicht auf die Konzentrationsbestrebungen		[Jena]	1905

Number of citations	Author	Book/Article Title	Periodical/Multivolume	Place of Publication	Year of Publication
	Roos	Additional Notes on the History of the Jews of Surinam	Publications of the American Jewish Historical Society		[1905]
	Sofer	Über die Entmischung der Rassen	Zeitschrift für Demographie und Statistik der Juden		1905
2	Stähelin	Der Antisemitismus des Altertums in seiner Entstehung und Entwicklung		[Winterthur]	1905
	von Luschan	Zur physischen Anthropologie der Juden	Zeitschrift für Demographie und Statistik der Juden		1905
	Weissenberg	Das jüdische Rassenproblem	Zeitschrift für Demographie und Statistik der Juden		1905
	Ziegler	Die Vererbungslehre in der Biologie		[Jena]	1905
	Steinschneider	[Mathematik bei den Juden (1551–1840)]	Monatsschrift für Geschichte und Wissenschaft des Judentums		1905–1907
3	Bothe	Beiträge zur Wirtschafts- und Sozialgeschichte der Reichsstadt Frankfurt		[Leipzig]	1906
	Bondy	Zur Geschichte der Juden in Böhmen, Mähren und Schlesien von 906 bis 1620		[Prague]	[1906]
2	Brüll	Populär-Wissenschaftliche Monatsblätter			1906
3	Däbritz	Die Staatsschulden Sachsens in der Zeit von 1763 bis 1837		[Leipzig]	1906
2	Erbt	Die Hebräer: Kanaan im Zeitalter der hebräischen Wanderung und hebräischer Staatengründungen		[Leipzig]	1906
2	Fromer	Vom Ghetto zur modernen Kultur: eine Lebensgeschichte		[Heidelberg]	1906

#	Author	Title	Journal/Publisher	Place	Year
	Haddon	Ethnology: Its Scope and Problems	Congress Of Art and Science	[New York]	[1906]
	Jeremias	Das alte Testament im Lichte des alten Orients		[Leipzig]	1906
	Marshall	Address in the Two Hundred and Fiftieth Anniversary of the Settlement of the Jews in the United States		[New York]	1906
	Meyer	Die Israeliten und ihre Nachbarstämme: Alttestamentliche Untersuchungen		[Halle]	1906
	Meyer	Gedächtnis und Vererbung	Archiv für Rassen- und Gesellschafts-Biologie		1906
	Pardel	Address: The Two Hundred and Fiftieth Anniversary of the Settlement of the Jews in the United States	Jewish Historical Society	[New York]	1906
	Sofer	Zur Biologie und Pathologie der jüdischen Rasse	Zeitschrift für Demographie und Statistik der Juden		1906
2	Straus	The Two Hundred and Fiftieth Anniversary of the Settlement of the Jews in the United States	Jewish Historical Society	[New York]	1906
	Weismann	Semons "Mneme" und die Vererbung erworbener Eigenschaften	Archiv für Rassen- und Gesellschafts-Biologie		1906
3		The Two Hundred and Fiftieth Anniversary of the Settlement of the Jews in the United States	Jewish Historical Society	[New York]	[1906]
	Adler	Auto da Fé and Jew	[Jewish Quarterly Review]		1907
	Auerbach	Bemerkungen zu Fishbergs Theorie über die Herkunft der blonden Juden	Zeitschrift für Demographie und Statistik der Juden		1907
	Bardenhewer	Biblische Studien			1907
	Bauer	Die Nationalitätenfrage und die Sozialdemokratie		[Vienna]	1907
2	Bock	Le Journal à travers les âges		[Brussels]	1907
	Bruck	Die biologische Differenzierung von Affenarten und menschlichen Rassen durch spezifische Blutreaktion.		[Berlin]	1907

Number of citations	Author	Book/Article Title	Periodical/Multivolume	Place of Publication	Year of Publication
	Dietz	Stammbuch der Frankfurter Juden: Geschichtliche Mitteilungen über die Frankfurter jüdischen Familien von 1349–1849		[Frankfurt am Main]	1907
	Doyle	The Colonies under the House of Hanover		[New York]	1907
	Fishberg	Zur Frage der Herkunft des blonden Elements im Judentum	Zeitschrift für Demographie und Statistik der Juden		1907
	Goldstein	Die Juden in der Amsterdamer Diamantindustrie	Zeitschrift für Demographie und Statistik der Juden		[1907]
	Hejcl	Das alttestamentliche Zinsverbot: Im Lichte der ethnologischen Jurisprudenz sowie des altorientalischen Zinswesens		[Freiburg]	1907
	Hilfman	Some Further Notes on the History of the Jews in Surinam	Publications of the American Jewish Historical Society		[1907]
	Hoppe	Die Kriminalität der Juden und der Alkohol	Zeitschrift für Demographie und Statistik der Juden		1907
	Italie	Geschiedenis der Israëlitischen Gemeente te Rotterdam	[Rotterdam in den loop der eeuwen]	[Rotterdam]	1907
	Kellen	[Die Entwicklung des Anzeigen- und Reklamewesens in den Zeitungen]	Studien über das Zeitungswesen Professor dr. Adolf Koch	[Frankfurt am Main]	1907
	Merx	Die Bücher Moses und Josua: eine Einführung für Laien		[Tübingen]	1907
3	Meyer	Die Literatur für und wider die Juden in Schweden im Jahre 1815	Monatsschrift für Geschichte und Wissenschaft des Judentums		1907
	Oppenheimer	An Early Jewish Colony in Western Guiana, 1658–1666	Publications of the American Jewish Historical Society		[1907]

	Author	Title	Journal	Place	Year
	Rosenfeld	*Die Sterblichkeit der Juden in Wien und die Ursachen der jüdischen Mindersterblichkeit*	Archiv für Rassen- und Gesellschafts-Biologie		1907
3	Schipper	*[Anfänge des Kapitalismus bei den abendländischen Juden im früheren Mittelalter]*		[Vienna/Leipzig]	[1907]
	Sofer	*Armenier und Juden*	Archiv für Rassen- und Gesellschafts-Biologie		1907
2	Sommer	*Familienforschung und Vererbungslehre*		[Leipzig]	1907
	Sommer	*Individualpsychologie und Psychiatrie: Bericht über den II. Kongreß für experimentelle Psychologie in Würzburg*		[Leipzig]	1907
	von Luschan	*Offener Brief an Herrn Dr. Elias Auerbach*	Archiv für Rassen- und Gesellschafts-Biologie		1907
2	Winckler	*[Die babylonische Geisteskultur in ihren Beziehungen zur Kulturentwicklung der Menschheit]*	Zeitschrift für Demographie und Statistik der Juden	[Leipzig]	[1907]
2	Aptowitzer	*[Josef Kohlers Darstellung des talmudischen Rechtes]*	Monatsschrift für Geschichte und Wissenschaft des Judentums		[1907]
2	Auerbach	*Die jüdische Rassenfrage*	Archiv für Rassen- und Gesellschafts-Biologie		1908
2	Bergmann	*Jüdische Apologetik im neutestamentlichen Zeitalter*		[Berlin]	1908
	Brakel	*De Hollandsche handelscompagnieën der seventiende euuw, hun ontstaan, hunne inrichtig*		[The Hague]	1908
2	Caro	*Sozial- und Wirtschaftsgeschichte der Juden im Mittelalter und der Neuzeit*		[Leipzig]	1908
2	Carqueja	*O capitalismo moderno e as suas origens em Portugal*		[Portugal]	1908

Number of citations	Author	Book/Article Title	Periodical/Multivolume	Place of Publication	Year of Publication
	Eisenstadt	Die Renaissance der jüdischen Sozialhygiene	Archiv für Rassen- und Gesellschafts-Biologie		1908
	Friedenthal	Arbeiten aus dem Gebiete der experimentellen Physiologie		[Jena]	1908
2	Fromer	Die Organisation des Judentums			1908
	Gomoll	Die kapitalistische Mausefalle: Katechismus für Privatkapitalisten		[Leipzig]	1908
	Hegemann	Die Entwicklung des französischen Großbankbetriebes		[Münster]	1908
12	Hyamson	A History of the Jews in England		[London]	1908
	Kohler	Darstellung des talmudischen Rechtes	Zeitschrift für vergleichende Rechtswissenschaft		1908
	Ruppin	Die Mischehe	Zeitschrift für Demographie und Statistik der Juden		[1908]
	Semon	Die Mneme als erhaltendes Prinzip im Wechsel des organischen Geschehens		[Leipzig]	1908
	Sofer	Über die Plastizität der menschlichen Rassen	Archiv für Rassen- und Gesellschafts-Biologie		1908
2	Sofer	Zur anthropologischen Stellung der Juden	Zeitschrift für Demographie und Statistik der Juden		[1908]
1	Strack	Einleitung in den Thalmud		[Leipzig]	1908
	Thon	Taufbewegung der Juden in Österreich	Zeitschrift für Demographie und Statistik der Juden		[1908]
	von Luschan		Archiv für Rassen- und Gesellschafts-Biologie		1908

Author		Title		Place	Year
Andréades		History of the Bank of England, 1640 to 1903			1909
Bölsche		Das Liebesleben in der Natur: eine Entwicklungsgeschichte der Liebe		[Jena]	1909
Breslauer		Die Abwanderung der Juden aus der Provinz Posen	Denkschrift im Auftrage des Verbandes der Deutschen Juden	[Berlin]	1909
Frese		Aus dem gräko-ägyptischen Rechtsleben		[Halle]	1909
Freud		Sammlung kleiner Schriften zur Neurosenlehre		[Leipzig]	1909
Hirsch	7	Versuche über Jissroëls Pflichten in der Zerstreuung		[Frankfurt am Main]	1909
Jaffé		Die Stadt Posen unter preußischer Herrschaft: ein Beitrag zur Geschichte des deutschen Ostens	Schriften des Vereins für Socialpolitik.	[Leipzig]	[1909]
Martius		Das pathologische Vererbungsproblem		[Leipzig]	1909
Schultz		Die Maschinentheorie des Lebens		[Göttingen]	1909
Sieveking		Die kapitalistische Entwicklung in den italienischen Städten des Mittelalters	Vierteljahrschrift für Soziale und Wissenschaft Geschicht		[1909]
Sombart		Der Kapitalistische Unternehmer	Archiv für soziale Wissenschaft und Soziale Politik		[1909]
Sommer		Die Beziehungen zwischen Psychologie, Psychopathologie und Kriminalpsychologie vom Standpunkte der Vererbungslehre	Wochenschrift für Soziale Hygiene und Medizin		1909
Ullmann	2	Studien zur Geschichte der Juden in Belgien bis zum 18. Jahrhundert		[Antwerp]	1909
Ward		[Reine Soziologie. Eine Abhandlung über den Ursprung und die spontane Entwicklung der Gesellschaft]		[Innsbruck]	1909
Weber		Agrargeschichte im Altertum	Handwörterbuch der Staatswissenschaften		[1909]

Number of citations	Author	Book/Article Title	Periodical/Multivolume	Place of Publication	Year of Publication
		Wochenschrift für soziale Medizin, Hygiene und Medizinalstatistik			1909
	Blau	*Judenwanderungen in Preußen*	Zeitschrift für Demographie und Statistik der Juden		1910
	Cheinisse	*Die Rassenpathologie und der Alkoholismus bei den Juden*	Zeitschrift für Demographie und Statistik der Juden		1910
2	Delitzsch	*Handel und Wandel in Altbabylonien*			1910
	Hirsch	*Das Warenhaus in Westdeutschland, seine Organisation und Wirkungen*		[Leipzig]	1910
	Hoffmann	*[Der Geldhandel der deutschen Juden während des Mittelalters bis zum Jahre 1350]*		[Leipzig]	[1910]
	Kaufmann	*Die Memorien der Glückel von Hameln*		[Vienna]	1910
3	Martius	*Die Bedeutung der Vererbung für Krankheitsentstehung und Rassenerhaltung*	Archiv für Rassen- und Gesellschafts-Biologie		1910
	Michaelis	*Die Rechtsverhältnisse der Juden in Preußen seit dem Beginne des 19. Jahrhunderts: Gesetze, Erlasse, Verordnungen, Entscheidungen*		[Berlin]	1910

	Nathanson	Die unehelichen Geburten bei den Juden	Zeitschrift für Demographie und Statistik der Juden		1910
	Rosenblüth	Zur Begriffsbestimmung von Volk und Nation		[Berlin]	1910
	Schallmayer	Vererbung und Auslese: Grundriss der Gesellschaftsbiologie und der Lehre vom Rassedienst, für Rassehygieniker, Bevölkerungspolitiker, Ärzte, Anthropologen, Soziologen, Erzieher, Kriminalisten, höhere Verwaltungsbeamte und politisch interessierte Gebildete aller Stände		[Jena]	1910
2	Wassermann	Die Entwicklung der jüdischen Bevölkerung in der Provinz Posen und das Ostmarkenproblem	Zeitschrift für Demographie und Statistik der Juden		1910
	Woodworth	Racial Differences in Mental Traits	Bulletin mensuel des Institut Solvay		1910
5	Zollschan	Das Rassenproblem unter besonderer Berücksichtigung der theoretischen Grundlagen der jüdischen Rassenfrage		[Vienna]	1910
	Löhr	Israels Kulturentwicklung		[Strasbourg]	1911
	Schrader	Die Indogermanen		[Leipzig]	1911

Note: Information in brackets is either added or corrected.

NOTES

Preface

1. *Financial Times*, April 21, 2010, emphasis mine.

2. Buffett's letter to his shareholders can be read in full at http://www.berkshirehathaway.com/letters/2002pdf.pdf (accessed July 9, 2018). The phrase had appeared in prominent media sources years before, but only after September 2008 did it go viral. See, e.g., "Buffet's 'time bomb' goes off on Wall Street," BBC News, September 18, 2008, http://news.bbc.co.uk/2/hi/2817995.stm (accessed July 9, 2018). The noted CBS News program *60 Minutes* aired an episode entitled "Financial Weapons of Mass Destruction" on October 26, 2008.

3. Marc Bloch, *The Historian's Craft*, trans. Peter Putnam (New York: Vintage Books, 1953 [1949]), 29–35. I cite English translations whenever they are available and give the original publication date within squared brackets. All other translations are my own.

4. Throughout the book, I purposefully avoid the casual use of the term *capitalism*, in spite of the new purchase it has acquired since 2008 and, especially, since the publication of Thomas Piketty's *Capital in the Twenty-first Century*, trans. Arthur Goldhammer (Cambridge: Harvard University Press, 2014 [2013]). I fear that to call the money markets of premodern Europe capitalistic would interfere with my quest to identify their specificities and link them to the cultural clashes that they generated. Consequently, in referring to the economy of the late medieval and early modern periods, I often resort to the label *preindustrial* because structural conditions that affected the working of credit markets, notably poor information technologies and the absence of notions of legal and political equality, can be found throughout the history of Europe from 1000 to 1800. Only in chapter 7 do I readily use the term *capitalism*, because there I engage with nineteenth- and early-twentieth-century social theories aimed at defining modern capitalism as a distinctive historical phenomenon.

5. Notable exceptions are Jonathan Karp, *The Politics of Jewish Commerce: Economic Ideology and Emancipation in Europe, 1638-1848* (Cambridge: Cambridge University Press, 2008) and David Nirenberg, *Anti-Judaism: The Western Tradition* (New York: W.W. Norton, 2014), in particular ch. 8, which is an abridged version of idem, "Shakespeare's Jewish Questions," *Renaissance Drama* 38 (2010): 77-113.

Introduction

1. Thomas Coryat, *Coryat's Crudities*, 2 vols. (New York: Macmillan, 1905), 1: 423.

2. Thomas Adams, *God's Anger; and, Man's Comfort: Two Sermons* (London: Tho. Maxey for Samuel Man, 1652), 32. I am grateful to Mordechai Levy-Eichel for passing on this reference.

3. Pat Hudson, "Slavery, the Slave Trade and Economic Growth: A Contribution to the Debate," in *Emancipation and the Remaking of the British Imperial World*, ed. Catherine Hall, Nicholas Draper, and Keith McClelland (Manchester: Manchester University Press, 2014), 36–59, at 46.

4. I borrow the expression from Aldo De Maddalena and Hermann Kellenbenz, eds., *La repubblica internazionale del denaro tra XV e XVII secolo* (Bologna: Il Mulino, 1986).

5. Joseph-Nicolas Guyot, *Répertoire universel et raisonné de jurisprudence civile, criminelle, canonique et bénéficiale*, 64 vols. (Paris: J. D. Dorez, 1775–1783), 103–159, at 117, s.v. "change." Whenever possible and relevant, I cite from the first edition of rare books. This jurisprudential compilation is better known through its second edition: Guyot, *Répertoire universel et raisonné de jurisprudence civile, criminelle, canonique et bénéficiale*, new ed., 17 vols. (Paris: Chez Visse, 1784–1785), 3: 125–148, at 129, s.v. "change."

6. Dana Štefanová, "Bankruptcy and the Bank: The Case of the 'kaiserlich königliche Wiener octroyierte Commercial-, Leih- und Wechselbank' of Vienna in the 18th Century," in *The History of Bankruptcy: Economic, Social and Cultural Implications in Early Modern Europe*, ed. Thomas Max Safley (London: Routledge, 2013), 126–140, at 129.

7. Benjamin Arbel, "Jews, the Rise of Capitalism and *Cambio*: Commercial Credit and Maritime Insurance in the Early Modern Mediterranean World" [in Hebrew], *Zion* 69, no. 2 (2004): 157–202. A revised English version expands the analysis of Jews' involvement in the trade of bills of exchange and rabbinical responses to it: idem, "Mediterranean Jewish Diasporas and the Bill of Exchange: Coping with a Foreign Financial Instrument (Fourteenth to Seventeenth Centuries)," in *Union in Separation: Diasporic Groups and Identities in the Eastern Mediterranean (1100–1800)*, ed. Georg Christ, Franz-Julius Morche, Roberto Zaugg, Wolfgang Kaiser, Stefan Burkhardt, and Alexander D. Beihammer (Rome: Viella, 2015), 527–553.

8. Building on the work of others and on his own interpretation of Iberian history, David Nirenberg has made the case that the events of 1391 provoked a crisis in European culture that had even graver repercussions than the expulsion ordered in 1492. Nirenberg, *Neighboring Faiths: Christianity, Islam, and Judaism in the Middle Ages and Today* (Chicago: University of Chicago Press, 2014), esp. 143–167. While the anxiety produced by baptized Jews was greatest in Iberia, it permeated all Christian societies, including those in the German-speaking regions, on which see Kenneth Stow, "Conversion, Apostasy, and Apprehensiveness: Emicho of Flonheim and the Fear of Jews in the Twelfth Century," *Speculum* 76, no. 4 (2001): 911–933.

9. The most comprehensive survey remains Jonathan I. Israel, *European Jewry in the Age of Mercantilism, 1550–1750*, rev. ed. (Oxford: Clarendon Press, 1989). My emphasis here is on themes that are tangential to Israel's synthesis and that I outline in "Jews and the Early Modern Economy," in *The Cambridge History of Judaism*, vol. 7: *1500–1815*, ed. Jonathan Karp and Adam Sutcliffe (Cambridge: Cambridge University Press, 2017), 139–167.

10. Jacques Savary, *Le parfait négociant, ou, Instruction generale pour ce qui regarde le commerce de toute sorte de marchandises, tant de France que des pays estranger* (Paris: Chez Louis Billaine, 1675), 121 (book 1, ch. 19).

11. Estienne Cleirac, *Us et coustumes de la mer, divisées en trois parties: I. De la navigation. II. Du commerce naval & contracts maritimes. III. De la iurisdiction de la marine. Avec un traicté des termes de marine & reglemens de la nauigation des fleuves & rivieres* (Bordeaux: Guillaume Millanges, 1647). "Estienne" is the archaic spelling of Étienne.

12. Albert O. Hirschman, *The Passions and the Interests: Political Arguments for Capitalism Before Its Triumph* (Princeton, NJ: Princeton University Press, 1977), 3.

13. Ronald Schechter ought to be mentioned here for his early and incisive use of online databases to highlight the relevance of themes concerning Jews and Judaism in the French Enlightenment: Schechter, *Obstinate Hebrews: Representations of Jews in France, 1715–1815* (Berkeley: California University Press, 2003). At the time, *The Making of the Modern World* did not exist, and his study does not take into account most of the legal and commercial compilations examined here.

14. "Distant reading" is what Franco Moretti calls his method of analyzing large-scale datasets of published titles in order to question our understanding of the canon of Western literature. For a short introduction, see his "The Slaughterhouse of Literature," *MLQ: Modern Language Quarterly* 61, no. 1 (2000): 207–227.

15. Clare Haru Crowston, *Credit, Fashion, Sex: Economies of Regard in Old Regime France* (Durham, NC: Duke University Press, 2013), 117–121.

16. Joel M. Podolny, *Status Signals: A Sociological Study of Market Competition* (Princeton, NJ: Princeton University Press, 2008).

17. The Deputies of Commerce asked that tax farmers and state financiers be allowed to accept bills of exchange drawn on Paris by merchants in Bordeaux and other areas as payments of their dues but prohibited from drawing their bills of exchange out of the kingdom, since that would harm the state. The request appealed to a protectionist stance averse to the export of specie that royal officials were likely to be sympathetic to. The citations come from Archives Nationales, Paris (hereafter ANP), "Mémoire des avantages et des abus qui présente le commerce des lettres de change en général," F12/641. Anne Ruderman kindly shared this document with me. On the Deputies of Commerce, see Sébastien Vosgien, *Gouverner le commerce aux XVIIIe siècle: Conseil et Bureau du commerce* (Paris: Comité pour l'histoire économique et financière de la France, 2017), 43–54.

18. William H. Sewell, Jr., "Connecting Capitalism to the French Revolution: The Parisian Promenade and the Origins of Civic Equality in Eighteenth-Century France," *Critical Historical Studies* 1, no. 1 (2014): 5–46, at 16.

19. Idem, "Connecting Capitalism"; idem, "The Empire of Fashion and the Rise of Capitalism in Eighteenth-Century France," *Past and Present* 206, no. 1 (2010): 81–120; Jürgen Habermas, *The Structural Transformation of the Public Sphere: An Inquiry into a Category of Bourgeois Society*, trans. Thomas Burger with Frederick Lawrence (Cambridge, MA: MIT Press, 1989 [1962]).

20. For a cultural analysis that differs from mine in topic more than in argument, see James H. Johnson, "The Face of Imposture in Postrevolutionary France," *French Historical Studies* 35, no. 2 (2012): 291–320.

21. Jonathan Sheehan and Dror Warman, *Invisible Hands: Self-Organization in the Eighteenth Century* (Chicago: University of Chicago Press, 2015).

22. It is not a coincidence that the scholar who denounced the "lachrymose conception of Jewish history" was also a pioneer of the social history of Jews: Salo Wittmayer Baron, *A Social and Religious History of the Jews*, 2nd ed., 17 vols. (New York: Columbia University Press, 1957–1983). The first volume of the first edition appeared in 1937.

23. For important analyses of late medieval conceptions of Jewish usury, I am particularly indebted to Lester K. Little, "The Function of the Jews in the Commercial Revolution," in

Povertà e ricchezza nella spiritualità dei secoli XI e XII (Todi: Accademia Tuderina, 1969), 272–287, and numerous works by Giacomo Todeschini, including: *La ricchezza degli ebrei: Merci e denaro nella riflessione ebraica e nella definizione cristiana dell'usura alla fine del Medioevo* (Spoleto: Centro italiano di studi sull'alto Medioevo, 1989); *I mercanti e il tempio: La società cristiana e il circolo virtuoso della ricchezza fra medioevo ed età moderna* (Bologna: Il Mulino, 2002), esp. 94–106, 227–238; "Christian Perceptions of Jewish Economic Activity in the Middle Ages," in *Wirtschaftsgeschichte der mittelalterlichen Juden: Fragen und Einschätzungen*, ed. Michael Toch (München: Oldenbourg, 2008), 1–16; and "Usury in Christian Middle Ages: A Reconsideration of the Historiographical Tradition (1949–2010)," in *Religion and Religious Institutions in the European Economy, 1000–1800*, ed. Francesco Ammannati (Florence: Firenze University Press, 2012), 119–130.

24. Israel, *European Jewry*, 56.

25. The expression "new paradigm" comes from Karp, *Politics of Jewish Commerce*, 94.

Chapter 1: The Setting: Marine Insurance and Bills of Exchange

1. The idea of a "posthumous invention" is obviously incongruous. The author probably meant to stress the longevity of that invention, but thus goes baroque prose. Estienne Cleirac, *Us et coustumes de la mer, divisées en trois parties: I. De la navigation. II. Du commerce naval & contracts maritimes. III. De la iurisdiction de la marine. Avec un traicté des termes de marine & reglemens de la nauigation des fleuves & rivieres* (Bordeaux: Guillaume Millanges, 1647), 224; idem, *Us et coustumes de la mer, divisées en trois parties: I. De la navigation. II. Du commerce naval & contracts maritimes. III. De la iurisdiction de la marine: auec un traicté des termes de marine & reglemens de la navigation des fleuves & rivieres: le tout reveu, corrigé & augmenté par l'autheur en cette derniere edition* (Bordeaux: Iacques Mongiron Millanges, 1661), 218. Since the 1661 edition of this book is far more easily accessible than the 1647 one, from here on out, I will give the page numbers from both editions, which I will refer to as *UCM 1647* and *UCM 1661*, respectively. A list of all Cleirac's books and their editions is provided in appendix 3.

2. The choice of the word *legend* requires a brief explanation, because the term does not appear in any of the texts that I examine. By most definitions, a legend, unlike a myth, has human rather than supernatural protagonists and is anchored in a kernel of historical truth. See William Harmon and C. Hugh Holmans, *A Handbook to Literature*, 7th ed. (Upper Saddle River, NJ: Prentice Hall, 1996), 288, s.v. "legend"; and M. H. Abrams, *A Glossary of Literary Terms*, 7th ed. (Fort Worth, TX: Harcourt Brace College Publishers, 1999), 170, s.v. "myth." The narrative I analyze here fits the definition of a legend insofar as it derives its purchase, at least in part, from its supposed historical setting. In another respect, however, it departs from legends' tendency to pivot on an individual rather than a collective: Karl Beckson and Arthur Ganz, *Literary Terms: A Dictionary*, rev. ed. (New York: Farrar, Straus and Giroux, 1975), 127–128, s.v. "legend." I occasionally also use the term *tale* in place of *legend*, since both describe an invented tradition. I am grateful to Diana Fuss for a stimulating discussion in this regard.

3. I say "loosely indebted" for several reasons: practitioners of symptomatic reading, an approach that reached its height in the 1980s and 1990s, were influenced by deconstruction, Marxism, and psychoanalysis to an extent that I am not; more generally, symptomatic reading has been applied to high-brow literature and thus to self-reflexive writing rather than to texts that,

for the most part, have normative and practical purposes, such as legal commentaries or merchant handbooks. For a concise introduction to the defining trends in literary criticism of the past three or four decades, including symptomatic reading, see Stephen Best and Sharon Marcus, "Surface Reading: An Introduction," *Representations* 108 (2009): 1–21.

4. Raymond de Roover, "The Organization of Trade," in *The Cambridge Economic History of Europe*, vol. 3: *Economic Organization and Policies in the Middle Ages*, ed. M. M. Postan, E. E. Rich, and Edward Miller (Cambridge: Cambridge University Press, 1963), 42–118.

5. The best synthetic introductions to bills of exchange and marine insurance remain, respectively, Raymond de Roover, *L'évolution de la lettre de change, XIVe–XVIIIe siècles* (Paris: Armand Colin, 1953); and L. A. Boiteux, *La Fortune de mer, le besoin de sécurité et les débuts de l'assurance maritime* (Paris: S.E.V.P.E.N., 1968). Late medieval European bills of exchange differed from earlier financial instruments that both Jewish and Muslims traders utilized in the Mediterranean, including the *suftaja*, a letter of credit used to remit funds between distant locations that is sometimes improperly referred to as a bill of exchange in English scholarship. See Abraham L. Udovitch, "Bankers Without Banks: Commerce, Banking, and Society in the Islamic World of the Middle Ages," in *The Dawn of Modern Banking* (New Haven, CT: Yale University Press, 1979), 255–275, at 268–269; Raymond de Roover, "New Interpretations of the History of Banking," *Cahiers d'histoire mondiale* 2 (1954): 38–76; S. D. Goitein, *A Mediterranean Society: The Jewish Communities of the Arab World as Portrayed in the Documents of the Cairo Geniza*, vol. 1: *Economic Foundations* (Berkeley: University of California Press, 1967), 230, 241–246; Nikolaus A. Siegfried, "Concepts of Paper Money in Islamic Legal Thought," *Arab Law Quarterly* 16, no. 4 (2001): 319–332, at 322; Mark R. Cohen, *Maimonides and the Merchants: Jewish Law and Society in the Medieval Islamic World* (Philadelphia: University of Pennsylvania Press, 2017), 25–27.

6. De Roover, *L'évolution*, 18.

7. The sea loan (*foenus nauticum*) allowed a ship captain or merchant to borrow a sum of money that would be returned only if the voyage was successfully completed. For this reason, lenders charged very high interest rates. A specific type of sea loan, known in Latin as *cambium maritimum*, combined credit with currency conversion and was declared usurious by a papal decree of 1236 known as *Naviganti*. See Raymond de Roover, "The *Cambium Maritimum* Contract According to the Genoese Notarial Records of the Twelfth and Thirteenth Centuries," in *Economy, Society, and Government in Medieval Italy: Essays in Memory of Robert L. Reynolds*, ed. David Herlihy, Robert S. Lopez, and Vsevolod Slessarev (Kent, OH: Kent State University Press, 1969), 15–33. Variants of the sea loan (known in English as *bottomry* when the collateral was the vessel or as *respondentia* when the cargo was pledged, and in French as *prêt à la grosse aventure*) were still in wide use in the eighteenth century.

8. Florence Edler de Roover, "Early Examples of Marine Insurance," *Journal of Economic History* 5, no. 2 (1945): 172–200; Federigo Melis, *Origini e sviluppi delle assicurazioni in Italia (secoli XIV–XVI)* (Rome: Istituto Nazionale delle Assicurazioni, 1975). Life insurance proper was a later development: Geoffrey Clark, *Betting on Lives: The Culture of Life Insurance in England, 1695–1775* (Manchester: Manchester University Press, 1999).

9. Giovanni Ceccarelli, *Un mercato del rischio: Assicurare e farsi assicurare nella Firenze rinascimentale* (Venice: Marsilio, 2012), 35–40.

10. Dave De ruysscher, "Antwerp 1490–1590: Insurance and Speculation," in *Marine*

Insurance: Origins and Institutions, 1300–1850, ed. A. B. Leonard (New York: Palgrave Macmillan, 2016), 79–105, at 95.

11. Violet Barbour, "Marine Risks and Insurance in the Seventeenth Century," *Journal of Economic and Business History* 1, no. 4 (1928–1929): 561–596, at 573.

12. Letter to Guillaume de Sève (*intendant* of Bordeaux) of March 3, 1673, in *Lettres, instructions et mémoires de Colbert*, 7 vols., ed. Pierre Clément (Paris: Imprimerie impériale, 1861–1873), 2:675.

13. Jeroen Puttevils and Marc Deloof, "Marketing and Pricing Risk in Marine Insurance in Sixteenth-Century Antwerp," *Journal of Economic History* 77, no. 3 (2017): 796–837.

14. Lorraine Daston, *Classical Probability in the Enlightenment* (Princeton, NJ: Princeton University Press, 1988), 119. See also Daston, "The Domestication of Risk: Mathematical Probability and Insurance, 1650–1830," in *The Probabilistic Revolution*, 2 vols., ed. Lorenz Krüger, Lorraine J. Daston, and Michael Heidelberger (Cambridge, MA: MIT Press, 1987), 1:237–260.

15. Barbour, "Marine Risks and Insurance," 579.

16. In 1612 the guild's total enrollment was set at 360, including a maximum of 10 Jewish brokers. Over time, unlicensed brokers became more and more numerous among both Jews and non-Jews. Christians' complaints against fellow Jewish guild members included the accusation that Jews violated the prohibition against trading on Sundays. Sabine Go, *Marine Insurance in the Netherlands 1600–1870: A Comparative Institutional Approach* (Amsterdam: Amsterdam University Press, 2009), 76–99.

17. Cátia Antunes, "Cross-Cultural Business Cooperation in the Dutch Trading World, 1580–1776: A View from Amsterdam's Notarial Contracts," in *Religion and Trade: Cross-Cultural Exchanges in World History, 1000–1900*, ed. Francesca Trivellato, Leor Halevi, and Cátia Antunes (New York: Oxford University Press, 2014), 150–168, at 155–156. On the institutional innovations enforced by Amsterdam magistrates in regard to foreign merchants, who were treated as equal before the law but were not allowed to set up their own corporate institutions, see Oscar Gelderblom, *Cities of Commerce: The Institutional Foundations of International Trade in the Low Countries, 1250–1650* (Princeton, NJ: Princeton University Press, 2013).

18. For the first printed edition, see Benedetto Cotrugli, *Della mercatura et del mercante perfetto libri quattro, scritti gia più di anni CX & hora dati in luce, utilissimi ad ogni mercante* (Venice: all'Elefanta, 1573), 34v. For an English translation, see idem, *The Book of the Art of Trade*, ed. Carlo Carraro and Giovanni Favero, trans. John Francis Phillimore (Cham, Switzerland: Springer, 2017), 66.

19. Lewes Roberts, *The Merchants Mappe of Commerce* (London: R. Oulton, 1638), 1. By his account, Roberts had learned most of what he knew from a merchant from Genoa and one from Lyon.

20. Sigismondo Scaccia, *Tractatus de commerciis et cambio* (Rome: Sumptibus A. Brugiotti, ex typographia I. Mascardi, 1619), 150–153 (sec. 1, question 2, nos. 11–18).

21. Bravard-Veyrières, *Traité de droit commercial*, 7 vols. (Paris: Marescq, 1862–1886), 3:1.

22. Alternatively, the bill could order that the payment be processed on sight. The ratio of postal times to *usance* between Venice and various cities around 1400 was 1:3: Reinhold C. Mueller, *The Venetian Money Market: Banks, Panics, and the Public Debt, 1200–1500* (Baltimore: Johns Hopkins University Press, 1997), 295. On the dependence of the trade in bills of exchange on postal services in seventeenth-century Antwerp, see Daniel Velinov, "Information et marché:

L'activité cambiaire et les services postaux à Anvers et en Europe au milieu du XVIIe siècle," *Revue d'histoire moderne et contemporaine* 63, no. 1 (2016): 85–109. In the eighteenth-century British Atlantic, bills of exchange with a sixty-day delivery date were crucial to the supply of credit to tobacco growers in the Chesapeake region: Jacob M. Price, *Capital and Credit in British Overseas Trade: The View from the Chesapeake, 1700–1776* (Cambridge, MA: Harvard University Press, 1980), 97. If a payer did not wish to pay a bill, whether for lack of funds or for other reasons, or if a beneficiary was not able to have the bill paid to him, it was possible to register a "protest" with a public official to certify that the transaction had not been completed.

23. For a detailed illustration of how these banking operations worked, see Nadia Matringe, *La banque en Renaissance: Les Salviati et la place de Lyon au milieu du XVIe siècle* (Rennes, France: Presses universitaires de Rennes, 2016), 56–64, 74–84.

24. Antoine Furetière, *Dictionnaire universel*, 3 vols. (The Hague and Rotterdam: Chez Arnout & Reinier Leers, 1690), s.v. "crédit" (emphasis mine).

25. Raymond de Roover, *The Rise and Decline of the Medici Bank, 1397–1494*, 2nd ed. (Cambridge, MA: Harvard University Press, 1968), 117–122.

26. Matringe, *La banque en Renaissance*, 109, 282–292, 373–376.

27. Eadem, "The Fair Deposit in the Early Modern Period: Credit Reallocation and Trade Finance," *Annales: Histoire, Sciences Sociales* 72, no. 2 (2017): 379–423.

28. Raymond de Roover, "What Is Dry Exchange? A Contribution to the Study of English Mercantilism," *Journal of Political Economy* 52, no. 3 (1944): 250–266, at 261–262, republished in idem, *Business, Banking, and Economic Thought in Late Medieval and Early Modern Europe: Selected Studies of Raymond de Roover*, ed. Julius Kirshner (Chicago: University of Chicago Press, 1974), 183–199.

29. Bernardo Davanzati, "Notizia de' cambi," in *Notizie mercantili delle monete e de' cambi*, ed. Luigi Carrer (Venice: Co' tipi del Gondoliere, 1840), 33–47, at 46. This treatise remained unpublished at the time. In *Lezione delle monete* (1588), Davanzati equated money (rather than bills of exchange) with blood circulation. That work was translated into English as *A Discourse upon Coins*, trans. John Toland (London: Awnsham and John Churchil, 1696), 18, 24. The bodily metaphor used by Davanzati remained common parlance throughout the eighteenth century. A German jurist wrote: "Sunt fere in commerciis cambia illud, quod circulatio sanguinis in corpore humano" ("Exchange dealings are to commerce almost what blood circulation is to the human body"). Johann Christian Hedler, *Positiones de origine cambiorum* (Wittenberg: Io. Guilielmus Bossegelius, 1744), 6.

30. Kenneth Stow, *Jewish Dogs: An Image and Its Interpreters; Continuity in the Catholic-Jewish Encounter* (Stanford, CA: Stanford University Press, 2006), 28.

31. For a synthetic introduction in English to the workings of these fairs, see Luciano Pezzolo and Giuseppe Tattara, "'Una fiera senza luogo?': Was Bisenzone an International Capital Market in Sixteenth-Century Italy?" *Journal of Economic History* 68, no. 4 (2008): 1098–1122. A lengthier examination is found in José-Gentil da Silva, *Banque et crédit en Italie au XVIIe siècle*, 2 vols. (Paris: Klincksieck, 1960).

32. Two scholars describe these operators as a "club." See Marie-Thérèse Boyer-Xambeu, Ghislain Deleplace, and Lucien Gillard, *Private Money and Public Currencies: The 16th Century Challenge*, trans. Azizeh Azodi (Armonk, NY: M. E. Sharpe, 1994), 17–18. The word used in the

French original is "caste": eidem, *Monnaie privée et pouvoir des princes: L'économie des relations monétaires à la Renaissance* (Paris: Editions du CNRS / Presses de la Fondation nationale des sciences politiques, 1986), 19.

33. Davanzati, "Notizia de' cambi," 40.

34. Da Silva, *Banque et crédit*, 88–93; Giuseppe Felloni, "All'apogeo delle fiere genovesi: Banchieri ed affari di cambio a Piacenza nel 1600," in *Studi in onore di Gino Barbieri*, 3 vols. (Pisa: IPEM Edizioni, 1983), 2:883–901, republished in idem, *Scritti di storia economica* (Genoa: Società ligure di storia patria, 1998), 551–568, at 556.

35. Giulio Mandich, *Le pacte de ricorsa et le marché italien des changes au XVIIe siècle* (Paris: Armand Colin, 1953).

36. Giuseppe Felloni, "Un système monétaire atypique: La monnaie de marc dans les foires de change génoises, XVIe–XVIIIe siècle," in *Études d'histoire monétaire*, ed. John Day (Lille: Presses universitaires de Lille, 1984), 249–260, republished in idem, *Scritti di storia economica*, 569–582. The value of the *scudo di marche* was first established on the basis of five foreign currencies issued by Spanish, Genoese, Venetian, Milanese, and Neapolitan governments and later modified to include other currencies that reflected the relative influence of other states as well: Mandich, *Le pacte de ricorsa*, 31. On monies of account in early modern Europe, see Fernand Braudel and Frank Spooner, "Prices in Europe from 1450 to 1750," in *The Cambridge Economic History of Europe from the Decline of the Roman Empire*, vol. 4: *The Economy of Expanding Europe in the Sixteenth and Seventeenth Centuries*, ed. E. E. Rich and C. H. Wilson (Cambridge: Cambridge University Press, 1967), 374–486, at 378–381.

37. A specialized literature discusses credit instruments that resembled early modern European bills of exchange but developed independently of them in other regions of the globe. See, in particular, Irfan Habib, "The System of Bill of Exchange (*hundis*) in the Mughal Empire," *Proceedings: Indian History Congress* 33 (1972): 290–303; E. S. Crawcour and Kozo Yamamura, "The Tokugawa Monetary System: 1787–1868," *Economic Development and Cultural Change* 18, no. 4 (1970): 489–518, at 495; Om Prakash, "The Cashless Payment Mechanism in Mughal India: The Working of the Hundi Network," in *Cashless Payments and Transactions from Antiquity to 1914*, ed. Sushil Chaudhuri and Markus A. Denzel (Stuttgart: Franz Steiner, 2008), 131–137. I omit any discussion of this important topic because it falls outside of my purview. Nothing analogous to the financial fairs of early modern Europe, however, existed outside of Europe at the time.

38. Mandich, *Le pacte de ricorsa*, 98.

39. De Roover, *Rise and Decline*, 122, paraphrasing a manual that remains unpublished: Biblioteca Nazionale, Florence, "Zibaldone di notizie utili a' mercanti" (c. 1443), Fondo palatino, 601.

40. Gio[vanni] Domenico Peri, *Il negotiante*, 4 vols. (Genoa: Pier Giovanni Calenzano, 1638–1665), 4:9–14. Peri included in his volume an epistolary exchange with a jurist of the University of Bologna, Antonio Merenda, who was even more critical than him of financial fairs and *ricorsa* exchanges (3:120–180). See also Rodolfo Savelli, "Modelli giuridici e cultura mercantile tra XVI e XVII secolo," *Materiali per una storia della cultura giuridica* 18, no. 1 (1988): 3–24, at 18n51.

41. Peri, *Il negotiante*, 4:49.

42. De Roover, *L'évolution*, 133; Herman van der Wee, "Anvers et les innovations de la tech-

nique financière aux XVIe et XVIIe siècles," *Annales E.S.C.* 22, no. 5 (1967): 1067–1089, at 1085–1089; idem, *The Growth of the Antwerp Market and the European Economy (Fourteenth–Sixteenth Centuries)*, 3 vols. (Louvain: Bureaux du Recueil, Bibliothèque de l'Université, 1963), 2:349–352.

43. Scaccia, *Tractatus de commerciis et cambio*, 205 (sec. 1, question 7, no. 25).

44. Jan de Vries and Ad van der Woude, *The First Modern Economy: Success, Failure, and Perseverence of the Dutch Economy, 1500–1815* (Cambridge: Cambridge University Press, 1997), 131–134.

45. The precise time and location of this innovation has been the object of animated scholarly debates: de Roover, *L'évolution*, 83–118; Federigo Melis, "Una girata cambiaria del 1410 nell'Archivio Datini di Prato," *Economia e storia* 5 (1958): 412–421; Henri Lapeyre, "Une lettre de change endossée en 1430," *Annales E.S.C.* 13, no. 2 (1958): 260–264; van der Wee, "Anvers," 1074–1085; idem, *Growth of the Antwerp Market*, 2:340–349; John Munro, "The Medieval Origins of the Financial Revolution: Usury, *Rentes*, and Negotiability," *International Journal Review* 25, no. 3 (2003): 505–562, at 545.

46. Isaac de Pinto, a Sephardi writer in Amsterdam and a strong proponent of the merits of commercial credit, claimed that bills of exchange often had ten endorsers: Pinto, *Traité de la circulation et du crédit* (Amsterdam: Chez M. M. Rey, 1771), 35.

47. Edhem Eldem, *French Trade in Istanbul in the Eighteenth Century* (Leiden: Brill, 1999), 145; Veronica Aoki Santarosa, "Financing Long-Distance Trade Without Banks: The Joint Liability Rule and Bills of Exchange in 18th-Century France," *Journal of Economic History* 75, no. 3 (2015): 690–719.

48. "Des changes," *Journal de commerce et d'agriculture*, May 1762, 49–56, at 51; Anne-Robert-Jacques Turgot, "Valeurs et monnaies (Project d'article, 1769)," in *Écrits économiques* (Paris: Calmann-Lévy, 1970), 231–250, at 237. Both are also cited by Thomas M. Luckett, "Credit and Commercial Society in France, 1740–1789" (Ph.D. diss., Princeton University, 1992), 9.

49. In France, quasi-paper money (*billets de monnaie*) circulated between 1701 and 1711 during the fiscal crisis provoked by the War of Spanish Succession. Between 1718 and 1720, banknotes (*billets-écus* backed by species and then *billets-livres* freed from real asset backing) were issued by John Law's General Bank, later the Royal Bank. Both experiments failed miserably. Antoin E. Murphy, *John Law: Economic Theorist and Policy Maker* (Oxford: Clarendon Press, 1997), 115–120, 223–226. The first European banknotes were issued in Sweden in 1661 but were discontinued three years later. The Bank of England, established in 1694, only issued banknotes of large denominations for much of the eighteenth century. As a result, ordinary people did not use them. John Clapham, *The Bank of England: A History*, 2 vols. (Cambridge: Cambridge University Press, 1944–1945), 1:3, 41–42, 59. Experiments with paper money in the British colonies of North America began as early as 1690. Dror Goldberg, "Massachussetts Paper Money of 1690," *Journal of Economic History* 69, no. 4 (2009): 1092–1106.

50. Some scholars still mistakenly equate bills of exchange with paper money. See, e.g., Markus A. Denzel, "The European Bill of Exchange," in *Cashless Payments*, 153–194, at 169; Robert Beachy, *The Soul of Commerce: Credit, Property, and Politics in Leipzig, 1750–1840* (Leiden: Brill, 2005), 35. On the relationship between banknotes and bills of exchange in England, see Jongchul Kim, "How Modern Banking Originated: The Londong Goldsmith-Bankers' Institutionalization of Trust," *Business History* 53, no. 6 (2011): 939–959; and James Steven Rogers, *The*

Early History of the Law of Bills and Notes: A Study of the Origins of Anglo-American Commercial Law (Cambridge: University of Cambridge Press, 1995), 186–193.

51. Rogers, *Early History*, 101. On the diffusion of the so-called "inland" or "domestic" bills in England, see Eric Kerridge, *Trade and Banking in Early Modern England* (Manchester: Manchester University Press, 1988).

52. Estien[n]e Cleirac, *Usance du négoce ou commerce de la banque des lettres change* (Bordeaux: Par Guillaume da Court, 1656) 153–154 (on discounting at the Lyon fairs); Henri Lévy-Bruhl, *Histoire de la lettre de change en France au XVIIe et XVIIIe siècles* (Paris: Siery, 1933), 103 (citing Cleirac regarding the transferability of bills of exchange); de Roover, *L'évolution*, 83–84; Pierre Jeannin, "De l'arithmétique commerciale à la pratique bancaire: l'escompte aux XVIe et XVIIe siècles," in *Banchi pubblici, banchi privati e monti di pietà nell'Europa preindustriale: Amministrazione, tecniche operative e ruoli economici; Atti del convegno, Genova, 1–6 ottobre 1990* (Genoa: Società ligure di storia patria, 1991), 95–116, republished in idem, *Marchands d'Europe: Pratiques et savoirs à l'époque moderne*, ed. Jacques Bottin and Marie-Louise Pelus-Kaplan (Paris: Editions Rue d'Ulm, 2002), 405–417; René Squarzoni, "L'arbitrage et les négociants banquiers, 1726–1735," in *Banque et capitalisme commercial: La lettre de change au XVIIIe siècle*, ed. Charles Carrière, Marcel Courdurié, Michel Gutsatz, and René Squarzoni (Marseilles: Institut Historique de Provence, 1976), 107–139.

53. The literature on the diffusion of bills of exchange across all social strata in France is more consistent for the eighteenth century than for the earlier period. See Claude-Joseph de Ferrière, *Dictionnaire de droit et de pratique contenant l'explication des termes de droit, d'ordonnances, de coutumes & de pratiques: avec les jurisdictions de France*, 2 vols. (Toulouse: Chez Marie Rayet, 1734), 1:290, s.v. "change"; Jean Hilaire, *Introduction historique au droit commercial* (Paris: Presses universitaires de France, 1986), 282–283; Romuald Szramkiewicz, *Histoire du droit des affaires* (Paris: Montchrestien, 1989), 173; Amalia D. Kessler, *A Revolution in Commerce: The Parisian Merchant Court and the Rise of Commercial Society in Eighteenth-Century France* (New Haven, CT: Yale University Press, 2004), 235.

54. Recent research has disproven Fernand Braudel's view that while the bill of exchange "moved freely throughout Christendom, [it] made only occasional appearances in Islam, so exceptional indeed as to suggest it was unknown in the East." Braudel, *The Mediterranean and the Mediterranean World in the Age of Philip II*, 2 vols., trans. Siân Reynolds (New York: Harper and Row, 1972–1973), 1:465. See, e.g., Eldem, *French Trade in Istanbul*, 124–147. This topic, however, requires further investigation.

55. Luckett, "Credit and Commercial Society," 20. More examples from the last quarter of the eighteenth century can be found in Kessler, *Revolution in Commerce*, 219–221; and Lynn Hunt, "The Global Financial Origins of 1789," in *The French Revolution in Global Perspective*, ed. Suzanne Desan, Lynn Hunt, and William Max Nelson (Ithaca, NY: Cornell University Press, 2013), 32–43, at 190–191n28.

56. Turgot, "Mémoire sur les prêts d'argent (1770)," in *Écrits économiques*, 251–296; Luckett, "Credit and Commercial Society," 14–15; idem, "Interest," in *Europe 1450 to 1789: Encyclopedia of the Early Modern World*, ed. Jonathan Dewald (New York: Charles Scribner's Sons, 2004), 280–283, at 280–281; Emma Rothschild, "An Alarming Commercial Crisis in Eighteenth-

Century Angoulême: Sentiments in Economic History," *Economic History Review* 51, no. 2 (1998): 268–293.

Chapter 2: The Making of a Legend

1. In this chapter and the next, whenever I cite from the text translated in appendix 2, I omit all bibliographical references. Those wishing to acquire a full appreciation of the pages penned by Cleirac that are dissected here may wish to read the entire appendix, which provides an annotated English translation of the full segment.

2. Elsewhere, Cleirac expands on the use of the terms *place, bourse,* and *marché* across various European cities but does not refer again to the "Lombard Square" of Amsterdam: *UCM 1661*, 224–226.

3. Myriam Yardeni, *Anti-Jewish Mentalities in Early Modern Europe* (Lanham, MD: University Press of America, 1990), 19. Modern historians doubt the expulsion ordered by Dagobert ever happened. Philip Augustus's order only applied to the region around Paris under direct royal domain: William C. Jordan, *The French Monarchy and the Jews: From Philip Augustus to the Last Capetians* (Philadelphia: University of Pennsylvania Press, 1989). Estimates of the number of Jews expelled in 1306 from the territories of the French monarchy range between 100,000 and 150,000: Céline Balasse, *1306: L'expulsion des Juifs du royaume de France* (Brussels: de Boeck, 2008), 60–61n14. Cleirac attended the prestigious Collège de Guyenne in Bordeaux before obtaining a law degree (chapter 4). On the marginal position that the teaching of history had in the curriculum of French *collèges* in the late sixteenth century, see Annie Bruter, *L'histoire einsegnée au Grand Siècle: Naissance d'une pédagogie* (Paris: Belin, 1997), 44–47.

4. I draw this quotation from the English translation of Francisco de Torrejoncillo's *Cantilena contra Judíos* (1674), in François Soyer, *Popularizing Anti-Semitism in Early Modern Spain and Its Empire: Francisco de Torrejoncillo and the Cantilena contra Judíos (1674)* (Leiden: Brill, 2014), 134. The seventeenth-century Spanish friar rehearsed the tenets of the expulsion ordered by Philip Augustus in 1182 as relayed by the contemporary French monk and chronicler Rigord, who had rationalized the anti-Jewish measures on the basis of four accusations: Jews ritually murdered a Christian infant on the eve of every Passover; they had amassed half of the wealth of the entire city of Paris; they illegally employed Christian domestic servants, who in turn took up the habit of "Judaizing"; and finally, they afflicted Christian borrowers with their usurious rates of interest: Rigord, *Histoire de Philippe Auguste*, ed. and trans. Élisabeth Charpentier, Georges Pon, and Yves Chauvin (Paris: CNRS, 2006), 130–133, 144–159.

5. On Bruges as the late medieval center of Italian banking and commerce in the Low Countries, see Raymond de Roover, *Money, Banking and Credit in Medieval Bruges: Italian Merchant-Bankers, Lombards and Money-Changers: A Study in the Origins of Banking* (Cambridge, MA: Mediaeval Academy of America, 1948).

6. H.A.J. Maassen, *Tussen commercieel en sociaal krediet: de ontwikkeling van de bank van lening in Nederland van Lombard tot gemeentelijke kredietbank 1260–1940* (Hilversum, the Netherlands: Verloren, 1994), 42, 52, 104–106; Jan de Vries and Ad van der Woude, *The First Modern Economy: Success, Failure, and Perseverence of the Dutch Economy, 1500–1815* (Cambridge: Cambridge University Press, 1997), 132. Mentions of the *Bank van Lening ofte Lombard* can also be

found in Caspar Commelin and Tobias van Domselaer, *Beschryvinge van Amsterdam*, 2 vols. (Amsterdam: Wolfgang, Waasberge, Boom, van Someren en Goethals, 1693), 640; and Thymon Boey, *Woorden-tolk of verklaring der voornaamste onduitsche en andere woorden* (Graavenhaage: Johannes Gaillard, 1773), 433–435, s.v. "Lombarden." The Dutch word *lommerd*, from *Lombard*, remains a colloquial term for pawnshops. Thanks are due to Anne Wegener Sleeswijk and Joost Jonker for correspondence on this topic.

7. At least one of Cleirac's readers underlined this passage in one of the surviving exemplars of *UCM 1647*, 224: Bibliothèque municipale, Bordeaux (hereafter BMB), P.F. 46485 Rés. A similar observation appears in numerous later texts: Jacques Savary, *Le parfait négociant* (Paris: Chez Louis Billaine, 1675), 121; Jean Moulinier, *Le grand tresor des marchands, banquiers et negocians, des financiers* (Bordeaux: Simon de la Court, 1704), 78; Paul Jacob Marperger, *Neu-eröffnetes Handels-Bericht* (Hamburg: Verlegts B. Schiller, 1709), 491; Jacques Savary des Brûlons and Philémon-Louis Savary, *Dictionnaire universel de commerce*, 3 vols. (Paris: Chez Jacques Estienne, 1723–1730), 2:503, s.v. "Lettre de change"; Thomas de Bléville, *Le banquier françois* (Paris: Chez Jean Musier, 1724), 22; Louis de Beausobre, *Introduction générale à l'étude de la politique, des finances, et du commerce* (Berlin: Chez Chretien Frederic Voss, 1764), 220n1; Honoré Duveyrier, *Rapport fait au Corps législatif sur le projet de loi intitulé Code du commerce, livre 1er, titre VIII (Séance du 11 septembre 1807)* (n.p: n.p., 1807), 3.

8. Sara Lipton links the development of new visual canons to identify Jews in Christian art during the thirteenth century to the expansion of the money economy, which intensified fears that Jews might not be easily distinguishable from the rest of the population: Lipton, *Dark Mirrors: The Medieval Origins of Anti-Jewish Iconography* (New York: Metropolitan Books, 2014), 158–167.

9. Written at the instigation of an English nobleman who also assisted in smuggling the manuscript out of Venice, *Historia de' riti hebraici* was first printed in Italian in Paris (1637) to avoid censorship. Reissued in an expurgated version in Venice the following year and later in multiple editions, it was translated into English (1650), French (1674), Dutch (1693), Latin (1694), and Hebrew (1867). Mark R. Cohen, "Leone da Modena's *Riti*: A Seventeenth-Century Plea for Social Toleration of Jews," *Jewish Social Studies* 34, no. 4 (1972): 287–321.

10. Henri Grégoire, *An Essay on the Physical, Moral, and Political Reformation of the Jews: A Work Crowned by the Royal Society of Arts and Sciences at Metz* (London: C. Forster, 1791), 199; French original: idem, *Essai sur la régénération physique, morale et politique des Juifs: Ouvrage couronné par la Société royale des sciences et des arts de Metz, le 23 août 1788* (Metz: Imprimerie de Claude Lamort, 1789), 160.

11. On Jews and coin clipping in the Middle Ages, see Willis Johnson, "Textual Sources for the Study of Jewish Currency Crimes in Thirteenth-Century England," *British Numismatic Journal* 66 (1996): 21–32; and Martin Allen, *Mints and Money in Medieval England* (Cambridge: Cambridge University Press, 2012), esp. 371–374. In the early modern period, minted coins continued to be the objects of manipulation and fraud. Specifically on France, see Jotham Parsons, *Making Money in Sixteenth-Century France: Currency, Culture, and the State* (Ithaca, NY: Cornell University Press, 2014); Rebecca L. Spang, *Stuff and Money in the Time of the French Revolution* (Cambridge, MA: Harvard University Press, 2015).

12. In canon law, "execrable crimes" referred to various forms of insubordination, including those against papal authority (as per Pius II's bulla *Execrabilis* of 1460).

13. Estien[n]e Cleirac, *Usance du négoce ou commerce de la banque des lettres de change* (Bordeaux: Par Guillaume da Court, 1656), 6. This work was reprinted in Paris in 1659 and again in Bordeaux in 1670. Note that its title played with the double meaning of the French word *usance*: in this context, it meant both commercial customs and the interval of time normally allowed for the payment of bills traded between two cities.

14. Cleirac, *Usance du négoce*, 29.

15. Originated in a liturgical context, the term became a staple of anti-Jewish Christian polemics and a synonym of Jewish religious and economic infidelity: Bernhard Blumenkranz, "Perfidia," *Archivum Latinitatis Medii Aevi* 22 (1952): 157–170; Giacomo Todeschini, "'Judas mercator pessimus': Ebrei e simoniaci dall'XI al XIII secolo," *Zakhor: Rivista di storia degli Ebrei d'Italia* 1 (1997): 11–24, esp. 16. The Good Friday liturgy of the Tridentine mass included a prayer for the conversion of "the Jewish unbelievers" that featured the word *perfidia* (*Oremus et pro perfidis Iudaeis*). Every churchgoing Catholic recited that prayer on a regular basis. The line referring to Jews' *perfidia* was taken out of the vernacular mass during the Second Vatican Council in 1962, at the same time that the Roman Church condemned blood libels and promulgated a conciliatory bull toward Judaism, *Nostra Aetate* (1965): "Declaration on the Church's Relation to Non-Christian Religions," in *Decrees of the Ecumenical Councils*, 2 vols., ed. Norman P. Tanner (London: Sheed & Ward and Georgetown University Press, 1990), 2:968–971. In 2007, however, in order to appease the followers of the Catholic schismatic priest Marcel Lefebvre, who had rejected the decrees of the Second Vatican Council, Pope Benedict XVI ruled that it was permissible to celebrate the older Latin version of the mass that included the prayer *Oremus et pro perfidis Iudaeis*. Following an outcry, the Vatican published an emended version of the said Latin prayer eliminating the word *perfidis* (now titled *Oremus et pro Iudaeis*) on the front page of the February 6, 2008, issue of *L'Osservatore romano*.

16. "Quanto amplius Christiana religio ab exactione compescitur usurarum, tanto gravius super his Iudaeroum perfidia insolescit . . .": Gregory IX's decretals (book V, title 19, ch. 18) in Aemilius Friedberg, ed., *Corpus iuris canonici*, 2 vols. (Graz, Austria: Akademische Druck-u. Verlagsanstalt, 1959), 2:816.

17. Sara Lipton, *Images of Intolerance: The Representation of Jews and Judaism in the Bible moralisée* (Berkeley: University of California Press, 1999), esp. 1–53.

18. In consultation with Giuseppe Porta, the editor of the most comprehensive and accurate modern edition of Villani's chronicle, Stephen Passamaneck reached the same conclusion: *Insurance in Rabbinic Law* (Edinburgh: University Press, 1974), 2–3, 27n19. In principle, one cannot exclude the possibility that an annotated copy of Villani's chronicle bore a version of the legend in its margins. But if such a manuscript or printed copy existed or still exists, neither Passamaneck nor I have located it. See also Giovanni Villani, *Nuova cronica*, 3 vols., ed. Giuseppe Porta (Parma, Italy: Ugo Guanda, 1990–1991).

19. Villani was even imprisoned for a brief period of time on account of complaints made by the creditors of one of his partnerships. Michele Luzzati, *Giovanni Villani e la compagnia dei Buonaccorsi* (Rome: Istituto della enciclopedia italiana, 1971), 60–61, 77–79, 97–101.

20. This manuscript is a rough draft of the published text and may be the one that was submitted to the censors for approval. To the extent that it is readable, the gloss reproduced in figure 2.3 says: "La pratique des letres de change qui s'obstine à present commença d'Italie et (. . .) et mise en credit lors et au temps que les sortis des Guelfes, c'est a dire Papistes, et Ghibel-

lins, qui estoit les Imperiaus, s'affarontheurent les uns contre les autres en Italie ou Lombardie notament soubz le pontificat de Clement 5 et des ses successeurs papes françois. Les faibles de l'un et de l'autre parti faisant plasse aux plus puissants, s'espandirent en France, Alemagne, Angleterre et ailleurs, et pour retirer leurs commodités d'Italie se servirent de letres de change sur leurs amis et corrispondents ausquels avant partir ilz avoit fit leur avoir et y ayant retrouvé[?] et fait naistre du lucre par l'affair et la grande intelligence que les Florentins et Genois avoit de la loy et bonté intrinsique des monayes, comme disent Villani et Giustiniano, pratiquerent le trafiq et commerce des letres de change [deletion] aveq toute sorte de Juifvctie et de usures. Les changeurs sont ordinairement nommés Juifs ou Lombards. La maison publique d'Amsterdam, en laquele les emprompts et les engagements se font a l'usure jusque aux moindrs fripeurs pour[?] quelles procreche la valeur de dix solz, a retenu jusque a present le nom de Lombarde et Maison des Lombards." BMB, Ms. 381, fol. 117v/p. 236. Cleirac also calls the handling of bills of exchange "friponne" in *Usance du négoce*, 29. On the ubiquity of the word *fripon* in early modern French characterizations of Jews, see chapters 5 and 6.

21. Cleirac's postmortem inventory lists an agreement between the deceased and "Monsieur Guillaume Millanges" regarding the printing of *Us et coustumes de la mer*, with the first payment dated January 27, 1646: Archives départementales de la Gironde, 3E3212, fol. 704r. The Millange printing press, the largest in town, was founded by a *converso* immigrant and routinely published Catholic religious books: Théophile Malvezin, *Histoire des Juifs à Bordeaux* (Bordeaux: Charles Lefebvre, 1875), 93–94, 137; Robert Boutruche, ed., *Histoire de Bordeaux*, vol. 4: *Bordeaux de 1453 à 1715* (Bordeaux: Delmas, 1966), 197–198, 411–416.

22. In recapitulating his works in the preface to *Usance du négoce*, Cleirac describes the long period of retreat from public life during which he wrote them. It is reasonable to assume that he tended to the revisions of *Us et coustumes de la mer* in person. The first edition must have been completed after 1644, since it cites an edict of August 20, 1644 (*UCM 1647*, 431). The second edition includes such changes as the mention of a January 1639 ordinance about public education in maritime matters that is not mentioned in the first edition (*UCM 1661*, 480). On the composition of these works, see chapter 4.

23. Cleirac, *Usance du négoce*, 6, with explicit reference to the author's lengthier explanation in his earlier work.

24. "Histoire Universelle di Giovanni Villani, Lib. 6, cap. 54," in Cleirac, *Usance du négoce*, 151 and 178. Cleirac likely had access to the sixteenth-century Venetian edition of Villani, of which today we find an exemplar in the municipal library of Bordeaux. See the chapter titled "Come si comincio di prima abattere il Fiorino delloro in Firenze" (book 6, ch. 54), in *Croniche di messer Giovanni Villani* (Venice: Bartholomeo Zanetti Casterzagense, 1537), fol. 52v, which corresponds to "Come di prima si fecino in Firenze i fiorni dell'oro," in Villani, *Nuova cronica*, 1:345 (book VII, ch. 53).

25. For example: "Ben si dice per molti antichi che l'uscita de' Guelfi di Firenze di Lucca fu cagione di loro ricchezza, perciò che molti Fiorentini usciti n'andarono oltremonti in Francia a guadagnare, che prima non erano mai usati, onde poi molte ricchezze ne reddiro in Firenze; e cadeci il proverbio che dice: 'Bisogno fa prod'uomo.'" Villani, *Nuova cronica*, 1:392 (book VII, ch. 85). In the sixteenth-century *Croniche di messer Giovanni Villani*, this passage corresponds to book 6, ch. 87.

26. Salient examples can be found in Villani, *Nuova cronica*, 1:613–615 (book VIII, ch. 140,

"Come i Fiorentini colloro amistà feciono la terza oste sopra la città d'Arezzo"), 2:333 (book X, ch. 132, "Come i Bolognesi cacciarono di Bologna Romeo de' Peppoli il ricco uomo e' suoi seguaci"), 2:488–489 (book X, ch. 319, "Come Castruccio con Azzo di Milano ritornò colloro oste a la città di Firenze"), 3:165–167 (book XII, ch. 77, "Come la nostra oste di Lombardia andarono infino alle porte di Verona, e corsonvi il palio, ed ebbono Montecchio"), 3:191–194 (book XII, ch. 92, "Entrata del Comune di Firenze"), 3:424–426 (book XIII, ch. 55, "Del fallimento della grande e possente compagnia de' Bardi").

27. Villani, *Nuova cronica*, 1:481–482 (book VIII, ch. 43, "Come papa Ghirigoro fece concilio a Leone sopra Rodano"). The canon *Usurarum voraginem* (*The Abyss of Usury*) of the Second Council of Lyon mandated that secular authorities expel foreign Christian usurers. The full text can be read in Tanner, *Decrees of the Ecumenical Councils*, 1:328–330. For a comprehensive analysis of this decree, including its doctrinal reasoning and impact across Europe, see Rowan William Dorin, "Banishing Usury: The Expulsion of Foreign Moneylenders in Medieval Europe, 1200–1450" (Ph.D. diss., Harvard University, 2015).

28. ". . . il re Filippo di Francia fece pigliare tutti i prestatori italici di suo reame, e eziando de' mercanti, sotto colore che usura non s'usasse in suo paese, accomiatandogli dal reame per lo divieto che aveva fatto papa Ghirigoro al concilio di Leone." Villani adds that the king was motivated by greed more than by honesty, judging from the funds he confiscated. Villani, *Nuova cronica*, 1:494 (book VIII, ch. 53, "Come il re Filippo di Francia fece pigliare tutti i prestatori italiani"). The passage is also noted in Rowan W. Dorin, "L'expulsion des usuriers hors de France à la fin du XIIIe siècle," *Hypothèses* 17, no. 1 (2014): 157–166, at 157n3, 165.

29. Cleirac's text only survives in a nineteenth-century manuscript copy, but there is no reason to believe this copy differs from the original: "Coustumier de Guyenne, nommé Roolle de la ville de Bordeaux, contenent partie des privileges, franchises, lois, moeurs et formes de vivre des anciens Bordelais, sur lequel la coustume reformée en l'an 1520 a été extraite. Tiré de l'Estude de Messire Michel de Montaigne, autheur des essais avec quelques notes pour l'intelligence et l'explication tant du langage que de l'histoire, adjoutées par Monsieur Estienne Clierac, advocat en parlement," Bibliothèque de l'Université de Bordeaux-4 (hereafter BUB), Ms. 5. The product of multiple revisions and redactions, these ancient *coutumiers* formed the object of intense study in the sixteenth and seventeenth centuries, when they became a bone of contention in the monarchy's efforts to expand its legal and jurisdictional authority at the expense of seigniorial rights. French kings began to mandate the written compilation of all *coutumiers* after the end of the Hundred Years' War. See Donald R. Kelly, " 'Second Nature': The Idea of Custom in European Law, Society, and Culture," in *The Transmission of Culture in Early Modern Europe*, ed. Anthony Grafton and Ann Blair (Philadelphia: University of Pennsylvania Press, 1990), 131–172; Martine Grinberg, *Écrire les coutumes: Les droit seigneuriaux en France, XVIe–XVIIIe siècle* (Paris: Presses universitaires de France, 2006). On the nineteenth-century copy of Cleirac's manuscript, see Henri Barckhausen, ed., *Livres de coutumes* (Bordeaux: G. Gounouilhou, 1890), xxxii; and André Tournon, *Montaigne: La glosse et l'Essai* (Lyon: Presses Universitaires de Lyon, 1983), 196–197.

30. BUB, Ms. 5, fol. 188r: "io ti renderò il tuo pegno sanza denari, disse il giudeo." The passage is a citation from *Croniche di messer Giovanni Villani*, fol. 94r (book 7, ch. 136). Porta's edition includes a minor variant: "Se tu mi rechi il corpo del vostro Cristo, io ti renderò i tuoi panni senza danari," in Villani, *Nuova cronica*, 1:616 (book VIII, ch. 143).

31. Miri Rubin, *Gentile Tales: The Narrative Assault on Late Medieval Jews* (New Haven, CT: Yale University Press, 1999), 41–48, 146–148; Dana E. Katz, *The Jew in the Art of the Italian Renaissance* (Philadelphia: University of Pennsylvania Press, 2008), 22–32; Giacomo Todeschini, "Jewish Usurers, Blood Libel, and the Second-Hand Economy: The Medieval Origins of a Stereotype (from the Thirteenth to the Fifteenth Century)," in *The Medieval Roots of Antisemitism: Continuities and Discontinuities from the Middle Ages to the Present Day*, ed. Jonathan Adams and Cordelia Heß (London: Routledge, 2018), 341–351. Caroline Walker Bynum places the associations between Jews and blood in the broader context of fifteenth-century blood cults in her *Wonderful Blood: Theology and Practice in Late Medieval Northern Germany and Beyond* (Philadelphia: University of Pennsylvania Press, 2007), esp. 48, 68–73, 79–81, 242–244.

32. Adrienne Gros, *L'oeuvre de Cleirac en droit maritime: Thèse pour le doctorat* (Bordeaux: Imprimerie de l'Université, 1924), 185.

33. See note 18 in this chapter. In the early nineteenth century, the Italian author of a booklet on the origin of bills of exchange wondered why Villani attributed the inventions of those instruments to Jews rather than Florentines but did not provide an answer. Giovanni Davide Weber, *Ricerche sull'origine e sulla natura del contratto di cambio da piazza a piazza* (Venice: Torchi Palesiani, 1810), 25. Many before and after him continued to reference Villani as the source of the legend even when they expressed doubt about the story he supposedly relayed. Thus, for example, the *Encyclopædia Britannica*'s eleventh edition maintained that "Villani, a 14th-century Florentine historian, speaks of marine insurance as having originated in Lombardy in 1182." *Encyclopædia Britannica*, 29 vols. (Cambridge: University Press, 1910–1911), 14: 674, s.v. "insurance." See also chapter 7, note 31.

34. Cited in Raymond de Roover, *Gresham on Foreign Exchange: An Essay on Early English Mercantilism with the Text of Sir Thomas Gresham's Memorandum for the Understanding of Exchange* (Cambridge, MA: Harvard University Press, 1949), 176.

35. Diane Owen Hughes, "Distinguishing Signs: Ear-Rings, Jews and Franciscan Rhetoric in the Italian Renaissance City," *Past and Present* 112, no. 1 (1986): 3–59.

36. Joseph Schatzmiller, *Shylock Reconsidered: Jews, Moneylending and Medieval Society* (Berkeley: University of California Press, 1990); Julie L. Mell, *The Myth of the Medieval Jewish Moneylender*, 2 vols. (London: Palgrave Macmillan, 2017), 2:113–146.

Chapter 3: The Riddle of Usury

1. The bibliography on these topics is vast, and I will draw from it liberally throughout this chapter. Particularly informative are the two-sequence study by Thomas P. McLaughlin, "The Teaching of the Canonists on Usury (XIIth, XIIIth, and XIVth Centuries)," *Mediaeval Studies* 1 (1939): 81–147 and 2 (1940): 1–22; Lester K. Little, *Religious Poverty and the Profit Economy in Medieval Europe* (Ithaca, NY: Cornell University Press, 1978); Giacomo Todeschini, *I mercanti e il tempio: La società cristiana e il circolo virtuoso della ricchezza fra Medioevo ed età moderna* (Bologna: Il Mulino, 2002); idem, *Franciscan Wealth: From Voluntary Poverty to Market Society*, trans. Donatella Melucci (Saint Bonaventure, NY: Franciscan Institute, Saint Bonaventure University, 2009 [2004]); idem, "Franciscan Economics and Jews in the Middle Ages: From a Theological to an Economic Lexicon," in *Friars and Jews in the Middle Ages and Renaissance*, ed. Steven McMichael and Susan E. Myers (Leiden: Brill, 2004), 99–117. Throughout his work,

Todeschini contests the long-held notion that late medieval merchants devised clever new financial instruments to bypass strict church anti-usury prohibitions and demonstrates instead how church teachings shaped the growth of market society in medieval Europe.

2. The expression "science of commerce" became common in the mid-eighteenth century but had already figured in earlier texts. In his defense of the legitimacy of lending at interest, a French clergyman spoke of "the science of the commerce in interest rates" ("la science de commerce des interests") in 1675: André de Colonia, *Eclaircissement sur le légitime commerce des interests* (Lyon: Chez Antoine Cellier, 1675), 5, 11.

3. The cases were brought starting in 2003: *In re Currency Conversion Fee Antitrust Litigation*, 265 F. Supp. 2d 385 (S.D.N.Y. 2003), http://law.justia.com/cases/federal/district-courts /FSupp2/265/385/2459416/ (accessed July 9, 2018). Settlement payments continued to be distributed at least through 2012.

4. Editor's introduction in Stephen J. Grabill, ed., *Sourcebook in Late-Scholastic Monetary Theory: The Contributions of Martín de Azpilcueta, Luis de Molina, S. J., and Juan de Mariana, S. J.* (Plymouth, UK: Lexington Books, 2007), xvi.

5. "Quicquid supra datum exigitur, usura est": Gratian's *Decretum* (XVI.III.II) in Aemilius Friedberg, ed., *Corpus iuris canonici*, 2 vols. (Graz, Austria: Akademische Druck-u. Verlagsanstalt, 1959), 1:735. See also "usura est ubi amplius requiritur quam datur" (XIV.III.IV), that is, "wherever more than it is given is required, there is usury."

6. Odd Langholm, *Price and Value in the Aristotelian Tradition: A Study in Scholastic Economic Sources* (Bergen, Norway: Universitetsforlaget, 1979); and idem, *The Legacy of Scholasticism in Economic Thought: Antecedents to Choice and Power* (Cambridge: Cambridge University Press, 1998).

7. For Ambrose, all usury is theft. Chapter 3 of his *De Tobia*, cited by Cleirac, ends with a strong and often-cited tirade about what today we would call predatory lending: "He pays usury who lacks food. Is there anything more terrible? He asks for medicine, you offer him poison; he begs for bread, you offer him a sward; he begs for liberty, you impose slavery; he prays for freedom, you tighten the knot of the hideous snare." Lois Miles Zucker, ed., *S. Ambrosii: De Tobia; A Commentary, with an Introduction and Translation* (Washington, D.C.: Catholic University of America, 1933), 30–31. Elsewhere Cleirac paraphrases Deuteronomy 15:3–6 and 23:19–20, as well as chapter 15 of Ambrose's *De Tobia* to say not only that "Jews can take large usuries from foreigners," but also that they do so "in order to ruin them": Cleirac, *Usance du négoce*, 84.

8. The full text of Canon 67 can be read in Tanner, *Decrees of the Ecumenical Councils*, 1:265–266. Contemporary interpreters and modern scholars are divided over how to interpret the meaning of "excessive interest." Some insist that the church refused to put a price on usury, if nothing else, to retain its free hand: McLaughlin, "Teaching of the Canonists" (1939), 99; Benjamin N. Nelson, *The Idea of Usury: From Tribal Brotherhood to Universal Otherhood* (Princeton, NJ: Princeton University Press, 1949), 16–18. Others interpret the expression "excessive interest" as leaving the door open to the possibility that something akin to moderate usury might be condoned: Léon Poliakov, *Jewish Bankers and the Holy See: From the Thirteenth to the Seventeenth Century*, trans. Miriam Kochan (London: Routledge & Kegan Paul, 1977 [1965]), 24. Kenneth Stow even suggests that Gregory IX allowed James I of Aragon to set an interest rate of 20 percent: Stow, "Papal and Royal Attitudes Toward Jewish Lending in the Thirteenth Century," *Association for Jewish Studies Review* 6 (1981): 161–184, at 165. Only in 1918 did the Roman Catho-

lic Church's code of canon law officially permit the charging of "legal interest, as long as it did not appear immoderate" (Canon 1543): Auguste Dumas, "Intérêt et usure," in *Dictionnaire de droit canonique*, 7 vols. (Paris: Letouzey et ané, 1935–1965), 5:1475–1518, at 1518.

9. Poliakov, *Jewish Bankers*, 20–22; David B. Ruderman, *The World of a Renaissance Jew: The Life and Thought of Abraham ben Mordecai Farissol* (Cincinnati: Hebrew Union College Press, 1981), esp. 87–89, 94, 210n8.

10. Cited in Dennis Romano, *Markets and Marketplaces in Medieval Italy, c. 1100 to c. 1440* (New Haven, CT: Yale University Press, 2015), 11, paraphrasing the original in Bernardino da Siena, *Prediche volgari sul campo di Siena 1427*, 2 vols., ed. Carlo Delcorno (Milan: Rusconi, 1989), 2:1131. On Bernardino's opposition between industrious merchants and usurious Jews, see Giacomo Todeschini, *La ricchezza degli ebrei: Merci e denaro nella riflessione ebraica e nella definizione cristiana dell'usura alla fine del Medioevo* (Spoleto, Italy: Centro italiano di studi sull'alto Medioevo, 1989), 152.

11. Gregory IX's decretals (book V, title 19, ch. 19) in Friedberg, *Corpus iuris canonici*, 2:816; John T. Noonan, *The Scholastic Analysis of Usury* (Cambridge, MA: Harvard University Press, 1957), 137–138; Giovanni Ceccarelli, "Quando rischiare è lecito: Il credito finalizzato al commercio marittimo nella riflessione scolastica tardomedievale," in *Ricchezza del mare, ricchezza dal mare, secc. XIII–XVIII (Atti della XXXVII settimana di studi, Istituto Francesco Datini, Prato)*, ed. Simonetta Cavaciocchi (Florence: Le Monnier, 2006), 1187–1199.

12. Odd Langholm, *Economics in the Medieval Schools: Wealth, Exchange, Value, Money, and Usury According to the Parish Theological Tradition, 1200–1350* (Leiden: Brill, 1992), 408, 416.

13. Noonan, *Scholastic Analysis of Usury*, 203; Giovanni Ceccarelli, "Risky Business: Theological and Canonical Thought on Insurance from the Thirteenth to the Seventeenth Century," *Journal of Medieval and Early Modern Studies* 31, no. 3 (2001): 607–658, at 620–621.

14. "Assecurationes quas quotidie in magnam Reipublicae utilitatem fieri videmus." Cleirac, *UCM 1661*, 215, citing Navarrus's *Enchiridion*, ch. 17, no. 284, on which more in note 22 to this chapter.

15. Ceccarelli, "Risky Business," 626. See also Rudolf Schüssler, "The Economic Thought of Luis de Molina," in *A Companion to Luis de Molina*, ed. Matthias Kaufmann and Alexander Aichele (Leiden: Brill, 2014), 257–288. Innocent IV had already deployed this argument in the mid-thirteenth century for the census contract, declaring it a sale (*venditio*) rather than a loan (*mutuum*): Joel Kaye, *A History of Balance, 1250–1375: The Emergence of a New Model of Equilibrium and Its Impact on Thought* (Cambridge: Cambridge University Press, 2014), 39.

16. Sigismondo Scaccia, *Tractatus de commerciis et cambio* (Rome: Sumptibus A. Brugiotti, ex typographia I. Mascardi, 1619), 34–35 (sec. 1, question 1, no. 128), also cited by Giovanni Cassandro, "Assicurazione," in *Enciclopedia del diritto*, 46 vols. (Milano: Giuffré, 1958–1993), 3:420–427, at 425, republished as "Genesi e svolgimento storico del contratto di assicurazione," in idem, *Saggi di storia del diritto commerciale* (Naples: Edizioni Scientifiche Italiane, 1974), 239–253, at 249–250. By the late sixteenth century, practice matched doctrine, and disputes over insurance contracts rarely raised questions about usury. See Vito Piergiovanni, "The Rise of the Genoese Civil Rota and the 'Decisiones de Mercatura' Concerning Insurance," in *The Courts and the Development of Commercial Law*, ed. Vito Piergiovanni (Berlin: Duncker & Humblot, 1987), 23–38.

17. "First Article: *Insurance* is a contract through which one promises the indemnity of the

goods that are transported from one country to another, especially when they are transported by sea; and it works by means of a price calculated as a percentage of the insured goods' value and agreed upon between the insured, who carries the goods or has them transported by a third party, and the insurer, who promises the indemnity" (appendix 2).

18. *De mercatura decisiones, et tractatus varii, et de rebus ad eam pertinentibus* (Cologne: Apud Cornelium ab Egemont de Grassis, 1622), 21, 27–28 (dec. 3, no. 28, "Assicuratio quis contractus sit") and 148–149 (dec. 39, no. 9, "Differentia inter socios et participes"). First published in 1582, these sentences intentionally excluded theologians' opinions and, even if they did not constitute a legal precedent in the same way as they would have in a common law country, exerted enormous influence on commercial and maritime jurisprudence across the Continent. They remained the standard references on the subject through the early modern period. See, e.g., Jean-Baptiste Denisart, *Collection de décisions nouvelles et des notions relatives à la jurisprudence actuelle*, new ed., 9 vols. (Paris: Chez la Veuve Desaint, 1783–1790), 2:485, s.v. "assurance." On the far-reaching influence of the sentences of the Genoese Rota on early modern Europe's legal and mercantile culture, see Rodolfo Savelli, "Between Law and Morals: Interest in the Dispute on Exchanges During the 16th Century," in Piergiovanni, *Courts and the Development*, 39–102; Vito Piergiovanni, "Genoese Civil Rota and Mercantile Customary Law," in *From Lex Mercatoria to Commercial Law*, ed. Vito Piergiovanni (Berlin: Duncker & Humblot, 2005), 191–206.

19. The first author to equate bills of exchange to purchase-and-sale contracts was probably the Roman law commentator Baldo de Ubaldi (c. 1327–1400). See his *Consiliorum*, 5 vols. (Venice: apud Hieronymum Polum, 1575), 1:113r (consilium 348, no. 6). Early modern jurists were introduced to Baldo's opinion primarily via Raffaele della Torre, *Tractatus de cambiis* (Genoa: Excudebat Petrus Ioannes Calenzanus, 1641), 40 (disputatio I, quæstio IX).

20. On Aristotle's legacy, see Langholm's works *Economics in the Medieval Schools*, *Price and Value*, and *Legacy of Scholasticism*. On loans in Roman law, see Reinhard Zimmermann, *The Law of Obligations: Roman Foundations of the Civilian Tradition* (New York: Oxford University Press, 1990), 154.

21. Thomas de Vio Cardinalis Caietanus, *Scripta Philosophica: Opuscola œconomico-socialia*, ed. P. P. Zammit (Rome: ex Typographia missionaria dominicana, 1934), 91–133, at 110–113 (ch. 5). See also Noonan, *Scholastic Analysis of Usury*, 313–331; Raymond de Roover, "Cardinal Cajetan on *Cambium* or Exchange Dealings," in *Philosophy and Humanism: Renaissance Essays in Honor of Paul Oskar Kristeller*, ed. Edward P. Mahoney (New York: Columbia University Press, 1976), 423–433.

22. First published in Portuguese (1549), Azpilcueta's handbook was translated into Castilian (1556), Italian (1569), Latin (1573), and French (abridged version, 1602), as well as reissued in many more expanded and revised editions. I consulted Martín Azpilcueta, *Enchiridion sive manuale confessariorum et poenintetium* (Paris: Apud Franciscum Huby, 1611), 538–540 (ch. 17, no. 284). Even more pertinent to Cleirac's reasoning was Azpilcueta's *Comentario resolutorio de usuras* (1556), which appeared as one of the four appendices to *Enchiridion* and not only recognized the legitimacy of four-party bills of exchange as purchase-and-sale contracts but also included an extensive commentary on the decretal *Naviganti*. For an English translation, see *Commentary on the Resolution of Money*, trans. Jeannine Emery, introduction by Rodrigo Muñoz, *Journal of Markets and Morality* 7, no. 1 (2004): 171–312. For further indictments of dry exchange, Cleirac turned to Romualdo Coli, *Trattato de' cambi* (Lucca: Appresso Ottaviano Guidoboni,

1619), 34–35 (ch. 27, "Se si può cambiare da fiera a fiera") and 42–44 (ch. 35, "Del cambio secco"), reprinted in idem, *Trattati de cambi, dell'usura, de censi* (Florence: Per Bartolomeo Sermatelli, 1619), 66–68 and 82–86.

23. Jacques Chauvet, *Méthodiques institutions de la vraye et parfaicte arithmétique* (Paris: Charles Roger Imprimeur, 1585), 338, also mentioned in Natalie Zemon Davis, "Sixteenth-Century French Arithmetics on the Business Life," *Journal of the History of Ideas* 21, no. 1 (1960): 18–48, at 24n18.

24. Mathias Maréschal, *Traicté des changes et rechanges licites et illicites* (Paris: Chez Nicolas Buon, 1625), 27.

25. Cleirac, *Usance du négoce*, 96. The fifth edition of the dictonary of the Académie Française registered both the literal definition of the term *Juiverie* (from the Spanish *Juderia*), an urban quarter, and its metaphorical meaning, "a usurious deal" (*un marché usuraire*). It gave the example of two common sentences: "*C'est une franche juiverie. Il m'a fait une juiverie.*" *Dictionnaire de l'Académie française*, 5th ed. (1798). From now on, whenever no place of publication or publisher is given for an old French dictionary, the citation comes from the online resource ARTFL, https://artfl-project.uchicago.edu/content/dictionnaires-dautrefois (accessed July 9, 2018).

26. Raymond de Roover, *Money, Banking and Credit*, 99; Yves Renouard, "Les Cahorsins, hommes d'affaires français du XIIIe siècle," *Transactions of the Royal Historical Society* 11 (1961): 43–67; Kurt Grunwald, "Lombards, Cahorsins and Jews," *Journal of European Economic History* 4 (1975): 393–398; Pierre Racine, "Paris, rue des Lombards, 1280–1340," in *Comunità forestiere e "nationes" nell'Europa dei secoli XIII-XIV*, ed. Giovanna Petti Balbi (Naples: Liguori, 2001), 95–111; Renato Bordone, "Lombardi come 'usurai manifesti': Un mito storiografico," *Società e storia* 100–101 (2003): 256–272; Renato Bordone and Franco Spinelli, eds., *Lombardi in Europa nel Medioevo* (Milan: Franco Angeli, 2005).

27. Iris Origo, *Merchant of Prato, Francesco di Marco Datini, 1335–1410* (Harmondsworth, UK: Penguin, 1963 [1957]), 150.

28. Jean Boucher, *L'usure ensevelie, ou, Défence des monts de piété de nouveau erigez aux Pais-Bas* (Tourney: Adrien Quinque, 1628), 70. See also Myriam Greilsammer, *L'usurier chrétien, un juif métaphorique? Histoire de l'exclusion des prêteurs lombards (XIIIe–XVIIe siècle)* (Rennes, France: Presses universitaires de Rennes, 2012), 238–245, 270–279.

29. To add rhetorical force to this passage, the second edition of *Us et coustumes de la mer* includes a long list of terms in Old French that describe those who cheat, a group that Dante condemns to inhale sulfide in the same circle of the *Inferno* to which he relegates those who engage in sodomy. The analogy between usurers, Jews, and sodomites is repeated in Cleirac, *Usance du négoce*, 7–8. Variants of the term *Cahorsin* continued to appear in French dictionaries of the nineteenth century with the meaning of usurer: e.g., Émile Littré, *Dictionnaire de la langue française* (1872–1877), s.v. "Corsin." A keyword search in *The Making of the Modern World*, however, suggests that the term had already fallen out of use during the seventeenth century—another confirmation that Cleirac had a predilection for archaic terminologies.

30. John Muddiman, *A Commentary on the Epistle to the Ephesians* (London: Continuum, 2001), 222. See also Giacomo Todeschini, " 'Soddoma e Caorsa': Sterilità del peccato e produttività della natura alla fine del medioevo cristiano," in *Le trasgressioni della carne: Il desiderio omosessuale nel mondo islamico e cristiano, secc. XII–XX*, ed. Umberto Grassi e Giuseppe Marcocci (Rome: Viella, 2015), 53–80.

31. The citation comes from the chapter entitled "Caursinorum pestis abominanda" in *Chronica Majora: Matthaei Parisiensis, Monachi Sancti Albani, Chronica Majora (1216–1239)*, 7 vols., ed. Henry Richards Luard (London: Longman & Co., 1872–1883), 3:329; and Matthew Paris, *English History from the Year 1235 to 1273*, 3 vols., trans. J. A. Giles (London: H. G. Bohn, 1852–1854), 1:2. See also Sophia Menache, "Matthew Paris's Attitude Toward Anglo-Jewry," *Journal of Medieval History* 23, no. 2 (1997): 139–162.

32. Vicente da Costa Mattos, *Breve discurso contra a heretica perfidia do Iudaismo* (Lisbon: Pedro Craesbeeck, 1622), 119. This work spread more widely in its Spanish translation: *Discurso contra los Judios*, trans. Diego Gavilan Vela (Salamanca: Antonia Ramirez, 1631), 152 ("como perros o caballos desenfrenados"). Note that in his original title, which the Spanish translation rendered even closer to the name of the old Christian genre of anti-Jewish polemics, *contra Iudeos*, Mattos used the word "perfidia" (see chapter 2, notes 15–16). Very little is known about this author, but his writings were popular across the Iberian world. See Soyer, *Popularizing Anti-Semitism*, 79. On the theological roots of the Christian trope of "Jewish dogs," see Kenneth Stow, *Jewish Dogs: An Image and Its Interpreters; Continuity in the Catholic-Jewish Encounter* (Stanford, CA: Stanford University Press, 2006).

33. No English translation of Aristoso's comedy *I supposti*, first performed in Ferrara in 1509, exists. A modern edition can be read in Ludovico Ariosto, *Opere minori*, ed. Cesare Segre (Milan: Ricciardi, 1954), 97–349. Cleirac's citation from *Orlando Furioso* is a slight variation on an octave in which Ariosto asks rhetorically: "If the same ardour, the same urge drives both sexes to love's gentle fulfilment, which to the mindless commoner seems so grave an excess, why is the woman to be punished or blamed for doing with one or several men the very thing a man does with as many women as he will, and receives not punishment but praise for it?" Idem, *Orlando Furioso*, trans. Guido Waldman (Cambridge, MA: Harvard University Press, 2010), 38.

34. The 1347 expulsion of Lombards from the kingdom of France is little researched, but we know that it was diligently implemented: William Dorin, "Banishing Usury: The Expulsion of Foreign Moneylenders in Medieval Europe, 1200–1450" (Ph.D. diss., Harvard University, 2015), 323.

35. Cleirac writes that "Pasquier in his *Recherches*, book 2, chap. 3, claims to have seen among the records of the accounting chamber of Paris the order sent to that court by King Philip of Valois, dated 12 August 1347, for the trials of the Lombard usurers." The reference is to Estienne Pasquier, *Recherches de la France*, rev. ed. (Paris: Chez Iamet Mettayer et Pierre L'Huillier, 1596), 34 (book II, ch. 3), and subsequent editions. In this work, Pasquier mentioned medieval Jews only once, in reference to their obligation to wear a distinctive yellow badge. See Yardeni, *Anti-Jewish Mentalities*, 24.

36. Adam Théveneau, *Commentaire de M. Adam Theveneau, advocat en parlement, sur les ordonnances contenant les difficultez meues entres les docteurs du droict canon et civil et decidées par icelles ordonnances tant en matière bénéficialle, que civile et criminelle, instructions des procez, iugemens, et exectuions d'iceux* (Paris: M. Ballagny, 1629), 948–969. In this work Théveneau recapitulated and commented on several French laws passed between 1311 and 1586 regarding usury, including the prohibition issued by Saint Louis against Jews practicing usury. No mention is made of bills of exchange and their origins. Théveneau, however, cited the Old Testament, various theologians and canonists, and Charles du Moulin's treatise on usury. Written in 1542 and

published four years later as *Tractatus commerciorum et usurarum* (Paris: Apud Ioannem Lodoicum Tiletanum, 1546), du Moulin's treatise offered a partial justification of usury before Calvin did, arguing, like Calvin, that no interest should be charged when lending to the poor or to those temporarily in need, but that interest was acceptable when lending to the rich, because they would reinvest the money. The Roman Church declared him a heretic and added his treatise to the index of prohibited books. See Jean-Louis Thireau, *Charles Du Moulin (1500–1566): étude sur les sources, la méthode, les idées politiques et économiques d'un juriste de la Renaissance* (Geneva: Droz, 1980); Rodolfo Savelli, "Diritto romano e teologia riformata: Du Moulin di fronte al problema dell'interesse del denaro," *Materiali per una storia della cultura giuridica* 23, no. 1 (1993): 291–324; idem, *Censori e giuristi: Storie di libri, di idee e di costumi (secoli XVI–XVII)* (Milan: Giuffrè, 2011), 93–147.

37. Poliakov, *Jewish Bankers*, 14.

38. Epistola 363: "Taceo quod sicubi desunt, peius iudaizare dolemus christianos feneratores, si tamen christianos, et non magis baptizatos Iudaeos convenit appellari," in J. Leclercq and H. Rochais, eds., *Sancti Bernardi Opera*, 8 vols. (Rome: Editiones Cistercienses, 1957–1977), 8:316. Bernard borrowed the Latin verb *iudaizare* from the Vulgate translation of Paul's letter to the Galatians (2:14): "Si tu, cum Iudaeus sis, gentiliter vivis, et non Iudaice, quomodo Gentes cogis Iudaizare?" ("If thou, being a Jew, live in the manner of the Gentiles and not of the Jews, how do you compel the Gentiles to live as the Jews do?"): *Biblia Sacra iuxta Vulgatae editionnis Sixti V Pont. Max. iussu recognita et Clementis VIII auctoritate edita* (Ratisbona, Germany: Friderici Pustet, 1929), 1133. Medieval preachers often incorporated variants of this passage into their sermons. See, e.g., Girolamo Savonarola's *On the Art of Dying Well* in *A Guide to Righteous Living and Other Works*, ed. Konard Eisenbichler (Toronto: Centre for Reformation and Renaissance Studies, 2003), 131.

39. Lipton, *Images of Intolerance*, 31–54.

40. Cited in David Nirenberg, *Anti-Judaism: The Western Tradition* (New York: W. W. Norton, 2014), 274.

41. For Giacomo Todeschini, this late medieval construct of usury not only extended to a host of other marginalized groups, including the poor and the migrants, but to this day still exerts a powerful influence on Western representations of reputable and disreputable market actors. Todeschini, *Visibilmente crudeli: Malviventi, persone sospette e gente qualunque dal medioevo all'età moderna* (Bologna: Il Mulino, 2007); idem, *Come Giuda: La gente comune e i giochi dell'economia all'inizio dell'epoca moderna* (Bologna: Il Mulino, 2011).

42. Idem, "Eccezioni e usura nel Duecento: Osservazioni sulla cultura economica medievale come realtà non dottrinaria," *Quaderni storici* 131 (2009): 443–460.

43. Obviously, the hierarchy of sins and crimes changed over time in response to broader shifts, including the expansion of credit markets. See Lester K. Little, "Pride Goes Before Avarice: Social Change and the Vices in Latin Christendom," *American Historical Review* 76, no. 1 (1971): 16–49.

44. No distinction between moderate and excessive usury was made in the comprehensive 1579 ordinances of Blois, which condemned usury and outlined severe punishments for interest-bearing loans (art. 202, confirmed in 1629 [art. 151]): Jean-Baptiste Denisart, *Collections de décisions nouvelles et de notions relatives à la jurisprudence actuelle*, 6 vols. (Paris: Chez Savoye et Leclerc, 1754–1756), 6:423–424, s.v. "usure"; Joseph-Nicolas Guyot, *Répertoire universel et raisonné de jurisprudence civile, criminelle, canonique et bénéficiale*, 2nd ed., 17 vols. (Paris: Chez Visse,

1784–1785), 9:458–478, at 463 and 473, s.v. "intérêt," and 17:417–419, at 418, s.v. "usure"; Dumas, "Intérêt et usure," 1489–1494. There is no comprehensive study of the legal history of usury in Old Regime France. See the brief recapitulation in Marcel Courdurié, *La dette des collectivités publiques de Marseille au XVIIIe siècle: Du débat sur le prêt à intérêt au financement par l'emprunt* (Marseilles: Institut historique de Provence, 1974), 62–66.

45. Philip T. Hoffman, Gilles Postel-Vinay, and Jean-Laurent Rosenthal, *Priceless Markets: The Political Economy of Credit in Paris, 1660–1870* (Chicago: University of Chicago Press, 2000), 15–19.

46. Guyot, *Répertoire*, 9:470, s.v. "intérêt"; Courdurié, *La dette*, 64. The usury statutes passed in England between 1571 and 1624 imposed a 10 percent ceiling. Afterward, the legal rate of interest on private money markets declined to 8 percent under statutes passed between 1625 and 1651 and to 6 percent under those issued between 1651 and 1714: Norman Jones, *God and the Moneylenders: Usury and Law in Early Modern England* (Oxford: Basil Blackwell, 1989).

47. The word *interesse* had been used in contrast to usury since the thirteenth century to refer to contracts in which risks involved the potential loss of gains (*lucrum cessans*) or the potential bearing of losses (*damnum emergens*). It appeared in the provisions made for the fairs of Lyon in the 1420s. More consistent edicts passed from the 1580s to the 1770s referred to transactions "among merchants and for the purpose of commercial matters" ("entre marchands & pour causes de marchandises"): Paul Joseph Nicodème, *Exercice des commerçans* (Paris: Valade, 1776), 20–21; Guyot, *Répertoire*, 9:463, s.v. "intérêt"; Jacques Antoine Sallé, *L'esprit des ordonnances de Louis XIV*, 2 vols. (Paris: Veuve Rouy, 1755–1758), 2:393–395.

48. Henri Lévy-Bruhl, "Un document inédit sur la préparation de l'Ordonnance sur le Commerce de 1673," *Revue historique du droit français et étranger* 10 (1931): 649–681.

49. Étienne Bonnot de Condillac, *Le commerce et le gouvernement, considérés rélativement l'un à l'autre*, 2 vols. (Paris: Chez Jombert & Cello, 1776), 1:136–150 (ch. 18); Turgot, "Mémoire sur les prêts d'argent [1770]," in *Écrits économiques* (Paris: Calmann-Lévy, 1970), 251–296. Arnaud Orain shows that Turgot followed closely a Jansenist criticism of Scholastic theories of usury: Étienne Mignot, *Traité des prêts de commerce*, 4 vols. (Paris: Chez P. Mathon, 1738); Orain, "The Second Jansenism and the Rise of French Eighteenth-Century Political Economy," *History of Political Economy* 46, no. 3 (2014): 463–490, at 481–484; Orain and Mazine Menuet, "Liberal Jansenists and Interest-Bearing Loans in Eighteenth-Century France: A Reappraisal," *European Journal of the History of Economic Thought* 24, no. 4 (2017): 708–741.

50. For a dispute heard in 1785, see Kessler, *Revolution in Commerce*, 211–212.

51. *Dictionnaire de théologie catholique*, 15 vols. (Paris: Letouzey et Ané, 1908–1950), 15, pt. II: 2379, s.v. "usure."

52. Several cases are summarized in Denisart, *Collections*, 4:424–425, s.v. "usure"; Guyot, *Répertoire*, 17:418–419, s.v. "usure." More examples are in Kessler, *Revolution in Commerce*, 205–208. On the persistence of the problem after the Revolution, see Erika Vause, "A Subject of Interest: Usurers on Trial in Early Nineteenth-Century France," *French History Review* 24, no. 1 (2017): 103–119.

53. *L'Aritmétique de Ian Trenchant départie en trois livres, ensemble un petit discours des changes, avec l'art de calculer aux getons* (Lyon: Pas Michel Iove, 1561), 269–295 ("Ensuit un petit discours des changes"); Maréschal, *Traicté des changes*, 6–25. Trenchant's work was particularly well known, with ten editions issued between 1561 and 1647. Other arithmetic manuals described

the calculations behind bills of exchange without commenting on their legitimacy. See, e.g., *L'arithmetique de Pierre Savonne, dict Talon, natif d'Avignon, comté de Venisse* (Lyon: Benoist Rigaud, 1571), 116–144.

54. Cleirac, *UCM 1661*, 230.

55. Ibid., 228–229.

56. Cleirac, *Usance*, 21; Ludovico Guicciardini, *Descrittione . . . di tutti i Paesi Bassi, altrimenti detti Germania inferiore* (Antwerp: Appresso Gugliemo Silvio, 1567), 117.

57. "Although on the surface bills of exchange are simple and innocent in their formula, they nevertheless produce terrible and ruinous effects for those who do not take the necessary precautions. In order to prevent disastrous consequences, to the extent that it is possible and that the conditions of the market allow it, it is necessary to combine human prudence with *usance*, that is, the practice of banking." Cleirac, *Usance du négoce*, 24.

58. Ibid., 88, citing "Giovan Lioni Africano, prima parte, capitolo ultimo" to say that "Turks and Saracens" had no knowledge of bills of exchange and could only make spot transactions "from a Turk to a Moor." The reference corresponds to the chapter titled "Delli vitti e cose nephande che hanno li Africani," which does not mention bills of exchange in particular but describes the inhabitants of the cities of the Barbary coast as ignorant and brutish, mostly pagan, and lacking any cognizance of trade or banking ("banchi de cambia"): Giovanni Leone Africano, *La cosmographia de l'Affrica (Ms. V.E. 953, Biblioteca nazionale centrale di Roma, 1526)*, ed. Gabriele Amadori (Rome: Aracne, 2014), 174–176. Here we have an example of a reader, Cleirac, drawing inspiration not from Leo Africanus's ecumenism but rather from his most disparaging clichés about Africans. For a more optimistic assessment of the impact of this sixteenth-century text, see Natalie Zemon Davis, *Trickster Travels: A Sixteenth-Century Muslim Between Worlds* (New York: Hill and Wang, 2006).

59. Cleirac, *Usance du négoce*, 80–81. The choice of 12 percent may not have been arbitrary. It was stipulated in an ordinance issued by Charles V in Antwerp on October 4, 1540, on the basis of the principle of *lucrum cessans*. Higher rates of 30 to 50 percent, however, were tolerated from Lombards in the city. J. A. Goris, *Étude sur les colonies marchandes méridionales (portugais, espagnols, italiens) à Anvers de 1488 à 1567: Contribution à l'histoire des débuts du capitalisme moderne* (Louvain, Belgium: Librairie Universitaire, 1925), 348, 350.

60. Cleirac, *Usance du négoce*, 58.

61. From the Latin *tortio*, meaning "torture," *tortionaire* meant something unjust: *Dictionnaire de l'Académie Française* (1694).

62. Rodolfo Savelli, "Modelli giuridici e cultura mercantile tra XVI e XVII secolo," *Materiali per una storia della cultura giuridica* 18 (1988): 3–24.

63. Umberto Santarelli, *La categoria dei contratti irregolari: Lezioni di storia del diritto* (Turin, Italy: G. Giappichelli, 1984); Andrea Massironi, *Nell'officina dell'interprete: La qualificazione del contratto nel diritto comune (secoli XIV–XVI)* (Milan: Giuffré, 2012), 344–362.

64. As an innominate contract, premium-based marine insurance was reducible to the formulas cited by the Genoese Rota to indicate the transfer of risk in exchange for a premium: *facio ut des* ("I will do something so that you can give me something") from the insurer's perspective and *do ut facias* ("I will give you something so that you can do something for me") from the insured's perspective. See also Luis de Molina, *De justitia et jure*, 6 vols. (Mainz: Sumpt. haered. Joh. Godofredi Schönwetteri, 1659 [1592]), 2:5–7 (disputatio 253: "Contractibus nominatis et

innominatis"); and J. P. van Niekerk, *The Development of the Principles of Insurance Law in the Netherlands from 1500–1800*, 2 vols. (Kenwyn, South Africa: Juta, 1998), 1:177, 185. On the "legal convulsions" of continental jurists to conceive marine insurance in relation to Roman law, see Guido Rossi, "Civilians and Insurance: Approximations of Reality to the Law," *Tijdschrift voor Rechtsgeschiedenis / Revue d'histoire du droit / Legal History Review* 83, nos. 3–4 (2015): 323–364.

65. Paolo Prodi, *Settimo non rubare: Furto e mercato nella storia dell'occidente* (Bologna: Il Mulino, 2009), 73–74.

66. The phenomeon is usually described with regard to England and the United Provinces: Sheilagh Ogilvie, *Institutions and European Trade: Merchant Guilds, 1000–1800* (Cambridge: Cambridge University Press, 2011), 182–184. In fact, it affected other regions as well, France included (chapter 5).

67. Greilsammer, *L'usurier chrétien.*

Chapter 4: Bordeaux, The Specter of Crypto-Judaism, and the Changing Status of Commerce

1. Roland Barthes, "The Author Is Dead," in *Image-Music-Text*, ed. and trans. Stephen Heath (New York: Hill and Wang, 1977 [1968]), 142–148, at 146.

2. Ibid., 147.

3. The 1550 edict is reproduced in Gérard Nahon, ed., *Les "Nations" juives portugaises du sud-ouest de la France (1684–1791): Documents* (Paris: Fundação Calouste Gulbenkian, Centro Cultural Português, 1981), 21–26. It was only ratified by the *parlement* of Bordeaux in 1580. The same privileges were granted again in 1574 and 1656 (26–35).

4. Frances Malino, *The Sephardic Jews of Bordeaux: Assimilation and Emancipation in Revolutionary and Napoleonic France* (Tuscaloosa: University of Alabama Press, 1978); Gérard Nahon, *Juifs et Judaïsme à Bordeaux* (Bordeaux: Mollat, 2003).

5. A contemporary historian regarded the nobility of the robe as "bastard nobility": Estienne Pasquier, *Recherches de la France*, rev. ed. (Paris: Chez Iamet Mettayer et Pierre L'Huillier, 1596), 80. After 1604, with the introduction of the *paulette* tax, certain venal offices could be passed on from generation to generation, together with the noble titles they conferred.

6. Jay M. Smith, *The Culture of Merit: Nobility, Royal Service, and the Making of Absolute Monarchy in France, 1600–1789* (Ann Arbor: University of Michigan Press, 1996). Ellery Schalk has gone further than other specialists in identifying a growing separation between virtue and birth in concepts of nobility during the first half of the seventeenth century: Schalk, *From Valor to Pedigree: Ideas of Nobility in France in the Sixteenth and Seventeenth Centuries* (Princeton, NJ: Princeton University Press, 1986), 115–144.

7. Adrienne Gros, *L'oeuvre de Cleirac en droit maritime: Thèse pour le doctorat* (Bordeaux: Imprimerie de l'Université, 1924), 4–5.

8. *Le livre des bourgeois de Bordeaux, XVIIe et XVIIIe siècles* (Bordeaux: G. Gounouilhou, 1898), 32.

9. Estien[n]e Cleirac, *Usance du négoce ou commerce de la banque des lettres de change* (Bordeaux: Par Guillaume da Court, 1656), preface, 4; Gros, *L'oeuvre de Cleirac*, 183–184. On the Ormée, see Robert Boutruche, ed., *Bordeaux de 1453 à 1715* (Bordeaux: Fédération historique

du Sud-Ouest, 1966), 333–345; Christian Jouhaud, *Mazarinades: La Fronde des mots* (Paris: Aubier, 1985); William Beik, *Urban Protest in Seventeenth-Century France: The Culture of Retribution* (Cambridge: Cambridge University Press, 1997), 228–249.

10. Regrettably, the scribe charged with compiling the postmortem inventory failed to jot down the book titles and merely indicated that the collection comprised 32 works of medicine, 84 of mathematics, 23 of history, 36 of political theory, 24 Italian or Spanish texts, 26 travel accounts, and 446 others: Archives départementales de la Gironde (hereafter ADG), 3E3212, fols. 690r–715r. My count differs from that in Laurent Coste, *Mille avocats du grand siècle: Le barreau de Bordeaux de 1589 à 1715* (Lignan-de-Bordeaux, France: S.A.H.C.C., 2003), 72.

11. The scholar to whom we owe the most comprehensive studies of early modern French commercial literature, Pierre Jeannin, merely mentions Cleirac's works in passing: Jeannin, "Les manuels de pratique commerciale imprimés pour les marchands français (XVIe–XVIIIe siècle)," in *Le négoce international (XIIIe–XXe siècle)*, ed. François Crouzet (Paris: Economica, 1989), 35–57, at 44, republished in idem, *Marchands d'Europe: Pratiques et savoirs à l'époque moderne*, ed. Jacques Bottin and Marie-Louise Pelus-Kaplan (Paris: Editions Rue d'Ulm, 2002), 377–395, at 390.

12. Starting in 1597, the city of Amsterdam issued compilations of local customs to be applied in commercial and maritime disputes, including the Laws of Visby, the Customs of Antwerp, ordinances issued by Charles V and Philip II, and procedural norms. Judging from the number of expanded editions that were subsequently issued, these publications enjoyed a large readership, but they were also more local in their purview than Cleirac's work. A list of editions appears in Oscar Gelderblom, *Cities of Commerce: The Institutional Foundations of International Trade in the Low Countries, 1250–1650* (Princeton, NJ: Princeton University Press, 2013), 137n157–158. For a fuller analysis of Cleirac's *Us et coustumes de la mer*, see Francesca Trivellato, " 'Usages and Customs of the Sea': Étienne Cleirac and the Making of Maritime Law in Seventeenth-Century France," *Tijdschrift voor Rechtsgeschiedenis / Revue d'histoire du droit / Legal History Review* 84, nos. 1–2 (2016): 193–224.

13. The number of copies printed in 1661 is recorded in a notarial deed involving the printer transcribed in *Archives historiques du département de la Gironde* 25 (1887): 419–420. Since the same publisher prepared two issues of the revised 1661 edition, it is unclear whether the number refers to the sum of both impressions or to only one of them. See appendix 3 for a complete list of Cleirac's works, in all their editions and issues.

14. Peter Burke, *The Fortunes of the Courtier: The European Reception of Castiglione's Cortegiano* (Cambridge, UK: Polity Press, 1995), 40–41.

15. Jean-Pierre Perret, *Les imprimeries d'Yverdon aux XVIIe et au XVIIIe siècle* (Lausanne: F. Roth, 1945), 45–46; Lucien Febvre and Henri-Jean Martin, *The Coming of the Book: The Impact of Printing 1450–1800*, trans. David Gerard (London: NLB, 1976 [1958]), 219; Leon Voet, ed., *The Plantin Press (1555–1589): A Bibliography of the Works Printed and Published by Christopher Plantin at Antwerp and Leiden*, 6 vols. (Amsterdam: Van Hoeve, 1980–1983), 2:726–727, 739–741; Angela Nuovo, *The Book Trade in the Italian Renaissance*, trans. Lydia G. Cochrane (Leiden: Brill, 2013), 99–116.

16. In the two Rouen editions, Cleirac's dedication to the regent queen is replaced by a dedication to the president of the *parlement* of Normandy, and eighty-seven pages of pertinent royal and regional legislation are added. The 1788 edition reproduces the Rouen versions. The few

copies of it that exist in today's rare book libraries suggest that the print run of the 1788 edition must have been lower than the previous ones.

17. Jean-Marie Pardessus, *Collection de lois maritimes antérieures au XVIIIe siècle*, 6 vols. (Paris: Imprimerie royale, 1828–1845). Note that when issuing a second edition of this work, Pardessus adopted Cleirac's title: *Us et coutumes de la mer, ou Collection des usages maritimes des peuples de l'antiquité et du Moyen Age*, 2 vols. (Paris: Imprimerie Royale, 1847).

18. Barnabé Brisson, ed., *Code du roy Henry III Roy de France et de Pologne* (Paris: Chez Sebastien Nivelle, 1587), 452r–458v (book XX, titles 8–12).

19. The booklet had previously appeared separately as Estienne Cleirac, *Explication des termes de marine employez dans les edicts, ordonnances, & reglemens de l'Admirauté. Ensemble les noms propres des navires, de leur parties, & l'usage d'icelles, l'artillerie navale, les livrees ou couleurs des estendards & pavillons de ceux qui voguent sur les mers* (Paris: Chez Michel Brunet, 1636). When he included *Explication* at the end of *Us et coustumes de la mer*, Cleirac complained that the Jesuit and naval chaplain Georges Fournier had borrowed generously from his work in order to compose a more systematic treatment of the subject: Fournier, *Hydrographie contenant la theorie et la pratique de toutes les parties de la navigation* (Paris: Chez Michel Soly, 1643). On a rare propagandist of French overseas colonization in the early seventeenth century, see Grégoire Holtz, *L'ombre de l'auteur: Pierre Bergeron et l'écriture du voyage au soir de la Renaissance* (Geneva: Droz, 2011). Later in the century, French works on all aspects of navigation became more common. See, e.g., C. R. Dassié, *L'architecture navale, contenant la manière de construire les navires, galères et chaloupes et la définition de plusieurs autres espèces de vaisseaux* (Paris: J. de La Caille, 1677); and idem, *Le routier des Indes orientales et occidentales, traitant des saisons propres à y faire voyage, une description des anchrages, profondeurs de plusieurs hâvres et ports de mer* (Paris: J. de La Caille, 1677).

20. Guy Miege, *The Ancient Sea-laws of Oleron, Wisby and the Hanse-towns Still in Force: Taken out of a French Book, Intitled, Les Us & Coustumes de la Mer* (London: J. Redmayne for T. Basset, 1686). Starting in 1686, Gerard Malynes's handbook was printed together with a number of accompanying "tracts," including the English rendition of Cleirac's compilation of maritime laws. The first edition of this work was Malynes, *Consuetudo, vel, Lex Mercatoria, or, The Ancient Law-Merchant* (London: Adam Islip, 1622).

21. Cleirac attributed the redaction of the Judgments of Oléron to Eleanor of Aquitaine (d. 1204), while English authors claimed that her husband Henry II of England and her son Richard I, who ruled over the Guyenne region, had issued them from across the Channel. Cleirac (*UCM 1647*, 3; *UCM 1661*, 2) borrowed his conclusion from Claude Barthélemy de Morisot, *Orbis maritimi, sive, Rerum in mari et littoribus*, 4 vols. (Dijon: apud Petrvm Palliot, 1643), 3:457 (book II, ch. 28), and disputed the English theory put forth by John Selden, *Mare clausum seu de domino maris libri duo* (London: W. Stanesbeius pro R. Meighen, 1635), 254–255 (book II, chap. 24).

22. Cleirac, *UCM 1661*, 8. The Qur'an had appeared in French translation in the same year as the first edition of *Us et coustumes de la mer*: *L'Alcoran de Mahomet, translaté d'arabe en français par le sieur Du Ryer* (Paris: A. de Sommaville, 1647). On the status of Qur'anic studies in seventeenth-century France, albeit with a focus on Orientalist circles, to which Cleirac did not belong, see Alastair Hamilton and Francis Richard, *André du Ryer and Oriental Studies in Seventeenth-Century France* (Oxford: Arcadian Library and Oxford University Press, 2005). The

medieval collection of prophecies attributed to Merlin had circulated widely in manuscript form before being printed as *Les prophéties de Merlin* (Paris: A. Vérart, 1498). See also Catherine Daniel, *Le prophéties de Merlin et la culture politique (XIIe–XVIe siècles)* (Turnhout, Belgium: Brepols, 2006).

23. I located one copy of this printed list in the Bibliothèque Nationale de France, Paris (FP-2710): "Table alphabétique des livres et des auteurs cités par Cleirac, dans les *Us et Coustumes de la Mer*." It is unbound and lacks any information about the date and place of publication.

24. Here and elsewhere I cite the earliest edition I was able to consult: Benvenuto Stracca, *De mercatura seu mercatore tractatus* (Venice: n.p., 1553); Pedro de Santarém, *Tractatus de assecurationibus et sponsionibus mercatorum* (Venice: Apud Baltassarem Constantinum ad signum divi georgi, 1522); Sigismondo Scaccia, *Tractatus de commerciis et cambio* (Rome: Sumptibus A. Brugiotti, ex typographia I. Mascardi, 1619); Raffaele della Torre, *Tractatus de cambiis* (Genoa: Excudebat Petrus Ioannes Calenzanus, 1641); Hugo Grotius, *De iure belli ac pacis* (Paris: apud Nicolaum Buon, 1625); idem, *De mari libero* (Leiden: Ex officina Elzeviriana, 1609); Selden, *Mare clausum*.

25. The *coutumes* of Amiens, Arc, Bordeaux, Bayonne, Bourgogne, Labour (Normandy), Nivernais, Orléans, Paris, and Tours are mentioned. Recall that Cleirac cites the jurist Charles du Moulin in spite of the Roman Catholic Church's condemnation of his ideas about usury (see chapter 3, note 36).

26. *L'Arithmétique de Ian Trenchant départie en trois livres, ensemble un petit discours des changes, avec l'art de calculer aux getons* (Lyon: Chez Michel Iove, 1561); Juan de Hevia Bolaños, *Curia filipica* (Madrid: por la viuda de Alonso Martin, 1619); idem, *Segunda parte de la Curia filipica* (Valladolid: por Iuan Lasso de las Peñas, 1629); Mathias Maréschal, *Traicté des changes et rechanges licites et illicites* (Paris: Chez Nicolas Buon, 1625); *V. Cl. Petri Peckii in titt. Dig. & Cod. ad rem nauticam pertinentes, commentarii* (Leiden: Ex officina A. Wyngaerden, 1647); Santarém, *Tractatus de assecurationibus; De mercatura decisiones, et tractatus varii, et de rebus ad eam pertinentibvs* (Cologne: Apud Cornelium ab Egemont de Grassis, 1622).

27. "The Florentines . . . were the first innovators to experiment with" bills of exchange: Benedetto Cotrugli, *The Book of the Art of Trade*, ed. Carlo Carraro and Giovanni Favero, trans. John Francis Phillimore (Cham, Switzerland: Springer, 2017), 66. For the original French translation to which Cleirac could have had access, see *Traicté de la merchandise, et du parfaict marchant . . . traduict de l'Italien de Benoît Cotrugli Raugean, par Jean Boyron* (Lyon: Par les heritiers de François Didier, 1582), 66v.

28. *Le Livre du Consulat . . . nouvellement traduict de language espaignol & italien en françois*, trans. François Mayssoni (Aix-en-Provence: Chez Pierre Roux, 1577). The first edition was printed in 600 copies. See Wolfgang Kaiser, "*Ars Mercatoria:* Möglichkeiten und Grenzen einer analytischen Bibliographie und Datebank," in *Ars Mercatoria: Eine analytische Bibliographie*, 3 vols., ed. Jochen Hoock, Pierre Jeannin, and Wolfgang Kaiser (Paderborn: Schöningh, 1991–2001), 3:6n35. A second edition appeared with the title *Le Consulat . . . traduict de language espaignol & italien, en françois*, trans. François Mayssoni (Aix-en-Provence, France: Estienne David, 1635). Cleirac references the *Consulat* in his commentary on multiple occasions and probably possessed a copy of the Catalan version. That a French translation already existed and that the Barcelona statutes were regarded as an authoritative source of law in the Mediterranean,

rather than in the Atlantic, explains why the Bordeaux lawyer did not try to include the *Consulat* in his compilation.

29. Peter N. Miller, *Peiresc's History of Provence: Antiquarianism and the Discovery of a Medieval Mediterranean* (Philadelphia: American Philosophical Society, 2011), 38–48; idem, *Peiresc's Mediterranean World* (Cambridge, MA: Harvard University Press, 2015), 41.

30. On Morisot's tome, which addressed contemporary doctrines and military conflicts and was dedicated to Louis XIII, see Guillaume Calafat, *Une mer jalousée: Souverainetés et juridictions des mers dans la Méditerranée du XVIIe siècle* (Paris: Seuil, in press).

31. Dom Francisco Manuel de Melo, "Epanáfora trágica segunda," in *Epanáforas de vária história portugueza*, 3rd ed., ed. Edgar Prestage (Coimbra, Portugal: Imprensa da Universidade, 1931), 118–209, at 202. The quip was repeated by the Portuguese historian Manuel de Faria e Sousa (1590–1649) in his *Ásia Portuguesa*, 3 vols. (Lisbon: H. Valente de Oliueira, 1666–1675), 3:399 (part IV, ch. 2, no. 13); *The Portuguese Asia*, 3 vols., trans. John Stevens (London: C. Brome, 1695), 3:339. The next paragraphs in the body of the text build on Marcel Gouron, *L'Amirauté de Guienne depuis le premier amiral anglais en Guienne jusqu'à la Révolution* (Paris: Sirey, 1938), 262–263; Yves-Marie Bercé, "L'affaire des caraques échouées (1627) et le droit de naufrage," in *État, marine et société: Hommage à Jean Meyer*, ed. Martine Acerra , Jean-Pierre Poussou, Michel Vergé-Franceschi, and André Zysberg (Paris: Presses de l'université de Paris-Sorbonne, 1995), 15–24; Jean-Yves Blot and Patrick Lizé, eds., *Le naufrage des portugais sur les côtes de Saint-Jean-de-Luz et d'Arcachon (1627)* (Paris: Chandeigne, 2000); Francesca Trivellato, "'Amphibious Power': The Law of Wreck, Maritime Customs, and Sovereignty in Richelieu's France," *Law and History Review* 33, no. 4 (2015): 915–944.

32. Elliott, *Richelieu and Olivares* (Cambridge: Cambridge University Press, 1984), 89–96. The Spanish–French alliance against the Protestant powers was signed on March 20, 1627.

33. In 1626 Richelieu attributed to himself the title of *Grand-maître, chef et surintendant général de la Navigation et du Commerce de France* (Grand Master, Head, and Superintendent of the Navy and Commerce of France), and in January 1627 he abolished the office of the admiral of France.

34. Both Fortia and Servien were members of the King's Council. Servien replaced Fortia in April 1627 and went on to be appointed *intendant* of Guyenne in 1628, to become president of the *parlement* of Bordeaux in 1630, and later to hold various higher-profile diplomatic and military positions in the kingdom, culminating in his service as a diplomat at the negotiations of the Treaty of Westphalia in 1648. Pierre Grillon, ed., *Les papiers de Richelieu: Section politique intérieure, correspondence et papiers d'État*, 6 vols. (Paris: Pedone, 1975–1997), 2:225–226.

35. Every admiralty was headed by a military officer (*lieutenant*) and a legal official (*procureur du roy*). Cleirac's appointment to the admiralty of Bordeaux is mentioned in his *Usance du négoce*, preface, 4. His involvement in the extensive inquiry (*procès-verbal*) into the fate of the shipwreck is reflected in his writing. Cleirac cites depositions made by surviving mariners before Fortia in Bordeaux in January 1627 and a report about the conflicts between royal officials and local lords contained "in a green book of Bordeaux's comptroller, call number C, fol. 221": Cleirac, *UCM 1647*, 42, 124; and idem, *UCM 1661*, 40, 122.

36. Théodore Godefroy, "Du droit de naufrage et que c'est un droit royal," ANP, AB XIX, 3192, dossier 3. More papers by Godefroy are preserved in the library of the Institut de France. See Bercé, "L'affaire des caraques échouées," 22; Erik M. Thomson, "Chancellor Oxenstierna,

Cardinal Richelieu, and Commerce: The Problems and Possibilities of Governance in Early-Seventeenth Century France and Sweden" (Ph.D. diss., Johns Hopkins University, 2004), 284–285; idem, "Commerce, Law and Erudite Culture: The Mechanics of Théodore Godefroy's Service to Cardinal Richelieu," *Journal of the History of Ideas* 68, no. 3 (2007): 407–427. Godefroy's younger brother, Jacques (1587–1652), a jurist of international stature who did not abandon the family's Calvinist persuasion and remained in his native Geneva, published a commentary on the Roman law of wreck: Jacques Godefroy, *De imperio maris deque jure naufragii* (Geneva: Stamp. Ioannis Antonis & Samuelis de Tournes, 1637). Cleirac cites from the latter but does not appear to have had access to Théodore's manuscript dossier.

37. For other episodes, see Alain Cabantous, *Les côtes barbares: Pilleurs d'épaves et société littorals en France (1680–1830)* (Paris: Fayard, 1993), 121–150.

38. Cleirac, *UCM 1647*, 98, 116, 122; and idem, *UCM 1661*, 94–95, 111, 120. D'Épernon's biographer described the villagers who looted the goods that survived the 1627 tempest as "a barbarous and inhuman people": Guillaume Girard, *The History of the Life of the Duke of Espernon, the Great Favourite of France*, trans. Charles Cotton (London: E. Cotes and A. Clark, for Henry Brome, 1670), 442. Montesquieu later identified the Romans as those who began to devise "humane" laws that curbed "the rapine" and "the rapacity" of coastal rulers and inhabitants: Charles-Louis de Secondat baron de La Brède and of Montesquieu, *The Spirit of the Laws*, 2 vols., trans. Thomas Nugent, with an introduction by Franz Neumann (New York: Hafner, 1949), 1:363 (book XXI, ch. 17).

39. Archivo General de Simancas (hereafter AGS), *Secretaría de Estado* (hereafter *SEF*), K.1443.105 (Diego de Irarraga to Juan de Villale, Bordeaux, June 15, 1627). Perhaps to downplay the duke's recalcitrance, d'Épernon's biographer maintains that little more than 7,000 or 8,000 small rough diamonds of modest value were recovered and dutifully placed in the hands of the merchants administering the salvaged goods. Girard, *History of the Life*, 447.

40. James C. Boyajian, *Portuguese Trade in Asia under the Habsburgs, 1580–1640* (Baltimore: Johns Hopkins University Press, 1993), 136.

41. See Blot and Lizé, *Le naufrage des portugais*, 53–57, 261n3, for the estimate of the *São Bartolomeu's* and *Santa Helena's* cargo; see Boyajian, *Portuguese Trade*, 44, for the educated guess of the value of the precious stones carried on Portuguese ships returning from India.

42. Ibid., 206.

43. Idem, *Portuguese Bankers at the Court of Spain, 1626–1650* (New Brunswick, NJ: Rutgers University Press, 1983); Carlos Álvarez Nogal, *El crédito de la monarquía hispánica en el reinado de Felipe IV* (Castilla y León: Consejería de Educación y Cultura, 1997), 125–132, 181–261.

44. AGS, *SEF*, King's order to don Juan de Villela, February 15, 1627, K.1434.47; report of the Council of State to the Spanish king, March 13, 1627, K.1434.65; report of the Council of State to the Spanish king, March 20, 1627, K.1434.70; Irarraga to the Spanish king, June 1628, K.1445.58; Irarraga to the Spanish king, September 26, 1627, K.1444.62; Joran de Freytas to the Spanish king, September 29, 1627, K.1435.68; report of the Council of State to the Spanish king, June 7, 1628, K.1434.44; Irarraga to the the Spanish king, July 29, 1628, K.1481.74. See also ADG, C.3877, fols. 44v–45r, and C.3904, fols. 55r-v, 57r-v, 116. Lopez often claimed to be a Morisco, and he is represented as such in a letter sent by Freytas to his king from Bordeaux on September 29, 1627: AGS, *SEF*, K.1435.68. In reality, he was of Jewish descent. In 1610 he settled in Paris as a diamond

cutter and dealer. See I. S. Révah, *Le cardinal de Richelieu et la restauration du Portugal* (Lisbon: Ottosgráfica, 1950); Elliott, *Richelieu and Olivares*, 116; Françoise Hildesheimer, "Une créature de Richelieu: Alphonse Lopez, le 'Seigneur Hebreo,' " in *Les Juifs au regard de l'histoire: Mélanges en l'honneur de Bernhard Blumenkranz*, ed. Gilbert Dahan (Paris: Picard, 1985), 293–299; Mercedes García-Arenal and Gerard Wiegers, *A Man of Three Worlds: Samuel Pallache, a Moroccan Jew in Catholic and Protestant Europe*, trans. Martin Beagles (Baltimore: Johns Hopkins University Press, 2002 [1999]), 116–119.

45. AGS, *SEF*, K1445.57, Irarraga to the Spanish king, June 10, 1628; K.1434, fol. 60, report of the Council of State to the Spanish king, July 8, 1628.

46. Blot and Lizé, *Le naufrage des portugais*, 184.

47. Ernest Gaullieur, *Histoire de Collège de Guyenne d'après un grand nombre de documents inédits* (Paris: Sandoz et Fischbacher, 1874), 387–389; Théophile Malvezin, *Histoire des Juifs à Bordeaux* (Bordeaux: Charles Lefebvre, 1875), 100–101; William Harrison Woodward, *Studies in Education During the Age of the Renaissance, 1400–1600* (Cambridge: University Press, 1906), 139–166; Boutruche, *Bordeaux de 1453 à 1715*, 188–191; Richard H. Popkin, *The History of Scepticism: From Savonarola to Bayle*, rev. ed. (Oxford: Oxford University Press, 2003), 38–39, 45–46.

48. Pierre Charron (1541–1603), a close friend of Montaigne, published his sermons on the Eucharist upon request of the archbishop of Bordeaux, Cardinal François d'Escoubleau de Sourdis: Michel Adam, *L'eucharistie chez les penseurs français du dix-septième siècle* (Hildesheim, Germany: Georg Olms, 2000), 30. Cleirac dedicated the first edition of his *Explications des termes de la marine* (1636) to de Sourdis's younger brother, Henri d'Escouleau de Sourdis, who followed his elder sibling in the post of archbishop of Bordeaux and, as a leading figure of the Catholic party, acted as commander-in-chief of the royal navy during the siege of La Rochelle. On the latter figure, see Boutruche, *Bordeaux de 1453 à 1715*, 376–379; Alan James, *The Navy and Government in Early Modern France, 1572–1661* (Suffolk, UK: Royal Society and Boydell Press, 2004), 11.

49. Richard H. Popkin, *Isaac La Peyrère (1596–1676): His Life, Work and Influence* (Leiden: Brill, 1987).

50. Two such city ordinances were issued in 1603 and 1612: Xavier Védère, ed., *Inventaire sommaire des registres de la Jurade, 1520–1783*, 8 vols. (Bordeaux: G. Gounouilhou & E. Castera, 1896–1947), 8:244. The *lettres patentes* allowing the open practice of Judaism in 1723 referred to the Jews of Bordeaux as "known and established in our kingdom under the title of Portuguese or New Christians": Nahon, *Les "Nations" juives portugaises*, 37.

51. This exception was noted by contemporary scholars of the crown's prerogatives. See, e.g., Jean Bacquet (d. 1597), *Des droicts du domaine de la couronne de France* (Geneve: Pour Pierre Aubert, 1625), 24.

52. For the number of Portuguese and Spanish New Christians in Bordeaux in 1636, see Malvezin, *Histoire des Juifs*, 129. The population of all French cities, including Bordeaux, is relayed in Philip Benedict, "French Cities from the Sixteenth Century to the French Revolution: An Overview," in *Cities and Social Change in Early Modern France*, ed. Philip Benedict (London and New York: Routledge, 1992), 1–66, at 24.

53. Jean Cavignac, *Les israélites bordelais de 1780 à 1850: Autour de l'émancipation* (Paris: Publisud, 1991), 15. On the eve of the French Revolution, Bordeaux and Bayonne had populations

of 110,000 and 13,000 and counted some 1,500–2,000 and 2,500–3,500 Jews, respectively: Benedict, "French Cities," 24–25; Simon Schwarzfuchs, *Les Juifs de France* (Paris: Albin Michel, 1975), 146. Most of the poor members of the Jewish community of Bordeaux were immigrants from Avignon. On the conspicuous consumption of the Sephardim of Bordeaux, see Richard Menkis, "Patriarchs and Patricians: The Gradis Family of Eighteenth-Century Bordeaux," in *From East and West: Jews in a Changing Europe, 1750–1870*, ed. Frances Malino and David Sorkin (Cambridge, MA: Basil Blackwell, 1990), 11–45.

54. Malvezin, *Histoire de Juifs*, 131–132. On Colbert's policies of commercial expansion in Bordeaux, though with no reference to Jewish traders, see Frederic C. Lane, "Colbert and the Commerce of Bordeaux," in *Venice and History: The Collected Papers of Frederic C. Lane* (Baltimore: Johns Hopkins University Press, 1966), 311–330.

55. Letters of June 11, 1686, September 7, 1686, and September 26, 1686, all in ANP, *Correspondence des intendants avec le contrôleur général des Finances*, G7, 133.

56. Malvezin, *Histoire des Juifs*, 171–175.

57. David Graizbord, *Souls in Dispute: Converso Identities in Iberia and the Jewish Diaspora* (Philadelphia: University of Pennsylvania Press, 2003).

58. Jonathan I. Israel, "Spain and the Dutch Sephardim, 1609–1660," *Studia Rosenthaliana* 12, nos. 1–2 (1978): 1–61, republished in idem, *Empires and Entrepôts: The Dutch, the Spanish and the Jews, 1585–1713* (London: Hambledon, 1990), 355–415.

59. These particular examples come from Arquivo Nacional da Torre do Tombo (hereafter ANTT), *Tribunal do Santo Ofício: Inquisição de Lisboa* (hereafter *IL*), processos 4512 and 1008 (Simão Rodrigues, 1595–1604), 5101 (Diogo Rodrigues, 1668–1669), 2383 (Manuel Nunes Chaves, 1664–1671), 2336 (Gaspar Fernandes Marques, 1684–1685), 3660 (Maria Soares, wife of the marchant Jacinto de Flores, 1684–1690).

60. I. S. Révah, "Les Marranes," *Revue des études juives* 118, no. 1 (1959–1960): 29–77, at 66, English translation in *Jews in Early Modern Europe*, ed. Jonathan Karp and Francesca Trivellato (London: Taylor and Francis, forthcoming).

61. Julio Caro Baroja, *Los Judíos en la España moderna y contemporánea*, 3 vols. (Madrid: Arion, 1961), 2:66–67.

62. Ibid., 3:336–344.

63. ANP, *Correspondence des intendants avec le contrôleur général des Finances*, G7, November 2, 1686.

64. *Requête des marchands et négociants de Paris contre l'admission des Juifs* (Paris: P.-A. Le Prieur, 1767), 15.

65. Pierre de l'Ancre, *L'incredulité et mescréance du sortilège pleinement convaincue* (Paris: Chez Nicolas Buon, 1622), cited in Nahon, *Juifs et Judaïsme*, 49–50.

66. Guy Saupin, *Nantes au XVIIe siècle: Vie politique et société urbaine* (Rennes, France: Presses universitaires de Rennes, 1996), 248.

67. Arthur Hertzberg, *The French Enlightenment and the Jews* (New York: Columbia University Press, 1968), 17. For the mixture of political and religious antipathy toward the Sephardim of southwestern France more generally, see Malvezin, *Histoire des Juifs*, 113–114; Myriam Yardeni, "Antagonismes nationaux et propagande durant les guerres de religion," *Revue d'histoire moderne et contemporaine* 13, no. 4 (1966): 273–284, 277–280; J. N. Hillgarth, *The Mirror of Spain, 1500–1700: The Formation of a Myth* (Ann Arbor: University of Michigan Press, 2000), 328–350, esp.

336; Gayle K. Brunelle, " 'À la Ruine totale de la France': A French Assessment of Portuguese and Spanish Immigration in Seventeenth-Century France," paper presented at the Western Society for French History 45th Annual Conference, Reno, Nevada, November 4, 2016.

68. The motto, written in both Latin (*Undarum terraeque potens*) and Greek (ΤΗΝ ΓΗΝ ΚΑΙ ΘΑΛΑΣΣΑΝ ΥΠΗΚΟΩΝ ΕΚΟΝ), is lifted from the laude of Roman emperor Domitian in the Latin poem *Thebaid* (1.30-1), written by Statius in the first century CE: "May you remain content with the governance of mankind, potent over sea and land, and waive the stars" ("maneas hominum contentus habenis, undarum terraeque potens, et sidera done"); Statius, *Thebaid*, ed. and trans. D. R. Shackleton Bailey, Loeb Classical Library 207 (Cambridge, MA: Harvard University Press, 2004), 40–41.

69. Cleirac, *UCM 1647* and *UCM 1661*, dedication. In the 1671 and subsequent editions, this dedication is replaced by one to the president of the *parlement* of Normandy (see note 16 above).

70. Amalia D. Kessler, "A 'Question of Name': Merchant-Court Jurisdiction and the Origin of the *Noblesse Commerçante*," in *A Vast and Useful Art: The Gustave Gimon Collection of French Political Economy*, ed. Mary Jane Parrine (Stanford, CA: Stanford University Libraries, 2004), 49–65.

71. The edict is reproduced in François-André Isambert, ed., *Recueil général des anciennes lois françaises, depuis l'an 420 jusqu'à la révolution de 1789*, 29 vols. (Paris: Berlin-Leprieur, 1821–1833), 14:153–158.

72. Laurent Coste, "Le recrutement des juges et consuls de la Bourse des marchands de Bordeaux, des origines au gouvernement de Richelieu," in *Les tribunaux de commerce: Genèse et enjeux d'une institution* (Paris: Association française pour l'histoire de la justice, 2007), 45–53.

73. Daniel Jousse, *Nouveau commentaire sur les ordinances des mois d'août 1669, & mars 1673*, new ed. (Paris: Debure, l'aîné, 1775), 411–412. We still know little about the actual functioning of these courts. Partial accounts of their institutional development are offered in Ernest Genevois, *Histoire critique de la juridiction consulaire* (Paris and Nantes: Durand et Pedone/Forest et Grimaud, 1866); Jacqueline-Lucienne Lafon, *Les Députés du commerce et l'Ordonnance de Mars 1673: Les jurisdictions consulaires; principe et compétance* (Paris: Cujas, 1979); *Les tribunaux de commerce*.

74. Citation from article 6 of the edict of November 1563 in Isambert, *Recueil général*, 14:155. All sentences up to 500 livres tournois issued by the *juges-consuls* were executable across the kingdom; only those above this sum could be appealed, normally before a *parlement*. The presence of lawyers in commercial courts became more frequent in the eighteenth century.

75. Isambert, *Recueil général*, 14:154.

76. On the administration of justice by the admiralty of Guyenne, housed in Bordeaux, see Gouron, *L'Amirauté de Guienne*. The 1673 *ordonnance de commerce* initially put all maritime affairs under the jurisdiction of the *juges consuls* until the admiralties protested and obtained the reversal of that norm: Lafon, *Les Députés du commerce*, 39n5.

77. Mathias Maréschal, *Traicté des iuge et consuls des marchands, et de leur iurisdiction* (Paris: Chez Iulian Iacquin, 1651), 27–28.

78. André de Colonia, *Eclaircissement sur le légitime commerce des interests* (Lyon: Chez Antoine Cellier, 1675), 96–97.

79. Joseph Vaesen, *La jurisdiction commerciale à Lyon sous l'Ancien Régime: Étude historique*

sur la Conservation des privilèges royaux des foires de Lyon (1463–1795) (Lyon: Mougin-Rusand, 1879), 6–7. In 1655, the court came under municipal control and changed its name to *Tribunal de la Conservation des privilèges des foires de Lyon*.

80. Joseph-Nicolas Guyot, *Répertoire universel et raisonné de jurisprudence civile, criminelle, canonique et bénéficiale*, 17 vols., new ed. (Paris: Chez Visse, 1784–1785), 4:535–544, at 538 and 541, s.v. "Conservation de Lyon"; Isambert, *Recueil général*, 18:211–217, at 213; Vaesen, *La jurisdiction commerciale à Lyon*, 108–111; Lafon, *Les Députés du commerce*, 60–63.

81. Erika Vause, "Disciplining the Market: Debt Imprisonment, Public Credit, and the Construction of Commercial Personhood in Revolutionary France," *Law and History Review* 32, no. 3 (2014): 647–682.

82. George Huppert, *Les Bourgeois Gentilshommes: An Essay on the Definition of Elites in Renaissance France* (Chicago: University of Chicago Press, 1977); Arlette Jouanna, *Ordre social: Mythes et hiérarchies dans la France du XVIe siecle* (Paris: Hachette, 1977).

83. Boutruche, *Bordeaux de 1453 à 1715*, 365–367.

84. Charles Loyseau, *A Treatise of Orders and Plain Dignities*, ed. and trans. Howell A. Lloyd (Cambridge: Cambridge University Press, 1994), 110–111 (my emphasis). *Lois de dérogeance* were reissued frequently in the sixteenth century, an indication of the growing challenges to them, as least in some locales. A royal decree of 1560 forbade all noblemen or legal officials from engaging in any trade at the risk of losing their titles and suffering the imposition of the chief direct tax (*taille*): *Ordonnance d'Orléans*, art. 109, cited in Jean Domat, *Le droit public, suite des lois civiles dans leur ordre naturel* (Paris: Chez Jean-Baptiste Coignar, 1697), 366–367. Brittany was an anomaly in the kingdom for its so-called *nobless dormante*, a local custom that permitted nobles to engage in trade without losing their privileges. In keeping with this tradition, in 1543 the *parlement* of Brittany allowed noblemen to become judges and lawyers: Isambert, *Recueil général*, 12, pt. 2: 869–873. But the extent to which the Breton nobility took advantage of these local exceptions before they were generalized remains unclear: Olivier Pétré-Grenouilleau, "La noblesse commerçante nantaise (XVIIe–XIXe siècles): Une noblesse ouverte?" in *Noblesse de Bretagne du Moyen Âge à nos jours*, ed. Jean Kerhervé (Rennes, France: Presses universitaires de Rennes, 1999), 197–209.

85. Isambert, *Recueil général*, 16:223–344, at 280 (art. 198) and 339 (art. 452). Marxist scholars traditionally attributed to Richelieu a leading role in initiating the bourgeois transformation of seventeenth-century French society: Henri Hauser, *La pensée et l'action économiques du Cardinal de Richelieu* (Paris: Presses universitaires de France, 1944), 48–73. More recently, historians have emphasized the contingent and opportunistic nature of Richelieu's commercial politics as well as the rivalry between the cardinal and Michel de Marillac, the primary architect of the Code Michau, as elements that undermined the reform's success. See Laure Chantrel, "Notion de richesse et de travail dans la pensée économique française de la seconde moitié du XVIe et du début du XVIIe siècle," *Journal of Medieval and Renaissance Studies* 25, no. 1 (1995): 129–158; James, *Navy and Government*; Thomson, "Chancellor Oxenstierna"; Lauriane Kadlec, "Le 'Code Michau': La réformation selon le garde des Sceaux Michel de Marillac," *Les Dossiers du Grihl: La Vie de Michel de Marillac et les expériences politiques du garde des sceaux* (2012), http://dossiersgrihl.revues.org/5317#ftn1 (accessed July 9, 2018); Caroline Maillet-Rao, *La pensée politique des dévots Mathieu de Morgues et Michel de Marillac: Une opposition au ministériat du cardinal de Richelieu* (Paris: Honoré Champion, 2015), 54–56.

86. Isambert, *Recueil général*, 18:217–218. The immediate goal of this edict was to encourage the nobility to invest in the newly created state companies devoted to trade with the West and East Indies (1664). In 1701, the same prerogative was extended to all noblemen who were not magistrates and who engaged in wholesale trade, whether overseas or overland (20:400–402). That the 1701 provision had to be repeated in 1727 suggests that its implementation was not without resistance (21:306). See also Kessler, " 'Question of Name,' " 62n12.

87. Jousse, *Nouveau commentaire*, 365.

88. Couchot, *Le traité du commerce de terre et de mer à l'usage des marchands, banquiers, agens de change & gens d'affaires avec la pratique suivie dans les jurisdictions consulaires, & dans les autres tribunaux, où les contestations pour le fait du commerce sont portées*, 2 vols. (Paris: Chez Jacques Le Febvre, 1710), 1:46–47, 58.

89. *Le praticien des juges et consuls, ou traité de commerce de terre et de mer à l'usage des marchands, banquiers, négocians, agens de change & gens d'affaire*, new ed. (Paris: Chez Saugrain, 1742), 12 (book 1, ch. V).

90. *Instruction générale sur la jurisdiction consulaire*, new ed. (Bordeaux: Chez Jean Chappuis, 1769), esp. 3–7; Lafon, *Les Députés du Commerce*, 92n10, 100–103.

91. Amalia D. Kessler, *A Revolution in Commerce: The Parisian Merchant Court and the Rise of Commercial Society in Eighteenth-Century France* (New Haven, CT: Yale University Press, 2004), 254–255.

92. Denis Diderot and Jean le Rond d'Alembert, eds., *Encyclopédie, ou dictionnaire raisonné des sciences, des arts et des métiers*, 28 vols. (Paris: Chez Briasson, David l'aîné, Le Breton, Durant, 1751–1772), 10:83, s.v. "marchand." Hereafter all citations from the *Encyclopédie* will be given in abbreviated form and will come from the University of Chicago's ARTFL Encyclopédie Project (spring 2016 edition), available at http://encyclopedie.uchicago.edu/.

93. Abbé (Gabriel François) Coyer, *La noblesse commerçante* (London [Paris]: Chez Duchesne, 1756). On the debate sparked by Coyer's short treatise, see John Shovlin, "Toward a Reinterpretation of Revolutionary Anti-Nobilism: The Political Economy of Honor in the Old Regime," *Journal of Modern History* 72, no. 1 (2000): 35–66; and Jay M. Smith, "Social Categories, the Language of Patriotism, and the Origins of the French Revolution: The Debate over Noblesse Commerçante," *Journal of Modern History* 72, no. 2 (2000): 339–374. Even after the French Revolution, by social convention if not by law, commerce was deemed incompatible with the highest public offices: Jean-Marie Pardessus, *Cours de droit commercial*, 4 vols. (Paris: H. Plon, 1814–1816), 1:64.

94. Henry C. Clark, "Commerce, the Virtues, and the Public Sphere in Early Seventeenth-Century France," *French Historical Studies* 21, no. 3 (1998): 415–450.

95. Cleirac, *UCM 1647*, 492; idem, *UCM 1661*, 479.

96. Ibid., 487–489.

97. Ibid., 486.

98. Tom[m]aso Garzoni, *La piazza universale di tutte le professioni del mondo, e nobili et ignobili* (Venice: Appresso Gio. Battista Somascho, 1586), 552–561. The author was a clergyman of modest background. The most successful of his works, this volume enjoyed remarkable editorial fortune.

99. Cleirac, *Usance du négoce*, 15–19.

100. Ibid., preface, 2. In the dedication of *Us et coustumes de la mer*, Cleirac similarly praises commerce and navigation for promoting "the maintenance of ties among all different people of the globe and the reciprocal and peaceful exchange between them of the graces and riches that God has endowed each one of them." Cleirac, *UCM 1647*, dedication, 6; idem, *UCM 1661*, dedication, unnumbered pages. On the legacy of Aristotle's leitmotif in sixteenth- and seventeenth-century economic thought, see Jacob Viner, *Essays on the Intellectual History of Economics*, ed. Douglass A. Irwin (Princeton, NJ: Princeton University Press, 1991), 39–43, 203–204; and David Harris Sacks, "The Blessing of the Exchange in the Making of the Early English Atlantic," in *Religion and Trade: Cross-Cultural Exchanges in World History, 1000–1900*, ed. Francesca Trivellato, Leor Halevi, and Cátia Antunes (New York: Oxford University Press, 2014), 62–90, at 76–77.

101. Émeric Crucé, *Le nouveau Cynée, ou, Discours des occasions et moyens d'establir une paix generale & la liberté du commerce par tout le monde* (Paris: Chez Iacques Villery, 1623); René Pintard, *Le libertinage érudit dans la première moité du XVIIe siècle*, new ed. (Geneva: Slatkine, 2000), 13–14.

102. Cleirac, *Usance du négoce*, preface, 2.

103. Bernardo Davanzati, *Lezione delle monete e notizie de' cambj*, ed. Sergio Ricossa (Turin: Fògola Editore, 1988), 54.

104. A fuller discussion of this point can be found in Trivellato, " 'Usages and Customs.' "

105. Cleirac, *UCM 1647*, 411–412, 416–417; idem, *UCM 1661*, 385–386, 389; idem, *Usance du négoce*, 36.

106. Cleirac, *UCM 1661*, 386. On the word *Iuifveries*, see chapter 3, note 25.

107. Ibid., 386. Guy Rowlands, *The Financial Decline of a Great Power: War, Influence, and Money in Louis XIV's France* (Oxford: Oxford University Press, 2013), 95, summarizes various estimates of bullion imports and settles on 200–250 million livres.

108. Cleirac, *Usance du négoce*, 93.

109. Daniel Dessert, *Argent, pouvoir et société au Grand Siècle* (Paris: Fayard, 1984), 83–86. On the institutional and social profile of state contractors and financiers in seventeenth-century France, see also Françoise Bayard, *Le monde de financiers au XVIIe siècle* (Paris: Flammarion, 1988).

110. Père Mathias de Saint-Jean (alias Jean Eon), *Le commerce honorable ou considerations politiques* (Nantes: Guillaume le Monnier, 1646), 111; Jean-François Melon, *Essai politique sur le commerce* ([France?]: n.p., 1734), 219–220; Jean Larue, *Bibliothèque des jeunes négociants*, 2 vols. (Paris: Chez Briasson, 1747–1758), 1:587. *Cabale* is also how Turgot described the clique of financiers who robbed local people in Angoulême during the 1760s and 1770s (chapter 1, note 56). More examples of the usage of this term in relation to credit fraud are cited in Emma Rothschild, "Isolation and Economic Life in Eighteenth-Century France," *American Historical Review* 119, no. 4 (2014): 1055–1082, at 1066. See also see the entry for "cabale" in *Dictionnaire de l'Académie française*, 1st ed. (1694), and Jean-François Féraud, *Dictionaire critique de la langue française* (1787–1788). Montesquieu employed the word in reference to political manoeuvring ("la cabale du Parlement"): *Pensées, Le Spicilège*, ed. Louis Desgraves (Paris: Laffont, 1991), 350 (pensée 800); an English translation is *My Thoughts*, trans. and ed. Henry C. Clark (Indianapolis: Liberty Fund, 2012), 243 (no. 800). As a conspiratorial group, *cabale* was also how the French police and others referred to artisans' revolts in the eighteenth century: Steven Kaplan, "Ré-

flexions sur la police du monde du travail, 1700–1815," *Revue historique* 261, no. 1 (1979): 17–77, at 30–33.

111. Cleirac, *Usance du négoce*, 94. He mentions in passing Alain Chartier (1385–1430), who was known principally for his *Quadrilogue inventif,* a treatise that urged the three estates of the French monarchy to unite against foreign enemies. See Jean-Claude Mühlethaler, "Alan Chartier, Political Writer," in *A Companion to Alain Chartier (c. 1385–1430): Father of French Eloquence,* ed. Daisy Delogu, Joan E. McRae, and Emma Cayley (Leiden: Brill, 2015), 163–180. To drive home his criticism of self-interest as inimical to the public good, Cleirac cites Seneca's tragedy *Hercules Furens,* "Prosperum ac felix scelus // virtus vocatur" (II: 251–252), and an Italian proverb, "Più preme il proprio amor ch'el commun bene, l'util proprio è velen del commun bene." Both citations were made popular by Renaissance *florilegia.* They are included in *Lucii Annei Senecae cordubensis Flores, sive Sententiæ insigniores, excerptae per Desid. Erasmum Roterodamum* (Paris: Apud Mathæum Dauidem, 1547), 211; and Janus Gruter, ed., *Florilegium ethico-politicum* (Frankfurt: Bibliopolio Jonae Rhodii, 1561), 280, respectively.

112. See also article 358 of the ordinance of Blois of 1579 in Boucher, *Institutions commerciales traitant de la jurisprudence marchande et des usages du négoce, d'aprés les anciennes et nouvelles lois* (Paris: Chez Levrault frères, 1801), 38.

113. Cleirac, *UCM 1647,* 416–417; idem, *UCM 1661,* 389. As a result, in 1644 this brokers' guild was abolished, and jurisdiction was transferred to the municipal council of aldermen (*jurade*): Cleirac, *UCM 1647,* 411; idem, *UCM 1661,* 384–385. Cleirac mentions the same example in *Usance du négoce,* 36.

114. Cleirac, *Usance du négoce,* preface, 2. The numeration of pages 1 through 8 is repeated twice in the 1656 and 1659 editions, while in the 1670 edition the preface appears on unnumbered pages.

115. Ibid., preface, 1.

116. Idem, *UCM 1647,* 417; idem, *UCM 1661,* 390.

117. Idem, *Usance du négoce,* preface, 2.

118. Luis Suárez Fernández, ed., *Documentos acerca de la expulsión de los judíos* (Valladolid, Spain: Consejo Superior de Investigaciones Científicas, Patronato Menéndez Pelayo, 1964), 391–395, at 394. The standard English translation of the March 1492 decree appears in the appendix to Edward Peters, "Jewish History and Gentile Memory: The Expulsion of 1492," *Jewish History* 9, no. 1 (1995): 9–34, at 23–28, but omits the reference to bills of exchange.

119. George-Herbert Depping, *Les juifs dans le moyen âge: Essai historique sur leur état civil, comercial et littéraire* (Paris: Treuttel et Würtz, 1834), 427; Suárez Fernández, *Documentos acerca de la expulsión,* 479–481; Haim Beinart, *The Expulsion of the Jews from Spain,* trans. Jeffrey M. Green (Portland, OR: Littman Library of Jewish Civilization, 2002 [1994]), 118–206, 218–223, 291–294, 317–318; Miguel Ángel Ladero Quesada, "Después de 1492: Los bienes e debdas de los judíos," in *Judaísmo Hispano: Estudios en memoria de José Luis Lacave Riaño,* 2 vols., ed. Elena Romero (Madrid: Junta de Castilla y León, Diputación Provincial de Burgos, Rich Foundation, and Consejo Superior de Investigaciones Científicas, 2002), 2:727–747; Javier Castaño, "La encuesta sobre las deudas debidas a los judíos en el arzobispado de Toledo (1493–96)," *En la España Medieval* 29 (2006): 287–309.

120. Nadia Matringe, *La banque en Renaissance: Les Salviati et la place de Lyon au milieu du XVIe siècle* (Rennes, France: Presses universitaires de Rennes, 2016), 227.

121. In 1599, Diego Londrade, a Portuguese merchant and *bourgeois* of Bordeaux, was a correspondent of a Florentine merchant residing in Lyon, Raffaello Bartoli, and sued another Florentine merchant, Matteo Cerretani, who lived in Bordeaux: Malvezin, *Histoire des Juifs*, 113–114.

122. Examples can be found in the business letters sent by David Lindo (1730–1741) from Bordeaux, whose microfilmed copies Frances Malino kindly shared with me (ADG, 7B1590-1612), as well as in Richard Menkis, "The Gradis Family of Eighteenth Century Bordeaux: A Social and Economic Study" (Ph.D. diss., Brandeis University, 1988), 154–245; and José do Nascimento Raposo, "Don Gabriel de Silva, a Portuguese-Jewish Banker in Eighteenth Century Bordeaux" (Ph.D. diss., York University, Toronto, 1989), 204–211, 250–261. The de Silva and Gradis families belonged to the top echelon of Bordeaux's Jewish society in the mid-eighteenth century: Cavignac, *Les israélites bordelaise*, 219.

123. Poggio Bracciolini, "On Nobility," in *Humanism and Liberty: Writings on Freedom from Fifteenth-Century Florence*, trans. and ed. Renée Neu Watkins (Columbia: University of South Carolina Press, 1978), 121–148, at 123.

124. Artistotle, *Nicomachean Ethics*, in *The Complete Works of Aristotle: Revised Oxford Translation*, 2 vols., ed. Jonathan Barnes (Princeton, NJ: Princeton University Press, 1984), 2: esp. 1732 (I: 1096a6–1096a10), 1779 (IV: 1127b10–1127b22), 1787 (V: 1132b22–1133a6); Aristotle, *Politics*, in *The Complete Works of Aristotle*, 2: esp. 1992 (I: 1256a1–1256b25) and 1994 (I: 1257a7–1257a41); Cicero, *On Duties*, ed. M. T. Griffin and E. M. Atkins (Cambridge: Cambridge University Press, 1991), 57–59 (I: 150–152).

125. Simona Cerutti, *Étrangers: Étude d'une condition d'incertitude dans une société d'Ancien Régime* (Montrouge, France: Bayard, 2012).

Chapter 5: One Family, Two Bestsellers, and the Legend's Canonization

1. Diderot and d'Alembert, *Encyclopédie*, 3:296, s.v. "Cherafs."

2. In eighteenth-century Marseilles, all major merchants owned a copy of Savary's *Parfait négociant* and other texts discussed in this chapter, even if we cannot determine what they used them for: Charles Carrière, *Négociants marseillais au XVIIIe siècle: Contribution à l'étude des économies maritimes* (Marseilles: Institut Historique de Provence, 1973), 765–770.

3. The six ancient *corps des marchands* were textile traders (*drapiers*), apothecaries (*épiciers*), mercers (*merciers*), leather and fur makers (*pelletiers*), hosiers (*bonnetiers*), and jewelers (*orfévres*). An additional guild was created in the 1570s for wine merchants, but it never acquired the same prestige as the six older guilds. François Olivier-Martin, *L'organisation corporative de la France d'ancien régime* (Paris: Sirey, 1938), 120–122. In 1597, at the end of the Wars of Religion, an edict that reestablished order within the guilds paired together "merchants" and "artisans": François-André Isambert, ed., *Recueil général des anciennes lois françaises, depuis l'an 420 jusqu'à la révolution de 1789*, 29 vols. (Paris: Berlin-Leprieur, 1821–1833), 15:135–141.

4. An earlier use of the term in Italian figures in the title of Giovanni Domenico Peri's merchant manual *Il negotiante*, 4 vols. (Genoa: Pier Giovanni Calenzano, 1638–1665). The first edition of the *Dictionnaire de l'Académie française* (1674) distinguished between *marchand* and *négociant*. See also Carrière, *Négociants marseillais*, 243–244; Pierre Jeannin, "La profession de négociant entre le XVIe et le XVIIIe siècle," in *Il mestiere dello storico dell'età moderna: La vita economica nei secoli XVI–XVIII*, ed. Philippe Braunstein (Bellinzona, Switzerland: Casagrande,

1997), 81–120, republished in idem, *Marchands d'Europe: Pratiques et savoires à l'époque moderne*, ed. Jacques Bottin and Marie-Louise Pelus-Kaplan (Paris: Editions Rue d'Ulm, 2002), 281–293.

5. Raymond de Roover famously equated *communis aestimatio* with market competition for the purpose of depicting Scholastic thought as a precursor to economic liberalism in his "The Concept of the Just Price: Theory and Economic Policy," *Journal of Economic History* 18, no. 4 (1958): 418–434. A less anachronistic examination of the meaning of this concept appears in Monica Martinat, *Le juste marché: Le systéme annonaire romain aux XVIe et XVIIe siècles* (Rome: Ecole française de Rome, 2004), esp. 73–76.

6. On the political economy of Colbert, his legacy, and a historiographical revision of both, see Philippe Minard, *La fortune du colbertisme: État et industrie dans la France des Lumières* (Paris: Fayard, 1998); idem, "'France colbertiste' versus 'Angleterre libèrale'? Un myth du XVIIIe siècle," in *Les idées passent-elles la Manche? Savoirs, représentations, pratiques (France-Angleterre, Xe–XXe siècles)*, ed. Jean-Philippe Genet and François-Joseph Ruggiu (Paris: Presses de l'Université Paris-Sorbonne, 2007), 197–209.

7. Benjamin Braude, "The Myth of the Sephardi Economic Superman," in *Trading Cultures: The Worlds of Western Merchants*, ed. Jeremy Adelman and Stephen Aron (Turnhout, Belgium: Brepols, 2001), 165–194; and idem, "Christians, Jews, and the Myth of Turkish Commercial Incompetence," in *Relazioni economiche tra Europa e mondo islamico, secc. XIII–XVIII (Atti della XXXVIII settimana di studi, Istituto Francesco Datini, Prato)* ed. Simonetta Cavaciocchi (Florence: Le Monnier, 2007), 219–239.

8. Jochen Hoock, "Le phénomène Savary et l'innovation en matière commerciale en France aux XVIIe et XVIIIe siècles," in *Innovations et renouveaux techniques de l'Antiquité à nos jours: Actes du colloque international de Mulhouse (septembre 1987)*, ed. Jean-Pierre Kintz (Strasbourg, France: Oberlin, 1989), 113–123, at 117.

9. In his preface, Savary spoke of "us & coustumes de la mer" as one of his subjects. The expression was not exclusive to Cleirac, but his was the only book by that title in Old Regime France. Jacques Savary, *Le parfait négociant, ou, Instruction generale pour ce qui regarde le commerce de toute sorte de marchandises, tant de France que des pays estranger* (Paris: Chez Louis Billaine, 1675), unpaginated preface, last page. Because multiple editions of both this and other texts by Savary and his sons exist, I include the publication date in parentheses in the second citation of each.

10. Savary, *Le parfait négociant* (1675), 121 (book 1, ch. 19: "De l'origine des lettres de change, & de leur utilité pour le commerce"). This chapter was reprinted without any changes in all of the book's subsequent editions and translations. A translation is provided in appendix 4. Further citations of this chapter omit the relevant bibliographical details.

11. Maréschal contested the assertion of "Cynus docteur de delà de Mons" ("doctor Cynus from the other side of the Alps"), who, finding these bills impious, apparently attributed their invention to the French. Mathias Maréschal, *Traicté des changes et rechanges licites et illicites* (Paris: Chez Nicolas Buon, 1625), 25. He was likely referring to Cinus de Pistorio (1270–1336), but I have not been able to identify any specific passage that might support this assertion. I appreciate Lawrin Armstrong's guidance in canvassing the relevant literature.

12. Henri Hauser, "Le 'parfait négociant' de Jacques Savary," *Revue d'historie économique et sociale* 13 (1925): 1–28, at 2–3.

13. Like other guilds, mercers did not formally distinguish between retail and wholesale

merchants in the same trade but operated on the basis of an oligarchic structure dominated by the latter: Ronda Larmour, "A Merchant Guild of Sixteenth-Century France: The Grocers of Paris," *Economic History Review* 20, no. 3 (1967): 467–481, at 471. In eighteenth-century Lyon, a town dominated by silk manufacturing and financial fairs, the drapers' guild, which included both wholesale and retail traders, was the richest and most influential of the guilds: Maurice Garden, *Lyon et les Lyonnais au XVIIIe siècle* (Paris: Les Belles-Lettres, 1970), 189, 198.

14. Hauser, "Le 'parfait négociant' de Jacques Savary," 11.

15. Estien[n]e Cleirac, *Usance du négoce ou commerce de la banque des lettres change* (Bordeaux: Par Guillaume da Court, 1656), 15; Père Mathias de Saint-Jean [Jean Eon], *Le commerce honorable ou considerations politiques* (Nantes: Guillaume le Monnier, 1646).

16. Savary, *Le parfait négociant* (1675), 3, 1 (book 1, ch. 1: "De la necessité et utilité du commerce").

17. François Marchetty, *Discours sur le négoce des gentilshommes de la ville de Marseille* (Marseilles: Chez Charles Brebion & Iean Penot, 1671), 7. For the context of these debates, see Junko Thérèse Takeda, *Between Commerce and Crown: Marseille and the Early Modern Mediterranean* (Baltimore: Johns Hopkins University Press, 2011), 15, 50–51.

18. Cited in ibid., 36.

19. Savary, *Le parfait négociant* (1675), 1 (book 1, ch. 1).

20. Ibid., unpaginated preface.

21. The term *mercantilism* was introduced into the English vocabulary via Gustav von Schmoller's 1896 translation of a chapter from his *Studien über die wirthschaftliche Politik Friedrichs des Grossen*: Schmoller, *The Mercantile System and Its Historical Significance in Prussian History* (New York: Macmillan and Co., 1896). For a recent engagement with the usages of this term, especially in relation to the history of British trade but with relevance for early modern Europe at large, see Philip J. Stern and Carl Wennerlind, eds., *Mercantilism Reimagined: Political Economy in Early Modern Britain and Its Empire* (Oxford: Oxford University Press, 2014).

22. Guy Rowlands, *Dangerous and Dishonest Men: The International Bankers of Louis XIV's France* (New York: Palgrave Macmillan, 2015). The term *financier* was used to indicate tax farmers and royal agents charged with tax collection and carried more negative connotations than *banquier*, which referred to those engaged in private finance rather than commodity trade: Herbert Lüthy, *La banque protestante en France de la révocaion de l'Edit de Nante à la Révolution*, 2 vols. (Paris: S.E.V.P.E.N., 1959), 1:10.

23. Savary, *Le parfait négociant* (1675), 122 (book 1, ch. 19).

24. Idem, *Parères ou avis et conseils sur les plus importantes matieres du commerce* (Paris: Chez Jean Guignard, 1688), 129 (Parère XIV).

25. Ibid., 128 (Parère XIV).

26. Ibid., 145 (Parère XIV).

27. Ibid., 693–701 (Parère LVIII).

28. The same logic informed the writing of several sixteenth-century Spanish authors: Michael Thomas D'Emic, *Justice in the Marketplace in Early Modern Spain: Saravia, Villalón, and the Religious Origins of Economic Analysis* (Lanham, MD: Lexington Books, 2014), 136.

29. Savary, *Le parfait négociant* (1675), 34 (book II, ch. 47).

30. Idem, *Le parfait négociant* (Geneva: Chez Jean Herman Widerhold, 1676), 66 (part II, ch. 47). The same formulation figures in idem, *Le parfait négociant . . . seconde ed., reveuë, corrigée, & augmentée par l'auteur* (Geneva: Chez Jean Guignard, 1679), 118 (part II, book 1, ch. 8).

31. Idem, *Le parfait négociant* (1679), 157 (part II, book 2, ch. 4).

32. Ibid., 447–448, 492–493 (part II, book 5, ch. 3).

33. Ibid., 493 (part II, book 5, ch. 3).

34. Gaston Rambert, ed., *Histoire du commerce de Marseille*, 6 vols. (Paris: Plon, 1949–1959), 4:11–13; Carrière, *Négociants marseillais*, 319–330.

35. Ina Baghdiantz McCabe, *Orientalism in Early Modern France: Eurasian Trade, Exoticism, and the Ancien Régime* (Oxford: Berg, 2008), 188–189. On Armenians and the silk trade, see Rudolph P. Matthee, *The Politics of Trade in Safavid Iran: Silk for Silver, 1600–1730* (Cambridge: Cambridge University Press, 2006); and Sebouh David Aslanian, *From the Indian Ocean to the Mediterranean: The Global Trade Networks of Armenian Merchants from New Julfa* (Berkeley: University of California Press, 2011).

36. Adolphe Crémieux, "Un établissement juif à Marseille au XVIIe siècle," *Revue des études juives* 55 (1908): 119–145; Carrière, *Négociants marseillais*, 283.

37. David Hume, "On National Characters," in *Essays, Moral, Political, and Literary*, ed. Eugene F. Miller (Indianapolis, IN: Liberty Classics, 1987), 197–215, at 205. Hume offered no justification for these two divergent characterizations. In an accompanying footnote, he called attention to the self-policing of minority groups and developed an argument that foreshadowed Max Weber's theory of "pariah capitalism" (chapter 8): "A small sect or society amidst a greater are commonly most regular in their morals; because they are more remarked, and the faults of individuals draw dishonour on the whole. The only exception to this rule is, when the superstition and prejudices of the large society are so strong as to throw an infamy on the smaller society, independent of their morals. For in that case, having no character either to save or gain, they become careless of their behaviour, except among themselves" (205n7).

38. For a comparison with other genres in which a tendency toward more dispassionate descriptions of Jews has been detected, particularly in eighteenth-century Germany, see R. Po-Chia Hsia, "Christian Ethnographies of Jews in Early Modern Germany," in *The Expulsion of Jews: 1492 and After*, ed. Raymond B. Waddington and A. H. Williamson (New York: Garland, 1994), 223–235; Yaacov Deutsch, *Judaism in Christian Eyes: Ethnographic Descriptions of Jews and Judaism in Early Modern Europe*, trans. Avi Aronsky (Oxford: Oxford University Press, 2012).

39. Charles D. Tékéian, "Marseille, la Provence et les Arméniens," *Mémoires de l'Institut Historique de Provence* 6 (1929): 5–65, at 12–15.

40. Savary, *Le parfait négociant* (1679), 532 (part II, book 5, ch. 8).

41. Ibid., 534–535 (part II, book 5, ch. 8). Demographic data about the inhabitants of Egypt are extremely scarce for the period before the nineteenth century. Reasonable estimates place Cairo's population at 385,000 around 1550 and describe a demographic decline thereafter: André Raymond, *Grandes villes arabes à l'époque ottomane* (Paris: Sindbad, 1985), 54. Egypt's Jewish residents were concentrated in Alexandria and Cairo, and even the highest figures put them at no more than 5,000 in the late fifteenth century: Abraham David, "Jewish Settlements from the 16th Century to the 18th Century" [in Hebrew] and Sergio Della Pergola, "Jewish Population in the 19th and 20th Centuries" [in Hebrew], both in *Jews in Ottoman Egypt (1517–1914)* [in Hebrew], ed. Jacob M. Landau (Jerusalem: Misgav Yerushalaim, 1988), 13–26 and 27–62, respectively. I am grateful to Phillip Ackerman-Lieberman and Alan Mikhail for helping me canvass the secondary literature.

42. Philippe Bornier, *Conférences des nouvelles ordonnances de Louis XVI*, 2 vols. (Paris: Chez les Associez choisis par ordre de Sa Majesté pour l'impression de ses nouvelles Ordonnances,

1681), 2:341. A first edition of 1678 is sometimes cited, but I was not able to locate it. At least five editions of this compilation appeared between 1681 and 1755.

43. Ibid., 2:341, 412.

44. Jean Toubeau, *Les institutes du droit consulaire, ou, La jurisprudence des marchands* (Bourges: Chez Jean Guignard, 1682), 180. This work is mentioned by Jean Hilaire, *Introduction historique au droit commercial* (Paris: Presses universitaires de France, 1986), 80; and Amalia D. Kessler, *A Revolution in Commerce: The Parisian Merchant Court and the Rise of Commercial Society in Eighteenth-Century France* (New Haven, CT: Yale University Press, 2007), 99 and passim.

45. Toubeau, *Les institutes*, 545, 547.

46. Ibid., 586–587, 647–648.

47. Antoine Furetière, *Dictionnaire universel*, 3 vols. (The Hague and Rotterdam: Chez Arnout & Reinier Leers, 1690), s.v. "assurance" and "change." Both entries were reproduced verbatim in *Dictionnaire universel françois et latin*, better known as *Dictionnaire de Trévoux*, which the Jesuits promoted after Furetière's work had been expanded by a Huguenot refugee, Henri Basnage de Bauval, author of *Tolérance des religions* (Rotterdam: H. de Graef, 1684). The *Dictionnaire de Trévoux* became one of the most colossal publications of the eighteenth century, with as many as seven new in-folio editions and one abbreviated in-quarto issue. Isabelle Turcan, ed., *Quand le dictionnaire de Trévoux rayonne sur l'Europe des lumières* (Paris: Harmattan, 2009), 139. On the borrowings between language dictionaries and the *Encyclopédie*, see Marie Leca-Tsiomis, *Écrire l'Encyclopédie: Diderot, de l'usage des dictionnaires à la grammaire philosophique* (Oxford: Voltaire Foundation, 1999).

48. Toubeau's conclusions were imprecise because he failed to make an accurate distinction between third-party premium insurance and earlier risk-sharing contracts cited by ancient Greek and Roman authors: *Les institutes*, 647–648.

49. *Journal des sçavans*, May 11, 1682, 91.

50. Jacques Dupuis de la Serra, *L'art des lettres de change suivant l'usage des plus célèbres places de l'Europe* (Paris: Chez l'auteur, A. Vvarin, 1690), unnumbered preface. Nothing is known about this author except for his works. Savary described him as "one of the most knowledgeable" in matters of commerce: Savary, *Parères*, unnumbered preface.

51. Dupuis de la Serra, *L'art des lettres*, 6–7.

52. Ibid., 7. In support of this idea, Dupuis de la Serra quoted a recent history of the city of Lyon penned by a royal official named Claude de Rubys (1533–1613). In reality, Rubys merely paraphrased Villani's account of the thirteenth-century conflicts between the Guelfs and the Ghibellines in Florence and how wealthy Guelfs fled to Lyon, where they established the banks from which they sent remittances back to Florence. "Et ie ne veux obmettre ce qu'escrit d'eux leur historien Gio. Villani. Si dice (dict-il) che l'uscita che fecero i Guelphi di Fiorenza fu cagione & principio de la lor richezza. Per che à l'hora molti usciti Fiorentini andavano ultra i monti in Francia, che mai non vi erano usati, onde poi molte ricchezze, ne tornarono in Fiorenza": Claude de Rubys, *Histoire véritable de la ville de Lyon* (Lyon: B. Nugo, 1604), 289–289, citing *Croniche di messer Giovanni Villani* (Venice: Bartholomeo Zanetti Casterzagense, 1537), fol. 60r (book 6, ch. 87). On de Ruby, see "Rubys, Claude, de," in *Biographie universelle ancienne et moderne*, 52 vols. (Paris: Chez L. G. Michaud, 1811–1828), 39:248–249.

53. Judging from how rare the 1690 reprint is in today's library collections in comparison to

later editions, its publisher initially did not realize how much demand there was for a treatise on bills of exchange in vernacular French.

54. *Commentaire sur l'ordonnance du commerce du mois de mars 1673 par Jousse avec des notes et explications . . . par V. Bécane suivi du Traité du contrat de Change par Dupuy de la Serre* (Poitiers: Mesdames Loriot, 1828).

55. Pierre Jeannin, "Les manuels de pratique commerciale imprimés pour les marchands français (XVIe–XVIIIe siècle)," in *Le négoce international (XIIIe–XXe siècle)*, ed. François Crouzet (Paris: Economica, 1989), 35–57, at 36, republished in idem, *Marchands d'Europe*, 377–395, at 378. Claude Naulot was a merchant from Lyon and the author of three short treatises on measurements, currencies, and accounting: Naulot, *Le vray tarif par lequel on peut avec une grande facilité faire toutes sortes de Comptes* (Lyon: Aux dépens de l'Auteur, 1681); *La manière de faire les comptes par les premières règles de l'arithmétique* (Lyon: Aux dépens de l'Auteur, 1686); *Nouveau traité des changes étrangers, qui se font dans les principales places de l'Europe*, new ed. (Paris: Chez Jacques Lyons, 1700). All Naulot's works were reprinted more than once.

56. Samuel Ricard, *Traité general du commerce* (Amsterdam: Chez Paul Marret, 1700), 89. The debt to Savary is evident in the phrasing of the legend as well as in the detail attributing to Ghibellines the invention of re-exchange. The treatise was well received, and the legend is repeated in all of its first five editions through 1732. It was, however, omitted from the 1781 edition, which is also the version that was translated into German: idem, *Handbuch der Kaufleute*, 3 vols., trans. Thomas Heinrich Gadebusch and Christian Wichmann (Greifswald: Anton Ferdinand Röse, 1783–1801). The chapter on the origins of bills of exchange is also omitted from the English adaptations (chapter 7, note 28). Ricard quoted his previous work when he repeated the legend in *L'art de bien tenir les livres de comptes en parties doubles a l'italienne* (Amsterdam: Chez Paul Marret, 1709), ix. Beginning in 1722, his son, Jean Pierre Ricard, edited several expanded editions of Jacques Le Moine de L'Espine's 1694 *Le negoce d'Amsterdam*, but curiously, he included no mention of the legend (chapter 7).

57. Ricard, *Traité general* (1700), 88. *Smous/smousen* was a derogative epithet used in reference to Ashkenazim across the Dutch world: Lynn Hunt, Margaret C. Jacob, and Wijnand Mijnhardt, *The Book that Changed Europe: Picart and Bernard's Religious Ceremonies of the World* (Cambridge, MA: Harvard University Press, 2010), 177; Natalie Zemon Davis, "Creole Languages and Their Uses: The Example of Colonial Suriname," *Historical Research* 82 (2009): 268–284, at 278.

58. Ricard, *Traité general* (1700), 95.

59. Pierre Gobain, *Le commerce en son jour* (Bordeaux: Chez Matthieu Chappuis, 1702), 1–2, opened his treatise with an account of the origins of bills of exchange that gave equal weight to the legend and to the alternative story relayed by Rubys, which arguably derived from Dupuis de la Serra (see note 52 in this chapter).

60. Jacques Savary des Brûlons and Philémon-Louis Savary, *Dictionnaire universel de commerce*, 3 vols. (Paris: Chez Jacques Estienne, 1723–1730). On this text's composition and editorial success, see Jean-Claude Perrot, *Une histoire intellectuelle de l'économie politique, XVIIe–XVIIIe siècle* (Paris: École des Hautes Études en Sciences Sociales, 1992), 102–103. The German and English versions of this work, compiled by Carl Günther Ludovici and Malachy Postlethwayt, respectively, are discussed in chapter 7.

61. Perrot, *Une histoire intellectuelle*, 100.

62. Whereas the elder Savary's treatment of the legend had omitted marine insurance, the *Dictionnaire universel de commerce* affirmed without a shadow of a doubt that Jews had invented both. Savary des Brûlons and Savary, *Dictionnaire universel de commerce* (1723–1730), 1:180, s.v. "assurance," and 2:503, s.v. "lettre de change." See appendix 4 for a translation of both entries.

63. Ibid., 2:443, s.v. "Juif." No companion entry for "Armenian," for example, figures in the first edition of this work, and only a descriptive five-line entry devoted to the subject appears in later ones: Jacques Savary des Brûlons and Philémon-Louis Savary, *Dictionnaire universel de commerce . . . Nouv. ed., exactement revûe, corrigée, et considerablement augmentée*, 5 vols. (Copenhagen: C. & A. Philibert, 1759–1765), 1:216, s.v. "Armeniens."

64. In the second edition of the *Dictionnaire universel de commerce*, Jews even appear in the definition of a plant similar to chicory, from which the ancients are said to have extracted oil for their lamps and which both Jews and the poor are said to use as nourishment in order to survive: Savary des Brûlons and Savary, *Dictionnaire* (1759–1765), 2:1, s.v. "Cicus." No edition of this dictionary includes an entry on usury.

65. All citations in this paragraph come from Savary des Brûlons and Savary, *Dictionnaire universel de commerce* (1723–1730), 2:444–445, s.v. "Juif." The word *fripon* and its cognates became inseparable from most mentions of Jews in the course of the eighteenth century (see note 86 below and chapter 6 more generally).

66. Ibid., 1:608, s.v. "boul."

67. Antoyne de Montchrestien, *Traicté de l'economie politique: dédié en 1615 au roy et à la reyne mère du roy* (Rouen: Jean Osmont, 1615; anastatic reprint: Geneva: Slatkine Reprints, 1970), 191–192, also mentioned in Jonathan I. Israel, *European Jewry in the Age of Mercantilism, 1550–1750*, rev. ed. (Oxford: Clarendon Press, 1989), 56.

68. The highest modern estimate puts the Spanish and Portuguese Jewish population of Amsterdam at 5,000 in the early eighteenth century but has been contested: Hubert P. H. Nusteling, "The Jews in the Republic of the United Provinces: Origins, Numbers and Dispersion," in *Dutch Jewry: Its History and Secular Culture (1500–2000)*, ed. Jonathan Israel and Reinier Salverda (Leiden: Brill, 2002), 43–62, at 52.

69. Savary des Brûlons and Savary, *Dictionnaire* (1723–1730), 2:444, s.v. "Juif."

70. Francesca Trivellato, *The Familiarity of Strangers: The Sephardic Diaspora, Livorno, and Cross-Cultural Trade in the Early Modern Period* (New Haven, CT: Yale University Press, 2009), 71.

71. Savary des Brûlons and Savary, *Dictionnaire* (1759–1765), 5:230, s.v. "Commerce de la Provence."

72. Lucette Valensi, *The Birth of the Despot: Venice and the Sublime Porte*, trans. Arthur Denner (Ithaca, NY: Cornell University Press, 1993[1987]).

73. Jean-Baptiste Tavernier, *The Six Voyages . . . Through Turky into Persia and the East-Indies Finished in the Year 1670*, trans. J. P. (London: R. L. and M. P., 1678), 202. The French original described Jews as "cette peste et cette gangraine": Tavernier, *Les six voyages . . . en Turquie, en Perse et aux Indes*, 2 vols. (Paris: Chez Gervais Clouzier et Claude Barbin, 1676), 1:527 (book 5, ch. 2).

74. Savary des Brûlons and Savary, *Dictionnaire* (1759–1765), 1:327, s.v. "Banians."

75. Louis de Beausobre, *Introduction générale à l'étude de la politique, des finances, et du commerce* (Berlin: Chez Chretien Frederic Voss, 1764), 340. Already the Savary brothers had drawn

the same equivalence: "The Chinese are in Asia like the Jews are in Europe: they can be found wherever there is a profit to make, they are cheaters, usurers, untrustworthy, skilled and subtle when handling a propitious business; and all this under the appearance of simplicity and good faith that can surprise even those who are most attentive and mistrustful": Savary des Brûlons and Savary, *Dictionnaire universel de commerce* (1723–1730), 1:1175, s.v. "commerce." For the presence of such analogies among the Dutch, who ruled Batavia (modern-day Jakarta), where Chinese traders had a significant presence, see Blake Smith, "Colonial Emulation: Sinophobia, Ethnic Stereotypes and Imperial Anxieties in Late Eighteenth-Century Economic Thought," *History of European Ideas* 43, no. 1 (2017): 1–15.

76. The description appeared in the second edition of Jacques Savary des Brûlons and Philemon-Louis Savary, *Dictionnaire universel de commerce*, 2 vols. (Amsterdam: chez les Jansons à Waesberge, 1726), 1:701, s.v. "Cherafs." It was reproduced unchanged in all subsequent editions, including *Dictionnaire universel de commerce*, 3 vols. (Paris: Chez la veuve Estienne, 1741), 2:267, s.v. "Cherafs"; *Dictionnaire universel de commerce*, 3 vols. (Paris: Chez la veuve Estienne et fils, 1748), 2:267, s.v. "Cherafs"; *Dictionnaire universel de commerce*, 4 vols. (Paris: Chez la veuve Estienne, 1750), 1:898, s.v. "Cherafs"; *Dictionnaire universel de commerce* (1759–1765), 1:1041, s.v. "Cherafs." The term *cheraf* was introduced into French, or at least popularized, by Tavernier, *Les six voyages*, 2:11–13.

77. Shamakhi was located along one of the routes by which Europeans travelers, merchants, and adventurers reached Iran. Most of its inhabitants spoke Turkish, but some also spoke Persian, Armenian, and Georgian. André Thevet had called attention to its diverse population in *La cosmographie universelle*, 2 vols. (Paris: Chez Guillaume Chaudiere, 1575), 1:280 (book VIII, ch. 15). The city remained a locus of French Orientalism in the nineteenth century, as illustrated by Gobineau's short story *La danseuse of Shamkha* (*The Dancer of Shamakhi*): Arthur, Comte de Gobineau, *Les nouvelles asiatiques*, 10th ed. (Paris: Gallimard, 1949), 19–80. I thank Abbas Amanat for bringing this text to my attention.

78. The term *cheraf* appeared more and more frequently in the French travel literature of the eighteenth century. In one such text, an Indian merchant (*cheraf*) was described alternatively as "an official appointed to issue or to receive bills of exchange" or as a "money-changer"—in both cases he was said to be potentially unreliable: Rousselot de Surgy, *Histoire générale des voyages*, 20 vols., new ed. (Paris: Chez Pierre de Hondt, 1746–1801), 13:36, 175 (see also 496–497 for the currency conversions operated by "cherafs").

79. See the section titled "Juifs condamnés pour un crime enorme qui revolte l'humanité" in François Gayot de Pitaval, ed., *Causes célebres et intéressantes, avec les jugemens qui les ont decidées*, 20 vols. (Paris: Chez Charles Nicolas Poirion, 1734–1743), 18:289–435. The section appeared in every subsequent edition, in either extended or abbreviated form. An abridged edition, compiled by François Richer (1718–1790), a prolific translator and editor, included the Metz trial of 1670 but not the commentary that relayed the legend: Gayot de Pitaval, *Causes célebres et intéressantes, avec les jugemens qui les ont decidées*, 2 vols. (London: Chez H. Hughs, 1777), 2:248–263. Sarah Maza includes Gayot de Pitaval's work among the "courtroom literature" that she argues shaped the political culture of prerevolutionary France, although she notes that its audience was not as large as that of more scandalous publications in the genre: Maza, *Private Lives and Public Affairs: The Causes Célèbres of Prerevolutionary France* (Berkeley: University of California Press, 1993), 25–26.

80. Gayot de Pitaval described Jewish history since the advent of Christianity as a sequence of punishments of Jews' crimes at the hands of God and Christian authorities. In his narrative, the Jewish invention of bills of exchange followed a discussion of Philip Augustus's persecutions, even if, in keeping with the standard narrative, it was said to have occurred during the implausibly long stretch of time spanning the reigns of Dagobert I, Philip Augustus, and Philip the Tall. Gayot de Pitaval, *Causes célebres*, 18:413–414.

81. Ibid., 18: 328–329.

82. Philip T. Hoffman, *Growth in a Traditional Society: The French Countryside, 1450–1815* (Princeton, NJ: Princeton University Press, 1996); Philippe Minard and Denis Woronoff, eds., *L'argent des campagnes: Échanges, monnaie, credit dans la France rurale d'Ancien Régime; Journée d'études tenue à Bercy, le 18 décembre 2000* (Paris: Comité pour l'histoire économique et financière, 2003). For a detailed study on the peasant credit economy in the eighteenth (rather than seventeenth) century, see Gilles Posterl-Vinay, *La terre e l'argent: L'agricolture et le crédit en France du XVIIe au début de XXe siècle* (Paris: Albin Michel, 1998).

83. Sharon Kettering, *Patrons, Brokers, and Clients* (New York: Oxford University Press, 1986); Jonathan Dewald, *Pont-St-Pierre, 1398–1789: Lordship, Community, and Capitalism in Early Modern France* (Berkeley: University of California Press, 1987); and idem, *Aristocratic Experience and the Origins of Modern Culture: France, 1570–1715* (Berkeley: University of California Press, 1993), esp. 146–173.

84. The secondary literature on French Atlantic port cities is tilted heavily toward the eighteenth century. Two notable exceptions are Gayle K. Brunelle, *The New World Merchants of Rouen, 1559–1630* (Kirksville, MO: Sixteenth Century Journal Publishers, 1991); and André Lespagnol, *Messieurs de Saint-Malo: Une élite négociante au temps de Louis XIV*, 2 vols. (Rennes, France: Presses universitaires de Rennes, 1997).

85. Julie Hardwick, *Family Business: Litigation and the Political Economies of Daily Life in Early Modern France* (Oxford: Oxford University Press, 2009), 10.

86. Furetière, *Dictionnaire universel*, s.v. "Juif." In Latin, *faluppa* was an object of little value. Jews in many areas were confined to the selling of secondhand clothing (*fripes*). See also chapter 6, note 63. A Catholic, Furetière held orthodox religious views: in his dictionary, Jesuits were praised, Calvinists were deemed heretics, Mohammed was a false prophet, and Lutherans were omitted altogether. See Walter W. Ross, "Antoine Furetière's *Dictionnaire universel*," in *Notable Encyclopedias of the Seventeenth and Eighteenth Centuries: Nine Predecessors of the Encyclopédie*, ed. Frank A. Kafker (Oxford: Voltaire Foundation at the Taylor Institution, 1981), 53–67, at 62–63.

87. Furetière, *Dictionnaire universel*, s.v. "usure." An eighteenth-century dictionary of trade followed suit: "In [the language of] commerce, we sometimes resort to the word 'Jew' to designate a usurious merchant or to speak of excessive interest." Jean Paganucci, *Manuel historique, géographique et politique des négocians*, 3 vols. (Lyon: Chez Jean-Marie Bruyset, 1762), 2:225–226, s.v. "Juif."

88. Pertinent examples appear in Couchot, *Le practicien universel, ou le droit françois, et la pratique de toutes les jurisdictions du Royaume*, 3 vols. (Paris: J. Lefevre, 1697–1707), 1:95–100, 279–282; idem, *Le traité du commerce de terre et de mer a l'usage des marchands, banquiers, agens de change & gens d'affaires avec la pratique suivie dans les jurisdictions consulaires, & dans les autres tribunaux, où les contestations pour le fait du commerce sont portées*, 2 vols. (Paris: Chez Jacques Le Febvre, 1710); Jacques-Pierre Brillon, *Dictionnaire civil et canonique contenant les etimologies,*

définitions, divisions & principes du droit françois (Paris: Chez Augustin Besoigne et Jerome Bobin, 1687), 546–549; idem, *Dictionnaire des arrests, ou Jurisprudence universelle des Parlemens de France et autres tribuaux*, 3 vols. (Paris: Chez Guillaume Cavelier, 1711), 2:596–599.

89. The lawsuit is recounted in Joseph-Félix-Guillaume Martin, *Traité des impétrations, ou Lettres qu'accordent les chancelleries établies près les cours souveraines du royaume* (Toulouse: D. Desclassan, 1786), 129–138.

90. Herbert Lüthy, *La banque protestante en France de la révocation de l'édict de Nantes à la révolution*, 2 vols. (Paris: S.E.V.P.E.N., 1959), 1:121–125, 188–226; Andrea Addobbati, "Le banquier juif du Roi Soleil: Notes de recherche sur l'anecdote entre le XVIIe et le XVIIIe siècle," *Rives méditerranéennes* 49 (2014): 35–60; Rowlands, *Dangerous and Dishonest Men*. Prone to outlandish identifications of all devious speculators as Jewish, some 200 years later Werner Sombart spread this mischaracterization of Bernard—and even hinted at the possibility that John Law might have been Jewish on the spurious grounds that his last name derived from Levy: Sombart, *The Jews and Modern Capitalism*, trans. M. Epstein (London: T. F. Unwin, 1913 [1911]), 92.

91. Rambert, *Histoire du commerce de Marseille*, 4:301–330.

92. Tékéian, "Marseille, la Provence," 53; Olivier Raveux, "Entre réseau communautaire intercontinental et intégration locale: la colonie marseillaise des marchands arméniens de la Nouvelle Djoulfa (Ispahan), 1669–1695," *Revue d'histoire moderne et contemporaine* 59, no. 1 (2012): 83–101.

93. Cited in Takeda, *Between Commerce and Crown*, 99.

94. Simone Luzzatto, *Discorso circa il stato de gl'hebrei et in particular dimoranti nell'inclita città di Venetia* (Venice: Gioanne Calleoni, 1638), esp. 28r–30v. On the context of this work, see Benjamin Ravid, *Economics and Toleration in Seventeenth-Century Venice: The Background and Context of the Discorso of Simone Luzzatto* (Jerusalem: Central Press, 1978). On the demographics of the Jews of Venice, see Giovanni Favero and Francesca Trivellato, "Gli abitanti del ghetto di Venezia in età moderna: Dati e ipotesi," *Zakhor: Rivista della storia degli ebrei in Italia* 7 (2004): 9–50.

95. "The Humble Addresses," in *Menasseh ben Israel's Mission to Oliver Cromwell: Being a Reprint of the Pamphlets Published by Menasseh ben Israel to Promote the Re-admission of the Jews to England, 1649–1656*, ed. Lucien Wolf (London: Macmillan, 1901), 82–89. See also Benjamin Ravid, " 'How Profitable the Nation of the Jewes Are': The Humble Addresses of Menasseh ben Israel and the Discorso of Simone Luzzatto," in *Mystics, Philosophers, and Politicians: Essays in Jewish Intellectual History in Honor of Alexander Altmann*, ed. Jehuda Reinharz and Daniel Swetschinski (Durham, NC: Duke University Press, 1982), 159–180.

Chapter 6: Between Usury and the "Spirit of Commerce"

1. The absence of any discussion of Jewish emancipation even in recent works is telling: David Andress, ed., *The Oxford Handbook of the French Revolution* (Oxford: Oxford University Press, 2015); Alan Forrest and Matthias Middell, eds., *The Routledge Companion to the French Revolution in World History* (New York: Routledge, 2016). Truncated accounts of Jewish emancipation appear in Peter McPhee, ed., *Companion to the French Revolution* (Malden, MA: John Wiley & Sons, 2012).

2. Londa Schiebinger, *Nature's Body: Gender in the Making of Modern Science* (Boston:

Beacon Press, 1993); Silvia Sebastiani, *The Scottish Enlightenment: Race, Gender, and the Limits of Progress*, trans. Jeremy Carden (New York: Palgrave Macmillan, 2013[2008]).

3. David Sorkin, "The Port Jew: Notes Towards a Social Type," *Journal of Jewish Studies* 50, no. 1 (1999): 87–97, at 97. See also Lois Dubin, *The Port Jews of Habsburg Trieste: Absolutist Politics and Enlightenment Culture* (Stanford, CA: Stanford University Press, 1999), esp. 198–214; and David Sorkin, "Port Jews and the Three Regions of Emancipation," in *Port Jews: Jewish Communities in Cosmopolitan Maritime Trading Centres, 1550–1950*, ed. David Cesarani (London: Frank Crass, 2002), 15–46.

4. The most recent recasting of emancipation as a moment of rupture because of the legal revolution and the makeover in political thought that it entailed is articulated in Kenneth Stow, *Anna and Tranquillo: Catholic Anxiety and Jewish Protest in an Age of Revolutions* (New Haven, CT: Yale University Press, 2016).

5. Amid the flurry of publications timed to coincide with the Revolution's bicentenary in 1989, few treated economic subjects. A rare exception was a special issue of *Revue du Nord* also printed as a standalone volume: Gérard Gayot and Jean-Pierre Hirsch, eds., *La Révolution française et le développement du capitalism: Actes du colloque de Lille, 19–21 novembre 1987* (Villeneuve d'Ascq, France: Revue du Nord-Collection Histoire, 1989). Soon after, Jean-Claude Perrot collected his pioneering studies of French economic thought in *Une histoire intellectuelle de l'économie politique, XVIIe–XVIIIe siècle* (Paris: École des Hautes Études en Sciences Sociales, 1992). A partial list of recent English-language works on eighteenth-century French commerce broadly conceived would include Emma Rothschild, *Economic Sentiments: Adam Smith, Condorcet, and the Enlightenment* (Cambridge, MA: Harvard University Press, 2001); John Shovlin, *The Political Economy of Virtue: Luxury, Patriotism, and the Origins of the French Revolution* (Ithaca, NY: Cornell University Press, 2006); Michael Sonenscher, *Before the Deluge: Public Debt, Inequality, and the Intellectual Origins of the French Revolution* (Princeton, NJ: Princeton University Press, 2007); Henry C. Clark, *Compass of Society: Commerce and Absolutism in Old-Regime France* (Lanham, MD: Lexington Books, 2007); Paul Cheney, *Revolutionary Commerce: Globalization and the French Monarchy* (Cambridge, MA: Harvard University Press, 2010); William H. Sewell, Jr., "The Empire of Fashion and the Rise of Capitalism in Eighteenth-Century France," *Past and Present* 206, no. 1 (2010): 81–120; idem, "Connecting Capitalism to the French Revolution: The Parisian Promenade and the Origins of Civic Equality in Eighteenth-Century France," *Critical Historical Studies* 1, no. 1 (2014): 5–46; Liana Vardi, *The Physiocrats and the World of the Enlightenment* (Cambridge: Cambridge University Press, 2012); Anoush Fraser Terjanian, *Commerce and Its Discontents in Eighteenth-Century French Political Thought* (Cambridge: Cambridge University Press, 2013); Emma Rothschild, "Isolation and Economic Life in Eighteenth-Century France," *American Historical Review* 119, no. 4 (2014): 1055–1082; Rebecca L. Spang, *Stuff and Money in the Time of the French Revolution* (Cambridge, MA: Harvard University Press, 2015); Lauren R. Clay, "The Bourgeoisie, Capitalism, and the Origins of the French Revolution," in Andress, *Oxford Handbook of the French Revolution*, 21–39.

6. The point applies to the scholarship on "port Jews" (see note 3 above), but also to the most capacious study of the representations of Jewish commerce in European thought at the crossroads of early modernity and postemancipation, a work that gives limited consideration to the French Revolution but generally argues for a positive link between pro-commercial at-

titudes and emancipation: Jonathan Karp, *The Politics of Jewish Commerce: Economic Thought and Emancipation in Europe, 1638–1848* (Cambridge: Cambridge University Press, 2008).

7. Daniel Gordon offers a probing account of how the idea of *société* emerged in connection with allegorical meanings of *commerce*, including a sobering account of Montesquieu's *doux commerce*, but omits any treatment of how Jews figure in the texts he examines: Gordon, *Citizens Without Sovereignty: Equality and Sociability in French Thought, 1670–1789* (Princeton, NJ: Princeton University Press, 1994). See also Céline Spector, *Montesquieu: Pouvoir, richesses et sociétés* (Paris: Presses universitaires de France, 2004), esp. 145–166; and, more generally, the classic essay by Keith Michael Baker, "Enlightenment and the Institution of Society: Notes for a Conceptual History," in *Civil Society: History and Possibilities,* ed. Sudipta Kaviraj and Sunil Khilnani (Cambridge: Cambridge University Press, 2001), 84–104.

8. I say "Christian discourses" even if influential protagonists of the debates I review, including Montesquieu, Voltaire, and Dohm, were neither believers nor practicing Christians, because most of their ideas about Jews and Jewish economic roles stemmed from well-established Christian views.

9. Charles-Louis de Secondat baron de La Brède and of Montesquieu, *The Spirit of the Laws,* 2 vols., trans. Thomas Nugent (New York: Hafner, 1949), 1:364–366. Hereafter all citations from *The Spirit of Laws* come from this edition and are indicated solely by book and chapter number. The one exception is in note 32 below, where another translation is cited.

10. For three examples, chosen from classic and recent studies, see Melvin Richter, *The Political Theory of Montesquieu* (Cambridge: Cambridge University Press, 1977); Alan Macfarlane, *The Riddle of the Modern World: Of Liberty, Wealth and Equality* (New York: St. Martin's Press, 2000); Annelien de Dijn, *French Political Thought: From Montesquieu to Tocqueville; Liberty in a Levelled Society?* (Cambridge: Cambridge University Press, 2008).

11. The expression *doux commerce* owes as much to Montesquieu as to Albert Hirschman, who notes that it does not appear as such in Montesquieu's writings but argues, quite persuasively, that it is fair to treat Montesquieu as its main interpreter: Albert O. Hirschman, *The Passions and the Interests: Political Arguments for Capitalism Before its Triumph* (Princeton, NJ: Princeton University Press, 1977). Montesquieu used the terms *doux* and *douceur* in *The Spirit of the Laws* to characterize moderate government and cultural dispositions and was familiar with the expression *doux commerce,* which was in usage during his time. An early example of its use appears in Michel de Montaigne's *Essais* (1588): Terjanian, *Commerce and Its Discontents,* 12.

12. A nonexhaustive list of such incidental references includes Diana J. Schaub, *Erotic Liberalism: Women and Revolution in Montesquieu's Persian Letters* (Lanham, MD: Rowman & Littlefield, 1995), 127; Claude Morilhat, *Montesquieu: Politique et richesses* (Paris: Presses universitaires de France, 1996), 100; Euleggero Pii, "Montesquieu e l'*esprit de commerce,*" in *Leggere l'Esprit des lois: Stato, società e storia nel pensiero di Montesquieu,* ed. Domenico Felice (Naples: Liguori, 1998), 165–202, at 196; Catherine Larrère, "Montesquieu on Economics and Commerce," in *Montesquieu's Science of Politics: Essays on* The Spirit of Laws, ed. David W. Carrithers, Michael A. Mosher, and Paul A. Rahe (Lanham, MD: Rowman & Littlefield, 2001), 335–373, at 357, 363; Pierre Manent, *Cours familier de philosophie politique* (Paris: Fayard, 2001), 151–152, translated in English by Marc LePain as *A World Beyond Politics: A Defense of the Nation-State* (Princeton, NJ: Princeton University Press, 2006), 91; Pierre Force, *Self-Interest Before Adam Smith: A Genealogy of Economic Science* (Cambridge: Cambridge University Press, 2003), 151–152; Robert

Howse, "Montesquieu on Commerce, Conquest, War and Peace," *Brooklyn Journal of International Law* 31, no. 1 (2005–2006): 698–708, at 706; Céline Spector, *Montesquieu et l'émergence de l'économie politique* (Paris: Honoré Champion, 2006), 173–175; Paul Anthony Rahe, *Montesquieu and the Logic of Liberty: War, Religion, Commerce, Climate, Terrain, Technology, Uneasiness of Mind, the Spirit of Political Vigilance, and the Foundations of the Modern Republic* (New Haven, CT: Yale University Press, 2009), 182; Cheney, *Revolutionary Commerce*, 60; Andrew Scott Bibby, *Montesquieu's Political Economy* (New York: Palgrave Macmillan, 2016), 85.

13. Hirschman, *Passions and the Interests*, 72–74. Before Hirschman, it was rare for scholars of Montesquieu's economic thought to consider the role of Jews in it. See, e.g., Alain Cotta, "Le développement économique dans la pensée de Montesquieu," *Revue d'histoire économique et sociale* 35 (1957): 370–415; and Nicos E. Devletoglou, "Montesquieu and the Wealth of Nations," *Canadian Journal of Economics and Political Science* 29 (1963): 1–25. In a detailed summary of Montesquieu's chapters on commerce, Thomas L. Pangle, for whom, "with minor exceptions, Montesquieu's economic theory is an endorsement of laissez-faire economics *avant la lettre*," omits any mentions of Jews and bills of exchange: Pangle, *Montesquieu's Philosophy of Liberalism: A Commentary on* The Spirit of the Laws (Chicago: University of Chicago Press, 1973), 242. A fierce critic of John Law and his short-lived experiment with paper money, Montesquieu praised private credit at the same time that he decried the public debt: Montesquieu, *Persian Letters*, trans. Margaret Mauldon, introduction and notes by Andrew Kahn (Oxford: Oxford University Press, 2008), letters 22 and 138; and idem, *The Spirit of the Laws*, II, 4; XXII, 10; XXII, 17. The point has already been noted by Hirschman, *Passions and the Interests*, 75–76; and Spector, *Montesquieu et l'émergence*, 283–284.

14. Samuel Ettinger, "The Economic Activities of the Jews" [in Hebrew], in *Jews in Economic Life: Collected Essays in Memory of Arkadius Kahan (1920–1982)*, ed. Nachum Gross (Jerusalem: Zalman Shazar Center for the Furtherance of the Study of Jewish History, 1984), 13–24, at 17, English translation in *Jews in Early Modern Europe*, ed. Jonathan Karp and Francesca Trivellato (London: Taylor and Francis, forthcoming); Karp, *Politics of Jewish Commerce*, 92–93; Jerry Z. Muller, *Capitalism and the Jews* (Princeton, NJ: Princeton University Press, 2011), 20. A subtler reading is proposed by Maurice Kriegel, "Juifs," in *Dictionnaire raisonné de l'Occident médiéval*, ed. Jacques Le Goff and Jean-Claude Schmitt (Paris: Fayard, 1999), 569–586, at 575–576.

15. Arthur Hertzberg, *The French Enlightenment and the Jews* (New York: Columbia University Press, 1968), 10, 70, 267, 287, 290, 292, 295–296, 307, 312–313.

16. Ronald Schechter, *Obstinate Hebrews: Representations of Jews in France, 1715–1815* (Berkeley: University of California Press, 2003); Adam Sutcliffe, *Judaism and Enlightenment* (Cambridge: Cambridge University Press, 2003), 213–246. Sutcliffe's anti-Hertzberg stand is even more pronounced in his "The Enlightenment, French Revolution, Napoleon," in *Antisemitism: A History*, ed. Albert S. Lindemann and Richard S. Levy (Oxford: Oxford University Press, 2010), 107–120.

17. In addition to the general contours of the story, specific textual comparisons suggest that Montesquieu consulted the work of fellow Bordelais Étienne Cleirac and Jacques Savary, even if neither appears in his library's catalogue: Louis Desgraves, Catherine Volpilhac-Auger, and Françoise Weil, *Catalogue de la bibliothèque de Montesquieu à la Brède* (Oxford: Voltaire Foundation, 1999), now available at http://montesquieu.huma-num.fr (accessed July 9, 2018). The

expression "secret letters," in Montesquieu's footnote, appeared in Cleirac but not in Savary's *Parfait négociant*, which spoke of "letters and bills of very few words and little substance," although it also figures in the Savarys' *Dictionnaire*" (appendix 4). Other textual and contextual clues suggest that Montesquieu likely knew Cleirac's work. Another comment in *The Spirit of the Laws* (XXI, 17) concerning the ancient Roman law of wreck appears to be derivative of Cleirac (chapter 4, note 38). Note that Montesquieu commended the usefulness of marine insurance to sustain seafaring trade but still called it "maritime usury" (XXII, 20), a telling linguistic relic of a medieval past that Cleirac perceived as proximate.

18. The introduction of bills of exchange, without reference to Jews, was also mentioned in discussions of the relationship between merchants and the state in Charles-Louis de Secondat baron de La Brède and of Montesquieu, *Considerations on the Causes of the Greatness of the Romans and Their Decline*, trans. David Lowenthal (New York: Free Press, 1965), 199 (ch. 21).

19. Patrick Riley, "Introduction," in François de Fénelon, *Telemachus, Son of Ulysses*, ed. and trans. Patrick Riley (Cambridge: Cambridge University Press, 1994), xiii–xxxi, at xvi.

20. Paolo Rossi, *Philosophy, Technology, and the Arts in the Early Modern Era*, trans. Salvator Attanasio (New York: Harper Torchbooks, 1970 [1962]), 82. Montesquieu himself noted that "the compass opened, if I may so express myself, the universe" (XXI, 21).

21. *Code de commerce avec le rapprochement du texte des articles du Code Napoléon et du Code de Procédure Civile, qui ont un rapport direct, suivi d'une table analytique et raisonée des matieres par un jurisconsulte qui a concouru à la confection de ces codes*, 2 vols. (Paris: F. Didot, 1807), 2:34.

22. Chapter 20 in Book XXI was among those targeted by censors for its condemnation of the Scholastic doctrine on usury: Larrère, "Montesquieu on Economics and Commerce," 373n45.

23. On the possible friendship between Montesquieu and the *converso* physician Cardoso in Bordeaux, see Hertzberg, *French Enlightenment*, 276. Montesquieu recorded his meeting with the Jewish scholar and rabbi Giuseppe Attias in Livorno in *Spicilège* no. 472: Charles-Louis de Secondat baron de La Brède and of Montesquieu, *Pensées, Le Spicilège*, ed. Louis Degraves (Paris: Laffont, 1991), 803–804.

24. Hertzberg, *French Enlightenment*, 276.

25. Richard Menkis, "Patriarchs and Patricians: The Gradis Family of Eighteenth-Century Bordeaux," in *From East and West: Jews in a Changing Europe, 1750–1870*, ed. Frances Malino and David Sorkin (Cambridge, MA: Basil Blackwell, 1990), 11–45; Silvia Marzagalli, "Limites et opportunités dans l'Atlantique français au 18e siècle: Le cas de la maison Gradis de Bordeaux," *Outre-Mers* 362–363 (2009–2011): 87–110.

26. See chapter 4, note 110.

27. Schechter, *Obstinate Hebrews*, 46. A balanced assessment can be found in Arnold Ages, "Montesquieu and the Jews," *Romanische Forschungen* 81 (1969): 214–219.

28. Elsewhere, Montesquieu criticized the Inquisition with no reference to its crimes against Jews (XXVI, 11). The Jews of Brazil were explicitly mentioned as targets of the Portuguese Inquisition in *Spicilège* no. 459: Montesquieu, *Pensées, Le Spicilège*, 797–798.

29. Other passing references include those to Judaism and Islam as religions of practice (XXV, 2), to the "stupidity" of those Jews who did not defend themselves when militarily attacked on a Saturday (XXVI, 7), and to the Visigoths' "ridiculous request" that Jews eat pork (XXIX, 16).

30. The salient passages are in letter 58 (*Persian Letters*, 78–79): "Wherever there is money, there are Jews"; "Nothing resembles an Oriental Jew more than a European Jew"; and "Jews in Europe have never before experienced such peace as they now enjoy. Christians are beginning to abandon that spirit of intolerance which formerly inspired them." Intent on offering a bleak picture, Hertzberg lifts damning statements from Montesquieu's notebooks, the famous *Pensées*, including some in which the philosophe rails against rabbinical Judaism (*French Enlightenment*, 275). But passages of the opposite tenor could also be highlighted. An even more contradictory conception of commerce can be found in Montesquieu's unpublished notes: Montesquieu, *My Thoughts*, trans. and ed. Henry C. Clark (Indianapolis: Liberty Fund, 2012).

31. Pangle's liberal reading (*Montesquieu's Philosophy of Liberalism*, esp. 204) is exemplary in this respect, and far less subtle than Hirschman's. See also note 13 above.

32. Charles-Louis de Secondat baron de La Brède and of Montesquieu, *The Spirit of the Laws*, trans. and ed. Anne M. Cohler, Basia Carolyn Miller, and Harold Samuel Stone (Cambridge: Cambridge University Press, 1989), 53.

33. For Hirschman (*Passions and the Interests*, 58), "the evaluation of commerce and money-making pursuits as harmless and innocuous can be understood as an indirect consequence of the long-dominant aristocratic ideal." By contrast, for Robert Boesche, Montesquieu maintained an aristocratic disdain for commerce that he justified theoretically by stressing not only the self-restraint that commerce could generate but also "the self-interest, luxury, and license that seemed to be the inseparable companions of the new commercial classes": Boesche, "Fearing Monarchs and Merchants: Montesquieu's Two Theories of Despotism," *Political Research Quarterly* 43 (1990): 741–761, at 744. Céline Spector also curbs classic and recent enthusiasm for Montesquieu as the voice of "liberalism before liberalism," showing that "the liberal reading of Montesquieu risks . . . omitting the subtleties and nuances of his work," particularly when it comes to the interpretation of *doux commerce*: Spector, "Was Montesquieu Liberal? The *Spirit of the Laws* in the History of Liberalism," in *French Liberalism from Montesquieu to the Present Day*, ed. Raf Geenens and Helena Rosenblatt (Cambridge: Cambridge University Press, 2012), 57–72, at 59, 68.

34. "Mémoire . . . au sujet du rétablissement de la noblesse dans la premiere place de l'Administration municipale" (1759), cited in Junko Thérèse Takeda, *Between Commerce and Crown: Marseille and the Early Modern Mediterranean* (Baltimore: Johns Hopkins University Press, 2011), 187.

35. Montesquieu, *Persian Letters*, 78 (letter 58).

36. Pierre Aubery, "Montesquieu et les Juifs," *Studies on Voltaire and the Eighteenth Century* 87 (1972): 78–99, at 99.

37. Cited in Sutcliffe, *Judaism and Enlightenment*, 242. Original in Voltaire, *Lettres philosophiques*, ed. Frédéric Deloffre (Paris: Gallimard, 1986), 60 (letter VI).

38. Erich Auerbach, *Mimesis: The Representation of Reality in Western Literature*, trans. Willard R. Trask, fiftieth-anniversary ed. (Princeton, NJ: Princeton University Press, 2003[1946]), 402–403; Carlo Ginzburg, "Tolerance and Commerce: Auerbach Reads Voltaire," in *Threads and Traces: True False Fictive*, trans. Anne C. Tedeschi and John Tedeschi (Berkeley: University of California Press, 2012 [2002]), 96–114, at 97.

39. Voltaire borrowed from Joseph Addison, who in turn echoed Spinoza's iconic descrip-

tion of Amsterdam and adapted it to the London Royal Exchange. See Thomas J. Schlereth, *The Cosmopolitan Ideal in Enlightenment Thought: Its Form and Function in the Ideas of Franklin, Hume and Voltaire, 1694–1790* (Notre Dame, IN: University of Notre Dame Press, 1977), 100–103; Steven Smith, *Spinoza, Liberalism, and the Question of Jewish Identity* (New Haven, CT: Yale University Press, 1997), 165.

40. The attribution of the invention of marine insurance to Jews appears only once and is lifted from the Savary brothers' *Dictionnaire* (chapter 5): Diderot and d'Alembert, *Encyclopédie*, 1:774, s.v. "assurance."

41. Ibid., 9:418. On Calas and Boucher d'Argis, see Sarah Maza, *Private Lives and Public Affairs: The Causes Célèbres of Prerevolutionary France* (Berkeley: University of California Press, 1993), 94–96; David A. Bell, *Lawyers and Citizens: The Making of a Political Elite in Old Regime France* (New York: Oxford University Press, 1994), 131–134.

42. The passage in Boucher d'Argis's entry was reprinted in Joseph-Nicolas Guyot, ed., *Répertoire universel et raisonné de jurisprudence civile, criminelle, canonique et bénéficiale*, 64 vols. (Paris: Chez J. D. Dorez, 1775–1783), 9:103–160, at 123, s.v. "change"; J.B.R. Robinet, ed., *Dictionnaire universel des sciences morale, économique, politique et diplomatique, ou Bibliotheque de l'homme-d'état et du citoyen*, 30 vols. (London: Chez les libraires associés, 1777–1783), 23:145–146. Montesquieu's version of the legend, paired with offhand remarks about Jews' proclivity to charge usurious interest rates, is repeated in Honoré Lacombe de Prézel, *Dictionnaire du citoyen, ou, Abrégé historique, théorique et pratique du commerce*, 2 vols. (Paris: Chez Jean-Thomas Herissant fils, 1761), 1:468, s.v. "Juifs," and 2:12–13, s.v. "lettre de change." This entire dictionary was subsequently reprinted as *Nouveau dictionnaire abrégé du commerce*, 2 vols. (Amsterdam: n.p., 1768). Other dictionaries, including those that compiled lists of inventors, absorbed the legend without questioning it: Augutin Roux, *Dictionnaire domestique portatif*, 3 vols. (Paris: Chez Vincent, 1762–1764), 2:535, s.v. "lettre de change"; Antoine Jean Baptiste Abraham d'Origny, *Dictionnaire des origines*, 6 vols. (Paris: Chez Jean-François Bastien, 1777), 1:66–67, s.v. "assurance," and 4:163, s.v. "lettre de change."

43. Diderot and d'Alembert, *Encyclopédie*, 3:693, s.v. "Commerce," and 9:24–25, s.v. "Juif." Even though Forbonnais criticized other aspects of Montesquieu's thought, he derived the meaning of the legend from him. The legend was the only mention of Jews in his entry, which dated the invention of bills of exchange to their expulsion from France in 1182. See also François Véron de Forbonnais, *Élémens du commerce*, 2 vols. (Leiden: chez Briasson, 1754), 25. Even more than Voltaire in his depiction of the Royal Exchange, Jaucourt leaned on Joseph Addison when exalting Jews' ability to connect the entire globe via commercial links. Compare Diderot and d'Alembert, *Encyclopédie*, 9:25, s.v. "Jews," with Addison: Jews "are, indeed, so disseminated through all of the trading parts of the world, that they are become the instruments by which . . . mankind are knit together in a general correspondence. They are like the pegs and nails in a great building, which, though they are but little valued in themselves, are absolutely necessary to keep the whole frame together." *Spectator*, no. 495, September 27, 1712.

44. "Those who practice a religion tolerated by the state make themselves, as a rule, more valuable to their homeland than do those who belong to the state's dominant religion; barred from consideration from public honours, and able to achieve distinction only by an affluent lifestyle and their own prosperity, they tend to acquire wealth by hard work, and seek out the most arduous occupation in a society": Montesquieu, *Persian Letters*, 116 (letter 83).

45. "We everywhere see violence and oppression give birth to a commerce founded on economy, while men are constrained to take refuge in marshes, in isles, in the shallows of the sea, and even on rocks themselves. Thus it was that Tyre [in Lebanon], Venice, and the cities of Holland were founded. Fugitives found there a place of safety. It was necessary that they should subsist; they drew, therefore, their subsistence from all parts of the world" (XX, 5).

46. Diderot and d'Alembert, *Encyclopédie*, 9:25, s.v. "Juif" (my emphasis). The debt to *The Spirit of the Laws* in this section is evident not only in the words "elude violence," but also in the choice of anecdotes, including that of the horrific treatment of the rabbi and financier Aaron of York (XXI, 20; "Aaron, juif d'Iorck" in the *Encyclopédie*). Christian polemicists and apologists became acquainted with the figure of Aaron of York (d. 1253) via the chronicles of Matthew Paris (chapter 3, note 31).

47. Robert Darnton, *The Business of Enlightenment: A Publishing History of the Encyclopédie, 1775–1800* (Cambridge: Belknap Press, 1979). See, e.g., *Le grand vocabulaire françois ... par une société de gens de lettres*, 30 vols. (Paris: Hôtel de Thou, 1767–1774), 15:157–162, s.v. "Juifs"; Guyot, *Répertoire*, 33:361–383, at 363, s.v. "Juifs"; Jaques-Philibert Rousselot de Surgy, ed., *Encyclopédie méthodique: Finances*, 3 vols. (Paris and Liège: Chez Panckoucke & Chez Plomteux, 1784–1787), 2:666–668, s.v. "Juifs"; Robinet, *Dictionnaire universel*, 23:144–147, s.v. "lettre de change"; Philippe-Antoine Merlin, *Répertoire universel et raisonné de jurisprudence*, 18 vols., 3rd ed. (Paris: Chez Bertin et Daniel & Chez Garnery, 1807–1825), 6:574–614, at 574, s.v. "Juifs."

48. No entry titled "Juifs" figures in the modern critical edition of Voltaire's *Dictionnaire philosophique*, ed. Christiane Mervaud, in *The Complete Works of Voltaire*, 143 vols., ed. Theodore Besterman (Oxford: Voltaire Foundation, 1994), vols. 35–36. That is because no such entry appeared in the first clandestine publication of *Dictionnaire philosophique portatif* in 1764 or in the revised versions issued through 1769, although there were numerous mentions of Jews throughout these texts. However, in 1756 Voltaire had published an essay titled "De Juifs" in the *Mélanges de littérature, d'histoire et de philosophie*. This is the text that inspired a rebuttal by the Amsterdam Jewish writer Isaac de Pinto (see chapter 7, note 126). Some early editions of Voltaire's complete works reproduced the 1756 essay: e.g., *Collection complette des œvres de Mr. de Voltaire*, 5 vols., new ed. (n.p.: n.p., 1772), 5:5–22. It was also included in the earliest English translation of his works: *The Works of M. de Voltaire*, trans. T. Smollett, 34 vols. (London: J. Newbery, 1761–1770), 16:1–20. For a modern critical edition, see Voltaire, "De Juifs," ed. Marie-Hélène Cotoni, in Besterman, *Complete Works of Voltaire*, 45B:79–138. More importantly for us, the 1756 essay became the first of the four sections that made up an extended spurious entry titled "Juifs" that figured in many versions of the *Dictionnaire philosophique* from the 1780s onward. The passage lifted from Jaucourt's entry in the *Encyclopédie* was cited in the third section of this expanded entry, which was assembled on the basis of Voltaire's sparse notes: e.g., *Dictionnaire philosophique*, in *Oevres completes de Voltaire*, 70 vols. (Paris: Société littéraire-typographique, 1784–1789), 41:136–182, at 158; Voltaire, *Dictionnaire philosophique*, 8 vols., new ed. (Amsterdam: Chez Marc-Michel Rey, 1789), 5:314–362, at 338; *Dictionnaire philosophique*, in *Œvres complètes de Voltaire*, 52 vols., new ed. (Paris: Garnier frères, 1877–1885), 19:511–541, at 526. The expanded entry concluded by exhorting Jews to make the most of their superior skills in matters of commerce and to take them back to Palestine. In his *Histoire générale*, Voltaire exploited the cliché of Jews' commercial dexterity in order to lament their excessive influence on the Spanish economy and to decry the "proud idleness" of Polish noblemen who left commerce in the hands of

Jews: Schechter, *Obstinate Hebrews*, 51. On Voltaire's views of Jews and commerce, see more generally Harvey Mitchell, *Voltaire's Jews and Modern Jewish Identity: Rethinking the Enlightenment* (London: Routledge, 2008).

49. Guillaume-Thomas Raynal, *Histoire philosophique et politique des établissemens & du commerce des européens dans les deux Indes*, 6 vols. (Amsterdam: n.p., 1770), 1:10–11. Raynal, a Jesuit renegade, was the principal author of this work, which first appeared anonymously. A large cast of authors contributed to it, notably Denis Diderot and the Baron d'Holbach. On Raynal's liberal views about Jews and his calls to end discrimination toward them, see Jonathan I. Israel, *Democratic Enlightenment: Philosophy, Revolution, and Human Rights 1750–1790* (New York: Oxford University Press, 2011), 495.

50. *Histoire universelle, depuis le commencement du monde jusqu'à présent, [traduite] d'après l'anglois par une Société de Gens de Lettres, &c.*, 46 vols. (Amsterdam and Leipzig: Chez Artistée et Merkus, 1742–1802), 41 [1779]: 188. This multivolume work also enjoyed a second edition printed in France. On ritual murder in Germany, and the 1285 episode specifically, see Helmut Walser Smith, *The Butcher's Tale: Murder and Anti-Semitism in a German Town* (New York: Norton, 2002), 97.

51. Examples in Charles Geneviève Louis Auguste André Timothée d'Eon de Beaumont, *Les Loisirs du Chevalier d'Eon de Beaumont*, 13 vols. (Amsterdam: n.p., 1774), 4:149–150; Charles Mayer, *Voyages . . . en Suisse*, 2 vols. (Amsterdam: n.p., 1784–1787), 1:27.

52. René-Josué Valin, *Nouveau commentaire sur l'ordonnance de la marine, du mois d'août 1681*, 2 vols. (La Rochelle: Chez Jerôme Legier, Chez Pierre Mesnier, 1760), 2:25, 45; Franz Stypmann, *Tractatus de jure maritimo et nautico*, new ed. (Stralsund, Sweden: Ottonis Reumanni, 1661), 103 (part IV, ch. 7, nos. 8–9).

53. For Cleirac, a lunar monthly interest was equivalent to one *sou* per *livre* (i.e., 5 percent a month, or 60 percent a year): Estien[n]e Cleirac, *Usance du négoce ou commerce de la banque des lettres de change* (Bordeaux: Par Guillaume da Court, 1656), 82–83. Jean Paganucci borrowed the association between Jews and "lunar interests" in his *Manuel historique, géographique et politique des négocians*, 3 vols. (Lyon: Chez Jean-Marie Bruyset, 1762), 2:251, s.v. "lettres de change," and 2:28, s.v. "interêts lunaires." See also Rousselot de Surgy, *Encyclopédie méthodique*, 3:56, s.v. "lunaire."

54. In a debate on the Roman origins of credit instruments, which occupied German and Italian legal scholars in particular, Pothier corrected the misreading of Cicero's letters to Atticus as evidence of the existence of bills of exchange in antiquity. Insisting on the uncertainty surrounding the emergence of these instruments, he also pointed to a 1357 Venetian law as evidence of their use at that time. See the chapter on the origins of bills of exchange in Robert Joseph Pothier, *Traité du contrat de change: de la négociation qui se fait par la lettre de change, des billets de change, & autres billets de commerce* (Paris: Debure l'aîné, 1763), 5–6, citing from Niccolò Passeri, *De scriptura privata tractatus novus plenissimus* (Venice: Apud T. Balionum, 1611), 187. A portion of Pothier's chapter was reprinted in *Code de l'humanité, ou La législation universelle, naturelle, civile et politique*, 13 vols. (Yverdon: impr. de M. de Félice, 1778), 8:386–390. The editor of Pothier's treatise on marine insurance inserted a reference to the legend in his introduction, replacing bills of exchange with marine insurance: Pothier, *Traité du contrat d'assurance . . . avec un discours préliminaire, des notes et un supplément, par Estrangin* (Marseilles: Sube et Laporte, 1810), x.

55. Balthazard-Marie Émerigon, *Traité des assurances et des contrats à la grosse*, 2 vols. (Marseilles: Chez Jean Mossy, 1783), 1:2.

56. Ludovico Guicciardini, *Descrittione . . . di tutti i Paesi Bassi, altrimenti detti Germania inferiore* (Antwerp: Guglielmo Silvio, 1567), 117. See also chapter 7, note 142.

57. Paul-Joseph Nicodème, *Exercice des commerçans* (Paris: Valade, 1776), 388.

58. Hertzberg, *French Enlightenment*, 276. Paul H. Meyer offers a strong, though not entirely fair, rebuttal of Hertzberg's reading of Montesquieu in his "The Attitude of the Enlightenment Toward the Jews," *Studies on Voltaire and the Eighteenth Century* 26 (1963): 1161–1205.

59. On the Alsatian Jews' successful campaign for the abolition of the personal transit tax (*péage*) in 1783 and their economic status more generally, see David Feuerwerker, *L'émancipation des Juifs en France de l'Ancien Régime à la fin du Second Empire* (Paris: Albin Michel, 1976), 3–15. On the elimination at the end of the Old Regime of all transit taxes more generally, see Denis Woronoff, "Lassez-passer? La politique de suppression des péages à la fin de l'Ancien Régime," in Gayot and Hirsch, *La Révolution française*, 101–110.

60. Lacretelle defended, in vain, two Jews of Metz before the *parlement* of Nancy in 1775 after the merchants' guild of Thionville, Lorraine, refused them admission in spite of recent royal legislation that had opened membership of all French guilds to foreigners. Jews were denied entrance because they were neither Catholic subjects nor foreigners. In his closing argument, Lacretelle described the trial as concerning "public order, the rights of humanity": Pierre-Louis Lacretelle, *Plaidoyer pour Moyse May, Godechaux & Abraham Lévy, Juifs de Metz, Contre l'hôtel-de-ville de Thionville & le corps des marchands de cette ville* (Bruxelles: n.p., 1775), 26. A revised version, which omits this passage, is included in Lacretelle, "Mémoire pour deux Juifs de Metz," in *Œuvres*, 6 vols. (Paris: n.p., 1823–1824), 1:213–235. Excerpts of Lacretelle's 1775 closing arguments appeared anonymously in *Mercure de France*, February 11, 1786, 76–84. In the *cahiers de doléance*, the merchants of Thionville continued to denounce "the exorbitant usuries charged by Jews" (see note 69 below).

61. On the keyword "regeneration," and specifically on Lacretelle's use of the expression "arrêt de régénération" and its misinterpretations, see Alyssa Goldstein Sepinwall, *The Abbé Grégoire and the French Revolution: The Making of Modern Universalism* (Berkeley: University of California Press, 2005), 57–59, 262n19. Given Grégoire's conversionist aims (see note 97 below), it is worth remembring that for Catholic canon lawyers, "regeneration" could only be achieved through baptism: Stow, *Anna and Tranquillo*, 108.

62. Lacretelle, *Plaidoyer*, 28–29; and idem, "Mémoire," 230.

63. In middle French, *friperie*, from the Latin *faluppa* ("chip, splinter, straw, fiber"), meant rags and old clothes. By definition, those involved in the sale of these garments were of lowly extraction. Jews' engagement in the secondhand clothing trade further strengthened the association. Randle Cotgrave, *Dictionarie of the French and English Tongues* (London: Adam Islip, 1611), s.v. "fripon."

64. Antoine Furetière, *Dictionnaire universel*, 3 vols. (The Hague and Rotterdam: Chez Arnout & Reinier Leers, 1690), s.v. "fripon" and "Juif." See also *Dictionnaire de l'Académie française* (1762), s.v. "fripon."

65. Lacretelle, *Plaidoyer*, 30; and idem, "Mémoire," 233–234.

66. Ibid., 232–233.

67. Ibid., 230. An earlier formulation of this phrase appears in his *Plaidoyer*, 28–29.

68. Jean Daltroff, *Le prêt d'argent des Juifs de Basse-Alsace : d'après les registres de notaires roy-aux strasbourgeois, 1750–1791* (Strasbourg: Société savante d'Alsace et des regions de l'Est, 1993). Some Jews also owed money to Christians: Zosa Szajkowski, "Alsatian Jewish Inventories in the Hebrew Union College Library," *Studies in Bibliography and Booklore* 4 (1959): 96–99, at 97.

69. Hell was ultimately found guilty, but only after having achieved his goal, since Jewish creditors were not given full compensation: Zosa Szajkowski, *Jews and the French Revolutions of 1789, 1830 and 1848* (New York: Ktav, 1970), 174–175, 202–219; Hertzberg, *French Enlightenment*, 287–289; Schechter, *Obstinate Hebrews*, 67–73. Ten years later, the *cahiers de doléance* from Alsace, Lorraine, and Metz were still railing against Jewish usury: François Delpech, "La Révolution et l'Empire," in *Histoire des juifs en France*, ed. Bernhard Blumenkranz (Toulouse, France: E. Privat, 1972), 265–304, at 274–276; Feuerwerker, *L'émancipation des Juifs*, 262–267; Maurice Liber, *Les Juifs et la convocation des États généraux (1789)*, ed. Roger Kohn and Gérard Nahon (Louvain-Paris: Peeters, 1989), 2–45.

70. Christian Wilhelm von Dohm, *De la réforme politique des Juifs*, trans. Jean Bernoulli, ed. Dominique Bourel (Paris: Stock, 1984). The work appeared in German, titled *Über die bürgerliche Verbesserung der Juden*, first in 1781 and then in a slightly revised edition in 1782. The second edition took notice of some revisions introduced in the authorized French translation by Bernoulli (also entitled *De la réforme politique des Juifs*). Cerf Berr had initially solicited Moses Mendelssohn (1729–1786), the renowned Berlin rabbi and voice of *Haskalah* (Jewish Enlightenment), to pen the defense, but Mendelssohn suggested that he enlist Dohm in his place on the grounds that a non-Jewish advocate would be more effective. Mendelssohn later took issue with Dohm's negative portrait of the Jews' involvement in commerce. In the preface to his German translation of Menasseh ben Israel's 1655 call for the readmission of Jews to England, Mendelssohn posited a stronger link between economic and civic freedom, and advocated "civic acceptance" (*bürgerliche Aufnahme*) for the Jews, in contrast to Dohm's call for "civic improvement" (*bürgerliche Verbesserung*): David Sorkin, *Moses Mendelssohn and the Religious Enlightenment* (Berkeley: University of California Press, 1996), 114; Sorkin, *The Religious Enlightenment: Protestants, Jews, and Catholics from London to Vienna* (Princeton, NJ: Princeton University Press, 2008), 197–198.

71. Claude Fleury, *Les moeurs des Israelites* (Paris: V.ve G. Clouzier, 1681), 341. Fleury made traditional Catholic views of Jews accessible to a large public within and beyond the church. Hertzberg (*French Enlightenment*, 41) describes this text as "the single most widely known book on ancient Judaism to appear in France before the Revolution." Dohm borrowed more from the noted Orientalist Johann David Michaelis (1717–1791), who depicted the ancient Jewish state as agrarian but also harbored profound hostility toward the Jews whom he studied. Dohm, *De la réforme politique des Juifs*, 162nan.

72. Representing a dissenting voice, a Prussian anticlerical deist and Jacobin described as "new and dignified" his idea that "the ancient colonies of the Jews were commercial and not agricultural." Following Montesquieu in arguing that "Christianity quenched all spirit of commerce," he celebrated the Jews' ingenious invention of bills of exchange as "a seal of immortality" that benefited both Jews and humanity at large. Anacharsis Cloots, *Lettre sur les juifs* (Berlin: n.p., 1783), 4, 54–55.

73. Dohm, *De la réforme politique des Juifs*, 69.

74. Ibid., 77–78 (emphasis in original).

75. Karp, *Politics of Jewish Commerce*, 103. For a different reading that sees Dohm as opposed to both the physiocrats' idealization of agriculture and the English valorization of commerce, see Robert Liberles, "Dohm's Treatise on the Jews: A Defence of the Enlightenment," *Leo Baeck Institute Year Book* 33 (1988): 29–42, at 38.

76. Dohm, *De la réforme politique des Juifs*, 51.

77. Ibid., 49. In several other passages, Dohm blurred the lines between commerce and usury, understanding the latter as excessive gain, whether in moneylending or in trade more generally (36–37, 58, 68–69, 76).

78. Ibid., 158n*ac*, citing Jacob Rodrigues Péreire, *Recueil de lettres patentes et autres pièces en faveur des Juifs portugais concernant leurs privilèges en France* (Paris: Chez Moreau, 1765). In fact, Péreire offered only generic praises for the commercial aptitude of Portuguese Jews, which he regarded as evidence of their distinctiveness from the rest of the Jewish people (see notes 89, 93, and 116 below). On this text, see also Hertzberg, *French Enlightenment*, 59–61. Note that Dohm knew well Montesquieu's *Spirit of the Laws*, from which he cited the account of the 1745 Jewish expulsion from Russia (*De la réforme politique des Juifs*, 161n*ah*) but not the legend. His translator adopted Montesquieu's language in rendering the passage that claimed that the Jews of Italy were treated in a gentler fashion than coreligionists elsewhere: "avec plus de douceur" (61). A more literal rendering of the German original, "mit wiserer Politik," would have emphasized the wiser policies of Italian rulers rather than the gentler mores of the Italian people: Christian Wilhelm von Dohm, *Über die bürgerliche Verbesserung der Juden*, 2 vols. (Berlin: F. Nicolai, 1781–1783), 1:82.

79. Hertzberg, *French Enlightenment*, 328. These essay competitions in the second half of the eighteenth century epitomized what a historian has called "the Enlightenment in practice": Jeremy L. Caradonna, *The Enlightenment in Practice: Academic Prize Contests and Intellectual Culture in France, 1670–1794* (Ithaca, NY: Cornell University Press, 2012). The author notes that the Metz contest is one of the few still discussed by historians but part of a much wider phenomenon (106).

80. For a discussion of the term "regeneration" in this context and a comparison between the first and second submissions of Grégoire's essay, see Sepinwall, *Abbé Grégoire*, 57–59, 66–74. On Hourwitz, see Frances Malino, *A Jew in the French Revolution: The Life of Zalkind Hourwitz* (Oxford: Blackwell, 1996).

81. Zalkind Hourwitz, *Apologie des Juifs en réponse à la question: Est-il des moyens de rendre les Juifs plus heureux et plus utiles en France?* (Paris: Chez Gattrey, 1789), 15, 24, anastatic reprint in Gayot and Hirsch, *La révolution française*, vol. 4. Before Hourwitz's defense, a young and vocal leader of the Metz Jewish community, Isaïe Berr-Bing (1759–1805), rebutted a libel written by an infantry captain, Philippe-Francois de Latour-Foissac, who portrayed Jews as insatiably hungry for gold, nourished by hatred for gentiles, and incapable of feeling pity for others because of their "greed" and "scandalous commerce": Latour-Foissac, *Le cri du citoyen contre les Juifs de Metz par un capitaine d'infanterie* (Lausanne: n.p., 1786), 6–7. Latour-Foissac later authored a lengthier denunciation titled *Plaidoyer contre l'usure des Juifs des Évechés, de l'Alsace et de la Lorraine* (n.p.: n.p., n.d.). Berr-Bing denounced the corrupting power of commerce and praised the virtues of rural life but also borrowed from the noted Amsterdam Sephardic writer Isaac de Pinto a complex (if scripturally inaccurate) distinction in Jewish law between usury and interest and described Jews as "the engines of commerce, the agents of circulation more than the real

proprietors of gold." Pinto, *Traité de la circulation et du crédit* (Amsterdam: Chez Marc Michel Rey, 1771), 211; Isaïe Berr-Bing, *Lettre . . . à l'auteur anonyme d'une écrit intitulé: Le cri du citoyen contre les Juifs* (Metz: impr. de J.-B. Collignon, 1787), 18–19. The same distinction and arguments were repeated in 1788 by Isaac Ber[r]-Bing, *Mémoire particulier pour la communauté des Juifs établis à Metz* (Metz: n.p., 1789), 15n5, reprinted in *Archives Parlementaires de 1787 à 1860 . . . 1re série (1787 à 1799)*, 7 vols., 2nd ed. (Paris: P. Dupont, 1867), 1:445–449. See also Jay R. Berkovitz, *Rites and Passages: The Beginnings of Modern Jewish Culture in France, 1650–1860* (Philadelphia: University of Pennsylvania Press, 2004), 97–98. On Isaac de Pinto, see chapter 7, notes 126–129.

82. Henri Grégoire, *Essai sur la régénération physique, morale et politique des Juifs: Ouvrage couronné par la Société royale des sciences et des arts de Metz, le 23 août 1788* (Metz: Imprimerie de Claude Lamort, 1789), 37, 47, 73, 75, 79, 80, 82 (here in relation to Christian usurers), 89, 94, 97, 107, 146, 184. These terms were rendered in English variably as "deception" (46, 117), "selling old cloths" (57–58, 178–179), "the art of committing fraud" (90), "cheats" (92), "deceitful" (98), "fraud" (99), "knaves" (102), "villainy" (110, 182), "villain" (121, 229), and "criminals" (134): idem, *An Essay on the Physical, Moral, and Political Reformation of the Jews: A Work Crowned by the Royal Society of Arts and Sciences at Metz* (London: C. Forster, 1791).

83. Thiéry dated this transformation of Jews from peasants to merchants to the destruction of the Second Temple by Herod: Claude-Antonie Thiéry, *Dissertation sur cette question: Est-il des moyens de rendre les Juifs plus heureux et plus utiles en France? Moyens de rendre les Juifs plus heureux et plus utiles* (Paris: Knapen fils, 1788), 7, anastatic reprint in Gayot and Hirsch, *La Révolution française*, vol. 2.

84. Grégoire, *An Essay*, 106.

85. Ibid., 103. Grégoire cited both Dupuis de la Serra and Fischer for the two alternative hypotheses: Jacques Dupuis de la Serra, *L'art des lettres de change suivant l'usage des plus célèbres places de l'Europe* (Paris: Chez l'auteur, A. Vvarin, 1690); Friedrich Christoph Jonathan Fischer, *Geschichte des deutschen Handels*, 4 vols. (Hannover: In der Helwingschen Hofbuchhandlung, 1785–1792), 1:297. Grégoire offered no textual or empirical evidence to support the legend but mentioned Giovanni Villani's chronicle, to which Cleirac had mistakenly attributed the legend.

86. Grégoire, *Essai*, 83 (my emphasis and my translation). Note that the period English translator rendered the sentence differently: Jews utilized bills of exchange to "elude *vigilance*" (not *violence*) and to acquire "riches almost invisible . . . which leave no traces behind them." Grégoire, *An Essay*, 102–103 (my emphasis). Either he made a mistake or he purposefully corrected Grégoire's original to render the *Essay*'s overall message more faithfully.

87. Sepinwall links Grégoire's life and thought in *Abbé Grégoire*, 15–55.

88. Grégoire, *An Essay*, 101.

89. Ibid., 101, 102, 106. Admittedly, the Sephardic apologetic literature also used some of these terms: "Their talent for commerce & their genius for opening up new branches of trade." Péreire, *Recueil*, 4.

90. Grégoire, *An Essay*, 105.

91. Ibid., 104–106.

92. Ibid., 104, 101. The trope informed politics at the local level as well. In 1759, when the nobility of the sword demanded that they be reinstated in the municipal government of

Marseilles (a privilege they obtained in 1767), aristocrats denigrated the *négociants* who monopolized civic government, arguing that merchants' "transient habits rarely produce a patriotic spirit." The *négociants* responded by stressing that their commerce was "useful to the state . . . and beneficial to the public good." Citations from Takeda, *Between Commerce and Crown*, 185, 188.

93. *Requête des marchands et négociants de Paris contre l'admission des Juifs* (Paris: Imprimerie de P. Al. Le Prieur, 1767), 38, 38n12. The text was signed by a certain "avocat Goulleau" and prompted a reply from a prominent Portuguese Jew in Bordeaux, who rebutted the argument in print by citing the royal decrees that welcomed Portuguese New Christians and later Jews to France starting in 1550: Jacob Rodrigue Péreire, "Première lettre circulaire en défense des Juifs portugais" (BNF, Richelieu, Joly de Fleury-585, fol. 288), and idem, "Seconde lettre circulaire en défense des Juifs portugais" (BNF, Richelieu, Ms. Joly de Fleury-425, fol. 31).

94. On December 24, 1789, the Prince de Broglie described Jews as "a sort of transient population, or rather as cosmopolitans who have never enjoyed, nor have ever demanded the title of French citizens": "Opinion de M. le prince de Broglie, deputé de Colmar, sur l'admission des Juifs à l'etat civil," 3, anastatic reprint in Gayot and Hirsch, *La révolution française*, vol. 7. On the Catholic connotations of eighteenth-century French patriotism, see David A. Bell, *The Cult of the Nation in France: Inventing Nationalism, 1680–1800* (Cambridge, MA: Harvard University Press, 2001).

95. Grégoire, *Essai*, 83; and idem, *An Essay*, 103.

96. "Speaking of the Jews, one has to speak of usury . . . : during the Middle Ages, their genius for calculation [*génie calculateur*] led to the invention of bills of exchange, useful to protect commerce and enhance it in every corner of the globe; but their rapacity has offset the benefits of this contribution . . . and this vice has long been gangrenous for the Jewish people." Henri Grégoire, *Motion à faveur des Juifs*, 28–29, anastatic reprint in Gayot and Hirsch, *La révolution française*, vol. 7.

97. On Grégoire's conversionist aims, see Hertzberg, *French Enlightenment*, 265; and Sorkin's chapter on the Reform Catholic theologian and Grégoire's teacher, Adrien Lamourette, in his *Religious Enlightenment*, 263–309, esp. 273. Grégoire remains a polarizing figure in current scholarship, reflecting contrasting assessments of the long-term stance of French republicanism with regard to Jews. Opposite views are presented in Alyssa Goldstein Sepinwell, "A Friend of the Jews? The Abbé Grégoire and Philosemitism in Revolutionary France," in *Philosemitism in History*, ed. Jonathan Karp and Adam Sutcliffe (New York: Cambridge University Press, 2011), 111–127; and Rita Hermon-Belot, "The Abbé Grégoire's Program for the Jews: Social Reform and Spiritual Project," in *The Abbé Grégoire and His World*, ed. Jeremy D. Popkin and Richard H. Popkin (Dordrecht: Kluwer, 2000), 13–26, esp. 16–17. Maurice Samuels, unlike Sepinwall, stresses that once in Paris, Grégoire abandoned the language of "regeneration" in favor of unconditional equality. Compare Sepinwall, *Abbé Grégoire*, 91, 95, with Maurice Samuels, *The Right to Difference: French Universalism and the Jews* (Chicago: Chicago University Press, 2016), 33.

98. Hourwitz, *Apologie des Juifs*, 36.

99. Ibid., 37. On the notorious difficulty of translating the term *police*, see Gordon, *Citizens Without Sovereignty*, 19–21. Poorly informed and repeating Dohm's advice (*De la réforme politique des Juifs*, 82), Hourwitz also proposed that Yiddish no longer be used in business contracts and account books in order to enhance transparency and Jews' reputation (*Apologie des Juifs*,

37). In reality, at least in Metz, Jews had been obliged to keep their business records documenting transactions with Christians in French since 1670, and by the time that Hourwitz was writing, the Jews of Alsace rarely signed their documents in Hebrew letters: Szajkowski, *Jews and the French Revolutions*, 177, 202. On the widespread association of Yiddish with conniving Jewish businessmen in central Europe, see Aya Elyada, *Goy Who Speaks Yiddish: Christians and the Jewish Language in Early Modern Germany* (Stanford, CA: Stanford University Press, 2012), 81–98.

100. Hourwitz, *Apologie des Juifs*, 72. At the same time, he maintained that Jewish merchants were more upstanding than other merchants, as shown by the infrequency of Jews' inclusion in the weekly printed lists of merchants who had gone bankrupt in London and Amsterdam (171n1). Hourwitz insisted that Jews were "the most sober & most industrious of all people" and claimed that "usury and fraud" were the only vices they shared with other nations (34).

101. Frances Malino, "Zalkind Hourwitz, juif polonais," *Dix-huitième siècle* 13 (1981): 78–89, at 87–88; and eadem, *Jew in the French Revolution*, 72.

102. Liber, *Les Juifs*, 86.

103. "Lettre adressé à M. Grégoire . . . par les députés de la Nation Juive portugaise de Bordeaux," in Richard Ayoun, *Les juifs de France de l'émancipation à l'intégration (1787–1812): Documents, bibliographie et annotations* (Paris: L'Harmattan, 1997), 89.

104. The authors of the document were David Silveyra, Jacob Louis Nunez, and Abraham Furtado. It can be read in full in Gérard Nahon, ed., *Les "Nations" juives portugaises du sud-ouest de la France (1684–1791): Documents* (Paris: Fundação Calouste Gulbenkian, Centro Cultural Português, 1981), 322–327, at 325.

105. Cerf Berr, "Mémoire sur l'etat des Juifs d'Alsace," in Dohm, *Über die bürgerliche Verbesserung*, 1:155–200, esp. 186–189.

106. Ber[r]-Bing, *Mémoire particulier*, 11. By contrast, his brother Isaïe had attributed the absence of Jewish wholesale merchants in Metz to external constraints: Berr-Bing, *Lettre*, 28.

107. *Lettre d'un Alsacien sur les Juifs d'Alsace* (Paris: Impr. de Savy le jeune, 1790), 13–15.

108. "Men who only own liquid assets can only live off the profits their money generate, and you have always forbidden them from owning any other property": Ayoun, *Les juifs*, 106–107. A proponent of emancipation, the Count of Mirabeau, whose earlier writings will be discussed in the chapter's conclusion, said little on the subject during the incendiary debates in the National Assembly in December 1789 and January 1790.

109. Ibid., 108. On Barbary pirates and the making of French collective identity, see Gillian Weiss, *Captives and Corsairs: France and Slavery in the Early Modern Mediterranean* (Stanford, CA: Stanford University Press, 2011).

110. I. H. Hersch, "The French Revolution and the Emancipation of the Jews," *Jewish Quarterly Review* 19, no. 3 (1907): 540–565, at 544 and 551. The author was assistant master at the elite Perse School in Cambridge, United Kingdom, and an amateur Jewish historian who aimed at countering rising antisemitism in France and England by memorializing a high point in French history. A brief profile of Hersch appears in *The Jewish Literary Annual for 1908*, ed. Cecil A. Franklin (London: George Routledge & Son, 1908).

111. Hertzberg, *French Enlightenment*, 314, 325–327; Szajkowski, *Jews and the French Revolutions*, 235–266; Delpech, "La Révolution et l'Empire," 266, 276, 280; Marcus Arkin, *Aspects of Jewish Economic History* (Philadelphia: Jewish Publication Society of America, 1975), 129–130;

Frances Malino, *The Sephardic Jews of Bordeaux: Assimilation and Emancipation in Revolutionary and Napoleonic France* (Tuscaloosa: University of Alabama Press, 1978), 27–64; Paula E. Hyman, *The Jews of Modern France* (Berkeley: University of California Press, 1998), 22, 29–30. A lone dissenting voice is Gérard Nahon's analysis of Jewish advocacy in Paris, which emphasizes the commonality of the cause advanced by the Jews of southwestern and northeastern France and Paris: Nahon, "Séfarades et ashkenazes en France: La conquête de l'emancipation (1789–1791)," in *Les Juifs dans l'histoire de France*, ed. Myriam Yardeni (Leiden: Brill, 1980), 9–145. Evidence of this commonality of causes is a letter signed by four Sephardic leaders in Bordeaux ("Furtado-Lainé, Azevedo, David Gradis, Lopes Du Bec") urging Abbé Grégoire to promote civil and religious liberties for all Jews of France: *Lettre adressée à M. Grégoire, curé d'Emberménil, député de Nancy, par les députés de la nation juive portugaise de Bordeaux, le 14 août 1789* (Versailles: Chez Baudouin, 1789). Ongoing research by Evelyne Oliel-Grausz confirms that while Jews actively lobbied for their own rights, commerce was not a touchstone of their advocacy. I thank her for sharing with me the unpublished paper she presented at the "Documents of Modern Jewish Political History" workshop, held at Yale University, May 31–June 2, 2016.

112. Allan Arkush, "Montesquieu: A Precursor of Emancipation?" in *L'antisémitisme éclairé: Inclusion et exclusion depuis l'époque des Lumières jusqu'à l'affaire Dreyfus*, ed. Ilana Y. Zinguer and Sam W. Bloom (Leiden: Brill, 2003), 45–59.

113. Schechter, *Obstinate Hebrews*.

114. "Moderate" is the revisionist label that Jonathan Israel uses to describe key figures of the mainstream French Enlightenment, including Montesquieu, in his *Radical Enlightenment: Philosophy and the Making of Modernity, 1650–1750* (Oxford: Oxford University Press, 2001).

115. Forbonnais, *Élémens du commerce*, 1:1.

116. Péreire, *Recueil de lettres patentes*, 4. Péreire published this collection to prove that the Sephardim of Bordeaux had been loyal subjects of the crown for more than 200 years at a time when they had come under attack by the guilds of Paris, which aimed to prevent them from obtaining additional privileges or rights (see note 93 above). An admiring biographical profile of Péreire, a neglected figure in mainstream histories of Jewish emancipation, is offered in Emílio Eduardo Guerra Salgueiro, *Jacob Rodrigues Pereira: Homem de bem, judeu português do séc. XVIII, primeiro reeducador de crianças surdas e mudas em França* (Lisbon: Fundação Calouste Gulbenkian, 2010).

117. Israël Bernard de Vallabrègue, *Lettre ou réflexions d'un milord* (London: n.p., 1767). My reading of this work is closer to that articulated by Schechter, *Obstinate Hebrews*, 116–119, than that offered by Sepinwall, *Abbé Grégoire*, 62–63.

118. "Across all times and by all nations Jews have been reproached for their bad faith, a capital flaw especially given that commerce was their only means of subsistence." Dohm, *De la réforme politique des Juifs*, 48.

119. Both decrees are reproduced in Gayot and Hirsch, *La révolution française*, vol. 7.

120. Lisa Leff uses the expression "cacophony of arguments for emancipation" to denote the absence of a single or even a predominant argument (let alone one built on economic grounds) in the debates that preceded the two decrees of 1790 and 1791: Lisa Moses Leff, *Sacred Bonds of Solidarity: The Rise of Jewish Internationalism in Nineteenth-Century France* (Stanford, CA: Stanford University Press, 2006), 19–20, 27.

121. Hertzberg, *French Enlightenment*, 120, 265, 287, 293–294, 334, 338. In his indictment of physiocrats as "anti-Jewish," Hertzberg regards Dohm and Mirabeau as "more generous spirits" (76) but gives a reductionist account of the economic theories underpinning Christian representations of Jewish economic roles.

122. Honoré-Gabriel de Riqueti, Comte de Mirabeau, *Dénonciation de l'agiotage à l'assemblée des notables* (n.p.: n.p., 1787). "Climactic pamphlet" is a quotation from Robert Darnton, *George Washington's False Teeth: An Unconventional Guide to the Eighteenth Century* (New York: Norton, 2003), 147. See also Robert D. Harris, *Necker and the Revolution of 1789* (Lanham, MD: University Press of America, 1986), esp. 58, 111, 461–464, 550–554, 641–642; Shovlin, *Political Economy of Virtue*, 159–172; Lynn Hunt, "The Global Financial Origins of 1789," in *The French Revolution in Global Perspective*, ed. Suzanne Desan, Lynn Hunt, and William Max Nelson (Ithaca, NY: Cornell University Press, 2013), 32–43, at 40–42.

123. Honoré-Gabriel de Riqueti, Comte de Mirabeau, *Sur Moses Mendelssohn, sur la réforme politique des juifs* (London: n.p., 1787), 88. Mirabeau mentioned the unwillingness of the Bank of England to discount bills of exchange by Jews as an example of patriotism that the French crown should imitate: idem, *Dénonciation de l'agiotage*, 75–76.

124. Joan Wallach Scott, *Only Paradoxes to Offer: French Feminism and the Rights of Man* (Cambridge, MA: Harvard University Press, 1996). Wendy Brown incorporates Scott's insights into a comparison of the battles for Jewish emancipation and women's equality in her *Regulating Aversion: Tolerance in the Age of Identity and Empire* (Princeton, NJ: Princeton University Press, 2006), 48–77.

125. In English translation, see Jean-Antoine-Nicolas de Caritat, Marquis de Condorcet, "On the Admission of Women to the Rights of Citizenship (1790)," in *Condorcet: Selected Writings*, ed. and trans. Keith Michael Baker (Indianapolis: Bobbs-Merrill, 1976), 97–104; and idem, "On Slavery: Rules of the Society of the Friends of Negroes (1788)," in *Condorcet: Political Writings*, ed. Steven Lukes and Nadia Urbinati (Cambridge: Cambridge University Press, 2012), 148–155. Pretending to have received the manuscript from a certain "pastor Joachim Schwartz," Condorcet was the real author of the widely circulated *Réflexions sur l'esclavage des nègres*, which contained an oblique reference to Jews as "a horde of oriental thieves" who were once guilty of killing married women as Africans also did: *Réflexions sur l'esclavage des nègres* (Neufchatel: Chez la Société typographique, 1781), 4. Condorcet nevertheless favored Jews' emancipation. On Condorcet's views of equality and, implicitly, the scarce attention he paid to Jews, see Rothschild, *Economic Sentiments*, 195–217; and David Williams, *Condorcet and Modernity* (Cambridge: Cambridge University Press, 2004), 139–171.

126. Sepinwall, *Abbé Grégoire*, 93–94, 97–102, 210–211.

127. Henri Grégoire, *On the Slave Trade and on the Slavery of Blacks and Whites* (London: Josiah Conder, 1815), 4; The French original appears as idem, *De la traite et de l'esclavage des noirs et des blancs* (Paris: Adrien Égron, 1815), 8–9.

128. Idem, *On the Cultural Achievements of Negroes*, trans. Thomas Cassirer and Jean-François Brière (Amherst: University of Massachusetts Press, 1996), 74. This is a modern English translation of *De la littérature des Nègres, ou Recherches sur leurs facultés intellectuelles, leurs qualités morales et leur littérature; suivies de notices sur la vie et les ouvrages des Nègres qui se sont distingués dans les sciences, les lettres et les arts* (Paris: Chez Maradan, 1808), which had previously appeared in English as *An Enquiry Concerning the Intellectual and Moral Faculties, and Literature of Negroes:*

Followed with an Account of the Life and Works of Fifteen Negroes & Mulattoes, Distinguished in Science, Literature and the Arts (Brooklyn: Thomas Kirk, 1810).

129. Sepinwall, *Abbé Grégoire*, 94.

130. Grégoire, *On the Cultural Achievements*, 40, 48, 63.

131. Idem, *Essay*, 34, 36. In the 1760s, the Amsterdam Sephardic merchant and scholar Isaac de Pinto had rebutted Voltaire's anti-Jewish sentiments not by defending all Jews, but by accusing Voltaire of generalizing about the basis of the religious traditionalism and poverty of Ashkenazim while ignoring the acculturated and sophisticated Sephardim. See Hertzberg, *French Enlightenment*, 284–285; Adam Sutcliffe, "Can a Jew Be a Philosophe? Isaac de Pinto, Voltaire, and Jewish Participation in the European Enlightenment," *Jewish Social Studies* 6, no. 3 (2000): 31–51.

132. Joan Wallach Scott, "The Vexed Relationship of Emancipation and Equality," *History of the Present* 2, no. 2 (2012): 148–168.

133. Samuels, *Right to Difference*, 30–49. The point is crucial to Samuels' overall reassessment of the historical trajectory of French universalism and his insistence on moments of greater inclusivity toward Jews than others (myself included) normally recognize.

134. Ronald Schechter, "Translating the 'Marseillaise': Biblical Republicanism and the Emancipation of Jews in Revolutionary France," *Past and Present* 143, no. 1 (1994): 108–135.

135. Idem, "The Trial of Jacob Benjamin, Supplier to the French Army, 1792–93," in *The Jews of Modern France: Images and Identities*, ed. Zvi Jonathan Kaplan and Nadia Malinovich (Leiden: Brill, 2016), 35–61.

136. Berkovitz, *Rites and Passages*, 104–105.

137. M. Diogene Tama, *Transactions of the Parisian Sanhedrim, or, Acts of the Assembly of Israelitish Deputies of France and Italy, Convoked at Paris by an Imperial and Royal Decree, Dated May 30, 1806*, ed. F. D. Kirwan (London: C. Taylor, 1807), 106. Furtado's report on the status of usury among the Jews of northeastern France is discussed in Robert Anchel, *Napoléon et les Juifs* (Paris: Presses universitaires de France, 1928), 108–110. For the historical background, see Delpech, "La Révolution et l'Empire," 290–297; Berkovitz, *Rites and Passages*, 121–136.

138. *Requête des marchands et négociants de Paris contre l'admission des Juifs* (Paris: de l'imp. de P.-A. Le Prieur, 1767), 25.

139. Grégoire, *Histoire des sectes* (1810), cited in translation by Sepinwall, *Abbé Grégoire*, 207.

140. In a classical study, Guy Chassinand-Nogaret maintains that "in 1789 nobles were the kingdom's Jews." Chassinand-Nogaret, *The French Nobility in the Eighteenth Century: From Feudalism to Enlightenment*, trans. William Doyle (Cambridge: Cambridge University Press, 1985 [1976]), 1. This offhand remark led Jonathan Karp to offer a subtler analysis of how Jews came to be regarded as covert aristocrats in postrevolutionary France: Karp, *Politics of Jewish Commerce*, 135–196.

Chapter 7: Distant Echoes

1. Languages and sovereign states were not homologous in the eighteenth century but were beginning to converge. In appendices 5 and 6, I use language (rather than place of publication or author's birthplace) as the ordering criterion of all printed volumes in which the legend appeared. At least two important works were written in French by non-French authors (Bielfeld

and Beausobre). I discuss them in this chapter, rather than in the previous one, which is devoted to eighteenth-century French thought. Samuel Ricard, by contrast, is discussed in chapter 4 and only referenced in passing here, although his treatise in French was printed in Amsterdam. While somewhat arbitary, these choices were made with the twin purpose of appreciating the legend's dissemination and outlining its local declensions. Obviously, there was no country in Europe at this time where Latin was a spoken language. Needless to say, neither appendix is exhaustive.

2. I am referring to the Universal Short Title Catalogue (USTC), which is currently being completed and digitized. The website is hosted by the University of Saint Andrews at http://www.ustc.ac.uk/.

3. Neither the corpus known as *Ars mercatoria* nor Kenneth E. Carpenter's "The Economic Bestsellers Before 1850" (both described in appendix 1) are helpful: the former ends in 1700, while the inadequacy of the latter as a point of reference is confirmed by the cross-references in appendix 6. Note that appendix 6 only lists the earliest edition of any text in which the legend is mentioned. In the Dutch case, the vehicle of the story was a single merchant manual that was reprinted multiple times. In one interpretation, early modern economic writing was scarcer in commercially vibrant countries, such as the Venetian and Dutch republics, than in countries like France, which sought to imitate their more commercially successful rivals: Étienne Laspeyres, *Geschichte der volkswirthschaftlichen Anschauungen der Niederländer und ihrer Litteratur zur Zeit der Republik* (Leipzig: S. Hirzel, 1863), cited in Erik S. Reinert, "Emulating Success: Contemporary Views of the Dutch Economy Before 1800," in *The Political Economy of the Dutch Republic*, ed. Oscar Gelderblom (Surrey, UK: Ashgate, 2009), 19–40, at 21. This observation, however, fails to explain why economic writing flourished in seventeenth- and eighteenth-century England/Britain.

4. Recently, a scholar has attempted to identify which texts among those listed in the *Ars mercatoria* can be defined as "merchant manuals." By his count, the *Ars mercatoria* catalogues 1,151 merchants manuals printed across Europe from 1474 to 1600 but misses over 100 publications of the same genre in the USTC. Jeremiah Dittmar, "New Media, Competition and Growth: European Cities After Gutenberg" (London School of Economics, Center for Economic Performance, Discussion Paper No. 1365, 2015), 11.

5. Ann M. Carlos, Erin Fletcher, and Larry Neal, "Share Portfolios in the Early Years of Financial Capitalism: London, 1690–1730," *Economic History Review* 68, no. 2 (2015): 574–599. The authors of this study, however, stress that the vast majority of those who invested in the equity market held shares in only one company.

6. I have not encountered figures of Jews in the heated debates surrounding the Great Recoinage crisis of 1696, which concerned the metallic value of English money rather than the intangible quality of paper credit instruments. Rhetorical appeals to Jews became more frequent after the South Sea Bubble burst in 1720. An anonymous pamphlet published soon after the creation of the Bank of England decried unsavory practices involving the stock market and the public debt but made no mention of Jews: *Angliae Tutamen: or, The Safety of England, Being an Account of the Banks, Lotteries, Mines, Diving, Draining, Lifting, and Other Engines, and Many Pernicious Projects Now on Foot; Tending to the Destruction of Trade and Commerce, and the Impoverishing This Realm* (London: printed for the author, 1695).

7. Wyndham Beawes, *Lex Mercatoria Rediviva, or, The Merchant's Directory* (London:

J. Moore, 1751), 362; Norman Jones, *God and the Moneylenders: Usury and Law in Early Modern England* (Oxford: Basil Blackwell, 1989), 19, 65.

8. Francis Bacon, "Of Usury," in *The Essays of Francis Bacon*, ed. Mary Augusta Scott (New York: Charles Scribner's Sons, 1909), 187–193, at 187. A few years earlier, the travelogue of an Englishman, Thomas Coryat, depicted Jews in the ghetto of Venice as wearing red hats: *Coryat's Crudities*, 2 vols. (New York: Macmillan, 1905), 1:371–372. One scholar has noted that throughout Elizabethan merchant manuals, plays, and satirical poems, "the idea that usurers were an especially intensified form of Jew is commonplace": David Hawkes, *The Culture of Usury in Renaissance England* (New York: Palgrave Macmillan, 2010), 68. See, more generally, James Shapiro, *Shakespeare and the Jews* (New York: Columbia University Press, 1996).

9. Thomas Wilson, *A Discourse upon Usury* (London: G. Bell and Sons, 1925), 232, 283.

10. Cited in Robin Pearson, "Moral Hazard and the Assessment of Insurance Risk in Eighteenth- and Early-Nineteenth Century Britain," *Business History Review* 76, no. 1 (2002): 1–35, at 31.

11. Julian Hoppit, "The Use and Abuse of Credit in Eighteenth-Century England," in *Business Life and Public Policy: Essays in Honour of D. C. Coleman*, ed. Neil McKendrick and R. B. Outhwaite (Cambridge: Cambridge University Press, 1986), 64–78, at 65. Carl Wennerlind, *Casualties of Credit: The English Financial Revolution, 1620–1720* (Cambridge, MA: Harvard University Press, 2011), is also relevant, although more focused on the contemporary discourse about public rather than private credit.

12. Daniel Defoe introduced the figure of Lady Credit in his periodical *Review* in January 1706: Sandra Sherman, *Finance and Fictionality in the Early Eighteenth Century: Accounting for Defoe* (Cambridge: Cambridge University Press, 1996), 40–53. See also Catherine Ingrassia, *Authorship, Commerce and Gender in Early Eighteenth-Century England: A Culture of Paper Credit* (Cambridge: Cambridge University Press, 1998); Laura Brown, *Fables of Modernity: Literature and Culture in the English Eighteenth Century* (Ithaca, NY: Cornell University Press, 2001), 95–131.

13. Julian Hoppit, "Attitudes to Credit in Britain, 1680–1790," *Historical Journal* 33, no. 2 (1990): 305–322, at 322.

14. Ibid., 313–314.

15. Numerous bills were introduced in Parliament between 1693 and 1773, but only five became law, including one regulating the number of Jewish brokers who could operate in the city: Anne L. Murphy, "Financial Markets: The Limits of Economic Regulation in Early Modern England," in *Mercantilism Reimagined: Political Economy in Early Modern Britain and Its Empire*, ed. Philip J. Stern and Carl Wennerlind (Oxford: Oxford University Press, 2014), 263–281, esp. 267, 274.

16. Although he did not refer to Jews when discussing bills of exchange, Defoe worried about their potential perils. He called bills of exchange "sacred in trade" and advised tradesmen "to pay them always punctually and honorably" but also warned about their mishandling: Daniel Defoe, "Letter XXIV: Of Credit in Trade," in *The Complete English Tradesman* (London: Charles Rivington, 1726).

17. Idem, *The Anatomy of Exchange-Alley* (London: E. Smith, 1719), 41. For an earlier condemnation of the stock exchange that does not invoke Jews, see idem, *The Villainy of Stock-jobbers Detected* (London: n.p., 1701). On Jews as manipulators of coins and foreign speculators,

see idem, *An Essay, on Ways and Means for the Advancement of Trade* (London: T. Warner, 1726), 19, 38. At the same time, adopting a different cliché used also in French commercial literature, Defoe singled out Jews as the only industrious people in the Ottoman Empire: idem, *A Plan of the English Commerce* (London: Charles Rivington, 1728), 14.

18. For more examples of Jews as stockjobbers, in both serious and satirical works, see *The Broken Stock-jobbers: or, Work for the Bailiffs; A New Farce as It Was Lately Acted in Exchange-alley* (London: T. Jauncy, 1720), 6; William Rufus Chetwood, *The Stock-jobbers: or, the Humours of Exchange-alley; A Comedy, of Three Acts* (London, J. Roberts, 1720), 23; *An Essay in Praise of Knavery* (London: Sam. Briscoe, 1723), 17; Alexander Montgomerie, Earl of Eglinton, *An Inquiry into the Original and Consequences of the Public Debt* (London: M. Cooper, 1754), 23; Thomas Mortimer, *Every Man His Own Broker: or, A Guide to Exchange-alley*, 4th ed. (London: S. Hooper, 1761), xvii. The latter was reissued in four editions in its first year, with a total of fourteen editions by 1807.

19. Michael Ragussis, *Theatrical Nation: Jews and Other Outlandish Englishmen in Georgian Britain* (Philadelphia: University of Pennsylvania Press, 2010), 89–90, 97.

20. Jonathan Karp, *The Politics of Jewish Commerce: Economic Thought and Emancipation in Europe, 1638–1848* (Cambridge: Cambridge University Press, 2008), 70–71. On the influence of party politics on the London stock market and the alignment of Jewish investors with Whigs, see Bruce G. Carruthers, *City of Capital: Politics and Markets in the English Financial Revolution* (Princeton, NJ: Princeton University Press, 1996), esp. 157.

21. David Hume, "Of Public Credit," in *Essays, Moral, Political, and Literary*, ed. Eugene F. Miller (Indianapolis, IN: Liberty Classics, 1987), 349–365; Wennerlind, *Casualties of Credit*, 241–243.

22. Adam Smith, *An Inquiry into the Nature and Causes of the Wealth of Nations*, ed. Edwin Cannan (New York: Modern Library, 1994), 330, 350 (book II, ch. 2).

23. John Adams to Thomas Jefferson, June 6, 1786, in *The Papers of Thomas Jefferson*, ed. Julian P. Boyd, 42 vols. (Princeton, NJ: Princeton University Press, 1950–2016), 9:612, partially cited in Woody Holton, "Abigail Adams, Bond Speculator," *William and Mary Quarterly* 64, no. 4 (2007): 821–838, at 826.

24. John Marius, *Advice Concerning Bills of Exchange*, 2nd ed. (London: William Hunt, 1655); John Scarlett, *The Style of Exchanges* (London: John Bringhurst, 1682). Note that Marius's booklet was published after Cleirac's *Us et coustumes de la mer* but before Savary's *Le parfait négociant*. Starting in 1656, it appeared together with other tracts at the end of Gerard Malynes's *Consuetudo, vel, Lex Mercatoria*, as did Cleirac's compilation in abridged English translation (chapter 4, note 20).

25. The English translation of Cleirac's *Us et coustumes de la mer* did not include the section in which the legend appeared (chapter 4, note 20).

26. John Barrow, *A New and Universal Dictionary of Arts and Sciences* (London: Printed for the proprietors, 1751), s.v. "bill of exchange"; Richard Rolt, *A New Dictionary of Trade and Commerce* (London: T. Osborne and J. Shipton, 1756), s.v. "bill of exchange"; John Tisdall, *Laws and Usages Respecting Bills of Exchange, and Promissory Notes* (Philadelphia: T. Stephens, 1795), 1 (though an early American print, the latter describes its author on the frontispiece as a "notary public of Belfast"). Two encyclopedias offered entries particularly close to Cleirac's rendering of the legend: Ephraim Chambers, *Cyclopaedia, or, An Universal Dictionary of Arts and Sciences,*

2 vols. (London: James and John Knapton, 1728), 1:102, s.v. "bill of exchange"; William Henry Hall, *The New Royal Encyclopædia*, 3 vols. (London: C. Cooke, 1788), s.v. "bill of exchange."

27. Malachy Postlethwayt couched his highly successful work as a translation of the Savarys' dictionary, even if he departed from that work in many ways, including in his depiction of the history of both marine insurance and bills of exchange. Postlethwayt claimed that Jews introduced dry exchange to England and described the practice as the equivalent of "usury": *The Universal Dictionary of Trade and Commerce Translated from the French of the Celebrated Monsieur Savary . . . with Large Additions and Improvements*, 2 vols. (London: John and Paul Knapton, 1751–1755), 1:254, s.v. "bills of exchange." Shortly thereafter, a booklet on bills of exchange repeated Postlethwayt's claim but also followed the Savarys closely with regard to the Jewish invention of marine insurance: Timothy Cunningham, *The Law of Bills of Exchange, Promissory Notes, Bank-notes and Insurances* (London: W. Owen, 1760), 7, 145.

28. Samuel Ricard, *A General Treatise of the Reduction of the Exchanges, Moneys, and Real Species of Most Places in Europe*, trans. Alexander Justice (London: J. Matthews, 1704). Although presented as a translation of the 1700 *Traité général du commerce* by Ricard, the English version was a very different work (chapter 5, note 56). Two-thirds shorter, *A General Treatise* was essentially devoid of the French original's narrative sections and only included tables of currency conversions. Ricard's translator, Alexander Justice, the author of a reputable introduction to maritime law, likely took it upon himself to introduce these emendations: Justice, *A General Treatise of the Dominion and Laws of the Sea* (London: J. Matthews, 1705).

29. Wyndham Beawes, *Lex Mercatoria Rediviva, or, The Merchant's Directory* (London: J. Moore, 1751), 261. Beawes's title is obviously indebted to Malynes. The work began as a translation of the Savarys' dictionary and continued with addenda by Thomas Mortimer (a former English consul in Cadiz) and Joseph Chitty (a jurist).

30. Ibid., 410–411. Savary had emphasized the role of Ghibellines rather than Guelfs. Like Beawes, William Forbes was also agnostic: Forbes, *A Methodical Treatise Concerning Bills of Exchange* (Edinburgh: Heirs and successors of Andrew Anderson, 1703), 17–18. Mortimer followed Beawes nearly word for word in his *A New and Complete Dictionary of Trade and Commerce* (London: Printed for the author, 1766), s.v. "bill of exchange" and "insurance."

31. Sir William Blackstone, *Commentaries on the Laws of England*, 4 vols. (Oxford: Clarendon Press, 1765–1769), 2:466–467. The second edition of the *Encyclopædia Britannica* incorporated the lemma "bill of exchange" and repeated Blackstone verbatim: *Encyclopædia Britannica, or, A Dictionary of Arts, Sciences, &c. on a Plan Entirely New*, 10 vols. (Edinburgh: J. Balfour and Co., 1778–1783), 2:1152.

32. John Millar, *Elements of the Law Relating to Insurances* (Edinburgh: J. Bell, G.G.J. & J. Robinson, 1787), 8. Millar cited Bornier and Savary as the sources for the legend and Cleirac as the source of specific elements of commercial law. In this, he was not unusual. John Weskett cited "Cleirac's *Guidon*" as saying that "the contract of marine insurance passed from the Italians amongst the Spaniards, afterwards into Holland" and attributed instead to "Mons. Savary" the idea that "Jews were the first who introduced the practice of insurance about 1183." Weskett, *A Complete Digest of the Theory, Laws, and Practice of Insurance* (London: Frys, Couchman, & Collier, 1781), 290.

33. James Allan Park, *A System of the Law of Marine Insurances* (London: His Majesty's law printers for T. Whieldon, 1787), iii.

34. William Stevenson, *A Full and Practical Treatise upon Bills of Exchange* (Edinburgh: John Robertson, 1764), 7, 9.

35. Johann Beckmann, *A History of Inventions and Discoveries* (London: J. Bell, 1797), 1:387, a translation of *Beyträge zur Geschichte der Erfindungen*, 5 vols. (Leipzig: Paul Gotthelf Kummer, 1783–1805), 1:209–210.

36. Thomas Mortimer, *The Elements of Commerce, Politics and Finances* (London: Printed for the author, 1772), 350. Montesquieu's *Spirit of the Laws* was published in at least seven English editions in the second half of the eighteenth century: Alison K. Howard, "Montesquieu, Voltaire and Rousseau in Eighteenth-Century Scotland: A Check List of Editions and Translations of their Works Published in Scotland before 1801," *Bibliotheck* 2, no. 2 (1959): 40–63, at 43–45. On Beccaria, see the section on the Italian peninsula in this chapter.

37. Stewart Kyd, *A Treatise on the Law of Bills of Exchange* (London: S. Crowder and B. C. Collins, 1790), 2; Joseph Chitty, *A Treatise on the Law of Bills of Exchange, Checks on Bankers, Promissory Notes, Bankers' Cash Notes, and Bank Notes* (London: P. Byrne, 1803), 11.

38. Keith Tribe, *Governing Economy: The Reformation of German Economic Discourse, 1750–1840* (Cambridge: Cambridge University Press, 1988), 133, 140.

39. James Steuart, *An Inquiry into the Principles of Political Oeconomy*, 2 vols. (London: A. Millar and T. Cadell, 1767), 2:353 (book IV, part IV, ch. II: "Of the Rise and Progress of Public Credit"). For his debt to Montesquieu, see his comments on the Jewish dominance of English trade in the Middle Ages (1:443 [book II, ch. 30]) and the preponderance of Jews in medieval moneylending (2:113 [book IV, ch. 1]). His book was translated into French at the start of the Revolution: *Recherche des principes de l'économie politique*, 5 vols. (Paris: De l'imprimerie de Didot l'aîné, 1789). Like most of the authors who absorbed Montesquieu's lesson, Steuart did not explicitly cite his source. The success of *The Spirit of the Laws* may be a better explanation for this omission than the censorship to which Montesquieu was subjected. For a brief introduction to Steaurt's work, see Andrew S. Skinner, "Sir James Steuart, *Principles of Political Oeconomy*," in *A History of Scottish Economic Thought*, ed. Alexander Dow and Sheila Dow (London: Routledge, 2006), 71–101. On his work more generally, see Ramón Tortajada, ed., *The Economics of James Steuart* (London: Routledge, 1999).

40. John Toland, *Reasons for Naturalizing the Jews in Great Britain and Ireland on the Same Foot with All Other Nations* (London: J. Roberts, 1714). Toland rejected the classical republicanism of James Harrington's *Oceana*, which only conceded a place in the commonwealth to Jews once they had converted and become farmers. For a fuller analysis of this pamphlet and the context of its publication, see Karp, *Politics of Jewish Commerce*, 43–66; Adam Sutcliffe, "The Philosemitic Moment? Judaism and Republicanism in Seventeenth-Century European Thought," in *Philosemitism in History*, ed. Jonathan Karp and Adam Sutcliffe (New York: Cambridge University Press, 2011), 67–89.

41. Karp, *Politics of Jewish Commerce*, 67–93.

42. Ira Katznelson, "Regarding Toleration and Liberalism: Considerations from the Anglo-Jewish Experience," in *Religion and the Political Imagination*, ed. Ira Katznelson and Gareth Stedman Jones (New York: Cambridge University Press, 2010), 46–69, at 57. A fuller analysis of the association of Jews with reckless financiers appears in Avinoam Yuval-Naeh, "The 1753 Jewish Naturalization Bill and the Polemic over Credit," *Journal of British Studies* 57, no. 3 (2018): 467–492. See also G. A. Cranfield, "The 'London Evening-Post' and the Jew Bill of 1753," *Historical*

Journal 8, no. 1 (1965): 16–39; Thomas Perry, *Public Opinion, Propaganda, and Politics in Eighteenth Century England: A Study of the Jew Bill of 1753* (Cambridge, MA: Harvard University Press, 1962); Frank Felsenstein, *Anti-Semitic Stereotypes: A Paradigm of Otherness in English Popular Culture, 1660–1830* (Baltimore: Johns Hopkins University Press, 1995), 187–214.

43. Arthur Murphy, "The Temple of Laverna: Scene II," *Gray's Inn Journal*, no. 18, Feb. 17, 1752, reprinted in *The Craftsman*, June 16, 1753; *A Collection of the Best Pieces in Prose and Verse Against the Naturalization of the Jews* (London: M. Cooper, at the Globe, 1753), 17–25; and Roy S. Wolper, ed., *Pieces on the "Jew Bill" (1753)* (Los Angeles: William Andrews Clark Memorial Library, University of California, 1983), unnumbered pages. The sketch was first published before the Jew Bill but was later incorporated into the propaganda that surrounded it.

44. Henri Grégoire's essay was published in English translation the year of the emancipation of all French Jews (1791) but fell on deaf ears in England because the stakes were different there than they were in France: Grégoire, *An Essay on the Physical, Moral, and Political Reformation of the Jews: A Work Crowned by the Royal Society of Arts and Sciences at Metz* (London: C. Forster, 1791).

45. The translator's name does not appear anywhere in this text, but he produced a literal translation of the work: Jacob Savary, *Der vollkommene Kauff- und Handelsmann*, 2 vols. (Geneva: J. H. Widerhold, 1676), 134–135 (book 1, ch. 19).

46. In 1682, a special ordinance regulated the use of bills of exchange at the Leipzig fairs and included provisions for the role that Jews could play in these gatherings: Carl Günter Ludovici, *Eröffnete Akademie der Kaufleute, oder, Vollständiges Kaufmanns Lexicon* (Leipzig: B. C. Breitkopf, 1752–1754), 3:1259; Robert Beachy, "Fernhandel und Krämergeist: Die Leipziger Handelsdeputierten und die Einführung der sächsischen Wechselordnung 1682," in *Leipzigs Messen 1497–1997: Gestaltwandel, Umbrüche, Neubeginn*, 2 vols., ed. Hartmut Zwahr, Thomas Topfstedt, and Günter Bentele (Cologne: Böhlau, 1999), 1:135–147.

47. Stefi Jersch-Wenzel, "Jewish Economic Activity in Early Modern Times," in *In and Out of the Ghetto: Jewish-Gentile Relations in Late Medieval and Early Modern Germany*, ed. R. Po-Chia Hsia and Hartmut Lehmann (Cambridge: Cambridge University Press, 1995), 91–101.

48. Johann Heinrich Gottlob von Justi, *Grundsätze der Policey-Wissenschaft* (Göttingen: Wittwe Vandenhoeck, 1759), 196–197.

49. Jonathan M. Hess, "Johann David Michaelis and the Colonial Imaginary: Orientalism and the Emergence of Racial Antisemitism in Eighteenth-Century Germany," *Jewish Social Studies* 6, no. 2 (2000): 56–101. Eisenmenger's *Entdecktes Judenthum* was banned from circulation because of its extremism but went on to "serve as a leading source book for anti-Jewish polemicists": Adam Sutcliffe, *Judaism and Enlightenment* (Cambridge: Cambridge University Press, 2003), 176. Eisenmenger's book was translated into English in the early eighteenth century together with the works of an earlier German Hebraist, Johann Buxtorf the Elder, whose *Synagoga Judaica* (1603) was a less than sympathetic proto-ethnography of Jewish rituals (ibid., 26–28).

50. John W. Van Cleve, *The Merchant in German Literature of the Enlightenment* (Chapel Hill: University of North Carolina Press, 1986), esp. 123–124.

51. Moseh Zimmerman, "The Man Who Preceded Sombart: Ludolf Holst (1756–1825)" [in Hebrew], in *Jews in Economic Life: Collected Essays in Memory of Arkadius Kahan (1920–1982)*, ed. Nachum Gross (Jerusalem: Zalman Shazar Center for the Furtherance of the Study of Jewish History, 1984), 245–256.

52. Ari Joskowicz, "Toleration in the Age of Projects: Cameralism, German Police Science,

and the Jews," *Jewish Social Studies* 22, no. 2 (2017): 1–37. On the German precursors and contemporaries of Dohm, see also Robert Liberles, "The Historical Context of Dohm's Treatise on the Jews," in *Das deutsche Judentum und der Liberalismus / German Jewry and Liberalism* (Sankt Augustin, Germany: Comdok-Verlagsabteilung, 1986), 44–69; Jonathan M. Hess, *Germans, Jews and the Claims of Modernity* (New Haven, CT: Yale University Press, 2002), 25–49.

53. Not coincidentally, the German title *Über die bürgerliche Verbesserung der Juden* (*On the Civic Improvement of Jews*) was rendered in French as *De la réforme politique des Juifs* (*On the Political Reform of Jews*), with an emphasis on the word "political" that signaled higher ambitions. See chapter 6, note 70.

54. Hans Jaeger, "Marperger, Paul Jacob," and Peter Koch, "Ludovici, Carl Günter," in *Neue Deutsche Biographie*, 26 vols. (Berlin: Duncker & Humblot, 1953–2013), 16:234–235 and 15:305–306, respectively.

55. Franz Schnorr von Carolsfeld, "Zedler, Johann Heinrich," in *Allgemeine Deutsche Biographie*, 56 vols. (Leipzig: Duncker & Humblot, 1875–1912), 44:741–742.

56. Paul Jacob Marperger, *Neu-eroeffnetes Handels-Gericht* (Hamburg: B. Schiller, 1709), 490–491 (ch. XVI: "Von den Wechseln und deren Recht"). In support of the legend, Marperger cited accurately from the second edition of Ricard's *Traité general du commerce* (Amsterdam: Paul Marret, 1705), 122. Ricard had lifted the legend from Savary (chapter 5, note 56). Marperger's *Neu-eroeffnetes Handels-Gericht* also included excerpts from Savary's *Le parfait négociant* and Friedrich Gladov, *Speranders sorgfältiger Negotiant und Wechssler* (Rostock and Leipzig: Johann Heinrich Russworm, 1706). In the abridged translation of Savary's *Parères*, however, Marparger omitted references to the legend: Paul Jacob Marperger, *Zulänglicher Vorrath unterschiedlicher von denen berühmtesten Universitäten und Handels-Plätzen über allerhand die Kauffmannschafft betreffende Vorfälle eingeholten Responsorum und kauffmannischer Pareres* (Hamburg: Benjamin Schiller, 1709), 17–29.

57. Paul Jacob Marperger, *Beschreibung der Banquen was und wie vielerley derselben seyn als nehmlich Land- Lehn- und Deposito-Wechsel- und Giro- oder kauffmännische Ab- und Zuschreib- wie auch Billets- oder so genannte Müntz-Zettels- und Actien-Banquen* (Halle and Leipzig: Felix du Serre, 1717), 4.

58. Johann Heinrich Zedler, *Grosses vollständiges Universallexicon aller Wissenschafften und Künste*, 64 vols. (Leipzig: n.p., 1732–1754), 5:351–352, s.v. "cambium," and 28:1487–1488, s.v. "Assecuranz/Police." The same lexicon defined Jews as children of the devil rather than God (14:1499, s.v. "Juden").

59. The entry for "cambium reale" was the same as in Zedler (and thus contained no references to Jews), while the Jewish invention of bills of exchange was given as one among several hypotheses in the entry "Exchange, Cambium, Change." Carl Günter Ludovici, *Allgemeine Schatz-Kammer der Kauffmannschafft*, 5 vols. (Leipzig: Johann Samuel Heinsius, 1741–1743), 1:1027 and 4:850, respectively. Savary's name did not figure on the title page, yet Jean-Claude Perrot calls this work Ludovici's first "rewriting" of Savary: Perrot, *Une histoire intellectuelle de l'économie politique, XVIIe–XVIIIe siècle* (Paris: École des Hautes Études en Sciences Sociales, 1992), 103. This German work was reissued in three more editions in 1752–1756, 1767–1768, and 1797. In a related compendium, the entry "Assecuranz" included a verbatim translation from the equivalent entry in the Savary brothers' *Dictionnaire* (appendix 4) and therefore left no doubt that Jews fleeing France beginning in 1182 invented marine insurance, but the section on bills of

exchange rejected the Jewish origin of those instruments on account of the many Italian words that defined the language of banking. Ludovici, *Eröffnete Akademie der Kaufleute, oder, Vollständiges Kaufmanns Lexicon*, 5 vols. (Leipzig: B. C. Breitkopf, 1767–1768), 1:969–970, s.v. "Assecuranz," and 5:67, s.v. "Wechselbrief."

60. Paul Jacob Marperger, *Nothwendig und nützliche Fragen über die Kauffmannschafft* (Leipzig and Flensburg: B. O. Bosseck, 1714), 208.

61. Carl Günter Ludovici, *Grundriß eines vollständigen Kaufmanns-Systems, nebst den Anfangsgründen der Handlungswissenschaft* (Leipzig: Bernhard Christoph Breitkopf und Sohn, 1768), 166, 194, 384. His last revisions to the *Eröfnete Academie* incorporated the findings of two then-recent works by Beckmann and Fischer that further disputed the Jewish invention of marine insurance: Ludovici, *Neu eröfnete Academie der Kaufleute*, 6 vols. (Leipzig: Breitkopf und Härtel, 1797–1801), 6:1385–1409, s.v. "Wechselbriefe"; Beckmann, *Beyträge zur Geschichte der Erfindungen*, 1:209–210; Friedrich Christopher Jonathan Fischer, *Geschichte des teutschen Handels*, 4 vols. (Hannover: In der Helwingschen Hofbuchhandlung, 1785–1792), 4:282, 820.

62. Wolfgang Adam Lauterbach, *De iure in curia mercatorum usitato* (Tübingen: Typis Johanni Alexandri Celli, 1655), 18 (art. 98: "Pecunia non est sterilis"). For a biographical sketch, see Klaus Luig, "Lauterbach, Wolfgang Adam," in *Neue Deutsche Biographie*, 13:736–738.

63. E.g., Johann Gottlieb Heineccius, Johan Loccenius, Reinhold Kuricke, and Franz Stypmann, *Scriptorum de iure nautico et maritimo* (Halle: Magdeburgicae Orphanotropheum 1740); Heineccius, *Elementa juris cambialis* (Amsterdam: Apud Iansoinio Waesbergios, 1742); Johann Gottlieb Siegel, *Corpus juris cambialis* (Leipzig: Heinsius, 1742); Johann Christian Hedler, *Positiones de origine cambiorum* (Wittenberg: Io. Guilielmus Bossegelius, 1744), 3–5; Johann Melchior Gottlieb Beseke, *Thesaurus iuris cambialis* (Berlin: Christ. Fried. Voss et fil., 1783), 1–3. A mere hint at the debate over whether Jews or other groups might have been the first to use bills of exchange appeared in the section that contested Heineccius's account in Georg Heinrich Ayrer, *De cambialis instituti vestigiis apud Romanos* (Amsterdam: Jansonius & Waesberg, 1743). Because of the polemical exchange contained in it, from then on Ayrer's treatise was often reprinted in a single volume together with Heineccius's. Elsewhere Ayrer discussed the terms of Jewish residence in a Christian polity: Ayrer, *Tractatio iuridica de iure recipiendi Iudaeos tum generatim tum speciatim in terris Brusvico-Luneburgicis* (Göttingen: Apud Abram. Vandenhoeck, 1741), esp. 16–21 (ch. I, sec. VII) and 29–32 (ch. II, sec. IV).

64. Johann Andreas Engelbrecht, *Corpus iuris nautici* (Lübeck: Christian Gottfried Donatius, 1790), e.g., drew from Cleirac for the text of the Laws of Oléron. A rare eighteenth-century mention of Cleirac as the textual source for the legend, accompanied by a dismissal of the fanciful tale, appeared in Beckmann, *Beyträge zur Geschichte der Erfindungen*, 1:209–210.

65. Montesquieu, *Das Geist der Gesetze*, 2 vols. (Altenburg: Richter, 1782). Scholars like Johann Heinrich Gottlob von Justi absorbed Montesquieu in French. In a compendium of writings on matters mercantile, Montesquieu's statement about the Jewish invention of bills of exchange was taken to be common knowledge: Friedrich von Deym, *Kurzgefaßte gründliche Einleitung in die Commerz und Handlungswissenschaft* (Frankfurt and Leipzig: Zeh, 1779), 133. In any case, Antonio Genovesi's *Lezioni di commercio* had hinted at Montesquieu's tale and was already available in German: *Grundsätze der bürgerlichen Oekonomie* (Leipzig: Paul Gotthelf Kummer, 1776). See also note 78 below.

66. Jakob Friedrich von Bielfeld, *Institutions politiques*, 3 vols. (The Hague: Chez Pierre

Grosse Junior, 1760–1772), 1:275–276. This work appeared in as many as twelve editions. What Tribe describes as the "French cultural hegemony" in eighteenth-century German Cameralism accounts for why Bielfeld wrote in French and why he was the most successful of German political economists abroad: Tribe, *Governing Economy*, 79 and passim.

67. Martin Euler, *Allgemeine Wechselencyclopädie*, 2 vols. (Frankfurt am Main: In der Andreäischen Buchhandlung, 1787) 1:1.

68. J.L.E. Püttmann, *Der Stadt Leipzig Wechselordnung* (Leipzig: bei Johann Samuel Heinsius, 1787), 3; idem, *Grundsätze des Wechsel-Rechts* (Leipzig: Paul Gotthelf Kummer, 1795), 2–3; Johann Georg Kruenitz, *Oeconomische Encyclopädie*, 242 vols. (Berlin: Pauli, 1773–1858), 218:416, s.v. "Vertrag [Versicherungs]," and 235:267–268, s.v. "Wechsel."

69. Johann Daniel Heinrich Musäus, *Anfangsgründe des Handlungs- und Wechsel-Rechts* (Hamburg: Carl Ernst Bohn, 1799), 108–110.

70. In citing multiple hypotheses, Büsch once made an explicit reference to Montesquieu (XX, 20) in his *Handlungsbibliothek*, 3 vols. (Hamburg: n.p., 1785–1797), 3:381–382, which was reprinted as *Sämmtliche Schriften über die Handlung*, 8 vols. (Hamburg: Campe, 1824–1827), 6:11. Later he rejected the same theory as "empty gibberish" and attributed the invention of bills of exchange solely to the growth of trade: Büsch, *Theoretisch-praktische Darstellung der Handlung in deren mannigfaltigen Geschäften*, 2 vols. (Hamburg: B. G. Hoffmann, 1791–1792), 1:58, 73. Following Büsch, the jurist Georg Friedrich von Martens derided those who still believed in the legend: Martens, *Versuch einer historischen Entwicklung des wahren Ursprungs des Wechselrechts* (Göttingen: J. C. Dieterich, 1797), 4. See also Manfred Friedrich, "Martens, Georg Friedrich v.," in *Neue Deutsche Biographie*, 16:269–271.

71. Fischer, *Geschichte des teutschen Handels*, 1:297. On marine insurance, see 4:282. Abbé Grégoire had disputed Fischer's claim when reaffirming the Jewish invention of bills of exchange (chapter 6, note 85).

72. Raffaele della Torre, *Tractatus de cambiis* (Genoa: Excudebat Petrus Ioannes Calenzanus, 1641), 20 (disputatio I, quæstio IV: "De origine, progressu, & augmento cambij secundum tempus," sec. 20). Della Torre stated that bills of exchange grew out of earlier forms of currency exchange (sec. 24). In an encyclopedia that was never completed, the Franciscan cartographer Vincenzo Maria Coronelli noted that writers debated the origins and first appearance of bills of exchange at length: Coronelli, *Biblioteca universale sacro-profana, antico-moderna*, 7 vols. (Venice: Antonio Tivani, 1701–1706), 7:548–550, at 548, s.v. "cambj locali, o letterali."

73. Jacques Dupuis de la Serra, *Trattato delle lettere di cambio secondo l'uso delle più celebri piazze d'Europa*, trans. Pietro d'Albizzo Martellini (Florence: nella stamperia di S.A.R. a spese di G.A. Mornini, 1718). The work was reprinted five more times in Venice (1750, 1761, 1772, 1785, and 1803). The Latin translation had already left a mark on contemporary Italian authors: Dupuis de la Serra, *Tractatus de arte litterarum cambii* (Cologne: Sumptibus Jacobi Promper, 1712) was cited as an authority by Domenico Maria Manni, *De Florentinis inventis commentarium* (Ferrara: Bernardini Pomatelli, 1731), 99–101 (ch. 52). Unknown to Dupuis de la Serra but likely familiar to some Italian authors was Benedetto Cotrugli's hypothesis that "the Florentines . . . were the first innovators to experiment with" bills of exchange (chapter 4, note 27).

74. Giuseppe Lorenzo Maria Casaregi, *Discursus legales de commercio*, 3 vols., 2nd ed. (Venice: Balleoniana, 1740), 2:357 (discorsus CCXVIII, no. 1, September 27, 1733). See also chapter 5, note 52.

75. Giovan Francesco Pagnini, *Della decima e di varie altre gravezze imposte dal comune di Firenze della moneta della mercatura de' Fiorentini fino al secolo XVI*, 4 vols. (Florence: G. Bouchard, 1765–1766), 1:126 (part III: "Sul commercio de' Fiorentini), citing the legend as re-layed by Bielfeld (see note 65 above) and Ricard (chapter 5, note 56). His discussion of bills of exchange was part of an argument, borrowed from French physiocrats, in favor of liberalizing the grain trade in Tuscany. Together with this text, Pagnini also published a new edition of two key merchant manuals from the late Middle Ages: Francesco Balducci Pegolotti's *La pratica della mercatura* (c. 1340) and Giovanni di Antonio da Uzzano's *La pratica della mercatura* (1442). In those two manuals, between which Pagnini failed to draw explicit comparisons, bills of exchange were the exclusive province of Christian international bankers, untainted by the operations of Jewish pawnbrokers.

76. Pompeo Baldasseroni, *Leggi e costumi del cambio che si osservano nelle principali piazze di Europa e singolarmente in quella di Livorno* (Pescia: Masi, 1784), xii, paraphrasing Casaregi, cited in note 73 above.

77. Ascanio Baldasseroni, *Delle assicurazioni marittime trattato*, 3 vols. (Firenze: Bonduc-ciana, 1786), 1:12.

78. Giovanni Francesco Muzio, *Principj di artimetica e commercio: Opera divisa in due tomi utilissima a negozianti*, 2 vols. (Genoa: Stamperia Gesiniana, 1790), 1:133.

79. Antonio Genovesi, *Delle lezioni di commercio, o sia, d'economia civile*, 2 vols. (Naples: Fratelli Simone, 1765–1767), 2:60 (part II, ch. 5). Full German and Spanish translations ap-peared within the next twenty years: *Grundsätze der bürgerlichen Oekonomie*, 2 vols., trans. August Witzmann (Leipzig: Paul Gotthelf Kummer, 1772–1774); *Lecciones de comercio*, 3 vols., trans. Victorian de Villanova (Madrid: Joachín Ibarra, 1785–1786). A partial French translation was published in the *Journal de l'agricolture, du commerce, arts et finances* in 1770, as explained in idem, *Delle lezioni di commercio o sia di economia civile con elementi del commercio*, ed. Maria Luisa Perna (Naples: Istituto Italiano per gli Studi Filosofici, 2005), 902.

80. Genovesi, *Delle lezioni di commercio* (1765–1767), 2:61.

81. Cesare Beccaria, *A Discourse on Public Oeconomy and Commerce* (London: J. Dodsley and J. Murray, 1769), 35–36 (emphasis mine). "Made use of" would be a more accurate English translation of the original. For the Italian and French versions, see *Prolusione letta il giorno 9 gennaio 1769 nell'apertura della nuova cattedra di scienze camerali nelle scuole palatine di Milano*, in his *Elementi di economia pubblica*, 2 vols. (Milan: G. G. Destefanis, 1804), 2:185; and idem, *Discours ... pour le commerce & l'administration publique* (Lausanne: Chez François Grasset & Comp., 1769), 35–36, respectively.

82. Beccaria, *Discourse on Public Oeconomy*, 35.

83. In his more extensive treatise on political economy, Beccaria discussed the difference between "interest" and "usury" but made no mention of bills of exchange: *Elementi di economia pubblica*, 2:118.

84. In principle, Cleirac's and Savary's chronology was not incompatible with Fibonacci's manuscript, but in Tozzetti's reading of Montesquieu, the alleged Jewish invention had occurred between the late twelfth and the early fourteenth century: "Il celebre autore de *l'Esprit des Loix* L. 21, Ch. 16 ne attribuisce l'invenzione agli Ebrei cacciati di Francia sulla fine del Secolo XII, e di nuovo al principio del XIV, e vi è chi l'attribuisce ai *Mercanti Fiorentini*, cacciati dalla Patria per le maledette Fazioni." Targioni Tozzetti, *Relazioni d'alcuni viaggi fatti in diverse parti della*

Toscana per osservare le produzioni naturali, e gli antichi monumenti di essa, 12 vols., 2nd ed. (Florence: Stamperia Granducale, per G. Cambiagi, 1768), 2:62. This passage did not appear in the first edition of this work.

85. Domenico Alberto Azuni, *Dizionario universale ragionato della giurisprudenza mercantile*, 2 vols. (Nice: Presso la Società Tipografica, 1786–1788), 1:xii–xiii. On this work and its vast diffusion in French and English translation, see Luigi Berlinguer, *Domenico Alberto Azuni, giurista e politico, 1749–1827: Un contributo bio-bibliografico* (Milan: Giuffrè, 1966).

86. Federica Francesconi, *Invisible Enlighteners: Modenese Jewry from the Renaissance to Emancipation* (forthcoming).

87. Giovanni Battista Gherardo D'Arco, *Dell'influenza del commercio sopra i talenti e sui costumi* (Cremona: per L. Manini, 1782), 61–64. D'Arco borrowed his argument against oligopolies from Montesquieu, who, however, did not associate them with Jews.

88. Idem, *Della influenza del ghetto nello stato*, 2 vols. (Venice: Gaspare Storti [vol. 1] and Tommaso Bettinelli [vol. 2], 1782–1785), 1:96. On Sessa's *Tractatus de Judæis* (1717) and its influence on D'Arco, see Kenneth Stow, *Anna and Tranquillo: Catholic Anxiety and Jewish Protest in the Age of Revolutions* (New Haven, CT: Yale University Press, 2016), esp. 218–219n3.

89. Benedetto Frizzi, *Difesa contro gli attacchi fatti alla nazione ebrea* (Pavia: Nella stamperia del R.I. Monistero d. S. Salvatore, 1784), 105–106.

90. Cristóbal de Villalón, *Provechoso tratado de cambios y contrataciones de mercaderes y reprovacion de usura . . . Visto y de nuevo añadido y emēdado* (Valladolid: n.p., 1542), lv; Thomas de Marcado, *Tratos y contratos de mercaderes* (Salamanca: Mathias Gast, 1569), 76r–80r. The latter treatise, by a Dominican friar, was addressed to confessors and lay readers and was promptly translated into Italian: *De' negotii et contratti de mercanti et de negotianti* (Brescia: Pietro Maria Marchetti, 1591).

91. Antonio de Capmany y Montpalau, *Memorias históricas sobre la marina, comercio y artes de la antiqua ciudad de Barcelona*, 4 vols. (Madrid: de Sancha, 1779–1792), 1:386.

92. Miguel Gerónimo Suárez y Núñez, *Tratado legal theórico y práctico de letras de cambio*, 2 vols. (Madrid: En la Imprenta de Joseph Doblado, 1788–1789), 1:2–3.

93. Bernardo J. Danvila y Villarrasa, *Lecciones de economía civil, o de el comercio* (1779), ed. Pablo Cervera Ferri (Zaragoza, Spain: Institución Fernando el Católico, 2008), 148.

94. José da Silva Lisboa, *Principios de direito mercantil e leis de marinha* (Lisbon: Na Regia officina typografica, 1798), v–vi.

95. Antonio Muñoz, *Discurso sobre economía política* (Madrid: Por D. Joachin de Ibarra, 1769), 302–304.

96. José Alonso Ortiz, *Ensayo económico sobre el sistema de la moneda-papel y sobre el crédito público* (Madrid: Imprenta real, 1796), 63–65.

97. Cited in Albert Hyma, "Commerce and Capitalism in the Netherlands, 1555–1700," *Journal of Modern History* 10, no. 3 (1938): 321–343, at 334.

98. Simon Schama, *The Embarrassment of Riches: An Interpretation of Dutch Culture in the Golden Age* (Berkeley: University of California Press, 1988), esp. 289–371.

99. Jacques Savary, *De volmaakte koopman* (Amsterdam: Hieronymus Sweerts, 1683), 134–135 (ch. 19: "Van den oorspronck der wissel-brieven, en der zelver nuttigheid in de koophandel").

100. I base this observation on an educated guess, since no comprehensive corpus exists for

the period beyond 1700 to support quantitative comparisons. I cite only a few Dutch titles of the most practical sort that I have consulted: Nicolaus Petri, *Practicque om te leeren reeckenen, cypheren, ende boeckhouwen* (Amsterdam: Voor Hendrick Laurentsz, 1635); Jeronimo Matthaeus Barels, *Advysen over den koophandel en zeevaert,* 2 vols. (Amsterdam: Hendrik Gartman, 1780–1781); Thymon Boey, *Woorden-tolk of verklaring der voornaamste onduitsche en andere woorden* (Graavenhaage: Johannes Gaillard, 1773); *Verzameling van casus positien, voorstellingen en declaratien, betrekkelijk tot voorvallende omstandigheden in den koophandel, van tijd tot tijd binnen Amsteldam beoordeeld en ondertekend* (Amsterdam: P. H. Dronsberg, 1793–1804).

101. Jacques Le Moine de L'Espine, *Den koophandel van Amsterdam,* 2nd ed. (Amsterdam: Wed. J. van Dijk and Pieter Sceperus, 1704), 1–2. Le Moine de L'Espine borrowed the story from Samuel Ricard (whose treatise had been written in French but published in Amsterdam), who in turn had borrowed it from Savary (chapter 5, note 56). Unfortunately, the editor to whom we owe the revisions in the second edition of *Den koophandel van Amsterdam* is not known. He may or may not have been the same editor who curated all the subsquent editions starting in 1714, Isaäc Le Long (1683–1762). Curiously, the legend appeared in all later Dutch editions (1704, 1714, 1715, 1719, 1724, 1727, 1734, 1744, 1753, 1763, 1780, 1801–1802), but in none of the French editions (1694, 1710, 1722). On this work and its publishing history, see Lucas Jansen, *"De koophandel van Amsterdam": Een critsche studie over het koopmanshandboek van Jacques le Moine de l'Espine en Isaac le Long* (Amsterdam: Nieuwe Uitgevers-Maatschappij, 1946).

102. *De koopman, of, Bydragen ten opbouw van Neerlands koophandel en zeevaard,* 6 vols. (Amsterdam: Gerritbom, 1768–1776), 3:90. Only the first volume of this work was translated into German.

103. Only the Dutch translation of Heineccius's *Elementa juris cambialis* included in a footnote the passage from Georg Heinrich Ayrer's *De cambialis instituti vestigiis apud Romanos,* which mentioned the possibility that either Jews, Florentines, Goths, or Longobards might have invented bills of exchange. Johann Gottlieb Heineccius, *Grondbeginselen van het wisselrecht in 't Latyn saamgesteld* (Middelburg, The Netherlands: Christian Bohemer, 1774), 14n7. On Heineccius and Ayrer, see note 62 above.

104. Cited in Sutcliffe, *Judaism and Enlightenment,* 215. The anonymous writer added that he hoped all Jews could be converted.

105. *Several Remarkable Passages Concerning the Hollanders since the Death of Queen Elizabeth until the 25 of December 1673* (n.p.: n.p., 1673), 38.

106. Anne Goldgar, *Tulipmania: Money, Honor, and Knowledge in the Dutch Golden Age* (Chicago: University of Chicago Press, 2007).

107. Jonathan I. Israel, *Diasporas Within a Diaspora: Jews, Crypto-Jews and the World Maritime Empires (1540–1740)* (Leiden: Brill, 2002), 450. New research shows that 1671–1672 may have been an even worse year for the Amsterdam stock market, but scholars have yet to examine the impact of that crisis on the public perception of Jews. Lodewijk Petram, "The World's First Stock Exchange: How the Amsterdam Market for Dutch East India Company Shares Became a Modern Securities Market, 1602–1700" (Ph.D. diss., University of Amsterdam, 2011), 178–179.

108. On the role of Jews in the Dutch stock exchange, see J. G. van Dillen, "De economische positie en betekenis der Joden in de Republiek en in de Nederlandse koloniale wereld," in *Geschiedenis der Joden in Nederland,* ed. Hendrik Brugmans and A. Frank (Amsterdam: Van Holkema & Warendorf, 1940), 561–616; Petram, "World's First Stock Exchange," 40–47.

109. Inger Leemans, "Verse Weavers and Paper Traders: Financial Speculation in Dutch Theater," and Julie Berger Hochstrasser, "Print Power: Mad Crowds and the Art of Memory in *Het groote tafereel der dwaasheid*," both in *The Great Mirror of Folly: Finance, Culture, and the Crash of 1720*, ed. William N. Goetzmann, Catherine Labio, K. Geert Rouwenhorst, and Timothy G. Young (New Haven, CT: Yale University Press, 2013), 175–189, at 182, and 191–195, at 195 and 204n31, respectively.

110. Pieter Langendyk, *Arlequyn Actionist* (Amsterdam: de Erven van J. Lescailje en Dirk Rank, op de Beurssluis, 1720), 19–20.

111. *De Koopman*, 5:243.

112. Lynn Hunt, Margaret C. Jacob, and Wijnand Mijnhardt, *The Book that Changed Europe: Picart and Bernard's Religious Ceremonies of the World* (Cambridge, MA: Harvard University Press, 2010), 185–189.

113. Petram, "World's First Stock Exchange," 159–165.

114. Josef Penso de la Vega, *Confusión de confusiones: Dialogos curiosos entre un philosopho agudo, un mercante discrete, y un accionista erudite descrivendo el negocio de las acciones, su origen, su ethimologia, su realidad, su juego y su enredo* (Amsterdam: n.p., 1688). Only a partial English translation exists: Josef Penso de la Vega, *Confusión de confusiones, 1688: Portions Descriptive of the Amsterdam Stock Exchange*, ed. and trans. Hermann Kellenbenz (Boston: Baker Library, Harvard Graduate School of Business Administration, 1957). A full Dutch translation is provided in M.F.J. Smith, ed., *Confusión de confusiones, van Josseph de la Vega; herdruk van den spaanschen tekst met nederlandsche vertaling* (The Hague: M. Nijhoff, 1939).

115. Jonathan Israel, "Een merkwaardig literair werk en de Amsterdamse effectenmarkt in 1688: Joseph Penso de la Vega's *Confusión de confusiones*," *De zeventiende eeuw* 6 (1990): 159–165. De la Vega would later dedicate to William III of England his *Retrato de la prudencia y simulacro del valor* (Amsterdam: Joan Bus, 1690). See also Daniel M. Swetschinski, *Reluctant Cosmopolitans: The Portuguese Jews of Seventeenth-Century Amsterdam* (Portland, OR: Littman Library of Jewish Civilization, 2000), 145–147; and Harm den Boer and Jonathan I. Israel, "William III and the Glorious Revolution in the Eyes of Amsterdam Sephardi Writers: The Reactions of Miguel de Barrios, Joseph Penso de la Vega, and Manuel de Ledo," in *The Anglo-Dutch Moment: Essays on the Glorious Revolution and Its World Impact*, ed. Jonathan I. Israel (Cambridge: Cambridge University Press, 1991), 439–461, esp. 451–454.

116. Petram, "World's First Stock Exchange," 188.

117. Yosef Kaplan, "The Portuguese Community of Amsterdam in the 17th Century Between Tradition and Change," in *Society and Community (Proceeding of the Second International Congress for Research of the Sephardi and Oriental Jewish Heritage 1984)*, ed. Abraham Haim (Jerusalem: Miśgav Yerushalayim, 1991), 141–171, at 166–167.

118. De la Vega, *Confusión de confusiones, 1688*, 41. The word "caba'la" appears three times in this work, always in segments that are not available in the abridged English translation: twice in reference to a business company (idem, *Confusión de confusiones*, 290, 302) and once as part of a comparison between certain trading practices and the mystical theory itself (293–294).

119. His name did not appear among those of Amsterdam Sephardic merchant-bankers in the 1680s: Petram, "World's First Stock Exchange," 187–188.

120. Penso de la Vega, *Confusión de confusiones, 1688*, 8, 11.

121. Ibid., 3.

122. Simone Luzzatto, *Discorso circa il stato de gl'hebrei et in particular dimoranti nell'inclita città di Venetia* (Venice: Gioanne Calleoni, 1638), 19v–23v, 27v–28v.

123. Benjamin Arbel, "Jews, the Rise of Capitalism and *Cambio*: Commercial Credit and Maritime Insurance in the Early Modern Mediterranean World" [in Hebrew], *Zion* 69, no. 2 (2004): 157–202, at 191; idem, "Mediterranean Jewish Diasporas and the Bill of Exchange: Coping with a Foreign Financial Instrument (Fourteenth to Seventeenth Centuries)," in *Union in Separation: Diasporic Groups and Identities in the Eastern Mediterranean (1100–1800)*, ed. Georg Christ, Franz-Julius Morche, Roberto Zaugg, Wolfgang Kaiser, Stefan Burkhardt, and Alexander D. Beihammer (Rome: Viella, 2015), 527–553, at 539–540.

124. "How Profitable the Nation of the Iewes Are," in *Menasseh ben Israel's Mission to Oliver Cromwell: Being a Reprint of the Pamphlets Published by Menasseh ben Israel to Promote the Readmission of the Jews to England, 1649–1656*, ed. Lucien Wolf (London: Macmillan, 1901), 81–103, at 81. See also Karp, *Politics of Jewish Commerce*, 34. In the preface to his 1782 German translation of Menasseh ben Israel's *The Salvation of Israel*, Moses Mendelssohn praised the utility of commerce and posited a strong link between economic freedom and "civic acceptance" (*bürgerliche Aufnahme*) for Jews: Mendelssohn, "Worrede zu Menasseh Ben Israels Rettung der Juden," in *Sammlung* (Leipzig: G. Wolbrecht, 1831), 71–103, at 73. David Sorkin draws attention to Mendelssohn's choice of words in contrast to Dohm's (chapter 6, note 70). Note that Mendelssohn shied away from any reference to the alleged Jewish invention of bills of exchange.

125. David S. Katz, *Philo-Semitism and the Readmission of Jews to England, 1603–1655* (Oxford: Oxford University Press, 1982); Avinoam Yuval-Naeh, "England, Usury and the Jews in the Mid-Seventeenth Century," *Journal of Early Modern History* 21, no. 6 (2017): 489–515.

126. Richard H. Popkin, "Hume and Isaac de Pinto," *Texas Studies in Literature and Language* 12, no. 3 (1970): 417–430; Adam Sutcliffe, "Can a Jew Be a Philosophe? Isaac de Pinto, Voltaire, and Jewish Participation in the European Enlightenment," *Jewish Social Studies* 6, no. 3 (2000): 31–51. Pinto's reputation in Enlightenment circles is best captured by a comment that David Hume made about him to a correspondent: "Allow me to recommend to your patronage M. Pinto, whom I venture to call my Friend, tho' a Jew." Hume to Thomas Rous, August 28, 1767, cited in Richard Popkin, *The High Road to Pyrrhonism*, ed. Richard A. Watson and James E. Force (San Diego: Austin Hill, 1980), 259n17.

127. When Pinto dissected the causes of growing poverty among Amsterdam Jews, he wrote in Portuguese: Isaac de Pinto, *Reflexoens politicas tocante a constituição da Nação Judaica: exposição do estado de suas finanças, causas dos atrasos e desordens que se experimentão, e meyos de os prevenir* (Amsterdam: n.p., 1744).

128. Idem, *Essai sur le luxe* (Amsterdam: n.p., 1762); English translation: *An Essay on Luxury* (London: T. Becket and P. A. De Hondt, 1766).

129. Idem, *Traité de la circulation et du credit* (Amsterdam: Chez Marc Michel Rey, 1771), 201; English translation: *An Essay on Circulation and Credit* (London: J. Ridley, 1774), 167. Note that the second French edition appeared under the title of *Traité des fonds de commerce, ou, Jeu d'actions* (London: Chez J. Nourse, 1772). Pinto also sought to distinguish between usury and interest on the basis of Jewish law—a fallacious argument that Ashkenazic French writers nev-

ertheless borrowed on the eve of the Revolution to defend their fellow moneylenders (chapter 6, note 81).

130. An early sign of change is noticeable in a letter sent around 1760 by a French poet and translator born in Tuscany to his Jewish friend living in Livorno, a certain Cesare Monselles. The letter listed the many accomplishments of the Jewish "nation." Following Montesquieu, Monselles compared the invention of bills of exchange to the breakthrough of the compass. The comparison was intended as a compliment. Giovanni Salvatore de-Coureil, *Opere*, 5 vols. (Livorno: Dalla Stamperia della Fenice, 1818–1819), 5:4, also quoted in Francesca Bregoli, " 'Two Jews Walk into a Coffeehouse': The 'Jewish Question,' Utility, and Political Participation in Late Eighteenth-Century Livorno," *Jewish History* 24, nos. 3–4 (2010): 309–329, at 311 and 325n19.

131. Isaac D'Israeli, *Vaurien, or, Sketches of the Times: Exhibiting Views of the Philosophies, Religions, Politics, Literature, and Manners of the Age* (London: T. Cadell, Junior et alii, 1797), xiv–xv. The title is a play on the French word for "rascal." Isaac D'Israeli renounced his membership in the Jewish community of London and baptized his children, although he did not convert. See Todd M. Endelman, *The Jews of Georgian England, 1714–1830: Tradition and Change in a Liberal Society* (Philadelphia: Jewish Publication Society of America, 1979), 125, 152–154, 258; David B. Ruderman, *Jewish Enlightenment in an English Key: Anglo-Jewry's Construction of Modern Jewish Thought* (Princeton, NJ: Princeton University Press, 2000), 130–134.

132. D'Israeli, *Vaurien*, 223.

133. Ibid., 232. Vaurien also denounced discrimination against "every Indian Negro and every European Jew" (218). In the historical notes added to his fiction, D'Israeli castigated Edmund Burke for portraying Jews as "moneylenders, clippers, and coiners" (222n) and paired Voltaire with the Tory leader Bolingbroke (226).

134. Ibid., 233.

135. Jeremy Cohen and Richard I. Cohen, eds., *Jewish Contribution to Civilization: Reassessing an Idea* (Portland, OR: Littman Library of Jewish Civilization, 2008).

136. Isaac D'Israeli, *The Genius of Judaism* (London: E. Moxon, 1833), 228–230.

137. Archivio Storico "Giancarlo Spizzichino," Comunità Ebraica, Rome, 1Za, fasc. 17, 2 inf3. I am indebted to Kenneth Stow for passing on this reference.

138. Michael Toch, *The Economic History of European Jews: Late Antiquity and Early Middle Ages* (Leiden and Boston: Brill, 2013).

139. Johann Wolfgang von Goethe, *Italian Journey*, trans. Robert R. Heitner (Princeton, NJ: Princeton University Press, 1989), esp. 214 , 256; Ernst Cassirer, "The Idea of Metamorphosis and Idealistic Morphology: Goethe," in *The Problem of Knowledge: Philosophy, Science, and History since Hegel*, trans. William H. Woglom and Charles W. Hendel (New Haven, CT: Yale University Press, 1950), 137–150; Ronald H. Brady, "Form and Cause in Goethe's Morphology," *Boston Studies in the Philosophy of Science* 97 (1987): 257–300. In assessing the advantages and drawbacks of morphology in assisting historians interested in tracing ideas and cultural practices across seemingly disconnected contexts, I have drawn insights in particular from Carlo Ginzburg, *Ecstasies: Deciphering the Witches' Sabbath*, trans. Raymond Rosenthal, ed. Gregory Elliot (London: Hutchinson Radius, 1990 [1989]) and Caroline W. Bynum, "Avoiding the Tyranny of Morphology; Or, Why Compare?" *History of Religions* 53, no. 4 (2014): 341–368.

140. For a synthesis of this important literature, see Christopher J. Berry, *The Idea of*

Commercial Society in the Scottish Enlightenment (Edinburgh: Edinburgh University Press, 2013), esp. 71, 91. Hume listed "the use of bills of exchange" alongside "the discovery of new worlds" and "the establishment of posts" as the "later improvements and refinements" that contributed to everyone's prosperity. He did not, however, elaborate on the sources of "these new inventions." David Hume, "Of the Populousness of Ancient Nations," in *Essays, Moral, Political, and Literary*, 377–464, at 420.

141. Gerard Malynes, *Consuetudo, vel, Lex Mercatoria, or, The Ancient Law-Merchant* (London: Adam Islip, 1622), 378.

142. Ludovico Guicciardini, *Descrittione . . . di tutti i Paesi Bassi, altrimenti detti Germania inferiore* (Antwerp: Appresso Guglielmo Silvio, 1567), 117; de Villalón, *Provechoso tratado de cambios*, fol. lv.

143. "Cambia introduxerunt Jus gentium & necessitas, Jura civilia confirmarunt, & consuetudo approbavit": Matthias Bode, *Dissertatio de cambiis* (Marpurgi: ex officina typographica Chemliniana, 1646), 14–15. The need to transfer money from one region to another more securely was cited as the reason for the appearance of bills of exchange in Christoph Achatius Hager, *Formular teütscher Missiven oder Sände-Schreiben* (Hamburg: gedruckt bey J. Rebenlein, 1642), 274–282.

144. Martin Wagner, *Idea mercaturae* (Bremen: In Verlegung Erhardt Bergers, Gedruckt bey Berthold und Henrich de Villiers, 1661), 24. See also *Speranders Sorgfältiger Negotiant und Wechßler* (Leipzig and Rostock: Rußworm, 1706).

145. Johann Adolph Krohn, *Tractatus de jure assecurationum / Vom Assecurantz-Recht* (Rostock and Parchim: apud Georg. Ludov. Fritsch, 1725), 1–2.

146. Louis de Beausobre, *Introduction générale à l'etude de la politique, des finances, et du commerce* (Berlin: Chez Chretien Frederic Voss, 1764), 220n1.

147. Myriam Yardeni, *Anti-Jewish Mentalities in Early Modern Europe* (Lanham, MD: University Press of America, 1990), 246. See also eadem, *Huguenots et juifs* (Paris: Honoré Champion, 2008), 99–142.

148. See chapter 5, note 38.

Chapter 8: A Legacy that Runs Deep

1. Charles Dickens, *David Copperfield* (Oxford: Oxford University Press, 1999), 872 (ch. 54).

2. "Der Wechsel ist der wirkliche Gott des Juden. Sein Gott ist nur der illusorische Wechsel." Karl Marx, *Zur Judenfrage* (1844), in Karl Marx and Friedrich Engels, *Werke*, 43 vols. (Berlin: Dietz Verlag, 1956–1990), 1:347–377, at 374. My translation differs slightly from the English text I will use throughout the chapter: Karl Marx, "On the Jewish Question," in *Early Writings*, trans. Rodney Livingston and Gregor Benton (New York: Vintage Books, 1975), 211–241, at 238.

3. An earlier example is Walter Scott's *Ivanhoe*, published in 1820 and set in twelfth-century England, which condemned both Jewish avarice and Christian persecution. It relayed the usual story: "The Jews increased, multiplied, and accumulated huge sums, which they transferred from one hand to another by means of bills of exchange—an invention for which commerce is said to be indebted to them, and which enabled them to transfer their wealth from land to land, that when threatened with oppression in one country, their treasure might be secured in an-

other." Walter Scott, *Ivanhoe*, ed. Graham Tulloch (London: Penguin Books, 2000), 62 (vol. 1, ch. 6).

4. The noted antisemite Édouard Drumont denied that Jews invented bills of exchange, the usage of which he traced back to ancient Athens: Drumont, *La France juive: Essai d'histoire contemporaine* (Paris: C. Mapron & E. Flammarion, 1886), 9n1. Reviewing this work, the French Jewish poet Gustave Kahn rebutted Drumont's accusations but defended the idea that Jews invented bills of exchange as evidence of not only the commercial dexterity that past Christian persecution had forced them to acquire but also their recent propensity to embrace the practical and scientific ideas propagated by the Christian socialist Henri de Saint-Simon: Kahn, "*La fin d'un monde*, par Édouard Drumon," *La revue indépendante de littérature et d'art* 9, no. 25 (1888): 309–314, at 310. Maurice Kriegel generously pointed out Kahn's article to me.

5. Here I wish to single out a French treatise on bills of exchange that devoted more pages than any other to the arguments of those who endorsed and those who refuted those bills' Jewish invention: Louis Nouguier, *Des lettres de change et des effets de commerce en général*, 2 vols. (Paris: Charles Hingray, 1839), 1:38–52. Reprinted in several editions, this text was also translated into Italian: Luigi Nouguier, *Delle lettere di cambio e degli effetti di commercio in generale* (Bologna: Giuseppe Tiocchi, 1843).

6. Werner Sombart, *The Jews and Modern Capitalism*, trans. Mordecai Epstein (London: T. F. Unwin, 1913[1911]).

7. In France, "the law does not force an active infringement of their law on them [the Jews], but if they want to observe their Sabbath as conscientiously as the Christians observe their holidays they are put at a material disadvantage." Bruno Bauer, *The Jewish Problem*, trans. Helen Lederer (Cincinnati, OH: Hebrew Union College–Jewish Institute of Religion, 1958), 69.

8. Marx, "On the Jewish Question," 229, 230.

9. Ibid., 216–217.

10. Ibid., 241, 236.

11. Ibid., 237. "Cash nexus" is how commentators normally abbreviate Marx's and Engel's famous statement that in a capitalist bourgeois order, "no other nexus between man and man [exists] than naked self-interest, than callous 'cash payment.'" Karl Marx and Friedrich Engels, *The Communist Manifesto* (London: Pluto Press, 2008), 37.

12. Marx, "On the Jewish Question," 237. A residual dualism, typical of Christian thought, between "the practical Jewish spirit" and "Christian society" can be detected in Marx's "On the Jewish Question," but it is resolved in the claim that "the Jew, who is a particular member of civil society, is only the particular manifestation of the Judaism of civil society" (238). See also 240 in that work.

13. Honoré de Balzac, "Gobseck," in *The Human Comedy: Selected Stories*, trans. Linda Asher, Carol Cosman, and Jordan Stump, ed. Peter Brooks (New York: New York Review of Books, 2014), 225–282, at 231, 241. The first version of the novella, titled *L'usurier*, appeared in a French periodical in 1830 and then as part of *La comédie humaine* in 1842. On the ambiguity of Jewish characters in a later Balzac novel, including Nucingen, who unlike Gobseck is a banker and stock speculator, see Maurice Samuels, "Metaphors of Modernity: Prostitutes, Bankers, and Other Jews in Balzac's *Splendeurs et misères des courtisans*," *Romanic Review* 97, no. 2 (2006): 169–184.

14. Marx, "On the Jewish Question," 239.

15. A detailed and judicious account appears in Gareth Stedman Jones, *Karl Marx: Greatness and Illusion* (Cambridge, MA: Harvard University Press, 2016), 7–30.

16. Alphone Toussenel, *Les juifs, rois de l'époque: Histoire de la féodalité financière* (Paris: École sociétaire, 1845).

17. For Stedman Jones (*Karl Marx*, 166), the move to Paris in late 1843 made Marx aware of the use of antisemitic language by French republican socialists, and he slowly "abandoned the terminology of the 'Jew' and shifted to the more capacious notion of the 'bourgeois.'" Pierre Birnbaum, by contrast, compiles a list of disparaging epithets that Marx continued to use in reference to Jews as proof of his persistent proclivity to resort to antisemitic language, although he recognizes that this language did not figure in *Capital*: Birnbaum, *Geographies of Hope: Exile, the Enlightenment, Disassimilation*, trans. Charlotte Mandell (Stanford, CA: Stanford University Press, 2008 [2004]), 65–73. Julie Kalman notes that in *The Class Struggles in France* (1850), Marx denounced the July Monarchy as a nation dominated by "stock-exchange Jews": Kalman, *Re-thinking Antisemitism in Nineteenth-Century France* (Cambridge: Cambridge University Press, 2010), 136. The only Jewish metaphor in *Capital* (vol. 1, ch. 4) described money as "circumcised Jews": "All commodities, however tattered they may look, however badly they may smell, are in faith and in truth money, are by nature circumcised Jews, and, what is more, a wonderful means for making still more money out of money." Karl Marx, *Capital: A Critique of Political Economy* (New York: Modern Library, 1936), 172. The reference to the smell of money may also have been a hint at the disparaging connection that existed at the time between Jews and garlic odor or, more generally, the traditional notion of *foetor Judaicus* ("Jewish stench"), on which a great deal is said in Jay Geller, *The Other Jewish Question: Identifying the Jew and Making Sense of Modernity* (New York: Fordham University Press, 2011).

18. Adam Smith, *An Inquiry into the Nature and Causes of the Wealth of Nations*, ed. Edwin Cannan (New York: Modern Library, 1994), 440 (book III, ch. 4).

19. Marx, *Capital*, 91 (ch. 1), 163 (ch. 4).

20. This characterization remained unchanged from the first to the second edition of Werner Sombart, *Die moderne Kapitalismus*, 2 vols. (Leipzig: Duncker & Humblot, 1902); idem, *Die moderne Kapitalismus*, 3 vols., 2nd ed. (Munich: Duncker & Humblot, 1916–1928).

21. Wilhelm Roscher, "The Status of the Jews in the Middle Ages Considered from the Standpoint of Commercial Policy," *Historia Judaica* 6, no. 1 (1944): 13–26, at 16 and 20. Roscher expanded on an earlier insight by Otto Stobbe about the deterioration of Jews' legal and material conditions in the later Middle Ages but rejected Stobbe's argument that the religious fanaticism of the Crusades was responsible for the worsening of Jews' status. Stobbe, *Die Juden in Deutschland während des Mittelalters in politischer, socialer und rechtlicher Beziehung* (Braunschweig: C. A. Schwetschke und sohn, 1866). In 1875 Roscher's essay appeared in both German and Italian: "Die Stellung der Juden im Mittelalter, betrachtet vom Standpunkte der allgemeinen Handelspolitik," *Zeitschrift für die gesammte Staatswissenschaft* 31 (1875): 503–526; "La situazione degli ebrei nel Medio Evo considerata dal punto di vista della generale politica commerciale," *Giornale degli economisti* 1, no. 2 (1875): 87–109. The English version, from which I cite, appeared much later and omitted the last section of the essay, in which Roscher outlined an embryonic comparative approach, putting Jews alongside other minorities devoted to niche commercial activities. It was published during World War II by Guido Kisch, a Czech-born Jewish scholar of medieval Jews for whom Roscher's piece demonstrated the integration of Jews into German

society (another reason why he did not care to include in the translation the section dedicated to non-Jewish middleman minorities). Other scholars, by contrast, described Roscher as "the grandfather of Nazi Jewish science" for his "folk-psychological theories" of Jews' economic roles and stressed that Heinrich von Trietschke, one of Sombart's teachers, easily reconciled Roscher's thesis with his own rabid antisemitism: Toni Oelsner, "William Roscher's Theory of the Economic and Social Position of the Jews in the Middle Ages," *YIVO Annual of Jewish Social Science* 12 (1958–1959): 176–195, at 176–177, 184n31. See also her "The Place of the Jews in Economic History as Viewed by Scholars: A Critical-Comparative Analysis," *Leo Baeck Institute Year Book* 7 (1962): 183–212. On Rocher's thesis and its contested legacy, see also Julie L. Mell, *The Myth of the Medieval Jewish Moneylender*, 2 vols. (London: Palgrave Macmillan, 2017), 1:31–75 and passim.

22. Roscher, "Status of the Jews," 19–20.

23. Anthony Grafton, *The Footnote: A Curious History* (Cambridge, MA: Harvard University Press, 1997).

24. Sombart, *Jews and Modern Capitalism*, 61. With the author's agreement, the English translator omitted certain passages from Sombart's original text and sanitized the last section in which the question of whether Jews constituted a race was discussed. All the citations I give from the English translation are faithful to the German original: Sombart, *Die Juden und das Wirtschaftsleben* (Leipzig: Duncker & Humblot, 1911). However, I have also chosen to use a more literal translation of the original book title (*The Jews and Economic Life*) than the published one.

25. Leon Goldschmidt, *Universalgeschichte des Handelsrechts* (Stuttgart: Ferdinand Enke, 1891), 107–112, 409. This was the first volume of a planned trilogy that was never completed.

26. Sombart, *Jews and Modern Capitalism*, 64 (emphasis in the original).

27. Ibid., 65, citing Goldschmidt, *Universalgeschichte des Handelsrechts*, 452 (who, in fact, weighed competing evidence and sources), and Georg Schaps, *Zur Geschichte des Wechselindossaments* (Stuttgart: Ferdinand Enke, 1892), 92 (which discussed Italian, but not Venetian, examples). The petition that Sombart cited in support of his hypothesis was addressed to the Senate in 1550 by Christian merchants who had extensive credit relations with crypto-Jews and feared losing their business if the republic went ahead with its plan to expel the latter. The petition cited by Sombart simply stated that its signatories used bills of exchange in trading with crypto-Jews ("Il medesimo comertio tegniamo con loro etiam in materia di cambia, perché ne rimettano continuamente i loro denari"): David Kaufman, "Die Vertreibung der Marranen aus Venedig im Jahre 1550," *Jewish Quarterly Review* 13, no. 3 (1901): 520–532, at 530. Of all of the previous versions of the legend attributing to medieval Jews the invention of bills of exchange, Montesquieu's was certainly known to Sombart, because it appeared in Théophile Malvezin, *Histoire des Juifs à Bordeaux* (Bordeaux: Charles Lefebvre, 1875), 35–36, a book that Sombart cited six times. But for reasons that should be obvious, Sombart did not embrace Montesquieu's version of the legend.

28. Moritz Steckelmacher, *Randbemerkungen zu Werner Sombarts "Die Juden und das Wirtschaftsleben"* (Berlin: Leonhard Simion, 1912), 7. This is not the place to review all the many outlandish statements made by Sombart. The few I mention here should suffice to give readers unfamiliar with this text a taste of his rhetoric.

29. Sombart, *Jews and Modern Capitalism*, 73.

30. Heinrich Graetz, *Geschichte der Juden von den ältesten Zeiten bis auf die Gegenwart*, 11 vols.

(Leipzig: O. Leiner, 1853–1876). An abbreviated English translation appeared in many editions, beginning with *History of the Jews*, 6 vols. (Philadelphia: Jewish Publication Society of America, 1891–1898). To provide a full-fledged evaluation of Sombart's citation practices would exceed the purposes of this chapter, but I have included all bibliographical references from the German edition of *The Jews and Economic Life* in appendix 7 to illustrate the range of authors and texts he mentions and provide others with the opportunity to dig deeper into his referencing practices.

31. Sombart, *Jews and Modern Capitalism*, 288, 300. To demonstrate that the Jewish diaspora's involvement in commerce was neither coerced nor an exclusively medieval phenomenon, for example, Sombart cited from a book by Rabbi Levi Herzfeld, *Handelsgeschichte der Juden des Alterthums* (Braunschweig: Joh. Heinr. Meyer, 1879), showing Jews' propensity in the Hellenistic period to settle in wealthy commercial towns (*Jews and Modern Capitalism*, 298).

32. Meyer Kayserling, *Geschichte der Juden in Spanien und Portugal*, 2 vols. (Berlin: Julius Springer, 1861–1867), 2:87–88; idem, *Christopher Columbus and the Participation of the Jews in the Spanish and Portuguese Discoveries* (New York: Longmans, Green, 1894), 109; idem, "The Jews in Jamaica and Daniel Israel Lopez Laguna," *Jewish Quarterly Review* 12, no. 4 (1900): 708–717; idem, "The Colonization of America by the Jews," *Publications of the American Jewish Historical Society* 2 (1894): 73–76.

33. Today's scholarly consensus that Jews lived in considerably better conditions in Iberia than northern Europe during the Middle Ages owes more than something to this nineteenth-century romanticization: Maurice Kriegel, *Les Juifs dans l'Europe méditerranéenne à la fin du Moyen Age* (Paris: Hachette, 1979), 9. On the Orientalist and romantic view of medieval Iberian Jewry in nineteenth-century Ashkenazic culture, see Ivan Marcus, "Beyond the Sephardic Mystique," *Orim* 1, no. 1 (1985): 35–53; Ismar Schorsch, "The Myth of Sephardic Supremacy," *Leo Baeck Institute Year Book* 34, no. 1 (1989): 47–66, republished in idem, *From Text to Context: The Turn to History in Modern Judaism* (Hanover, NH: University Press of New England, 1994), 71–92; Paul Mendes-Flohr, "Fin de Siècle Orientalism, the *Ostjuden*, and the Aesthetics of Jewish Self-Affirmation," *Studies in Contemporary Jewry* 1 (1994): 96–139, republished in idem, *Divided Passions: Jewish Intellectuals and the Experience of Modernity* (Detroit: Wayne State University Press, 1991), 77–132; Daniel Schroeter, "From Sephardi to Oriental: The 'Decline' Theory of Jewish Civilization in the Middle East and North Africa," in *The Jewish Contribution to Civilization: Reassessing an Idea*, ed. Jeremy Cohen and Richard I. Cohen (Portland, OR: Littman Library of Jewish Civilization, 2008), 125–148; John M. Efron, *German Jewry and the Allure of the Sephardic* (Princeton, NJ: Princeton University Press, 2016).

34. Eisenmenger's influence is detected by Oelsner, "Place of Jews," 198.

35. On this literature, see Derek J. Penslar, *Shylock's Children: Economics and Jewish Identity in Modern Europe* (Berkeley: University of California Press, 2001), 90–123.

36. Examples include an article by Zecharias Frankel (1801–1875), editor of the *Monatsschrift für die Geschichte und Wissenschaft des Judentums* (hereafter *MGWJ*), the main publication associated with the movement that took its name, *Wissenschaft des Judentums* (the academic study of Judaism), on Talmudic laws of the marketplace and related social policies, which belonged to a larger scholarly effort to highlight concerns with public good and philanthropy in Jewish history: Frankel, "Über manches Polizeiliche des talmudischen Rechts," *MGWJ* 1 (1851–1852): 243–261. An accessible 1894 survey denied that Jews in antiquity were a commercial people:

Isidore Loeb, "Rôle social des Juifs," *Revue des études juives* 28 (1894): 1–31. In 1905, a Zionist journalist admitted that Jews had been involved in protocapitalist activities during the early Middle Ages but attributed those activities to external pressure rather than a supposedly Jewish "commercial spirit" (*Handelsgeist*) and thus stayed closer to Roscher's original thesis: Lazar Felix Pinkus, *Studien zur Wirtschaftsstellung der Juden* (Berlin: Louis Lamm, 1905). Sombart cited none of these texts. Two learned studies, one by the Orthodox rabbi Moses Hoffmann (which Sombart cited) and one by Bruno Hahn (which may have appeared too late to be incorporated into Sombart's volume), challenged Roscher by showing that he had overestimated the scope of Jews' commercial activities in the period before the Crusades: Hoffmann, *Der Geldhandel der deutschen Juden während des Mittelalters bis zum Jahre 1350* (Leipzig: Duncker & Humblot, 1910); Hahn, *Die wirtschaftliche Tätigkeit der Juden im fränkischen und deutschen Reich bis zum zweiten Kreuzzug* (Freiburg: Hammerschlag & Kahle, 1911). See also Penslar, *Shylock's Children*, 88, 167.

37. Ibid., 125, 146–147.

38. *Jewish Chronicle* (London), March 24, 1848, 475, also cited in Penslar, *Shylock's Children*, 148; Dov Aryeh Fridman, "Over le-sokhar" [in Hebrew], *Knesset Yisrael* 1 (1886): 189–214, at 189, with thanks to Cornelia Aust for the reference.

39. Jehuda Reinharz, *Fatherland or Promiseland: The Dilemma of the German Jew, 1893–1914* (Ann Arbor: University of Michigan Press, 1975), 165, 191–193; Penslar, *Shylock's Children*, 165–166; Adam Sutcliffe, "Anxieties and Distinctiveness: Werner Sombart's *The Jews and Modern Capitalism* and the Politics of Jewish Economic History," in *Purchasing Power: The Economics of Modern Jewish History*, ed. Rebecca Kobrin and Adam Teller (Philadelphia: University of Pennsylvania Press, 2015), 238–257. The noted painter Max Liebermann was among the few assimilated Berlin Jews to praise Sombart as a philosemite: Friedrich Lenger, *Werner Sombart (1862–1941): Eine Biographie* (München: C. H. Beck, 1994), 210.

40. Ismar Schorsch, *Jewish Reactions to German Anti-Semitism, 1870–1914* (New York: Columbia University Press, 1972), 197.

41. Werner Sombart, *Die Zukunft der Juden* (Leipzig: Duncker & Humblot, 1912). A Hebrew translation of this book, prepared by a group of young Zionists, appeared in Kiev in 1912 (no English version exists): Gideon Reuveni, "Prolegomena to an 'Economic Turn' in Jewish History," in *The Economy in Jewish History: New Perspectives on the Interrelationship Between Ethnicity and Economic Life*, ed. Gideon Reuveni and Sarah Wobick-Segev (New York: Berghahn Books, 2011), 1–20, at 5–6. More critical responses to *Die Zukunft der Juden* by the Berlin intelligentsia appeared in Werner Sombart, Matthias Erzberger, Fritz Mauthner, Friedrich Naumann, Max Nordau, Franz Wedekin, Hermann Bahr, et al., *Judentaufen* (Munich: Georg Müller, 1912), which is discussed in Paul Mendes-Flohr, "Werner Sombart's *The Jews and Modern Capitalism*: An Analysis of Its Ideological Premises," *Leo Baeck Institute Year Book* 21 (1976): 87–107, at 105–106. By 1911, David Ben-Gurion, the future first prime minister of the state of Israel, had already translated Sombart's *Sozialismus und soziale Bewegung im 19. Jahrhundert* (*Socialism and the Social Movement in the Nineteenth Century*) into Hebrew: Penslar, *Shylock's Children*, 163.

42. Sombart, *Jews and Modern Capitalism*, 130, 382n324, and 317, 400n571, citing George Caro, *Sozial- und wirtschaftsgeschichte der Juden im Mittelalter und der Neuzeit*, 2 vols. (Leipzig: Gustav Fock, 1908–1920), 1:222 and 83. Caro died soon after Sombart's volume appeared and did not have the opportunity to react to it. Schipper had authored a book on the economic

history of Jews from antiquity to the Middle Ages. A leftist Zionist, he downplayed religion more than Graetz and Caro, but, like them, he stressed oppression as the key factor in funneling Jews into trade. While embracing Roscher's thesis of Jews' turn to moneylending in the late Middle Ages, he highlighted the occupational diversity of all Jewish societies and the many instances in which Jews were employed in agriculture rather than international trade: Schipper, *Anfänge des Kapitalismus bei den abendländischen Juden im früheren Mittelalter* (Wien and Leipzig: Wilhelm Branmuller, 1907). Characteristically, Sombart did not contend with Schipper's thesis but only quoted his book to say that "in the later Middle Ages the Jews were wealthy" and to sprinkle his narrative with one more anecdote: Sombart, *Jews and Modern Capitalism*, 296, 317, 397n544, 399n571, 400n572. Schipper responded by challenging Sombart's notions that Judaism as a religion was conducive to capitalism and that Jews possessed a "predisposition" (*Urveranlagung*) to it. He was particularly critical of Sombart for depicting the Jews as a socially and economically homogeneous group and failing to discuss the relationship between Jewish "patrician" families and Jewish society at large: Schipper, "Der jüdische Kapitalismus (zur Sombart-Brentano-Kontroverse)," *Der Jude: Eine Monatsschrift* 1–2 (1918): 130–137. Other German historians also took Sombart to task for his overblown statements about Jews' economic influence: Felix Rachfahl, "Das Judentum und die Genesis des modernen Kapitalismus," *Preussischer Jahrbücher* 147 (1912): 13–86, at 60–62; Hermann Wätjen, *Das Judentum und die Anfänge der modernen Kolonisation: Kritische Bemerkungen zu Werner Sombarts "Die Juden und das Wirtschaftsleben"* (Berlin: Kohlhammer, 1914).

43. In an article first published in 1818, a prominent figure in the so-called academic study of Judaism, Leopold Zunz, hinted at the possibility that Jews might have invented paper money (*Papiergeld*) but also stressed the need for more thorough studies of rabbinic texts to illuminate this and related topics: Zunz, "Etwas über die rabbinische Literatur: Nebst Nachrichten über ein altes bis jezt ungedrucktes hebräisches Werk," in *Gesammelte Schriften* (Berlin: Louis Gerschel Verlagsbuchhandlung, 1875), 3–31, at 15. Hoffmann called out Sombart for his preposterous reading of Baba Bathra 172 and the apocryphal book of Tobit as textual evidence that Jews used bills of exchange in antiquity: Hoffmann, *Juden und Kapitalismus: Eine kritische Würdigung von Werner Sombarts "Die Juden und das Wirtschaftsleben"* (Berlin: H. Itzkowski, 1912), 12–19. Steckelmacher, *Randbemerkungen*, 7–8, also singled out those mistakes. Julius Guttmann (1880–1950), later a professor of Jewish philosophy at Hebrew University in Jerusalem, questioned Sombart's understanding of rabbinics, including the sixteenth-century legal code composed by Yosef Caro, *Shulhan Arukh*, but was generally more sympathetic: Guttmann, "Die Juden und das Wirtschaftsleben," *Archiv für Sozialwissenschaft und Sozialpolitik* 36, no. 1 (1913): 149–212. Franz Oppenheimer (1864–1943), a leading sociologist and vocal opponent of racial theories in the German academic community of the time, had harsher words for his colleague: Oppenheimer, "Die Juden und das Wirtschaftsleben," *Neue Rundschau* 22 (1919): 889–904. On the more forceful impact of the *Wissenschaft des Judentums* on the exposure of the factual mistakes made by Sombart in comparison to the rather muted response by German Jewish historians, see also Giacomo Todeschini, "Una polemica dimenticata: Sombart e 'Die Juden und das Wirtschaftsleben' nella discussione storiografica (1911–1920)," *Società e storia* 10, no. 35 (1987): 139–160; idem, *La ricchezza degli ebrei: Merci e denaro nella riflessione ebraica e nella definizione cristiana dell'usura alla fine del Medioevo* (Spoleto: Centro italiano di studi sull'alto Medioevo, 1989), 24–25, 36–38; idem, "Les historiens juifs en Allemagne et le débat sur l'origine du capitalism avant 1914," in

Écriture de l'histoire et identité juive: L'Europe ashkénaze, XIXe–XXe siècle, ed. Delphine Bechtel, Évelyne Patlagean, Jean-Charles Szurek, and Paul Zawadzki (Paris: Les Belles Lettres, 2003), 209–228.

44. Max Weber, *The History of Commercial Partnerships in the Middle Ages*, ed. Lutz Kaelber (Lanham, MD: Rowman and Littlefield, 2003 [1889]).

45. In his *General Economic History*, Weber stressed the Roman origins of several contracts involved in the medieval commercial revolution that were known from Italian, sources but noted that bills of exchange evolved from earlier forms found in "Arabic, Italian, German and English law": Max Weber, *General Economic History*, trans. Frank H. Knight (New York: Greenberg, 1927), 342, see also 258–263.

46. Some consider *The Protestant Ethic* to have been a response to a passage in the first edition of Sombart's *Der moderne Kapitalismus* (1902), in which Protestantism was described as the outcome, rather than the engine, of modern capitalist reason: Hartmut Lehmann, "The Rise of Capitalism: Weber Versus Sombart," in *Weber's Protestant Ethic: Origins, Evidence, Contexts*, ed. Hartmut Lehmann and Guenther Roth (Cambridge: Cambridge University Press, 1987), 195–208, at 198. What is uncontroversial is that Weber incorporated several rejoinders to Sombart, including the statement that "Jewish capitalism was speculative pariah-capitalism, while the Puritan was bourgeois organization of labor," in the revised edition of *The Protestant Ethic* (1920), which is also the one available in English: Weber, *The Protestant Ethic and the Spirit of Capitalism*, trans. Talcott Parsons (New York: Charles Scribner's Sons, 1958), 271n58.

47. Weber, *General Economic History*, 217. In *Economy and Society*, Weber admitted that Jews had played an important historical role in medieval moneylending and finance but argued that the types of securities and other obligations handled by Jews rarely displayed "the forms, both legal and economical, characteristic of modern Occidental capitalism": Max Weber, *Economy and Society: An Outline of Interpretative Sociology*, 2 vols., ed. Guenther Roth and Claus Wittich (Berkeley: University of California Press, 1968), 613.

48. Idem, *Ancient Judaism*, trans. and ed. Hans H. Gerth and Don Martindale (New York: Free Press, 1952 [1921]), 3.

49. Ibid., 345. See also idem, *Economy and Society*, 492–499, 611–623, 1200–1204; and idem, *General Economic History*, 196, 358–361.

50. Idem, *Economy and Society*, 378 (emphasis in the original).

51. Wallace K. Ferguson, *The Renaissance in Historical Thought: Five Centuries of Interpretations* (Boston: Houghton Mifflin, 1948); Charles Homer Haskins, *The Renaissance of the Twelfth Century* (Cambridge, MA: Harvard University Press, 1927); Jacob Burckhardt, *The Civilization of the Renaissance in Italy*, trans. S.G.C. Middlemore (London: G. Allen & Unwin, 1921 [1860]).

52. Henri Pirenne, "The Stages in the History of Capitalism," *American Historical Review* 19, no. 3 (1914): 494–515, at 495–496. This article is an abridged translation of idem, "Les périodes de l'histoire sociale du capitalisme," *Bulletin de la classe des lettres et des sciences morales et politiques*, May 6, 1914, 258–299. An expanded version is the highly influential Pirenne, *Medieval Cities: Their Origins and Revival of Trade*, trans. Frank D. Halsey (Princeton, NJ: Princeton University Press, 1925). Before Pirenne, a German scholar had already set capitalism's birth date as 1396: Jacob Strieder, *Zur Genesis des modernen Kapitalismus* (Leipzig: Duncker & Humblot, 1904). For an explicit refutation of Sombart, see idem, *Studien zur Geschichte kapitalistischer Organisationsformen: Monopole, Kartelle und Aktiengesellschaften im Mittelalter u. zu Beginn der*

Neuzeit (Munich and Leipzig: Duncker & Humblot, 1914); idem, "Origin and Evolution of Early European Capitalism," *Journal of Economic and Business History* 2 (1929): 1–19.

53. Lujo Brentano, *Die Anfänge des modernen Kapitalismus: Festrede gehalten in der öffentlichen Sitzung der K. Akademie der Wissenschaften am 15. März 1913* (Munich: Akademie der Wissenschafte, 1916), 42. Subsequent German studies of medieval economic history predictably gravitated toward the Hansa. See, e.g., Fritz Rörig, *Hansische Beiträge zur deutschen Wirtschaftsgeschichte: mit einem Plan des Marktes von Lübeck* (Breslau: F. Hirt, 1928).

54. Henri Sée, "Dans quelle mesure puritans et juifs ont-ils contribué aux progrès du capitalisme moderne?" *Revue historique* 52, no. 65 (1927): 57–68; idem, *Modern Capitalism: Its Origin and Evolution*, trans. Homer B. Vanderblue and Georges F. Doriot (New York: Adelphi, 1928 [1926]); André-E. Sayous, *Structure et évolution du capitalisme européen, XVIe–XVIIe siècles*, ed. Mark Steele (London: Variorum Reprints, 1989); Henri Hauser, "Les origines du capitalisme moderne en France," *Revue d'économie politique* 16 (1902): 193–205, 313–333; idem, *Les débuts du capitalisme* (Paris: Félix Alcan, 1927). Of these three authors, Sayous was the most instrumental in identifying new archival documents that helped scholars trace the historical evolution of bills of exchange and deny their Jewish origins.

55. Ercole Vidari called redundant (*oziosa*) the controversy over whether Jews or Ghibelline refugees had invented bills of exchange: Vidari, *La lettera di cambio: Studio critico di legislazione comparata* (Florence: G. Pellas, 1869), 8. Arturo Segre explicitly denied that either Jews expelled from France by King Dagobert I or Florentine exiles to France could have invented bills of exchange and insisted instead on the slow evolution of the contract, pointing to Muslim merchants in tenth-century Sicily as possible precursors: Segre, *Manuale di storia del commercio*, 2 vols. (Turin: S. Lattes & C., 1915), 1:83–84; revised edition: *Storia del commercio*, 2 vols. (Turin: S. Lattes & C., 1923), 1:103–104. See also Enrico Bensa, *Il contratto di assicurazione nel medio evo* (Genoa: Tipografia Marittime Editrice, 1884); French translation: *Histoire du contrat d'assurance au Moyen Age*, trans. Jules Valéry (Paris: Albert Fontemoing, 1897). Giuseppe Salvioli admitted that Jews may have known bills of exchange since antiquity but stressed that they could not possibly have played an important role in those bills' development, because during the Middle Ages and the Renaissance their economic influence paled in comparison to that of merchants and bankers from Florence, Genoa, Venice, and Pisa: Salvioli, *I titoli al portatore nella storia del diritto italiano: Studi* (Bologna: Nicola Zanichelli, 1883), 109.

56. Amintore Fanfani, ed., *L'opera di Werner Sombart nel centanario della nascita* (Milan: Giuffrè, 1964). See also idem, *Catholicism, Protestantism and Capitalism* (New York: Sheed & Ward, 1935 [1934]). Fanfani was influenced by Giuseppe Toniolo (1845–1918), the leading theorist of the Catholic social doctrine that sought to offer an alternative to both liberalism and socialism, with whom Sombart had studied during a brief stay in Pisa in 1883. Sombart's book on Jews and capitalism is one of his very few writings that has not been translated into Italian; Gino Luzzatto was the Italian translator of *Der modern Kapitalismus*. Armando Sapori did not identify as a Catholic, and his work focused more on Italian medieval merchants' business techniques than spiritual life, but he too assumed a synthesis between early capitalism and Christian morality. His earlier writings focused on Florentine merchant houses: Sapori, *La crisi delle compagnie mercantile dei Bardi e dei Peruzzi* (Florence: Leo S. Olschki, 1926); idem, *La compagnia di Calimala ai primi del Trecento* (Florence: Leo S. Olschki, 1932). His most influential

text originated from his university lectures, which he expanded for publication in the prestigious French series "Affaires et gens d'affaires," with a preface by Lucien Febvre: idem, *The Italian Merchant in the Middle Ages*, trans. Patricia Ann Kennen (New York: Norton, 1979 [1952]).

57. These broad patterns were apparent in the *Economic History Review* (founded by Eileen Power in 1927) and the volumes on the Middle Ages of *The Cambridge Economic History of Europe* (a joint endeavor of Power and her husband, Michael Postan, himself a Jewish refugee to England). In the United States, the major synthesis of that period paid only scant attention to Jews but noted their role in the late medieval boom of urban economies and commerce to counter the notion that medieval wealth was locked up in landholdings: James Westfall Thompson, *Economic and Social History of Europe in the Later Middle Ages (1300–1530)* (New York: Century Co., 1931), esp. 10.

58. Lopez took issue with Pirenne's famous "thesis" about the decline of Europe's economy as a result of the Muslim expansion in North Africa and the western Mediterranean: Henri Pirenne, "Mohamet et Charlemagne," *Revue belge de philosophie et d'histoire* 1 (1922): 76–86; idem, *Mohammed and Charlemagne*, trans. Bernard Miall (New York: W. W. Norton, 1939); Robert S. Lopez, "Mohammed and Charlemagne: A Revision," *Speculum* 18, no. 1 (1943): 14–38. Lopez's work, however, was in line with Pirenne's earlier insistence on the late medieval urban revival: idem, *Genova marinara nel Duecento: Benedetto Zaccaria, ammiraglio e mercante* (Messina: Giuseppe Principato, 1933); idem, *Storia delle colonie genovesi nel Medierraneo* (Bologna: Nicola Zanichelli, 1938).

59. Idem, *The Commercial Revolution of the Middle Ages, 950–1350* (Cambridge: Cambridge University Press, 1976), vii.

60. Ibid., 60–61. Lopez's debt to Roscher in these pages should be clear by now, but his brief overview of Jewish commerce in the Middle Ages represented the consensus, as summarized by his contemporary Israel Abrahams, *Jewish Life in the Middle Ages* (London: Edward Goldston, 1932), 229–272.

61. The expression first figured in a reply that Raymond de Roover offered to a paper by N.B.S. Gras titled "Capitalism: Concepts and History": "Discussion by Raymond de Roover," *Bulletin of the Business Historical Society* 16, no. 2 (1942): 34–39; and later as the title of the reprint of those comments as a standalone article: de Roover, "The Commercial Revolution of the Thirteenth Century," in *Enterprise and Secular Change: Readings in Economic History*, ed. Frederic C. Lane and Jelle C. Riemersma (Homewood, IL: R. D. Irwin, 1953), 80–85.

62. Julius Kirshner, "Raymond de Roover on Scholastic Economic Thought," in *Business, Banking, and Economic Thought in Late Medieval and Early Modern Europe: Selected Studies of Raymond de Roover*, ed. Julius Kirshner (Chicago: University of Chicago Press, 1974), 15–36.

63. Among a vast literature, the following interventions stand out in current debates about why by the late eighteenth century Europe (or at least Britain) was richer than the rest of the world: Douglass C. North and Barry R. Weingast, "Constitutions and Commitment: Evolution of Institutions Governing Public Choice," *Journal of Economic History* 49, no. 4 (1989): 803–832; Kenneth Pomeranz, *The Great Divergence: China, Europe, and the Making of the Modern World* (Princeton, NJ: Princeton University Press, 2000); Robert C. Allen, *The British Industrial Revolution in Global Perspective* (Cambridge: Cambridge University Press, 2009).

Coda

1. George Eliot, *Daniel Deronda* (London: Penguin Books, 1967), 35.

2. Anthony Grafton, *What Was History? The Art of History in Early Modern Europe* (Cambridge: Cambridge University Press, 2007).

3. Raymond de Roover, *Money, Banking and Credit in Mediaeval Bruges: Italian Merchant Bankers, Lombards and Money-changers; A Study in the Origins of Banking* (Cambridge, MA: Mediaeval Academy of America, 1948); idem, *The Medici Bank: Its Organization, Management, Operations and Decline* (New York: New York University Press, 1948); idem, *L'évolution de la lettre de change, XIVe–XVIIIe siècles* (Paris: S.E.V.P.E.N., 1953); idem, *The Rise and Decline of the Medici Bank, 1397–1494* (New York: W. W. Norton, 1966); Julius Kirshner, ed., *Business, Banking, and Economic Thought in Late Medieval and Early Modern Europe: Selected Studies of Raymond de Roover* (Chicago: University of Chicago Press, 1974).

4. A recent exception is Veronica Aoki Santarosa, "Financing Long-Distance Trade: The Joint Liability Rule and Bills of Exchange in Eighteenth-Century France," *Journal of Economic History* 75, no. 3 (2015): 690–719. Three leading economic historians have devoted a very important study to eighteenth-century French credit markets, but they examine almost exclusively debt contracts in which land functioned as collateral and thus do not address the questions raised by commercial credit, the subject with which I am most concerned: Philip T. Hoffman, Gilles Postel-Vinay, and Jean-Laurent Rosenthal, *Priceless Markets: The Political Economy of Credit in Paris, 1660–1870* (Chicago: University of Chicago Press, 2000).

5. A short but illustrative list would include Avner Greif, "On the Interrelations and Economic Implications of Economic, Social, Political, and Normative Factors: Reflections from Two Late Medieval Societies," in *The Frontiers of the New Institutional Economics*, ed. John N. Drobak and John V. C. Nye (New York: Academic Press, 1997), 57–94; idem and Guido Tabellini, "Cultural and Institutional Bifurcation: China and Europe Compared," *American Economic Review* 100, no. 2 (2010): 135–140; Luigi Guiso, Paola Sapienza, and Luigi Zingales, "People's Opium? Religion and Economic Attitudes," *Journal of Monetary Economics* 50, no. 1 (2003): 255–282; Timur Kuran, *The Long Divergence: How Islamic Law Held Back the Middle East* (Princeton, NJ: Princeton University Press, 2011). Greif is unusual among recent social scientists for his dating of Europe's so-called Great Divergence from Asia to the late Middle Ages. Avner Greif, *Institutions and the Path to the Modern Economy: Lessons from Medieval Trade* (Cambridge: Cambridge University Press, 2006).

6. Exemplary of this trend are Istvan Hont, *Jealousy of Trade: International Competition and the Nation-State in Historical Perspective* (Cambridge, MA: Harvard University Press, 2005); Isaac Nakhimovsky, *The Closed Commercial State: Perpetual Peace and Commercial Society from Rousseau to Fichte* (Princeton, NJ: Princeton University Press, 2011); Sophus A. Reinert, *Translating Empire: Emulation and the Origins of Political Economy* (Cambridge, MA: Harvard University Press, 2011). Andrew Sartori offers an important critique of this overemphasis on statehood and international competition and redirects our attention to the commercialization of English domestic markets as a source of inspiration for early theorists of commercial society: Sartori, "From Statehood to Social Science in Early Modern English Political Economy," *Critical Historical Studies* 3, no. 2 (2016): 181–214.

7. Dubnow's multivolume *World History of the Jewish People* appeared in German, Russian,

Hebrew, and other languages in the 1920s and 1930s. See Simon Dubnow, *History of the Jews*, 5 vols., trans. Moshe Spiegel (South Brunswick, NJ: T. Yoseloff, 1967–1973).

8. Salo W. Baron, *A Social and Religious History of the Jews*, 3 vols. (New York: Columbia University Press, 1937); idem, *A Social and Religious History of the Jews*, 20 vols., 2nd ed. (New York: Columbia University Press, 1952–1993).

9. Idem, "Modern Capitalism and Jewish Fate," *Menorah Journal* 30, no. 2 (1942), republished in idem, *History and Jewish Historians: Essays and Addresses*, ed. Arthur Hertzberg and Leon A. Feldman (Philadelphia: Jewish Publication Society of America, 1964), 43–64, at 47. Baron, it should be noted, displayed even fewer sympathies toward Marxism and socialism.

10. The discomfort was somewhat less pronounced in the United States, although it was not until much later that the writings of economics Nobel laureate Simon Kuznets (1901–1985) on Jewish economic history were first collected in two volumes: *Jewish Economies: Development and Migration in America and Beyond*, ed. Stephanie Lo and E. Glen Weyl (New Brunswick, NJ: Transaction Publishers, 2011–2012). An economist at the University of Chicago, Arcadius Kahan (1920–1982), was rare in his interest in the economic history of European Jews. In addition to his studies of tsarist and Soviet Russia, he co-edited with Baron and others an unusual highbrow textbook on the subject: Nachum Gross, Salo W. Baron, and Archadius Kahan, eds., *Economic History of the Jews* (Jerusalem: Keter, 1975). The same year another brief synthesis appeared: Marcus Arkin, *Aspects of Jewish Economic History* (Philadelphia: Jewish Publication Society of America, 1975). Nothing of the sort has been attempted since.

11. *The Jewish Encyclopedia*, 12 vols. (New York: Funk & Wagnalls, 1901–1906), 5:284, s.v. "exchange, bill of." Consider that in the nineteenth century, a number of Jewish authors had endorsed or commented on the legend, including Charles-Joseph Bail, *État des Juifs en France, en Espagne et en Italie* (Paris: Alexis Eymery, 1823), 101; Joseph Salvador, *Histoire des institutions de Moïse, et du peuple hébreu*, 3 vols. (Paris: Ponthieu et Cie., 1828), 1:337–338; Jsraéle Bédarride, *Les Juifs en France, en Italie et en Espagne* (Paris: M. Lévy frères, 1859), 179.

12. Baron, *Social and Religious History* (1937), 2:177. In the much-expanded second edition of this work, Baron included a description of divergent attitudes toward commercial papers among Palestinian and Babylonian rabbinic scholars in the Tannaim period (first and second centuries CE): *Social and Religious History* (1952–1993), 2:302.

13. Isaac Samuel Emmanuel, *Histoire des Israélites de Salonique (140 av. J.-C. à 1640)* (Thonon: Lipschutz, 1936), 56. On this author and the intellectual milieu in which he composed this work, see Julia Phillips Cohen and Sarah Abrevaya Stein, "Sephardic Scholarly Worlds: Toward a Novel Geography of Modern Jewish History," *Jewish Quarterly Review* 100, no. 3 (2010): 349–384; Devin E. Naar, *Jewish Salonica Between the Ottoman Empire and Modern Greece* (Stanford, CA: Stanford University Press, 2016), 219–225.

14. The anecdote is relayed in Sasha Abramsky, *The House of Twenty Thousand Books* (London: Halban, 2014), 268. I owe the reference to Maurice Kriegel.

15. Shmuel Ettinger, "The Economic Activities of the Jews" [in Hebrew], in *Jews in Economic Life: Collected Essays in Memory of Arcadius Kahan (1920–1982)*, ed. Nachum Gross (Jerusalem: Zalman Shazar Center for the Furtherance of the Study of Jewish History, 1984), 13–24, English translation in Jonathan Karp and Francesca Trivellato, eds., *Jews in Early Modern Europe* (London: Taylor and Francis, forthcoming).

16. The course was "Introduction to English Law," taught by Avigdor V. Levontin. Dr. Michal Shaked, personal communication, Tel Aviv, December 22, 2015.

17. Jonathan I. Israel, *European Jewry in the Age of Mercantalism, 1550–1750*, rev. ed. (Oxford: Clarendon Press, 1989), 1.

18. Pertinent reflections can be found in Gideon Reuveni, "Prolegomena to an 'Economic Turn' in Jewish History," in *The Economy in Jewish History: New Perspectives on the Interrelationship Between Ethnicity and Economic Life*, ed. Gideon Reuveni and Sarah Wobick-Segev (New York: Berghahn Books, 2011), 1–20; Jonathan Karp, "Can Economic History Date the Inception of Jewish Modernity?" in *Economy in Jewish History*, 23–42; idem, "An Economic Turn in Jewish Studies?" *AJS Perspectives: The Magazine of the Association of Jewish Studies*, Fall 2009, 8–14; Rebecca Kobrin and Adam Teller, eds., *Purchasing Power: The Economics of Modern Jewish History* (Philadelphia: University of Pennsylvania Press, 2015), esp. 1–24; Liliane Hilaire-Pérez and Evelyne Oliel-Grausz, "L'histoire économique des Juifs: Institutions, communautés, marchés," *Archives Juives* 47, no. 2 (2014): 4–9.

19. Yuri Slezkine, *The Jewish Century* (Princeton, NJ: Princeton University Press, 2004), 56.

20. For Slezkine, "Sombart was able to attribute the rise of capitalism to the Jews by dramatically overstating his case (and thus seriously compromising it)": *Jewish Century*, 42. He summarizes the problem as follows: "Sombart did not like capitalism . . . ; Jews excelled under capitalism; so Sombart did not like the Jews" (55).

21. Botticini and Eckstein cite Sombart as one of the "scholars" who "maintained that the Jews . . . preferred to invest in education rather than in land because human capital is portable and cannot therefore be expropriated." Maristella Botticini and Zvi Eckstein, *The Chosen Few: How Education Shaped Jewish History, 70–1492* (Princeton, NJ: Princeton University Press, 2012), 59.

22. Sutcliffe, "Anxieties and Distinctiveness," 239, 240.

23. Arthur Mitzman, *Sociology and Estrangement: Three Sociologists of Imperial Germany* (New York: Afred A. Knopf, 1973), 135.

24. This double impetus informs Natalie Zemon Davis, "Religion and Capitalism Once Again? Jewish Merchant Culture in the Seventeenth Century," *Representations* 59 (1997): 56–84.

25. Albert O. Hirschman, *The Passions and the Interests: Political Arguments for Capitalism Before Its Triumph* (Princeton, NJ: Princeton University Press, 1977).

26. In sixteenth-century Spain, the forced conversion of Muslims generated fears about the pollution of Christian society that were specific byproducts of Christian ways of understanding Islam and its outward practices but also structurally similar to the fears inspired by forced Jewish converts. See Olivia Remie Constable, *To Live Like a Moor: Christian Perceptions of Muslim Identities in Medieval and Early Modern Spain*, ed. Robin Vose (Philadelphia: University of Pennsylvania Press, 2018).

Appendix 1: Early Modern European Commercial Literature

1. Jochen Hoock, Pierre Jeannin, and Wolfgang Kaiser, eds., *Ars Mercatoria: Handbücher und Traktate für den Gebrauch des Kaufmanns, 1470–1820 / Manuels et traités à l'usage des marchands, 1470–1820*, 3 vols. (Paderborn: Schöningh, 1991–2001). The first three of the projected six vol-

umes have appeared (the first two are bibliographical instruments covering the period 1470–1700, while the third is a collection of essays analyzing aspects of the material inventoried in the first two volumes). No other work titled *Ars Mercatoria* appears in WorldCat. The expression *Lex Mercatoria* is the object of a similar reinvention.

2. Carpenter, "The Economic Bestsellers Before 1850: A Catalogue of an Exhibition Prepared for the History of Economics Society Meeting, May 21–24, 1975, at Baker Library," *Bulletin of the Kress Library of Business and Economics* 11 (1975), available at http://www.othercanon.com /uploads/AJALUGU%20THE%20ECONOMIC%20BESTSELLERS%20BEFORE1850.pdf (accessed July 9, 2018).

3. Sophus A. Reinert, *Translating Empire: Emulation and the Origins of Political Economy* (Cambridge, MA: Harvard University Press, 2011), 52–60.

4. Jean-Claude Perrot, *Une histoire intellectuelle de l'économie politique, XVIIe–XVIIIe siècle* (Paris: Éditions de l'École des hautes études en sciences sociales, 1992). John Shovlin has since calculated that between 1760 and the Revolution, French printing houses issued more works related to political economy than novels: Shovlin, *The Political Economy of Virtue: Luxury, Patriotism, and the Origins of the French Revolution* (Ithaca, NY: Cornell University Press, 2006), 2.

5. Antoyne de Montchrestien, *Traicté de l'economie politique: dédié en 1615 au roy et à la reyne mère du roy* (Rouen: Jean Osmont, 1615; anastatic reprint: Geneva: Slatkine Reprints, 1970).

6. Calculations based on http://gdc.gale.com/products/the-making-of-the-modern-world -the-goldsmiths-kress-library-of-economic-literature-1450-1850/evaluate/customer-list/ (accessed December 28, 2015). This information, originally posted as part of a marketing campaign by Gale, was removed from the website after a relaunch and no longer appears online.

7. The endowment ranking for fiscal year 2016 is reported in Farran Powell, "10 Universities with the Biggest Endowments, *U.S. News & World Report*, September 28, 2017, https://www .usnews.com/education/best-colleges/the-short-list-college/articles/2016-10-04/10-univer sities-with-the-biggest-endowments (accessed July 9, 2018).

Appendix 2: The Legend's Earliest Formulation (1647)

1. The original title of this compilation is *Guidon, stile et usance des marchands qui mettent à la mer*. The English translation of Robert Joseph Pothier's 1810 French treatise on marine insurance (*A Treatise on Maritime Contracts of Letting to Hire* [Marseilles: Sube et Laporte, 1821]) refers to this compilation as *The Standard of the Sea*. In the nautical vocabulary of the time, *guidon* was a pennant or burgee, that is, a type of flag flown on ships. The *Guidon* was a collection of norms about marine contracts and navigation first issued in Rouen in the mid- to late sixteenth century. The earliest extant copy was printed in Rouen in 1608 and is identical to the one reproduced by Cleirac. A transcription of the French original is published in the appendix to Francesca Trivellato, "La naissance d'une légende: Juifs et finance dans l'imaginaire bordelais du XVIIe siècle," *Archives Juives* 47, no. 2 (2014): 47–76.

2. *De mercatura decisiones, et tractatus varii, et de rebus ad eam pertinentibus* (Cologne: Apud Cornelium ab Egemont de Grassis, 1622), 21, 27–28 (dec. III, no. 28: "Assicuratio quis contractus sit"), 148–149 (dec. 39, no. 9: "Differentia inter socios et participes").

3. No such statement appears in the chronicle by Giovanni Villani (c. 1280–1348).

4. The French word is "retaillés," literally those who suffered a surgical amputation and, by extension, those who were circumcised—that is, Jews. The French word was used with this meaning by the poet Joachim de Bellay (c. 1522–1560), who may have borrowed it from the classical scholar Henri Estienne (c. 1530–1598): Louis Becq de Fouquières, ed., *Oeuvres choisies des poètes français du XVIe siècle, contemporains de Ronsard* (Paris: Charpentier, 1876), 163. It remained in currency in the eighteenth century: "RETAILLÉ, adj. *terme de Chirurgie* dont Ambroise Paré s'est servi pour dénommer celui qui a souffert une opération, dans la vue de recouvrer le prépuce qui lui manquoit. Cette opération est décrite par Celse, *lib. VII. c. xxv.* (…) Les Juifs engendrent des enfans, & connoissent les femmes comme les autres hommes; il en conclut que cette opération n'est pas nécessaire, & qu'on ne doit point la pratiquer." Diderot and d'Alembert, *Encyclopédie*, 14:198.

5. Dagobert ruled from 629 to 634, Philip Augustus from 1180 to 1223, and Philip the Tall from 1316 to 1322.

6. The expression *le pair & la touche* referred to the proper bullion content of gold and silver coins. Cleirac uses it also in another section of his commentary: "The doctrine of Jews and bankers called *le pair & la touche.*" UCM 1647, 329; UCM 1661, 313. An authoritative dictionary of the late seventeenth century noted that the saying "a man is known *au pair & à la touche*" indicated someone who was known for his intrinsic goodness in the same way that metallic coins were known to be fine and pure: Antoine Furetière, *Dictionnaire universel*, 3 vols. (The Hague and Rotterdam: Chez Arnout & Reinier Leers, 1690), 3, s.v. "touche."

7. "Cloaking their usury under the shadow of trade." The citation comes from a chapter entitled "Caursinorum pestis abominanda" in Matthew Paris's medieval *Chronica Majora* (1216–1239). See Henry Richards Luard, ed., *Matthaei Parisiensis, Monachi Sancti Albani, Chronica Majora*, 7 vols. (London: Longman & Co., 1872–1883), 3:329; *Matthew Paris's English History from the Year 1235 to 1273*, 3 vols., trans. J. A. Giles (London: H. G. Bohn, 1852–1854), 1:2. Cleirac may have consulted *Matthæi Paris monachi Albanensis Angli, historia major* (London: Excusum apud Reginaldum Vuolfium, Regiæ Maiest. in Latinis typographum, 1571). His knowledge of this author is confirmed by other passages in the text. See notes 11, 16, 20, 45, and 50.

8. *De cambiis*, by Tommaso de Vio, also known as Cardinal Cajetan (1469–1534), was written in 1499 and first published in 1506. It can now be read in *Thomas de Vio Cardinalis Caietanus (1469–1534): Scripta Philosophica; Opuscola œconomico-socialia*, ed. P. P. Zammit (Rome: ex Typographia missionaria dominicana, 1934), 91–133 (ch. 5 is at 110–113).

9. "Mutuum quodvis cum pacto, ut mutuans assecuret usura." Martín Azpilcueta, *Enchiridion sive manuale confessariorum et poenintetium* (Paris: Apud Franciscum Huby, 1611), 538–540 (ch. 17, no. 284). Chapter 17 is a commentary on the seventh commandment, "Thou shalt not steal." Entry no. 284 in chapter 17 is the first of a series devoted to usury in exchange dealings ("De usura circa cambia") that only appears in the revised and extended Latin editions and focuses on the difference between dry exchange and the classic four-party bill of exchange.

10. Cleirac's imprecise statement points to the fact that during the Great Schism (1378–1417), Europe was divided between countries loyal to the Avignon papacy (France and Spain) and those loyal to Rome (Italy, England, and the Holy Roman Empire).

11. "[A.D. 1235] Per idem tempus ex partibus ultramarinis venerunt Londonias quidam ignoti, qui se esse domini papae mercatores vel scambiatores asserebant, cum tamen manifesti existerent usurarii. Quorum usurae duriores erant conditionis quam Judeorum." I cite from

Matthew Paris, *Abbreviatio chronicorum Angliae*, in *Matthaei Parisiensis, Monachi Sancti Albani, Historia Anglorum*, 3 vols., ed. Sir Frederic Madden (London: Longmans, Green, Reader, and Dyer, 1866–1869), 3:272.

12. *In foro conscientiæ*, as opposed to the obligations enforced by legal tribunals.

13. *De usuris extra* refers to the section on usury added by Pope Gregory IX to the *Corpus iuris canonici* (book V, title 19). See also note 49. Canon 67 of the Fourth Lateran Council of November 1215, known as *Quanto amplius*, corresponds to book V, title 19, ch. 18 in *Corpus iuris canonici*, 2 vols., ed. Aemilius Friedberg (Graz: Akademische Druck-u. Verlagsanstalt, 1959), 2:816.

14. Slight variation of Ariosto, *Orlando Furioso* (first published in Italian in 1516), IV.66.5–8: "Perché si de' punir donna o biasmare, / che con uno o più d'uno abbia commesso / quel che l'uom fa con quante n'ha appetito, / e lodato ne va, non che impunito?" English translation: "If the same ardour, the same urge drives both sexes to love's gentle fulfillment, which to the mindless commoner seems so grave an excess, why is the woman to be punished or blamed for doing with one or several men the very thing a man does with as many women as he will, and receives not punishment but praise for it?" Ludovico Ariosto, *Orlando Furioso*, trans. Guido Waldman (Cambridge, MA: Harvard University Press, 2010), 38.

15. This comedy, *I supposti* (of which no English translation exists), was first performed in Ferrara in 1509. A modern edition can be read in Ludovico Ariosto, *Opere minori*, ed. Cesare Segre (Milan: R. Ricciardi, 1954), 97–349. The citation is from Act III, Scene I (319): "*Dolio:* Come siamo a casa, credo ch'io non ritrovarò de l'uova, che porti in quel cesto un solo intiero. Ma con chi parlo io? Dove diavolo è rimasto ancora questo ghiotto? Sarà restato a dar la caccia a qualche cane o a scherzare con l'orso. A ogni cosa che truova per via, si ferma: se vede facchino o villano o giudeo, non lo terrieno le catene che non gli andasse a fare qualche dispiacere. Tu verrai pure una volta, capestro: bisogna che di passo in passo ti vadi aspettando. Per Dio, s'io truovo pure un solo di quelle uova rotte, ti romperò la testa." In this passage Dolio, a cook, complains that his young assistant is distracted by anything he encounters in the street—whether a porter, a peasant, or a Jew—and warns him against breaking any of the eggs he is carrying. The gist of the story is that the servant takes it for granted that Jews are among those who can be harassed in the street. It should also be noted that in several of his comedies, including *La Lena*, Ariosto satirized the worship of money in contemporary society.

16. "Caursinorum pestis abominanda" is the title of a chapter in Matthew Paris' *Chronica Majora*: Luard, *Matthaei Parisiensis, Monachi Sancti Albani, Chronica Majora*, 3:328; *Matthew Paris's English History*, 1:2. See also notes 7, 11, 20, 45, and 50.

17. Boccaccio used the word *caorsino* only once, in his vernacular commentary on Dante's *Inferno*, XI.46–51, the same canto cited by Cleirac (see below and note 35). In his *Genealogy of the Gentile Gods* (book I, ch. XXI), Boccaccio defined fraud as an "infanda pestis," mentioning Dante as an authority. I am grateful to David Lummus for help with the latter reference.

18. *Commentaire de M. Adam Theveneau, advocat en parlement, sur les ordonnances contenant les difficultez meües entres les docteurs du droict canon et civil et decidées par icelles ordonnances tant en matière bénéficialle, que civile et criminelle, instructions des procez, iugemens, et exectuions d'iceux* (Paris: M. Ballagny, 1629), 948–969.

19. Here Cleirac plays with the phonetic assonance between the Italian words for pocket (*scarcella*) and for scarcity (*scarcità*).

20. Since at least the fourteenth century, the word "cahorsin" or "caursin" had meant a usurer. Cleirac invokes a common etymology by which the word meant "an inhabitant of Cahors," a small town in southern France whose merchants and bankers were apparently ill reputed for their moneylending practices. The thirteenth-century English monk Matthew Paris, whose work Cleirac cites repeatedly, suggested an alternative etymology, noting that "Caursines" may derive from "*causor*, to cheat, or *capio*, to take, and *ursine*, bearish." *Matthew Paris's English History*, 1:4. An early use of *caorsino* to denote a usurer is found in Boccaccio, *Esposizioni sopra la Comedia di Dante* (1373–1374), ch. XI, par. 39, cited in *Tesoro della lingua Italian dalle origini*, s.v. "caorsino" (http//tlio.ovi.cnr.it/TLIO/). The word continued to appear in French dictionaries of the nineteenth century: e.g., *Émile Littré: Dictionnaire de la langue française* (1872–1877), s.v. "corsi." But a full-text keyword search for "ca(h)orsin/s" in *The Making of the Modern World* shows that the term was rarely used in Cleirac's times or thereafter.

21. "Barateurs," for cheaters, from "*BARAT*, m. acut. Est tromperie, fraude, principalement en marchandise, Fraus, dolus malus, deceptio. Ainsi l'on dit, Contracter sans fraude, barat ne malengin, Bene pacisci ac sine fraudatione, Bona fide conuenire. C'est un mot grandement usité és pays de Languedoc, Provence, et adjacents. Lesquels en font un verbe actif en leur langue, Barator, c'est Barater, qui signifie tromper autruy en fait mesmement de marchandise, vendant, acheptant ou trocquant, et en usent aussi pour trocquer ou eschanger une chose à autre. Et outre encores en font un nom adjectif, Baratier, et Baratiere, pour celuy ou celle qui est coustumier de frauder autruy, Fraudulentus, Fraudator, Fraudulenta, Fraudatrix." Jean Nicot, *Thresor de la langue françoyse, tant ancienne que modern* (1606).

22. "Triquoteurs" (a variant of "tricoteur") literally meant someone who wove threads to produce a tissue or a lace. Cleirac appears to use the word in an unusual metaphorical sense to indicate those who made up stories and were thus dishonest.

23. Judges condemned insolvent debtors who were not incarcerated to wear a green hat as a mark of infamy, although some authors recommended that this sentence be moderated for certain individuals on account of their character and the nature of their debts: Gabriel Bounyn, *Traité sur les cessions et banqueroutes* (Paris: Chez Pierre Chevillot, 1586), 111–115 (ch. 14). In Bordeaux, this custom remained in place into the eighteenth century: Robert Joseph Pothier, *Traité de la procédure civile*, 2 vols., new ed. (Lyon: Chez Joseph Duplain, 1776), 2:370. "Bonnet: (…) On dit, *Prendre le bonnet vert*, pour dire, Faire cession, faire banqueroute, Et, *Porter le bonnet vert*, pour dire, Avoir fait cession, avoir fait banqueroute." *Dictionnaire de l'Académie française*, 1st ed. (1694).

24. "Stellionates" (from the Latin *stellio*, trickster) were those guilty of selling an inheritance that they had mortgaged or, more generally, something they did not own. Joseph-Nicolas Guyot, *Répertoire universel et raisonné de jurisprudence civile, criminelle, canonique et bénéficiale*, 17 vols., new ed. (Paris: Chez Visse, 1784–1785), 16:404–406, s.v. "stellionat."

25. "Usuriers par mois & par livres."

26. "Rongeurs."

27. "Laveurs."

28. "Maltôtiers porteurs de quittances" indicated those who requested payments on the basis of illegal receipts. "Maltôtier, s.m. Celui qui exige des droits qui ne sont point dûs, ou qui ont été imposés sans autorité légitime. C'est un Maltôtier. Il se dit aussi par abus De ceux qui

recueillent toute sorte de nouvelles impositions." *Dictionnaire de l'Académie française*, 4th ed. (1762).

29. "Acquereurs, exacteurs des remises, & de non valoirs."

30. "Guichetier. s. m. Valet de Geolier qui ouvre & ferme les guichets, & a soin d'empescher que les prisonniers ne se sauvent. *Les Guichetiers de la Conciergerie, du Chastelet, &c.*" *Dictionnaire de l'Académie française*, 1st ed. (1694).

31. "Geheineurs" perhaps from "Géhenne, s. f. Mot hébreu, qui se dit quelquefois, dans l'Écriture sainte, pour l'enfer. *La géhenne de feu. Le feu de la géhenne.*" *Dictionnaire de l'Académie française*, 6th ed. (1835).

32. "Comites, sou-comites."

33. "Arioli, arusipices, vaticinatores."

34. Ephesians 5:3–5 reads: "(3) But let fornication and all uncleanness or covetousness not even be named among you, as is fitting with saints, (4) and obscenity, frivolity and facetiousness which are hardly appropriate, but rather thanksgiving. (5) For you should know this, that no fornicator, unclean or covetous person, idolaters in other words, has any inheritance in the kingdom of Christ and of God." John Muddiman, *A Commentary on the Epistle to the Ephesians* (London: Continuum, 2001), 222.

35. Dante, *Inferno*, XI.49–52: "E però lo minor giron suggella / del segno suo e Soddoma e Caorsa / e chi, spregiando Dio col cor, favella. / La frode, ond'ogne coscienza è morsa, / può l'omo usare in colui che 'n lui fida / e in quell che fidanza non imborsa." English translation: "And so the imprint of the smallest ring / falls on Cahorsian bankers, as on Sodom, / and those who speak at heart in scorn of God. / As for deceit—which gnaws all rational minds— / we practice this on those who trust us, / or those whose pocket have no room for trust." Dante Alighieri, *The Divine Comedy: Inferno*, trans. and ed. Robin Kirkpatrick (London: Penguin, 2006), 92–93. The entire canto deals with the sins of fraud and usury, among others. In lines 91–115, Virgil explains the sin of usury as follows: nature is an emanation of God; men follow nature when they derive their source of income from work; by contrast, usurers derive their income from money alone.

36. "Griveleries" from "Grivelée. s.f.v. Profit qu'on fait en grivelant. *Il s'est enrichi par ses gri-velées. Faire des grivelées.*" *Dictionnaire de l'Académie française*, 1st ed. (1694).

37. Louis IX, later proclaimed a saint, ruled from 1226 to 1270, and Philip the Fair from 1285 to 1314.

38. Guillaume de Breuil, *Stilus antiquus supremae curiae amplissimi ordinis Parlamenti Parisiensis* (Paris: Apud Galeotum, 1558), 216. I owe this reference to Rowan Dorin.

39. Philip IV, the first French king from the house of Valois, ruled from 1328 to 1350.

40. Cleirac here paraphrases Gilles: "En ces temps aussi furent prins tous les Lombards, banquiers, & usuriers qui estoyent en France, & furent chassez & bannis du royaume, pour la grande evacuation qu'ils faisoyent des finances de France, dont le Royaume estoit appauvry: & par proces faict contr'eux fut ordonné que quinconque seroit tenu envers eux en aucunes usures, en baillant au Roy le sort principal, il ne payeroit rien des arrerage. Et qui feroit de present ainsi ce seroit bien faict, car ils font beaucoup de mal en France: & quand ils y viennent iamais n'y apportent un ducat, mais seulement une feuille de papier en une main, & une plume en l'autre, & ansi tondent aux François la lain sur le dos, & leur font gabelle de leur propre argent. Il fut

lors trouvé que les debtes qu'on leur devoit montoient oultre vingt & quatre cens mil livres d'usures, desquelles le fort principal ne montoit point oultre douze vingt mil livres." Nicole Gilles, *Les chroniques et annales de France dès l'origine des François, & leur venuë és Gaules* (Paris: M. Sonnius, 1617), 216v.

41. "Supliques" from "Supplique, subst. fem. Terme de la Daterie de la Cour de Rome, Requeste qu'on presente au Pape. *Presenter sa supplique. Une supplique tendant &c.*" *Dictionnaire de l'Académie française,* 1st ed. (1694).

42. "Chambre de comptes de Paris."

43. The 1347 "procés aux Lombards Usuriers" is discussed in Éstienne Pasquier, *Recherches de la France,* rev. ed. (Paris: Chez Iamet Mettayer et Pierre l'huillier, 1596), 34 (book II, ch. 3).

44. "Contracts pignoratifs" were contracts by which buyers rented a title that they purchased to the sellers for a fixed interest rate. "PIGNORATIF. adj. Terme de Jurisprudence. Il se dit en parlant d'Un contrat par lequel on vend un héritage à faculté de rachat à perpétuité, & par lequel l'acquéreur loue ce même héritage à son vendeur pour les intérêts du prix de la vente. *Ces contrats tolérés dans quelques Coutumes qui les admettent, ne sont qu'une voie détournée de tirer intérêt d'un principal non aliéné; ce qui les fait rejeter dans toutes les autres.*" *Dictionnaire de l'Académie française,* 4th ed. (1762).

45. "Circumveniebant enim in necessitatibus indigentes, urusam sub specie negotiationis palliantes, (...) non ut alienae succurrant inediae, sed ut suae consulant avaritiae." Luard, *Matthaei Parisiensis, Monachi Sancti Albani, Chronica Majora,* 3:328–329.

46. Chapter 3 in Saint Ambrose's *De Tobia* ended with a strong and often-cited tirade: "He pays usury who lacks food. Is there anything more terrible? He asks for medicine, you offer him poison; he begs for bread, you offer him a sward; he begs for liberty, you impose slavery; he prays for freedom, you tighten the knot of the hideous snare." ("Usuras soluit qui victu indigent, An quidquam gravius? Ille medicamentum quaerit, vos offertis venenum: panem implorat, gladium porrigitis: libertatem obsecrat, servitutem inrogatis: absolutionem precatur, informis laquei nodum stringitis.") Lois Miles Zucker, ed., *S. Ambrosii: De Tobia; A Commentary, with an Introduction and Translation* (Washington, D.C.: Catholic University of America, 1933), 30–31.

47. The expression "excroissances de parties honteuses" implied a sexual innuendo.

48. The first part of this quote ("quanto perditior quisque est, tanto acrius urget") comes from Horace's *Satires* (I.2.15), which ridicules Fufidius, a rich man who lends at usury: "And the nearer a man is to ruin, the harder he presses him." Horace, *Satires; Epistles; The Art of Poetry,* trans. H. Rushton Fairclough (Cambridge, MA: Harvard University Press, 2014), 19.

49. *Decretals,* from the Latin *epistola decretalis,* are papal decrees collected in the *Corpus Iuris Canonici.* The first were added by Pope Gregory IX (1227–1241) as part of the so-called *Liber extra* (see also note 13). Usury is dealt with in book V, title 19, chs. 1–19. *Clementines* are the decrees issued by Pope Clement V (1305–1314) and published after his death in 1317. They include a decree against usury (*Ex gravii*) issued in 1311, which condemned Christian rulers who protected usurers.

50. "[A.D. 1253] quae conditio gravior est quam Judæorum, quia quandocunque sortem Judæo attuleris, recipiet benigne, cum tanto lucro quod tempori tanto se commensurate." Luard, *Matthaei Parisiensis, Monachi Sancti Albani, Chronica Majora,* 5:405.

51. "En ce temps avoit un marchand Turquois à Paris: qui estoit moult puissant homme, &

grand marchand, & auquel tous les faits d'autres Lombards se rapportoient: & estoit congnu, à parler par raison, par tout le monde, là ou marchands vont, viennent, & hantent." *Histoire et chronique memorable de messire Iehan Froissart, reveu et corrige* (Paris: Pour Robert Granjon, 1574), 238 (book 4, ch. 85). The citation is taken from a chapter describing how the Duke of Burgundy and his wife hired some influential merchants to rescue their child and others whom the Turks had taken captive; it shows the persistence of the term *Lombards*.

52. "Dardanaires" from "DARDANAIRE. s.m. Ancien nom qu'on donnoit à un monopoleur." *Dictionnaire de l'Académie française*, 4th ed. (1762).

Appendix 4: The Legend in the Works of Jacques Savary and His Sons

1. There existed a variety of *billets*. So-called *billets à l'ordre* were essentially IOUs or promissory notes. By contrast, *billets de change* expressed the obligation to either pay or remit a bill of exchange. Their function is described later in this section by Savary. The section of the 1673 *Ordonnances de commerce* regulating bills of exchange was entitled "Des lettres et billes de change" (title V, arts. 27–32). See also Joseph-Nicolas Guyot, *Répertoire universel et raisonné de jurisprudence civile, criminelle, canonique et bénéficiale*, 17 vols., new ed. (Paris: Chez Visse, 1784–1785), 2:382–385, s.v. "billets"; Jean Hilaire, *Introduction historique au droit commercial* (Paris: Presses universitaires de France, 1986), 283–284.

2. "Pour le fait de la marchandise." This technical expression is important because it signals the tension between commercial jurisdiction as determined by personal status and as determined by subject matter, an issue discussed in chapter 4.

3. The word used here is *procureurs*, i.e., legal practitioners who prepared the written evidence to be submitted before the court. They were hierarchically inferior to lawyers but indispensable to the proceedings of all legal suits.

INDEX

Abramsky, Chimen, 222

The Abyss of Usury (church canon, 1274), 56

Adams, John, 170

agriculture, Jews and, 137, 146–48, 150–52, 221–23

Alciato, Andrea, 73, 112

Alembert, Jean le Rond d', *Encyclopédie*, 99, 120, 139, 156

Alonso Oritz, José, 184

Alsace and Lorraine, 128, 144–46, 152, 156, 159

Alvarez, Enrique, 80

Ambrose of Milan, 51, 311n7

Amsterdam, 23–24, 32, 34, 37–38, 48, 68, 71, 83, 110, 113, 116, 119, 126, 150, 169, 174, 185–87, 189, 195, 320n12

ancient Israelites, 137, 146–48

Anne of Austria, Regent Queen of Austria, 84

antisemitism, 12, 45, 133, 203, 206, 209–10, 224

Aquinas, Thomas, 53

Arbel, Benjamin, 4

Arco, Giovanni Battista Gherardo d', 182

Ariosto, Ludovico, 20, 56, 72

aristocracy. *See* nobility

Aristotle, 18, 30, 50, 55, 96, 118

Armenians, 10, 102, 109–11, 118, 120, 125–27

ars mercatoria (writings on commerce and economy), 9, 50, 71, 99, 103, 113, 115, 117, 124, 185

artillery, 79

Ashkenazi Jews: in England, 167; negative

perceptions of, 116, 150, 153, 167–68; Sephardic Jews compared to, 6, 116, 129, 150, 153, 155, 157, 167, 186, 199, 208

Assembly of Jewish Notables, 159

assimilation, 6–7

Auerbach, Erich, 139

Augustus Ferdinand, Prince of Prussia, 178

Austrian School, 218

Azpilcueta, Martín. *See* Navarrus, Doctor

Azuni, Domenico Alberto, 181

Bacon, Francis, 136, 167

Baldasseroni, Pompeo and Ascanio, 179

Balzac, Honoré de, *La comédie humaine*, 203

bankers, 91–92, 147, 176

banknotes, 34, 169, 206, 210, 303n49. *See also* paper money

Bank of England, 169

Bank of Loan or Lombard (*Bank van lening ofte Lombard*), 38

"baptized" Jews, 58–59, 65, 68

Baron, Salo W., 220–21

Barthes, Roland, 66

Basnage de Beauval, Henri and Jacques, 195

Bauer, Bruno, 201

Bayle, Pierre, 195

Bay of Biscay, 75, 76

Bayonne, 81, 147, 150, 156, 325n53

Bazin de Bezons, Louis, 82

Beausobre, Louis de, 194–95

Beawes, Wyndham, 171, 179

Beccaria, Cesare, 172, 180, 181, 194

Ben Israel, Menasseh, 126–27, 151, 188–89

Berlin, 120, 150, 158, 194–95, 379n39, 379n41

Bernard, Jean-Frédéric, *Ceremonies et coutumes religieuses de tous les peuples du monde*, 187

Bernard, Samuel, 124–25

Bernardino da Siena, 51

Bernard of Clairvaux, 58, 64

Berr, Cerf, 146, 152

Berr-Bing, Isaac, 152

Berr-Bing, Isaïe, 352n81

Besançon, 30

Bielfeld, Jakob Friedrich von, 178, 183, 194

bills of exchange, 193; analogies between Jews and, 97–98; apprehension about, 14, 24, 26, 32, 53, 106–7, 136; assurances behind, 2–3; Catholic acceptance of, 52–54; classic (four-party), 25, 26, 27; complexity/opacity of, 3, 21, 24–26, 28, 38–39, 50, 108, 113–14; discounting of, 32–34; in economic history, 218; endorsable, 33–34, 206–7; function of, 2; historical development of, 21, 165, 170–71, 176–78, 178–79, 193, 206; impact of, 1–2, 35; interest rates on, 50; Jews credited with invention of, xiii–xiv, 4, 8, 13, 19, 21, 28, 36–38, 75, 95, 107, 112, 132–34, 148, 171–72, 181, 184, 190–91, 195, 197, 200, 221; marine insurance linked to, 20–21; material and abstract qualities of, 13–14; mercantilist role of, 106; and modernity, 136; money compared to, 3, 34; Montesquieu on, 132–33, 155; as nameless contracts, 63; overview of, 24–30, 34–35; Savary on, 103–4; speculative use of, 2, 28–33, 92; transferability of, 32–33, 33; transparency in use of, 3, 26; ubiquity of, 1, 48; utility of, 14, 21, 32, 106, 136

blacks, 110, 129, 152–54

Blackstone, William, 171

Bloch, Marc, xii

blood libel. *See* ritual murder

Boccaccio, Giovanni, 72

Bolaños, Juan de Hevia, 73

Bolingbroke, Lord, 169

Bordeaux, 17, 23, 66, 81–84, 95, 136, 150–51, 155–57

Borgherini, Niccolò, 25

Bornier, Philippe, 112, 113

Botticini, Maristella, 223

Boucher d'Argis, Antoine-Gaspard, 139–40

Bourgeoisie, fiscal privileges of, 69, 88

Bracciolini, Poggio, 96

Braudel, Fernand, 304n54

Brentano, Lujo, 211

brokers, 93–94, 107

Bubble Act, 173

Buffett, Warren, xi, xi–xii, 1

Burckhardt, Jacob, 211

Büsch, Johann Georg, 178

Caeser, Claudio, 171

Cahorsins, 55–56, 58

Cajetan, Tommaso de Vio, Cardinal, 53, 61

Calas, Jean, 139–40

Calvin, John, 316n36

Calvinism, 81, 124, 324n36

Cambridge School, 219

Cameralism, 175–76, 178

capitalism: credit and, 206; Jews in relation to modern, 198–215; Marx on, 204–5; meaning of, 295n4; in medieval period, 211–13; Sombart on, 200

Capmany y Montpalau, Antonio de, 183

Cardano, Gerolamo, 72

Caro, Georg, 209

Casaregi, Giuseppe Lorenzo Maria, 179

Castiglione, Baldassare, *Courtier*, 71

Catherine of Aragon, Queen of England, 53

Catholic Church: and commerce, xiii, 18, 49–53, 87, 135, 149, 211–13; conversion and allegiance of Jews to, 5, 58–59, 66–68, 81–82; and prejudices/stereotypes concerning Jews, 68, 307n15; on usury, 49–51, 59. *See also* Christianity

Central Union of German Citizens of Jewish Faith, 209

Cerutti, Simona, 97

Chamber of Commerce, Bordeaux, 83, 138

Chamber of Commerce, Marseilles, 109, 110, 125–26

chambers of commerce, France, 151

Chartalism, 193

Christ, Jews' denial of divinity of, 16, 39, 40, 45

Christianity: Jews in the imagination of, xiv, 4–5, 10, 15–18, 64–65, 131–32, 200, 225; moneylending and usury associated with, 55–59. *See also* Catholic Church

Cicero, Marcus Tullius, 105, 113, 177, 348n54

civil law, on usury, 59–61, 184

Clark, Henry C., 91

Cleirac, Étienne: in Bordeaux, 17, 23, 66–71, 67, 78, 81, 323n35; on Christian money-lenders, 54–58; on commerce, 60–62, 91–94; *Explication des termes de marine*, 72, 321n19, 325n48; Iberian reception of, 183; on Jews and usury, 49–57, 59, 62; Jews as target of, 39–40, 46–51, 56–57, 61–62, 94, 96, 121; on Jews' invention of credit in-struments, 19–20, 34, 36–41, 45–48, 75, 95, 134, 139–40, 198, 205; on law and jurispru-dence, 86, 93–94, 177; life of, 69, 78, 323n35; on maritime law and marine in-surance, 52, 61, 69–75, 78–79, 84, 86, 91–93; and merchant tribunals, 86; Savary and, 103–7; sources used by, 73, 74, 75; *Usance du négoce*, 40, 41, 61, 307n13; *Us et coustumes de la mer* (*Usages and Customs of the Sea*), 8–9, 19–20, 41, 42, 43, 44, 45, 52, 61–62, 65, 69–73, 74, 75, 78, 84, 85, 86, 92, 95, 103, 112, 134, 139–40, 177, 183, 198, 205, 308n22

Clermont-Tonnerre, Count, 152

Code Henri, 72

Code Michau, 89

Colbert, Jean-Baptiste, 22–23, 60, 69, 82, 88, 89, 90, 92, 96, 98, 100, 101, 104, 106, 109, 111, 112, 118–19, 125–27

Coli, Romualdo, 61

Collège de Guyenne, 81

Columbus, Christopher, 208

commerce: Catholic Church and, xiii, 18,
49–53, 87, 135, 149, 211–13; commercial revolution of the Middle Ages, xiii, 20, 21, 51, 58, 63, 212–13, 381n45, despotism coun-tered by, 133–34, 137, 139, 145, 160, 172, 203; emancipation of Jews linked to, 143–61, 164; historical discourses on role of Jews in, 16–18; Jews' participation in, 16–18, 66–68, 82–83, 121, 125–27, 132, 134, 136, 145–47, 157–59, 174–75, 189, 206; mean-ings of, xiii, 130; Montesquieu and, 199; Montesquieu on, 132–39, 206; nobility in relation to, 86, 88–90, 96–97, 105, 111–13, 138; regulation of, 101, 106, 109, 159; role of images/representations in, 10–11; Savary on, 105–7; social changes in rela-tion to changes in, 63–64, 68–69, 84–90, 95, 96–97, 100, 127, 129, 134–35, 225; social norms underlying, 124; toleration in rela-tion to, 130, 137, 138, 155; usury linked to, 131–32, 135, 145–52, 155. *See also* merchants

Compagnie de la Nouvelle France, 89

Condillac, Étienne Bonnot de, 60

Condorcet, Marie Jean Antoine Nicolas de Caritat, Marquis of, 153

Confraternity of the Corpus Domini, Ur-bino, 45

Conservation des privileges royaux des foires, Lyon, 87–88

contracts, 63–64

conversions, of Jews, 5, 58–59, 66–68, 81–82, 201. *See also* New Christians

Costa, Diego da, 80

Cotrugli, Benedetto, 26, 367n73; *Della mer-catura*, 73, 75

Court, de la, brothers, 185

courtroom literature, 121

coustumier de Guyenne, 45

coutumiers, 309n29

Coyer, Gabriel-François, 90

credit: analogies between Jews and, 98; cap-italism and, 206; in England, 166–68; meanings of, xiii; reputation as basis for, 28, 34, 59, 64

credit default swaps, 1

Cromwell, Oliver, 127, 189
crypto-Judaism, 5, 68, 83, 95–96, 126, 136, 161, 179, 215
Cujas, Jacques, 73, 112

Dagobert, King of France, 36–37, 104
Dante Alighieri, 20, 72; *Inferno*, 55
Danvila, Bernardo, 183
Darnton, Robert, 141
Daston, Lorraine, 23
Datini, Francesco, 55
Davanzati, Bernardo, 29, 30, 45, 73, 92
Declaration of the Rights of Man and of the Citizen (1789), 153, 201
Defoe, Daniel, 168, 169
Della Torre, Raffaele, 73
diamonds, 79–80
Dickens, Charles, 197
Diderot, Denis, *Encyclopédie*, 90, 99, 120, 139, 156
discounting, of bills of exchange, 32–33
D'Israeli, Isaac, 165; *The Genius of Judaism*, 191; *Vaurien*, 190
Dohm, Christian Wilhelm von, 146–47, 150, 152, 158, 175, 182, 343n8, 351n70
doux commerce, 98, 106, 133, 135, 137, 145, 152, 156, 343n11
dry exchange, 29–31, *30*, 53, 107
Dubnow, Simon, 220
Duns Scotus, John, 52
Dupuis de la Serra, Jacques, *L'art des lettres de change*, 113–15, 124, 134, 140, 171, 177, 179–81, 183, 194

early modernity, 15–16, 38, 135–36, 199
East India Company (England), 166
East India Company (Holland), 187
Eckstein, Zvi, 223
economic history, xii, 48, 218–20
economy, as field of study, 8–10
Edict of Nantes (ratified in Bordeaux), 81
Edict of Toleration (1782), 175, 182
Eisenmenger, Johann Andreas, 175, 208
Eliot, George, 216

emancipation of Jews: commerce as factor in, 143–61, 164; debates over, 143–52, 155, 199, 200–1; in German Empire, 201; historiographical accounts of, 129–30, 133; in Holy Roman Empire, 175; limits on, 150, 152–54, 161; opposition and backlashes evoked by, 144, 158–61; prelude to, 6, 18, 39, 129–30; Sephardim vs. Ashkenazim as factor in, 155–57. *See also* naturalization of Jews, in England
Emmanuel, Isaac Samuel, 221
Encyclopædia Britannica, 171
endorsable bills, 32–34, *33*, 200, 206–7
England: reception of legend in, 72, 166–73
Enlightenment: commerce championed by, 3, 17, 130, 193; Italian, 180; Jews as subject of, 133, 140, 155–56; on Jews' role in commerce, 17, 120, 130, 140; limitations of, 129; on women and, 11
Enrique, Antonio, 80
Eon, Jean, 105
Épernon, Jean-Louis Nogaret de La Valette, duc d', 78–80
Ettinger, Shmuel, 222
Exchange Bank (*Wisselbank*), 32–33
exchange rates, 3, 25, 31
expulsions, of the Jews, 4, 5, 36–37, 39, 94, 104, 110, 182, 305n4

Fabri de Peiresc, Nicolas-Claude, 75
Fanfani, Amintore, 212
farming. *See* agriculture
Fénelon, François de Salignac de La Mothe-, Archbishop of Cambrai, *The Adventures of Thelemachus*, 135, 160
Ferguson, Wallace, 211
Feuerbach, Ludwig, 203
Fibonacci, Leonardo, 181
finance. *See* credit
financial fairs, 30–32
Fischer, Friedrich Christoph Jonathan, 178, 191, 206
Fleury, Claude, 146
Florence and Florentines, 41, 165, 179

Forbonnais, François Véron de, 140, 156

Fortia, François de, 78

Fouquet, Nicolas, 104

Fourth Lateran Council (1215), 16, 40, 51, 121; Canon 67, 40, 51, 122, 311n8

France: chambers of commerce and Jews, 151; Fronde, 69; *lois de dérogeance*, 89–90, 328n84; *parlements'* jurisdictions in, 70; rights for Jews in, 129–30, 143–52; royal ordinances, 70, 72. *See also* French Revolution; nobility; Wars of Religion

Franciscan friars, 16, 51

Francis I, King of France, 68

French Revolution, 6, 60, 128–30, 151–53, 157–59, 204

friponnerie (roguery), 118, 144, 147, 150, 157, 308n20

Frizzi, Benedetto, 182

Froissart, Jean, 57

Fronde, 69. *See also* Ormée

Fuchs, Eugene, 209

Furetière, Antoine, 123, 144

Furtado, Abraham, 159

Galiani, Ferdinando, 180

Garzoni, Tommaso, 91

Gellert, Christian Fürchtegott, 175

Genovesi, Antonio, 180, 183

German Historical School, 178, 205, 218

Germany. *See* Holy Roman Empire

Ghibellines, 36–37, 41, 104, 113, 114–15, 171, 176, 179

Giacomini & Gondi, 25

Gilles, Nicole, 57, 72

Giraud, Guillaume, 75

Godefroy, Jacques, 324n36

Godefroy, Théodore, 78, 324n36

Goethe, Johann Wolfgang von, 192

Goldschmidt, Levin, 206, 210, 214

Govea, André, 81

Graetz, Heinrich, 207–10

Grand Sanhedrin, 159

Gratian, *Decretum*, 50

Greeks, 10, 102, 118, 119

Grégoire, Henri, 147–51, 153–54, 160

Gregory IX, Pope: *Naviganti*, 51–52

Grotius, Hugo, 73, 185

Guelfs, 36–37, 41, 57, 115, 179

Guicciardini, Ludovico, 61

Guidon de la mer (*The Standard of the Sea*), 20, 40–41, 52, 63, 72

guilds, 6, 13, 24, 63–64, 69, 93–94, 100–101, 149, 158–60, 332n3

Habermas, Jürgen, 14

Hanseatic League, 71–72, 93

Hauser, Henri, 212

Hegel, G. W. F., 203

Hell, François-Joseph-Antoine, 146

Henry III, King of France, 72

Henry VIII, King of England, 53

Hertzberg, Arthur, 133, 143, 147

Hirschman, Albert O., 8–9, 133; *The Passions and the Interests*, 154–55, 157, 224

historiography: disappearance of legend from, 217–26; of Jewish emancipation, 129–30, 133, 155; Marx and, 204; medievalists and, 211–13, 215; methods in, 10, 13–15; Montesquieu and, 135; stadial conception of history, 192–93, 204. *See also* Jewish history

Holocaust, 221

Holst, Johann Ludolf, 175

Holy Roman Empire, 165, 173–78

honesty, in marine insurance, 23

Hoppit, Julian, 168

host, profanation of, 45, 121–22

Hourwitz, Zalkind, 147, 150

Huguenots, 125, 168, 195

Hume, David, 110, 169, 172, 190, 192, 335n37, 372n126, 374n140

Iberia, 164, 183–84. *See also* Portugal

infamous decree (1808), 159

information: bills of exchange as conveyors of, 13–14, 25; costs of acquiring, 34; guilds are conveyors of, 100–101; Savary's *Le parfait négociant* as compendium of, 103,

information (cont.)
123; scarcity of, 2, 10–11, 28; unequal distribution (asymmetry) of, 22, 23, 101, 104; verifiability of, 28
Inquisition, 5, 65, 68, 80, 81, 83, 122, 137
insider trading, 31
interest (finances), 50, 51, 59–60, 311n8
Isnard family, 33
Israel, Jonathan, 17, 186, 187, 222–23
Italian peninsula, 178–82, 211

Jaucourt, Louis de, 140–41
Jefferson, Thomas, 170
The Jewish Encyclopedia, 221
Jewish history, 7, 48, 129, 198, 207, 215, 220–23
Jews: in Alsace and Lorraine, 128, 144–46, 152, 156; analogies between credit instruments and, 97–98; anxieties/fears associated with, 4, 6–7, 13–14, 68, 84, 97, 102, 110, 126, 130–31, 159–61, 201, 224–25; assimilation of, 6–7; "baptized," 58–59, 65, 68; in Bordeaux, 82–84, 95, 136, 150, 151, 155–56; and capitalism, 198–215; Christian conceptions and representations of, xiv, 4–5, 10, 15–18, 64–65, 131–32, 200, 225; clothing stipulated for, 51, 56; conversions of, 5, 58–59, 66–68, 81–82, 201; crypto-, 5, 68, 83, 95–96, 126, 136, 161, 179, 215; denial of Christ's divinity by, 16, 39, 40, 45; distinctions between non-Jews and, 6, 22, 51, 56, 68, 84, 95–96, 131, 167, 215, 306n8; diversity of, 128, 170; economic activities and roles of, 16–18, 47–48, 132, 134, 136, 145–47, 159, 165, 174–75, 189, 206, 222; economic utility of, 17, 66–68, 82–83, 121, 126–27, 132, 134, 151–52, 172–73, 186, 189–91, 209; in England, 166–68; expulsions of, 4, 5, 36–37, 39, 94, 104, 110, 182, 305n4; and farming/agriculture, 137, 146–48, 150–51, 221–23; financial knowledge ascribed to, 39–40; in Holy Roman Empire, 174; Iberian émigrés, 68, 81–82; invisibility of, 5–7; on Italian peninsula, 179, 181–82; linked to private finance, 4; in Marseilles, 110; Marx's conception of, 202–4; Montesquieu and, 132–39, 145–46, 148, 154–55, 199; Orientalist discourse applied to, 119–20; perceptions of, 12–13; as presence in early modern commerce, 107–8; usury linked to, 16–18, 40, 47, 50–51, 54, 56, 58–59, 102, 108, 118, 140, 142, 145–50, 155, 156–59, 167; Voltaire on, 137, 138–39, 141, 156, 348n48. *See also* ancient Israelites; emancipation of Jews; stereotypes and prejudices concerning Jews
Joseph II, Emperor, 175
Josephus, 137
Jousse, Daniel, 115
Judaizing, 58, 167, 170, 202–3, 305n4
Judgments of Oléron, 71–72, 177, 321n21
juridictions consulaires (merchant tribunals), 86–88, 90

Kamer von assurantie en avarij (Chamber of Insurance and Average), 22–23
Karp, Jonathan, 146, 169
Kayserling, Meyer, 208
Kessler, Amalia, 86
De koopman (*The Merchant*) [anonymous], 186, 187

Lacretelle, Pierre-Louis, 144–45, 154, 157, 204
laïcité, 154
Lamourette, Adrien, 354n97
La Peyrère, Isaac, 81
La Rochelle, 79
Lattes, Alessandro, 212
Latour-Foissac, Philippe-François de, 352n81
Lauterbach, Wolfgang Adam, 177
Law, John, 124, 158
Laws of Wisby, 71–72
legend about Jews and finance: credibility of, 37, 102, 113–15, 132–40, 163–65, 171–72, 176–77, 179–81, 214; cultural and moral

significance of, xiii–xiv, 4–5, 7, 11–13, 20, 35, 48, 59, 64, 97–98, 111, 124, 160, 217; disappearance of, 217–26; dissemination of, 115–22, 164; English reception of, 72, 170–73; exemplary nature of, 195; factual elements of, 37–38; falsity of, xiv, 4, 19, 20, 36–38, 41; formulation of, 36–48, 72; German reception of, 173–78; Iberian reception of, 183–84; Italian reception of, 178–82; Jewish responses to, 188–91; legacy of, 197–215; Montesquieu and, 102, 131–42, 145, 147–49, 154, 160, 162–66, 170, 171–72, 190, 194, 222; obscurity of, 4–5, 8–9; printed references to, 358n1, 359n3; propagation of, 99, 102, 111–13; reception of, 162–65; skepticism concerning (*see* credibility of) split transmission of, 139–43; terminological clarification, 46–47, 298n2; United Provinces' reception of, 184–88; Villani as source of, 19, 20, 40, 46, 183, 307n8, 310n33, 353n85

Le Moine de L'Espine, Jacques, *La négoce d'Amsterdam/Den koophandel van Amsterdam*, 185–86

Lessing, Gotthold Ephraim, 175

Levi, Raphäel, 121

Libre del consolat de mar, 75

Lipton, Sara, 306n8

Livorno, 119

Locke, John, 192

lois de dérogeance, 89–90, 328n84

Lombardy and Lombards, 36–37, 45, 55–58, 104, 222

Lopez, Alphonse, 80

Lopez, Robert Sabatino, 212–13

Louis, Saint, 57

Louis XIV, King of France, 99, 135

Louis XV, King of France, 99

Loyseau, Charles, 73, 89

Ludovici, Carl Günter, 176, 177

Luther, Martin, 53

Luzzatto, Gino, 212

Luzzatto, Simone, 126, 151, 188–89

Lyon, 30–31, 60, 87–88

Machiavelli, Niccolò, 136

Malesherbes, Chrétien Guillaume de Lamoignon de, 151

Malynes, Gerard, *Consuetudo, vel Lex Mercatoria, or, The Ancient Law-Merchant*, 72, 193, 321n20

Manchester School, 218

Mandeville, Bernard, *Fable of the Bees*, 144

Mantua, 181–82

Marchetty, François, 105

Maréschal, Mathias, 60, 73, 104, 113, 333n11

Maria Theresa of Austria, 182

marine insurance: bills of exchange linked to, 20–21; Catholic acceptance of, 51–52; Cleirac on, 52, 61, 71; historical development of, 21, 142–43, 171, 178, 194; institutions connected with, 22–23; Jews credited with invention of, xiii–xiv, 19, 21, 36–38, 75, 95, 112, 142–43; as nameless contract, 63; overview of, 22–24; premiums for, 22; suspicion of, 23; utility of, 21, 23

maritime law, 69–75, 84, 92–93

Marperger, Paul Jacob, 176, 177

Marseilles, 109–10, 125–27

Marx, Karl, xiv, 153, 197, 198, 201–5, 214; "On the Jewish Question," 201–2

Maury, Abbé, 152

medieval period, 15–16, 38, 47, 199, 205, 211–13, 215

Mendelssohn, Moses, 153, 158, 190, 208, 351n70, 372n124

Mendes, Beatriz. *See* Nasi, Gracia

mercantilism, 106, 109, 118, 145

merchant manuals, xi, 10, 60, 103, 116, 124, 170, 178–79, 359n4

merchants: attitudes toward, 91, 96; conceptions of, 69; foreign, 93–94; liability of, 27–28; self-organization/self-regulation of, 3–4, 14, 21, 31, 35, 93–94, 101, 106. *See also* commerce; *négociants*

merchant tribunals. See *juridictions consulaires*

Metz, 66, 121–22, 144, 147, 150, 154

Michaelis, Johannes David, 175

Middle Ages. *See* medieval period

middleman minorities, 140–41

Millanges, Guillaume, 41

Mirabeau, Honoré-Gabriel de Riqueti, Count of, 158, 189–90, 218, 355n108, 357n121, 357n123

Mirabeau, Victor de Riqueti, Marquis of, 189

Modena, Leon, *The History of the Rites, Customes, and Manners of Life, of the Present Jews*, 39, 306n9

Molière, *Bourgeois gentilhomme*, 88

Molina, Luis de, 52

money. *See* banknotes; paper money

moneylending: Christians engaged in, 37, 55–59, 64–65; Jews associated with, 38, 39, 47–48, 51, 64–65, 180. *See also* usury

money of account (*écu de marc* or *scudo di marche*), 31

Montaigne, Michel de, 45, 69, 325n48, 343n11

Montchrétien, Antoine de, 118–19

Montesquieu, Charles-Louis de Secondat, Baron de La Brède and of: on commerce, 98, 106, 135–38, 145, 156, 199, 206; English reception of, 171–72; German reception of, 173–74, 177–78; influenced by Christian ideas of Jews, 343n8; influence of, 15–16; Italian reception of, 180–81; and Jews, 132–39, 145–46, 148, 155–56, 199; and legend about Jews' invention of credit instruments, 102, 131–42, 147–49, 154–56, 158, 160, 162–66, 170, 171–72, 190, 194, 222; *Persian Letters*, 119, 136–37, 140; *The Spirit of the Laws*, 132–35, 137–38, 141, 154–55, 172, 177–78, 206–7

Monti di Pietà, 38, 55, 180

morality: and credit, 28; and economic principles, 16, 18; and financial speculation, 29–30; of merchant activity, 12

Morisot, Claude Barthélemy de, 75

Mortimer, Thomas, 172

Moulin, Charles du, 73, 315n36

Muslims, 102, 221, 224

nameless contracts (*contracti innominati*), 52, 63

Napoleon Bonaparte, 159, 204

Napoleonic Code of Commerce, 136

Nasi, Gracia (Beatriz Mendes), 95

naturalization of Jews, in England, 172–73

Naulot, Claude, 115

Navarrus, Doctor (Martín Azpilcueta), 53, 61

Necker, Jacques, 124

négociants (wholesale and overseas merchants): characteristics of, 100–101, 105; Savary's focus on, 100, 105

New Christians, 5, 66–68, 79–84, 95, 97–98, 136, 215

nobility: criteria for determining, 68, 96–97; in relation to commerce, 86, 88–90, 96–97, 105, 111–13, 138, 328n84

nobility of the robe, 68, 88, 105

notaries, 21

Novi Ligure, 31

Núñes, Juan Saraiva, 68

Old Regime France: commercial activity in, 7, 35; social change in, 7, 88–90, 97; social hierarchy in, 11, 14, 68, 86, 88–89, 97

Olivares, Count-Duke, 80

ordonnance de commerce (1673), 86, 90, 103, 107, 112, 115, 123–24

ordonnance de la marine (1681), 142

Orientalism, 10, 102, 110, 119–20, 214

Ormée, 69

Ottoman Empire, 109, 110, 119, 125

Pacioli, Luca, 47

pactes de ricorsa, 31–32

Pagnini, Giovan Francesco, 179

paper money, 34, 169–70, 180, 303n49. *See also* banknotes

Pardessus, Jean-Marie, 71

pariah capitalism, 335n37
Paris, Matthew, 20, 56, 167
Pasquier, Étienne, 57, 72
Paul, Saint, 20
Paulson, John Alfred, xi
pawnbroking: in Amsterdam, 38; Jews
    linked to, 13, 15, 16, 108, 145, 168
Peck, Peter, 73
Penso de la Vega, Joseph, *Confusión de con-
    fusiones*, 187–88
perfidy (*perfidia*), 40, 307n15
Peri, Giovanni Domenico, 32, 73; *Il nego-
    tiante*, 103
periodization, 15–18
personal-status law (*ratione personae*), 86
Philip II, King of Spain, 71
Philip IV, King of Spain, 78
Philip IV (the Fair), King of France, 37, 45,
    57
Philip V (the Tall), King of France, 36–37,
    104, 134, 171
Philip VI of Valois, King of France, 57
Philip Augustus, King of France, 36–37, 104,
    134, 171
Philippson, Ludwig, 209
philosemitic mercantilism, 17
Piacenza, 30–31
Picard, Bernard, *Ceremonies et coutumes reli-
    gieuses de tous les peuples du monde*, 187
Pinto, Isaac de, 153, 189–90, 220, 352n81
Pirenne, Henri, 211, 212
Pitaval, François Gayot de, *Causes célèbres et
    interessantes*, 121–22
pogroms, 59
Poliakov, Léon, 58
political economy, 118, 180
Portugal, 66–68, 75, 77–81
"Portuguese merchants," 5, 68, 80, 82–84,
    96, 156–57
Pothier, Robert Joseph, 143
predatory lending, 31, 311n7
premium-based insurance, 22–23, 52, 63,
    318n64

private finance: advantages and disadvan-
    tages of, 3; anxieties about, reflected in
    legend about Jews, 4, 7, 13–14
The Prophecies of Merlin, 72
Protestant Black Legend, xii

Qur'an, 72

rank. *See* nobility
re-exchange contracts, 28, 29, 53, 104, 106, 113
Reformation, 53
religious toleration: and attitudes toward
    Jewish commerce, 17, 84, 97–98, 175, 182,
    195; commerce in relation to, 130, 137, 138,
    156; in France, 68, 81, 97–98
reputation: credit linked to, 28, 34, 59, 64; in
    preindustrial commerce, 11, 34
Ricard, Samuel: *Négoce d'Amsterdam*, 117;
    Traité general du commerce, 116
Richelieu, Cardinal Armand du Plessis,
    Duke of, 75, 78–80, 89, 110, 323n33, 328n85
Ridolfi, Lorenzo, 52
rights. *See* emancipation of Jews
Rise of the West, 4, 196, 211, 215
ritual murder, 45, 121–22
Rodrigues Péreire, Jacob, 156
Rogers, James Steven, 35
Roman jurisprudence, 19, 36, 52, 62–63, 73,
    177
Roover, Raymond de, 213, 218
Roscher, Wilhelm, 178, 198, 205–6, 208–10,
    214
Rota (high civil court of Genoa), 52, 63, 73,
    313n18
royal ordinances, 70, 72
Royal Society of Arts and Sciences, 147

Salviati, Averardo, 25
Samuels, Maurice, 154
Santa Helena (ship), 75, 77–78, 79
Santarém, Pedro de, 73
São Bartolomeu (ship), 75, 77–78, 79
Sapori, Armando, 212

Savary, Jacques, 73; on commerce, 99–100; English reception of, 170; German reception of, 173, 176; Iberian reception of, 183; Italian reception of, 179; and Jews, 99,

Savary, Jacques (cont.) 103–4, 107–11, 123; and legend about Jews' invention of credit instruments, 99, 103–13; life of, 104; *Parères*, 107; *Le parfait négociant*, 8, 9, 99–100, 103–13, 115, 116, 117, 134, 139–40, 164, 166, 170, 173, 185

Savary, Philémon-Louis, 99, 117; *Dictionnaire universel de commerce*, 117–20, 176

Savary des Brûlons, Jacques, 99, 117; *Dictionnaire universel de commerce*, 117–20, 176

Savelli, Rodolfo, 62

Sayous, André-E., 212

Scaccia, Sigismondo, 26, 32, 52, 73, 112

Scaliger, Joseph, 69, 72

Schama, Simon, 185

Schechter, Ronald, 137, 155, 297n13

Schipper, Ignaz, 209, 379n42

Schmoller, Gustav von, 205

Scholasticism, 18, 100. *See also* Second Scholasticism

scientific racism, 7, 215

sea loans, 22, 299n7

Second Council of Lyon, 45

Second Scholasticism, 53

Second Vatican Council, 307n15

Sée, Henri, 212

Segre, Arturo, 212

Selden, John, 73

Sephardic Jews: in Amsterdam, 83; Ashkenazi Jews compared to, 6, 116, 129, 150, 153, 155, 157, 167, 186, 199, 208; and emancipation, 155–57; in England, 167; Iberian émigrés, 68; as merchants, 6, 145, 147, 150–51, 153, 158, 174; Sombart on, 200; status of, 6, 129–30, 154, 155; in stock market, 187

Sernigi, Rinieri, 25

Servien, Abel de, 78, 323n34

Sessa, Giuseppe, 182

Sewell, William, Jr., 13–14

Shamakhi, 120, 339n77

Sheehan, Jonathan, 14

Silva Lisboa, José da, Baron and Viscount of Cairu, 183

Slezkine, Yuri, 223

Smith, Adam, 3–4, 30, 98, 154, 168, 169–70, 192, 204

social change, commerce in relation to, 63–64, 68–69, 84–90, 95, 96–97, 100, 127, 129, 134–35, 225

sodomy, 55–56

Sombart, Werner, xiv, 198, 200, 205–12, 214–15, 218, 222–24, 341n90, 377n21, 377n24, 379n42, 380n43; *Die Juden und das Wirtschaftsleben* (*The Jews and Economic Life*), 198, 206, 209, 210, 212, 223–24; *Die Zukunft der Juden* (*The Future of the Jews*), 209, 379n41

Sorbonne University, 60, 136

Sorkin, David, 129

Soto, Domingo de, 52

South Sea Bubble, 169, 186

speculation, financial, 158, 168–70. *See also* bills of exchange: speculative use of

stereotypes and prejudices concerning Jews, 123; antisocial behavior, 40, 56, 120–21, 144–45, 149, 157, 202; Catholic Church and, 307n15; cognitive value of, 12, 124; commerce-oriented, 10, 12, 62, 101–2, 107–11, 123, 175; competence and power, 17, 39, 102, 109–10, 118–21, 125–26, 191; exemplary nature of, 16–17, 18, 47, 54, 59, 62, 64–65, 94, 101–2, 107–8, 111, 120, 123–25, 131, 168–69; German, 175; insularity, 160, 210–11; interrelation of social and economic, 12–13, 16, 39, 48, 62, 123, 125, 131–32, 159, 225–26; life-sapping powers, 30, 45, 121; negative, 13; opacity and secretiveness, 38; permanence and adaptability of, 15, 102, 124, 192; speculation and greed, 140, 164, 169–70, 173, 186–87; un-

fairness/deceitfulness, 18, 24, 35, 107, 118, 125, 131
Steuart, James, 172, 194
stock market, 166, 169, 185–88
Stoicism, 96
Stracca, Benvenuto, 73
Stypmann, Franz, 142
subject-matter law (*ratione materiae*), 86, 88, 90
Suetonius, 171
Sutcliffe, Adam, 223
symptomatic reading, 20, 298n3

Tavernier, Jean-Baptiste, 120
tax farmers, 93
Théveneau, Adam, 57, 315n36
Thiéry, Claude-Antonie, 147
Toch, Michael, 191
Toland, John, 172–73
toleration. *See* religious toleration
Tory Party, 169
Toubeau, Jean, *Les institutes du droit consulaire*, 112–13
Toussenel, Alphone, *Les juifs, rois de l'époque* (*The Jews, King of the Time*), 204
Tozzetti, Giovanni Targioni, 181
transparency: in bills of exchange use, 3, 26; in marine insurance, 23
Trenchant, Jean, 60, 73
tribunals. See *juridictions consulaires*
Tucker, Josiah, 173
Turgot, Anne-Robert-Jacques, 35, 60, 172, 330n110
Twelve Years' Truce (1609–1621), 83

Uccello, Paolo, Miracle of the Profaned Host, 45, 46–47
United Provinces, 83, 89, 164, 169, 184–88
University of Salamanca, 52
usury: analogy between desecration of the host and, 121–22; Catholic Church on,

49–51, 59, 316n36; Christians associated with, 55–59; civil law on, 59–61, 184; commerce linked to, 131–32, 135, 145–52, 157; conceptions of, 16, 49–54, 61–62, 108, 123; in England, 166–67; Jews linked to, 16–18, 40, 47, 50–51, 54, 56, 58–59, 102, 108, 118, 140, 142, 145–50, 157, 159, 167; at junction of medieval and early modern periods, 49–50; sodomy synonymous with, 55–56; Villani on, 41, 45. *See also* interest; moneylending

Vallabrègue, Israël Bernard de, 156
Villani, Giovanni, 19, 20, 40–41, 45–46, 56, 112–15, 121–22, 183, 307n18, 308n20, 310n33, 336n52, 353n85; *Nuova Cronica*, 40–41, 308n24
Vitoria, Francisco de, 52
Voltaire, 125, 133, 137, 138–39, 141, 149, 156, 189, 343n8, 348n48; *Dictionnaire philosophique*, 141

Warman, Dror, 14
War of Mantua Succession, 78
Wars of Religion (1562–1598), 68, 222
Weber, Max, xiv, 198, 205, 210–11, 214, 218, 335n37; *Ancient Judaism*, 210; *Economy and Society*, 210; *The Protestant Ethic and the Spirit of Capitalism*, 210
Whig Party, 169, 173
William III (William of Orange), King of England, 187
Wilson, Thomas, *A Discourse upon Usury*, 167
women, 11, 129, 152–53, 168

Yardeni, Miriam, 195
Yiddish language, 39, 144

Zedler, Johann Heinrich, 176
Zionism, 209

A NOTE ON THE TYPE

This book has been composed in Arno, an Old-style serif typeface in the classic Venetian tradition, designed by Robert Slimbach at Adobe.